THE CLOSED CIRCLE

David Pryce-Jones has traveled widely throughout the Arab world and was a war correspondent in the Middle East in 1967 and 1973. He
is the author of nineteen books of fiction and
nonfiction, including *The War That Never Was,
Paris in the Third Reich, The Face of Defeat,* and
The Hungarian Revolution, as well as novels and
literary biography. *The Closed Circle* is the fruit
of a lifelong interest in the subject, which
began with childhood experiences in Morocco
and continued, over the course of his career, to
draw him back to the Middle East to study
Arab history and culture. Mr. Pryce-Jones lives
in London.

THE CLOSED CIRCLE

An Interpretation of the Arabs

DAVID PRYCE-JONES

With a New Preface by the Author

IVAN R. DEE
Chicago

for Adam

www.ivanrdee.com

The Library of Congress has cataloged the 1989 Harper & Row edition as follows:
Pryce-Jones, David, 1936–
  The closed circle.
  "An Edward Burlingame book."
  1. National characteristics, Arab. 2. Civilization, Arab. 3. Arab countries—Politics and
government. 4. Arab countries—Social life and customs. I. Title.
DS36.77.P79   1989
909'. 0974927
ISBN 0-06-016047-0   88-45546

This Ivan R. Dee paperback edition carries the ISBN 978-1-56663-826-5.

To thank all those who have helped me to find my way through this subject—either on the ground or in libraries—is impossible and perhaps invidious, but I should like to single out Professor Elie Kedourie for his kindness in reading this book in manuscript.

Contents

Note to the Reader

Until the early years of this century, almost all Arabs were subjects of the Ottoman Empire, in its day the preeminent Muslim power. Islam and the sultan-caliph, as well as public and private codes of conduct, were common to the two peoples. When drawing on the Ottoman background and heritage, I have not paused each time to spell out the distinction between Turks and Arabs, a distinction often anachronistic in any case. The transformation of the Ottoman Empire into Turkey and the successor Arab states has posed questions of national identity, modernization, and secularization for Turks and Arabs alike to resolve. How the Turks have fared is the subject of Chapter 6, included not just for its own sake but because otherwise the Arab context is incomplete.

The Persians had also acquired Islam and corresponding codes and values from the Arabs. Perennial adversary of the Ottomans, the former Persian empire was another Muslim power. In the course of their transformation into present-day Iranians, Persians are in the same predicament as Turks and Arabs in having to decide what sort of adaptations to make to the world outside the House of Islam, and to what ends, and by what means. Whenever it illuminates the Arab context, I have also referred without ado to what has been said and done in Iran.

Arab names and place-names sometimes have letters represented in English by apostrophes and other grammatical signs. These affect pronunciation and have been omitted throughout on the simple ground that this book is intended for the general reader, who in thought and speech is bound to anglicize, as best may be, all such proper nouns. Following the same reasoning, a few words have always been used in the form already standardized in English: for instance, sheikh, emir, Koran or Koranic, sharia, ulema, and above all Muslim instead of Moslem or Mohametan and the like. In quotations from other authors, alternative spellings which may have been either more correct or more quaint have been brought into conformity with this simplification. Help to the general reader, it is believed, counts for more than shock to the specialist and purist.

Preface to the 2009 Edition

The Closed Circle is an attempt to come to grips with the phenomenon of violence that characterizes the Arab and Muslim world. Twenty years have passed since the book was first published, and in that time the violence has been constant in intensity and scope. The Arab and Muslim world almost without exception is dissipating its hopes and creative energies in destruction.

Just consider a selection of recent events: civil wars in Algeria and Sudan; Saddam Hussein's invasion of Kuwait in 1991 and his subsequent repression of the Shias and Kurds who rose against his rule, their corpses discovered afterward in mass graves; the Palestinian *intifada* of 2000 following the failure of the Oslo Accords and President Clinton's abortive attempt to broker peace at Camp David; the murder of Lebanese Prime Minister Rafiq Hariri and other prominent personalities in car bombings for which Syria is supposedly responsible; the war launched by Hizbollah against Israel in 2005; the takeover by Hamas of the Gaza Strip, leading to rival Palestinians brutalizing and killing each other.

No longer local or regional, the violence is also inescapably devolving upon the West in a globalized form. The al-Qaeda attack of 9/11 against landmark targets in New York and Washington was in effect a declaration of war. Such acts of terror on battlefields in the West are met on Muslim battlefields by the incursion of Western armies and open-ended occupation. Invading Iraq in 2003, a coalition of Western countries led by the United States then overthrew Saddam Hussein and his regime. In response to the attempted empowerment of the Taliban in Afghanistan and Pakistan, NATO forces have moved against them in a conflict that is already long-drawn. Muslim suicide bombers have killed Westerners in cities such as London, Madrid, Bali, and Jerusalem, and have killed far more Muslim victims in many of the principal cities in the Muslim world.

The primary source of violence, so I concluded while researching and writing this book, is the absolutism of the political order.

The Arab and Muslim Middle East exemplifies Lord Acton's re-sounding observation that absolute power corrupts absolutely. The present is all of a piece with the historic past, indeed a seamless extension of it. In the formative years after the Second World War, a few powerful personalities, mostly military men, led nationalist movements whose outcome was their own one-man rule, as though they were medieval despots. In the absence of the rule of law and the institutions to protect it, conflicting interests become tests of strength. Violence is the instrument to hand. At every level, the strong win and the weak go to the wall. When power is at stake, he who has the ambition and the capacity eliminates by any means, however brutal, whoever stands in the way. Statecraft and the daily conduct of business alike require funding and followers who form a militia or secret-police apparatus, in practice or in embryo. Those defending the possession of power, and those aspiring to it, engage in the selfsame acts of violence.

Other elements of course contribute, for instance some of the prescriptions of the Qur'an and sacred texts to which faithful Mus-lims adhere, or the cultural values of shame and honor that on the one hand lead to unrealistic and anti-social self-assertion on the part of the individual, and on the other hand shut out self-criti-cism.

The politicization of Islam might seem different, a novelty. A number of Muslim intellectuals in the past have resented what they perceive as Muslim weakness in relation to the West. Muslims, they have held, form a united community. Transcending and displacing nationalism, religious faith is what will mobilize the Muslim masses and give them the primacy and preeminence that is their due. Ayatollah Khomeini was the first to construct a political ideology out of these beliefs and emotions, and in 1979 to seize hold of Iran, a state with the resources to put this Islamism into practice.

Like any nationalist one-man ruler, Khomeini made sure to kill his opponents, whether political or sectarian, or otherwise repress and persecute them. Floggings, stonings, and judicial executions are commonplace in Iran (as also in Saudi Arabia). And it turns out that the absolutism of the man in a turban and robes is identical to the absolutism of the man in khaki uniform and a peaked cap. Osama bin Laden and al-Qaeda, Moqtada al-Sadr and his Mahdi army in Basra, Khalid Maashal of Hamas and Sheikh Nasrallah of Lebanese Hizbollah—all proclaim a version of Islamism but none-theless employ the same old absolutist tactics of enrolling them-selves as clients of paymasters and recruiting the requisite paramilitary apparatus. Islamist animus against the West also has its quotient of aggressive nationalism. Innumerable chorus masters of absolutism speak in the idiom of one typical Hamas representative who promised his listeners, "The approaching victory . . . is not limited to Palestine. You are creating the ethos of victory for all Arabs and Muslims, and Allah willing, even on the global level." Extraneous factors in the wider world allowed the Islamism of Khomeini and his imitators to take hold. The Soviet Union invaded Afghanistan. Muslim volunteers went there to resist, and were to boast in the end that they alone had defeated a superpower, as though funding and weaponry furnished by the United States in pursuit of the Cold War had nothing to do with it. Almost fortuitously, Islamism rushed into the geopolitical vacuum left by the fall of the Soviet Union.

Also in 1979, a Saudi extremist by the name of Juhayman al-Utaibi and several hundred followers seized the Great Mosque in Mecca. They claimed that the country's ruling royal family were bad Muslims and deserved to be overthrown. Most of the rank-and-file were shot dead in gun battles, and the ringleaders were captured and executed. Here is a classic illustration of the violence that even a small-time careerist is able to wreak in the absolute order. Osama bin Laden is only Juhayman writ large, richer and therefore better able to recruit others to do his will. He seems to have imagined that the 9/11 attack on the United States would easily topple the last superpower to stand in the way of Islam's universal victory, and bring down the immoral rulers of Saudi Arabia into the bargain.

In panic, the Saudi rulers responded by turning defense into aggression, allocating huge amounts of petrodollars to spread their brand of Islamism, building mosques around the world, financing thousands of madrasas or religious schools, endowing chairs in Western universities, and so on. So rival brands of Islamism are now struggling for supremacy, the one Arab and Sunni, the other Persian and Shia.

Although Sunni and Shia Islamism seem set to confront each other, they nevertheless have in common an emotional resentment against the West. They like to repeat with many a rhetorical flourish that the United States and Israel are one and the same diabolical entity, and neither can be allowed a presence in the Middle East. The overthrow of Saddam Hussein and his Sunni regime opened an unexpected opportunity for Shia Iran to extend its reach throughout the Middle East. It is not by accident that on the gallows Saddam Hussein's reported last words were, "Death to the Persians!" Sunni Arabs are the first to believe that Iran's nuclear program is not designed for peaceful purposes but in order to have a weapon that will place Shia Islamism and its ideology beyond challenge. As Libyan President Mu'ammar Gaddhafi put it, "What Iran is doing stems simply from arrogance."

9/11 obliged the United States to take a position toward Islamism in all in its manifestations. President George W. Bush expressed the view that in past decades American policy had sought to maintain stability in the Middle East, but this has only perpetuated violence. Democracy is the sole hopeful alternative, and its imposition by force of arms in Afghanistan and Iraq are experiments to replace absolutism, the like of which have never happened before in the Muslim world.

The Closed Circle was duly banned in the Arab and Muslim world. Nonetheless reviews have appeared here and there in the Arab press, mostly consisting of extensive quotations purporting to show that the book is misguided but actually presenting its arguments about the systemic and instrumental nature of violence to the public. In a bookshop in Cairo, I found copies that had been smuggled in and were being sold surreptitiously. The number of dissidents steadily grows, and many are no longer afraid to express their opinions and even to demonstrate in the street. Again to give just one example, Khalil Ali Haider is a Kuwaiti, not a household name but representative of the many thoughtful and courageous people who protest at the conditions they have to endure. In May 2008 he posted on a website entitled Middle East Transparent a passionate cry from the heart addressed to those who perpetuate violence in the name of resistance, anti-Americanism, honor, facing conspiracies, and other "false catchwords," in his phrase.

I want to say [he writes] that people in the Arab world and in the countries of the Muslim world have had enough bloodshed, violence, murder, scenes of explosions and destruction, and of wailing women, striking themselves [as a sign of mourning]. I would like to shout to the Arabs and the Muslims: O people! Enough! O [champions] of war, struggle, jihad, and honor! Enough! Life in our homeland has been destroyed. . . . We do not want to have our lives destroyed, our homes reduced to ruins, our children killed, our bridges torn down, our wives widowed, our blood spilled in your incessant wars, which you launch rashly and from which you withdraw without having learned any lessons. . . . We don't want it.

There is no mistaking the wish for peace, reform, and a civil society, since otherwise absolutism and violence must extend not just for another twenty years but into the indefinite future.

THE CLOSED CIRCLE

Wa lā yaslamu as-sharafu al-rafī'u min al-adha
hatta yurāqu 'ala jawānibihi al-damu

High honour is not safe from injury
until blood is spilt over its flanks

al-Mutanabbi (915–965)

Introduction

In the course of 1941, I reached Morocco, coming from Vichy France. I was in the care of an aunt and uncle, the latter a Spanish diplomat who had been accredited to the government of Marshal Pétain but was now posted consul in Larache. We were to live in Tangier. I well recall the blue sky, the imposing block of the hotel to which we first arrived, the extraordinary relief of being able at last to eat enough to feel full. The man who carried the trays was extremely fat and his laughter at the sight of the appeasement of hunger was itself a pleasure. At night, the room converted into an excitingly whitened tent as the mosquito net was lowered over the bed. It was not long before we moved into a house with a view over the Mediterranean to Gibraltar, a chunk of a silhouette on the skyline. Next door (but rarely in residence) was the Glaoui, the great Berber chieftain from the south, and friend of France. Soon I was discovering the local witch doctor, who dyed her hands and feet with henna, and who burnt crows' feathers in awesome magical rites. Soon I was having my scalp examined for the lice which it was assumed I would have caught as a result of associating with Arab boys of my age. I was spellbound by the long twist of hair in the center of their otherwise shaven heads, on to which, I was informed, God would grip if he should wish to raise them up to heaven. In the garden, I followed around Mohammed Driss, master of cactuses and specialist of arum lilies.

The Arab world, then, to me primarily meant safety, food, color. Other dimensions were in the distance. One day we were driving into the Petit Socco of Tangier. The big black car was pushing through the flow of the crowd, when a hooded face stooped at the window and a man spat right at the glass between him and me. As the phlegm slid down the pane, the indignant grown-ups tried to prevent me looking and asking why this had happened. Years were to pass before I acquired perspectives on these experiences of my five- and six-year-old self. Grown-up and returning to Tangier, I found the house as I remembered it. The Glaoui had long since died, humbled and disgraced on account of his friendship with the French; he and his family had been dispossessed, and Morocco was independent. I walked through familiar gates where the witch doctor had squatted on her haunches, past the graceful arum lilies, and there was Mohammed Driss, unchanged, still bent over his work. Straightaway recognizing me from afar, he arrived at a run. When he embraced me, his cheeks were wet with tears, and neither of us could speak for a while.

Morocco, like the majority of Arab states, reached its independence in the aftermath of the Second World War. For thirty years now (in some cases longer, but in the Gulf a little less), the Arab states one and all have been free to make whatever political or social arrangements they choose.

To an Englishman of my generation, this evolution appeared only right and proper. Chance alone had brought the British into the Middle East in the first place. The Industrial Revolution had been developed in England. In consequence, a new order, based upon science and technology, had spread throughout the world, and in the course of this widening process, peoples everywhere were expected to adapt, just as the English themselves had done. It was not supposed that the adaptation would be straightforward, but it was rational and therefore in time everybody would accept it.

Colonialism, we were taught, had no other justification than the establishment of this coming international order. Within itself, colonialism contained its expiry date. A stage would be reached in the spread of modern communications and education and facilities when the Arabs, like everyone else, would be on an equal footing with the colonial powers. To be sure, we heard about the strategic demands of empire, the overland route to India, the imperatives of coaling stations and ports and garrisons. These were the requirements of keeping the peace. Such is the English temperament that we tended to admire those who resisted us. Recent history had provided schoolboy idols in such figures as the Mahdi and his dervishes heroically throwing themselves at the thin red line at Omdurman, the "Mad Mullah" of Berbera, Abdul Krim defying the French and the Spanish in the Rif, Sultan el-Atrash leading the Druze revolt in Syria—all no doubt romanticized because doomed to enter our own modern world.

As in so much else, the First World War had proved the major disruption to smooth or normal evolution. The Ottoman Empire had fatally allied itself to Germany. Whether or not they liked it, the British and the French had then become responsible for the Arabs in the successor states of the defeated Ottoman Empire. Under the colonial aegis, the institutions prerequisite to independence were devised, such as a constitution, legislative assemblies, political parties, armed forces, a judiciary practicing a civil code fitting the new circumstances.

The test of the effectiveness of these institutions lay in the Arabs proclaiming that they were ready and able to manage them. Between the wars, progress had seemingly been perceptible. In Egypt, as in Iraq and Syria and north Africa, Arabs were indeed to be heard proposing self-government. These countries, it could truthfully be said, were a good deal better prepared to rule themselves than Saudi Arabia or Yemen, regions which were both so backward and out of reach that they had slipped into independence almost unseen, in the hiatus between the drawn-out decline of the Ottoman Empire and the arrival of Western influences.

Arab voices reaching Europe at the time of the Second World War and afterward were in the European idiom. Nationalism for the Arabs, these voices said, was the same as nationalism for Europeans: the right to one's own country, one's past and present, one's liberties. A slogan like "Egypt for the Egyptians" had its unarguable logic in the West. In one country after another, moreover, public movements began to oppose colonialism with rising nationalism, in demonstrations and riots. Violence of the kind in turn brought down upon itself colonial policing. This spiral was evidently futile and self-defeating. When a nationalist leader like Abd al-Rahman al-Bazzaz in Iraq declared that "The national movement is 'democratic,' 'socialist,' 'popular,' and 'cooperative,' " it seemed reasonable to assume that the angry mob on the street proved the point. No post-1945 European was likely to question the value of these adjectives nor to doubt the sense in which they were being applied. The hour of independence had arrived. The Arabs would resume the acknowledged place that was theirs in the international order. This was the received wisdom with which a twenty-year-old like myself met the Suez crisis in 1956. I was a very junior officer in a regiment standing by for operations in Egypt. I lectured my platoon on the necessity of recapturing the Suez Canal, even if this meant overthrowing Colonel Nasser, and I did not believe what I was saying. Nasser seemed to be exercising legal rights in doing what he thought was best for his country. Those few who argued that this was an incomplete understanding of Egyptian society and politics were dismissed without a hearing; they said that Nasser was not concerned with what he could do for Egypt but with what Egypt could do for him, and this cynicism could not be squared with what we had heard of Egyptian independence. In the event, the political failure of the British and the French surely defined the reality of Arab nationalism. The resignation of Prime Minister Anthony Eden, subdued and silent and ill, appeared to certify that Egypt and Egyptians had rights and values like those of any Western country.

The Suez crisis marked the end of colonialism, British as well as French. Fighting in a last gasp to hold Algeria from 1954 to 1962, the French were destroying everything for which they had worked. Peace brought relief, even if a million French people were to be dispossessed and exiled. Everywhere the independence had arrived for which Arab nationalists had been pleading and fighting. Their new men had won through, not only Nasser in Egypt and Ben Bella in Algeria but also Bourguiba in Tunisia, young military officers in Syria and their counterparts overthrowing dynastic regimes in Yemen and in Iraq, and finally Libya. "Give me five years," the new military ruler of Syria, Husni Zaim, had vaunted in 1949, "and I will make Syria as prosperous and enlightened as Switzerland." Michel Aflaq, perhaps the leading theorist of Arab nationalism, wrote an essay as early as 1940 under the title "Nationalism Is Love before Everything Else." In his opinion, nationalism was all things to all Arabs, it was spiritual and would not clash with religion, it was racial "in the sense that we hold sacred this Arab race," it spread "hope in the soul," and it was even revolutionary as well. Thanks to nationalism, then, Arabs might expect to be observant Muslims and progressive, free, and happy. How nationalism might become embodied in something more substantial than these warm emotions was not spelled out. At the same time, nobody denied that enormous wealth and power were amassing in the hands of the few while the huge majority were destitute, that injustice and corruption were general, that violence was an everyday occurrence. These blots survived from the past, it was explained by Arab and Western apologists alike, the "feudal" or colonial past, and perhaps had even been perpetuated by Westerners for purposes that were not clear but could only have been malign. The new rulers were soldiers, said to be an elite, a class of their own, eager and efficient, "in a hurry," and moreover with an ideology. Socialism was to be their modality for ushering in the great and undoubted benefits of nationalism.

What socialism might be, what institutional form it could have or what program it might adopt, whether or not it was applicable to Arab societies and traditions, and if so which, who exactly was to practice it and according to what models or theories, were practicalities not under discussion. Whenever such questions were raised, the language of debate rose loftily. Michel Aflaq again: "When I am asked to give a definition of socialism, I can say that it is not to be found in the works of Marx and Lenin. I say: socialism is the religion of life, and of its victory over death. By giving work to everyone and helping them to develop their talents it keeps the patrimony of life for life, and leaves for death only dried up flesh and scorched bones." How was this to be translated into policy? Yet an informed commentator like the French sociologist Jacques Berque, sympathetic to the Arabs as well as to socialism, could write in 1964, "Almost everyone professes adherence to Socialism in the Middle East." He could go further: "Liberalism is deeply rooted in the urban life of the Arab East."

Such assertions were taken at face value. If true, then these Arab socialists and deeply rooted urban liberals, these successful nationalists, were in a recognizable Western mold, apparently responsible politicians acting for responsible constituents. In theory, they had open horizons before them, a world to make, in which the Arab spirit of which they were indubitably proud would find its contemporary expression. Coming into their own, they ought to be the equal of Britain and France, even able to patronize them a little, forgiving them more in sorrow than in anger for any past mistakes, gratified by any past achievements. In addition, the nationalists had the unexpected good fortune to attain power at the height of the Cold War between the United States and the Soviet Union. This geopolitical confrontation of two super powers offered leverage to everyone in-between. No longer at the bidding of a single colonial power, the Arab leaders could now play off two massive blocs, both offshoots of European history but nonetheless political rivals, sidling between the one and the other in order to obtain the highest favors, up-to-date arsenals, the most preferential treatment.

Truly the moment appeared propitious. In an unprecedented transfer of resources, capital flowed in from the entire West to develop oil fields in Saudi Arabia, the Gulf, north Africa, to build airports and steel mills and public utilities and communications. Places which hitherto had known subsistence agriculture and barter trade were now the object of Five Year Plans. The most remote oasis in the Sahara or the Empty Quarter of Arabia acquired a generator for electricity. Computation is impossible but it is certain that the Arab world since 1945 has received billions upon billions of dollars in the form of aid, grants, loans, and investments from Western governments and private sectors alike, as well as goods, and free or subsidized services of a general or technical kind, not to mention the immense sums received from the sales of oil and natural gas.

Yet the Arabs did not take their due place in the modern international order. Something was still amiss. Money and opportunity and goodwill were to little or no avail. In the years since independence, the Arabs have instead been creating an order all their own, owing nothing to the structures or values of the West, nothing to nationalism or socialism, justice or equality, as generally understood.

Censuses and statistics are not reliable enough to show exactly how many Arabs there are, but the figure is between 160 and 200 million. Some fifty million of these are Egyptians, making them far and away the most substantial of Arab populations, outmatched numerically in the Middle East only by Turkey (which is not Arab). Arab annual per capita income in the early 1980s varied from $100 to $15,000, according to Samir Amin, the political economist, although the latter figure is somewhat notional, reached by dividing national oil revenue by population figures. Amin noted the more meaningful figure of $370 as average per capita consumption. Sixty percent of all Arabs are under nineteen years old and therefore have known nothing but the postindependence sociopolitical system. One and all, in a score of countries, they have grown up amid an uninterrupted sequence of wars, both national and civil, with coups and assassinations, and they are familiar with every trauma of war, massacre, terror, and sudden death.

I am no Arabist, no orientalist, no social or political scientist, or indeed specialist of any kind but only a writer concerned to make sense of what I see and hear. It was 1962 before I returned to the Middle East. What could be observed was already stark enough. Nasser and his imitators had laid violent hands on their countries. The institutions and resources of the state were entirely at their disposal, the army and the bureaucracy, the treasury, education, and above all the secret police and intelligence services. Socialism had become qualified as Arab socialism, which in practice was only absolute rule, everywhere an exercise of untempered autocratic power. Switzerland indeed! Husni Zaim had long since been murdered, and his successors had been removed and usually murdered too by rivals themselves destined to disappear in the same bloody whirlpool. In Iraq, a similar succession of rivals for power were engaged in murder and massacre. Slogans in praise of unity and progress were overwhelmingly loud but did not translate into reality. In 1958, Egypt and Syria had declared themselves to be a political unity, only to separate three years later in recrimination.

Most extraordinary was the example of Algeria, which French intellectuals and others had been heralding as the torchbearer of socialism and progress. In 1962 Ahmed Ben Bella, leader of the liberation movement against the French, had proclaimed himself premier of a Democratic and Popular Republic, transforming his supporters into a government and a National Assembly. A series of compulsory measures of confiscation then placed the state and its resources in their hands. Within a year, Ben Bella was executing as "counterrevolutionaries" colonels and others who thought that they too had claims upon these resources. Eighteen more months, and Ben Bella was overthrown and imprisoned by his colleague Houari Boumedienne. Algeria was declared an Islamic state. Algerian women, famed as freedom fighters equal or superior to their menfolk, returned to the veil. Evidently Algerian nationalism and socialism could not be what their European supporters had imagined.

It was during the Six Day War in June 1967 that the discrepancy between what was done in the Arab world and what was said about it in the West became so bewildering that I wanted to get to grips with it. As a war correspondent, I found myself in the Sinai Desert. Somewhere near Abu Agheila, I came upon Egyptian trenches. Sprawled over the sand were soldiers who had fought and died there, more like boys in their youthfulness. What political process, what self-delusion in the leadership, could have ordered such vulnerable troops into so wretched a battle? A wave of pity shook me, and then anger against Nasser.

Captured Egyptian prisoners were willing to speak of their ordeal. Mostly they knew little or nothing about Israel and had hazy or antique conceptions of the Jew. Hatred was not one of their emotions. In the usual Egyptian manner, they were gregarious and friendly. Like all soldiers after battle, they were glad to be alive. At Kantara on the east bank of the Suez Canal, they were eventually loaded into boats and ferried across in parties of fifty at a time, and this continued for several days. Supervising, a doctor was obliging them to sign a register, and one by one they pressed their thumb on to a purple ink-pad and then on to the floppy pages of a book. These were conscripts, and illiterate. On the other bank, under the sun, waited mothers in immobile and resigned lines, assembled from all over the country to learn the fate of their sons. Behind the serried mothers ran the barbed-wire fencing of an officers' enclosure in a barracks and four or five officers were reclining in striped deck chairs, scrutinizing the masses through field glasses. Why did the mothers and returning sons not storm those lounging and staring officers, and curse at them and cry for humane treatment? No less unimaginable was Nasser's announcement on Egyptian television that the war had ended in catastrophe, whereupon millions of Egyptians had crowded into the streets to weep and cheer and implore him not to resign (which he accepted without ado, in revealing contrast to Eden's earlier departure). Today I stand by the sense of moral outrage that so upset me at the time, but I have since perceived how essentially Eurocentric this reaction is. Like those who were so seized by their own concepts of nationalism and socialism that they transposed them by an act of utter imagination into an Arab world which has no place in it for anything so alien, so I too was forming judgments according to a scale of values which could not apply in those circumstances. Nonetheless, somewhere in the frozen immobility of those officers and the frightened mothers at the Canal was born the impulse to understand and interpret for myself a society in which such a scene was possible.

There have been other moments too. That same week of June 1967, Israel had captured the West Bank, the territory of the old British Mandate of Palestine which had been incorporated into Jordan in 1948 after the first round of Arab-Israeli fighting. Hearing that the inhabitants of the West Bank were fleeing in a mass exodus, I drove in haste to the Allenby Bridge, then a narrow and broken-down footbridge, and the crossing-point between the West Bank and Jordan. Sure enough, refugees were swarming down to cross over. Until then, the majority of them had not seen an Israeli soldier, let alone been caught up in the war. The fighting had been brief, and it was over. Their faces stiffly wooden and inexpressive, they passed across, whole families with small children, babies in arms, possessions tied in bundles. If precedent were a guide, they were unlikely to be returning. It seemed obvious that they must be exchanging their homes and land for a future which could only be more uncertain and hopeless. Ready to stop and talk, they were nevertheless unable to explain their motivation. Fear was not moving them. In the grip of a collective response, they were obeying codes of their own, inviting comparison to the mothers of Egypt waiting for their sons.

That evening I wandered by myself in the Jordan Valley, at Aqabat Jaber, a complex of refugee houses from which some 60,000 people had fled. Too old or ill to leave, a few very elderly people lingered in that ghostly place. Abandoned hens and goats wandered into open rooms. On house walls and doors were superstitious signs painted in bright blue to ward off the evil eye and all bad spirits, and to promote fertility. Here, it seemed clear to me, a whole community had committed a mistake which it could not help committing. Something in the culture more powerful than either self-interest or common sense had worked upon these people.

The twenty years that have elapsed since that war offer more and more examples of self-inflicted and almost suicidal injury. Victims in the Middle East have become statistics to be estimated in round numbers rather than counted. After the Six Day War, Nasser sought to recover by launching the so-called War of Attrition, consisting of artillery exchanges across the Suez Canal, during which Ismailia and Port Said were virtually destroyed and hundreds of thousands of refugees swarmed into a Cairo that could not accommodate them. A further round of Arab-Israeli fighting occurred in 1973, with an extension in 1982 when Israel invaded Lebanon. The Arab-Israeli conflict, according to a senior Egyptian diplomat in 1985, "has been the most important single factor in the shaping of history in the Middle East during the past four decades. Had it not been for that conflict, we would have been able to see in that area a much more stable order, the orientation of which would have been liberal and rational." This sentiment is repeated so often that it seems a truism, but it is superficial: plenty of other wars have broken out to defy liberalism and rationality, and they owe nothing to the presence of Israel in the Middle East. Morocco and Algeria have fought, and for years Algeria has financed a proxy, the Polisario movement, to continue its feuding against Morocco. Libya has raided across the Egyptian and Tunisian borders and interfered militarily in Sudan. Syria has twice invaded neighboring Lebanon, and once neighboring Jordan, and it has mobilized against neighboring Iraq. Iraq has threatened neighboring Kuwait and Syria and has twice sent forces into Jordan, and under Saddam Hussein has fought one of the longest wars of the century against neighboring Iran. Jordan, Yemen North and South, and Oman have experienced civil wars. In South Yemen, Ali Nasser Muhammed and Abdul Fattah Ismail, both nominally Marxists, fought in 1986 to decide which of them should rule; perhaps 13,000 people died, and fifty years of development in the port of Aden and along the shore were shelled to ruins. For over a decade now, the world has watched in impotence and horror the death-agony of Lebanon, as its component communities, Maronite, Druze, Sunni, Shia, Palestinian, have been each in turn victim and victimizer in the accelerating cycle of massacre and countermassacre. Lebanese villages, city quarters, refugee camps, refineries and hospitals, have been destroyed indiscriminately. Beirut, once one of the most agreeable of Mediterranean cities, has become a mass of rubble and no-go areas. Over the years, Beirutis have been obliged to endure nights of random bombardment, to emerge pale and shaking in the dawn. Truces are no sooner made than broken. Rooftop snipers fire at any person visible in the streets below, women and children included. Churches and mosques are the object of sacrilege, and the living, and even the corpses of the dead are regularly defiled. In a country of about 3.5 million, a tenth have become refugees, perhaps 150,000 have been killed, and countless more maimed and wounded.

Mercilessness to external enemies is matched by mercilessness to the internal population under rule. In 1982 President Hafez Assad of Syria directed his artillery upon people in his own town of Hama who threatened his absolutist hold on power, and in the ensuing carnage killed several tens of thousands. A million and a half foreign workers live in Saudi Arabia, and in 1982 some of them demanded better living conditions. Six hundred police surrounded one particular camp. The Security Forces selected three Koreans at random, put them on a truck, drove them away and executed them without any due process of justice, as Said Aburish, a Palestinian by origin, describes it in his book. Raising the matter with a Saudi prince, Aburish was told that guilt or innocence was immaterial. The example was enough. Neither Korean nor any other workers would now dare contemplate disturbing the authorities. An assassination attempt in November 1986 on the head of state in Kuwait led to the deportation of 26,898 people. Some 32,000 Tunisians were expelled from Libya and had their assets seized, for no other reason than that a proposed merger between the two countries had come to nothing.

The Palestine Liberation Organization has killed some tens of thousands of people by now, only a relatively small number of whom are Israeli or Jewish, though these include many schoolchildren and a sixty-nine-old cripple thrown in his wheelchair off a liner at sea. Hijackings and hostage-takings have been so many affronts in the Arab world and abroad, involving politicians, academics, businessmen, tourists, clergymen, journalists, who happened to provide available targets. The world has grown accustomed to pictures on television and in the newspapers of Arabs strewing corpses in their wake, throwing bodies out of aircraft on runways, driving cars loaded with high explosives to kill anyone who might happen to be within reach, placing bombs in markets and shops.

Nothing appears too inhuman. Nizar Hindawi, a Jordanian in London but in fact a Syrian agent, over a long period deceived an Irish girl into thinking that he loved her, made her pregnant, bought her a ticket to Tel Aviv and placed in her luggage a bomb to blow up in midflight, which would have killed her and his own unborn child as well as all the passengers. Having put the plan into effect, as he thought (wrongly, thanks to security measures), he returned to the Syrian embassy in London, where the ambassador masterminding this operation "greeted him warmly," in the evidence later given in the British court which sentenced Hindawi to life imprisonment.

These two typical newspaper items speak for themselves, the first on the conduct of Syrian soldiers in Lebanon, the second a report from Iraq.

In Tripoli on December 18, Syrian soldiers arrested a leader of the fundamentalist Islamic Unification Movement, also known as the Tawheed. All its members are Sunni Muslims. In response Tawheed killed 15 Syrians. That night members of the pro-Syrian Arab Democratic, Lebanese Communist, Baath and National Syrian Socialist parties cordoned off the suburbs of Tabbaneh. Syrian intelligence officers then named more than 200 people for summary execution. All were shot in the head. The massacre is taken to be a warning to other groups that Syria rules in Lebanon.

Fifty-seven boxes were recently returned to the Kurdish city of Sulaimaniya in Zeit trucks—large Russian military vehicles—by the Iraqi government authorities. Each box contained a dead child, eyes gouged out and ashen white, apparently drained of blood. The families were not given their children, were forced to accept a communal grave and then had to pay 150 dinars for the burial.

The fifty-seven children were among several hundred taken hostage by their own government in order to bring the rebellious Kurdish minority into line by means of this atrocity.

Public executions are frequent in Syria and Iraq, and criminals also suffer amputation in Saudi Arabia, Libya, Sudan, and Iran. Between 1983 and 1985, according to a newspaper report, religious courts in Sudan approved over a hundred amputations, sometimes for petty theft, and thousands of floggings, even an unconfirmed crucifixion. A doctor, Kamal Zaki Mostapha, apparently British-trained, is quoted as saying that he was preparing executioners for this task, teaching them how to dislocate the wrist from the forearm. "There was never any cutting of the bone. I attended the first seven or eight cases and when I was satisfied with the standard of chopping, I didn't go back." In Saudi Arabia, offenders are decapitated or have a limb amputated in public on a Friday, the day of prayer. Now and again, a shocked Westerner describes in the press how during his stay in Saudi Arabia he has stumbled upon such a sight, witnessed by a large crowd. *Death of a Princess* was a film shown on British television in 1982 about the execution of Mishal, a young Saudi princess whose offense was to wish to live abroad with a young man of her choice. The Saudi regime admitted that the execution had occurred for the reasons given, but the mere fact of screening this film led to diplomatic tension and, of all paradoxical things, an apology to the Saudis from the British foreign minister of the day. In Libya, the execution of offenders has been lengthily shown on television. In one instance, Muammar Gaddhafi, who is responsible, offered the explanation that those hanged were "terrorist groups," although none of them had perpetrated any attack, and none had been before a court of law. Whether a country declares itself secular or religious has less bearing on the level of cruelty than on the methods of its implementation.

A single news item can sometimes give a more telling insight than any number of frightening generalities.

Kuwait's State Security Court is to put on trial Mohammad Ahmed Al Kandari, on charges of promoting baseless news and deceptive rumours of the country's internal situation in other countries.

The inference is that on some journey this man was overheard, denounced and then arrested on his return home, to be brought before a special court with plenary powers, where he will be judged all the more harshly if what he is alleged to have said happens to be true. Nothing more is known of the man, nor is it likely ever to be; nobody has to account for the likes of him.

In the years of independence, the Arabs have so far made no inventions or discoveries in the sciences or the arts, no contribution to medicine or philosophy. Among those millions of quick and gifted people of individualistic outlook, and heirs to one of the world's civilizations, hardly a single Arab has earned an international reputation except as the beneficiary of his country's politics or his country's oil extraction. Sucking in Western goods out of all proportion to their capacity to absorb them, the Arabs are returning only oil, the Middle East's commodity par excellence. Oil alone now permits Arabs to feed themselves. In 1985 the Arab states imported foodstuffs to the value of $22.5 billion. At a conference held in Abu Dhabi in February 1986, Saif Ali Al-Jarwan, the Minister of Economy and Trade in the Emirates of the Gulf, explained that 60 percent of Arab food was now imported. As he put it, "This means that we have to import six out of ten loaves of bread from abroad."

Instead of construction, destruction; instead of creativity, wastefulness; instead of a body politic, atrocities. The Moroccan intellectual, Abdallah Laroui, has summed up what ought to have been the new and positive era of independence as "The long winter of the Arabs." This self-critical tone is now occasionally to be heard, at least among intellectuals. The Algerian writer Malek Bennabi entitled a section of his book on contemporary events, "The Chaos of the Modern Muslim World." The prominent Palestinian novelist, Jabra Ibrahim Jabra, wrote, "From the Arab Gulf to the Atlantic Ocean I heard a cry, I heard weeping and the sound of sticks and plastic hoses. Capitals and casbahs, the secret police was everywhere, on mountain tops and in the valleys below; men in neat civilian suits walking to and fro like a thousand shuttles on a thousand looms, hauling off to the centres of darkness people by the tens and hundreds." In *The Arab Predicament,* a sustained attempt at a truthful reckoning of these Middle East realities, Fouad Ajami, originally a Lebanese Shia, called the material of his book "a chronicle of illusions and despair, of politics repeatedly degenerating into bloodletting."

An Iraqi writer in exile, Khalid Kishtainy, writing to an English newspaper, offered one explanation for this dereliction. Even from a London address, it took courage to say openly in print that he could see from the latest news of horrors in Lebanon that the Arabs have given their leaders and politicians the valid title "sons of a bitch," and he concluded, "That is, Sir, what they are." The rulers, then, are alone to blame for whatever is done. But is it likely that "sons of a bitch" have been thrown up in every Arab country simultaneously but coincidentally, without exception? To ascribe everything to bad character in this way begs the further question of what kind of people the Arabs must be first to throw up and then to tolerate as their leaders such "sons of a bitch." If it were so simple, the good-hearted many could easily overcome the degenerate handful.

Another explanation has resonated in the speeches of Nasser and his colleagues and imitators over the Arab world. To them, "imperialism" has been the reason why their societies were making so little headway. Blame was directed away from themselves on to "imperialism." In this proposed "imperialism," Arab self-esteem vanishes and the relations of Arabs with the rest of the world at large are twisted and poisoned. There was no external reference for the idea. Neither British nor French garrisons, nor even stores, had been permitted to remain in any Arab country, as though their mere presence was conducive to backwardness. Yet at the same time, postwar Germany and Japan contained foreign bases with large numbers of foreign troops, and both countries were spectacularly recovering from a wartime devastation on a scale fortunately never experienced anywhere in the Middle East. In this usage, "imperialism" derived from the Cold War and was promoted and borrowed from the Soviet Union as a code word for the United States (a country not notably impeded from progressing by its own colonial past). The American presence in the Middle East was associated almost entirely with the extraction of oil for which the market price was negotiated and paid, with aid and development projects, and with its support for Israel. How this translated into "imperialism" was never explained in the speeches of Nasser and his followers. "Imperialism" was something other, happening like a fate, blind, occult, often to be detected in strange euphemisms like "external forces" or "vested interests." This was a shorthand for some psychological state of mind akin to an inferiority complex.

For me, it was soon evident that words like "socialism," "democracy," and "revolution" had no meaningful application to Arab societies but were serving a purpose as metaphors for an absolute rule that could not be declared openly as such. Merely mystifying, these metaphors were for export only. It was abroad, in Western conferences and congresses, in learned journals and in fashionable reportage by no means always or necessarily Marxist, that Arab socialism and revolution thrived. The realization that "imperialism" was another such metaphor, in this case for the failure or evanescence of Arab nationalism, came more slowly. I resisted the conclusion because it was painful to accept that Britain and France had so misconceived the nature and intent of Arab nationalism. Supposing themselves to be acceding to natural and popular demands, Britain and France had actually handed over whole populations to the tyranny of the ambitious few among them.

For at least a generation, "imperialism" as a metaphor hid the extent to which nationalism lacked political or social foundations in reality. Nationalism, as rhapsodized by Aflaq and his like and manipulated with supreme skill by Nasser and others, served to legitimize aspiring one-man rulers in their bid for power. Listening, approving, conceding, the colonial powers released themselves from their responsibilities to the Arab masses—those masses, who according to the American social scientist Morroe

Berger, "really believe in their inalienable right to be exploited by people of their own nationality." Perhaps there was nobody in the ruling circles of the West who sympathized sufficiently with the Arab masses to foresee what would happen to them. Frantz Fanon, the Marxist agitator from the West Indies who supported the Algerian independence movement, will hardly be accused of residual colonialist urges, but he was quick to detect cynicism in the attitude of his opponents. "In plain words, the colonial power says: 'Since you want independence, take it and starve.' " A far better writer and a more rounded personality than Fanon, the Algerian Mouloud Feraoun, felt that his countrymen were being dismissed to "manage as best they can."

Here speaks a Moroccan, a small street trader, Al-Hajj Muhammad, voicing disappointments common to Arabs who were his contemporaries:

> In those days, we thought that once we obtained independence everything would be wonderful. We thought we Muslims would live the way Christians live, with villas, cars, and servants. But now we are no better off than we were under the Christians. Now the Fassis [men from the city of Fez who led the nationalist movement] rule as the Christians used to. *They* have villas, cars, and servants. But those of us who toil for a mouthful of bread have gained nothing since independence.

Quite what the relationship should be between Arabs and modern civilization, as epitomized in villas and cars, is hard if not impossible to define, but the ending of colonial rule could do nothing to clarify or rationalize it. If anything, the Arabs were left more haplessly than before to make what they could of this civilization. Many even began to turn their backs on their own countries. Europe today has between six and eight million Muslim immigrants, the majority from North Africa. Millions more ask little better for themselves than to abandon their own societies for a European one, so much so that Sweden, Denmark, West Germany, and Switzerland are among countries legislating against further Arab or Iranian immigration.

The passage of the years and the unfolding of the wars between the newly independent states has revealed how misleading it was to suppose that the violences of the Arab world were momentary maladjustments, as it were the teething troubles of nationalism. To me as to many, the Middle East for a while seemed in anarchy; here was the war of every man against the other, in which the frightening phrase of Thomas Hobbes had come true, and life was "poor, nasty, brutish and short." Life for the Arabs is certainly that, but it is also displaying a pattern, much more fundamental, recurrent, rooted in the past.

"For all the indisputable diversity, the remarkable thing is the extent to which Muslim societies resemble each other," Ernest Gellner has observed. "One has the feeling that the same and limited pack of cards has been dealt." Here again, slogans of "imperialism" widened the discrepancy between what was done in the Arab world and what was said about it, creating artificial distinctions where actually none existed. Like Algeria, Egypt since Nasser, Iraq since 1958, Syria, Sudan, North Yemen and South Yemen are nominally republics, nominally "progressive." Jordan and Morocco, Oman, Qatar and the United Arab Emirates, Bahrain, Kuwait and Saudi Arabia have dynastic ruling families and are nominally "conservative." All have had varied historical experiences and yet now common to all is the rule of a single power holder around whose ambitions the state has been arranged. Set up by Muslims for Muslims, every Arab state is explicitly Islamic in confession. Religious and ethnic minorities have been persecuted everywhere. Nowhere is there participation in the political process corresponding to any conception of representative democracy. No parliament or assembly except by appointment of the power holder, no freedom of expression throughout rigidly state-controlled media, no opinion polls, nothing except a riot to determine what public opinion might be. Nowhere in the Arab world is there security guaranteed under the law for persons and property. The same is true for non-Arab and Shia Iran, where the difference between the rule of the late Shah and his successor Ayatollah Khomeini may be posed as a question of who is persecuting whom and according to what principle. Lebanon, which until 1975 had maintained participatory institutions, has also become a truly Hobbesian example of social and political disintegration.

Time after time, another bout of intra-Arab fighting produces a flurry of further metaphors about socialism and revolution, which fade out as yet another absolute ruler takes power exactly as his predecessor had done. National interests are not at stake. Territorial adjustments do not follow. In all the many wars of the Middle East, Israel alone has gained on the ground, notably in 1967. Yet the Sinai Desert, far the largest of the captured territories, was returned by Israel to Egypt after the Camp David settlement of 1977. Other captured parts may be restored to Syria and Jordan in the event of peace being extended. Otherwise no state boundary in the Middle East has changed during the period of Arab independence.

To a Westerner, the conclusion that political instability and violence are all of a piece with continuity is almost too paradoxical to be credited, in too great a conflict with the obvious assumption that orderly politics can be produced only by an orderly society. It is difficult for a Westerner to jettison every one of his deceptive slogan-metaphors as worthless, to make the imaginative leap of abandoning his universe and his institutions, and so enter the Arab collectivity of tribe and kin and religious affiliation.

Familiar organizing principles are missing. Does the Arab have an Oedipus complex, for instance, when his concepts of father and mother are not those postulated by Freud? Can he belong to a class, be a "bourgeois" or a "proletarian" in Marx's layered design, when the industrial and occupational base hardly exists for such categorization? It is merely fanciful for Gaddhafi to refer to illiterate desert tribesmen in preindustrial Libya as "workers." North Yemen is a country in which the tribesmen feel no inclination even to license their vehicles and the government has no means to compel them to do so, yet an official brochure states that "the Governmental System is republican, Democratic and cooperative." Iraq, a country, as despotic as any in the world, is described in a comparable official booklet as "a people's democratic republic."

Eurocentricity, in other words the application of Western idioms and values to an Arab context, is a falsification, an attempt at apologetics. Similarly, "right-wing" and "left-wing," originally parliamentary expressions, relate to the central democratic issue of what degree of control over the individual the state has or ought to have. If there is no elected parliament, and absolute rule submerges state and individual alike, the terms are notional. Nonetheless, commentators habitually apply them to Arab rulers and even groups, for example alleging that Maronites in Lebanon are "right-wing," or Shia and Palestinians are "left-wing," when the latter fight among themselves and all alike are engaged in one and the same self-defense for survival as a group. "Puritan," a Christian term of strictly limited application, is invariably applied to the Saudis, followed in the next breath by evocation of their lavishness, their sexual and other extravagances and surreptitious drinking. "Fundamentalist," that Western phrase with its suggestion of a scale for intensity of religious belief, is no less inappropriate to countries in which secularism has as yet no institutional form. Those who fit the Arabs into Western organizing principles and vocabularies ignore or misrepresent the quite other principles upon which the Arabs in fact organize. This condescension is most probably unconscious and unintentional. In the Eurocentric view, it is supposedly to their credit that the Arabs are becoming like Westerners, that they are "modernizing," as though Western standards in these matters were as positive as they are universal. By now, many Arabs have been educated in the West, where they too have learned the techniques for judging themselves and their background in Eurocentric perspectives. Those who adopt these organizing principles and vocabularies place themselves in an awkward and uncomfortable position of implicitly criticizing their own societies insofar as these are not yet Westernized. A peculiar alienation arises, compounded of complacency at mastering these techniques and the self-rejection they seem to imply. Not surprisingly, it becomes an escape from self-hatred to swing to Islamocentric emotions, to deny and to misrepresent Western values, to pretend that Muslims inhabit one world and Christians quite another, to lose any embarrassing comparisons of the cultures in apologetic metaphors of "imperialism."

Far from creating approximations of Western social and political norms, the Arab order in its post-1945 independence has been reverting to basic tribal and kinship structures, with their supportive group values, as they were in precolonial days—with hindsight, perhaps it was only natural that this should have been so, a defiant assertion of that special and persistent sociopolitical system which in the last resort makes them Arabs. To the limited extent that Arab power holders over the last thirty years tried to alter old structures and values and to introduce participatory institutions, they all failed. On the contrary, the older structures and values absorbed and so denatured "nationalism," "socialism," and "revolution."

Taken at face value, nationalist or revolutionary rhetoric may lead Westerners to bizarre and ignorant conclusions. Where Arabs are actually asserting their identity as Arabs, in the Eurocentric view they are backward; where they are adjusting relationships among themselves in the customary manner, they seem violent; where they are justifying themselves and their values, they seem irrational. What is normal procedure within the system of tribe and religious affiliation looks to those outside it like evidence of bad or vicious character. To suppose that the Middle East today is in a state of special and almost inexplicable turbulence, that the wars of the Arabs are somehow Western-induced, and in any case a general threat to the peace of the world, is a Eurocentric misreading of the nature of these conflicts. Tribes and religions do not have institutional mechanisms for compromise and mediation. Instead they resort to war in a perpetual process of adjudicating issues outstanding between them. What might look like volatility or willful self-damage is customary, normal on its own terms. But to describe the continuing cruelty of custom as "progress" is truly to patronize the Arab masses who still have no say in deciding their fate.

1

Tribal Society and Its Legacy

Tribal society is a closed order. Those within the tribe are deemed to be relations by blood, a family, by virtue of which they are to be protected and secured; those outside are strangers, and therefore suspected to be enemies. Blood-relationship provides the closest social binding, greatly simplifying the common purpose. Aggrandizement and perpetuation of the tribe are ends requiring no justification. Living in proximity, tribal members have no choice but to share resources more or less equitably.

As the tribe multiplies, so more and more families develop within it over a period of time. The common identity and descent are questioned when one family makes a demand of another, over some changing circumstance, to do with land or grazing or water or women. Vital issues of the sort contain potential for quarrels. The danger is at once perceptible. Every person interferes as by right in the affairs of every other person. Spokesmen for the parties involved put their cases and a carefully delineated web of shifting alliances and intrigues builds up, leading to adjudication through a procedure of protracted argument and lobbying by the elder and more experienced men of the tribe.

Disputes arising between neighboring tribes follow the same lines, but of course are more fraught as more is at stake. As a kinship or tribal group disputes an issue with outsiders, gain and loss has to be calculated with the greatest care. It is a zero-sum affair. Pursuit of ambition by one family or tribe is necessarily loss and restriction to another. Delicate and long-drawn arbitration may be necessary to avoid unacceptable loss to one side, over-weening gain to the other. Once passions have been aroused, arbitration by elders may not have the power to compel obedience. Failure threatens tribal identity. The response will be violent and immediate. Indeed, violence is an essential ingredient in the pro-cess of decision making, it is proof of serious intention, of the will to proceed in the group interest, no matter what the rights and wrongs. In tribal society, violence is therefore a mechanism of social control. The only way to discover a shift in the balance of forces is to test it. Tribal history tends to be a series of skirmishes in which offense and defense are inextricable. Should life be lost, the tribe is diminished and must exact retribution. The blood feud begins. The feud is not simply primitive barbarism, as Gellner explains, but also a mediating process "by which groups constrain each other to constrain their own members, by wreaking ven-geance indiscriminately, anonymously, on *any* members of the rival group."

Since violence is a necessary instrument in these processes, hate is rapidly inflamed but just as rapidly extinguished once its purpose has been achieved. Mental reservation is prudent, as today's enemy may easily transform into tomorrow's ally against some third party. One authority, Black-Michaud, emphasizes the extent to which feuding is politics rather than war. "Once victory has been achieved, the identity of the adversary may be forgotten: the victory as such is more often exploited than the defeat of a given player. Similarly, the reason for indulging in feuding rela-tions is not so much the desire to inflict a loss on a given section, as to use this victory to enhance individual and group prestige within the home community and in the eyes of the world. The prestige acquired is a foremost ingredient of leadership."

Isabel Burton, wife of the explorer, gives an account of the impulsiveness of feuding and then its strict procedural logic, in this case in the Syrian village of Zebedani a hundred years ago. Two families were feuding, and Hasan, a twenty-two-year-old, belonged to one of them. Seeing Mrs. Burton riding through the village one day, he said, "What fools you Fellahin [peasants] are to salute this Christian woman; I will show you how to treat her." The other villagers tried to appease him and to apologize to Mrs. Burton for the insult. Hasan fired his gun, and the bullet hit a wall behind Mrs. Burton's head. She complained to the authorities, and Turkish soldiers arrived to arrest Hasan and eleven members of his family.

Mrs. Burton then decided to play the role of the elder and reconcile the two families. She summed up:

Hasan and I also became great friends. After doctoring him for weak eyes, I asked, "What made you want to hurt me, O Hasan?" He replied, "I don't know—the devil entered my heart; the excitement of all that was going on made me want to begin a quarrel, and I was mad to see you always with the Sheikhs and never noticing us, and Kasim [an unruly relation] set me on, but since I have got to know you I could kill myself for it."

This is how an Egyptian woman, Om Naeema, describes her village in Upper Egypt today.

There are many ways in which these feuds are begun, but one major source of violence is jealousy. People think, "How can your son walk around well dressed and well fed," for example, "and mine go hungry while yours mocks or insults him?" Or they might think, "How can your field be more resplendent and prosperous than mine?" The good fortune of one man causes ill feeling in another.

A young man might come asking to marry another's daughter, for example, and the parents will choose the richer of the two suitors. The poorer one will be vexed and say to himself, "If I had been richer or better, they would have chosen me." In his anger at being rejected, he might sneak into the field belonging to the girl's father and pull up the man's plants. He might poison the man's buffalo. Anything is possible. The fiancé of the bride would then intervene, now being a part of that family, and another feud will begin. That's the villagers for you.

In 1975 a dispute began in a café in Zahleh, in Lebanon.

A Syrian tried to throw a bomb at another man and was either shot dead by a third party before he managed to throw it, or was killed when the bomb exploded in his own hand. Three other men, who were accompanying the Syrian, were wounded as a result of the explosion. Two Christians from Zahleh—one of whom had shot at the Syrian—were arrested by the Lebanese Security authorities, who proceeded to investigate the incident. Two days later, the Christians of Zahleh staged a demonstration, blocking the main roads and demanding the release of the two arrested men. The authorities complied. . . . Thereupon the Shiites living in the suburbs of Zahleh, backed by Palestinian commandos, took up arms against the Christians of the town, on the grounds that some of the men wounded in the café incident were Shiites from the locality and that the Syrian who was killed was in some way their political associate. The two sides fired at one another with heavy machine guns and rockets, and the fighting continued for several days.

Sectarian zeal, which more profoundly here is social identity, drove the participants in these affrays to separate into their various family, tribal, or religious groups. However strong their individuality, nonetheless group impulses proved stronger. Anyone within such a group cannot judge it objectively, let alone critically, and cannot condemn what might be errors or crimes committed by his group members. He may fall out with them and be ostracized, or choose to live elsewhere through marriage or job prospects, but it is still virtually unknown for such a man to take any distance from his background. Neither Hasan in Mrs. Burton's incident, nor Om Naeema and her villagers, nor the fighters of Zahleh are acculturated to enlarge their identities into any wider form of citizenship.

The strengths of tribal society are inseparable from the weaknesses. This is particularly evident in the matter of leadership, where tribalism is completely at the mercy of its lack of organizing principle other than custom. Ruthless and cruel and ambitious men exist everywhere, of course, and societies everywhere are judged by the success with which they restrain those who have these characteristics. In tribal society, all male members are theoretically equal and capable of exercising authority. Those who esteem themselves to be likely leaders must therefore set about establishing their credentials, acquiring standing and respect, heroic enough to gather supporters but also frightening enough to deter critics. Ruthlessness and cruelty come into their own; ambition is a prerequisite for reward. Someone will duly emerge beyond question as superior, perhaps exclusively through the exercise of these characteristics. Should tribal ceremony be involved in any form of recognition, this man's position as leader or sheikh will have been accepted beforehand. A tribal meeting would not be for electoral purposes but for certification. In due course, the sheikh will grow old, his sons will hope to succeed, and each of them will challenge the other, being themselves challenged by others with similar aspirations. Leadership itself acquires the characteristics of feuding, with implicit violence. Each aspirant to power holding must make unmistakably clear his determination to win, if need be by eliminating those in his way.

In this manner, there develops a dialectic which determines the history and the politics of the group. Challenge leads to power, power invites challenge. This power-challenge dialectic in itself is stable, its practice most unstable. Theoretically each power holder embodies the wishes of his group and to that extent is endorsed by it. Should such endorsement be withheld for any reason, then the power holder is diminished and the possible challenger may emerge. From the outset, this can only be a test of strength, with a winner and a loser. In the search for endorsement, the power holder will also mount challenges to other power holders within reach, his equals in the region, in the hopes that victory over them will substantiate his own position in the eyes of his group. Power challenging by its nature has offensive and defensive aspects. Whoever mounts a challenge upon "rights," "just claims," "hereditary territory," will be met by their reversal into "aggression," "arrogance," "expansionism." In the absence of institutional checks, this pattern runs from top to bottom. What the social scientist Andrea B. Rugh wrote in the context of Egypt has general political validity throughout the Arab world:

> The fabric of life requires that people constantly are involved in assessing their relationships with others, in strengthening some, in developing others, in shoring up reciprocal obligations, in letting some lapse, in mobilising others, and in other ways keeping their networks operational. Conflicts are as much a way of activating and assessing relationships as are pleasant exchanges.

In a constitutional democracy, those elected to office are obviously as prone as everyone else to follow misconceived policies, to make miscalculations and self-serving errors; but over a period of time this will become evident and even scandalous, and representative institutions will oblige them to pay the price of losing an election and therefore office. No such correction is possible for the Arab power holder or challenger, whose miscalculations and self-serving errors must be worked through to the bitter end, which more often than not is his death.

This drive to violence has a constantly degrading effect upon power holder and challenger alike. No matter what his hopes and idealism, the moment a would-be challenger embarks upon his course of action, he is constrained. Eliminating rivals as he rises, he realizes what the price of failure must be. The stakes increase until failure to deal decisively with a rival or with a power holder becomes tantamount to his own death warrant. Transforming himself into a successful power holder, he has no choice, if he is to survive, but to put into practice the very methods of his predecessor. In order to justify what otherwise would seem naked careerism, group values must then be formulated. Doctrine is a prime careerist tool, to be sharpened, altered, dispensed with, and reversed according to the requirements of mounting challenges or of strengthening defenses.

A member of the Moroccan elite has described with candor how doctrine must be accommodated to the rewards of power, and what he says about his own country is also valid throughout the Arab order.

We are all members of a big family; perhaps there are two hundred of us. Some call themselves progressives, UNFPistes, others Istiqlalis [respectively the anti-monarchist opposition and nationalist parties], others monarchists. But we all know one another, and one shouldn't take our public name-calling very seriously. Today we need support from the U.S., so the monarchists are in power. But if our relations with France sour even more, and the U.S. does not aid us, all we have to do is bring in a UNFP or UMT government and start knocking on the door of Russia or China.

In unadulterated form, tribal life today is to be found only in remoter parts of the Arab world, especially in Arabia. Arabs have of course formed into states, each with its flag, its passport, its army, its airline, its postage stamps, and other appurtenances of sovereignty. Surviving as a tribal legacy down the centuries, the power-challenge dialectic has everywhere perpetuated absolute and despotic rule, preventing the evolution of those pluralist institutions that alone allow people to participate in the processes of the state and so to identify with it, making of it a living reality.

The further effect of the power-challenge dialectic is to have left intact the family as the basic social building block of the Arab world, and that too is a tribal legacy. Families, their loyalties and affections, are the same the whole world over. The successful state generates larger loyalties and affections to which the entire society willingly subscribes. Arab power holders and challengers alike can hope to rely only upon their own families, to which they seek to associate in ever-widening circles others of their kin and of their religious confession.

Among Arabs, in the words of Pierre Bourdieu,

The family is the alpha and omega of the whole system: the primary group and structural model for any possible grouping, it is the indissoluble atom of society which assigns and assures to each of its members his place, his function, his very reason for existence and, to a certain degree, his existence itself.

Commenting on the persistence of basic modes of tribal ties in family relations, Hisham Sharabi and Mukhtar Ani find that every child grows up feeling that his prime responsibility is not toward society but toward his family. "When faced with conflicting social and family demands, the individual finds it easier to reconcile the two by doing his duty towards his family." Society merely represents "the external world of strife where one makes one's career." As the individual steps out into that external world, he feels insecure: "He feels cheated and pushed around and discovers that if he is not aggressive, he will be trampled upon. His experience of the outside world repels him, and he gravitates to the haven of the family." This, Sharabi and Ani conclude, "keeps him from going over to the side of society."

What remains remarkable is the conformity with which throughout Arab history the power-challenge dialectic has absorbed external influences that might have threatened it, dealing with them on its own terms, apparently resistant to reform and preserving intact the ancient tribal structure. Islam was originally such a threat. Teaching that men were equal before God, Islam was a creed carrying reformist implications for tribalism. To join the community of the faithful, a man had only to bear witness to God, to pray as ordained, to give alms and to fast for the prescribed month, and to make a pilgrimage to Mecca. Inspiring this creed in the seventh century A.D., the Prophet Muhammad was both religious leader and temporal power holder, rising to supremacy from a position of humble birth in an example of unparalleled tribal power challenging. At the time of the Prophet's revelation of Islam, Arab tribes were either pagan or in syncretistic contact with Judaism and Christianity. The welding of the community of Islam released human energies which had been hitherto suppressed in scattered tribalism. The impact spread in conquests over an area ultimately extending from the Iberian peninsula to Persia, India, and what is now Soviet Asia. Muslims believed themselves to be enlarging the community of the faithful until it covered the earth, and observing the Holy Law. No part of the House of Islam, as conquered territory was called, could be surrendered. As opportunity arose, the House of War, where unbelievers lived, would fall to the faithful. Here was a doctrine of justification. Most of the subdued peoples accepted Islam, and the rest were either put to the sword or became minorities tolerated on condition that they acknowledged Muslim supremacy and paid discriminatory taxes. On those terms, the Eastern Christian churches and the Jews of the Middle East survived. Other non-Arab indigenous people, such as the Berbers of north Africa and the Kurds across what is now the Iraq-Iran border and in southern Turkey, converted to Islam but retained ethnic particularities.

Absence of an agreed institutionalized method for establishing succession perpetuates tribal power challenging, and the Prophet had not resolved that dilemma by the time of his death. The Prophet left only a daughter as family heir. Leadership of the community might pass through her and her descent, or through the Prophet's companions who were best qualified. A majority, known as Sunni, preferred election. A minority, known as Shia, preferred the principle of heredity, devolving through Ali, the cousin and husband of the Prophet's daughter, and those descendants of his specifically designated for the succession by their own immediate predecessor. Disputed authority made for the fragmentation of Islam. Three of Muhammad's four immediate successors, known as caliphs, were murdered. Turning upon legitimacy, the quarrel between Sunni and Shia became irreconcilable. Through the centuries, Muslims have tended to divide further into sects, each legitimized in its own eyes by other lines of descent. Where there ought to have been one undisputed divinely directed leader, there were instead caliphs, first in Damascus, then in Baghdad, themselves challenged by rivals, descending in time into a variety of local power holders, sultans, emirs, kings, and finally presidents. Splitting into Sunni and Shia, Islam had provided doctrines for power holders to use in challenges against one another. In either case an aspiring ruler might appeal for support to those whom he had reason to believe to be his own kind. To this day, a man takes it for granted that his birth as a Sunni or a Shia, or into some other sect or grouping, lays an obligation upon him greater than any he might have as a member of his state. The Islamic vision of equality was thus shattered.

The Islamic vision of justice also failed to be translated into practice from its inception. Islam, even in its early and self-absorbed upsurge, could hardly fail to follow the example and the influences of surrounding empires, most notably the Sassanids and the Byzantines. The tradition of oriental despotism was transmitted from these societies. Without exception, the caliphs and their heirs were oriental despots who demanded from their subjects the most absolute obedience, military service, and taxation enforced at sword point. The ruler ordained as he saw fit, his subjects complied, no other relationship was entertained, and this entailed a passivity among the masses whose historic shadow overcasts the present. No institution could evolve either for purposes of reshaping the tribal order or to realize Islamic ideals. In the words of the historian Bernard Lewis, "There are no parliaments or representative assemblies of any kind, no councils or communes, no chambers of nobility or estates, no municipalities in the history of Islam; nothing but the sovereign power, to which the subject owed complete and unwavering obedience as a religious duty imposed by the Holy Law." For the last thousand years, then, "the political thinking of Islam has been dominated by such maxims as 'tyranny is better than anarchy. . .'"

Another wider community to which the Arabs as a whole have belonged was the Ottoman Empire. Early in the sixteenth century, the Ottoman Turks conquered the Mameluke power holders of Egypt and Syria and then subjected what is now Iraq and Arabia, as well as the southern Mediterranean shore up to Algiers. A nomadic warrior people from Asia, converted from Shamanism to Islam, the Turks adopted from the Arabs some particulars such as their script and their language, though the latter only for purposes of worship. As peoples, Arabs and Turks were to remain separate and distinct within the empire.

At the farthest reach of the Arab world, Morocco under its sultan escaped Ottoman rule. Morocco at the time was a power vigorous enough to initiate its own conquests. A Moroccan army, complete with artillery, undertook the feat of crossing the Sahara to overthrow empires such as the Songhai deep in Africa. Persia, under the Safavid rulers (1500–1722), also resisted the Ottomans. The Safavids had adopted Shia doctrines, campaigning to impose them upon the neighboring Arabs of Baghdad and then on the Turks. Turks and Arabs were Sunni in the huge majority. Here were two oriental despotisms championing two different creeds, both Islamic. Once neither side proved able to subjugate the other, the doctrinal divide became embodied on the ground in the respective frontiers of Turkey and Persia, with Iraq awkwardly strad-dled between Sunni and Shia. With the passage of time, this divide also served to mark an ethnic frontier. In general, the Ottoman Turks left their subject peoples as they found them. Obedience was the important characteristic of citizen-ship. The Ottomans had no interest in preserving (or destroying) the identity of any group under their rule—"identity" itself in the context is an anachronism. They resolved the inherent problem of the treatment of conquered minorities by the so-called *millet* sys-tem, whereby each religion was deemed to constitute a social entity in itself, entitled to its own religious head or authority, worship-ping according to its rites, tolerated in return for the payment of taxes, including one in lieu of military service. Tax inducements to convert to Islam had little effect. Seventeen *millets* were eventually recognized within the empire. Muslims, among whom the Arabs were naturally included, were exempt from such minority taxation and the pressures that went with it, able to enroll in the army and state bureaucracy and to rise in a way prohibited to non-Muslims, such as Christians or Jews. Ottoman rule thus preserved Arab identity, stabilizing and perpetuating, however unwittingly, the tribal order and its customs.

Those who have primary tribal or religious allegiances implic-itly believe in the virtues of their own group and defensively flatter themselves, while tending to ascribe ill to those in other group-ings, whom they denigrate as an offensive measure. Protectiveness of this kind is one of the demands of identity. Isabel Burton ob-served a century ago:

They hate one another. The Sunnis excommunicate the Shia and both hate the Druzes; all detest the Ansariyyehs [better known as Alawis, who are Muslim schismatics in Syria, at that time disowned even by the Shia]; the Maronites do not love anybody but themselves, and are duly abhorred by all; the Greek Orthodox abominate the Greek Catholics and the Latins; all despise the Jews.

A hundred years later, a British colonial administrator could write of the tribes in the interior of Aden, "But they will remain Saar and Rashid and Mahra, and hate each other to the end of time."

In *Farewell to Arabia,* the journalist David Holden gave this sum-mary of contemporary local tribalism:

The Ruler of Bahrain, for instance, is not on speaking terms with the Ruler of Qatar, to part of whose territory he maintains an ancient family claim; while the Ruler of Qatar has prudently married a daughter of Sheikh Rashid of Dubai, to the disgust of Sheikh Shakhbut, who happens to be a neighbour of both of them. Sheikh Rashid dislikes Sheikh Shakhbut, the Ruler of Sharjah is suspicious of Sheikh Rashid, and the Sheikhs of Ajman, Fujairah, Ras al Khaima and Umm al Qawain, being the rulers of the four smallest and poorest territories of the lot, are steeped in suspicion of practically everybody.

Sheikh Hafiz Wahba, originally from Egypt but for years the Saudi ambassador in London, in speaking of Arabia described how tribal preconceptions stretch to human qualities.

Kuwaitis think the people of Bahrain stupid, or at best simple, and Bahrain women do acknowledge those of Kuwait to be their superiors in beauty, good management and housekeeping; in fact, most Nejdis are prepared to concede this much to the Kuwaitis, as also to the inhabitants of Enaiza and Hail. But the Nejdis tend to look down on the inhabitants of Kuwait, Bahrain and Hasa.

Nationalism simply adds what might be called an outer ring to this style of passing tribal judgments. Said Aburish, for instance, writes that "The Palestinians loathe the Lebanese, considering them sticky-fingered Phoenician traders, not to be trusted. Of course, the Lebanese hate and despise the Palestinians, and they accuse each other of atrocious social crimes. . . . They unite, however, in looking down on the Egyptians and Syrians."

In this perspective, killing in pursuit of a quarrel elides into protection of tribe or religion, and so becomes obligatory, if not virtuous. Sir Edwin Pears, one of the best-known foreign correspondents in the final decades of the Ottoman Empire, described how he had witnessed simple Ottoman villagers fleeing from Bulgaria in the war of 1877. As refugees, these people then became victims of a cholera epidemic. A doctor, or hekim, visited a Turk dying of cholera, to be told how this Turkish family had lived amicably next door to Christians and their children had played together.

Then one night [as Pears reports the dying man's wife], my husband came home and told me that the padisha had sent word that we were to kill all the Christians in our village, and that he would have to kill our neighbours. I was very angry, and told him that I did not care who gave such orders, they were wrong. These neighbours had always been kind to us, and if he dared to kill them Allah would pay us out. I tried all I could to stop him, but he killed them—killed them with his own hand, Hekim. Then, when the war began, we came here.

As a child in Isfahan early in this century, the Persian writer Mohammad Ali Jamalzadeh was traumatized by encountering a crowd lynching two men who happened to be Babis, or Shia schismatics. These two were paying the penalty for belonging to a minority which was heretical, and furthermore defenseless. Jamalzadeh witnessed someone shouting, "It's a Babi-killing! Hit them!" and then throwing himself like a madman into the pandemonium. "The sashes of those two wronged and helpless bareheaded men had been thrown around their necks and they were being dragged along, bleeding, as degradingly as possible." In one of the innumerable atrocities committed by both sides during the Algerian war of independence, three Algerian teenagers murdered a thirteen-year-old French boy whom they had previously befriended. Why had they picked on him? "Because he used to play with us. Another boy wouldn't have gone up the hill with us." Friendship weighed less in the balance than the fact of belonging to an outside group. A pitched battle broke out in Cairo in 1981 between Muslims and Copts. "Atrocious crimes were committed by people who had earlier lived together peacefully: men and women were slaughtered; babies were thrown from windows, their bodies crushed on the pavement below; there was looting, killing, and arson. At the same time, leaflets were distributed elsewhere in the city urging each community to take up arms."

Such deeds, such certainties in the name of tribe or religion are brought into question by exposure to people organized on other principles. The West has provided quite another dimension against which to observe and to judge the customs and practices of the old order. Releasing the energies of its citizens by means of voluntary participation in social and political institutions, the Western nation-state appeared in the colonial age to be irresistible, therefore to be imitated. At the practical and instrumental level, some modifications proved possible. Sunshine hours became clock time. The caravan adapted to wheeled traffic. The room in which the tribal elders sat and received guests proved more comfortable with armchairs. Bedding on the floor was easily replaced by a bed with springs and a mattress, and the use of fingers for eating by forks and spoons. The merits of a toothbrush or eye ointment needed no arguing over the remedies of the local barber and tooth drawer. A decree was enough to convert tribal land into a commodity, and subsistence agriculture into a market venture. The tribesman could become a tenant or a sharecropper, even a city dweller with a paid job. Dignitaries and sheikhs lost nothing through appointments to be officials.

At the emotional level, identity and custom join in mutual defense. Loyalty to tribe and religious affiliation obliges the Arab and the Muslim to defy and to reject true understanding and acceptance of the outsider and the unbeliever. The power-challenge dialectic continues to prevent the transformation of the collectivity of separate families into an electorate, of group values into rights and duties, of obedience into choice and tolerance, of arranged marriage into romantic love, of the power holder into a party system with a loyal opposition.

2

Shame and Honor

Like other peoples in the Mediterranean basin, the Arabs use concepts of shame and honor to sanction their conduct. This shame-honor ranking—to borrow a term from the social sciences—stems from the ancient tribalism of the region and predates Islam, though in the course of time merging with it in some respects. Acquisition of honor, pride, dignity, respect and the converse avoidance of shame, disgrace, and humiliation are keys to Arab motivation, clarifying and illuminating behavior in the past as well as in the present.

Among Westerners, the extraordinarily persistent pattern of Arab conduct has often been ascribed to Islam. This line of argument goes far back into the past, but it was memorably formulated toward the end of the last century by Ernest Renan, the French scholar and originator of the study of comparative religions. Because Islam unites the spiritual and the temporal and makes a dogma of both, Renan wrote, it was "the heaviest chains which have ever shackled humanity," an engine of despotism and persecution, oblivious to everything but itself. Yet on the face of it, simplicity and lack of institutionalization ought to facilitate change in Islam rather than block it. Christianity and Judaism are religions similarly based on God-given revelation. Political and social changes nonetheless obliged their absolutist theology to become relative in a universe which was better explored and more factually delineated. Attitudes or doctrines historically fostered by Islam no doubt have hitherto deterred the establishment of scientific or rational enquiry into the universe. For instance, it is an orthodoxy in Islamic theology that everything happening in the world, in each particular and in each occasion, is decreed at that very moment by God. Hence there is no scope for natural law, God-given yet accessible to human reason—and this doctrine is responsible for the accusation of fatalism so often leveled at Muslims. No reason exists why Islam should not adapt to the scientific and rational outlook as Christianity and Judaism have done; and its supposedly peculiar and total intractability in this respect remains to be proven.

Islamic revival or no, there is no scale upon which to measure whether the man who says his prayers as a Muslim is motivated by genuine religious devotion, by custom, or by psychological demands of identity. There are no measurements of hypocrisy either, to spot the man who proclaims himself a sincere Muslim because he seeks some advantage out of it, thinking it fitting or impressive within the context of his own life. Today an Arab travels and compares, and if he inwardly decides to be indifferent to religious demands, let alone to become a skeptic or a cynic, he may still prefer for any number of reasons to keep his opinions to himself. In every Arab country, an ever-larger and more educated and worldly wise public is indeed indifferent to Islam and its practices, though not necessarily to the identity that it offers. Such a public pays lip service to Islam because anything less risks being shameful.

Occupying the center of social and moral value judgments, shame and honor are a good deal harder to ignore or repudiate than Islam: because they coincide, the two codes enforce identity and conformity of behavior. What otherwise seems capricious and self-destructive in Arab society is explained by the anxiety to be honored and respected at all costs, and by whatever means. For a would-be leader in any sphere, honor occupies a place akin to balloting or favorable public opinion polls in a democracy, and it is the value which above all others certifies power and careerism.

Honor is what makes life worthwhile: shame is a living death, not to be endured, requiring that it be avenged. Honor involves recognition, the openly acknowledged esteem of others which renders a person secure and important in his or her own eyes and in front of everyone else. Honor may derive from a variety of sources: genealogy or lineage (descent from the Prophet, for example), acquired standing, old age, piety, hard work, reliability, the possession of money, courage, and generosity. Honor and its recognition set up the strongest possible patterns of conduct, in a hierarchy of deference and respect. Honor commands politeness. A man may be observed kissing the hand of another, or his shoulder, or the hem of his robe. A conversation may be broken off, never to be resumed, because a more estimable third party has entered into the proceedings. Those within this hierarchy display unmistakable indication of their ranking: the turban of the religious leader, the suit and tie of the dignitary, the full Arab dress of the power holders of Arabia and the Gulf. Such classification of relative superiority and inferiority goes to substantiate the importance of manners, for fear of giving offense and thereby slighting honor. Everyday life is ritualized accordingly.

Explaining this to a Western audience, the Egyptian Mansour Khalid wrote:

> To an Arab, honor and respect by the community are interchangeable concepts. Honorable behaviour can be reflected in manifestations of manliness, attitudes towards the old and weak, sexual conduct, particularly in the case of women, and so on. But here again there is a strong correlation between honor and group cohesion and group survival. Honorable behaviour is that "which strengthens the group . . . while shameful is that which tends to disrupt, endanger, impair or weaken. . . ."

Shame derives from being a "bad" man, losing esteem through cowardice or meanness, having no money, being in a humble occupation, being menial, remaining unmarried or appearing "womanly," letting down one's own kind, failing in obligations to the family or the group. Some shame associations are merely customary. "It is shameful for a man to live in his wife's house," the Moroccan trader Al-Hajj Muhammad says. Also, "It is shameful for a Muslim woman to sell anything in the street. A woman should stay at home, hidden from the eyes of men." The passing of judgments instinctively attributes shame or honor, as when the same Moroccan says picturesquely, "If the rich man farts, for them it is as though a canary had sung. If the poor man farts, they insult him and add to that a beating."

Shame and honor closely define the roles of men and women and all transactions between them, validating and dramatizing them unforgettably and at all times. Honor for the male lies in fulfilling traditional masculine virtues, from being a "warrior" to fathering children, sons above all. Honor for the female consists in modesty and faithfulness, the bearing of children, sons once

again above all. Immodesty or unfaithfulness forfeits her honor
and shames the men in the family in whose keeping this honor is
vested. Men must put the lapse right at all costs, if need be killing
the dishonored woman. Such tragic occurrences are commonplace, reported in the daily newspapers. In 1964, President Aref
of Iraq amnestied as many as forty-three men who had murdered
their sisters. Regulation of conduct between men and women derives from innate awareness that sexuality is the greatest disturber
of the peace, as well as from the demand in tribal society to be
certain that those who inherit what property there is are entitled
to do so. "The world of the Arab is indeed a strange world," Khalid
Kishtainy remarks, in describing the apportioning of shame between the sexes. "A man is not supposed to complain when they
pull him by the genitals, but he should cry if they call his mother's
genitals names!" A man who kills his wife or daughter for her
unfaithfulness, real or supposed, goes to prison glad to have preserved his family's honor. If he did not really wish to punish her,
his only alternatives are to be dishonored himself or to leave the
community altogether. The community thinks well of him as he
pays whatever the penalty may be, valuing his action and disre-
garding the flagrant breach of the law.

In daily life, actions are prompted and governed by the positive
acquisition of honor and the negative avoidance of shame. Suda,
for example, a simple village woman, telling the story of her life
to a sociologist, reveals the sort of pitfalls into which the unwary
might fall. Her brother worked in a garage whose owner "raised
his voice and was unpleasant," until the brother was obliged to ask,
"Why should you humiliate us?" and walked out. Suda's comment
on this is, "By humiliating my brother he was humiliating the
whole family." As a maid, she herself walked out because the lady
of the house asked about the cleanliness of Suda's clothes. To
Suda, "a woman's honor is her most important asset," and on
those grounds she refused to give a photograph of herself to a man
she once loved because of possible future embarrassment: "he
could use it to humiliate me if there was disagreement between us.
Egyptians are no good in this way and are always trying to get the
better of each other. A woman must be very careful." One day, she
visited the house of a family in which one of the sons had taken a
liking to her. Going down the stairs, this man's younger brother
had tried to take her hand, whereupon Suda had no alternative but
to insult him. "May God curse you, you disgusting beast. Are you

a child acting this way?" Verbal violence was a protection of her marriage prospects.

Shame-honor ranking effectively prohibits the development of wider, more socialized types of human relationship. Status considerations of the kind are impervious to Western concepts of contractual relationships. In Sicily too, according to the writer Leonardo Sciascia, himself Sicilian, the family is the state, a be-all-and-end-all in itself. To any Sicilian, "the exact definition of his rights and duties will be that of the family." The Mafia, the Camorra of Naples, the Corsicans, people in Provence and in Spain, share with the Arabs self-regulatory group concepts wholly opposed to the workings of a state with norms legally defined and voluntarily obeyed. Equality under the law, that central constitutional pillar, cannot be reconciled with codes of shame and honor. On the contrary, the individual finds honor-justification in whatever will promote his career, and shame-justification for not compromising in anything that might lessen his advantages over other people. Pierre Bourdieu, the French social anthropologist, has pointed out that no dishonor attaches to such primary transactions as selling short weight, deceiving anyone about quality, quantity or kind of goods, cheating at gambling, and bearing false witness. The doer of these things is merely quicker off the mark than the next fellow; owing him nothing, he is not to be blamed for taking what he can.

Anyone embarking upon a challenge, then, has a ready excuse for whatever will advance him; he is merely self-aggrandizing, acquiring status, a careerist whose only restraint lies in unlucky or inept miscalculation that will bring shame or ridicule through exposure. Such a challenger is absolved from conscience as well as the law. The killing of enemies is a careerist instrument, not different in kind from any other, but only in degree. Marwan, a sixteen-year-old enrolled in the Shia militia in Beirut, explained to the French journalist Patrick Meney how murdering the innocent in the Lebanese civil war actually enhanced him. A friend of his had been shot in the day's fighting. For the sake of revenge, Marwan simply approached a crowd of bystanders and shot one of them dead. Afterward he told Meney, "Everyone knew I'd killed this man, for nothing, point-blank. Many people witnessed it. . . . Later that was a help. They were all afraid of me, they respected me. I'd proved my will publicly. I was a real warrior. I was able to boast of my prowess, knowing I'd get away with it."

By the same token, any power holder orders torture or massacre, or declares war without reference to his subjects, and without a qualm. Far from being some kind of bloodstained beast, he is only a supreme careerist and would feel himself shamed or lacking in manly and warriorlike qualities if he were to treat his challengers on the merits of their case. Leniency or the admission that he might have been wrong in his own decisions would prove dishonorable and thus advance someone else's careerism.

Shame-honor considerations reinforce power challenging from the top to the bottom of Arab society. A tiny elite of family heads or patrons everywhere disposes of the available patrimony. In Syria between 1946 and 1958, 208 ministerial positions were filled by only 90 individuals. In Iraq, according to one authority, a group of 175 men and two women comprised the entire ruling elite between 1958 and 1975. In both Syria and Iraq, subsequent one-man rule has further narrowed even this power base. Referring to the final years of the Shah, one authority wrote, "There are 40 national elite families in Iran today." John Waterbury put the ruling elite of contemporary Morocco at a thousand people. "The whole political history of Lebanon may be viewed as the history of a handful of leading families competing to affirm their name, power and prestige in their respective communities," writes the historian Salah Khalaf about his own country. "Over the entire span of 50 years of parliamentary life, only 359 deputies, representing 210 families, have won parliamentary seats." Khalaf goes on to quote Sami as-Solh, a postwar Lebanese prime minister.

Every sultan [used idiomatically here, to mean a notable with access to patronage] had an entourage and a group of followers, relatives, in-laws, in-laws of in-laws, associates, middle-men, and hangers-on from every faction and class and every village and street. Whichever of us should come to power, to the crematorium of cabinet office, found himself obliged to pay homage to those sultans and their followers and the followers of their followers. It is they who govern and direct, plan, and execute policies, while we are only the instruments which they set up before the eyes of the public to bear responsibility for their errors and misdeeds.

To take the everyday matter of wanting to obtain a job, a young man approaches the head of his family or clan, his patron. The head of the family is under obligation to do his very best to make sure that his kinsman is given what he asks for. The honor of the whole family is at stake. If the job is in the gift of someone from another clan or religion, complicated bargaining ensues, and a quid pro quo is sought. In the event of the job going to someone else, the patron becomes the object of shame, and his standing is under threat until such time as he can reestablish it by whatever means, and his young kinsman is satisfied. Placing him, the patron has the right to expect allegiance and loyalty in return, and so he himself is also taking a personal careerist step forward. Whether or not the young man deserved the job is no kind of consideration. Civic spirit, the good of the community, or mere consideration of who could best perform the job in hand has no part in these proceedings. Jobbing and dealing, even in the most sophisticated Arab circles, remains an essential business of promoting and protecting one's own kind.

By definition, honor and shame involve publicity. There can be no honor without show and even swagger. Display has priority over reticence and self-control. Whoever judges that honor is due to him must demand it; he must brook no interference or delay in his affairs. A power holder must lay claims to a heroic past and strike attitudes accordingly, ascribing nobility to himself and his supporters, wearing a uniform with rows of medals, traveling in an entourage which forces oncoming vehicles off the road and if necessary into the ditch, the equal of other power holders with his private aircraft and palaces. Anyone who claims honor will never wait for service, never be seen jostling at a counter like ordinary mortals; he drives a Mercedes, he impresses women with his seductiveness, he may grow the nail of his little finger long to prove that he is exempt from manual labor, he will insist on being a lavish host and abuse his inferiors and servants to impress upon them the distance from him at which they stand, and he would not be caught in some lowly activity like sweeping the path or repairing the broken table even as a hobby. Should he prefer to wear blue jeans, to stay at home and be himself, either he must be so high in the social scale that it would be shameful to criticize him at all, or else he risks being misunderstood and therefore shamed. Dropouts, eccentrics, the inspired inventor, the truly modest, or genuine nonconformist have no place here.

Between the poles of honor and shame stretches an uncharted field where everyone walks perilously all the time, trying as best he can to interpret the actions and words of others, on the watch for any incipient power-challenging response that might throw up winners and losers, honor and shame.

In the West, what is said and done more or less corresponds to the intentions of the speaker and the doer. Liars and cheats abound, of course, but generally they can go only so far before being caught out in the contractual relationships of their society. Lying and cheating in the Arab world is not really a moral matter but a method of safeguarding honor and status, avoiding shame, and at all times exploiting possibilities, for those with the wits for it, deftly and expeditiously to convert shame into honor on their own account, and vice versa for their opponents. If honor so demands, lies and cheating may become absolute imperatives. In Shia practice, a man is allowed what is called "precautionary dissimulation," a recognition that truth may be impossible in some contexts.

In response to a demand at the simplest level, a man will promise to finish a piece of work, say, or to obtain a license from a ministry within a specific time, or to act as escort on a visit to some notable. Actually he may not be in a position to perform any of these tasks, but since he has been asked to, he would feel ashamed to reveal that too much honor has been done to him, and he has no recourse but to prevaricate, to invent excuses, or simply to fail to appear. For the same reason, he may be generous, expansive, knowing, obsequious, all the while cursing inwardly at whoever has been able to take advantage of him, and planning how to bring about that person's downfall. Fear of humiliation, not malice, is inhibiting him.

Since everybody (except the foreigner) is well aware that any interlocutor is responding exactly as he is, due process begins. Other people have to be sounded out about when the work will be finished, or under what circumstances the officials will grant the license, and what arrangements must be made before the notable can be visited. Time passes. Decisions are delayed until it is safe for everybody concerned to take them. The whole interplay creates frustration (particularly for the uncomprehending foreigner), but humor too, as each man's performance is evaluated. The man who does actually cheat or lie maliciously is penalized probably more effectively than he would be in the West. Shame-honor demands that he be paid back in his own coin. Arab television comedies often seem impenetrable to a Westerner, as he watches how the perpetrator of a deliberate bad turn is repaid for it with interest in some climax of lengthily but carefully plotted pain and humiliation. The more convoluted the equalizing trick or cunning proves to be, the more the audience approves of it and laughs in pleasure. Western-type humor based on retort or satire is incompatible with the risk of humiliation, so that there cannot be the Arab equivalent of a crusading playwright or a talk-show comedian. One of Arab literature's favorite and most poignant themes concerns the employee who feels insulted by his superior and can neither swallow his pride nor level the score.

Confronted by examples of Arab lying and cheating, Westerners have often complained as though these were arts practiced for their own sake. Far from seeing what a fascinating and ritualized play was in progress, unfolding what amounts to a narrative as opaque as it is controlled, Westerners usually reached the opposite and false conclusion that the Arabs were willful children, not quite responsible for themselves. "In many respects they are more unprejudiced than we are, and very intelligent, and very good in many ways; and yet they seem so strangely childish," wrote a sensitive English woman, Lucie Duff Gordon, of the Egyptian fellahin among whom she was living in the 1860s. Typical of his kind, Sir John Drummond Hay, a British diplomat of long standing in Morocco, wrote, "The Moors are children, vain children."

An American academic writes of today's Egyptian peasant:

> The narrowness of his experience has made possible his apparent cheerfulness and contentment and contributed to his seemingly childlike qualities—his jokes and sudden irrepressible gaiety that can change suddenly into anger and rage. . . . The small circle of the village probably generates those personal animosities, often as irrational as schoolboy fights, that flare up so easily in an Egyptian community.

In his justly celebrated book *The Diary of a Country Prosecutor,* Tewfik el-Hakim describes just such a village and one of its fights. "What sparked off this bloody battle in the course of which adults had behaved themselves like children? . . . They rose up at a word, and calmed down at another." An Egyptian sociologist, Hamad Ammar, in a study of his own village, pointed out how children were socialized through "techniques of fear," forcing them to resort to lies and deception, all of which is reflected later "in the prevailing atmosphere of adult life which is charged with suspicion, secrecy and apprehension." Sami al-Jundi, a Syrian politician, a typical victimizer who then fell victim in a power-challenge play, applied this language to himself. "Society persecuted us, and so we defied it and began to destroy all institutions with much intelligence and much stupidity, like children growing up who with time become more childish."

Unni Wiken, a Norwegian sociologist, one day had free clothes to give to the poverty-stricken women among whom she was conducting research in Cairo. Stealing resulted, then lying about which woman had what. She analyzed what really had happened.

What is produced are myths expressing and confirming collective ideas about the character of the woman in question. Her problem in any attempt to affect this myth-creation is that there is no way in which she can control the perspective which others apply to her action. This limitation is a direct result of the demand that all those who are friends have to humor each other. Consequently, no versions can be corrected by any possible information the listeners may possess, and no objective arguments of plausibility can serve as a brake on the person telling the story.

Information control, which might or might not include lying, is the only effective strategy for arbitrating between shame and honor—and, Unni Wiken might have added, for cutting short the power-challenge response instantly set in motion by even such a humble allocation of resources as the gift of secondhand clothes.

Shame-honor ranking works its way through private and public life in unseen attendance wherever there is a human encounter. Inequality through performance may be regretted by Westerners, but it can be accepted nonetheless, whereas inequality through honor and shame seems to them arbitrary and cruel. In the past, Europeans commonly misconceived shame-honor among Arabs as some sort of elusive national characteristic evolving out of history. Hundreds of years of oppression and suffering made the Egyptian very suspicious, wrote a French director of veterinary services in Cairo in 1900, in a perfect illustration of this line of thought: "He mercilessly tyrannizes over those below him in station, he is arrogant towards those equal to him, while towards those above him he is submissive and humiliates himself to the very limit of abasement." In his memoirs, the Egyptian author Salama Musa described how in his youth, "It was quite normal that we should not feel anything disagreeable or wrong in having a peasant going behind us for an hour or so while we were riding on the back of

a donkey; if the man was thirsty and out of breath, what was the
difference between him and the donkey?"
A psychiatrist in Lebanon, Haig Khatchadourian, concluded
that shame-honor led to such subterfuge and evasion in matters of
etiquette that a man's adopted "mask" in the end was actually
indistinguishable from his true "face." The majority "cannot express their pent-up resentment of their superiors and the entire
social structure. They are driven to an outward servility, often
exaggerated into sickening sycophancy. Resentment, dislike, even
hate are masked by outward compliance," and the exactly opposite
tendency is manifested by these same servile persons in dealing
with their inferiors. The net result was the decay of individuality.

Even after long experience of the contemporary Middle East,
the French writer Péroncel-Hugoz, oblivious to the shame-honor
component, could be caught in a false interpretation of a scene. At
Cairo airport, he happened to observe a policeman mistreating
poor workers returning from the Gulf, and he was unable to bear
the wantonness of it. Reproaching the policeman, he was told,
"But they are slaves, as stupid as animals." Péroncel-Hugoz made
the practical retort that their remittances actually provided his
salary. Characteristically Western, this social linkage between policeman and poor workers is true but irrelevant, because it neglects
the policeman's ascription of honor to himself by virtue of his
office and uniform and revolver. This honor had to be recognized
by the workers in whatever form he chose to assert it, forcing the
issue with verbal violence about "animals"; and they had to submit, for failure to recognize his authority would be shameful to
them. Not particularly a thug, the policeman was impervious to the
guilt that Péroncel-Hugoz was hoping to instill in him as a first step
to reformation.

Arabs themselves may fail to perceive how deceptive shame-
honor appearances can be, and what toils they are caught in. Michael Gilsenan, the social anthropologist, has a telling illustration.
Over twenty years ago, while still an untrained teacher, Gilsenan
found himself in a small town in the Hadhramaut, in southern
Arabia, therefore off the beaten track. There he met two young
men of sherifian family (meaning that they traced their descent to
the Prophet). "The green band around their turbans, their flowing
cream-coloured outer garments, and their trim beards all signified
the holiness and precedence of their position." He was impressed
when in the street another student whom he knew stooped to kiss

the hands of his two acquaintances, and he interpreted this as a mark of respect. The two then invited him home, whereupon they closed the windows and shutters, switched on the lights and played Western pop music on a Grundig tape recorder. "Turbans were quickly doffed, and there was no talk of religion but only of stifling boredom, the ignorance of local people, the cost of alcohol." Splendid externals, then, in no way corresponded to the inner personality.

The shock of this discovery was enormous. Worse was to follow next day, when the hand-kissing student privately explained to Gilsenan that he was a Nasserist and had revolutionary ambitions, hoping to cut down not only the two privileged sherifians but also the "imperialist" Gilsenan himself. "The handkissing was a show, but a show with diametrically opposed meanings for the actors. It secreted hidden interpretations, reversals and denials."

The greater the stakes, the more urgent the caution and the need for a safety screen. Kenneth Pendar, an American intelligence officer whose task it was to persuade Moroccans to side with the Allies during the last war, expressed the difficulties of conducting a negotiation in which he expected a yes or a no from people unable to commit themselves to either, because they could not tell who would win the war and acquire honor or who would lose and be shamed. Pendar wrote:

Arab psychology is a fascinating study. . . . Much of what goes on in places like Syria or North Africa must seem utterly confusing to anyone who has not lived with Arabs and been in close contact with their subtle and indirect ways of thought. At first I was completely baffled by some of the conversations I had with them. As I carefully recorded my notes afterwards, I would find that my written record of the conversation was quite different from the *impression* I had of it. Sometimes it seemed exactly the opposite.

Conversation took place on a series of different planes: the upper stratum that seemed to be the main subject, with underneath four or five planes or subjects on which the Muslim was also communicating. "They appear, glance, and retreat, or are only felt, like lights in a prism. It is on these planes that the real exchange of ideas is made." Such obliquity, in Pendar's judgment, accounted for the political inefficiency he ran into. Recently, Dr. Henry Kissinger, as Secretary of State and therefore in a position to frustrate and to be frustrated in the power-challenge dialectic, observed the same phenomenon in the case of the Saudis. He could not penetrate a style "at once oblique and persistent, reticent and assertive." Success or failure in public negotiation is all the more fraught in that an attentive Arab audience is eagerly anticipating the allocation of honor or shame.

In one last example of the style dictated by these considerations, a journalist in Lebanon confronted Abd al-Mohsin Fadlallah, cousin of the leader of Hizbollah, the Iranian-backed militia, and in standard Western manner he asked directly whether Fadlallah advocated an Islamic Republic in Lebanon. The reply was, "People who believe in God and see things in the long term, they will win. People who think only of the next hour, of their immediate surroundings, they will not win." The utterance is marvelously oracular. Fadlallah cannot exactly be accused of promoting violence in the name of Islam, nor certainly of distancing himself from Hezbollah and his friends, but he reveals nothing of his thoughts or intentions. Forfeiting no honor, he shames nobody.

As with people, so with what they have created. The world is modernizing, and so the Arabs must; it would be shameful not to do so. Again, no standards are available to measure modernization. Nobody can be quite positive about its alleged but elusive benefits. Nobody can say where, how or why, past honor acquired present shame. Everywhere the Arab heritage, its cities and achievements alike, is either in ruins or monumentally preserved, in a kind of limbo that will neither die nor be reborn: a panorama of medinas, casbahs, souks or markets, mosques and minarets, citadels long since converted into museums. Around ancient cities like Fez, Algiers, Tunis, Cairo, Damascus, Baghdad, spread European-type developments, out into what lately was open country or desert. Like Pendar's conversations, these externals are to be interpreted at several levels.

There are unities, suggestive cultural detail—neon lights in pink and chemical blues and greens, or strings of colored lightbulbs sometimes even profiling a mosque; cafés where men assemble at all hours without women. Honor is symbolized architecturally in triumphal arches of plywood blazoned with heroic military slogans; in the larger-than-life portraits of the country's power-holder in a martial or benevolent pose, his uniform bright with medals and badges, or perhaps all-wise in a civilian suit; in a massively laid-out Liberation Square usually adorned with a statuesque but deteriorating tank and arrayed flags fraying in the wind;

a Tomb of the Unknown Warrior, embellished with Italian marble and washed down all day long by laborers under the eyes of bored soldiers in body-hugging uniforms, fingering their side-arms and stroking the moustaches which complete the warrior's image. Along the main streets of every Arab capital is a civilian chaos of cars whose drivers prefer to use the continual horn rather than the occasional brake, and have no intention of stopping for mere pedestrians. On the sides and bumpers of chaotic buses cling the passengers for whom there is no more room inside. Traffic fatalities feature significantly in mortality rates.

The Westerner steps out of a familiar hotel, around which stand other steel-framed glass and concrete buildings. In Dubai, the International Trade Center staged the World Chess Federation championship in 1986. A National Gallery opened in Jordan in 1980, and a National Museum in Doha. Boy scouts are to be found as far away as Oman. Kuwait has a skating rink and a stock exchange which notoriously crashed amid spectacular bankruptcies; Tunis has a Horse Racing Club and a National Library; Cairo has learned societies which issue publications in French and English; in Casablanca, a clinic pioneers sex-change operations; and it is possible to play golf in Dubai and Muscat or in Morocco at Rabat and Marrakesh, and to ski at Ifrane. Research councils have been set up in Damascus, Cairo, Riyadh, Beirut. Kuwait invests its petro-dollars through an Investment Office. Saudi Arabia contributes to the International Monetary Fund, and a Prize for Science commemorates King Faisal. Soccer was introduced into the Ottoman Empire as long ago as 1908, and the national teams of Algeria and Morocco reached the 1986 finals of the World Cup in Mexico City. Back in 1907, the Red Crescent Society was founded as a counterpart to the Red Cross. Inter-Arab organizations exist: such as the Arab League, founded in 1945 and which now has offices abroad and organized lobbies; the Fund for Arab Economic Development; and not least of all, the Organization of Arab Petroleum Exporting Countries.

The official or high-level visitor may well move within the exclusive orbit of the glass and concrete buildings and suppose that they are reality, and all else is folklore. He may hear that from time to time mobs have rioted and burnt down these hotels and casinos, nightclubs and bars and cinemas. Are there not underprivileged and discontented people everywhere, taking the law into their own hands? Imagination and experience are required before those scenes reveal another level of meaning. The mobs burn down these buildings because they very well understand these symbols for what they are: the buildings have not arisen out of the demands of the society, they are façades, imitating the West in order to ward off the charge of being "backward" and "uncivilized." Islamic pretexts about the sinfulness of selling alcohol or staging floor shows are handy, but what the rioters feel is alienation, shame at the discrepancy between the values represented by these buildings and their own lives. Arson articulates their sense that there is no organic link between these buildings and themselves, and besides, they wish to wipe out a shame for which they see no reason. Are they really expected to consider themselves "backward" or "uncivilized"?

When Volney, the famous French traveler, landed in Egypt in 1783, he found that Cairo had "the universal appearance of wretchedness and misery. The crowds which thronged the street, present [the sight of] nothing but hideous rags, and disgusting nudity." Two hundred years after Volney, Sami Nair, also arriving from Paris, can write in a travel book (in which he gives no indication of his origins but presumably they are Middle Eastern), "Cairo is apocalyptic. First and most fundamental impression. Attempted walk in the center, Midan el Tahrir [i.e. Liberation Square], the main square, everywhere in collapse: 'they' are trying to put in a subway, 'they' being French companies . . . this is a universe of high numbers. You have to learn to count in thousands. . . . Women dressed in European style, or wearing the religious costume, men in western suits or in a *galabiyeh*." The man in the suit is as likely as the man in the *galabiyeh* to be wearing a gold watch and to speak to the Westerner in his own language, but such details might surprise Volney less than the magnified scale of what he would find familiar.

Palgrave, eccentric even by the standards of English travelers, reached Riyadh in 1862, describing it as "divided into four quarters" which intersected in the marketplace, and on one side of which was a palace while on the other was a mosque. That was all. He thought it worth mentioning that soap was obtainable. Cairo and Riyadh alike now have dual-expressway approaches, overpasses, the latest lines of luxury Western goods, and international airports. Yet a century after Palgrave, another English rolling stone, Trevor Mostyn, describing himself as a technical consultant ("consulting who and what I did not really know"), could take his place among other Western businessmen "almost overcome by gloom" in a Riyadh where the air conditioning smelled of damp rats and the drainage ditch in the streets stank like a sewer. Calling on a deputy minister, he had a clear illustration of how business is done among the Saudis. The scene, as he describes it, has its prismatic levels of meaning. Twenty Bedouin suddenly rushed without warning into the deputy minister's office, brushing Mostyn aside. Cycles of formal conversation followed, with exchanges of mutual compliments, highly formal in style, until one Bedouin whispered to the minister that someone had put a fence across their land so that their sheep could no longer graze. "You could see from the Deputy Minister's face that he was carefully absorbing the laments, for these were cousins on whom his position within the extended family and power structure depended."

On the outskirts of Riyadh, writes another contemporary witness, an American doctor, were "junkyards of rotting automobile bodies, dozens of goats feasting on garbage, and shabby three-storey apartment houses, whose balconies were almost hidden by an assortment of ragged laundry hung out to dry. Farther on, we came upon countless groups of sheds thrown together haphazardly with pieces of corrugated metal, wood, and cardboard offering little protection from the elements. Sometimes a tiny yard extruded with metal sheeting extended from a dilapidated dwelling where goats wandered about bleating like children."

Behind the honor-façades is the plane of humiliating reality where the majority must spend their lives. In every city there still survive from the past some traditional houses, enclosed behind walls, around a courtyard; and there are still immemorial villages of white-washed houses in every country. More usual, though, is a range of crumbling apartments in flaking materials, of houses with wires and poles sticking above them for additional stories but where in the meantime goats are tethered and hens scratch, of shelters erected out of packing cases and corrugated iron and palm branches and even tenting, run up illegally but in areas where custom always has precedence over law. Women and children share the available space with the animals, leading the goats down to feed off the rubbish, amid scavenging dogs. Back streets, and certainly the alleys, are unpaved, muddy with slops. Garbage collection is virtually unknown. Plumbing and electricity are hazards. Fires break out. Unni Wiken, in her district of Cairo, found the stench almost beyond endurance. "A vast cloaca, the smell of carrion," Sami Nair says. A large Arab city conveys an impression of improvisation, of hazards, of encampment. In the cemeteries of Cairo, people fight for living space in tombs and sarcophagi and have become tourist attractions as they do so. The Cairo population in 1900 was 400,000, over two million in 1946, and today it is estimated to be approaching fifteen million. Parts of the sewage system have been known to back up and spill over the streets. Probably twenty million of the fifty million Egyptians have been born since 1973, and every nine months now adds another million. So much of the country is uncultivatable desert that 99 percent of the population live on 4.5 percent of the land, most of that consisting of the banks of the Nile. In this country whose prime resource is agriculture, in which some 4000 villages and their peasants support almost everybody, the ratio of productive land to each person has dropped to about one-seventh of an acre. In his fine autobiography, *Out of Egypt*, the Egyptian-born critic Ihab Hassan is unsure whether to mourn or to rejoice when he asks, "After a revolution, a presidential assassination, four wars and a tripled population growth within half a century, what has really changed there beyond some streets and squares renamed?"

Kuwait in the early 1950s had 35,000 inhabitants, and today over a million. Baghdad, with 3.8 million out of an Iraqi population of fourteen million, is expected to reach twelve million by the end of the century, while Damascus, today at two million, is projected to grow to five million. The cities of North Africa are expected to grow by a similar factor of two or three. In these extrapolations of current trends, the Arab urban population of the year 2000 could be altogether 250 million out of a total of 280–300 million. If so, four out of every five Arabs will be living in cities never designed to house or feed them.

European societies expanding during the previous century at comparable rates also had labor forces that were one-third to one-half industrialized. "Egypt, Iraq, Morocco and Tunisia in the 1970s," writes the Egyptian demographer Saad Eddin Ibrahim about four of the best-case countries, "had urban populations of 45, 43, 35 and 43 per cent respectively, but only 18, 10, 13 and 11 per cent of their labor force in industry." A European process of modernization is under way, in other words, without the European means of generating its financing.

Modernization as inherent degradation runs counter to the rationale of Western history; it is a paradox denying the scientific method which analyzes the nature of change in terms of problem and solution. Consistent within itself, shame-honor ranking is unsuited to a technical context because it prevents reason being an agreed value. Political and social decision-making in which the deciders are motivated by any shame and honor consideration is more than usually vulnerable to human accident. A modern pump, some ambitious local leader thinks, will improve agriculture in his village. Money will flow in, and the credit will be his, he will earn a reputation as a patron. Warning him of technical obstacles, a consultant succeeds only in making the local leader feel ignorant, provoking a shame reaction that makes him dig in his heels. When the local leader, in power-challenge style, moves the issue higher up the decision-making hierarchy, he has already attached his honor to it. Installed, the pump encourages overirrigation, which exacerbates the salinity of the soil, precipitating the ruin of the village agriculture, the uselessness of the pump, and the waste of that resource. Instead of being blamed for promoting an imperfectly analyzed project, the local leader will be honored for knowing how to get his way.

A road is built to a hitherto isolated community. A politician wants access to his land, or perhaps a plan specifies that better communications are wealth-producing. The adventurous and the able-bodied then emigrate down that road to the city, ceasing to contribute to the regional economy but adding to demand in the city. A block of apartments is erected in cement, and those who have to live in it stifle in the heat. In another example, cassette players are cheaply available, whereupon Ayatollah Khomeini ensures that the prerecorded tapes provide an attack upon the Western way of life that produces, among other goods, cassette players and tapes.

The Aswan Dam, Nasser's favorite project for modernizing Egypt, required external financing. The intention was to free the peasants of the Nile Valley from the vagaries of the river's annual flooding. Needless to say, Nasser did not consult them. The dam would permit year-round irrigation and also provide electric power that would further promote industrialization. As early as 1944, the controller general of the endemic disease department of the ministry of public health in Egypt had warned that perennial irrigation would increase bilharzia to a level of 75 percent. This debilitating disease is spread by parasites breeding in contaminated water in a complicated cycle. Moreover, the financing of the dam proved difficult. When the Eisenhower government reversed its decision to put up the money, Nasser appealed successfully to Moscow.

From the moment that Nasser had staked his prestige on the dam, practical considerations became irrelevant because the shame of abandoning the scheme would have made his position untenable. Nothing less than the nation's foreign policy was swung by a shame-honor response. Sure enough, the Aswan Dam has spread bilharzia in exact accordance with the 1944 warning. Other consequences of this planned and forcible freeing of the peasants from age-old living patterns were more incalculable. In a moving account of one particular peasant affected by it, Shahhat, from a traditional village in Upper Egypt, Richard Critchfield reached the general conclusion about the control of the Nile waters that "This increase in scientific and material power, instead of diminishing cultural turbulence, left the people of Upper Egypt far more vulnerable to it." Shahhat, a good-natured and popular character, had been at the center of the village and its activities. He cared for his widowed mother, he tilled the family small holding. Suddenly he became one of many who had no idea how to respond to the demands imposed by the dam on his way of life. He felt inadequate, drifting into crime, then abandoning his mother to take his doubtful chance in Cairo. The circumstances which Shahhat and millions like him could not understand and even less control had been conditioned by Nasser's need for prestige.

Public health measures in the Arab world stem directly from the period of colonialism. To give an illustration, in 1883, the year after the British occupation, the latest in a long and lethal series of cholera epidemics in Egypt claimed 100,000 lives. Greene Pasha, in charge of the new sanitary services, and a typically energetic Victorian reformer, introduced the building of free clinics, compulsory vaccination for smallpox, and a clean water supply. Throughout the Middle East, the British and the French administrations introduced the standards of public health to which they were themselves accustomed. Sir John Strathearn, a famous ophthalmologist and warden of the St. John's Ophthalmic Hospital in Jerusalem in mandated Palestine after the First War, used to say that a cursory walk through an Arab village was enough for him to be able to judge, from the state of the children's eyes, whether or not a government school had been established there by the British. "There are no doctors in Arabia," wrote a missionary, P. W. Harrison, in 1925. Instead of even elementary medicine, he found that behind all diseases was the superstitious fear of "the evil eye." He commented dryly that amputation of the hand for theft was the most common major surgical procedure.

Nasser pledged himself to provide health care "to every citizen in every corner of the country under conditions of comfort and service." Not many years were to pass before one expert was to conclude that planned social centers and health units had "largely failed to reach their projected aims." All across the Arab world, and especially in Saudi Arabia and the Gulf states, very large sums of money have been invested in hospitals and medical care. It remains noticeable that the rulers of Saudi Arabia and the Gulf states, and their relations and tens of thousands of their citizens prefer to place themselves in the hands of doctors in the West; that Nasser, when seriously ill, chose to be treated in the Soviet Union; that even Ayatollah Khomeini has sent members of his family and his entourage to the United States to be cured by the doctors of what he likes to call "the Great Satan."

Ian Young, an English doctor, served in the early 1970s as a gynecologist in a hospital in the Kabyle district of Algeria. Most of his colleagues were from Eastern Europe. He described conditions:

Pictures of dirt and fatigue, in stained robes and old sheets, the women stare up at us from their beds. Head to toe, taking turns on the pillow, a woman without a baby—strangled during delivery by its cord—shares with a woman who has no milk of her own. She's feeding her baby from an old yogurt carton, with cold mint tea brought in from home. The smell in the room is weeks old. Water-melon pips and flies, egg-shells in the corners, dry bread and broken vitamin ampoules, a half-finished packet of biscuits alive with red ants, newspaper soggy with meat juice on the floor. Dr. Kostov's provoked. He points to each item: "Look!" He grabs hold of the women and drives them to the window, to feel shame before the balcony thick with encrusted food and flies.

Provoked into a shame-honor response, the Algerian assistant, Djamila, had no choice but to refute the reality of the conditions and so she did with the irrelevant words, "We Arabs always wash." Her medical standards were such that she failed to detect that a patient's swollen belly was due to a tumor, not an embryo. When Young could bear it no longer, he did what he would have done in England, and complained in a report to the supervisor. This supervisor was not a doctor but held the post as a reward for his work as a nursing orderly during the war of Liberation. Little did Young realize the extent to which as a Westerner and a medical man he was shaming the supervisor for his ignorance and unfitness for his job. To rescue his position, the supervisor had to insult and shame Young, telling no matter what kind of lies for the purpose, altogether denying reality.

He shook me, and I didn't resist. . . . In my passivity, he seemed to discover new reserves of anger, and wilder inspiration. He knew all pathology, more than any doctor in the hospital, he knew "all the pathology in the world," all surgery and gynaecology too, and he gave me a shake with every subject. His knowledge was as limitless as his power. No hospital door was closed to him, no piece of paper was not his to do with as he wished. He walked the wards, the Theatres and the corridors. They were all his, and he had accounts to give to no one: "I run this place."

Dragging Young to an assistant director, he sought to establish what credentials he could by asking if it was not true that he had been an officer in the Algerian Liberation Army. What the assistant director had to say was also irrelevant to medical standards in the hospital and only affirmed the supervisor's honor. Reassured, he rounded on Young again.

How it pained him, that all the sacrifices of the black hours should be brought to nothing, by "white-coated saboteurs passing their hands from vagina to vagina, infecting my heroic people with syphilis!" He would never tolerate it, never! His voice became hysterical. "Get out!" he shrieked. "Leave this hospital immediately! Leave this country!"

Nobody could consider dismantling even such a hospital as that, though it was itself pro forma, not really a care center but a beacon to flash the message that Algeria must be like any other modern country because it has social institutions of the sort approved everywhere today. This impedes amelioration as certainly as the supervisor's shame-honor response frustrated effective care. In that sense, the women patients were victims of deception. Traditional medicine would have been no more harmful, and far less brutal.

Illiteracy, wrote Samuel M. Zwemer, an American missionary in 1915, "is well-nigh universal among Muslims." In no other social field has there been so much endeavor and investment as in education in the Middle East. Education has been perceived as the means for introducing the scientific method or objectivity in problem solving. Everywhere education is compulsory for boys and now for girls as well, and everywhere it is at state expense. Fifty-five universities now adorn the Arab world. A contemporary authority, Charles Issawi, can emend Zwemer's generalization about illiteracy. "In the last few years the Middle East has reached the level of primary education which some economists regard as the most important single factor in the absorption of technology and, consequently, in economic development—the level attained by Western Europe and the United States in the first half of the 19th century." Between 1970 and 1982, another authority, A. B. Zahlan, points out that around a trillion dollars have been spent on purchasing technical services and technology products, amounting to half of all food needs, weapons, factories, roads, petrochemical complexes, airports, and so on. Education has to succeed if these goods and services are to be produced locally, substituting for importation.

From the moment that Western-style education was introduced, resistance to it implied a cultural defense. Children who had been taught according to the ideas of foreigners and unbelievers would no longer be children in whom parents could take pride. On the contrary, they might well be shamed by them, treated with disrespect, exposed as ignorant, criticized as Muslims. One early reformer was Ismail Kemal Bey, an energetic official of the Ottoman Empire in the last century, who built schools in his province. His Grand Vizier, Ali Pasha, at the head of the state bureaucracy, asked him sarcastically, "What will become of all these people when they have received their instruction in the condition in which the country is at present? Will they all become lawyers and idlers as in Greece?" Zia Gokalp, who grew up to become the leading exponent of Turkish nationalism, was born and educated in the provinces. A guest suggested to his father, himself a teacher, that this clever boy should be educated in Europe. The father feared that in Europe his son might become an unbeliever. "And what will happen if he stays here?" the guest asked. "Then he will become an ass," the father replied.

At about the same time, a local ruler in the Sudan was arguing with the British district commissioner, Hugh Boustead. "Well now, if I educate my sons as you suggest they will be better than me and I will get no respect and no obedience from them. I would much rather keep them like myself and respectful and under my control until I die." The district commissioner answered that if he took this line he would merely have other people coming in over him to give the orders. "You will die and your sons will be the donkeys and the eastern Arabs will ride on them and they will curse you as being their stupid father, and they will curse me." Both men were sincere, and both were right. The sociopolitical condition has not permitted education to liberate people and ideas, as in the West. Control lost by fathers did not pass to the sons themselves but to the ruler of the state. No absolute ruler could possibly permit an educational system whose values would produce students who might shame him, destroy his prestige, finally form a power challenge to overthrow him. Education, like so many modern reforms, has evolved into a method of state control. Group-direction, not self-realization, has been the aim of Arab education.

Article 28 of the Iraqi constitution describes educational aims in that country, but the same applies to Arabs everywhere.

Education shall aim at raising and developing the general cultural level, developing the scientific thinking, kindling the spirit of research, fulfilling the requirements of economic and social development programs, creating a free nationalist and progressive generation solid in structure and character, which esteems its people, its homeland and its legacy, sympathises with the rights of all the nationalists, and struggles against the philosophy of capitalism, exploitation, reaction, Zionism, and colonialism for achieving Arab unity, freedom and socialism.

An Egyptian student, Mahmud Faksh, has depicted what it is like to have been put through the comparable course of indoctrination in Egypt. Through the study of secular and political ends, he felt separated from those who had received a religious education to the point where he can quote with approval a Western observer who said, "contact between the two cultures has been one of more bitter and protracted conflict, and has caused much pain, uncertainty, equivocation, and proneness to illusion and emotionalism." Covert but specific socialization was occurring. Students, always suspected for their disruptive potential, were being introduced to a bureaucratic atmosphere; they were expected to enroll for practical subjects, and they came to realize that the authority of the university was altogether subordinate to security officers assigned by the ministry of the interior.

Based on his own experience of socialization through education, Faksh went on to say that it would be safe to assume that such ceaseless efforts to bring about an identification with the regime have been somewhat successful. My classmates and I developed a strong sense of identification and pride with Arabism, anti-colonialism, and nationalist leaders of Nasser's calibre. On different occasions, as the government deemed it necessary, we were able to express these feelings and attitudes by demonstrating in support of regime causes and against anti-regime causes, domestic or foreign.

More children in more schools should mean higher literacy rates, but demography is suppressing achievement, and illiteracy is rising. To illustrate the literacy level, the 1976 census figures in Egypt showed that 43.5 percent of the population above the age of ten was literate, the men significantly more so than the women. Overcrowding is already such that in lecture halls in Egyptian universities, each tutor has an average of 294 students compared with the world average of between ten and twenty students.

In a rationally ordered world, these problems are open to solution, but education is not being pursued just as an end valuable for cultivating problem solving. In the words of the French Arabist Gilles Kepel, education has taught "the mannerisms of modern life but not its techniques or spirit." Education, like health, consists of arrangements to suit purposes predetermined by the decision-making power holder. The packed and ideologically guided universities and the new roads and the baking hot jerrybuilt apartments are so many impositions from above, for the show of it and for the honor, without reference to those intended to benefit from them. In themselves, these institutions and projects may or may not have been well conceived in the first place; they may or may not have been appropriate to the human situation for which they were designed. Materializing, these projects acquire certificates of unchallengeable rightness from the power holder who decreed them. Tied into prestige, a project loses scientific criteria of viability. If a project in fact proves to be misconceived, it becomes taboo, to be ignored, a pure waste.

Modernization, then, which in its nature is bound to disturb and dislocate, has to be suffered as oppression, a doom all the more unsettling to the masses because nothing allows them to predict how it will fall, nor gives a clue about how to deal with it. The more the Arabs modernize, the less Arab they become: the more they assert themselves as Arabs, the less they truly modernize. Definitions of progress, in the circumstances, are neither continuous nor coherent.

3

Western Approaches

In the heyday of the Ottoman Empire in the sixteenth century, it was easier to imagine the encroachment of the Turks on Europe than the reverse prospect of European supremacy over any part of the house of Islam. At that time, the great historian Guicciardini wrote with foreboding about the danger of the Turkish invasion of Italy. To Shakespeare, Turks and the Moors of Morocco were figures of power. The difference in religion between Christianity and Islam, however, did not give rise to what today would be called a Cold War, and it has been greatly exaggerated by modern nationalists anxious to falsify history to their benefit. European and Islamic rulers at the time belonged to the same state system and concluded treaties of mutual convenience across the religious barrier. François I of France persuaded the Ottoman sultan into an anti-Habsburg alliance. The British and the Safavid shah of Persia joined forces to expel the Portuguese from Hormuz and the Gulf. Politics, trade, and exploration in the long run would probably have dissolved Islamic exclusivity, where outright colonialism rather tended to reinforce it. More invisibly, the burgeoning development of scientific method throughout the seventeenth century laid the foundation of European dominance of the world of Islam.

"Original scientific ideas and concepts are basically the work of individuals rather than the collective effort of many, and the success of our world has for centuries now depended on the achievements of geniuses," Kurt Mendelssohn writes in his history of science, adding, "It is here perhaps, more than in any other respect that the West differs from the civilizations of the East." Galileo,

Newton, Descartes, Hooker, Leibnitz, the Royal Academy, the Berlin and the French Academies, form a constellation of personalities and institutions projecting their societies out of the fixed religious doctrines of the past and into the different harness of reason and discovery whose purpose, in famous words of Descartes, was the "mastery and possession of nature." A monk in Padua, Lodovico Marracci, in 1698 published the first accurate translation of the Koran into a European language. Using this text, George Sale produced an English version in 1734. By the end of that century, Sir William Jones, professor of Arabic at Cambridge, could write that the Arabs were a nation "who have ever been my favourite." Soon European explorers and scholars, such as the Swiss Jean-Louis Burckhardt and the Hungarian Armin Vambéry, were able to pass as Arabs or Turks and to survive triumphantly examinations of their Islamic learning in which failure would have meant instant death. In broad terms, such achievements are among the many which enabled European society to be the first in history to put human division and natural change to work to its own advantage by a process of objectifying and universalizing all knowledge.

Ibn Khaldun, the great historian of the fourteenth century, had already perceived that a contrary trend existed among his fellow Arabs. "The practice of the arts is in general very limited in the countries where the Arabs are indigenous and in the areas which they have conquered since the promulgation of Islam. Consider, on the other hand, how the arts are flourishing in the countries inhabited by the Chinese, the Hindus, the Turks and the Christians, and how the other nations derive goods and foodstuffs from them." In lands north of the Mediterranean, he wrote, "Philosophical thought is said to be revived, its instruction widespread, its books comprehensive, its scholars numerous, and its students many. But God alone knows what goes on over there!"

Nothing prevented a Muslim at any moment from going to find out. No record substantiates that a Turk or an Arab at that time traveled to Europe. No Turkish or Arab entrepots were built in European ports, no Turkish or Arab vessels ventured outside their coastal waters as once they had done. The pirates of the Barbary Coast and the Gulf continued to make themselves feared as they overpowered trading ships from Europe, but they took from them nothing but booty and slaves. In the absence of contact with European intellectual and social developments, the Muslims sealed the unequal relationship that was to come.

In 1683 the Turks failed to capture Vienna. Over the next

hundred years, they fought wars with an aggressive Russia, ending each time in unequal treaties, and the overall loss of what today are Soviet Muslim territories in the Caucasus and Armenia, and the Crimea. In similarly unequal wars with Persia from 1804 to 1813, and again from 1826 to 1828, Russia annexed what today are its possessions southwest of the Caspian sea. European perceptions shifted with the new balance of forces. The eighteenth-century style of *turquerie* domesticated the Ottomans by incorporating them into European arts and fashions. In 1748, art students in Rome staged a masquerade entitled "Caravan of the Grand Signor to Mecca." Implausibly, Mozart introduced Turkish women into the catalog of Don Juan's seductions, and both he and Rossini made Turks into playful operatic figures. *The Bedouins* was the title of nothing less than a comic opera in Dublin in 1802.

Eurocentric reactions on the one side were matched by Islamo-centric reactions on the other. Under the Ottoman Empire, the Arabs were settled, and it is another distortion of nationalist historians to describe this as stagnant. Material deprivation is one thing, but rooted identity and culture quite something else. The Arabs continued to live as they had always done, exploiting the challenges of tribe and of Islam to generate new leaders in the traditional manner. In Arabia, in Yemen, in the so-called regencies of Algiers, Tunis, and Tripoli along the Mediterranean coast were rulers who nominally acknowledged Ottoman sovereignty and paid tribute but in practice had wrested their independence. Personalities included the founder of the Saudi dynasty which today is ruling Saudi Arabia and his associate Muhammad Ibn Abdul Wahhab, preaching purist Islamic doctrines; Suleiman Pasha, the governor of Baghdad; Ali Bey el Kebir (meaning the Great), who had been sold to the Mamelukes or Ottoman soldiers in Cairo as a slave and rose to be a ruler; Abdel Ghani al-Nabulsi, the mystic theologian. In 1789 Muhammad bin Ali al-Sanusi was born in Algeria. Studying in Fez and in Mecca, he started the religious order known as the Sanusiyya at Jaghbub in Libya, and his sons and descendants converted this order into a kingdom for themselves. Continuing to maintain independence, the sultans of Morocco posted ambassadors abroad and signed treaties to accept foreign trading agents at home. Now and again, the Ottoman sultan in Istanbul estimated that an Arab vassal had overstepped the threshold of tolerance to become a challenge to his rule, and sent an expedition to compel obedience. Ordinary Arabs, familiar with the governing pasha and the tax collector, the tribal notables and sheikhs, defended themselves with time-honored stratagems against rapacities no less time-honored. As is the case with absolutist structures, a radical reform to any one part threatened to bring down the whole.

Selim III was the first Ottoman sultan to try to take the measure of the European performance. In his youth, the loss of the wars with Russia had seen such unprecedented events as a Russian fleet in the Mediterranean and Russian troops landing in Beirut. Turning to France as the foremost military power of the day, Selim invited assistance. In 1784 while still heir-presumptive to the throne, he had written to King Louis XVI, "We are meditating in secret on the proper means to repair the evils, damages, and losses that our enemies have caused us." Accordingly, with French technical help, the imperial engineering works and the artillery corps were relaunched. New factories produced muskets, equipment, and uniforms. The Arsenal of Istanbul, which 200 years earlier had been the basis of Ottoman naval supremacy in the Mediterranean, was rebuilt. Jacques Le Brun, a foremost naval architect of his day, entered the Sultan's service from 1793 to 1804, supervising the construction of forty-five ships of the latest design.

Reform of the kind depended on the Sultan and was imposed by decree, regardless of the absence of trained managers and a work force for the purpose. Those accustomed to precedent were simply overridden. Previously the Ottoman army had contained formations of free soldiers but its *corps d'élite* consisted of Janissaries, who were youths captured in the Caucasus, Georgia, or the occupied parts of Europe and forcibly converted to Islam. The Ottomans were not alone in conscripting in this way. The earlier Ayyubid rulers of Egypt had also relied on military slaves from the Caucasus and elsewhere, in their case known as Mamelukes. Behind this apparently bizarre system was the sound intention of raising and training soldiers without tribal or family allegiances that would override their loyalty to the Sultan. Bypassing tribal solidarities had proved efficacious until such time as the slave-soldiers themselves evolved into a caste with inherited privileges. Asserting their independence, the Mamelukes had converted themselves from slave-soldiers into the rulers of Egypt, as in the example of Ali Bey el Kebir. The Janissaries also had every intention of exploiting the old system. At their headquarters in Istanbul, the Janissaries were only one degree more controllable than in garrison in provincial cities of the empire. Introducing a different conscription, Sultan Selim raised an entirely new type of army, consisting by 1806 of 22,685 men and 1590 officers. Fearing for their future, the Janissaries rose in revolt, deposing and killing Selim III.

Elsewhere in the empire, local power holders had taken tentative steps to import European military technology. Suleiman Pasha, governor of Baghdad during the last twenty years of the eighteenth century, ordered arms and ammunition from the East India Company in Bombay, with requests for British instructors. In 1797, the Dey of Algiers asked for American aid to build and equip ships for piracy. Thomas Jefferson foresaw a danger in acceding to such a demand, but Congress voted the funds and the ships were duly delivered. Jefferson's caution was ignored everywhere. Spain in 1804 was providing carpenters to build gunboats for the Pasha of Tripoli. No Western government at any stage held the view that Muslim military inferiority ought to be encouraged as a safeguard of Western supremacy. From the outset, the transfer of arms and armament technology was considered a trade on equal terms, without preconceptions about how those receiving these resources might use them. No less obvious was the fact that the Ottoman Empire had already missed the chance to build the infrastructure for its own industry, military or otherwise. The Age of Enlightenment, for good and ill alike, had passed it by.

Napoleon's invasion of Egypt in 1798 was one of those strategic decisions with which the military mind so often bemuses the civilian. The aim was to attack England, for which purpose, more straightforwardly, Napoleon three years later assembled a flotilla in the Channel. Personally he appears to have had some attraction to the Orient. In 1795 he had applied for service in Turkey; and he had promoted the dispatch of a military mission to Persia. (James Morier's novel of 1824, *Hajji Baba*, based on firsthand experience, puts these words into the mouth of Persians: "But a few months ago an ambassador from Europe arrived at the gate of Empire, Tehran, and said he was sent by a certain Boonapoort . . . how this Boonapoort had become Shah not a single man in Persia could explain."). Long afterward, in defeat, Napoleon judged the Arabs to be "the picture of savage man in the most hideous form imaginable." Once in exile, he declared himself to have been disappointed by the Orient, harping on the image "savage man is a dog," which reveals his own prior romanticizing.

Brave but custom-bound as ever, the Mamelukes of Egypt

charged the soldiers of the French revolution as they had charged the army of Selim the Grim in 1516. There could be no recovery. Occupying Cairo, Napoleon adopted a turban, visited mosques, invited the notables, and let it be known that he supported Islam and was hoping to install a regime based on Islamic Law. What kind of country the French had occupied was examined by a scientific commission accompanying the army. *Description de l'Egypte,* published in twenty-four volumes between 1809 and 1824, still remains a tribute to the spirit of Enlightenment.

Liberty, Equality, and Fraternity, in the slogan of revolutionary France, had no equivalent in Islam. Al-Jabarti, a notable and the foremost Egyptian chronicler of the invasion, translated "the French republic" as "on behalf of the French," a wording which fails to grasp the political notion and so misses the whole point. Visiting the scientific mission at work, al-Jabarti registered "incomprehension and amazement." Another dignitary, Hassan al-Attar, the Sheikh of Al-Azhar—that thousand-year-old university in Cairo, which has always been at the core of the interpretation and teaching of Islam—also saw the scientists but he "delved into their books and learned from them." The daughter of one religious notable dressed like a French lady, and after the French evacuation she was executed for it. The native Christian minority, the Copts, responded confessionally. A Copt by the name of Muallem Jacob raised a Coptic legion on the side of the French, which led to accusations of Christian forwardness rather than of collaboration.

Military conquest as such brought Napoleon nothing but honor, and shame to the Mamelukes. A popular song in Cairo testified to it:

We longed for you, O General,
O you handsome one with the hanging cloak,
Your sword in Egypt made havoc
Of the Ghuz and the Urban [the Mamelukes and the bedouins]
Ya Salam!
O splendid republican,
With the lock on the head
You brought light into Egypt,
And came in like a crystal lamp,
Ya Salam!

Forty years later, Flaubert on his youthful travels in Egypt found that Napoleon was still regarded "almost as a demi-god."

British countermeasures on land and sea ousted the French

army of occupation. Far from proving stagnant or decadent, the immediate local response to the sudden power vacuum was in the historic pattern. Several contenders among surviving Mamelukes struggled for power, but an Ottoman officer, Muhammad Ali, emerged victorious. Born in 1770 at Kavala in Macedonia, he had arrived in Egypt with the Macedonian Brigade of the Ottoman army that had been sent to resist Napoleon. Through skillful intrigue and the murder of his commanding officer, and with promises offered to the ulema (as those learned in Islam, whether doctors of law or preachers, are called), Muhammad Ali assumed power. In 1811 he invited his Mameluke rivals to a banquet in the Cairo citadel, closed the doors, and massacred them almost to the last man. The state was then his until his death in 1849.

Speaking in 1826 to the British consul, Muhammad Ali made a classic statement of the motivation of such a power holder.

I came to this country an obscure adventurer, and when I was but a bimbashi [roughly, major] it happened one day that the keeper of the tents had to give to each of the bimbashis a tent. They were all my seniors, and naturally pretended to a preference over me; but the tent-keeper said, "Stand ye all by; this lad, Muhammad Ali, shall be served first." And I *was* served first; and I advanced step by step as it pleased God to ordain, and now here I am.

He concluded his boast with the words, "I never had a master." On another occasion, he gave the no less classic defense of a dictator, that his ambition was indispensable to the public good whether or not the public recognized it.

I collected all power into my hands in order to ensure efficiency. The question is one concerned with production, and if I fail to act, who else would? Who is going to provide the necessary funds, suggest the plans to be followed and the crops to be planted? Who is going to force the people to acquire knowledge and sciences which made Europe progress? I was forced to lead this country as children must be led because allowing it to function alone would only lead to chaos again.

One of his advisers was to reveal to the political economist Nassau Senior how autocracy of this kind conditioned social attitudes. "The Fellah is an animal—kind, docile, laborious: a higher sort of dog. The Bedouin, too, is kind and laborious after his fashion," and he continued, "When we are talking of political life on a great scale, the Fellah and the Bedouin must be left out of the question." In following through his power play, Muhammad Ali was distinguished from comparable rulers in the past by one new and incalculable factor: the unavoidable presence of Europe and Europeans. He and his overlord, the Ottoman sultan, were to adjust their relationship by the usual method of testing out their mutual strengths. Some blunder on his part, however, might well set off a European power response, possibly another military intervention, which would decisively wreck his ambitions. Shrewdly, he turned to the European powers for help, to France first and foremost, then to Britain. Experts and advisers took it for granted that he would want to modernize on European lines. In doing so, he was assuring himself of foreign goodwill and support. Illiterate until the age of forty, and probably afterward as well, he liked to listen to readings of the life of Alexander the Great and Machiavelli's *The Prince,* from which he declared that he had nothing to learn. Recasting traditional despotism into his own unique form of oriental Bonapartism, he had devised a brilliant guarantee of his absolutist hold of the state. No power challenges or even peasant troubles erupted under his rule, and his dynasty was ensconced at the end of it.

Rounding on the ulema who had helped him to power, Muhammad Ali confiscated the religious foundations that had been the sources of their wealth, in the end amassing almost all agricultural land in his own hands. Instinctively aware that wealth creation amounted to power, he initiated agricultural techniques and crops, notably cotton, and he undertook public works. From 1812 onward, he set up a centralized economy in which purchase and sale prices had been fixed for his benefit, "a system reminiscent of Soviet practices in the 1930s" in the words of the economist Charles Issawi. Monopoly of exports and foreign trade provided between a quarter and a third of his budget receipts.

Nothing in the previous experience of the population had taught them how to deal with the new forms of ruthlessness imposed by this ruler. One authority, quoting a contemporary witness, describes how Muhammad Ali and his state

inflicted terrible or harsh duties on women of poor areas, subjecting them to forced labor in which the "entire population of several villages, men, women, children and young girls, led by the sheikh al-balad [a man designated to be mayor], were taken, chained, and laboriously found their way to the appointed place." They were forced to buy the cloth of the state at a price fixed by the administration and were forbidden to weave their own clothes. All dresses had to bear a stamp attesting that the material came from government stores.

Under a system of unpaid labor known as the *corvée*, the fellahin were press-ganged into the fields or into repairing the Nile floodwater dykes. Conscription into the army was considered a virtual sentence of death. The objective was military strength, pure and simple. An Englishman, Galloway, built a foundry at Bulaq with eight furnaces turning out castings for machinery and arms. A Frenchman, de Cerisy, built the naval yards at Alexandria. Army training required manuals and dictionaries, which in turn called for translators and printing facilities. The first printing press in an Arab country was opened in 1822, in Cairo, and within twenty years it had published 243 books, two of which were volumes of Arabic poetry. To train translators, in 1826 Muhammad Ali paid for a party of forty-four students to go to Paris, to learn the language and to attend trade schools and workshops. In 1832, twelve medical students arrived. Two of his own sons were among those educated in Paris. The real objective, comments a historian of these missions, was not to encourage the penetration of Western ideas but to create a nucleus of loyal servants laying the foundation of an administrative structure geared to the military machine.

By 1833 Muhammad Ali was employing seventy Italian officers, another seventy French officers, and about a dozen British and Spanish. Octave Sève, his chief of staff, had been a lieutenant under Napoleon, later converting to Islam under the name of Suleiman Pasha (not to be confused with the earlier governor of Baghdad); his statue still dominates a square named after him in Cairo. By the end of his reign, Muhammad Ali had 130,000 men under arms. His campaigns had been successful in Sudan, in Arabia where Egyptians had reached the Holy Cities, and in Syria and Palestine, occupied for ten years under the rule of his son and heir, Ibrahim Pasha. Engaging and defeating his overlord, the Ottoman sultan, at the battle of Nezib in 1839, Muhammad Ali finally overreached himself. Britain and France had differing views about the consequences of the collapse of the Ottoman Empire, but nonetheless they imposed a peace treaty which established that Muhammad Ali's power challenge had reached its peak. Put another way, however, the British and the French stopped him by certifying that he could keep what he had won for himself in Egypt.

E. W. Lane had lived in Egypt during the latter years of the reign. Observing what drastic changes had been brought about by Muhammad Ali, Lane could not but lament the difference of the state of Egypt under his rule from what it might be; possessing a population of scarcely more than one quarter of the number that it might be rendered capable of supporting! How great a change might have been effected in it by a truly enlightened government; by a prince who (instead of impoverishing the peasantry by depriving them of their lands, by his monopolies of the most valuable productions of the soil, and by employing the best portion of the population to prosecute his ambitious schemes of foreign conquest, and another large portion in the vain attempt to rival European manufactures) would have given his people a greater interest in the cultivation of the fields, and made Egypt what nature designed it to be, almost exclusively an agricultural country!

Muhammad Ali's technique was not lost on his opponent and victim, the Sultan Mahmud II. Succeeding to the throne after the turmoil of the revolt of the Janissaries and the murder of Selim III, Mahmud appeared likely to preside over disintegration of the empire. While Muhammad Ali was building his power base in Egypt, the Arabs in the Hejaz had campaigned in the name of Wahhabism only to be crushed by an Egyptian expedition. Russia and Persia both opened hostilities, and Greek nationalists were preparing for independence, or sedition in the Ottoman perspective. Centralization and consolidation of power was the only hope in dealing with these challenges. The more ruthlessly Mahmud reformed, the greater the prospect of eventual power, and if that happened to be what the Europeans welcomed as necessary and overdue modernization, then he could allow himself a free hand. Mahmud began to take the steps which enabled the empire to survive for almost another century.

The defenders of the old order consisted of the Janissaries and the ulema (or Islamic divines), with the Grand Mufti at their head. Between them, they held the monopoly of force and education. If reform was to be on Western lines, then their dominant position would have to be destroyed, a most desirable achievement from an absolutist sultan's point of view. Mahmud reorganized the artillery corps into a bodyguard of 10,000 men, favored by better pay and new barracks. When in 1826, the Janissaries again objected, he loosed on them this bodyguard. The massacre was general. The survivors in provincial garrisons were disbanded, mostly without bloodshed. Euphemistically, the sultan's elimination of conservative opposition was referred to as the Auspicious Event.

* * *

Prince Metternich, the Austrian Chancellor, was one who foresaw that reform might prove more dangerous to the Turks in the long run than tradition. What was useful to them was too easily confused with what was harmful. Losing their Turkish identity, they would only become secondhand Europeans. Metternich's advice was, "Do not borrow from European civilization institutions that do not agree with your institutions, because Western institutions are based on principles that are different from those forming the bases of your Empire." Turks, he concluded, should stay Turks on a basis of Islamic Law.

The British, whose influence throughout the Middle East was in the ascendant, disagreed. Stratford Canning, lyricized by Tennyson as "the voice of England in the East," was on and off for some thirty years the dominant figure in Istanbul as British ambassador, part-adviser, part-viceroy. He had witnessed how fleeing Janissaries had been cut down, their blood turning the Bosphorus red. Not a squeamish man, he had earlier been present when the head of a rebellious Pasha of Baghdad was laid at Mahmud's feet. To Canning, a Victorian, progress was one and indivisible. In a dispatch of 1832, he stated what all through his life he believed the Turks ought to do and could do. "I want to see the Porte [as the government establishment was called] in a situation to receive the full tide of European civilization, to enlist the whole force of the country in support of its independence, to take her proper place in the general councils of Europe, and to base her military and financial systems on the only true foundations of security for persons and property." Otherwise, he thought, it would be better to revive the Janissaries and return to the old ways. "The choice lies between *fanaticism* and *discipline;* there is no middle line."

Fanaticism was a clear course at least. But where was the law, consent, rights, and duties to underpin and realize the discipline that went with security for persons and property? A superficial glance at the surroundings revealed the gap between reality and aspiration. In 1837, a fastidious English traveler and scholar, Robert Curzon, arrived in Istanbul in search of ancient manuscripts. He wrote to his parents that "the filth is not to be imagined by any one who has not particularly nasty notions, it only seems wonderful to me that the plague does not sweep away the whole population . . . old clothes hang out of the broken windows, dead animals remain in the streets, which are not wide enough for carriages, houses which have fallen remain as they fell, and the only scavengers of the city are the vultures, and a race of mangy, deformed and half-wild dogs."

Mahmud reformed the bureaucracy, and with it the administration of the provinces, including tax collection. In 1833 he summoned military advisers from Prussia. One of these was Helmut von Moltke, the future field marshal, and in 1840 he and his colleagues were reporting to Berlin how military and social reform must be inseparable. The weakest part of the army, they wrote, was the officers.

Two of the major-generals came from the harem of Muhammad Khusrau's palace [he was Grand Vizier], a third had been a porter ten years earlier, and a fourth had been a galley-slave taken off a ship. There were a few talented officers among the brigadiers and colonels, and these provided the momentum that kept things going, though they received almost no help from the officers junior to them. Often very young men were made majors. They might have been narghileh-tenders or coffee-makers to some pasha, and they were immediately given command of a battalion. Captains and lieutenants were usually the more elderly men . . . none had scientific training as we know it, and few had battle experience.

Technical schools were built, and some one thousand students enrolled in them by the end of Mahmud's reign. Translation offices were opened. Western clothes and uniforms were introduced. Nonetheless, the battle of Nezib in 1839 dramatically revealed the sultan's inability to withstand Muhammad Ali. Mahmud died shortly afterward.

Between 1839 and 1876, successive Ottoman sultans followed in the established Westernizing path, issuing a series of decrees generally known as the Tanzimat, or the reforms. Whether these reforms were genuinely desired by the rulers or carried through to propitiate Europe is impossible to decide. The 1839 edict concludes with a curse on those who might fail to observe the reforms, and indeed there was no other more effective enforcement. The general thrust was to introduce equality for all subjects, Muslims, Christians, and Jews, in contrast to the *millet* system. Such equality required supporting laws and institutions as prerequisite to a society whose subjects were to become citizens. Embryonic municipalities developed, and Councils of Ministers, creating a professional class capable of absorbing and reproducing Western ideas.

The rapidity of the changes concealed the extent to which received notions of identity and culture were in question. At stake was indeed what kind of confidence the inhabitants of the Ottoman Empire could have in themselves. Adolphus Slade, a perceptive Englishman, in 1836 was already describing what could only be a type of emotional defiance, in this case displayed by Tahir Pasha, the vice admiral of the Ottoman fleet. In his heart, Slade wrote, Tahir hated Westerners on account of their superiority, "hating them particularly because unable to carry on some works of the arsenal without them; hating them the more because not allowed to vent his wrath upon the bodies of those in his pay." Tahir's one wish, Slade concluded, would have been to have these "representatives of Christendom" at his mercy. (In fact, by the time Slade had published his book, Tahir Pasha had been strangled by order of the sultan, perhaps because he was held responsible for the failure to prevent the French from invading Algiers.) It was only 1854 when Vambéry arrived in Istanbul. He hoped to support himself by giving lessons to a young Bey, who was "trying to acquire the external attributes suitable to his wealth." These attributes were a suit of the latest cut, tight patent leather shoes, a small fez, and gloves. Vambéry's task was to ensure that his pupil acquired "an easy, graceful step" and French conversation. The household's attendant mullah, or man of religion, muttered in his beard, "This is the way in which the spirit of infidelity is being smuggled into our houses." He was right, but the young Bey was not necessarily wrong. The split between old values and new, between the Islamic heritage and the current upheaval, had already begun in the encounter with Europe, and the Tanzimat period of reform widened it into a painful and irreconcilable divide.

Unexpectedly, the destruction of the old monopolies of force and education strengthened the sultan's authority by eliminating ancient checks on it. In a somewhat similar contrary reaction, the undermining of the *millet* system aroused in the mind of the Muslim the suspicion that he was considered inferior to the infidel, and then the fear that he might actually be so. A sultan reforming to keep himself more and more absolutely in power might hope, it appeared, cunningly to combine discipline and fanaticism. The technology of the European Industrial Revolution, surging suddenly and massively into the Middle East, happened to coincide with the Tanzimat with more unforeseeable consequences: whoever was ruler could concentrate more power by means of these inventions and improvements.

Steam navigation appeared on the Tigris in 1839, on the Nile in 1841. In the latter year, as many as seventy-six steamboats were plying the Mediterranean, from England, France, the Habsburg Empire, Italy, and ports farther away, allowing a drop in freight costs of about 25 percent. In 1847 an American frigate was the first screw-propelled warship to enter the Mediterranean; soon afterward, propeller-driven and anthracite-fueled ships were general. The following year, an American mining engineer was engaged to survey mineral resources in Turkey, leading to the opening of the coal industry there. European companies laid the first Turkish railway from Izmir to Aydin between 1857 and 1866, and another from Izmir to Alaşehir between 1864 and 1872, with the effect of reducing costs and making new crops profitable. With the Crimean War in 1855, the first telegraph cables were laid overland, followed by submarine cables a year later. By 1860 Istanbul was linked by telegraph to the main provincial centers of the empire. The sultan was enabled at any moment to issue incontrovertible orders in writing to his governors, and by the same token could be informed of any disturbance on the day it broke out. The telegraph alone annulled the somewhat wishful attempts of the Tanzimat to limit autocracy. In the West, inventions of the kind arose from the culture and could be understood as improvements even if there were human and social readjustments to be made in taking the strain. Within the Ottoman Empire, these things were mere gadgetry falling out of the blue, the unsanctioned work of infidels, yet at once tools for the sultan.

In the wake of the inventions came men who could exploit them and teach how this was done. An extraordinary collection of Western adventurers and explorers, some of them idealists and others scoundrels, spread out through Muslim lands into the remotest corners where no such person had ever been seen. Either converts to Islam, "renegades" in the language of the day, or Christians still in name, they had an impact out of all proportion to their numbers, whether as exemplars or activists, sometimes spreading but often undermining their own original culture. Nassau Senior, the political economist, visiting Egypt in the 1840s, reported his conversation with an Armenian notable who told him how foreigners were "the objects of a mixture of envy, dread, hatred and contempt." The Christian missionaries were a caste apart, beginning with French or Portuguese Carmelites and Lazarists early in the seventeenth century, first along the Mediterranean and then up into Persia. Franciscans and Jesuits followed, with Protestants and Presbyterians from England and America as from the late 1820s. Each order tended to build its hospitals and schools, including in the end such well-known institutions as Robert College in Istanbul in 1840 and the Syrian Protestant College (later the American University of Beirut) in 1866.

Ibrahim Muteferrika was a Hungarian convert to Islam who in 1731 published a book, *Rational Bases for the Politics of Nations*, offering a rare European perspective to his Turkish compatriots. He pointed to Ottoman laziness and corruption, which he contrasted with European energy in opening up the world, for example, the colonizing of America. If the Ottomans would also acquire the useful sciences, military science especially, he said that they would defeat their enemies. He also had to import a printing press into Turkey to produce the book. His message seems to have gone unheeded; the printing press folded, to be started again only after a lapse of half a century. One French renegade organized the fire brigade in Istanbul, a largely wooden city; and another, a count, taught modern gunnery to the artillery corps. In 1772 Imam Abbas of Yemen crushed a rebellion in his capital of Sana with the aid of two renegades, a Scot called Campbell in command of his artillery and a Frenchman to produce the munitions. An English captain sold himself and his ship to help the Persian shah capture the port of Bander Abbas. A Frenchman in the 1780s constructed a drainage system in Fez. Europeans captured by the Barbary slavers often chose to enter service in Algiers or Tripoli, where another Scot rose to be an admiral. An English artilleryman accompanied Muhammad Ali's army under Ibrahim Pasha at the capture of Medina, while another officer, George Sadlier, rode alone across the desert to convey official congratulations on the campaign's success. (From his diary: "I have only to repeat that the procrastination, duplicity, falsity, deception, and fraudulence of the Bedouin cannot be described by one to an European in language which would present to his mind the real character of these hordes of robbers.") Passing himself off as Ali Bey, a Spanish officer, Domingo Badia, traveled through the Middle East between 1803 and 1807. In 1819, the Italian Vincenzo Maurizi published an account of Muscat, where he had been the private physician of the local sultan.

A former Harvard divinity student, George Bethune English,

otherwise Muhammad Effendi, commanded the Egyptian artillery on behalf of Muhammad Ali's expedition to Dongola and Sennar in 1823, and with him were two other Americans calling themselves Khalil Aga and Achmed Aga. John W. Cochrane of Boston entered the sultan's service in 1833 to manufacture cannon of his own design. Revolutions in 1848 and 1863 in Europe drove into exile in Turkey various Hungarians and Poles, notably Severin Belinski who ended up as an Ottoman administrator in Bulgaria, and Constantine Borzęcki, otherwise Mustafa Celaleddin Pasha, and author of *Les Turcs anciens et modernes,* in 1869, arguing that Turkish ethnic origins were European.

Few renegade careers were so unusual as that of Léon Roches, who at the age of twenty-two arrived in Algiers in 1830 with the French army of occupation. Converting to Islam, Roches made the pilgrimage to Mecca. In common with many European renegades, he was an artilleryman, an expert in explosives, with the skill for the technical upgrading of a Muslim army. Deserting to the Algerians as they rallied in self-defense under the Emir Abdel-Kader, Roches became his translator, adviser on foreign relations with Britain, Turkey, Morocco, and Egypt, and even go-between with Marshal Bugeaud, his former commander in chief at the head of the French expedition. An unofficial minister of defense, he also opened a munitions factory in Abdel-Kader's capital at Tagdempt. Eventually he returned to France, and in 1884 published a memoir *Trente Ans à travers l'Islam.*

The French invasion of Algeria is often ascribed to an incident in which the Dey of Algiers is supposed to have hit the French consul with a fly whisk. The French thus had no option but to invade—altogether a mythological rendering which provides the handy explanation that the French action was inspired by shame and therefore more comprehensible to Muslims. The invasion marked a historic turning point. Not since the Moors had fled from Andalusia had so central a portion of the House of Islam fallen so flagrantly to infidels, in violation of Islamic doctrine and sentiment. The motives of Charles X and his government remain obscure. The simplest explanation may also be the most convincing, that Algeria looked to be there for the taking. Between 1671 and 1818, fourteen of the thirty ruling Deys rose to power as a result of the murder of the incumbent. The writ of the Deys hardly ran over the tribes of the interior; and the French may have mistaken this condition for *fin de race* decadence. There was virtually no strategy for the expedition and much less a long-term imperial plan. For several years the French did little more than establish a bridgehead on the coast. Marshal Bugeaud went so far as to make a present to Abdel-Kader of the hundreds of muskets with which armed resistance began.

The resilience of the Muslim system of leadership emerging upward through the power challenges of the tribes once again proved itself. The Dey of Algiers surrendered almost at once to the French, but his place was taken by Abdel-Kader. The circumstances were right for an appeal to Islam in order to mobilize support. Son of a tribal chief, Abdel-Kader had been on a pilgrimage to Mecca, passing through Cairo. There he had been impressed by Muhammad Ali. Algeria lacked Egypt's resources. Léon Roches and a handful of other Europeans could not train a modern army. Many, perhaps most, Algerians also failed to see the French in nationalist or religious terms but rather in the traditional perspective of a challenger more powerful than any other. Shocked, Abdel-Kader was obliged to threaten them, to speak of conspiracy and betrayal, for instance declaring, "Any Muslim who revolts against my authority—I who accepted the title of sultan only in order to be able to chase the invaders from the land of the believers—by the sole fact of his rebellion gives help to our enemies and in consequence must be considered an enemy of Islam." Successfully withstanding the French for long years of fighting and intermittent truces, he was to end his life in honorable exile in Damascus, where in 1860 he helped to rescue Christians during widespread confessional massacres. A final revolt broke out in 1870. What with fighting and disease, about 100,000 Frenchmen had by then lost their lives in Algeria.

Truce-inspired peace in 1837 brought with it 25,000 colonizers, and two years later the first Bishop of Algiers was appointed. By 1847, 120,000 Europeans had already settled in the country, building in their own style, creating villages with a *mairie* and a *gendarmerie*, a post office and a school. The French Republican government of 1848 decreed that under French law Algeria was henceforward French territory divided into the three departments of Algiers, Oran, and Constantine. By 1865 the status of Algerians had acquired this definition: "The native Muslim is French; nonetheless he will continue to be ruled by Muslim law. He may be admitted to serve in the land or naval forces. He may be enrolled in tasks and civil positions in Algeria. On request he may be granted the enjoyment of the rights of French citizens."

An Algerian poet at the time of the occupation revealed the emphasis on military values governing the Muslim response in Algeria. The poet could have been speaking for any province in the Ottoman Empire in the face of Western encroachment.

O my God! Give the victory to our flags,
Revive our armies and humble the unbelievers!
O Creator of Slaves! O Master!
Send us a Sherif [descendant of the Prophet] who loves Muslims . . .
He will re-establish order,
The Christians will be extinguished,
And he will put to flight our corrupters.

To Karl Marx, the French were justified in invading Algeria because they were modern, while the Algerians, all feudal lords and marauding robbers, were in a "barbarian state of society." His was only one voice among others urging intervention for what were generally agreed to be civilizing purposes everywhere, in China, India, even in Lebanon, where Marx hoped in 1860 to see the suppression of "the high-pitched antagonism of the barbarous clans."

Lebanon offered a long history of local power challenges, some of which had been strong enough to result in an absolute ruler and a dynasty. Every *millet* was represented in Lebanon in an intense microcosm of the whole empire, and the mountains offered retreats and fortresses to power holders and challengers alike. Power holding in so small an area had overridden the religious barrier, with the result that Christian and Islamic sects were in alliance or opposition according to the political turns of the moment. Geography and human diversity and increasing links with Europe encouraged more and more challenges. Bashir II (1788–1840) was the last ruler able to crush opponents inside the country and even to extend his influence into Syria and Palestine. His fall opened a free-for-all.

In pre-Tanzimat days, the sultan would have dispatched a pasha and soldiers to control and arbitrate through procedures of divide-and-rule, mingling force and bribery. But this was harder in a Tanzimat atmosphere of equality decreed without means of institutionalizing that equality. Maronites and Druze, the country's predominant communities, interpreted any mitigation of their claims as a surrender of their identity, an outright attack upon their religious or sectarian status. Whatever the good intention, the Tanzimat reforms proved a cast-iron method of enforcing a defensive reaction of this tribal type. The Ottoman authorities, wrote Charles Churchill, a contemporary observer, had no jurisdiction whatever, as each of the great families ruled supreme in its district. In the absence of any commonwealth or civil structure, everyone exploited everyone else as much as possible. "Houses were built, lands purchased, crown property farmed, horses gorgeously caparisoned, all surreptitiously out of the coffers of the state."

The crumbling of central authority encouraged anyone with a mind to revolt, in other words to begin power challenging on his own scale. Here is an account of one particular peasant, in 1859, as described by a contemporary.

Tanyus Shahin gathered some of the sheikh's possessions from the coastal and mountain districts, including silk and wheat, and stored them in his house. . . . He opened the provisions in his house to people going and coming, provided rooms for them to sleep in, distributed arms and ammunition, and behaved as if he were the head of a great household, with the result that his name was spread far and wide. To every village that did not heed his words a crowd of people was sent from the other villages to oblige it to obey. He gave orders for the securing of rights and punishment of wrongdoers in whatever way he saw fit, without opposition, speaking with the authority of the "republican government." His prestige became considerable, and his commands binding on all.

As far back as the sixteenth century, the Christian communities had been in contact with Europe. A Maronite College was founded in Rome in 1584. The Maronite patriarch started modern schooling in 1789. By 1840, missionaries all over Lebanon had the means of relaying the news of events to the European public. Deteriorating conditions of civil war led to the intercommunal atrocities of 1860. At Hasbayya and Dayr al-Qamar, at least 5000 Christians were massacred by the Druze, and then as many again in Damascus. One hundred thousand more became destitute refugees, of whom about 4000 died. Europe was scandalized. French troops intervened. At the international conference then convened, an Organic Statute for Lebanon was signed. The country would remain an Ottoman province, guaranteed by the six signatory powers. The Christian governor was responsible to the sultan in Istanbul and under him was a council of four Maronites, three Druze, two Greek Orthodox, with the Greek Catholics, the Sunni and Shia having one member each. The *gendarmerie* was French-officered. Communal participation, though limited, was enough to stop the violence. Lebanon prospered as never before. These arrangements lasted until 1915. There was a portent here. What might have looked like the progress of destroying barbarous old forms in fact was the prelude to the unprecedented savagery of peoples who now felt themselves having to fight for survival. The absence of the discipline of political institutions could only foster fanaticism and massacres.

Tunisia was another country which had to adopt a view about military modernization for survival, with the example of Abdel-Kader's Algeria on the one hand, and Muhammad Ali's Egypt on the other. A somewhat similar course had to be steered between nominal Turkish sovereignty and the looming European presence. The ruler of Tunis, Ahmed Bey, was the son of an Italian woman captured and enslaved in a pirate raid. From his mother, he had learnt Italian and through her he came to rely on the services of Giuseppe Raffo, a Sardinian who stayed Christian and loyal to the Bey until 1860. In order to inherit, Ahmed had to kill contending cousins in his family. He invited a French military mission from 1842 to 1855. Starting the Bardo military school, he raised infantry and artillery regiments until the army had an establishment of 26,000, of whom 16,000 were on active service. Equipment imported from various European countries proved unsatisfactory, and some factories were built with the aim of self-sufficiency. In 1853 French engineers built and launched an iron-clad frigate, but she was never put to sea because the harbor mouth had not been widened.

Military modernization bankrupted the treasury. Ahmed's plight worsened when his treasurer absconded to Paris in 1852 with the funds and the files. Losing control of his army, Ahmed took the next logical step. In 1860, he and his minister Khayr ed-Din introduced a constitution, the first of such regulatory or legal constraints on his autocracy ever admitted by a Muslim ruler. European public opinion did not perceive what fears and political motives actuated Ahmed, and praised him as a liberal. The historian L. C. Brown writes, "Ahmed wanted so much the respect of his arrogant, and at times reluctant, European mentors that he was poignantly eager to take initiatives having no apparent benefit other than the possibility of winning that respect." His aspiration to honor appeared in the creation of a palace designed by an

Italian architect, with water gardens laid out by a Frenchman, in order to surpass the king of France at Versailles, as he told General Daumas, the French military representative and an Orientalist in his own right. In 1881 the French declared a protectorate over a Tunisia that seemed to them even more ready for it than Algeria in 1830.

Tunisia was the earliest example of a country where a ruler whose attempted survival through military modernization had destroyed his own authority and opened the way to the European occupation it was supposed to prevent. Yemen and Arabia had no sustained experience of modernization, retaining the tribal existence into the present. Access to the Arabian peninsula was difficult enough to exclude all but the boldest foreigners, but more importantly the retention of tribal life and custom preserved an inner confidence which the Algerian writer Malek Bennabi has called "uncolonizability." The Muslim who wished in some secret recess of his mind to be as good as a European, or to impress him, had imagined a scale upon which he was obliged to cede inferiority in advance. To such a person, the European ruling presence would be accepted in the natural order of progress; defiance itself would look hopelessly backward. Instead of articulating reasons for resistance and the defense of identity, the educated class, still small but growing, failed to separate admiration of Europe from self-contempt.

In Egypt, the race to modernize ended as in Tunisia, and only one year later. In 1882, the British protectorate was declared. William Gladstone, the Liberal Prime Minister, did so reluctantly, unable to explain satisfactorily to himself, let alone to others, why the government had taken this measure, and no opportunity was lost to stress how temporary it was. Turkey, culturally shattered by modernization and the Tanzimat, might very well also have been put under European protectorate. Rivalry among the European powers about which might be the protector, and of what, alone ensured the status quo. In addition, Abdul Hamid, ascending the throne in 1876, proved to be a man who sought to preserve the Ottoman Empire as it had been. Exactly tandem developments in Turkey and Egypt instructively led to continuing independence for the former and occupation for the latter.

That pioneering waterway, the Suez Canal, dug between 1856 and 1869, gave Egypt a wealth-creating asset and a footing in international affairs. The Khedive Ismail, Muhammad Ali's son, ruling from 1863 to 1879, sought to maximize connections with Europe. At the end of Muhammad Ali's reign, 3000 Europeans had lived in Egypt; by the end of Ismail's reign there were 70,000, half of them Greek, the remainder French or Italian. "My country is no longer in Africa, it is in Europe," Ismail famously proclaimed, and shame-honor can be detected in this reaction. To him as to Ahmed Bey, Europe was the standard by which to measure achievement; it was the source of good things; and it was temptation. As a young man, the Khedive had been notorious for his excesses in Paris, Rome, and Istanbul. Prisse d'Avennes, the French orientalist, commenting on the outlook and conduct of the first sons of pashas to appear in European capitals had observed, "They each exhausted their body by debauchery, acquired our defects, and none of our qualities or virtues."

In Egypt and in Turkey land laws passed in 1858 tended to concentrate estates in the possession of owners with Westernizing values. The Ottoman Penal Code of 1858 was followed by the comparable Egyptian Penal Code of 1875, both codes departing from Islamic Law in criminal matters. In 1871 Turkey and Egypt both passed laws to set up administrative and judicial councils in villages, towns, and provinces.

In the forceful manner of his father, Ismail constructed and transformed as he judged fit: railroads (the total railroad mileage of Argentina and Brazil overtook Egypt's only in the 1870s), port facilities, a postal service, the celebrated Cairo opera house and his several palaces, and the first stone bridge over the Nile. Between 1866 and 1873 were founded a Polytechnic, Schools of Accounting and Surveying and Veterinary Science, of Law, Egyptology, Military Science, and a national library. Elementary schools rose in number from 185 to 4000.

Whatever these institutions might one day hope to achieve, the army was the instrument on which Ismail relied for his independence. To that end, he built an iron-clad fleet; he purchased the newest models of guns from Germany and placed large orders for weapons and ammunition. In the aftermath of the American Civil War, qualified officers were available as mercenaries. The Khedive recruited almost fifty American officers, including his chief of staff General Charles P. Stone, Henry Sibley in charge of artillery, and Thaddeus Mott Pasha. As in Turkey, the army could only reflect the society at large and its familiar values. "Favouritism in promotion had led to the advancement of uneducated officers and to a corollary contempt for schooling," the historian James A. Field writes. "There was no brigade or divisional organisation, no uniformity of drill, no staff corps." An Englishman, Sir Samuel Baker, was engaged to suppress the slave trade in the south and to extend Egyptian domination into the Sudan. After four years and the waste of half a million English pounds, Baker was replaced by General Charles Gordon. A flamboyant personality, Gordon had made a career in China and skillfully promoted himself as the type of hero civilizing dark places. The rout of expeditions to the Sudan and to Ethiopia alienated support for Ismail in Europe. When in 1881 a Sudanese, Mohammed Ahmed, proclaimed himself the Mahdi or Messiah, the Egyptian army was unable to oppose him and the army he assembled under an Islamic banner. The prolonged drama of the Mahdi, in which eventually Gordon was to meet his death at Khartoum, more than anything else served to implant the attitude in ruling circles in Europe that if peoples in Africa and Asia would not keep the peace, then they would have to be taught to do so.

To finance his modernizing, the Khedive had raised foreign loans through banks in London and Paris. In the manner of Ahmed Bey in Tunisia, he overspent. Deficit financing was an unknown art. In Egypt and in Turkey, 1876 was the year in which extended financial crises broke. Egypt declared itself unable to repay its debts, and the Franco-British creditors insisted on control of the economy. Control in itself was hardly decisive. The future was to prove how smoothly the Khedive's debts, amounting to some one hundred million Egyptian pounds, were consolidated, rolled over, and repaid by sound management. The Egyptian economy's potential for growth was not in doubt. Out of panic, the Khedive miscalculated. He tried to follow the Tunisian example. Sending for his adviser, Nubar Pasha, an Armenian known to advocate a pro-European policy, he announced that constitutional rule would be introduced. An assembly of notables would be summoned, though it could only receive petitions and would meet in camera. To the British and French governments, the stratagem was unconvincing and did not placate.

To the army officers, however, the significance of the move was that the Khedive had lost his hold on power. Their turn to challenge had come. Because of the financial squeeze, the army budget had been cut, and salaries remained unpaid. In February 1879, in what was a Khedivial intrigue so complicated that it misfired, army officers mounted a demonstration for their pay. To the British and French governments unwittingly responsible for creating this turbulence, Egypt appeared to be falling into anarchy. That June, they forced the Khedive into exile as though he were a reprobate. His son and heir, Tewfik, could not avoid the shame and humiliation of succeeding to the throne in the circumstances. Thus it proved impossible for him to assert authority over the army officers. One of the colonels, Arabi Pasha, took the chance of extending the series of demonstrations into an attempted coup. Only the European powers could put a limit to his challenge. When the British in fact intervened in 1882, their first act was to reconstitute the army under senior British officers—not a Gladstonian Liberal priority under normal times, but a necessity if this example of power challenging was to be brought to an orderly end. International debts and military coups belonged to a new vocabulary, but the Khedive Ismail was neither the first nor the last Muslim power holder to discover that at the least sign of loss of control, the soldiery's ambitions were more conducive to his destruction than to his independence. Like Ismail, Arabi Pasha was also disgraced and exiled, neither the first nor the last Muslim challenger to discover that his pretensions ceased where superior power began.

In the disastrous 1878 war with Russia, Turkey lost another round of fighting. Neither the sultan nor the army had anything to be ashamed about, but on the contrary they rallied together against the aggressing unbelievers. In the final count, control of the army saved Abdul Hamid for some years longer from the fate of living in exile like the Khedive Ismail.

Very great difficulties impeded Muslims from a correct evaluation of the factors governing the ever more unequal relations between them and Europeans. Famous and ancient universities such as Al-Azhar in Cairo, Zeituna in Tunis, or Cairouan in Fez taught only Islam, its theology and related aspects. Only a select elite of Muslims had the opportunity for foreign travel and education. For an Arab, a Persian, or a Turk, the process of understanding European societies was usually through books, and few of any merit were available. To discover European institutions and habits and tastes was also to realize their absence in Muslim lands. Elements of self-analysis and comparison were unavoidable. Secondhand information, prejudice, and no doubt fear and shame obscured what might be the real relationship between objects such as a railroad or a cannon and the scientific method which had brought these objects into being, as well as the humanism within which science itself had grown. Ottoman ambassadors in European capitals failed to bring systematic understanding to their observations. In reports to the sultan, Louis XV's France had seemed to Celebi Mehmed in 1720 the discovery of "a new world," and in the Vienna of 1837 Sadik Rifat Pasha had picked up a phrase like "the proper application of the necessary rights of liberty." By 1845 a Turkish consulate was open in Boston. The first Muslim to publish a sustained account of European development seems to have been Sheikh Rifaa al-Tahtawi. Born in 1801, the son of a tax farmer, he had received an education at Al-Azhar. In 1826, as the religious leader of the party, he had accompanied the first students dispatched to Paris by Muhammad Ali. *The Book of the Distillation of Pure Gold, in a Summary Conspectus of Paris,* a travel book with reportage, appeared in Cairo in 1834. Tahtawi had the broadness of mind to like what he saw in France, the city and the countryside, the pretty women, the interior decors, the food and clothes, even the theater and dancing. There was a sense of release into a fresh and fascinating dimension. He had witnessed the revolution of 1830, attended the French parliament, and perceived a connection between politics and progress. The object of government seemed to be human welfare, and this very new thought implied a complete reordering of his own country. Egyptians, he realized, "had no channel by which they could oppose their rulers and no protection provided by the rules of holy law." This led to the conclusion that "what we call justice and good works, they call freedom and equality." Albert Hourani has summed up the important but partial message brought home by Tahtawi, namely the belief "that the secret of European strength and greatness lies in the cultivation of the rational sciences." Muslims, then, could enter the mainstream of modern civilization by adapting European sciences. The book's Turkish edition proved influential, and thirty-five years later Tahtawi covered the same ground in *The Programme or Paths for Egyptian Minds into the Joys of Modern Arts.*

Something of the same eager innocence is found in Assad Khayat's *A Voice from Lebanon,* written and published in English in 1847, the first book in a foreign language by an Arab. Born in 1811, a Christian from Beirut, Khayat had been taken up and educated by American missionaries, exchanging Arabic for English lessons with them. Afterward he established himself as a money changer, translator, and general factotum. Twice he journeyed to England, and his pleasure in the important and titled people he met there is infectious. Public and private proceedings at home contrasted unfavorably with those of the fortunate English. He was particularly impressed that £60,000,000 of revenue could be collected by the state without the use of a single musket.

Here we find a judge, with a salary equal to that of the grand vizier, whom the king himself cannot remove from his office; whereas, in some other places, we find a body of the servants of the state whose pay arises from what they can grind out of the people. Here the government borrows money, and must pay interest; and a man of the highest rank cannot touch the person of the meanest peasant. There the government seizes property at pleasure, and a man, without having committed any offence, can be sold in the market for a slave. However, by observing these contrasts, we may learn the benefits arising from civilisation, and hope that they will soon be extended to other parts of the globe.

Returning home from Europe, he wrote, an Eastern youth feels himself superior to his countrymen; with a natural anxiety to introduce all the improvements he has seen, "but he must not try to accomplish this at once, for his countrymen are too poor and too slow."

Peaceful and mutually agreed tax collection was a symbol of popular participation in the state, and it was also singled out with amazement by Muhammad Bin Diyaf, a Tunisian and secretary of Ahmed Bey, visiting Paris twenty years after al-Tahtawi, to whom he refers in his own chronicle. The secret of prosperity and lack of oppression in Europe, he wrote, "is that these taxes are not unfair. The inhabitants know exactly what is required, and the revenue collected is spent for the benefit of all without distinction." In Paris, Bin Diyaf found "all you could wish of sciences, industries wealth, good administration, elegance, civilization, and justice."

Sultan Abdul Aziz of Turkey visited Egypt in 1863 and Europe in 1867, accompanied by his nephew, the future Sultan Abdul Hamid; they were the first Ottoman rulers ever to leave their domains as tourists. Shah Nasir al-Din of Persia traveled to Europe in 1873 and 1879, publishing in the manner of a gazette delightful but rather unworldly accounts of his trips. He spoke in French to the Russian czar. The Prussian kingdom had "a very pretty soldiery." Queen Victoria was "very cheerful." The costs of building the Westminster parliament interested him more than the political attributes of the two-party system, which he saw as a mere division of the spoils. "Whenever the first-named set may go out of office, the whole of the Ministers and others must be changed and re-placed by others from the latter party."

Khayr Ed-Din, the Tunisian president of the Grand Council during the short constitutional interlude of 1860, made perhaps the first concerted attempt to grasp the causes of the Muslim-European inequality, for the purposes of redress. This remarkable man was born about 1810, in Georgia, reared as a Mameluke and reached Tunis in about 1840. More or less in exile, he lived in Paris from 1853 to 1857. When in 1867 he came to write *The Surest Path,* an outright political treatise, he made use of knowledge assidu-ously gleaned at firsthand about various European countries. European institutions and practices, he wrote, were often useful, but some were harmful, and all had to be reconciled in any case with Islamic Law. No reason prevented Muslims from enjoying a good administration. "I also assert openly the truth that any func-tionary who does not believe he should be held accountable in his public office lacks trustworthiness and sincerity to his state and country."

Visualizing society in the classic and static concept of the ruler and the ruled, he spoke of liberty in the sense of a man's freedom over himself, and not in the European sense of rights commonly accepted and legally protected. After the Tunisian constitutional experiment, he traveled once more in Europe, "to study the base and conditions of European civilisation" and to write. In 1873 the Sultan appointed him as Grand Vizier in Istanbul but then removed him almost at once.

Perhaps no Muslim statesman in his day was so well known and highly reputed as Midhat Pasha, the man upon whom turned the 1876 crisis in Turkey, and the architect of the short-lived constitu-tion that resulted from it. He and his fate exemplify the ambiva-lences inhering in the transfer of European ideas into a society without grounding for them. As a provincial governor in the Danube district, and then in Baghdad, Midhat had earned his reputation for such achievements as building schools, pulling down the walls of Baghdad and laying there the first streetcar line. These were changes for the likes of which over a period of forty years influential Englishmen such as Stratford Canning and others of a Westernizing mind had been pressing, and Midhat, an avowed "liberal," therefore became the subject of admiring articles in London and Paris.

During the 1876 constitutional debates, a member of the ulema pertinently asked, "How can you assemble those ignorant Turks of Anatolia and Rumelia and consult with them on the affairs of state?" That was not Midhat's intention. Islam, in his view, already quite sufficiently recognized the sovereignty of the people. Constitutionalism was to do with the disposition of power, not the bestowal of rights.

Ismail Kemal Bey, himself a member of the brief 1876 parliament, records how he used an argument about the principle of jury service to expose Midhat's shallow opportunism.

I maintained that it was totally unsuited to the people of Turkey, where it was necessary, first of all, to make the law felt and accustom the population to respect it. The jury system was suited to a country whose population were lovers of order, and who lived in awe and respect of the law. To establish the jury system in Turkey, where the mere idea of law had not yet taken root, would mean that crime would go unpunished. The first thing to be done was to take measures to prevent specific crimes in the various parts of the country, and especially to put down the different forms of crime that were rife in the various localities. In Albania, for instance, one would never have found a jury to condemn for murder in the case of a vendetta. Similarly, an Arab jury would never condemn a person accused of the "Razzia," or raids upon neighbours' belongings.

Skillfully deposing Sultan Abdul Aziz and then his nephew Murad in one palace coup on top of another, Midhat pushed through elections leading to a parliament. In June 1878, Midhat published an essay in the English intellectual journal *The Nineteenth Century,* under the title "The Past, Present, and Future of Turkey." The tone was judicious. He told his audience what it wished to hear. Constantly losing strength, the Ottoman Empire had fallen to the rank of a second-rate power, Midhat explained, "whilst European civilisation made growth and rose up beneath the shadow of liberties secured to it by new institutions." He went on, "In Turkey every one is desirous to see constitutional government acclimatised, established, and becoming at the same time the soul and mainspring of our institutions." How all this was to be implemented Midhat wisely did not try to explain. Only a small number of Turks would have understood Midhat's article, and they would have observed how he had omitted from it any mention of his role in disposing of two sultans and thereby levering himself into power.

Abdul Hamid, the third successive sultan in this crisis, could only draw the conclusion that constitutionalism was Midhat's brilliant and novel method of co-opting the Europeans into his power challenge and thereby guaranteeing its success. Rather than await his own imminent demise, he preferred to have Midhat exiled and after a while strangled. Abdul Hamid was reviled for this by European liberals for as long as he lived. None of these *bien-pensants* paused to wonder why a seemingly modern political approach had ended in the old way, in murder. Their indignation about Midhat, soon to be swelled by their sympathy for Arabi Pasha in Egypt, served for many years to mislead public opinion in the West into the Eurocentric and totally unfounded notion that a new wave of "progressive" Muslims was courageously battling against "reactionary" rulers. This was a false projection abroad of the class-warfare with which they were familiar at home. In fact, power holders and challengers alike were proving fully and inventively capable of adapting every European modernism to their own traditional purposes, just as long ago they had absorbed Islam itself.

In 1881 Husayn al-Marsafi published in Cairo a collection of essays called *The Eight Words,* which were respectively nation, fatherland, government, justice, despotism, politics, freedom, and education. For him, the key to European supremacy lay somewhere in that complex. Like Khayr Ed-Din in *The Surest Path,* he advocated expanding the scope of science and knowledge, as though this were an end that could be pursued in isolation from other ends. The implication was that Europeans could be resisted only by their own methods and skills. Yet it was already observable that the current importation of such methods and skills had worsened the situation by strengthening the hand of the few able to exploit them, and at a more general level weakening traditional skills and crafts and the culture that went with them.

If Muslim development was to be rational and free from shame-honor reaction, a thorough analysis of Western civilization had become imperative. Transmission of knowledge of visible factors such as science or patriotism or parliamentarianism was less crucial than the relating of the parts to the whole, to elucidate the spirit in which Western man conceived the ordering of the world—and his place in that world.

Instead of an intellectual analysis, the simplifications of Jamal al-Din al-Afghani proved irresistible. Over the last hundred years, Afghani has probably had more influence than any other Muslim in the shaping of ideas, earning a wide posthumous reputation. Born in 1838, in Shia Persia, Afghani, as his name suggests, found it expedient to pretend to have been an Afghan, and therefore belonging to the Sunni majority. His education in holy Shia cities in Iran and Iraq was religious. Some of the years between 1858 and 1865 he spent in India, in the aftermath of the Indian Mutiny. There he conceived what can only be called an obsession that the British were out to destroy Muslim culture as such, and that this pointless behavior could be explained by their inherent wickedness. Islam, he believed, was the only power now able to mobilize Muslims and challenge the British. All his life he searched for ways and means to translate this attitude into influence and power.

Strangely enough, he himself was hardly a sincere Muslim, but something of a freethinker and at one time the lover of a Dutch woman. In Egypt, he became a Freemason; the Emir Abdel-Kader, who used Islam as a rallying cry in Algeria, was another early Arab Freemason. Unoriginal as a thinker but familiar enough with names like Voltaire and Darwin to be able to insert them into his discourses, he wrote one short book, *The Refutation of Materialists,* which is by no means the full religious statement that might have been anticipated. In an exchange of opinions in 1883 with Ernest Renan, Afghani conceded that Islam stifled intellectual and other freedoms, but went on to claim that other religions were equally retrograde. A strong and compelling personality, he convinced a number of disciples who listened to him with fervor in private talks or in lectures. In the conduct of his life, he was nevertheless somewhat of a failure. Power holders in Afghanistan, Persia, Egypt, and Turkey all at one time or another saw him as an agitator, pure and simple, and expelled him from their countries. In exile, he traveled in Europe, including Russia and again in India, dying eventually in Istanbul at the age of fifty-nine.

Backwardness was a word which Afghani did not hesitate to apply to Muslims. This in itself set up the tension of self-pity, which he exacerbated by the call to Islam. More than anyone else, Afghani built into the definition of progress a contradictory regression to the Islamic past. What evolved was less a doctrine than a mood, swinging between unhappy nostalgia and fierce assertion, at all times volatile and emotional. The mood may be caught in a single sentence of his, from 1884: "It is amazing that it was precisely the Christians who invented Krupp's cannons and the machine gun before the Muslims." Characteristically, the pessimistic recognition that the Christians already had the guns invalidated any optimistic hope that Muslims have only to shoot their way to equality. It was also Islamocentric to link the invention of cannons to the supposed Christianity of the inventors. Nothing could come from such a perspective but the fanaticism of Muslim solidarity, fighting for honor and power. Afghani's painful sense of shame and apologia is reflected time and again in his depiction of Muslims prostrate and humbled before the West, wrongly, but through no fault of their own.

The Europeans have now put their hands on every part of the world. The English have reached Afghanistan; the French have seized Tunisia. In reality this usurpation, aggression, and conquest have not come from the French or the English. Rather it is science that everywhere manifests its greatness and power. Ignorance had no alternative to prostrating itself humbly before science and acknowledging its submission.

Islam, he asserted, was the religion closest to science—the incompatibility between Islam and science which he had allowed to Renan he concealed from his fellow Muslims. Should this be true, it still remained for Afghani to elucidate how Muslims were to invent their own cannon, and then whether or how Islamic and European cannons would differ, and finally what benefit would accrue to anyone from this rivalry by cannon. In this view, science was less an organic expression of a civilization than a magic by means of which Muslims might throw off the hold of Europe. The contemporary Muslim-European encounter had far too many facets for this one-dimensional approach, whose sole outcome could only be the legitimization of violence. Afghani's widening reputation as a great man in the Muslim world revealed how troubling was the sense of shame induced by European supremacy.

Afghani did not live long enough to see the experiment in constitutionalism in his native Persia in 1906, an equally brief and chaotic repetition of what had happened in Tunisia and Egypt and Turkey. Persia looked destined to disappear in the Anglo-Russian rivalry which pincered it. French occupation of Morocco in 1907 and the subsequent declaration of a protectorate in 1912, and the Italian invasion of Libya in 1911, brought further large portions of the Muslim world under European control.

Muslims who longed for an escape from the House of War into

the security of the House of Islam had only inviolate Arabia to which they could turn. The Dutch orientalist C. Snouck Hurgronje was one of the extremely rare Europeans ever to have lived in Mecca, able to pass as a Muslim under the name Abd al-Ghaffar and to research Islam there during the 1880s. In Mecca, he met a cultivated Egyptian who had emigrated, a virtual refugee, to avoid the unbelievers. One day the Egyptian was complaining about the stupid conceit of the English in Egypt and the rudeness of their soldiers. When Hurgronje put it to him that the English government had rendered good service, the man replied, "here a white dog, there a black dog, but they are all dogs, and sons of dogs." Hurgronje later described the resentment and distaste of such believing Muslims on coming into contact with Europeans, with their wide-brimmed hats, their loud laughter, and godless ways.

"How Can the East be True to Itself?" was the title of an article written by Abdallah al-Nadim, an Egyptian who had supported Arabi Pasha and who became one of the earliest and most celebrated Arab journalists, dying at the age of forty-three in 1896. Orientals, he wrote in this article, had no chance to better themselves, "as if their race had been created to serve the Europeans they are so obviously incapable of imitating." Unsure whom to blame, he cursed everyone.

> Accursed condition to which these phantoms called "knowledge" and "civilised ways" have reduced us! We have planted hatreds in our now starving and aggressive hearts. We have exhausted ourselves in pointless enmities through ignorance and stupidity. We have exposed our innermost selves to the scorn of others.

The alternatives seemed to him to be either "to mend this moth-eaten cloth" and to speak with a united voice, or else to be chased out altogether by the foreigner. What he took to be the scorn of others prevented him from a proper examination of his characteristic assertion, on the one hand to posit which measures were practical for effective self-defense, and on the other to assess rationally whether the foreigners were really nothing but predators, and their "civilised ways" only a cruel trick for seeking advantage.

European ignorance of Islamic culture was unfortunately exceeded by Muslim ignorance of European civilization. In a shadow play of things and images incompletely understood, Muslims inter-

nalized feelings which were to well up into doubt and self-hatred.
Demoralization fed xenophobia, once again to the point of fanaticism. The Turkish poet, Mehmed Akif, captured the attitude in this
stanza of his poem "Sermon from the Suleymaniye Pulpit," written
in 1912, which made a stir at the time.

> Look at Morocco, Tunisia, Algeria—
> They are all gone!
> Iran—they are dividing it too!
> This is most natural, the field is the runner's
> The right to live was given to the strong by God.
> Muslims! a nation afflicted with factional dissent,
> Will civilized Europe not eat them in three bites?
> O community, if only for God's sake, awake!

Gokalp injected more anger into the vein.

> We were defeated because we were so backward,
> To take revenge, we shall adopt the enemy's science.
> We shall learn his skill, steal his methods.
> On progress we will set our heart.
> We shall skip five hundred years
> And not stand still. Little time is left.

Looking back in 1935, barely a hundred years after the adventures
of Tahtawi and Assad Khayat, an elderly Turkish writer, Huseyin
Cahit, summed up the self-consciousness resulting from the interaction of Europe and the old Muslim order.

This talk of Oriental culture, Islamic civilization, the sciences of the
Arabs was repeated constantly in every writing, and on all occasions in
order to anaesthetize the nation, in order to prevent it from joining the
stream of life of the West passing us near by. In addition to the thick and
black shroud of ignorance laid upon the nation, we had the twofold
ignorance to boast of our condition and to despise Europe. It was impossible for anyone who could more or less sense the situation and who loved
his country not to be tormented by such a spectacle.

4

The Consequences of Careerism

A long line of Western travelers and diplomats have judged that bad government in the Ottoman Empire, and since then in the successor Arab states, has obstructed the civic fulfillment and personal welfare of the Muslim citizenry. Volney, that lucid observer, wrote that the art of governing in Egypt "consists only in taking money and giving blows with the sabre." Sir Henry Layard, excavator of Nineveh and Babylon and afterward ambassador in Istanbul, spoke of the honest, simple, and hospitable Turk "before he is corrupted by the temptation and vices of official life and power," and, he added, "by intercourse with Europeans and the Europeanised Turks of the capital." "Despotism tempered by assassination" was Richard Burton's description of government in the Near East. To Gladstone, ever the moralist, Turkey was "incorrigible in sin." The passionately muddle-headed poet Wilfred Scawen Blunt imagined himself to be campaigning for the Arabs and their freedom as Byron had once campaigned for the Greeks. A hundred years after Volney, Blunt was repeating the view that the Ottomans in their empire had "a government of force and fraud, corrupt and corrupting to the last degree." Without this government, he believed, the Arabs would be happy. On this topic, though on few others, Blunt spoke like a British official.

In an influential book first published in 1899, Sir Charles Eliot, who had been at the embassy in Istanbul, gave his account of the Turks.

No Turk dare associate with foreigners, or give a large dinner-party to his own people, and two or three Turks of eminence cannot safely meet in a private house. The whole city groans under the tyranny of the Minister of Police. It is inevitable that spies in their desire to show zeal should invent baseless accusations. The highest functionaries may be summoned in the middle of the night, and interrogated by persons much their inferiors in rank on utterly frivolous charges; and any one who should venture to oppose this regime would find his fortunes and perhaps his life imperilled. . . . The real evil is that all the joy of life, all freedom and originality, all political, intellectual, and social activity, are destroyed by the ubiquity of this espionage.

Eliot wondered why the Turks put up with it, when the majority were honest, patriotic, and God-fearing. Change, he decided, proved not for the better and only endangered the rule of Muslims over Christians. The system was intractable.

 Corruption was viewed in the Eurocentric perspective as an excrescence on the system, something unnatural and of course unjust, as much of an oppression as the ubiquitous espionage. Like lying and cheating, corruption was deemed to be malicious, evidence of poor character, and to this extent could be used to justify the European rule which would clean it up. Corruption in fact survived intact through the end of the Ottoman Empire and the colonial period and today flourishes as never before in every Arab state. Moralizing on the matter is irrelevant and Eurocentric. The ordinary Arab recognizes and approves of the principles of liberty and justice and equality as much as the Westerner does; but he is excluded from their means of achieving or enjoying these ends. In his value system these principles apply differently if at all. Corruption among Arabs is nothing more nor less than the daily functioning among everyone of the power-challenge dialectic, and it is registering individual advances and retreats everywhere and at all times. Corruption plays a role approximating to competition in a democracy. At the top of the social scale, corruption represents the power of the strong over the weak; at the bottom, however, it may soften the caprices of power and so promote tolerance.

In democracies, nepotism and jobbery have to submit to measurable or at least visible criteria of performance and merit. A man attaining high office through his connections rather than his competence becomes a cause of mockery and then scandal. No such criteria apply in the Arab world. There, every man sets out on a career by virtue of who he is, who his family are, what honor he is entitled to. The well-connected Arab not in high office would be the cause for scandal and shame to his family. Public examinations for admission to universities, government departments, the armed forces and particularly officer training colleges, the law, and institutions in general are therefore less meritocratic matters than a vast jockeying for place and influence. All manner of patrons, themselves also grandfathers and fathers and uncles, lobby behind the scenes in order to favor their children, their kinsmen, or anyone to whom they owe some obligation or for any reason wish to foster.

Needless to say, those promoted to executive or managerial level in Arab institutions such as government agencies, banks, newspapers, industrial companies, may very well be of a high caliber but one and all remain in the course of their lives at the mercy of power challenges swirling around them, and in which they cannot help being both active and passive. They have no means of predicting when or how the power challenge of someone else might sweep them away into disgrace or poverty, or worse. In self-preservation, they have to be alert to the least intention of attack, not because they may have proved unfitted for their responsibility but simply because they are standing in the way of the challenge of other patrons, other families, other tribal-religious interests, or most serious of all, an aspiring power holder. Challenges are secret, moreover. Nobody declares his ambition until certain of success because he risks exposure, antagonism, the mobilization of more powerful opponents against him, and perhaps murder. Instead, he intrigues, he influences as best he may, he conspires.

From the privileged down to the humblest, every man is in the posture of a challenger throughout his life. He can rely on nobody and nothing except the retinue of kinsmen and perhaps friends, of which he himself is a member. To begin with, he is likely to be challenging modestly, as a seller or buyer, as trade competitor or clerk, lowly enough to offer and to receive more or less harmless individual challenges. Advancing in experience, and perhaps in wealth and status, he begins to encounter other challengers with their kinsmen and friends. If he is to surmount and win, he has to enlist or to neutralize them. Either solution requires tactical handling. The choice is simple: force or favor. Force is most effective, but only if the agent can be certain that he will not arouse counterforce. Usually favor is preferable, and the simplest and most universal of favors is money. Generally speaking, money passes upward and favors in return pass downward, but obviously circumstances may dictate otherwise. Careerism as a whole is a money-favor nexus. Expressed another way, the money-favor nexus is the civilian idiom for the challenges of power.

In Western societies, licenses, passports, certificates of import and export, tax returns, legal judgments, bureaucratic documentation of every type represent contractual or defined dealings between the state and the individual and are negotiable only to the extent that the relevant law is imprecisely worded. If the bureaucrat or administrator or judge concerned with the paperwork is absent or retires, his replacement will apply the same impartial and impersonal standards and procedures until such time as the law may change. In Arab countries, every one of the signatures on those indispensable bureaucratic pieces of paper represents power to some particular holder. The decision to dispense or to withhold the signature vitally adjusts power between one person and the next and must be treated accordingly, well prepared, and paid for.

Lord Cromer was British agent and consul-general in Cairo from 1882 to 1907 and a believer in decent administration as the basis of public welfare. Describing the system that he had encountered, he was helplessly outraged.

The contractor bribed the Minister to obtain a contract on terms unduly advantageous to himself, and would then bribe the Clerk of the Works in order that he should not inquire too carefully as to whether the terms of the contract had or had not been strictly executed. The subordinate official bribed his superior in order to get promotion. The landowner bribed the engineer in order that he should obtain more water for his fields than was his due. The Kadis [Islamic judges] were paid by both the plaintiff and the defendant to any suit, the decision being usually given in favour of the highest bidder. The Government surveyors were bribed to make false measurements of land. The village Sheikhs were bribed to accord exemption from the corvée and from military service. The Police were bribed by everybody who had the misfortune to be brought in contact with them. The passenger by railway found it cheaper to give "bakshish" to the guard or to the ticket-collector than to pay for a ticket. As a preliminary to bribing a Moudir [provincial governor] to inquire into any alleged grievance, it was necessary for the petitioner to bribe the hungry satellites, who hang about the office of the Moudirieh, before the great man could be personally informed that any petition had been presented. The ramifications of the system were, in fact, endless. Egyptian official and social life was saturated with the idea that in Egypt personal claims and interests, however just on their own merits, could never be advanced without the payment of "bakshish."

To Cromer, corruption more than anything else impeded reform. Reform itself, he came to conclude, was like firing a cannonball into a mountain of mud. Here was another clash of value systems. Corruption did not saturate the system as though by pollution; on the contrary, the system required corruption as oil for its own workings; and was immune to Cromer's cannonballs. The French consul gave this picture of Baghdad in March 1891:

> Disorder has reached a new height: robberies are continuing and in the course of the last eight months, at least 200 murders have been committed in the city; not one effective sentence has been passed; the magistrates sell indemnities to the criminals and cases are reported of assassins who commit their crime in broad daylight only to be freed on the pretext that there were no witnesses . . . from the governor down to the lowest gendarme everyone steals and anarchy would be preferable to the regime now experienced.

Here is Unni Wiken on dealing today with one of the most common of demands in Cairo.

> To get paid while off sick, a man must obtain a certificate from one of the doctors employed by the company's health department. It is not easy for a poor man to get that certificate. However sick he is, he has to go to the health department, often several times, in the hope of finding the right person. Besides, the certificate costs bribes. One man I know had to pay £2 [perhaps a tenth of his monthly salary] for such a certificate and still did not receive it. In other words, he lost the bribe and a whole month's pay.

Desmond Stewart, a writer sympathetic to the Arabs, teaching in Baghdad in the 1950s, tells the story of an English-language textbook in Iraq. Another Englishman, John, has a conversation with a woman teacher who informs him that an Iraqi, Zeki, has written this new textbook. John is on a ministry of education committee to decide which textbooks will be adopted, and he replies lightly that reading textbooks is a bore. Two days later, he is telephoned and told that this remark has reached the ministry, and he is no longer on the committee. Desmond Stewart replaces John, reads the textbook in question, and observes that Zeki has a desk at the ministry of education. The committee meets for its decision but its two Iraqi members, carefully forewarned, do not attend as "we do not want to make enemies." Instead there is Zeki who screams at Stewart. The issue has to be referred to higher authority. Next day the committee is dissolved by ministerial edict and Zeki's textbook is then selected for use in all Iraqi primary schools. Invisible in this typical careerist ploy was the way that Zeki had paid bribes to a publishing house, fixed the committee, and prior to any formalities pushed a decision in his favor through the ministry where he worked.

Tewfik el-Hakim recounts how an idealistic doctor volunteered to work in a poor district of Upper Egypt. There he discovered that his assistant extracted the enormous sum of £300 a month from the peasants. After objecting to receiving this money, the doctor heard how his assistant would separate patients into those who could pay and those who had to have free care because they had no money. The doctor then was allowed to see only the former, while the assistant gave flasks of colored water to the latter. "You are not going to waste your time doing that for nothing!" the assistant scolded the doctor, explaining how he obtained all sorts of profitable authorizations from the authorities which had permitted the extortion of the £300. "Doctor, by ourselves we can't reform the world!"

John Waterbury, a scholarly observer of the Middle East, has sketched a scenario for a business deal, specifically in Morocco, though the example would serve for any Arab country.

X, Y and Z are prominent Moroccan businessmen with connections in the Palace and, more often than not, close relations or friends in the Ministry of Finance. They approach a thriving French textile plant and propose that they be allowed to acquire a certain proportion of the company's stock, let us say 15 per cent of all outstanding shares. It is understood that they will pay nothing for the shares but that dividends will accrue in their names until they are the equivalent to the value of the shares on the day of "purchase." The company can use those dividends as they accumulate, and, depending on the bargain, include interest in the purchase price. In the meantime, X, Y and Z will have been "elected" to the board of directors with salary. Without investing a penny, the three entrepreneurs can each pick up a salary and eventually a share of the company's assets. The more influential they appear to be, the more often they can repeat this gambit. In return for what is essentially protection money, they do favors for the company, such as arranging duty-free importation of machinery or keeping the labor inspector from closing the place down for violation of safety regulations.

Adaptation of ostensibly Western procedures for committees, boards of directors, and validation of certificates only perpetuates the money-favor nexus and even impressively opens new fields for old endeavors. Guided and planned by the regime in Morocco, Waterbury concludes, corruption is expected by everyone, replacing or dwarfing all other forms of politics.

There are even civil servants [wrote a Tunisian journalist in 1986, about his own country] who own villas worth hundreds of millions. Sometimes these are built thanks to loans that will not be repaid, if all goes well, for two or three centuries. Everybody sees to it that he's all right. For instance, there is the school or hospital administrator who uses his institutional account to purchase furniture, his television set or refrigerator, after which the goods are delivered, bit by bit, to his own home. Another man signs the authorisation for his wife, or for a cousin who is on the pay-roll, to take a year's leave of absence. She goes to work elsewhere, while he continues to pay her salary, because nobody does the accounting.

Louis Awad, an Egyptian writer and lifelong champion of the need for Egyptians to participate in the state, is almost alone in pointing out the reactionary resilience with which the money-favor nexus has overtaken and colonized, so to speak, all countervailing influences. No matter the outward changes of form in Egypt, he writes, "It is more or less the same conservative power and money elite of depoliticised professional deputies, technocrats and administrators whose families have ruled Egypt for more than a hundred years, surviving the quicksands of national and social revolutions and disasters."

Everybody has to develop the attitudes necessary for coping and surviving. In his book about modern Egypt, Gilles Kepel refers to the Egyptian sociologist Dr. Sayyid Uways who listed the outlets by means of which people manage to confront misfortune and oppression: "indifference," "hypocrisy," "raillery," "emigration," "rebellion and revolt." The humiliated and dominated strata, Kepel explains, resort day by day to the first three of these outlets, for instance addressing some clerk with the ludicrous title of "bey" or "pasha," or snapping to attention and muttering "at your service" to any superior. The defense mechanism is generalized. In Kepel's words:

This sort of popular release preserves a kind of social equilibrium: although he grows rich, the exploiter gains no prestige, but only ridicule and derisive nicknames. Meanwhile, everything the dominated layers do, they do badly. The underpaid *bawwab* [porter] who sleeps on a mat in the building's entrance-way deliberately scratches the bodywork of the tenants' automobiles, which it is his job to polish. The miserably paid teacher comes to class late and teaches the pupils nothing. The only students who pass their examinations are those who have paid for private lessons, the fees for which enable the teacher to survive. The whole dialectic is expressed in two famous words in the Cairo dialect: *ma'alesh* ["that's all right," "it doesn't matter"] and *bakshish*, which needs no translation. *Ma'alesh*, the car is scratched; *ma'alesh* the child is ignorant; *ma'alesh*, the machine is broken; *ma'alesh*, there is a three-day - or three-month - delay.

The attitude of *ma'alesh* contains what Kepel calls "a small but undeniable slice of freedom," but the acceptance of the corruption of *bakshish* both fulfills and annuls it self-perpetuatingly.

Programs for social development and amelioration may well be devised on scientific criteria by experts at the top level. The execution of these programs in accordance with such rationale then runs headlong into power challenging and the attached values of shame and honor. In the absence of open debate and accountability, the masses who have to implement the programs remain uninvolved, mere hands, sardonic witnesses of a superior person's hypothetical success or failure, cherishing *ma'alesh*. In his recent travel book *An Egyptian Journal*, the English writer William Golding gives a good example of the kind of practice which follows this systemic logic, but to a Westerner seems maddeningly wasteful and even evidence of vice. In the Fayoum, or desert east of Cairo, Golding one day came across an institute for the multiplication of mango and olive trees. The seedlings were there, suitable land existed, the minister had approved. But, said the European director of the project, "no matter what the minister says or tries to do, somewhere in the pyramid the order dies, is lost. I am quite simply giving up." In the end, Golding comments, "we did a lot of shrugging at each other and came away." Who were they to grasp—let alone to affect—the personal intrigues and power challenges whereby this worthwhile planting of trees would simply be lost in the sands?

Without a public forum, clashes of interest cannot be debated, assessed, and resolved by common, or at least majority, consent. Wealth, resources, property, even the bodies of men and women, the state itself, all become one huge money-favor nexus to be plundered by those who can. Human beings become instruments. The spoils for the successful careerist are irresistible. Public welfare is a concept without meaningful application; there is no common good. Long ago, a Turkish official whose duty it was to prevent Jews immigrating into Palestine, put the matter with amusing clarity when he took bribes from Jews arriving illegally at Jaffa harbor: "If it's a question of your interests and the Empire's—yours come first." A Druze emir, once asked how he and his kind spent their money, gave the equally clear but more tragic answer, "We spend it on injuring one another."

Power challenging survives unscathed because it is so harsh a process of natural selection. Great hardship and injustice are generated by the system. Generosity is suspect as a ploy for advantage. Idealism and sincerity are penalized. Self-sacrifice is akin to lunacy or martyrdom. At best, a kind of rueful cheerfulness may breed in the huge net of mutually concealed intentions. So low is the view of human nature that any altruistic impulse prompts tears and high emotion. Life is too dramatic to be staid. Privately, complaints are heard in Arab countries. Sometimes a newspaper will be permitted to criticize some particularly obstructive piece of bureaucracy. A privileged columnist may remark in rebuke or sarcasm that the Arabs are not the brothers they claim to be. Nonetheless it is obviously futile to pick out one part of what is a consistent whole. By definition, whoever complains is a loser in the power-challenge dialectic, and a loser has no recourse to appeal; he can only wring his hands and hope to engage in some other ploy in which he may emerge a winner.

The most successful challenger is obviously he who works his way through the elimination of every rival and seizes the supreme prize of the state. In form, his career starts like that of any civilian. Rising upon the energy of his ambition, he must seek to bind together a retinue of men on whose services he can rely, in all likelihood kinsmen or friends and associates since childhood. Then comes another circle of those connected by village or tribe. Beyond that extends a wider circle still, of those who share an ethnic or religious tie, as Sunnis or Shias, as Druze or Alawis in Syria, as Kurds in either Iran or Iraq, as Berbers in North Africa, as Christians or Jews. If a man is to aim for absolute power, he has no choice but to appeal to his own kind, to promote them in the expectation that they will promote him. Only the ulema (and hardly even them in Sunni Islam) and the senior commanders of the army can be said to have any other organized or institutionalized loyalties. Those two groupings are in a position significantly to authenticate and support a challenge or to oppose it; and they must be approached with due prudence. A challenger backed by representatives of Islam and of the armed forces may expect to broaden his retinue into a winning coalition. The prime incentive to lure potential allies is the promise of rewards in the event of success, with the complementary fear of deprivation and exclusion if they do not join.

The test of experience alone can determine where a challenge will end. Depending on the extent of the power holder's ambition, the boundary of the state itself expands into hopeful imprecision, in the profusion of territorial demands that every Arab state makes upon its neighbors, varying the approach in a rhythm of military attacks and protestations of brotherhood and unity. Those of his tribe or religion who happen to live upon the other side of some frontier as defined according to the accidents of history and geography will expect to participate in the triumph of one of their own kind. Declaring allegiance to him, or even merely invited from afar to do so, they risk reprisal and massacre from the power holder to whose rule they actually submit. Others may turn to the successful challenger as a sponsor, seeking to join his coalition at an inter-Arab level. This of course provokes a reaction of self-defense and militarization among those who perceive themselves now threatened by this reinforced challenge. Mobilizations follow, uprisings fomented across frontiers, "liberation" movements, raids and incursions and outright war. Force and favor, as determined among individuals through corruption, are writ large into the statecraft of fighting and inter-Arab conferences, with their in camera sessions which so occupy the calendars of Arab leaders.

Mohamed Heikal, the Egyptian journalist who was Nasser's mouthpiece, has given an example from a session at an inter-Arab conference called to discuss what policy to adopt toward King Hussein when in 1970 he destroyed the PLO bases in Jordan.

GADDHAFI: If we are faced with a madman like Hussein who wants to kill his people we must send someone to seize him, handcuff him, stop him from doing what he's doing, and take him off to an asylum.

KING FEISAL: I don't think you should call an Arab King a madman who should be taken to an asylum.

GADDHAFI: But all his family are mad. It's a matter of record.

KING FEISAL: Well, perhaps all of us are mad.

PRESIDENT NASSER: Sometimes when you see what is going on in the

Arab world, your Majesty, I think this may be so. I suggest we appoint a doctor to examine us regularly and find out which ones are crazy.

KING FEISAL: I would like your doctor to start with me, because in view of what I see I doubt whether I shall be able to preserve my reason.

Naturally none of the participants really believed that anyone was in need of a psychiatrist. Behind those interjections, each leader was mentally calculating personal profit and loss and possible honor and shame, each one as anxious to gain as he was fearful of the sudden thrust that might bind or commit him unexpectedly. Not one represented any genuine constituency or was accountable to anyone except himself. None of that could be stated openly. In such circumstances, a consensus is only a remote prospect, and King Hussein had little to fear but offensive propaganda. Decisions about whom to trust and whom to betray have to be fended off until there is the privacy in which to confide or conspire. What might sound like the most laughable farce is in fact the deadly serious constraint of these politics. Emerging from such a conference into the glare of modern publicity, the participants can only resort to the trite platitudes and turgid ideology that so enigmatically conceal the very vivid dangers of Arab politics.

Language in which to do justice to the political aspect of Arab careerism once again is inadequate. Interpreting the interminably repetitive and dreary speeches, attending to the conference resolutions, assessing the lengthy and interconnected chains of assassinations and coups and wars, historians and commentators are driven to blanket phraseology about one ruler after another "emerging after a struggle," "taking certain measures," "being a strong man," "depending on his right arm," "establishing links with the armed forces." Behind these links and measures and struggles is a reality which defies all but the greatest novelists: a lifelong questing for power, the gradual sensing and probing for potential allies of similar ambition, the conspiracy into which crucial friends are admitted and from which others have to be excluded, an ever-present awareness that the trusted friend is best placed as a mortal traitor, double-crossings and feints and denunciations, calculations over the smallest matters of promotion and demotion, the scrutiny for those imperceptible details of manner or facial cast which may reveal someone's inner purpose, the secret meetings at safe houses or abroad to escape the security services, the maps of key locations and the lists of rivals to be murdered, midnight flights, disguises, untraceable cars and guns whose serial numbers have been filed off, and perhaps above all, huge bundles of banknotes received from hands whose anonymity must be at all times safeguarded. Today as a thousand years ago, from high office to prison or the gallows is only a question of minutes. Knives and bullets remain the final arbiters between one line of action or policy and another.

Absolute rule engenders conspiracy, which alone can over-throw it. Yet absolute rule is also the final fulfillment of conspiracy, a gigantic plot of one man against everyone else. This is what keeps the power-challenge dialectic in perpetual motion.

Ever renewed in successive generations, ever dazzling in its limitless temptation, power challenging, like a vortex, sucks in all who approach close. Foreigners stand in the same relationship as Arabs to the power-challenge dialectic; they have the same choice of either surmounting it by superior force in order to emerge as power holder, or entering into it on its own terms, complete with money-favoring and shame-honor ranking. Europeans could never have appreciated this alternative at the moment when they might have reformed the system altogether, as their soldiers and ad-ministrators seemed to hold every field. The superiority of Euro-pean force was also a deterrent to its use. No prime minister could have declared in a European parliament that he was destroying Muslim customs in the interests of a new sociopolitical order and hoped to stay in office. No European ever advocated such a policy, nor could he have thought that title or will existed to do anything so drastic. By the same token, no European could have imagined that the power-challenge dialectic, if unchecked, would eventually deal with him as it dealt with the Arab masses. As a further brake on all such forecasts, virtually all nineteenth-century European statesmen lacked conviction in the ultimate social benefit of liber-ating their own masses to participate in political processes.

Democratic societies are always handicapped when dealing with closed and absolute systems. A government responsible to an elec-torate has no equivalence to a power holder accountable to no-body. Had European power been unitary in the nineteenth cen-tury, then perhaps the Middle East might have been integrated into the Western order after a period of time. But European power was instead split into competing centers, not only London and Paris, but Berlin, Rome, Vienna, St. Petersburg, with further possible alliances among lesser states at the margin. If Britain and France were already moving toward participatory democracy, the Central Powers and Russia preferred absolutism. Here the power-challenge dialectic had its opening. Challengers in the world of Islam could enlist European powers as well as provoke them, play one off against the other, conspire offensively and defensively, altogether co-opting the foreigners at a national level into their tribal and sectarian order. Richly endowed, technically equipped, but none too well instructed in these unfamiliar ways, the foreigners obliged by throwing themselves mindlessly into power challenging. Anxious to be loved and devoid of that will to be hateful which is indispensable to triumph, manipulated by reason of their diversity, the Europeans were to be outmaneuvered in less than a century, and much to their surprise.

Sometimes this is expressed the other way about, in accusations that the Arabs are servile flatterers of those in authority over them. A popular Turkish author, Burhan Cahit, put it into a novel in succinct sentences that would once have passed for wisdom among Europeans too. "The Arabs are always the same: sweet as lambs when faced with armed might. They care little whether they are governed by Muslim Turks, Roman Catholic Frenchmen, Protestant Englishmen or Buddhist Japanese. They are always ready to flatter the mighty." Interpreting behavior at face value, judgments of the kind ignore that a skillful and quasi-conspiratorial defense is in operation. Europeans also greatly encouraged their own illusions by taking their opinions from interlocutors like Afghani and his disciple Muhammad Abdu, later the Mufti of Egypt, from the likes of Arabi and Midhat similarly speaking in what were approved Western vocabularies of appeals to public opinion and national rights, which of course have no foundation in a power-challenging society. One and all, including their Westernized successors into the present, have actually been engaged as prime challengers for power, archconspirators, brilliantly incorporating into their schemes the novelty of Western doctrines and consolidating their chances, no matter how fleeting.

As the European impact shook the fabric of the Ottoman Empire, conspiracies fermented. A number of these secret societies affected grandiloquent titles in concealment of their true aims, and perhaps in imitation of *Illuminati* conspiracies in Italy or the *Philhel-*

lenes in Greece. Some Turkish conspirators chose the name "Young Ottomans" for themselves in 1865. In 1875 a Christian Arab Society was started in Beirut. At the center of each tiny secret society was usually an individual, and perhaps his brother or cousin or a kindred spirit, who had been in contact with Europe and its ideas. All were political. Here and there, a few ephemeral leaflets were published in which shame-honor phrases about "Arab pride" jostle strangely with European-influenced echoes about "degenerate Turks."

Under conditions of absolute rule, if the challenger is to make headway and not squander his time fantasizing and verbalizing, he must make the most judicious selection of a patron for the necessary money-favoring. The power holder is the primary patron of all, and a challenger may advisedly encourage the power holder himself to sponsor him, keeping secret, of course, that the ultimate goal is the destruction of that very man. If not the power holder, then a close contender, for instance an aggrieved brother or disinherited uncle, anxious to recruit helpers to his own challenge. The career of Afghani, for example, was a desperate search for a patron among the rulers of Persia, Afghanistan, Turkey, and Egypt, or then among English radicals like Blunt, and Russians like the publicist Katkov in St. Petersburg, all the while so maneuvering between British and Russian authorities that he may even be suspected of offering his services to them. How all this was financed is far from clear. To Afghani seems to go the credit for a clever exploitation of something original, namely European publicity methods. In 1883 Afghani and Muhammad Abdu, then his most admiring Egyptian disciple, founded *The Indissoluble Bond*, a paper in Paris that ran for eighteen issues. Hundreds of copies were shipped back into Egypt and Turkey.

In 1889 Turkish medical students started a secret society which recruited in the military and naval colleges in Istanbul. These conspirators were in touch with a similar handful of Turks already in exile in Paris. A prominent personality among them was Ahmet Riza, the son of an Austrian woman who had converted to Islam and of a Western-educated Turkish father. Ahmed Riza, nicknamed by his colleagues "Riza the Dreamer," reached Paris in 1889, started a paper and took over the conspiratorial group known as the Young Turks. Sultan Abdul Hamid broke up the group by the usual methods of bribery and cajolery. Ahmed Riza was nonetheless the organizer of a congress in Paris in 1902, attended by forty-seven delegates from all over the empire. Six years later, army officers in a military secret society which they called the Committee of Union and Progress staged a coup against Abdul Hamid, and then invited Riza to leave his Paris attic as the first President of the new Turkish Chamber of Deputies.

The atmosphere of these conspiracies was evoked by an English writer at the time.

> The form of initiation crystallised into a definite ritual. The man was blindfolded, and led to a secret place whose whereabouts was entirely concealed from him. The bandage was then removed from his eyes, and he found himself, perhaps in a darkened room, perhaps in a lonely hollow of the hills, in the presence of three strangers wearing black masks. These administered to him the oath which was to become the rule of his life. Swearing on the sword and on the Sacred Book [the Koran], he bound himself to devote his whole energies to the redemption of his country, to obey every order given to him through the channels of the Society, never to reveal its secrets, and to kill every person, however near and dear to him, whom it might condemn to suffer death. His eyes were again covered, and he was led back to the place from where he had started on the mysterious journey.

Challengers and the power holder both barred no holds.

> The Committee [of Union and Progress] developed a rival system; the spies became known, and were spied upon in their turn; the death penalty was sometimes ruthlessly applied. The despotism, in a word, was fought with its own weapons.

Conspiracy in Europe, with its prospect of arousing the interest of European sympathizers and journalists able to pressurize their own governments and public opinion, became a vital staging post for power challengers. A case in point was a Persian high official, Malkam Khan, who fell out with Shah Nasir al-Din and reached London, where in 1890 he demanded constitutionalism for Persia, which, he hoped, would make him the prime minister in the new dispensation. His newspaper was called *Qanun,* and he too was patronized by Blunt.

Mustafa Kamil was an Egyptian careerist of a type soon to become familiar. Born in 1874, the grandson of a rich grain merchant and son of an engineer educated in Muhammad Ali's schools, he entered government service. As a bureaucrat under British rule, he felt that he had not been promoted quickly enough. Lack of recognition sparked off a response of humiliation, and this could only be appeased if he received what he took to be his due. Turning secretly to the then Khedive, Abbas Hilmi, he found himself a patron.

Abbas Hilmi and Mustafa Kamil thought that they might start a nationalist party to oppose the British. Whether such a party was to be monarchist or republican was naturally left unspecified, but it could not be both. As Abbas Hilmi and Mustafa Kamil proceeded to the next step, each imagined himself to be outwitting and exploiting the other.

The Khedive and Mustafa Kamil, who were on the look-out for potential propagandists for the nationalist movement, soon heard about this secret society, and got in touch with Lufti [Lufti al-Sayyid, an intellectual, came to see that Egypt would have to develop over a long period its participatory institutions, and in the end bitterly opposed Kamil]. Kamil, who knew Lufti, told him that the Khedive had suggested that he join another secret society, having the same aims as his own, and headed by the Khedive. . . . This new secret society turned out to be *al-Hizb al Watani* [the Nationalist Party] which was still in its infancy, and which had only five members: the Khedive, Mustafa Kamil, Muhammad Faris, a pharmacist from Zagazig, and Lufti. They all had code names.

Funds were provided to launch a paper in 1900, *al-Liwa*, which soon had the large circulation of 10,000 copies a day. Through the paper, Mustafa Kamil preached Islamic solidarity against the British. Expulsion of the British was the beginning and ending of his policy. How the Egyptians would then organize was not his concern, but he supposed that it might somehow follow the example of Japan, about which he wrote an admiring book. "Nationalism," he wrote with the cloudiness that was the be-all and end-all of his political program, "is a sentiment before which all nations and all communities bow because it is the feeling of the worth and dignity of man, of the bounty of God and His care, of the meaning of existence itself." As Mustafa Kamil's reputation as a firebrand orator and journalist grew, the Khedive rightly saw in him the rival for power that he was. Patronage ceased. If he was to continue enlarging his power challenge, Mustafa Kamil had to look elsewhere, and he turned to France. Sponsors were to be found there, among politicians and journalists who supposed that the British in Egypt were the main threat to the French in North Africa. Grouped around the literary *salonière* Juliette Adam were publicists like

Henri Rochefort and W. T. Stead, an English radical crusading against the British Empire, and Léon Daudet and Edouard Drumont, both obsessive anti-Semites, the latter the author of *La France Juive*. Once again, this coalition comprised people who imagined themselves to be exploiting their partners.

A disastrous shooting accident occurred at Denshawai in 1906. Pigeon shooting by British officers in Egyptian villages was looked upon by the fellahin as poaching, and in an altercation in this village, one of several officers discharged his gun and wounded a woman. The fellow officer who ran for help died of sunstroke. Nobody doubted that the chain of events was accidental, but in a reaction out of all proportion the British set up a special tribunal to try the villagers. Four men were hanged in public, and sixteen condemned to prison, four for life. "When I read the verdict," the Egyptian Salama Musa says in his memoirs—he was then a young man but destined to become a prominent writer—"I felt as if I had to vomit." The shame had to be avenged. Here was a national blood feud. *Al-Liwa* had its cause. At the same time, Mustafa Kamil was writing:

> No truly patriotic Egyptian will ever consent that Egypt be ruled by His Highness the khedive alone, or by the British Commissioner, or by both of them. He demands that his beloved homeland be governed by the talented and sincere among its children and that the system of government be constitutional and representative.

Had Mustafa Kamil not died of a chest disease in 1907, it is possible that he might have been the talented and sincere Egyptian that he had in mind to wrest power from the Khedive and the British.

Another successful conspirator in this mold was Abd el-Rahman al-Kawakibi, a native of Aleppo. Instead of starting a paper, he published a book arguing that tyranny had caused the decline of Muslim society. True Islam was the remedy. *The Mother of Cities*, in 1900, was his second book. In structure the book has been shown to be plagiarized, but in content it described a secret society of twenty-two members, meeting, in the words of one critic, in "an atmosphere of political cloak-and-dagger like that of a modern thriller." These characters were discussing what was to be done about replacing tyranny with constitutionalism. Although a Syrian, Kawakibi was secretly in the pay of Khedive Abbas Hilmi, who sent him on a clandestine mission to Arabia, perhaps to initiate intrigues about wresting the Caliphate from the Ottoman sultan. At any rate, as conspirators often do, Kawakibi died young, mysteriously.

Syrian students founded a Young Arab Society in Paris in 1911. C. Ernest Dawn, analyzing the pre–1914 Arab movement for independence in Syria has found that "Only 126 men are known to have been public advocates of Arab nationalism or members of Arab nationalist societies before October, 1914," and even this may be too high a number, as some thirty of these men were doubtfully active. At a congress held in Paris in June 1913, twenty-four delegates from anti-Ottoman secret societies assembled, with some observers in addition. Signatures on telegrams of support to this congress amounted to 387 names (some of which of course overlapped with the Syrian 126). These numbers indicate what a task it is to convert the private purpose of a conspiracy into a mass movement. On the eve of the war, Aziz Ali el-Masri, an Egyptian and at the time an Ottoman officer stationed in Istanbul, founded Al-Ahd, recruiting a handful of other Arab officers.

At the beginning of the First World War, neither Britain nor France had any plan for the future of the Ottoman Empire. The impulsive Ottoman military alliance in 1914 with Germany had not been foreseen. British troops landed at the port of Basra in Iraq in November 1914, Egypt was declared a protectorate, and the army, in spite of the surrender of General Townshend and 10,000 men at Kut in Mesopotamia, mobilized in the Middle East against the Turks. As from 1916, government committees in London began seriously to study what the map of the Middle East should be in the coming peace. The Sykes-Picot agreement of 1916 delineated territories for the British in Palestine and in Iraq, for the French in Syria and Lebanon. The boundaries of these territories were duly settled after the war when the League of Nations awarded them to France and Britain, to be held not as colonies but as Mandates. In November 1917 the British government of its own accord issued the Balfour Declaration (so-called after A. J. Balfour, then just appointed foreign secretary), with its promise of a national home in Palestine for the Jews, not omitting a qualifying respect for the rights of the Palestinian Arabs. Authoritative work has been devoted to the elucidation of these arrangements, but it is still worth pointing out how Sherif Husein of Mecca, the leader of what has been called the Arab nationalist revolt against the Turks, acted as a typical challenger to the existing power holder.

Sherif Husein came from the Hashemite family whose claim to be guardians of the Holy Cities of Mecca and Medina was disputed by another branch of the same family. Unable forcibly to subject Arabia, at least until the construction of the famous Hijaz railway, the Ottoman sultan had resorted to keeping the peace there by promoting first one, and then the other, of the contending families. When nominated Sherif, or keeper of the shrines which are the objective of the annual pilgrimage, Husein was actually living in Istanbul and possibly under house arrest. His first act upon reaching the Holy Cities was to suppress as far as possible the rival family.

After the outbreak of war, the Ottomans had every reason to look for loyalty from their fellow Muslims and the Sherif in particular. The Ottoman caliph-sultan had proclaimed a holy war in 1914. But the Sherif rightly saw his chance for power challenging, in part through a calculation of the balance of forces, and in part through converting his own religious position into a rival monarchy. Outwardly Ottoman Turks and Sherifian Arabs engaged in polemics about which party was the more authentically Islamic. Inwardly the Sherif waited until he was convinced that the British would win the war. There was also an inducement of patronage. At a time when his revenues had dwindled to £8,000 a year, the British paid him a monthly subsidy of £125,000 in gold. Gradually, Arab officers, including Aziz Ali el-Masri and others from Al-Ahd, defected to the Sherif. Duly he crossed the confessional divide, or in other words revealed that he had recruited the British into his conspiracy to promote himself. The gold sovereigns were then paid out to tribal leaders in exchange for their help, which was sometimes given reluctantly, or even denied.

To the British wartime establishment in Cairo, the short-term advantage of such an ally seemed attractive. As presumed specialists and men of experience in Arab affairs, they might have been expected to understand how they were being exploited. British weapons and money and officers under secondment would permit the Sherif to gain independence once and for all from the Ottoman sultan. As part of his pretensions, the Sherif declared himself "King of the Arabs" and aimed to incorporate territory up to and including Damascus. Had he succeeded, he was certain to have found a pretext to break with the British, who would prove at best an embarrassment, at worst a threat to newly won independence. It was a consummate entrapment of British officials whose training and values did not equip them, indeed positively unfitted them, for this power challenging. The vain and insubstantial nature of the Sherif's challenge was proved shortly after the end of the war. In Saudi Arabia, the neighboring ruler, Abdul Aziz ibn Saud, in command of some thousands of camel-mounted tribesmen, completed a local power challenge of his own by raiding the Holy Cities, driving the Sherif away into exile by 1926.

Personal accounts of the Sherif and his habits call further into question what kind of conception British officialdom can ever have had of this curious ally-rival. One British diplomat, Laurence Grafftey-Smith, gave this firsthand portrait:

> In Mecca, below his Palace, was an underground dungeon called the *Qabu*, into which he threw peccant officials or other notables or business-men whom he feared or disliked. They were herded like beasts, and were only allowed up into the sunlight for thirty minutes each day. Some spent years there. When the impulse seized him, the king would take a great club and go down into this den, with a slave to carry the lantern, and there he would belabour one or other of his victims until he wearied.

Post–1918 treaties installed the British and French as power holders in the Middle East. Apparently nobody in ruling circles appreciated that the Mandate system, and the European rule resulting from it, would encourage challengers to turn by every possible means against them. Final arbitration lay with the British and French armies, but parliaments could never happily countenance in the pursuit of government abroad the use of force which was constitutionally illegal at home. The contradiction was too great. Would-be challenger-conspirators required less courage than ever. In other words, those who felt so minded were invited to dress up their ambitions and their grievances into causes for self-assertion.

In the colonial period, one conspiracy in particular, the Muslim Brotherhood, deserves to be singled out for its success, as it was virtually unique in enlarging itself into a genuine mass movement. This was the achievement of Hasan al-Banna, born in 1906 in a small town north of Cairo, the son of a preacher educated at Al-Azhar. In about 1927, al-Banna became a schoolteacher in Ismailia but soon devoted himself wholly to politics. It appears that in 1928 six Egyptians came to visit him, and the official account of this meeting quotes them as saying, "We know not the practical way to reach the glory of Islam and to serve the welfare of Muslims. We are weary of this life of humiliation and restriction. Lo, we see that the Arabs and the Muslims have no status and no dignity." Here was a shame-honor response to the British presence. It was al-Banna's inspiration that Islam would serve the twin purpose of restoring dignity and recruiting a following. In the manner of an Afghani or a Mustafa Kamil, here was a challenger basing himself upon the call of Islam. Soon the Muslim Brotherhood was organized into secret cells, and within twenty years claimed a membership of 40,000. It recruited a "Rovers" force for purposes of fighting and a "Special Secret Organisation" under Abdul Qadir Auda for sabotage and the killing of opponents. The Brotherhood published attacks on Westerners, especially missionaries. Its outlook remained characteristically conspiratorial:

At last it has become clear to us that there exists a widespread conspiracy plotted by religious and cultural imperialism against Islam. The purpose of this plot has been to destroy the position which Islam occupies in the heart of the faithful.

In his testament written in about 1942, al-Banna rejected all forms of Western political or social organization.

The Western way of life—founded in effect on practical and technical knowledge, discovery, invention, and the flooding of world markets with mechanical products—has remained incapable of offering to men's minds a flicker of light, a ray of hope, a grain of faith, or of providing anxious persons the smallest path toward rest and tranquillity. Man is not simply an instrument among others. Naturally he has become tired of purely materialistic conditions and desires some spiritual comfort. But the materialistic life of the West could only offer him as reassurance a new materialism of sin, passion, drink, women, noisy gatherings, and showy attractions which he has come to enjoy.

Islam, he asserts, is the complete answer, but he declined to be programmatic about its implementation. Quite why Westerners should have had so sterile and ridiculous an aim as the destruction of Islam in the hearts of the faithful is not explained. Presumably he was also satisfied that there was nothing more to Western values than the catalog of hedonistic trivialities he provided. In the event of the withdrawal of the Western presence from the Middle East, the advocated Islamic purity would still have to find a relationship with the abiding problems of modernization, but al-Banna did not look that far ahead. Inevitably the power holder confronted the challenger. In February 1949, al-Banna was summoned to a secret rendezvous in Cairo and shot dead in the street. It is presumed that King Farouk's secret service was responsible.

An incumbent Middle Eastern ruler after 1945 has tended to be pro-Western in education. He also possessed the immense advantage over his historic predecessors in the range of available equipment to extend absolutism, from telephones and telexes, copy machines and computers to surveillance devices. But plainly their international sponsors had failed them.

To the long line of murdered, deposed or exiled power holders, to Sultan Abdul Hamid and his successor, to Khedive Ismail and his heirs down to King Farouk, last of the descendency in 1952, were added Shah Reza Pahlavi of Iran, deposed in 1941; his son Shah Muhammad Reza, deposed in 1979; King Feisal II of Iraq, who was murdered with his family and his prime minister in 1958 and their corpses then defiled in the streets; the Imam of Yemen; the sultan of Oman, deposed by his son Qabus; King Idris of Libya; King Abdullah of Jordan, killed in 1951; and King Feisal of Saudi Arabia, shot dead in 1975 by a young relation. And to them was then added the next generation of power holders, Qassem in Iraq, shot by the brothers Aref, one of whom was then deposed and the other killed in a helicopter crash; Ibrahim Hamdi of North Yemen, murdered in 1977 with his brother Abdullah by Ahmed Hussein Ghashmi, who himself nine months afterward was blown up by a bomb in the briefcase of an envoy sent by the president of South Yemen; Husni Zaim and President Shishakli and Salah al-Bitar and dozens more in Syria; Riad as-Solh, prime minister of Lebanon; Anwar Sadat in Egypt; General Abboud in Sudan, where his successor General Nimeiri was in due course deposed—not to mention the twists and turns whereby King Hassan of Morocco and King Hussein of Jordan have both escaped more attempted assassinations than can be correctly counted, whereas General Oufkir or Mehdi Ben Barka, both Moroccan challengers, met strange deaths, and innumerable Arab officers everywhere have been hurried from specially convened tribunals to the firing squad.

This is an Iraqi bulletin, from 1962:

> To the honourable Iraqi people, while His Excellency the sole leader of the country, Major-General Abd al-Karim Qassem, was passing by car

through Rashid Street about 18.30 today, a sinful hand opened fire at his car. He received a very slight wound in the shoulder. His condition is very good and does not give cause for worry. We call on the honourable people to rest assured that our saviour is in excellent good health. We call on them to remain calm and pass on the news to the people that as soon as our sole leader saw the masses of the people thronging around the hospital to inquire about his health he went and greeted them in order to give them peace of mind.

Compare a Kuwaiti bulletin, of 1985:

At 09.15 today, the motorcade of His Highness the Amir of the Land was exposed to a sinful attack. As His Highness was travelling on his way to his office at Sif Palace, a car laden with explosives which was parked on the central division of the road tried to ram into the motorcade. This detonated the explosives, setting fire to a number of the cars. . . .

The former is said to be progressive, the latter reactionary, but these bulletins comment identically on a power challenge.

Saddam Hussein, holding power in Iraq since 1979, condemned some unsuccessful challengers as

people who had infiltrated the Party leadership and the Revolution and included traitors belonging to the Party. This group had for some years been preparing an ugly plot.

Ayatollah Khomeini, ostensibly Saddam Hussein's mortal enemy, shares precisely his view of how and why people conspire to challenge power.

A group of people came together, deliberated, made decisions, and then began to propagate their aims. Gradually the number of like-minded people would increase, until finally they became powerful enough to influence a great state or even to confront and overthrow it. . . . Such movements began with no troops or armed power at their disposal; they always had to resort to propagating the aims of their movement first. The thievery and tyranny practiced by the regime would be condemned and the people awakened.

Had there been wrongdoing of the kind punishable in law courts, the power holder would be expected to name names and specify charges. In reality, the power holder and the challenger are proceeding against each other with the same tactic of merciless conspiracy. Hence the element of fantastical absurdity in political discourse. In self-justification, the power holder, like the challenger, has resort to these vaguely self-righteous yet accusatory imprecations about the baseness of the other party. Each can truth-fully impute to the other the general habits of tyranny and thievery but cannot spell them out because he is demonstrably indulging in them as well. Nasser, overthrowing King Farouk's regime, de-scribed it in identical terms as "a limited liability company for theft and robbery in which the people had no share," at the same time declaring himself absolute ruler with the state at his full disposal. Where conspiracy is the norm, concepts such as the free play of ideas or of loyal opposition or even of mere compromise cannot be entertained.

It matters only in external details such as flags and uniforms whether the justifying principle of the power holder is supposedly religious, as in the case of Ayatollah Khomeini, or socialist and secular as with Nasser or Saddam Hussein. In the past, the capture of the state by an Ayatollah Khomeini or a Nasser would have required no justification—"What I have, I hold" in the proud boast of medieval monarchs. The Arab public, or the Iranian, naturally is under no illusion today when a power challenger comes to triumph and a new ruler declares himself head of state. The rele-vant public perceives who belongs to the new Revolutionary Com-mand Council, and whether these Free Officers and saviors are Sunni or Shia or Alawi, from this tribe or that, who is in their retinue and will be favored, and who must run for his life into exile.

Modern communications blur the otherwise clear profile of the winners and losers. The new ruler can hardly push his way past the tanks surrounding the television center in order to announce that he is in the process of satisfying his innermost ambitions and thankfully has killed his rivals from other tribes, sects, or religions. The whole world may now be watching and listening. A more constructive intention must be devised. To blacken his ousted predecessor as a thief and tyrant, to accuse him of generalized corruption, has the merit of being true and almost certainly prov-able. Announcing himself the savior of the nation, he gives assur-ances that there will be no more corruption. As a justifying princi-ple or doctrine appealing to as many people as possible, he then separately or in combination professes nationalism, democracy, socialism, revolution, Islam, although these abstractions have no more institutional reality than they did under his predecessor. The words are the coinage paid out in power challenging, to mobilize friends and to isolate opponents.

In fact, the leader of the successful challenge is at once projected into the place of the man he has dispossessed, now himself heir to the self-same anxieties about challengers, and he resorts to well-tried defenses. He too erects around himself the entire absolutist apparatus, refashioning his supporters as a congress of delegates who cheer and raise their hand in a display of solidarity at the appointed moment, placing men of proven loyalty in control of the secret police and the media. Accordingly, Arab memoirs tend to be catalogs of everyday oppression and victimization. To select one example among many, the Palestinian Fawaz Turki described how he had returned to Damascus after three years of study in England, to be met by his uncle, a leading member of the state-controlled Syrian Workers Union. First the uncle ordered him to remove his English college blazer, then warned him not to listen even accidentally to Radio Amman, and finally informed him that three union leaders were in prison without specific charges, and a fourth had been beaten and tortured before being released.

Soon after that, my uncle and the remaining men on the Board signed a secret petition condemning that action against their union colleagues and had one man take it to Cairo and hand it to Nasser personally. But the man, along with his document, was stopped at the airport by security police and taken into custody, somewhere in Damascus, although no one yet knew where. As the meeting which resulted in the decision to sign the petition was presumably secret, and as all the members had decried police intervention in their affairs and the arrest of their men, agreeing unanimously that action be taken to stop it, it was obvious they had a Deuxième Bureau [state security] plant in their midst who must have informed his superiors of these goings on.

Immediate danger threatens the leader from his fellow conspirators, whose chief personalities well realize how narrowly decided the issue was. Another twist of fate, perhaps the abstention or the inclusion of a sole conspirator, and power might have been in their hands. The successful leader's first move is prudently to neutralize his recent supporters, whether they are generals, royalists, communists, or ulema, even possibly his own kinsmen. Gratitude, the dispensing of the promised rewards, may only encourage latent tendencies in these close contenders to imagine themselves more powerful than they are.

The specter of civil war haunts these splits: in Iraq, Qassem versus Aref; in Syria, Hafez Assad versus Jedid; in Algeria, Boumedienne versus Ben Bella; in Egypt, Nasser versus Neguib; in Tunisia, Bourguiba versus Salah Ben Yussef; in Sudan, the Ansari versus the Khatmiyya; in Lebanon, on the Christian side, the rival families of Franjieh, Chamoun or Gemayel, and on the Muslim side the equivalent Sunni, Druze, and Shia factions. Contending dualities among those nominally defined as an entity in the power-challenge context are roughly what two-party politics are to a democracy.

Treason, said Talleyrand, is a matter of dates. Power challenging makes treason a matter of names. The power holder will accuse challengers, and especially those once in his own retinue, of betraying him or the justifying principle of his conspiracy, and challengers will throw back at him the very same accusations. Time and again, the words "treason" and "betrayal" mean no more than "difference of opinion." Their violent usage reveals the speaker's distance from constitutionality, his immersion in conspiracy.

At the time of the coup in 1952 which ended the monarchy in Egypt, the following broadcast was addressed by the new though temporary ruler, General Neguib, "To my brothers, the sons of the Nile":

You know that our country has been living through delicate moments, and you have seen the hands of traitors at work in its affairs. These traitors dared to extend their influence to the Army, imagining that it was devoid of patriotic elements. We have therefore decided to purify ourselves, to eliminate the traitors and weaklings.

At the time of the 1956 Suez war against Israel, Neguib's successor Nasser could say that "Egypt was now purged of traitors, and therefore victory was possible." In the 1967 war, he said, "We have not been beaten, only betrayed." To him, the Jordanian monarchy, at the moment of dissension, became "the family of traitors in Arab history, residing in Amman." In 1965, Bourguiba made a speech in which he floated the idea of negotiating with Israel. Ahmad Shuqairi, then leader of the PLO, replied, "Bourguiba is a traitor, and therefore I demand a punishment for the Tunisian President commensurate with the gravity of his crime," in other words, his assassination. Political manifestos regularly threaten and accuse in this style, as in this example from Syria: "The spirit of treason prevails in the current regime . . . which has made of this country a haven for conspirators and a centre for intrigue." In an example from Iraq, anyone associating with "foreign agents" is "a traitor to the Iraqi homeland, a traitor to the air and soil of Iraq and to the waters of the Tigris and Euphrates." Sadat's peace making drew him "into the ranks of traitors," according to the Syrians and their friends who disagreed with the policy. When Egypt staged military maneuvers with American forces, the Libyan government first revealed a shame-honor reaction by calling this "shameful" and then went on, "The traitors and mercenaries of the ruling regime in Egypt have placed Egyptian soil and territorial waters under the enemies of this proud people."

The accusation of being a traitor, then, is not to be seen as literal but metaphorical, fashioned in defense of group identity. Any encounter involving possible engagement or commitment to an outsider, however personal or momentary, may diminish group identity and so becomes "treason." The Englishman Trevor Mostyn has recorded how in the course of wooing an Algerian girl, he went for a walk openly with her in Algiers and overheard one man shouting to another, "Our sister is betraying us." When an armed group of Kurds attacked a village in southeast Turkey, killing thirty of its inhabitants, it came naturally to the non-Kurdish wife of one of the victims to say, "The traitors opened fire on the people as they fled." A meeting between King Hassan of Morocco and Shimon Peres, at the time the Israeli prime minister, was described as "a treacherous act" by the Iranian government.

This is from contemporary Iraq:

As to the existence in Syria or in Lebanon—mostly in Syria and in Egypt—of some traitors and plotters who plotted against this country, these traitors will be chased and eliminated by the Syrian people and the Egyptian people. The Syrian people and the Egyptian people can never agree to sheltering traitors assailing Iraq and working against its liberated structure. The Syrian people and the Egyptian people can never consent to provide shelter to such traitors [who] work against the immortal Iraqi Republic which is free from all ties and obligations, and which has become an independent and a fully sovereign country defending herself and defending her brethren. The end of these traitors is imminent. If they remain alive, they will be haunted by disgrace and dishonour. If they are eliminated, that will be the fate of all traitors.

Power holders, challengers, and the public know how to interpret the issuing and the reception of these vituperations and death threats, and whose names belonging to which sects or religions are to be read between the lines. The literally murderous intensity of the struggle obscures the lack of ideological substance. The difference between power holders and contenders is not actualized in principles but in the dispensation of favor. Ideology is not a belief system but a composition for purposes of power holding, a tool in constant need of revision and maintenance as new challenges appear.

The suspicious ruler of course offers bribes and promises which he hopes are more alluring than those of the challengers. Between power holder and challenger is a fierce and seething underworld of intermediaries, informants, spies, double agents, rumormongers, "traitors" in the making. Should he lose control of the military, the ruler loses everything. He needs to ensure their loyalty by every available means; he must study and digest the secret intelligence reports; he must have methods of his own for sifting truth from falsehood in what the informants and spies are relating. He lives in a constant dread of acting too hastily to make a clean sweep of the plotters or acting too late to be able preemptively to crush them. On the day that the ruler appears irresolute, abandoned by his sponsors abroad, losing charisma, ill, or unfortunate, everyone draws the conclusion and hastens to insure himself on the side of the challenger.

Opportunity arrives more often precipitately than planned, and usually because the ruler has made a blatant or crass misjudgment. A clash of arms follows. Tanks surround the official palace and the broadcasting station. Either the incumbent power holder is victorious and kills or exiles the challengers or he is himself killed or exiled.

The strain is enormous; it wears down endurance, it saps vitality. Devolving any decision-making to others, he only creates his rivals, what Sadat used to call "power centers." Each victor lives in the awareness that without a shadow of doubt other conspirators are somewhere at a secret meeting, seemingly innocent but in fact listening to informants and spies, collecting supporters as patiently and warily as he once did. A few years of this, and only the hardest-hearted power holder retains the appetite to outflank challengers, to supervise in person the career of every single officer down to quite junior ranks in order to be sure that the army can be trusted to fire at those mobilized by the conspirators and not at him in his palace, to bribe off challengers or shoot them down in cold blood. Lassitude creeps upon the ruler; he flinches or ceases to concentrate; and in another bloody spiral the state is then seized by someone else.

Considerations of shame and honor forbid crimes of careerism from being judged for what they are. Honor is accorded to the man who succeeds in capturing the state because he has truly proved his mastery, he has displayed ruthlessness beyond the imagination and capacity of the ordinary man. Rejoicing in his strength and virility according to the customary codes, the new leader himself feels that he has the right to be respected for the strong man he is. So it happens that the Arab masses come to accept and even to admire their oppressor. Time and again, the Westerner looking for mercy or human pity in the case of some brutality is at a loss when confronted instead by an Arab reaction of approval. To give an example from the past, Marmaduke Pickthall, an English convert to Islam, was in Damascus in 1913 at a time when twelve Arabs were hanged there in response to turmoil in Istanbul. Pickthall had a friend whom he described as "a very peaceful, law-abiding Syrian merchant" and whom he expected to be outraged by these executions of Arabs by the Ottoman authorities. Not at all. Going to inspect the bodies on the gibbet, the Syrian said with satisfaction that he felt more comfortable in the knowledge that "we had a government." He was grateful to be spared the violence that would have been caused by these would-be challengers. Commonly and wrongly, Westerners first fail to recognize an underlying shame-honor response, and then ascribe to degenerate character what is only a natural instinct of self-preservation. A famous example is Lord Cromer's lofty and much-quoted pronouncement upon Egypt: "A long enslaved nation instinctively craves for the strong hand of a master rather than for a lax constitutional regime."

However destructive the practice of the power-challenge dialectic may be, the wish endures that it could be fulfilled in the person of the idealized Islamic hero, the just and righteous leader or latter-day caliph, in the religious idiom. In his day Muhammad Abdu made the attempt to think through how Islamic forms and institutions ideally ought to develop. "The Orient needs a despot who would force those who criticize each other to recognize their mutual worth," he wrote, "a despot who would never take any step without his primary consideration being the effect on the people he governs, so that any personal good fortune which befell him would be quite secondary." Another of Afghani's disciples is quoted as saying "We felt in our souls that any one of us was capable of reforming a province or a kingdom"; the excitation that this political process has on the individual is strikingly revealed. In a history of modern Iraq, Majid Khadduri described the successful military coup of 1937, in the course of which General Bakr Sidqi horribly murdered Jafar al-Askari, the minister of defense. This crime notwithstanding, Khadduri is able to make the general comment, "The novelty of the procedure, and the masterly fashion in which the coup d'état had been carried out, brought to power a Government of unprecedented popularity and prestige." Elsewhere Khadduri could go further on these lines. "There is an almost nostalgic longing in the Middle East, common to all political groups, for a 'strong' regime which will tolerate neither multiplicity of political parties nor anarchy of ideas." Again he writes, "Arabs yearn for strong political leaders to preside over their destiny."

Support for this sentiment is to be heard on all sides. In 1946, at a time when many Arabs were able to foresee that the period of colonialism was reaching its end and wondering what might be in store, the Egyptian writer and an Al-Azhar sheikh Khalid Muhammad Khalid published an influential essay *From Here We Start.* Professing himself a socialist, Khalid nonetheless called for "the honest governor." Tewfik el-Hakim in a novel writes "The Worshipped One! This people needs only that man from its own ranks who would embody all its aspirations and feelings and serve for it as a symbol of the goal"; Nasser is said to have so much admired this passage that in office he sent for the writer to congratulate him. In *Days of Dust,* a novel in 1969 by Halim Barakat, a professor at the American University of Beirut, the young hero longs for a leader "who would glow with defiance, one who would inspire the people to use their minds and their emotions in a dialogue with themselves and their leaders." Remembering Nasser, Sadat declared, "We had called for a benevolent dictator, a just tyrant." The sociologist Daniel Lerner in the 1950s asked Syrian students what they would do to change the course of the national crisis. They felt themselves powerless, he reported, but most advocated their own dictatorship, and one said that "I would have a sword and kill all those in the big chairs in the government now." After that, "I could *set up a dictatorship* and strike with an iron hand on all who dare move—that is how our people understand—and then I would start improvement." Bourguiba, self-styled "President for Life" in Tunisia as well as "Supreme Warrior," was once asked about the country's system. "What system? I *am* the system," he replied. "Pluralism for us," said Hedi Nouira, a Tunisian prime minister, "is just the icing on the cake." The quest for power conditions but at the same time frustrates such aspirations.

5

Men and Women

Relationships between the sexes are matters of choice in Western societies. Choosing tends to the establishment of rights; and rights tend to equality. Things are not so in the Arab world, where women are unable to make their own life choices and are not on any sort of equal footing with men over rights or status. Westerners quickly interpret this to be evidence of bad faith and perhaps vice, or at least of the selfish assertion of masculine superiority with which they may be familiar in their own societies, and which must therefore be susceptible to change by popular pressure and legislation. Under such a misapprehension, for instance, a party of Western feminists flew in 1979 to the Ayatollah Khomeini's Teheran to demand women's rights as they understood them and an ending to cruel and discriminatory treatment. However well-intentioned and unconscious of what they were doing, this involved the risk of death, not for themselves of course, but for any Iranian woman who might have joined in the demonstration of Western values. Throughout the Muslim Middle East, the inferior status of women is integrally bound up with custom and therefore goes to the roots of historical identity. As such, this status is for the time being largely unreachable by the enactment of laws. Identity cannot be altered on request.

Those who suggest otherwise are often in the position of inviting cultural and psychological upheavals and alienations that very few people have the resources to endure. Although all Arab or Iranian women would accept that their status is different from that of men, only a Western-educated handful would then proceed to the Eurocentric judgment that it is "inferior." Mai Yamani is an adult daughter of Sheikh Yamani who for many years played his part in fixing the world's oil price. She was educated in Europe and nonetheless in an interview in 1986 she explained how she continued to value Saudi custom. Wearing the veil was a matter of belonging to her group, identifying herself with the domain of women. "I think it is a form of social distance," she told her interviewer, "like a barrier I have between me and men. I like my veil. I like to be a Saudi Arabian woman." Even in the case of someone educated to make objective choices, the demands of group identity overrode those of personal freedom and rights.

Margaret Luce, traveling in the 1960s in Arabia with her husband, an experienced British diplomat, and observing how soon after birth the segregation of small boys and girls began, had what may be called the standard Eurocentric response. Nothing could be done about this process of unequal socialization between the sexes except to regret it.

Two little girls watched us, too young to wear a batula [a black cloak-cum-veil], very pretty, rather shy, about a year or two of freedom still to go. The women were in their distant black herd. I think what one really longs for is just a single spirited one who would throw off her batula, jump on it, put out her tongue, and buy a dress in scarlet with yellow spots. One doesn't exactly feel sorry for them because they are unhappy. I don't think they are. The sadness is that they don't mind. And a certain sadness for the thought of hundreds of years of this black static unflowering unfeminine waste of spirit.

Ancient pre-Islamic custom dictates group practices like polygamy, male and female circumcision, the arrangement of marriages by parents for their children, with the payment of a bride-price, and much attendant ritual concerning virginity and the circumstances proper to its loss. Post-Islamic custom dictates the wearing of the veil and probably the seclusion of women as well. In broad terms, Koranic sanction is absent for these practices, although certain passages can be interpreted to suit and substantiate custom, as in a verse stating that a man may have four wives if he can be sure of treating them all fairly, or another verse to the effect that a man's mere verbal repudiation of his wife is enough to constitute divorce, without right of appeal. Down the centuries, custom and religion have interacted in mutual reinforcement.

Custom varies according to time and place. Harems with hundreds of women may be found, as in the royal households of Saudi Arabia today, and so may monogamous faithfulness, concubines, slave girls, the Shia practice of "temporary marriage" whereby a man takes on a wife for a period of time fixed by contract, and outright prostitution, which has been practiced everywhere and at all periods. Bedouin or desert women are more likely than urban women to escape the veil and seclusion. It is hardly possible to wear a full veil while doing agricultural work. Female circumcision is not practiced in Saudi Arabia, Iraq, Syria, Jordan, or among Palestinians, Turks, Iranians, and North Africans. Whether or not Islamic sanction exists in the popular mind, the purpose of custom is the maintenance of the family group, its honor and its values. Immemorially, the consequence has been the devaluation of women as individuals in their own right. Boys are regarded from birth as capital investment, in the phrase of the Egyptian sociologist Hamad Ammar, while girls are the fountainhead of shame, valued only because in due course they will develop into the producers of boys or of more capital. There can be no approximation here of a relationship freely and privately agreed between a man and a woman, which is the basis of Western romantic love and marriage, and therefore a prime determinant of Western values.

Marriage in the Arab world is by the arrangement and consent of the parents of the prospective bride and bridegroom. The heads of the families concerned are seeking mutual advantage by means of bringing together their children. Both parties aim to acquire honor and standing; neither will accept the shame of any liaison that might be deemed inappropriate or humiliating. Commonplace and anxiety-ridden themes in everyday life as well as in literature concern the girl who brings shame by losing her virginity inappropriately, and the young man who brings shame by refusing the bride selected for him by his family.

The Algerian novelist Djanet Lachmet writes in her autobiographical novel *Lallia:*

> I wouldn't play those games any more. I didn't want to be dishonoured. If I played at being a bride, I would lose my virginity. Like that poor girl from the mountains who played with her cousin when she was small, and when she got married properly she wasn't a virgin. Her in-laws were furious and disowned her. They put her on a donkey facing towards

its tail, with her head shaved and her arms tied, and they took her back to her family. Her elder brother stabbed her to death because she'd dishonoured the family.

Zahra Freeth, daughter of a well-known British colonial administrator, was born and brought up in Kuwait, and she tells the characteristic story of Hindal, a young man whose family selected for him a first cousin to be his wife. Hindal loved a girl from another tribe. During a family discussion about this, an older man seized his rifle and shot the stubborn Hindal dead, whereupon in blind rage every armed man present also fired recklessly into the family gathering. In the end, eight men and the girl from the other tribe were dead. In another of the tragedies so frequently evolving from Arab marriage customs, the twenty-five-year-old Fajar Salem al-Sabah, a niece of the Amir of Kuwait, committed suicide in London in 1987 by swallowing a mixture of alcohol and drugs. From her first marriage, she already had a daughter. Marrying again, she was obliged by law to leave this child with its father. Her second husband already had another wife. "A family feud" resulted, according to newspaper reports, and a witness at the inquest said that "no one was speaking to her."

Ommohamad, who has spent a lifetime in her Egyptian village, speaks for virtually all Arab mothers when she tells her son Shahhat, "Marriage means you are establishing a household. You must become a real man who looks to the needs of the house and the land, a man who fathers many children and raises them. It means to prosper and lead a decent life so that everyone must respect you." Shahhat proposed to marry a girl of his own choice, but she had a status unacceptably lower than his. Ommohamad, a widow as it happened, scotched her son's proposal of marriage with the words, "I would rather kill you than see our family so disgraced."

In his novel *Far from Jerusalem*, Ibrahim Souss, a senior PLO official, depicts a Palestinian hero with a Jewish wife. "My mother had tried everything to dissuade me from marrying Gabrielle," this rather sophisticated and custom-defying Palestinian is made to say, "explaining to me the shame she would feel at the sight of her son introducing a Jewess into our family which was Muslim and attached to the thousand-year-old tradition whereby mixed marriages were forbidden, and so such a union could not be tolerated." This tradition still applies (though not to both sexes) and in some countries has acquired the force of law: Muslim men may marry non-Muslim women, but Muslim women are legally prohibited from marrying outside their confession.

Under Islam, married partners retain their individual names and property, and as the social scientist Andrea B. Rugh has pointed out, for practical purposes they become a unity only after the birth of a child. Love comes to be valued not for itself but for its instrumentality. Arabs of both sexes pay a terrible price for this. The Algerian Abdelwahab Bouhdiba, author of *Islam and Sexuality,* draws the general conclusion that in Arab society love must always be restrained if it has any private or individual expression that does not conform to the interests of the group. Group defense is inseparable from Arab sexuality. Far from being an absolute and incontestable value, love is careerist aggrandizement and simply that part of the money-favor nexus which takes place in the domestic arena. In the words of the Egyptian feminist Nawal el Saadawi, referring to the payment of the bride-price, "the norms of buying and selling are the ones applied to marriage." The huge majority will speak like the Moroccan woman recorded by Hildred Geertz, "Arranging marriages is a highly serious matter, like waging war or making big business deals." The tiny minority will reply in the embittered and certainly Westernized phrases of the Syrian feminist Ghadah al-Samman, "Marriage today, in my opinion, is a corrupt institution" and even "a kind of human prostitution."

It is in the private forum, then, that careerist challenging begins and takes shape, and from there that it is perpetuated and radiated outward openly to become the primary social expression. Muslim life, private and public, social and political, secular and religious, is all of a piece and wholly consistent in this respect. The family, and all choices about the disposal of its members and its resources, is in the hands of an undisputed autocrat who judges himself fit to assess and extend the collective interest. As with the family, so with the state. It was in no light spirit of self-flattery that Sadat used to refer to Egyptians as his "children" and call himself "the father of the Egyptian family." Put differently, the leader who dominates the family and the leader who captures the state have in common their careerist behavior and group values, which compel their indifference to the realization of hopes or choices other than their own.

These are two recent news items, the first from Gaza, the second from Abu Dhabi:

The Gaza Strip's oldest resident, Haj Abdullah Kadurah, died last week at the age of 128. For the last 70 years he had served as muezzin [caller to prayer] of the Tufah neighbourhood mosque, located next to his home. Kadurah is survived by more than 240 children, grandchildren, great-grandchildren and great-great-grandchildren.

Forty-year-old Salem Jemaa Mabruk has 27 children, and aims to have 100. He said in an interview in the daily newspaper *Al-Ittihad* that he might have to divorce some of his four present wives and seek more energetic ones.

To local readers of those items, the numbers involved are self-evidently creditable, proof of the masculine virility of Haj Abdullah and of Salem. A local reader would hardly be likely to reflect on the role of the mothers involved or to sympathize with the predicament of Salem's wives, who apparently may be divorced simply because they do not meet the criterion for fertility that he decides to impose upon them, quite as though they were expected to give birth seasonally. Similarly, Al-Hajj Muhammad, the Moroccan street trader, had eight wives, and he speaks boastingly on behalf of all men when he says, "The Moroccan woman wants a big *zibb* [penis] or money from a man. Sometimes I have money. Sometimes I don't. But I have always had a big *zibb.*" (An honor-assertion, as it turns out, since in fact he proved impotent.) Abdelwahab Bouhdiba quotes an Egyptian colleague who knows of a great many men who have married twenty or thirty women in no more than ten years. By the same token, women of no great age have married more than a dozen men, one after the other. It is observable today, he adds, that some men are in the habit of changing their wife once a month. He goes on to write of "the almost obligatory character of the sexual act" as comprising the Islamic sexual ethic, and has even wondered whether "there is not something essential which frequently prevents the male in our societies from being a one-wife man." With pointed irony, the Iraqi writer Khalid Kishtainy has thrown out the aphorism that "Nothing can equal the disgrace of a woman indulging in illicit sex except the disgrace of a man unable to."

The cult of virility can be carried to lengths which in other circumstances would obviously be a debasement, and a brutalization of human feelings. This recent news agency report from Abu Dhabi speaks for itself:

An 85-year-old merchant married two teenage girls simultaneously and consummated both marriages the same night. Khafan Askour said he opted for a double wedding so his wives could keep each other company.

José Arnold was a Swiss steward in the household of King Saud of Saudi Arabia in the 1950s, and he described how one day the King fell ill and had to be flown for treatment to the Aramco hospital in Dhahran.

Before he would consent to leave Riyadh, however, he insisted on having his favourite wife, Umm Mansur, brought to his bed. With the assistance of four slaves, the sick King had intercourse with the woman. The next day, after the King's departure for Dhahran had been publicly announced, word of his "strength" of the night before was discreetly passed around Riyadh, and his people were thus assured that he was not too weak to rule.

Unni Wiken, setting about her fieldwork in the Cairo slums, had to travel on buses "where most of the passengers were men, and most of them tried to fondle me." That she was a European aggravated the fact that here was a woman visibly defying custom. The men could consider themselves challenged in their virility. Unni Wiken goes on:

But once I arrived at the bus stop by the poor neighbourhood the worst trial awaited me: to get into the area I had to run the gauntlet of the market street which was very crowded and included a large number of men who were a constant annoyance. I developed a defence technique, hitting my handbag against any man who came near me, and also acquired the greatest repertoire of invective in the area. It helped, but not enough to stop me dreading the trip each day. I did not know anyone in the streets I had to pass through, and as a result I was often bombarded with garbage, and naturally with foul names.

The French sociologist Juliette Minces, herself a militant progressive who cannot be accused of anti-Muslim sentiment, elaborates why such sexual obsession is more openly manifest toward a Western woman. "In such cases, sexuality combines with an almost racial form of nationalism. The idea is to prove not only one's own potency but also the sexual superiority of one's group. Furthermore, the Western woman is not a member of the clan, so everything is permissible. . . . Even more than an Arab woman, a Western woman is seen as potential prey."

In accordance with the values of group defense, then, in Arab countries an average 45 percent of girls aged fifteen to nineteen are already married, and again on average there will be seven live births per married woman. According to UNESCO figures of 1972, female illiteracy in the Arab world decreased during the 1960s from 90 percent to 85 percent (male illiteracy from 71 to 60 percent over the same span). Relatively few women are employed outside the home, and an average of only 1 percent of all married Arab women work in nonagricultural sectors of their economies. In Egypt, more emancipated than elsewhere, women make up 25 percent of the agricultural workforce, and another 23 percent of the nonagricultural workforce.

In their introduction to *Women in the Muslim World,* Lois Beck and Nikki Keddie give a general sketch of what is to be anticipated from an upbringing and way of life designed to preserve honor and other group values:

In most cases, a girl's parents decide whether and for how long she goes to school; the parents of both parties decide on the marriage partner (this limits the boy too, but he can often turn to other sexual partners or repudiate his spouse, which she cannot easily do); the mother-in-law and husband rule over much of the young wife's life, and the husband can, de jure or de facto, decide if the wife can work for wages, at what kind of job, and whether she can use any of her wages if she works. The husband, according to religious law, receives custody of children (after a certain age) after divorce; women are thereby suddenly cut off from those by whom their role as females is defined, and are denied the continuing satisfactions of the maternal role. Most women are not allowed to remain unmarried, even after an early divorce, or to live alone. Women are threatened with repudiation or with a second wife being brought into the house if they do not bear sons. Many women find considerable satisfactions in traditional family life, but their legal and customary status is often precarious.

Every one of these particulars conditions the assumption that women are to have their relationships dictated for them by men. Here are the conclusions about the relative attributes and capacities of the sexes, as drawn unquestioningly by an ordinary Moroccan:

A man will think. He sees a quarrel leading to [court]; he knows that the other man has more "pull" with the [court] than he does. He knows how to deal with people bigger and weaker than he is. A woman is light-headed. She doesn't know how to do these things. If she goes to the [government offices], who pays attention to her? Better that she stay at home, where she can teach her daughters to cook and sew. They don't know Islam like men do; they even have tricks to avoid fasting.

Tragedies regularly occur as girls do indeed try to make choices for themselves, seeking to elope or to refuse an arranged marriage, risking dishonor and its fatal consequences. In 1969, according to the Algerian feminist Fadela M'Rabet, in the disappointment that the Algerian war of independence had not offered women a better deal, the records of one single hospital in Algiers contained the names of 175 girls who had preferred to commit or to attempt suicide rather than accept the marriages arranged for them. Revolutions pass away, the French social scientist Germaine Tillion observed, "while grandmothers and elderly aunts abide."

Nawal el Saadawi rose to be director of health education in the Egyptian ministry of public health. Her autobiography, *The Hidden Face of Eve,* opens with the statement, "It is no longer possible to escape the fact that the underprivileged status of women, their relative backwardness, leads to an essential backwardness in society as a whole." With considerable courage, she proceeds to describe how at the age of six she was obliged to submit to circumcision, in spite of the fact that her father had been general controller of education for the province of Menoufia and her mother had been a teacher of French. In addition to the pain came the shock that her mother had stood by smiling during the cliterodectomy. Péroncel-Hugoz tells of an Egyptian villager who married a French wife and then felt that her introduction into his village would create shames with which he could not cope. Eventually his wife persuaded him otherwise, and over a period of time, she succeeded in making friends with the local women. One day, these village women noticed her body hair and overpowered her in order to discover if she was "clean." Then they thought it was a kindness to make her "clean" by circumcising her on the spot, and she died as a result.

An Egyptian theater director, Laila Abou Saif, has described in her autobiography *A Bridge Through Time* how she returned to her grandmother's village to film the circumcision of a little girl. "The midwife again delved between the thighs for flesh, the razor slicing gently and slowly at the nerves. The little girl screamed as if the screams could drown the agony." When the midwife finished, she turned to Laila Abou Saif to say, "Look, she's as clean as the palm of my hand now." Justification of the kind is simple, instinctive. It

is "a tradition" in the words of Om Gad, one of the Egyptian
women telling her life story in *Khul-Khaal:* "My people do this, and
so I must do like they do." Another Egyptian woman, quoted by
Juliette Minces, similarly says that the pain is beside the point: "It
is the custom. God wills it."

Female circumcision is considered by Abdelwahab Bouhdiba to
be "like a vaccination against the dangers of sexuality." To him,
practices of the kind and their supporting values create "a fundamental erotic anxiety." The image of the all-powerful father is
destructive. In reality, young Arabs have to resort "very frequently, if not almost entirely" to organized prostitution. Innocent
relations cannot develop between the sexes. "Whenever a man and
a woman meet together, their third is always Satan" is a much-
quoted proverb that shows how sexual fears and custom combine
to prevent even mere friendship between a man and a woman. The
cults of virginity on the one hand and virility on the other are
hardly likely to be the prelude to a mutual respect between the
married couple. Another Algerian, the author Rachid Boudjedra,
comes to this shattering conclusion:

> Brutally and swiftly deflowering his bride, the husband is responding
> to a social criterion of virility, which is still very widespread. Deflowering
> is not a means leading to the consummation of the sexual act, but a proof
> of power to engender, to be given to friends grouped about the bedroom.
> Above all, here is a matter of male pride whose consequences may well
> be disastrous for the couple's future harmony.

A psychiatrist, John Racy, with experience of Arab societies,
comments that little is known about the private and intimate aspects of Arab marriages; that whole issue is taboo; and anyone
outside the culture who raised it would touch upon honor and
shame so indelicately that his own life would be endangered. Like
others who have studied the Arab sexual ethos, he underlines how
it promotes in men and women a rising and threatening sense of
inadequacy. "Impotence and related problems in men are among
the commonest reasons for seeking psychiatric help in this area,"
and he goes on to add that in parts of the Arab world "homosexuality is said to be extremely common. It is not possible to tell
whether it is merely a substitute for unavailable heterosexual contacts (as local observers suspect) or a preferred method of gratification." Perhaps it is some indication of reality that the remote

town of Suhar in northern Oman provided the setting for research by Unni Wiken into male transsexual prostitution.

Arabic literature and sociological writing time and again raise complicated and neurotic questions of what is to be done about masculine inadequacy or the lack of opportunity in a society whose values do not admit of such a possibility. Shahhat, for example, is a normal young Egyptian villager who nonetheless one night went out with a friend into the fields in order to "see who was the strongest" with a female donkey. Richard Critchfield, recording Shahhat's life, goes on to explain that the two friends were then caught in this act of bestiality by small boys, who informed the other villagers. "Faruk and the others, when they heard about it, roared with laughter and took it as proof of Shahhat's sexual prowess." He then adds, "The prevalence of sodomy deeply mortified the village women." General Neguib, who came to power in Egypt in the 1952 coup, has described in his memoirs how he was once a young officer in a provincial garrison. A young husband complained to him of impotence, which General Neguib cured with some eggs, bully beef, and "two of my four remaining laxative pills." Seymour Gray, a distinguished American doctor, taking up an appointment in 1975 in a brand new hospital in Riyadh, noted that "we were inundated with Saudis complaining of 'impotence.'"

Raja Shehadeh is a Palestinian whose book *The Third Way* evokes daily life on the West Bank under Israeli occupation, and recommends a policy of ultimate triumph through endurance. In the book Shehadeh relates what happened when Kamil's eighteen-year-old cousin Khalil married Kamil's nineteen-year-old sister. The bridegroom found himself inhibited by the publicity involved in marriage custom, whereby his deflowering of his bride was a matter of general interest. "His penis won't rise. We have tried everything. Everything they told us to do, we have done. We rubbed his penis with hot oil, we gave him a massage, we brought the *Haj* [a man who has completed the pilgrimage to Mecca] to drive evil spirits away, the Qadi himself prayed over his head. But nothing has worked so far." Far from coming to terms with the psychological consequences of custom, popular wisdom reached the helplessly fatalistic group conclusion that the man's impotence was like the Israeli occupation, and God's will. "When God changes his mind, the Jews will go. When He changes his mind, Khalil's penis will rise."

Fear of sexuality is seen by Fatima Mernissi as the governing impulse behind custom, and in her pioneering book *Beyond the Veil* she shows how this fear is passed back and forth between the sexes to their mutual damage. Born in Fez in 1941, Fatima Mernissi belongs to a family of Moroccan notables, and she was educated at Rabat University, and then in Boston. ("My grandmother was kidnapped in Chaouia plain, sold in Fez and bore my mother as a concubine to a member of the landowning bourgeoisie," she writes in an aside that reveals startling contrasts in three generations of women. "This group was the main buyer of slaves for decades after the French occupation of 1912.") The Muslim system, she flatly states, is not so much opposed to women as to the heterosexual couple. "What is feared is the growth of the involvement between a man and a woman into an all-encompassing love." She speaks of "the conflict structure" imposed on husband and wife. To carry the argument to its end, women cannot be emancipated unless and until men are. A fulfilled marriage will be only a miniaturized version of a society with equal rights. Women's liberation among Arabs is not a separate issue amenable to piecemeal reform but an aspect of the far more intractable question of how a modern Muslim society ought to be ordered.

"Until a radical reform is effected in the social relations between men and women, true civilisation cannot be said to exist in any Muslim nation. Unfortunately, of all the necessary reforms, it is the one most difficult to carry out." That was written over a century ago by Sir Henry Layard and has since remained the standard view among Westerners and such Arabs as they succeed in convincing. Samuel M. Zwemer, an American missionary doctor, can be found commenting in 1915 on the Muslim girl and her fate:

> Because of early marriage she has no real childhood; she looks forward with fear and dread to marriage with a man whom she may never have seen; she is early trained in all those ways of deceit which are the protection of the weak and helpless against strength and authority, and jealousy is one of her ruling passions. Unwelcome at birth, always considered inferior to her brothers and father and husband, and surrounded by so much in this religion that means degradation and humiliation, who can blame her if she is not happy!

Arab children are still socialized early in this way, and with severity. There appears never to have been any such thing as an Arab toy or games for children, in the sense that Western children have had a ball or a hoop, a shuttlecock or boardgames. To this day, toys and games and bicycles are Western imports or imitations. Similarly, there are old and often striking folktales that Arab children may enjoy, but no classic such as *Robinson Crusoe* or *Black Beauty* conceived specifically for the imaginative child.

Under the modernizing influence of the West, one or two Muslims drew critical attention to the treatment of women in their societies. Among the earliest were a Turkish writer, Ahmet Midhat; and the Egyptian Qasim Amin, whose books were *The Emancipation of Women,* published in 1899, and *The New Woman* two years later. Like Abdu, who was a friend, Qasim Amin advocated reform on Western lines. Polygamy, he thought, was "nothing but a legal fiction designed to satisfy animal desires, an indication of corrupted morals." What he was saying had profound social and political implications.

Look at the eastern countries; you will find woman enslaved to man and man to the ruler. Man is an oppressor in his home, oppressed as soon as he leaves it. Then look at the European countries; the governments are based on freedom and respect for personal rights, and the status of women has been raised to a high degree of respect and freedom of thought and action.

More than thirty books were written at the turn of the century to attack and refute Qasim Amin. A similar storm arose against *Our Women in the Sharia and in Society,* by the Tunisian Taher Haddad, pleading for women's rights. Like Qasim Amin, Taher Haddad was accused of being anti-Islamic and heretical; and both men collapsed under the strain, dying young. In 1955 Salama Musa wrote a book with the self-explanatory title of *Woman Is Not the Plaything of Man.*

No Arab feminist has been so renowned as Huda Shaarawi, author of a memoir, *Harem Years.* Born in 1879, the daughter of an influential Cairo notable and a personality at the court of the Khedive Ismail, she was married at the age of thirteen to her cousin. This husband, Ali Shaarawi, was a friend and colleague of Saad Zaghlul's. Three French women, two of them social friends and the third a political radical named Marguerite Clement, westernized her. Visiting Paris, she judged that "intense love of country" was the secret of French advancement. Transferring these sentiments to Egypt, she supported Zaghlul after 1919 and caused a scandal by becoming the first woman to appear in public in Cairo without a veil. Her lasting achievement as a feminist was to create a charity, the Mabarat Muhammad Ali, which by 1961 was operating twelve hospitals and eighteen dispensaries or clinics, treating patients free or for a nominal charge.

Between 1920 and about 1960, laws were passed in almost all Arab countries, as well as in Turkey and Iran, which aimed to ameliorate the status of women in accordance with Western notions. Turkey and Tunisia are the only two Muslim countries to have abolished polygamy outright. In Jordan and Iraq, polygamy is restricted. Divorce by simple repudiation has been modified in Egypt, Syria, Morocco, Algeria, and Jordan. A minimum age for marriage has been established in a number of these countries. Property and inheritance rights have been nominally strengthened. Sultan Mohammad V of Morocco appointed one of his daughters as ambassador to England. Egypt was the first country to give women the right to vote, followed by Tunisia. Fatma Talib Ismail became the first woman to receive a university education in Sudan, and celebrated it in 1956 by joining a communist delegation to Moscow. In 1959 Dr. Naziha Dulaimi was Iraq's first female minister. Zhor Ounissi has been the first female minister of education in Algeria. In 1962 an Egyptian woman joined the government as minister of social affairs. Fethia Mzali has been minister of family and women's affairs in Tunisia. Even in Dubai, Ayysha Sayyar has been director of social services, "the Gulf's token Emancipated Woman."

Appointments of the kind may serve symbolic purposes, but little else. Nowhere in the Arab world is there a systematic attack on political power challenging and its social support through shame-honor ranking, which so combine to deny civic rights to men and women alike, defining their status and roles with such special inflexibility. What happens instead is that a very few critics of the caliber of Fatima Mernissi and Abdelwahab Bouhdiba acquire the Western education and values which permit them to stand at a distance from their own culture. Their very objectivity is the source of alienation. The more penetratingly and coruscatingly they write, the more they are perceived to have internalized a Western outlook. Insofar as the masses hear of them at all, they come to think of such critics as "traitors" rather than saviors. Instead of addressing a public in need of their analyses and judg-

ments, intellectuals of the kind have become more and more mar-
ginalized and westernized, and therefore a neglected coterie writing for itself in some helplessness.

During the past twenty years, the Western or colonial influence
underlying all legislation to emancipate women has been ebbing
and draining away fast, to be replaced by the former Islamic or
precolonial order. Underage marriage, divorce by simple repudiation, appropriation and abuse of a woman's property by males in
her family, even polygamy, are increasingly practiced and increasingly disregarded by the authorities, in the correct belief that it is
futile and unjust to pick on some man here or there who is only
doing what he believes is customary and sanctioned by Islam.
"Paper legislation," according to two specialists on the subject,
Noel Coulson and Doreen Hinchcliffe, "in many respects does not
represent the social reality." Even in Tunisia, once the most progressive of Arab countries, the prospect for women's rights has
been deteriorating. The clash of values can be observed starkly in
Israel, where Muslim practices often defy the state's legal codes.
To give a recent example, Salman Abu Jildan agreed with another
man that each would marry the other's teenage daughter. Abu
Jildan was forty-two. His own daughter, one of eight children by
his first wife, accepted the agreement, but his sixteen-year-old
designated bride did not. She fought for her rights and was advised
to complain to the police. When the case reached court, the defense lawyer pleaded, no doubt truthfully, that his client "had no
idea he was doing anything wrong." Nonetheless, Abu Jildan was
sentenced to prison for bigamy and for the rape of the sixteen-
year-old girl.

Andrea B. Rugh suggests in her recent and far-sighted book
The Family in Contemporary Egypt that the reversion to the
precolonial Islamic order is not only foregone by now but may also
at present be in the best interests of women. Since women are
actually living within this careerist sociopolitical order, they have
learned through immense and inherited experience how to benefit
from it, how to make their own careers accordingly. They too have
strategies, intrigues, conspiracies; they too treat other people, hus-
bands and sons included, as instruments, just as they are themselves so treated. In effect, women are using careerism within the
family to turn the tables upon men, and in so doing they become
very strong and masterful personalities, as often as not. Andrea
Rugh writes perceptively, "Women have an advantage, when fam-

ily is central to a society, that has been overlooked by those focusing on authority patterns. They are the central figures in the central institution of the society." Women, she continues, "control those things that are most valued by the men—sex, honor, children, a happy well-organised household" and so "they occupy valued, respected, and rewarded roles in society."

Once again, what might have looked to a Westerner like unreflecting deprivation, cruelty, and violence is actually a very much more profound assertion of the significance of being an Arab.

6

The Turkish Example

Turkey today is a republic of some 50 million people, projected to rise by the end of the century to 65 million. Eighty to 85 percent are Sunni, the remainder Shia or heterodox sects. Perhaps as many as eight million Kurds, mainly Sunni, are settled in the southeast. A minority of them have formed either separatist Marxist groups, meaning that they are sponsored by the Soviet Union, or separatist national groups, meaning that they are sponsored by fellow Kurds over the borders in Iraq and Iran. About 70 percent of the country is rural, living in 40,000 villages, half of which have no more than 300 inhabitants. About a third of Turks in jobs other than agriculture are employees of the state. About a third of the population over the age of eleven is illiterate. The Ottoman heritage and the continuing difficulties of adjusting to the West are responsible for this unbalanced social structure, as well as the educational and cultural cleavage between the elite and the masses. Shame-honor ranking remains general. Peasant women may still wear the veil; polygamy, the payment of the bride price, and the blood feud are practiced, though to a diminishing extent. Some authorities reckon that blood feuds run in most Turkish villages, with killings in about a third of the instances.

Whether or not Turkey becomes the first Muslim country to construct an urban industrial society on Western lines depends on the balance eventually reached between the army and the existing political institutions, which have been locked for most of this century in uncomfortable symbiosis. Turkey remains a country where alternating decrees create, and then ban and dissolve, political parties. The constitution is emended accordingly. The Turkish army is 600,000 strong, and those generals who can command its obedience are the final arbiters of power.

The military coup of 1908 remains the exemplar of events repeated subsequently throughout the Middle East. Officers of the Third Army stationed in Salonika had formed the conspiracy known as the Committee of Union and Progress (CUP), and when they declared themselves and their ambitions, they enjoyed a bloodless revolution. For the first time, Sultan Abdul Hamid had lost control of the army. In the despairing hope of regaining it, he decreed the recall of the parliament which he had suspended more than thirty years earlier, and the very mention of which had always been an anathema to him. Constitutionalism resurfaced; and the crowd cheering in the streets asked what it might be. According to Halide Edib, daughter of an ancien régime notable and herself a writer enthusiastic for the new style of nationalism and progress, a speaker told them that "Constitution is such a great thing that those who do not know it are donkeys." The crowd roared back "We are donkeys." When the speaker then said that their fathers had not known it either, the crowd roared again, "We are the sons of donkeys."

Opening a parliament, Sultan Abdul Hamid and the CUP appeared to have agreed ends, but each was privately seeking to take advantage of the other. The sultan was still the caliph. In the name of the preservation of Islamic unity, units stationed in Istanbul mounted a countercoup in April 1909. "We want the Holy Law!" shouted those who demonstrated on his behalf. Concealing their purposes for fear that they would be disobeyed, the officers rallied the soldiers, marched on Istanbul and brought Abdul Hamid to Salonika, where he remained, deposed, under house arrest, returning to the capital only to die in 1918. His successor was obliged to accept as a fait accompli this imposition at gunpoint of constitutionalism. The Ottoman ruling establishment in the main foresaw where these arrangements would lead, as in the skepticism of the governor of Jerusalem who reported that the concept of freedom would be regrettably misused. "The corrupt gangs of notables, who regard the ignorant local populations as their prey will regard the idea of freedom as an important means of disobedience and revolt." Pickthall, in Turkey in 1913, was pithy: "A parliament! A water-melon!"

The fact that it was not a genuine constitutional movement but only a successful conspiracy deprived the CUP of legitimacy. Helpless to deal with problems which they themselves introduced or exacerbated, the officers turned upon one another in free-for-all challenges. Point-blank assassinations and arrests followed, until a dictatorship of three of the CUP leaders was established in 1913. External attacks were mounted by Italy in Libya and by Serbia in the Balkans. To rally in the name of the sultan-caliph was no longer possible. Islam had provided one continuing identity, but another lay in the new prospect of nationalism. Seeking whatever means were available to strengthen their own hand, the CUP leaders alienated those peoples of the empire who were not Turks. Armenians, Greeks, Jews, Kurds, Albanians, and Bulgarians were invited to see themselves as such, no longer as belonging to one among equal *millets*. If so, then these peoples comprised separately identifiable nations and the Turkish empire had ceased to have a multicommunal structure, losing the rationale for its existence. Arab nationalism, in particular, began at this moment when the simple fact of being a Muslim within the Ottoman Empire brought no advantage.

Entering the war on the German side, the CUP sealed the fate of the empire for whose survival and modernization they so paradoxically claimed to have seized power. By the Armistice of 1918, British and French forces of occupation were in Turkey itself; and Russia, Greece, and Italy were claiming territory as spoils of war. A Greek army occupied Izmir in 1919 and began to advance inland. At the Peace Conference of Versailles, the Allies advocated the principle of self-determination, a euphemism in the Turkish perspective for dismemberment.

Quite as firmly as Abdul Hamid, the CUP intended to preserve the integrity of the empire. In the course of the century since the Greeks had first sought independence, Rumanians, Bulgarians, Serbs, and Macedonians had asserted themselves as nationalists, with a claim to a territory of their own. To an Ottoman sultan, these people seemed ungratefully disloyal but Christian, and therefore inevitably put up to sedition and treason by Christian powers and their agents. The Armenians were another such people, and their fate exemplifies how massacre comes to be the final adjudication of differences in tribe and religion. What had happened earlier to the Maronites of Lebanon in 1860 was repeated upon a terrible scale with the Armenians.

As a Christian *millet*, the Armenians had prospered. In the eighteenth century, Armenian priests had begun to revive the language and the literature. Unlike other Christian *millets* in the Balkans, the Armenians were nowhere a majority but scattered throughout the empire, with concentrations in the heartland, in eastern Anatolia and Cilicia. Many individual Armenians rose to prominence as bankers, customs' officials, and traders. Ismail Kemal Bey spoke for the Ottoman governing classes when he called them "the faithful people," comparing them favorably to the Greeks. Western doctrines of nationalism and independence threatened the traditional pluralist arrangements of the empire. The first Armenian secret society was formed in 1860. In 1872 an Armenian was writing in a patriotic paper in Tiflis, "Yesterday, we were an ecclesiastical community; tomorrow, we shall be a nation of workers and thinkers." Quoting this aspiration, the historian Elie Kedourie goes on to ask how the Armenians should have become such a nation. Without the prerequisites of political or geographical unity or a generally knowledgeable citizenry, the Armenians were at the mercy of those among them with ambitions. Careerist Armenians followed the well-trodden path into exile in Paris and Geneva, and there they published newspapers to promote their factions. Unscrupulous conspirators, these exiles accepted the sponsorship of czarist Russia, with its own Armenian minority and its imperialist aims of annexing Ottoman provinces. Returning home, the conspirators initiated in the 1890s violent clashes with the Ottoman authorities who, seeing their worst fears realized, responded in kind. Sultan Abdul Hamid let loose upon the Armenians the Kurdish tribes in whose land the Armenian autonomy was supposedly to be set up. Demands for independence reached a climax in the First World War, when in 1915 a local Armenian government, with Russian backing, was declared in the town of Van, followed by a republic of Armenia lasting for some months in 1919 and 1920. In reaction, the Turkish authorities virtually eliminated the community from the country; and amid scenes of horror, the remnants dispersed into a resentful and embittered exile. Along with the Armenians, Ottoman pluralism had finally died. In the new era, tribal and religious differences were not to be settled any differently or with less bloodshed simply by applying to them alien and far-fetched words like nationalism and self-determination.

Apparent disintegration is the supreme opportunity for the

power challenger, and Mustafa Kemal (not to be confused with the Egyptian Mustafa Kamil) was the man to seize it, rising from a modest background to earn the sobriquet of Ataturk, father of the Turks. Born in 1881 in Salonika, he was the son of a clerk in the Customs who died young. At the age of fourteen, he left home to enter a Military Training School, graduating a year later to the War College in Istanbul. Posted to the Fifth Army in Damascus, he took his first careerist steps by inviting two other officers to form a secret society with the purpose of inciting a revolution. Scenting the unrest in his hometown, he made his way there before the CUP coup but had no part in its inner council, instead widening his own conspiracy to half a dozen school friends and officers. One evening in this circle Kemal read out the articles of his secret society, which he had just jotted down.

After that a revolver was produced and laid on the table. The oath was to be sworn on this weapon, not on the Koran or on the honour of an officer as was the Ottoman practice. It symbolised their fidelity to the Revolution and their intention to resort to arms, if need be, to bring it about. One by one they kissed the revolver and swore. Afterwards Kemal remarked, "This revolver is now sacred. Keep it carefully, and one day you will give it to me."

At thirty-two, he was a staff officer. In 1915 he earned his reputation through his tactics and personal courage in opposing the Allied landings at Gallipoli. After the war, in disobedience of orders from the sultan, he traveled inland to Sivas and then Ankara, at the time an Anatolian village, to recruit a retinue of like-minded people. In careerist style, he enlarged his following into a movement of opposition both to the sultan and to the Allied forces of occupation and altogether superseding the defeated CUP. The appeal to defend the homeland mobilized the masses. His close followers became first a congress, then a national assembly, to do his bidding and legitimize his hopes and ambitions. In a war of independence, he routed the Greeks in a campaign of massacre and countermassacre as the two communities in their turn disengaged from historic involvement in the old empire. His success obliged the Allies to come to terms which maintained the territorial integrity of Turkey. Then he was in a position, in November 1922, to depose the sultan, closing that chapter of Ottoman history forever.

At the outset of this astonishing phase of imposing himself on his own people and the world at large, he had stated:

I shall follow no personal interest or ambition but the salvation and peace of my Fatherland and nation. I shall not try to revive the Union and Progress party. I shall not serve the interests of any political party. This I swear in the name of Allah.

What happened in Turkey was what he had decided would happen, and nothing else. "After the Greeks we will fight each other, we will eat each other," he told Halide Edib in an accurate insight into the power-challenge dialectic, at the same time promising to have lynched two men who were an immediate threat to him. To those who opposed abolishing the sultanate, he warned that "a few heads will probably have to be chopped off." An incipient Islamic revolt was mercilessly repressed, and his method with critics throughout his rule was simply to kill them. The founder of the Turkish Communist Party and his fourteen-man Politburo were among those done away with. An officially sanctioned opposition party lasted for all of four months in 1930. The National Assembly, supposedly embodying the will of the people, was a dictator's instrument for ratifying his decisions. An infrastructure of municipalities and Houses of Culture commanded popular obedience to the new order.

Between 1922 and his death in 1938, Ataturk refashioned Turkey down to the last detail. Modernization was posited on secularization. The old Islamic posts, the religious schools and foundations, the mystic and dervish orders were abolished. A new legal code, imitated from a Western model, was substituted for the Holy Law. Civil marriage became obligatory, the veil was officially discouraged, and traditional Turkish costume was declared illegal. Women were enfranchised. Alcohol was legalized. Arabic for purposes of worship was replaced by Turkish, and the script itself romanized. A modern system of compulsory education put the seal upon secular reform. Symbolizing modernism, Ataturk built Ankara into the new national capital. In accordance with the practice of other modernizing nations at the time, in 1927 he passed a law for the encouragement of industry with the first Five Year Plan and accepted foreign loans for development. Peace at home and abroad was his slogan, and perhaps the proof of his greatness lies in his restraint from seeking to enlarge and justify his power challenging by means of foreign adventure.

To the Turks, according to his early biographer H. C. Armstrong, Ataturk seemed their ideal of a conqueror-ruler, possibly "cruel, vicious, brutal and spiteful" but all the same strong and decisive. "I don't mean to be like the rest of you," Ataturk had boasted. "I mean to be somebody." Halide Edib heard him say, "I don't want any consideration, criticism, or advice. I will have only my own way. All shall do as I command." Like everyone, she kept her reservations to herself. Or again, "I don't act for public opinion, I act for the nation and my own satisfaction." In a psychobiography of the man, Volkan and Itzkowitz concluded that Ataturk had "an inflated and grandiose self-concept," believing that he had the right to assert his will. His admirers and followers were distinguished, as far as he was concerned, from the rest who had no existence.

Ataturk's resort to traditional despotic methods in order to compel his people to westernize without forms of voluntary association was a very great paradox and likely to cause dislocation and lasting strain. In effect, the Turks were ordered to reject their past and accept a future of Ataturk's choosing. Islam was no longer to be the vehicle of identity but a private system of belief like any other, separated from the state in the manner of worship in the West. To a devout Muslim, this was inconceivable heresy. Whether it is feasible to decree into existence a supposedly modern and democratically conceived state did not concern Ataturk, and he certainly sought no systematic or philosophic reconciliation between such a state and Islam.

In speeches and declarations, he kept insisting upon the need to modernize and civilize, as though these words contained self-evidently positive values to his listeners. The negative inference was that hitherto they had been neither modern nor civilized and so must change. "What does this word 'modern' mean?" an angry Islamic divine once asked him, to receive the reply, "It means being a human being." What did that make the divine? "We shall be civilised and proud of it." "We must prove that we are capable of becoming active members of the society of civilised peoples." Referring to wiping out the animosity of the Greeks, he said, "It is not by military victories that we shall do this, but only by attaining to everything which modern knowledge and civilisation demand." If women did not share in the nation's social life, he said, full development was impossible and "We shall remain irremedia-

bly backward, incapable of treating on equal terms with the civilizations of the West." He concluded this last speech,

And all that will still be nothing if you refuse to enter resolutely into
modern life, if you reject the obligations which it imposes. You will be
lepers, pariahs, alone in your obstinacy, with your customs of another
age. Remain yourselves, but learn how to take from the West what is
indispensable to an evolved people. Admit science and new ideas into
your lives. If you do not, they will devour you.

Heir to a nineteenth-century analysis by then more or less
standardized, yet a man of his times with the example of the Bolshevik government on the far side of his northern frontier, Ataturk
had absorbed the stream of feeling that Muslims were backward,
to be held in contempt for their customs and their lack of science.
These feelings hurt him and his pride. The strong language, the
insults like "lepers" and "pariahs" are raw with a sense of inferiority. Shame-honor ranking required that he be as good as a Westerner or better, in the very respects in which Westerners appeared
to excel. Why make it a crime to continue wearing a turban instead
of a hat?

Gentlemen [Ataturk said in a speech in October 1927], the Turkish
people, who founded the Turkish Republic, are civilized; they are civilized in history and reality. . . . A civilized, international dress is worthy
and appropriate for our nation, and we will wear it. Boots or shoes on
our feet, trousers on our legs, shirt and tie, jacket and waistcoat—and of
course, to complete these, a cover with a brim on our heads. I want to
make this clear. This head-covering is called "hat."

Resorting to all available means, including most uncomfortable
mockery, Ataturk incited and aroused the awareness of their own
humiliation that alone would force people to change their habits.

In some places I have seen women who put a piece of cloth or a towel
or something like it over their heads to hide their faces, and who turn
their backs or huddle themselves on the ground when a man passes by.
What is the meaning and sense of this behaviour? Gentlemen, can the
mothers and daughters of a civilized nation adopt this strange manner,
this barbarous posture? It is a spectacle that makes the nation an object
of ridicule. It must be remedied at once.

One of Turkey's most popular writers, Aziz Nesin, has described
in his memoirs how important it had become—a matter of pride—

to look modern. At the time, most of the intellectual young men sported a walking stick, pointed shoes, a bow tie or a cravat, and trousers revealing expensive socks. Instead of calling them "Sir" children yelled "Monsher" (from Monsieur) at such men and "Tango" (this dance was all the rage) at their women.

A small but significant incident in Ataturk's youth reveals susceptibilities all too easily bruised. On his first visit to Western Europe, to observe the French army on its annual maneuvers, he had bought in Salonika what he took to be Western clothes and a soft hat. Meeting him at the station in Paris, the military attaché had laughed at the sight. "The suit was dark green and the hat had a jaunty Tyrolean air to it." Paris-styled clothes then had to be procured. A shame-response also lay in later far-fetched theories he promoted to prove that Turkish was the mother of all languages and that the Turks were a white Aryan race.

Ataturk's westernizing thrust seemed to have reached a milestone in 1946 when Ismet Inönü, his successor as President, licensed an opposition, the Democratic Party. In 1950 the Democratic Party defeated the ruling People's Party in what so far has been the only fair and free election ever to be held in the Muslim Middle East. Coinciding with the Cold War and the heyday of Stalin, who viewed Turkey in the light of his czarist predecessors as an area into which to expand, this achievement was considerable. That same year, Turkey committed herself to support the United Nations forces in the war in Korea. In 1952, Turkey joined NATO and two years later the Baghdad Pact, conceived as an alliance to contain the Soviet Union. Geopolitical considerations appeared to consolidate Turkey's position in the democratic West. Policies of industrialization, with improving facilities for communications and transport, were maintained.

The Democratic Party limited landownership and distributed what had been expropriated to landless tenants and agricultural workers. In spite of its name, the Democratic Party, under its leader Prime Minister Adnan Menderes, was soon lapsing into mere money-favoring, taking land and possessions away from opponents in order to enrich friends, legislating and intriguing to establish supremacy. Here were what Ataturk had called "customs of another age." In office, in 1959, Menderes survived an airplane crash. He returned to the capital by train.

The platform was lined on both sides with hundreds of sacrificial animals, which were slaughtered in a ghastly carnage as the train stopped. Amid the dying groans of innumerable expiring beasts, Menderes stepped from his carriage. More creatures—sheep, oxen, even camels— were sacrificed in the streets as the Prime Minister's cortege drove by. Blood ran in torrents down the main boulevard, lapping the tyres of the smart limousines. The Prime Minister had been saved from death by divine intervention.

An army coup in 1960 revealed how weak a hold democratic institutions had on national life. The arrests of hundreds of Democratic Party supporters led to trials for corruption, and Menderes and two other ministers were hanged in 1961, just two years after the public sacrificing of animals in his honor. Relaunched, party politics have not lost all purpose, but leaders of every persuasion must expect attempts on their lives, spells of prison or house arrest, as dependent on the money-favor nexus as everyone else.

A further army intervention in 1971 ushered in a succession of power challenges for a decade. Some of these sought to mobilize around Islam. Necmettin Erbakan founded the National Salvation Party (NSP) in 1972 to reestablish an Islamic state, declaring the following year, "The only way out for us and for Westerners is to become Muslims." The NSP obtained about 10 percent of the vote in elections and entered government coalitions. Directly or indirectly sponsored by the NSP, and later by Iran and even Saudi Arabia, Islamic secret societies have sprung up, with names like "Islamic Turkish Fighters" and "Muslim Fighters." Out of this shadowy world emerged Mehmet Ağça, who attempted to kill Pope John Paul II in May 1981. Perhaps an unwitting agent of the Soviet Union, Ağça more probably was aware of this sponsorship and acted from motives of Marxism, Islam, and nationalism too confused to be articulated, even at the trial in which he was sentenced to life imprisonment.

Seeking to polemicize, a member of the Muslim Brotherhood summed up in a pamphlet twenty years ago the loaded question behind Islamic challenges of the kind. In Turkey, he wrote, "a miserable reactionary movement was started for the purpose of reviving the Turkic nationality. It succeeded in dissolving the Caliphate and in separating religion from the state." He went on, "Today, Turkey is a petty state which begs for its arms from America and lives in the orbit of the dissolute democracies. The Turks live under constant fear of the outside world and possess less than 10 per cent of their empire. To what good has their unbelief led them?" To show how the pendulum has swung, there were eleven religious associations and teaching institutions in Turkey in 1946, but 14,239 in 1968.

During the late 1970s, about thirty Marxist or Soviet-sponsored secret societies were operating clandestinely in Turkey. Thousands of people were killed in the gunfire on the streets between these rival conspirators and their opponents. Expressed more accurately, Turkey experienced a trial of strength between its military power holders, its internal Islamic challengers, and its external Soviet challengers. Twenty or thirty dollars a month seems sufficient pay to hire recruits to these secret societies, and there are said to be 10,000 members of them, glorified as political refugees, now in exile abroad. The army once more deposed the government in 1980, and a year later arrested and charged a former deputy prime minister, Alparslan Turkes, with attempting armed insurrection—he had also been prominent in the 1960 coup. Trade unionists and intellectuals were arrested, and by mid–1983 the military authorities still held arrest warrants against 5854 individuals. By 1984, political parties were again permitted, and martial law was mostly lifted. Despite rapid progress in recent times, a cautious English commentator noted in 1985, "economic and social evolution has not yet gone far enough to make it clear what the country will look like when it is fully urbanized and industrialized." Portraits and statues of Ataturk are visible everywhere in public places, and his memory is held in high esteem, but neither he nor anyone else has yet explained how Western life-styles and habits acquire meaning or coherence in the absence of their supporting institutions.

7

Colonialism

The colonial period pushed Westerners and Muslims into an encounter from which neither side could again disengage. In India, China, Japan, and Africa, parallel encounters were occurring, each of which would determine, in historical terms, how much of these ancient and autonomous cultures could be accommodated for better or worse with post-Enlightenment values stemming from Europe. The upheavals have proved dramatic, and every civilization, naturally including the European, interpreted them in the light of its own experiences.

Responsible Europeans were confident that the organizing principles of their societies fully accounted for their rule over other people. Seeing themselves as uniquely able to introduce undoubted improvements, responsible Europeans could never have concluded that other people might cling to a customary power holding that was tyrannical and murderous. Observing Middle Eastern society, no European administrator could believe that he should himself adopt Muslim practices of government nor conceive that he might have the duty to break such practices by force, in favor of his own.

Alexis de Tocqueville, one of the most far-sighted political minds of the age, visited Algeria in 1841. In Philippeville, he met a colonel who said to him and other Frenchmen present, "Only force and terror, my dear sirs, work with those fellows." For as long as colonialism lasted, the tiny number of men who spoke in that voice were invariably dismissed as bigots, fire-eaters, altogether a threat to civilized values. Through firsthand experience, this colonel and his kind had in fact grasped that the colonial powers had either to absorb and ingest the power-challenge dialectic and behave like any Muslim power holder, or else to break it once and for all and so integrate peoples of different religions and customs into one value system. Had the alternatives been understood, they would still have been unacceptable. Democracy is not conquest. De Tocqueville listened to the colonel with sadness and asked himself "what the future of the country in the hands of men such as these could possibly be, and how this cascade of violence and injustice could end but in the revolt of the native and the ruin of the Europeans." Example and persuasion, education and reason would have to serve, and so they did, yet these options ended just the same in cascading violence and injustice, and revolt and ruin.

A few Europeans, whose influence was always greater than their numbers, valued Islamic society for its own sake. Their hopes that Muslims would never change matched their fears for the Muslim future. One such was Ignaz Goldziher, a Hungarian Jew and the founder of modern orientalist studies. On a journey in the Middle East in 1874, he wrote a poem to complain that the Arabs were prostituting themselves to European values. "This good weak people" was being blinded by external things,

> the good old kernel expires,
> Never again to yield that fruit which made this people
> Achieve victory for three and a half millennia
> To the admiration of the entire world.

Three and a half millennia was of course a wild and wishful exaggeration. Colonial administrators easily shared nostalgia of the kind, but few could grasp that successful modernizing might introduce and generalize the bitterness captured in Goldziher's lines.

A shared outlook links the conservative Cromer, in 1889 informing the foreign secretary of the day, Lord Salisbury, that evacuation of Egypt would be irresponsible in view of "the utter incapacity of the ruling classes in this country," to the post–1945 socialist Prime Minister Attlee and his sweeping statement about Arab leaders, "I must say I had a very poor view of the governing classes." European administrators everywhere took pride and pleasure in initiating the social facilities which raised the level of prosperity and increased life spans. Cromer had the habit of appointing his advisers, about 250 in all, from the circle of his English friends and acquaintances, high-minded Victorians like himself. In 1903 public examinations were instituted for the Egyptian and Sudanese civil services. Humphrey Bowman, in memoirs written after a life spent as an administrator among Arabs, gives a thumbnail sketch of a character called Dr. Balfour, head of the Wellcome Tropical Research Laboratories. In Khartoum there was no water supply for sanitation, and night soil was removed in carts. If Balfour heard a complaint about the cleanliness of the carts' buckets, he would send for the Sudanese at fault and upbraid him in Scottish-accented Arabic. Colonialism has its symbolic image there. In every walk of life, men like Balfour were creating the stereotype of the European in the Arab mind, while transmitting to the European a corresponding stereotype of the Arab. "Egyptian hands and British heads" was the catchphrase for attitudes that died hard.

Behind European standards and values was the whole panoply of institutional instruments, censuses, surveys and maps, parliamentary debates, White papers, a free press, cabinet responsibility. Lord Rosebery, Gladstone's foreign secretary at the time of the occupation of Egypt, had remarked that he was determined to shield Egypt from the nightmare of "Commissions, reports and experiments." The certainty that these were in store for the British and the Egyptians gives this wish its humor. Realization came late and reluctantly that the values implicit in European constitutionality might not be universal.

Politicians like Disraeli and Charles Dilke, Paul Cambon and Jules Ferry, a certain number of generals and admirals, and a few eccentrics with firsthand knowledge of foreign regions further advanced a variety of arguments to the effect that colonization was the avenue to power and riches. Failure to occupy some territory, it might then be claimed, was only an opportunity abandoned to a more eagerly expansionist competitor. Arguments for expansion did not have practical ends in view, in the last resort capturing the imagination through myth and literature. Possession of territory did not consolidate power but diluted it. No money was ever taxed or levied abroad to be remitted home, if for no other reason than that surplus wealth did not exist to be extracted. Wealth, especially in the custom-bound lands of India, Africa, and the Middle East, had first to be created, which meant the extraction of minerals and other primary resources, trade and development, requiring the prior provision of European capital. The foreign debts of every Arab ruler who attempted this course of action spoke for themselves.

The Marxist-derived notion, spread by J. A. Hobson and other "imperialist" mythmakers, that colonialism was a stage in the necessary expansion of capitalism and therefore part of some great engine of exploitation, is not based in reality. As the economist Charles Issawi has pointed out, Spain, Italy, and France were impoverished rather than enriched by their colonies in the Arab world and so was Germany by its competitive attempts to gain a presence there. In North Africa, the French eventually had 1.7 million settlers and a total investment of $10 billion. For Britain, "the balance sheet shows a large surplus" in Issawi's estimation, but any such surplus did not end in the British Treasury but in building and maintaining the infrastructure of trade and development. Controversy at the time, and continuing into the present in nationalist circles, has centered on specifics such as the optimal size of budgets for education or health. No example can be adduced of expenditure that was deemed right in itself but postponed for fear of a consequent transfer of wealth and power into Arab hands. Nonetheless, to the Arabs the whole range of Western innovations—from the Middle East Anti-Locust Unit, the Inland Water Transport Board of Iraq, the Palestinian Matriculation Examination, the *Bureaux Arabes,* the Queen Elizabeth Hospital and Girls' College in Aden, the Banque de Suez et de l'Indochine, the Messageries Maritimes, and so on, down to foreign-language newspapers, cinemas, plumbing, cutlery, pharmaceuticals—did not appear only as the undoubted benefits that they were but also as physical intrusions into the landscape, perhaps therefore Western entrapments, and in any case calling for ambivalent psychological responses.

In London and Paris, colonial expansion was never a popular policy. Colonialism involved political and electoral risk, open-ended expense to the taxpayer, loss of life, dispersion of military strength vital in the European cockpit. The huge majority remained indifferent to colonialist issues, had no firsthand knowledge of any colony, and generally speaking, assumed that the apparently corresponding passivity of the Arabs endorsed complacent catchphrases such as "the white man's burden" and *"la mission civilisatrice."*

One of the intentions of the Entente Cordiale of 1904 was to check the danger of unwanted rivalry between Britain and France by defining spheres of influence. French aims in Morocco were recognized in exchange for a similar recognition of British aims in Egypt (a blow, incidentally, to Mustafa Kamil and the warmongering Juliette Adam circle). Abdel Aziz, the then sultan of Morocco, was one more in the succession of Muslim rulers to conclude that his country had to adapt and modernize in self-defense. Succeeding in 1894, at the age of twelve or thirteen, Abdel Aziz descended in a long line from a great-grandson of the Prophet. Traditionally, the sultan had ridden out twice a year, in the midst of tribal levies, to receive allegiance and taxes throughout the countryside. Modernizing, Abdel Aziz, like every Muslim ruler in his position, offended the upholders of custom, tribal chiefs, and the ulema. Borrowing abroad, by 1903 he had a debt of £800,000.

Walter Harris, for many years the renowned correspondent of *The Times* of London in Morocco and a close witness of these events, found the sultan well-intentioned but unable to control a whimsical extravagance. No distinction was yet drawn between his revenues and the country's. The palaces of the sultan were littered with packing cases, Harris wrote:

Grand pianos and kitchen-ranges; automobiles and immense cases of corsets; wild animals in cages, and boxes of strange theatrical uniforms; barrel-organs and hansom-cabs; a passenger lift capable of rising to dizzy altitudes, destined for a one-storied palace; false hair; cameras of gold and of silver with jewelled buttons; carved marble lions and living macaw parrots; jewels, real and false; steam-launches and fireworks; ladies' underclothing from Paris, and saddlery from Mexico; trees for gardens that were never planted, or, if planted, were never watered; printing presses and fire-balloons—an infinity of all that was grotesque, useless and in bad taste.

In response to the sultan's unpopularity among subjects upon whom he was imposing far-reaching changes for reasons that were not explained, power challengers appeared, including a pretender by the name of Bou Hamara, and Raisuli, who today would be called a terrorist. Raisuli held to ransom an American, Ion Perdicaris, in a cause célèbre of the day. Evidently the sultan's writ did not run far. Using as a pretext the sultan's lack of authority and his indebtedness, the French built up a presence in Morocco by seconding police officers and starting a state bank with financial inspectors. In 1907 an incident at the port of Casablanca led to the murder of nine Europeans. The French navy shelled Casablanca and then landed an expeditionary force. By 1912 Abdel Aziz had resigned in favor of his brother Hafiz, and a treaty was signed to formalize a French protectorate. The average Moroccan, in Harris's shrewd judgment, had looked upon the invaders as unwarlike Christians, ridiculous in appearance. When nonetheless these ludicrous infidels were victorious, the same Moroccan perceived how power had changed hands and simply picked up his rifle to offer himself and his services to the French. Like so many Europeans, Harris could not quite sort out the customs he admired from the barbarity he condemned, resorting to elegy to smooth over his contradictory feelings.

The advent of the French has put an end to the period that was really terrible. Yet when one lived among these great crimes—the sudden appearances and disappearances, the midnight burials in desert places, the carrying off of women; hate, love, revenge and now and again some great unselfishness—the exaggeration, in fact, of all qualities and all sentiments good and bad—one ceased to wonder. Whole families would fall—in wealth and luxury today, and gone tomorrow—to rise again perhaps a generation later, and carry on the blood-feud of revenge and hate—or perhaps, generally unwisely, to forgive.

The modernizer of Morocco was Marshal Lyautey, the French Resident, a famous soldier sympathetic to autocracy, whether Muslim or any other. He believed that it was possible to maintain the sultan as ruler, with the Residency as the power behind the throne, imposing first the requisite control over the tribes and then building a civic infrastructure. "The concept of the Protectorate," Lyautey declared, "is that of a country retaining its own institutions, governing itself with its own organs, but under the control of a European power which assumes control over its foreign relations, its army, its finances, and guides it in its economic development. What dominates and characterizes this conception is the notion of 'control' as opposed to that of direct rule." By 1913 the French population had reached 26,000. In spite of the intervening First World War, Lyautey developed the port of Casablanca, roads, and railroads; set up a French bureaucracy, complete with municipalities; and secularized the law. Europeans acquired just over 5 percent of the land, much of it the best available. But the school system separated the French from the Moroccans and then again divided the Moroccan elite from the masses. By 1930–1931,

European schools had 22,770 students of whom only 144 were Muslims.

In the protectorate of Tunisia, the Bey, descendant of Ahmed Bey, was also maintained as ruler. By 1895 the number of Europeans was 77,000, 40,000 of them Italians, the rest French or Maltese. Under the Residency, as in Morocco, a prime minister, in cooperation with French *directions* or technical services, ran finance and public works, education, post and telegraph, agriculture, commerce and colonisation. By 1939 Tunisia had 14,500 bureaucrats, 5,500 of whom were Tunisian. The Khaldouniya university had been founded in 1896, and a secret society of about a dozen students had formed there as Young Tunisians, in imitation of the Young Turks. Claiming to be inspired by the French, they spoke of national independence. The Young Tunisian leader was exiled in 1912. Throughout the First World War, Tunisia was under martial law. In that war, however, 100,000 Tunisians served in France in army or labor battalions.

In both Morocco and Tunisia, then, French ruling influence had the effect of substituting centralizing power for the old separatist tribal challenges. The French acted as though they were forming European-style entities, or states; if so, former tribesmen must be correspondingly Moroccans or Tunisians. The more conscious people grew of these definitions, the more they perceived that there was a demarcation between French nationality and their own. In the Residencies and *directions* it was assumed that the citizens of the protectorates would continue some of their ways as Muslims but yet somehow change other of their ways in the light of the indubitable benefits of French rule. Among those not required to change their ways were the ruler, the caids, and the notables who worked with the administration and drew from it new strength in patronage and money-favors. In this contradiction was born an awareness that the French could not be sincere. They appeared to have set up a scale of money-favoring with Europeans and their friends at the top; and Muslims had a well-tried experience of doing this for themselves. Those with the ambition for it would be able to build upon a sense of grievance and then a nationality, which might be secular in expression or Islamic, depending on their outlook and education. By the 1920s challengers were prominent in Tunisia in the person of Habib Bourguiba and those with him in the Destour Party, and in Morocco in the person of Allal al-Fassi and his friends forming the Istiqlal Party.

In Algeria, a more efficient and protracted centralization had consolidated the structure of the state, also at the expense of the tribes. Theoretically the incorporation of Algeria into metropolitan France gave its citizens the prospect of assimilation. In practice, the so-called *Code de l'Indigénat* demarcated Algerians from the French. About 250,000 Algerians had participated in French army and labor battalions during the First World War—around a tenth losing their lives. By 1923, 70,000 Algerians were already working in France. Yet by 1936 no more than 2500 Algerians had actually become French citizens and could be considered assimilated. Here too no institution had been created in which Algerians could participate on terms of equality. Under the governor-general were French prefects in the three departments, each of which sent French senators and deputies to the National Assembly in Paris.

One electoral college had been created for French Algerians and selected Muslims, and another for the remainder of the Muslims. In consequence, a million French or other settlers had the same voting rights and representation as eight million Algerians. This was not a policy of deliberate unfairness cunningly carried through in Paris, as nationalists liked to claim. The essential obstacle to French citizenship for Algerian Muslims was the simple fact that citizenship for Muslims necessarily placed them under French law, like the French themselves, precluding the recourse to Muslim religious law in matters of personal status. Only a very few Muslims were prepared for such complete assimilation, and they were known as *évolués*.

The difficulty of integrating peoples of different religion was further revealed as a result of the passing in 1870 of a law to confer full citizenship on Algerian Jews, in the expectation that this would encourage Muslims. Becoming French citizens, the Algerian Jews surrendered their customary recourse to Jewish religious courts in matters of personal status. Soon these Jews found themselves the object of anti-Semitism from those Frenchmen who did not welcome new citizens of the kind and also from Muslims who accused them of opportunism. In either case, French sincerity again became suspect.

To begin with, the *évolués* made the running. In 1911, a grandson of the long-deposed Emir Abdel Kader founded the Young Algerians. These were modern-educated doctors and lawyers, and unlike the Young Tunisians they asked for complete assimilation. Imposition of military service on Algerians, for example, was approved by them as a measure of equalization. "We are Frenchmen with Muslim personal status," declared Ferhat Abbas, a spokesman for those who pleaded for genuine assimilation and a man who preferred to use French rather than his halting Arabic. Born in 1899, Ferhat Abbas had grown up to take European values such as equality and secularism for granted. In sentences that were to be debated hard and long, he said, "If I had discovered an Algerian nation, I would be a nationalist and I would not blush for it as though it were a crime. . . . Yet I will not die for the Algerian homeland, because such a homeland does not exist. I have not found it." Unable to refute this logic, the French could only stand on privilege. Ferhat Abbas's Muslim challenger was a member of the ulema, Sheikh Ben Badis, who insisted that Ferhat Abbas's position was an impossible surrender. History, language, religion were different. "This Muslim population is not France; it cannot be France, it does not want to be France." An attempt in 1936 to enfranchise 20,000 Muslims failed in the National Assembly. When Ferhat Abbas was finally obliged against his instinct to join the Algerian nationalists, he was also conceding the force of Sheikh Ben Badis's challenge. Here was a tragic example of democratic impulse deprived of the structure to realize it.

The Cartesian clarity of thought for which the French are allegedly famous was not discernible in arrangements whereby a European republic declared that a part of Africa was actually integrated into metropolitan France, while the countries on either side of this odd African France were protected monarchies. In addition to these confusions, the French acquired Lebanon and Syria under Mandate from the League of Nations, as accorded by the post–1918 peace settlements. In Syria, at the outset, a challenger appeared in the person of Feisal, one of the sons of Sherif Hussein of Mecca. Feisal had himself proclaimed king in Damascus by his supporters, in the main either Syrians who had been at the Paris Congress in 1913 or who had joined the Sherifian retinue in the war. The French rightly perceived Feisal as first and foremost a British client. In a skirmish at Maysalun, near Damascus, the French dispersed this opposition. Some of their units were Muslim Algerians. Forty-two Frenchmen and approximately 150 Arabs were killed. Feisal departed for England.

Historically Syria and Lebanon had been an intricate agglomeration of tribes and religions and sects in a perpetual state of localized warring, either to seek domination or to ensure survival. In one generation after another, the balance of power was adjusted in violence and bloodshed as rivals formed coalitions to contain whoever among them might be emerging as a predominant power holder. If Lebanon was to have a central government, indeed any future as a state, the Organic Statute of 1861 had to be continued by some means. Ideas and experiments were explored by successive French governments for creating local identities and communities, in general building up the Lebanese province into the so-called "Grand Liban"—this of course was answered by nationalists and aspirants to power in Damascus with corresponding notions of a greater Syria. In 1926 Lebanon was declared a constitutional republic, with a constituent assembly. The former council was enlarged into a chamber of deputies, and notables were appointed by the French high commissioner to a senate or second chamber. In 1932 a census was held to establish how and in what proportion the offices of state, as well as parliamentary seats, were to be allotted between the sects and religions. Arranged democracy of the kind was fragile, likely to shatter into its separate elements at the first real pressure. Hardly were the arrangements in operation than the high commissioner had to suspend the constitution on the question of whether a Muslim rather than a Christian could be president. The French had a tendency to treat the Maronites as favored clients in government. Until the Second World War, the French nonetheless arbitrated between the multiple groups; and Lebanese resourcefulness and versatility saw to it that a pluralist society began to take shape, however imperfect or exotic.

Revolts in Syria between 1920 and 1922, and 1925 and 1927 were in the nature of power challenges, consisting sometimes of purely tribal uprisings on the part of the Druze, sometimes of local and personal assertions as in the revolt of Ibrahim Hananu in Aleppo or the revolt in Hama led by Fawzi al-Qawukji, a defector from the Syrian Legion, a force raised locally by the French. Dr. Abdel Rahman Shahbandar saw himself as the Syrian Zaghlul. Born in Damascus in 1880, he came from a fairly prosperous merchant family and had been educated at the American University in Beirut, studying medicine. Supporting first the Young Turks in 1908 and then Feisal, he also kept lines open to the British, gathering his fellow-conspirators into the so-called Iron Hand Society, which later enlarged into the National Bloc. The French found a pretext to deport Dr. Shahbandar and to hang five of his associates. Nonetheless, Dr. Shahbandar remained the guiding spirit of the National Bloc, a close analogy in its anti-French sentiments to the anti-British Wafd in Egypt. Obliged to resort to increasing use of power, the French shelled Damascus in 1925. A search followed for some means of regularizing politics at national level. The high commissioner, a civilian after 1925, resorted to a local variety of Organic Law, followed in 1928 by a constituent assembly. French optimism was dissipated once this assembly met. The spectacle, according to the historian Philip Khoury, was "something to behold."

Gathered together were members of what seemed to be two alien worlds: one was old and conservative, rural, and coarse; the other, by comparison, was modern and radical, urban and sophisticated. Here, traditionally attired rural notables and Bedouin chiefs sat across from their urban nationalist colleagues in fezzes and European business suits.

One and all, these members were strangers to the concept of a national interest and looked on the assembly as the area where spoils would be divided. Briefly, the high commissioner toyed with the appointment of a king on the lines of Iraq, then he prorogued the assembly. The next attempt at elections, in 1931, led to force and fraud. According to Khoury, in Damascus, "paid agents protected by local security forces appeared, stuffed the boxes with papers carrying the names of electors chosen by the government, and quickly disappeared. When nationalist leaders later appeared and tried to inspect the boxes they were told that this had already been done. They immediately called for a total boycott." In the fighting, five were killed and fifty injured. Similar scenes broke out in the other main cities. This parliament was suspended in 1934. After 1936, a Franco-Syrian Treaty to grant qualified self-rule was negotiated and signed but could then not be ratified in the French Assembly. To some extent this was a failure of the Popular Front government of the day, whose policies in general—and concerning foreign affairs in particular—were anathema to the French right. But more importantly, the National Bloc had succeeded in terrorizing and eliminating the many notables and tribal leaders who were willing to work with France, thus annulling and rendering ineffective whatever constitutional forms could be agreed. The power drive of the National Bloc prevented even the more primitive levels of compromise and power sharing. It was only the plain truth to argue in the French Assembly that those Syrians who were expecting to operate self-rule were also eager to tyrannize everybody else the moment they could, and especially any friends of France. The turbulence indicated that the French impact hardly disturbed traditional Syrian politics. In its first 184 years as an Ottoman city, Damascus had witnessed no fewer than 133 governors, of whom no more than 33 held office as long as two years. On the whole, and Syrian nationalist propagandists of the "Great Revolt" notwithstanding, French administrators romanticized Muslim customs and tribal diversity: "the Orient" was a cherished figment of imagination. *"Partant pour la Syrie,"* the most popular of French military tunes, evoked high adventure, as though Syria were an open-air playground for swashbucklers and *zouaves,* like their counterparts the *spahis* and *tirailleurs* of French North Africa. Orientalists of the caliber of Louis Massignon and Henri Laoust tended to defer to Muslim values and susceptibilities.

The British were no more disposed than the French to force upon the Arabs institutions and values that had to be honored and obeyed at all costs and, if need be, implemented by force. In accordance with the national temperament, they had a habit of revering custom and rejoicing in anomaly. In Arabia, men of this cast of mind found the most unlimited scope, and the wife of one administrator from the Gulf could truthfully generalize in speaking of "their deference to other religions, their courage, their determination to defend, against all-comers, the tribe or people for whom they were mainly responsible." In *Arabia and the Isles,* another administrator of legendary reputation, Harold Ingrams, describes with pride how he had negotiated peace and an end to feuding among more than a thousand tribes but left their customs otherwise intact. Wilfred Thesiger was a district commissioner in Sudan in the mid–1930s, and he captured the approach of his colleagues. "In the evenings, as we sat round a large fire over drinks, the others talked shop, ranging over the whole Province and every aspect of its administration. Listening, I realized how completely they had identified themselves with the people in their charge, and I sensed their misgivings about the changes that had inevitably to occur."

No less than the French, these Englishmen could visualize the Arabs and their world as a heightened experience of excitement, a flight from their own humdrum, mechanistic, and legalistic soci-

ety, an adoption of fancy dress and freedom. Even so prosaic a
soldier as Kitchener was to be found in unrecognizable disguise as
an Arab, priding himself in 1882 on going ashore in Alexandria
from the naval force as "a greasy Levantine." Disguised as Mirza
Abdullah of Bushire, a pilgrim to Mecca, Burton played a practical
joke by familiarly addressing a fellow officer who had failed to
recognize him. St. John Philby, T. E. Lawrence, Gertrude Bell in
Iraq (colloquially "Umm al-Muminin" or mother of the faithful),
all gloried in adopted Arab names and role-playing—Lawrence
had difficulty dispensing with Arab clothes even in Europe. That
unusual soldier-saint, Charles de Foucauld, destined to be murdered during the First World War in his hermitage in the southern
Sahara, had disguised himself alternately as an Arab or a Jewish
merchant in his earlier travels. Numerous memoirs, from ambassadors like Layard and the Persian enthusiast E. G. Browne down to
insignificant Christian missionaries, carry as a frontispiece a photograph of the author in native Arab or Persian costume. English
orientalists were at greater pains than the Arabs themselves to
recover the literacy and architectural heritage of Islam. Romantici-
zation of the Arabs bloomed in the most unlikely characters. Joseph McPherson, a hard-boiled head of the Secret Police in Cairo,
meeting the Grand Qadi, or supreme Muslim judge, in 1902 could
find him "one of the most remarkable and admirable characters
that I have met in my life" and "one of the most learned men in
the world, notwithstanding which, he understands neither the language nor the customs of the Europeans." McPherson occupied
his leisure studying popular religion, or Sufism. The same man
could write that Egyptians often asked him, "How is it that you, our
Friend, almost an Egyptian in many ways, would hesitate to give
us complete independence?" His reply was, "I love you too well
to give you what would harm you."

The average Egyptian was particularly singled out for admiration. As consul-general, Kitchener passed a land reform in favor
of the fellah, and the peasants' plight seems genuinely to have
moved him. Russell Pasha, a chief of police in Cairo between the
wars, considered the fellah "a peaceful, law-abiding and hard-
working fellow with an excellent sense of humour." Murder was a
private affair, in pursuit of the blood feud, "a thing that he cannot
escape; he did not cause it, but his code of honour compels him
to carry it on, and he is proud to do so." An Englishman with the
pseudonym of "Tawwaf," writing an angry pamphlet about the

1919 disturbances in which scores of Englishmen had been savagely killed, nonetheless generalized, "The Egyptian fellah is one of the most diligent and skilled day labourers in the world." Thousands of extrovert soldiers to whom Egypt was nothing but a temporary posting would probably have agreed with all the nuances in this passage from a letter by George Lambert, a genial Australian and successful artist who saw service in Egypt in the First World War:

> The Gypo as we call him, was properly managed, clothed, fed and very well paid and in a somewhat perfunctory manner he came in for an occasional clout of the ganger's whip. We of the white North, already too energetic, mentally whip and spur ourselves into greater efforts; the Gypo, with his natural indolence, prefers his whipping to be done by properly appointed officials. With the stimulus of weird singing, perfect unity of action, a physique equalling that of our finest athletes, and the aid of the whip, he performed almost miracles of labour.

During that war, for purposes of rallying support, the Allies made a number of statements about their peacetime intentions. One instance was the Anglo-French Declaration of 1918 to the effect that the sole role of the Allies in the liberated territories of the Ottoman Empire was "to ensure impartial and equal justice, to facilitate economic developments by evoking and encouraging indigenous initiative, to foster the spread of education, and to put an end to the divisions too long exploited by Turkish policy." Western ideals of the kind pointed to self-determination, which could only be incompatible with colonialism. In the immediate aftermath of the war, challengers naturally threw back at the Allies their own words, not only in the proposed Mandates, but also in Egypt and Tunisia. Mobilizing a retinue in the Arab careerist manner, a challenger was able to present himself as a patriot of the kind understood in the West, and was no less easily understood and approved when he simply labeled himself and his followers as a nationalist party.

The most successful challenger was Saad Zaghlul Pasha in Egypt. The son of a village notable, or *omdah*, Zaghlul was born either in 1857 or 1860 and educated at Al-Azhar and then in Paris. A pupil of Abdu, he had studied law and in 1892 became a judge in the Court of Appeals. Marrying the daughter of Mustapha Fahmi, a prime minister well-known for pro-British sympathies, Zaghlul also accepted British sponsorship, and it did him no harm. Mustafa Kamil, he declared, was "mad." Cromer praised him as a coming man. From 1906 to 1910, he was minister of education, then minister of justice. With his brother, Fathi, an intellectual and translator of several standard works, Zaghlul was one among the organizers of the so-called People's Party, with the hidden aim of exploiting constitutionalism in order to curb the power of the Khedive, and then perhaps to replace him altogether. Whatever his pronounced opinion about Mustafa Kamil, Zaghlul had set up exactly the same rival-ally challenge between himself and the ruler, with the British as arbitrator to both. King Fuad said of Zaghlul, "You can win him with a smile or a rose," and Zaghlul said of Fuad, *"J'ai encore besoin de la grâce de Sa Majesté"* (I still need His Majesty's favor). Competing with Adli Yegen and Rushdi Pasha and others for the royal favors, Zaghlul was quick to grasp that if the British really meant what they said in their grandiloquent declarations, then he had every chance of making a clean sweep of rivals, including the king and perhaps even the British themselves. Concerting the policy first with the king, he put the British to the test. He asked to be allowed to lead a delegation to London or to Paris· to discuss Egyptian independence.

This delegation was entirely self-constituted. The Egyptian people had as yet no notion of what was being proposed in their name. But Zaghlul had one unanswerable argument, that the war had already resulted in the independence of the most backward areas of the Arab world. Abandoned by the retreating Ottomans, Yemen, a mountainous region as sealed as Tibet and ruled by its Imam Yahya, was the very first Arab country to become independent. The next was the kingdom still without frontiers that Abdul Aziz ibn Saud was in the process of conquering in the Arabian Desert with his tribal warriors. A century previously, Muhammad Ali's Egypt had overrun this Saudi territory. If Imam Yahya and Abdul Aziz were now their own masters, then the continued British occupation of historic Egypt was truly humiliating, and every Egyptian could be made to feel it. Zaghlul also knew that resentment had gathered during the war at the forced conscription into the labor corps of fellahin and their animals. Egyptian and Islamic sentiment could be fired. Laurence Grafftey-Smith, at the time a young consular official, records how in 1918 he had overheard a peasant at Damanhour ask another which was better, the English or the Germans, to catch the answer, "They are both sons of dogs."

Nothing speaks louder about British assumptions than the fact that the authorities were utterly aghast at Zaghlul's demand, as though ambushed. Refusing permission to form a delegation, they were unprepared for the fanatical violence Zaghlul was able to unleash. Enlarging his friends and followers into the Wafd, or Delegation Party, he appealed for attacks on the British. In March 1919, the rivalry-alliance of King Fuad and Zaghlul came to a head, when the now frightened monarch complained to the British authorities that he was being insulted by Zaghlul. The British deported Zaghlul, which made him a household name, a focus of identity. The Judicial Adviser, Sir William Brunyate, made one of those remarks (it may be apocryphal) which immortalize fools, that "an Egyptian revolution can be drowned in a gob of spittle," clinching what could only be the shame-honor response.

During the course of 1919, revolution spread from the cities into the countryside. By the end of April, 60 Westerners had been killed, 29 of them British soldiers, and over 800 Egyptians. In the end, the dead numbered perhaps twice as many. As usual, power challenging was self-multiplying, without limits until somebody was prepared to stop it by force. An Egyptian writer, Fikri Abaza, witnessed peasants attacking the house of Muhammad Mahmud, a large landowner in Upper Egypt and an associate of Zaghlul's. When he tried to stop them, the peasants replied, "Has Mahmud Pasha Sulayman [this landowner's father] distributed bread to the hungry? We want bread!"

As the Wafd, Zaghlul and other associates became the first secret society to transform itself into a mass movement. At its core was a so-called Vengeance Society, a terrorist squad which planned to murder King Fuad and all former ministers and to seize power. Evidence implicated Zaghlul in this terrorism, but it was disregarded until the murder in 1924 of Sir Lee Stack, governor general of the Sudan and commander of the Egyptian Army. British indecisiveness at the unfolding of violence increased a hysterical sense that the future was beyond prediction. Russell Pasha, the police chief of Cairo, writing in April 1919, told his father of a mob,

composed of several thousands of the roughest elements of Cairo, all armed with something, some with knives and some with spearheads, chisels, adzes, tree-trunks, tree-props and so on, and those who had no weapons carried great jagged chunks of cast-iron gratings that they had torn up from around the trees; the only thing I did not see was fire-arms. The whole mob was shrieking and yelling and waving their weapons in the air. Many of the crowd, with their heads back and their mouths wide open, produced no sound from their throats except a sort of dry whistle. Others had their beards and chests white with dried saliva and I saw several fall spinning to the ground in fits of mad hysteria.

To restore order, General Allenby, recently the conqueror of the Ottoman armies in Palestine and Syria, was appointed special high commissioner. From a man of his reputation, the Egyptians anticipated the usual application of force with whatever brutality was required to arbitrate the issue. Allenby chose the alternative of releasing Zaghlul from exile and further proposing a constitution and a qualified independence by way of settlement. Egyptians could only conclude that Zaghlul had proved to have superior power to the British. The mob had mastery over soldiers. Zaghlul had only to remain as intransigent as possible, calling for further demonstrations, refusing compromises with other politicians like Adli Yegen and Rushdi Pasha. The 1923 constitution set him on the course well trodden by Midhat Pasha and Arabi and Mustafa Kamil of challenging the power holders by apparently modern means. Whether he would have triumphed is not clear, because after the murder of Sir Lee Stack and the arrest of Wafdists that followed, Zaghlul had to resign, and he died in 1927. The historian John Marlowe, a defender of Egyptians in the face of colonial policy, nonetheless concluded that the idea of service to his country was genuinely incomprehensible to Zaghlul. "It was not his business to advance his country's interests; it was his country's business to advance his interests."

Careerist violence had paid. In granting the new constitution, the British were not laying the foundations for the democracy in which they themselves might believe, but implementing the dialectic of power challenging. The sultan, now promoted king, had the right to dismiss cabinets and dissolve parliaments, the right to appoint the Sheikh of Al-Azhar and army officers and two-fifth of the Senate. Enough rights, in short, to frustrate genuine representation but not enough to make of him an undisputed autocrat. Nursing their respective grievances and ambitions, the king and the politicians were locked into a power challenge that could only be resolved one day by violence. The British had revealed themselves to be politically and temperamentally unable to deploy the superior force which alone could have blocked this outcome.

Here is Grafftey-Smith on the reality of the botch.

The 1923 constitution had provided for a two-degree system of election as being that most suitable to an electorate roughly 90 per cent illiterate: groups of 30 electors on adult suffrage each elected one delegate possessed of certain qualifications, and these in turn elected deputies to parliament. Zaghlul, to ensure the mob-vote for the Wafd, instituted the direct system of election in 1924. The elections under the new/old indirect system were held in May 1931, and were boycotted not only by the Wafd but also by the Liberals under Muhammed Mahmoud Pasha. The King's party of Ittehadists, and Sidqi Pasha with a new group he had formed called the Shaab (or People's) Party of Reform, had to prove that they, with such odds and ends of help as they could pick up, could produce a respectable majority of voters at the polls to refute the loud opposition claim that they represented nobody but themselves.

It was an unedifying spectacle. Every device of administrative authority was used to produce voters at the polls. Groups of unhappy men were led from polling booth to polling booth to make their mark. Sir Robert Greg [adviser at the Ministry of Foreign Affairs] recognized his gardener in one such gang and learned that he had voted 10 or 11 times already that morning, always under a different name. Anyone identified as spoiling a ballot paper, or voting for the Wafd, was patted amicably on the back by the policeman in the booth, and the chalk-marks thus left on his *gallabiya* earned him a severe beating-up by the policeman outside. There were over 50 deaths.

Electoral Laws were passed in 1925, 1930, and 1935, providing for supervisory commissions, but to no avail. Officials, or in the villages the *omdeh,* acted as a channel between the party leader and the voters to fix the result. From above, the officials and *omdehs* received money-favors, and from below they extracted votes. "I let people vote as they like," Tewfik el-Hakim quotes one official as saying, "right up to the end of the election. Then I simply take the ballot box and throw it into the river and calmly replace it with a box which we prepare ourselves." Democratic and electoral fraudulence became a favorite topic of Egyptian writers. The famous novelist Neguib Mahfouz wrote in *Midaq Alley,* one of his Cairo novels, that an election was so external a phenomenon that it "might as well be a storm or an accident." His imaginary candidate had accepted bribes in elections for supporting the Wafd, after which he became a supporter of whoever "paid most" and "he was content to be corrupt, absent-minded and beset by his own passions." Saying that "the days of empty talk and bribery are over," this candidate promises prosperity and hands out bribes himself. When it suited the king, as it did in 1931, he simply abrogated the constitution, calling out the police to shut the House of Assembly by placing a chain across the entrance, drafting another constitution, and ruling through his ministers. When it suited the British, as it did in 1942, they imposed on the king ministers friendly to them, by the no less simple expedient of surrounding the palace with soldiers. In the eyes of Egyptians, the British after 1923 appeared insincere and irresponsible. It could only be a matter of time before the British would evacuate on the terms of some power challenger taking Zaghlul's place, and blamed as justly for the political arrangements they had introduced as for those they had failed to introduce.

Egypt at least had the advantage of being a more or less homogeneous society with the Christian Copts as a minority of perhaps 10 percent or more. Iraq, the largest of the postwar Mandates, had a population half Shia, perhaps 20 percent Arab Sunni, the others Sunni Kurds, as well as other sects and Christians of several denominations, and Jews. Whole areas were inhabited by tribes, some of them Sunni, others Shia, long since accustomed to doing as they pleased, on the safe assumption that central government could only be an oppressor. Policy toward Ottoman Iraq had hitherto been a responsibility of the India Office; now it was about to fall to Whitehall and the colonial secretary. In 1918 Sir Arnold Wilson was appointed as a deputy civil commissioner, complete with secretaries for finance, law, agriculture and irrigation. Sir Ronald Storrs, supposedly one of the specialists in handling Arab affairs, exemplified the quite unjustified belief in bureaucratic rule-of-thumb when he wrote, "I seriously recommend that now, before anything is altered, an accurate illustrated description of the place be published in English, French, and Arabic so that they may not forget the pit from whence they were digged; so that future tar-bushed elastic-sided-booted patriots may not claim for themselves before all the world the exclusive credit for cleanliness, health, water, electricity and a hundredfold budget."

The Iraqi patchwork of tribes and religions, like the Lebanese, might conceivably have been brought into coherence under some contrivance similar to the 1861 Organic Statute in Lebanon, in order to allow representation, however primitive in form, in this equally baffling pluralist plight. No such compromise was considered. Whitehall's concern was to pare expenditure, not to devise ideal institutions. Astonishingly true to their traditions, the British discovered an Iraqi king in the person of Feisal, actually exiled now from his native Mecca as well as from Damascus. "The Iraqi wanted a Monarchy," Mrs. Steuart Erskine could state without apology in an authorized biography of Feisal in 1933.

Amid silence and incomprehension and opposition, Feisal arrived in Baghdad. There he was equipped by the high commissioner with a council of state consisting of a president and ministers. How to legitimize his position was awkward indeed. Feisal was a Sunni, and the Shia ulema resented what they perceived as their forcible subjection by the British to the Sunni minority. They formed a secret society with the purpose of rebellion. Seeing the trouble ahead, Sir Arnold Wilson asked Sunni leaders how they would cope with the more numerous Kurds and Shias, to be told that "both groups were ignorant peasants who could easily be kept in their place." A one-man one-vote plebiscite was out of the question in an area where subjects were not asked for their opinion. Notables were consulted and petitions circulated, until in a later referendum it was possible to assert that Feisal had 96 percent support from the population. Gertrude Bell, an adviser who had arrived there from Cairo in 1916, thought that "It doesn't happen often that people are told that their future as a State is in their hands and asked what they would like." Without irony, she expressed enthusiasm about "public opinion," as though certain that such a thing was the same in this Iraq of tribes and religions as in Britain. Those who labored to start the state, she conceded, had "an ungrateful task."

Shia and tribesmen together saw no reason to submit to a stranger who had yet to impose his authority. Rebellion was open and general in the summer of 1920. By the time order was restored, the British had spent the huge sum of £40 million, merely to prove what ought to have been the obvious fact that they were the arbiters of power. Sir Percy Cox succeeded Sir Arnold Wilson as high commissioner. The Shia leaders continued to forbid their congregation to participate in political processes, and Cox and Feisal, a bizarre Anglo-Sunni combination, then deported them to Iran. In three hectic years, the British could not hope to reconcile the centuries of hatred between Sunni and Shia, but this handling of the Iraqi Mandate could only harden and prolong the injustices and violence of tribal and religious separatism. Hardly had the Mandate been agreed and ratified in Iraq than the British began to argue that it might be less trouble to abandon it. Concession in Egypt led naturally to concession in Iraq. The Anglo-Iraq Treaty was signed in 1930, and an independent Iraq then joined the League of Nations.

King Feisal represented nobody but himself. As power holder he behaved in the traditional way, enriching himself, for instance expropriating land and an orchard of 40,000 trees which he coveted outside Baghdad; King Fuad of Egypt, likewise, had inherited 800 feddans of land but died leaving 39,000. Feisal appointed whom he pleased to public positions in a Sunni money-favor nexus. In Iraq between 1920 and 1958 there were twenty-one cabinets but only fifty-seven officeholders, and of these Nuri Said Pasha held office fourteen times. Born in 1888, the son of an official, Nuri attended school in Baghdad, and on graduation he went to Military College in Istanbul at the age of fourteen. There he had joined the Al-Ahd conspiracy. Defecting in the war to the Hashemites, he had selected Feisal as his particular sponsor. Feisal's own sponsors were the British, and he cultivated them in the most assiduous careerist style, without interest in British institutions.

"The true ruling elite of Iraq," the historian Reeva Simon has written, "could be said to have consisted of about 14 men who changed cabinet posts frequently and were constantly scheming to get back into power if they happened to be out. The king controlled the game of musical chairs." The old Ottoman governor and his notables, it might be said, were ruling as before, only in British-designed uniforms. Yet the British laid the basis for present and future Iraqi power holders through the training of a mechanized army and an air force and the formation in 1925 of an Army Staff College. Meanwhile a flow of British State Papers and parliamentary reports conjured up illusions about Iraq by referring to "sound public finance, and enlightened administration."

Dying in 1933, Feisal in his decade of rule had not revealed whether he had the ruthlessness to deal with the challengers biding their time. It was an ominous portent that toward the end of his life he did not prevent the massacre of a pitiful minority, the Assyrians, Christian refugees from the Ottoman Empire who had afterward enlisted in British service. The chance to initiate some sort of pluralist structure in Iraq had been dissipated before the British had understood that this was truly their responsibility.

Unlike the other Mandates, Palestine was internationally emotive. Jerusalem was a center of worship for Muslims, Christians, and Jews. Capturing the city in 1918, General Allenby had thought it right to dismount and enter on foot. Military administrations gave way to a high commissioner, Herbert Samuel, appointed because he was a Jew sympathetic to Zionist ideals and had played a part in the promulgation of the Balfour Declaration. A Liberal politician prominent in public affairs, Samuel was nothing if not a constitutionalist.

An illustrative episode marked the opening of the Mandate in Palestine. Abdullah, another of the sons of Sherif Hussein, marched out of Mecca at the head of some hundreds of tribal warriors, ostensibly on his way to assist his brother Feisal in recapturing Damascus. Halting at the station of Ma'an on the Hejaz railway, Abdullah half expected to be arrested by the British officer who greeted him. Styling himself Emir, he moved in March 1921 northward to Amman, then a small town. Hitherto there had been no state structure of any kind in the desert between Arabia and Palestine, merely Bedouin tribes such as the Rualla, the Shammar, the Howeitat and Aneizeh, in a pattern of annual migration interrupted by feuding. In a skillful power challenge in undemarcated and even unexplored territory, Abdullah reached an agreement with the British colonial secretary, then Winston Churchill, that he could indeed establish his rule in Amman and even receive a subsidy of £5,000 a month for doing so. Churchill's intention, genuinely imperialist, was to set a limit both to the French in Syria and to the Zionists in Palestine. What might have been the eastern portion of Palestine was instead drawn on the map as the emirate of Transjordan, and Jews were promptly forbidden from settling there.

By the standards of the region, the Palestine population was fairly homogeneous. On the eve of the First World War, 85,000 Jews lived there, two-thirds of them in Jerusalem. The 1922 census showed 589,000 Muslims, with a further 71,500 Christian Arabs and 7,500 Druze. In 1919, 1,806 Jews immigrated, followed by an average of 8000 for the next four years, rising in 1926 to 13,853.

Increasingly, Samuel and then all succeeding high commissioners found themselves in the position of arbitrator between Zionist pressure to immigrate and build the national home, and Arab resistance to it. Zionism was a voluntary association. A minority of Jews was Zionist; the rest were indifferent or outright hostile either on grounds that Zionism did not accord with the tenets of Judaism, or that it contained a political logic likely to hinder assimilation between Jews and Gentiles. From the outset Theodor Herzl, founding father of the Zionist movement, had created the appropriate organizations of a bank and a central fund and a world congress whose delegates met at regular intervals in parliamentary fashion. This more than anything else translated what initially seemed a romantic ideal of a Jewish state into a reality in which those who wished to do so could participate.

This institutional character set Zionism apart from Palestinian Arab society, at the time completely family-tribal in structure. Arab grievances against Zionism could be expressed only through violence, and in 1919 and 1920 Arab demonstrations had led to loss of life. Samuel tried to institutionalize the Arabs, setting up the Supreme Muslim Council in 1922 as well as supporting a proposal for a constitution with a legislative council, in which Arabs would be fairly and proportionately better represented than Jews. In the face of a flat rejection, Samuel next convened a meeting of twenty-six Arab notables, whom he hoped would form themselves into an "Arab Agency" on the lines of the Jewish Agency. This attempted institutionalization also failed.

The shadow of a single Arab personality, Haj Amin el Husseini, fell over these aborted searches for a pluralist future. The Husseini family had been prominent in Jerusalem since the seventeenth century, and traditionally had held the post of Mufti, the principal scholar pronouncing opinions on points of Holy Law. Records of birthdates were not reliably kept by the Ottomans, and it is uncertain whether Haj Amin was born in 1893 or 1896. In 1912 he studied at Al-Azhar in Cairo but does not seem to have had a truly religious bent. At the start of the First World War, he was at the Military Academy in Istanbul and served as an officer in the Ottoman army until 1917, when he returned to Jerusalem. There he incited the earliest anti-Zionist riots, fled abroad to escape arrest, and was sentenced in absentia to ten years imprisonment.

In 1922 the post of Mufti fell vacant. Long-established procedure existed for the selection of a new Mufti, and there were three more scholarly candidates than the still youthful and inexperienced Haj Amin. Samuel connived in setting aside the due procedures, pardoning Haj Amin from his sentence, and promoting him Mufti, and then president of the new Supreme Muslim Council as well. Far from creating any institution in which Palestinian Arabs might participate, and through which their legitimate demands might be articulated, Samuel had sponsored a single individual. In doing so, he had been badly advised and even browbeaten by his senior officials. Otherwise no good reason can be found for Samuel's promotion of Haj Amin; no doubt Eurocentric ignorance led him to suppose that a Mufti must be akin to an archbishop or a rabbi, in any case a man of the cloth. Dressed in the robes and turban of an Islamic divine, Haj Amin impressed many as a grave, capable, and deliberate man. In the 1920s the experienced foreign correspondent Vincent Sheean was by no means alone in thinking that Haj Amin had "great gifts." During his career as Mufti, Haj Amin carefully concentrated power in his hands. Power sharing was a concept outside his intellectual and moral framework. Sir Arthur Wauchope, a succeeding high commissioner, in 1934 established municipal councils in Palestine and hoped to advance to the next step in self-government, a legislative council. Haj Amin once more would not have it; and the intercommunal relationship was already so tense that the Zionists also rejected the last of such proposals to have any chance of bridging the Arab-Jewish divide.

Between 1920 and the mid–1930s, then, attempts to introduce representative institutions had been withdrawn almost as soon as they were proposed in the Arab countries for which Britain and France were responsible, or else denatured and voided of participatory significance upon contact with leaders concerned only to promote themselves and their own kind. Except in Lebanon, the worst of both worlds had been achieved: democracy appeared a sham, and the traditional system had acquired new methods of control that could be put to vicious and degrading use in the old context. Allenby, Samuel, Sir Percy Cox, had propelled forward power challengers whom they had been in a position to break for the sake of the greater good of the community. Like them, the other high commissioners and French residents and governors-general were not wicked men, but neither were they philosopher-kings. Respecting custom, supposing themselves in their conscience to be intruders, lacking the courage of their convictions, for all their high-minded intentions, these men and their superiors in London and Paris failed to construct political devices for pluralism, thus driving the Arab each into the refuge of his own tribe and religion, even encouraging such custom and tradition to survive and flourish with a vengeance. As responsible administrators, and in common humanity, no Englishman or Frenchman could possibly have argued that if persuasion and example were inadequate, then force would have to introduce pluralist accommodations in some form. Perhaps government for Muslims and Western democracy were two beautiful but incompatible ideals: nobody resolved that conundrum.

Referring to the politics of this period when the colonial power holders unknowingly sealed the fate not only of themselves but also of those for whom they were responsible, Walid Khalidi writes of the manifold Arab challengers that "The countless parties with pompous titles into which they divided were entirely meaningless except in terms of clashes of will and personality." In Syria there arose the National Bloc and the Syrian National Party, inflated names behind which lay the personal ambitions of Dr. Shahbandar and Adib Shishakli. In Iraq, the Istiqlal and the Liberals, the National Democratic Party, the National Union, the People's Party were so many secret societies within which the few dozen leaders conspired. In Egypt, the Ittihad Party was the king's, the People's Party was Ismail Sidqi's, the Wafd was Zaghlul's, and after his death disputed between Nahas Pasha and Ahmed Mahir and Nuqrashi Pasha. In Tunisia, the Destour Party was Bourguiba's; in Morocco and Algeria, each would-be nationalist leader tried to develop his own Independence Party.

Disputes within each party, and between parties, were in the nature of feuds and could only be settled accordingly by violence. Terrorism here is akin to a no-confidence vote. Murder is the instrument for calibrating the balance of forces. When Dr. Shahbandar was murdered in Damascus, the other National Bloc leaders were implicated, escaping to Baghdad. Shishakli took power in one coup, was overthrown in another and murdered in exile in Brazil. In Iraq, Nuri Said Pasha twice fled for his life, returning to pass death sentences on his political opponents, before being murdered himself. In Egypt, the king, the Wafd and the Muslim Brothers interacted in a pattern of mutual killings which grew in the 1940s into a terrorist crescendo, so that every public personality went in fear of his life. It is a rough-and-ready yardstick of reality that among the fifty-seven contributors to an anthology edited by the Egyptian Anwar Abdel Malek to illustrate Arab political thought in this century, two were executed, six were assassinated, twelve suffered imprisonment, and fifteen were exiled; a tally reached, moreover, by allowing each contributor only one of these fates, though some suffered a combination of them.

Thoughtful Arabs certainly perceived that the clash of value systems entailed by colonialism had implications for the future ordering of society. It was impossible for Egyptians to achieve constitutional government without European help and consent, according to Faris Nimr, a Syrian Christian who had emigrated to Cairo in Cromer's day and started a paper there. In his opinion, the burgeoning national movement was "a sort of trade in which self-seeking persons indulge. All they want is personal gain. If they were given the authority they are craving for, their voices would not have been heard. Given authority, they are capable of bigger injustices than the ones they are denouncing. The fellah would suffer far more under them." Such prophetic truth was answered not intellectually, but by denouncing its author as a Christian, therefore having interests coinciding with the British, therefore conspiring, and a spy. Muhammad Abdu, trying to reform Islamic practices down to such matters as permitting the opening of a post office savings account without infringing the religious prohibition on usury, could be dismissed as a tool of the British because he was indeed on dining terms with Cromer. Rival-allies of the British, including men ostensibly so far apart as Zaghlul (in his first stage, before 1914) and Nuri Said Pasha, had to take extreme pains to extract advantage from their sponsors while maintaining in public that they were not doing so. Muslim resistance to any reform that appeared a concession to Western values was revealed strikingly in 1925, when Ali Abd el-Raziq, a member of the ulema who had also been to Oxford University, published a book to argue that Islam as such did not prevent the faithful from choosing the form of state most suitable to them. He was dismissed from his post as a religious judge for heresy.

The number of westernized Muslims retaining confidence in themselves and their social practices was too restricted to be able to introduce to a larger audience the perceptions of which they were themselves eagerly persuaded. Writing at the turn of the century, the Egyptian Qasim Amin was among the very first Muslims to be able to pronounce so un-Islamic, indeed blasphemous, an opinion as "In a truly free country no one should be afraid to renounce his fatherland, to repudiate belief in God and his prophets, or to impugn the laws and customs of his people." The scandal was proportionate. Qasim Amin said openly that Egypt had never enjoyed so much freedom and justice as under the British. "The West is our teacher; to love it is to love science, progress, material and moral advancement," wrote the Turkish Abdulla Cevdet in 1913, blaming the plight of Muslims on inertia, ignorance, and fanaticism. "To be an industrious and thankful disciple of the West—that is our lot!" Against the grain of Muslim prejudice, he added, "To believe that the entire world of Christianity is working against us is a symptom of persecution mania." A typical westernizer, the Iranian Abdullah Razi declared in 1925 that "the people of the East had been long enough in the debt of the West, and it was time for repayment." Western legal codes should be adopted, and Muslims should approach the house of the heathen "and implore them to save us from our ignorance and misery." "What good would it do Muslims of the twentieth century," asked Abdel Djelil Zaouche, a Paris-educated Tunisian, "to return to the civilization of their ancestors if they had to remain strangers to scientific progress?"

Ahmad Lutfi al-Sayyid believed that Egypt had much to learn from Europe and European institutions, and he argued uncompromisingly that only constitutional arrangements guaranteed freedom. "The dominant civilization of today is European, and the only possible foundation for our progress in Egypt is the transmission of the principles of that civilization." Born in 1872, Lutfi al-Sayyid was the son of a landowner, and he founded a paper to promote his views. In his youth he had been an associate of Mustafa Kamil but came to see that the nationalist or anti-British cause was blind to the need for creating institutions, and was therefore flawed and sterile. During the 1920s he devoted himself to the essential task of writing about the kind of state, and what rights and duties, Egyptians might aspire to.

One of his disciples was Taha Husayn, a remarkable, not to say unique, man. Born in 1889, he came from a large family in a village and at the age of two went blind from ophthalmia. Educated at Al-Azhar, in 1915 he won a scholarship to a university in France and became the first Egyptian to receive a doctorate from the Sorbonne. Accompanied by a French wife, he returned to Cairo as professor of Arabic literature. In novels and memoirs and essays, he depicted the outworn traditions from which he thought that Egyptians suffered and the hope that lay in modern education. Retaining the confidence to analyze his own society, he could be objective about it and also explain what it had been like to acquire European manners and even European dress. His views often proved heretical, and he was condemned by the Al-Azhar ulema and forced to resign from public posts.

In 1938, he published *The Future of Culture in Egypt,* and one eminent orientalist has called this book nothing less than "a programme of national instruction." Taha Husayn considered that Egypt, a historic entity, was also linked by a common culture to the other peoples of the Mediterranean, Christian Europeans included, and that was for the good of all. The future lay with Europe, its ideals and its institutions, and Egypt would participate in it by right of heritage, even though as yet European ideals had touched only a few intellectuals and not the sentiments of the masses. In due course, this would occur. "Day by day," he said, "we are drawing closer to Europe and becoming an integral part of her."

Our real national duty, once we have obtained our independence and established democracy in Egypt, is to spend all we have and more, in the way of strength and effort, of time and money, to make Egyptians feel, individually and collectively, that God has created them for glory not ignominy, strength and not weakness, sovereignty and not submission, renown and not obscurity, and to remove from their hearts the hideous and criminal illusion that they are created from other clay than Europeans, formed in some other way, and endowed with an intelligence other than theirs.

Free spirits themselves, Lutfi al-Sayyid and Taha Husayn pinpointed that the impelling motivation of Egyptian behavior toward Europeans was the desire to lose the sense of shame and to recover honor. "Deep in their souls was a feeling of inferiority," is the way one authority has summarized how Lutfi al-Sayyid viewed some of his countrymen. Here was the invisible rock upon which progressive intentions, reason and education, persuasion and example, and in the end colonialism itself, were shipwrecked.

Everywhere and at all times, the solid achievements of colonial-

ism, its good order, its material improvements and scientific benefits, were vitiated by the sense of shame provoked in the supposed
beneficiaries. The shame-response long antedated the colonial
powers, as it was to outlast them as well. Called into account by
a superior, Egyptian fellahin had the habitual reply, "We are only
animals, sir." Removal of the element of protective exaggeration
still leaves the residue of self-abasement. "The cup of humiliation," writes Tewfik el-Hakim, "passes from the man at the top, to
his subordinates, in this country, before coming to rest with the
unfortunate populace, which swallows it down in a single
draught." Not estimating themselves according to this ranking,
French and British administrators did not perceive, or else neglected, the shame-response in the Arabs. Whether the Europeans
were assertive and commanding or tactful and accommodating
mattered less than the fact that they were giving the orders and
setting the standards, therefore undermining Arab self-respect. If
placed in a position of having to deprecate himself as an animal
before a European, anyone and everyone was certain to respond
by affirming his identity, first as a shame-sufferer, then as a Muslim
or nationalist.

Someone sensitive to shame-honor was Herzl, with his instinctive and personal reactions to anti-Semitism. In 1903, in Egypt on
a tour to inspect whether El-Arish in the Sinai Desert might be an
alternative to Palestine for a Jewish national home, he noticed how
education was producing a type of modern young Egyptians and
sensed how this would have a backlash.

They are the coming rulers of the country, and it is a wonder the
British don't see this, but think they are always going to deal with *fellahin*.
The role of the English here is superb: they are cleaning up the East,
letting air and light into its dens of filth, breaking old tyrannies and
destroying old abuses. But together with freedom and progress they are
teaching the *fellahin* the art of revolt. I believe that the English colonial
methods must either destroy England's colonial empire—or lay the foundations for England's world dominion. One of the most fascinating alternatives of our age! We would like to see, 50 years hence, how it all turned
out.

Colonialist thoughtlessness in daily matters revealed an inner
supercilious attitude that was shame-arousing to those subjected
to it. In a scandal at the royal palace, King Fuad was shot at by his
brother-in-law. The guard ran to help. When the English corporal

of the guard was called afterward to give his evidence in court, he stated, "I saw the nigger standing at the top of the marble steps and closed with him and overpowered him." Words and actions often seemed incomprehensibly insulting. Another celebrated case concerned the trial of Menshawi Pasha, who managed some of the royal estates. He accused some fellahin of having stolen a bull belonging to the Khedive and had them flogged in order to extract their confession. Well-known for pro-European sentiments, Menshawi was reputed to have saved Europeans from death during the Arabi troubles. Determined to make an example of the fact that there was one law for all, the British authorities sent Menshawi Pasha for trial, and he was sentenced to prison. To the Egyptians, this strict application of the law was itself an injustice. Any other Pasha would have behaved like Menshawi. Appearing despicable for not standing by their friend, the British in such a case dishonored themselves, Menshawi Pasha, and all Egyptians.

British insistence on British values was arrogance in Egyptian eyes. McPherson of the Secret Police allowed that arrogant officials played a part in fostering anti-British feeling, but with more insight he saw this as being on a par with "the laxity with which we allowed unscrupulous natives to abuse their powers." The British could not help narrowly projecting themselves and their values, and McPherson complained about

> our miserable kill-joy policy, which has interfered with innocent picturesque ancient native customs, which has spoilt the merry feast meetings (Moulids) for local saints, suppressed snake charmers, acrobats, wandering conjurors, and such-like Eastern accessories, which lend colour and charm to native life, and had it made an offence to sing at weddings, to weep at funerals, and to dance in native style at theatres, which has closed bars and cafés at absurdly early hours, and generally hustled the easy-going and good-tempered native, until he has become irritated and worried.

One of the most prolific journalists and writers of the time was the Syrian Muhammad Kurd Ali, of Kurdish origin as his name implies. For many years he was director of the Damascus Arabic Academy. In memoirs written at the end of his life, after the Second World War, he recorded that in his youth he had visited Europe four times, but "I never fully understood Western civilisation or really had a taste for it." But since the French had occupied Syria, the best thing in this unfortunate state of affairs had been "to try to make the best of it." "The French," he told a friend, "had accomplished some things in the villages; they had maintained public order, paved a few roads, reduced taxes, abolished forced labour, and reduced the exploitation of the weak by the strong." He felt that he could have confidence in them, as they had treated him "with respect and dignity." Yet even he, whose dignity had been respected, could feel that foreign values were too remote to be attained and in themselves were somehow negative. "A whole army of corrupt influences has invaded our land and received a warm welcome at the hands of the dissolute."

The Egyptian Ihab Hassan caught the psychological conflict that was so damaging. "Like some invisible worm, the colonial experience feeds on all those seeking redress for old wrongs and lacks. Self-hatred, self-doubt, twist in their bowels, and envy curls there with false pride." A poignant compression of years of shame-honor responses to colonialism came from Ferhat Abbas, in Algeria: "Help us to reconquer our dignity or else take back your schools." "We had freed ourselves from everything," wrote Mouloud Feraoun about this interaction, "but not from being despised by the French." Scorn ran through the heart, he went on, like showers over a raincoat. A popular Egyptian song had a couplet:

> I saw the British flag—
> A sight that humiliated me and made me cry.

In time, a handful of the rich, educated in Europe, became marvelously and eloquently adept at living with and shuttling between two value systems; true cosmopolitans and ornaments to their society. The Egyptian Jew, Georges Cattaoui, for example, was completely at ease in the rarified circle of Proust and his friends in Paris. To many ordinary Arabs, recipients of a scholarship to study abroad, Europe proved a mixed blessing, a temptation and a revelation, a standard against which to measure their own background, and often a place where they felt rejected, where some real or imagined slight or faux pas might sear everlasting shame into the soul. Such students returned to take revenge through nationalism. Grafftey-Smith recorded how a crowd had waited to kill some British officers at the railroad station in the riots of 1919. The crowd's leader had just arrived home from Wye Agricultural College in the south of England, where a month previously he had been awarded the prize for the most promising student of the year.

Salama Musa had "a boundless veneration for European literature." France made him "a European by thought and inclination."
During four additional years in London, he learned "the firm idea
of struggle against the English" but at the same time completely
rid himself "of any trace that might have remained of friendly
feelings for the East." Voltaire, Anatole France, Ibsen, Shaw, and
Wells were the models leading him not so much to self-fulfillment
as to dissatisfaction in more than one culture. Moreover, Elizabeth,
an Irish teacher whom he had met in London, hated the "imperialist" English, and on the basis of their common political approach,
"friendship quickly grew into love." Girls like Elizabeth, famous
European writers, anonymous teachers, and even agricultural colleges in rural England proved supremely efficient at alienating the
intelligent young like Salama Musa, who were longing for relief
from a shame they could hardly articulate, and for whatever
achievement might flood them with self-respect.

The same thing happened to Bourguiba in France, where, in
the words of a biographer, "he was attracted in particular to the
liberal atmosphere of the University of Paris, where he enrolled for
study, and to the Quartier Latin, where he lived. He found his
professors, as well as some French writers and politicians with
whom he had come into contact, quite willing to listen to his
account of French activities in Tunisia and was able to arouse their
sympathies for his country's national aspirations." He also married
a Frenchwoman. As president, he was still unable to drop shame-
honor ranking, accusing Tunisia of backwardness "that brings disgrace upon us in the eyes of the world. The only possibility to free
ourselves from the shame is continuous and assiduous work."

An Arab Tells His Story is a sensitive autobiography published in
1946 by a Lebanese Christian, Edward Atiyah. In his youth in
Beirut, he felt nothing less than hero worship for the West. "It was
taken for granted in the talk to which from my earliest days I had
listened that the East was inferior to the West in every way, especially in political matters, and would always be so." To his generation "the road to progress was the highway of Western civilisation." A scholar at Oxford University, he considered himself on an
equal footing with any Englishman—"I need no longer feel
ashamed of myself, inferior." Then he met and fell in love with a
left-wing English girl who persuaded him that his identity was still
in flux. It was all very well to be cultured and westernized, but
inside him "the shame of the East still burned fiercely." As a

teacher in Gordon College in Khartoum, he found himself segregated from the British staff during a visit by the governor-general. Now he could understand why the Egyptians hated the British: "My whole life went into reverse gear. I became myself an Arab nationalist." Quite simply, the British "wounded the feelings of the educated class." People like him felt

> mental and emotional instability, superficial imitativeness, confusion of standards and that combination of inward lack of assurance and outward assertiveness which is born of the inferiority complex. In their heart of hearts they recognised the superiority of the Englishman and his culture, and wished to emulate him. But this recognition itself, coupled with the fact that the Englishman was in a position of authority over them, caused them to resent and deny that superiority.

Émile Sage was a provincial schoolmaster from the south of France, thoroughly smug, and of no interest whatever except insofar as he typifies a facet of the European contact which was most puzzling for Arabs to come to terms with. Arriving for a tour in Egypt in 1899, Émile Sage was proud to boast that "The Egyptians always recall that we were the first to bring them civilisation." Everywhere he went, he hit upon evidence of British perfidy, hastening to inform the Egyptians of it, and they were eager to concur. One day, he rode out into the countryside with two Egyptian friends and a fellow Frenchman. Stopping for refreshments with a sheikh who told him that the village comprised his whole tribe of some 800 people, Sage reflected aloud how happily this world lived except for the presence of the British, whose very name was so hated that it could be mentioned only with "a reaction of disgust." Here was the growth of European sanction for hatred of Europeans.

Similarly, Salama Musa was one day in conversation with a Frenchman who suddenly burst out, "Don't argue, you! You have no right to do so. The English are your masters!" At first Salama Musa was unsure how to react, but then "I felt as if I had drunk poison, and experienced a sharp pain as if my intestines were being torn apart. I got up and went to my room, threw myself down upon the bed, and cried."

Previously, Europeans had been pressed into a reductive definition as Christians; now they were defined even more reductively as exploiters, or "imperialists." The Tunisian, Taher Haddad, was only one of the abler polemicists who accused all Frenchmen of being indistinguishable as exploiters, whether socialists, rightists or settlers.

"It is always the Frenchman who is the enemy," answered Joachim Durel, himself a socialist teacher in the Lycée Carnot in Tunis.

That rapacious and slothful feudalism which you have suffered for centuries and which has fabricated in you the souls of slaves, that mosque in whose shadow you eternalise your intellectual servitude and that "glorious past" whose delusion suffocates and empoisons you—these real causes of your misery and your downfall you do not want to see. It will be necessary, however, to choose between the slow but sure death in the abject poverty of your old traditions and a renewed life in a grand effort of intelligence and of collaboration with men of the West.

No doubt this was well-meant, but the underlying belief system was exclusively European. The supposition that collaboration with men like himself was a matter of choosing was itself superficial, ignorant of the mainsprings of Muslim society, egocentric. And after so many years of protection, what was the nature of their collaboration to be?

If Europeans themselves began to spread doubt and dissension about their own values, why should Arabs continue to believe in them? By 1913, Egypt enjoyed 282 newspapers and periodicals, freedom of speech and the presence of foreign correspondents for the major European organs of opinion. The outcry against the British after the Denshawai incident had been heard everywhere; Bernard Shaw, for one, used the occasion to rail against colonial policy. Freedom of speech had been introduced by the British and French throughout the Arab world, and the Syrian revolts or the Mufti's latest call to arms were headline news. By about 1920, the view that colonialism was nothing but exploitation of the natives had become an orthodoxy in the Fabian Society, among English radicals reaching out to the opinion-makers in Bloomsbury and the universities, to lawyers and lecturers and publicists, Jean Jaurès and the French socialists, those who adhered to the doctrines of Lenin and Trotsky. Arabs studying or traveling in Europe most frequently met these kinds of people and were enlisted into their psychological and social vanities and dissatisfactions. To this whole stratum, revolt appeared an act of absolving grace, no matter what it was directed at. Contemptuously oblivious to the very real difficulties of defining what a modern Muslim society ought to be, they did not treat Arabs as individuals from a vibrant and problematical background but as representatives, "anti-imperialist" spokesmen, raw material for a cause. From them, Arabs learned to apply to their own society concepts and language which were far-fetched and unfounded: twisting the inherited tribal-religious order into the grotesqueries of class struggle; positing non-existent "feudalism" as the reason for "backwardness," itself a Eurocentric yardstick; reducing all Western values and people into the indiscriminate abstraction of "colonialism." Flattered, agitated, the first generation of Arabs with the chance between the World Wars to explore and evaluate the West objectively, instead internalized what they were hearing, uncertain only who was the most shameful, the exploiters or those who let themselves be exploited.

8

The Impact of Nazism

Jews in the Middle East had been settled in communities dating back to early recorded history in Mesopotamia and Egypt, scattered more widely still after the Roman dispersal of Jewish Palestine. One of a number of separate ethnic or religious minorities under Muslim rule from the seventh century A.D., they had a special status, protected by the power holder in return for certain taxes not raised from Muslims, and enjoying freedom of worship subject to limitations. Public office was forbidden. Evidence against a Muslim in a lawsuit was not accepted. Muslim cities were divided into quarters, each of which was originally a family settlement, and it was no hardship—indeed a protection—that Jews also had a reserved quarter.

Evolving down the centuries, discriminatory practices were usually definitions of right conduct: what clothes could be worn, what sexual relations with Muslims were permissible, which occupations might be enjoyed. According to the attitude of the power holder, discrimination varied from country to country and from period to period. Discrimination was not a function of anti-Semitic cruelty, as so often in Europe, and more a matter of shame-honor than of religious persecution. The unbeliever, Christian or Jew, had only himself to blame for his refusal to convert to Islam; and therefore he merited his shame. Subject peoples had to be publicly and openly shamed in order to certify their inferiority to the conquering and honor-bearing Muslims. The shame-image of pigs applied to Christians, that of apes or dogs to Jews. Accepted shame on the one hand and acknowledged honor on the other was integral to the decent ordering of Muslim society.

Of all the peoples under the Ottoman dispensation, Jews alone had chosen to immigrate, in two distinct waves, the first in 1492 after expulsion from Catholic Spain, the second in the nineteenth century in flight from czarist Russia. As a *millet,* the Jews fared neither better nor worse than others. The Tanzimat era brought into the new public arena a community with a low cultural level, lower than that of contemporary European Jewish communities, producing few noteworthy rabbis, scholars, and commentators of the Law.

The Prophet Muhammad had sometimes praised Jewish tribes caught up in his power challenge in Arabia but more often had inveighed against greed and cunning as invariable Jewish attributes. He is also recorded as putting Jewish men to the sword and selling their women and children into slavery. Classical Arabic literature time and again reveals ingrained prejudices, such as this example from 1065, "Look at medicine, a noble art, which since she has been practised by vulgar Jews has been infected by their vulgarity while they have by no means acquired her nobility." A Jewish beard, Lane noted in the 1830s, would defile the executioner's sword, and in Cairo Jews were therefore hanged, not beheaded. Among formal curses listed by Daumas in the mid-nineteenth century in North Africa were many invoking Jews, for instance, "May God curse me like a Jew." A traditional belief in Morocco was "If a Jew enters the house of a Moor, the angels will desert it for 40 days." Discussing how fifty Jews had accompanied a Roman expedition to Yemen in 27 B.C., a modern Arab historian can reproduce this stereotype, however anachronistically, "It is characteristic of the Jews that they are agents of invaders and conquerors and sanctify the money in their money-boxes."

Bernard Lewis has traced in *The Jews of Islam* how in the course of the nineteenth century the influence of Europe activated Muslim persecution of Jews and altered its nature. Anti-Semitism in the vicious European mode began to seep in through Greece and the Balkan provinces, often deriving from some particular European, a missionary or a consul. In 1840 in Damascus, a Capuchin monk and his servant disappeared; a Jewish barber was accused of their murder and his confession extracted under torture. Other innocent Jews were then tortured to death. The French consul, Ratti-Menton, bore full responsibility because he had started to spread the calumny that the Jews had killed the missing men to use their blood for ritual purposes. Blood libel had sprung from medieval European fantasies, but until now had been unknown in the Middle East. Lewis gives instances of thirty-two repetitions of blood libels in Middle East cities between 1840 and 1908. Violent anti-Jewish rioting in Algeria during the years of the Dreyfus Affair was an extreme case of imitation of a malign European example.

Generally speaking, the Jewish reaction was to seek the protection of Europeans, usually those consuls, either English or French, from whom they could then hope to acquire European nationality. Otherwise, no identity existed outside their confession of Judaism.

From the Jewish point of view, Palestine might be physically and administratively an Ottoman province like any other, but emotionally it was inseparable from Judaism. The prophets and founders of the Law had lived in that landscape. The ruins of Solomon's Temple, the Western Wall, were in Jerusalem, and since at the end of days Jews would be gathered there, they aspired to pray, and to be buried, on the spot. Palestine carried associations of redemption, of messianism. At all times, a trickle of religiously inspired Jews had arrived, sometimes settling into the existing community. The Baal Shem Tov, reviver of orthodoxy and one of the great religious personalities of the eighteenth century, had set off from eastern Europe for Palestine but had abandoned the journey in Istanbul. His spiritual heir, Rabbi Nahman of Bratslav, had reached the Holy Land in 1798. There he visited his grandfather's tomb in Tiberias but became too depressed with a sense of his own unworthiness to proceed to Jerusalem. Napoleon's campaigning then obliged him to return home.

Among emancipated Jews who reacted against the torpor and obscurantism of the community in Palestine were Adolphe Crémieux; Heinrich Graetz the historian, Baron von Laemel, an Austrian industrialist; and the English philanthropist Sir Moses Montefiore. All were of one mind, that education had to be promoted. In 1860 the Alliance Israélite Universelle was opened in Paris, with the aim of working for emancipation and moral progress, aiding Jews and encouraging the publication of useful literature. Over sixty Alliance schools were to bring Jewish children in the Middle East into contact with European knowledge and skills. This was only one of many repercussions in the worldwide process of Jewish cultural and social assimilation.

Jewish redemption, secularized as a return to the land of Palestine, was appealing to anyone who had no very clear idea of what the Jewish place or role might be in a changing world. Thoroughly assimilated Jews would obviously no longer be Jews in any meaningful sense. In Palestine, according to opinion makers as diverse as Lord Palmerston, Disraeli, George Eliot the novelist, and Moses Hess, the early German socialist, Jews might become a people like any other and yet retain a valuable heritage and identity.

Political developments in Russia transformed this romantic or nationalist element of Zionism into a serious prospect. Trapped between oppression from above and revolution from below, Jews sought escape. Between 1880 and 1914, the majority of Jewish emigrants moved to the United States, though some stayed in Britain and France. A handful went to Palestine. In 1881, the Ottoman government decreed that Jews could settle anywhere in the empire except Palestine, and Jewish pilgrims could enter the country for no more than thirty days. The money-favor nexus ensured that these restrictions served mainly to enrich local officials. Inexpert, insufficiently funded, often ill with malaria, early Jewish pioneers and their collective settlements had a visionary air about them. Less than 5 percent of the population in 1882, Jews were 10 percent by 1908. In 1914, Zionist immigrants numbered 35,000. Herzl's pamphlet, *The Jewish State,* published in Vienna in 1896, read like fiction with its prophecy that a Jewish state would come into existence in fifty years. His second book, *Altneuland,* depicting the state and its Arab-Jewish harmony, was actually a novel.

In his diaries, Herzl gave free rein to an imagination racing away with him. Jews would create imitations of Paris and Florence; they would have a style of their own; language would pose no difficulty; Switzerland would be the model for federation; women would not work in factories; here would be a nation of thinkers and artists. Shaken by seeing the reality of Palestine on a visit in 1898, he still managed to salvage his optimism.

I would clear out everything that is not sacred, set up workers' houses beyond the city, empty and tear down the filthy rat-holes, burn all the non-sacred ruins, and put the bazaars elsewhere. Then, retaining as much of the old architectural style of possible, I would build an airy, comfortable, properly sewered, brand new city around the Holy Places.

By the time of Herzl's death in 1903, the Zionist movement had constructed organizing institutions for raising and spending money and for making all Zionist activity, financial and political, accountable to bodies constituted by election. There followed a bank, the Jewish National Fund to purchase land, an art school, a national library and a university, the Jewish Labour Federation or trade union movement, representatives such as Dr. Chaim Weizmann and David Ben-Gurion duly authorized by the Zionist movement to solicit help or to make official representations. A Jewish desire to use Jewish capital and labor to build the national home had within it the determination not to exploit the Arabs, but it also contributed to exclusivity and the separation of the two communities. Jews everywhere could decide for themselves whether or not this new Zionist identity was appealing. The Balfour Declaration, promulgated as part of the British war aims, acknowledged these facts and sought to exploit them, but it had little to do with creating them. Whatever the military and political outcome of the First World War might have been, the Zionist movement would still have originated in much the same form.

Herzl had put his proposals for a homeland to Sultan Abdul Hamid in person. The rejection in Istanbul was absolute. The sultan had already resisted separatist demands from Bulgarians, Rumanians, and Serbs; he was engaged in fighting Armenian nationalists, and he anticipated similar Arab reactions. To him, the Jews were in a well-set pattern of a community seeking independence, taking with it a portion of the empire as well. How could he be expected to sympathize with the process whereby religious and ethnic communities were tentatively seeking to transform themselves into nation-states? His own, and the empire's, destruction could only follow. That Zionists at the time were European confirmed to him that the movement was foreign inspired, a power-challenge plot against him. Were not the Armenians sponsored by Russia, the Maronites by France? In the belief system of that time and place, how could it have been perceived that Jews, and for that matter Armenians and Maronites, would of their own accord link the two different ideas of tribal or religious identity and territorial exclusivity?

Relations between Arabs and early Jewish pioneers were strained on occasion by quasi-tribal infringements of grazing rights or petty crime of no great consequence. A modernizing Ottoman official like Ismail Kemal Bey welcomed the Zionists. On a tour, he found the Arab villages in the province backward because they were "the private property of some influential persons or of some governor." To shield themselves from extortionate taxes, the villagers had sold their land and become peasants. Baron de Rothschild, spending millions to finance the Jews, in Ismail Kemal Bey's opinion, was "contributing to the development of the wealth of the country, and was giving the population an example and a stimulus by the establishment of wine and perfumery industries."

Land proved increasingly to be the key to the Arab-Jewish relationship. Before the Zionist immigration, most of the land lay uncultivated, including the fertile Jordan valley. The Ottoman Land Law of 1858 had attempted to regularize the highly involved system of landholding and tenure, but its contrary effect had been to concentrate holdings into the hands of a few tribal leaders and family heads. These landowners were willing to satisfy Zionist demands to purchase, and over the years were to do so.*

Land sales continued up to and beyond the creation of the Israeli state. The historian Y. Porath judges that the devastating effect of these sales on Palestinians cannot be overestimated, spreading "an atmosphere of suspicion, mistrust and mischief." He quotes a Palestinian newspaper of 1925, "The British government should not be blamed for their refusal to heed our demands. We are to be blamed since we charged with the running of our affairs the untrustworthy, the sellers, the brokers and office-seekers." The opinion, though true, was also an unfair application of Eurocentric standards to a situation where the power-challenge dialectic was running unchecked. No institution existed for the representation of Palestinian interests as a whole. A landowner who refused to sell was only depriving himself of the chance to profit from rapidly rising prices. In the absence of a formally defined common good, self-sacrifice could only appear a pointless injury to oneself.

In 1891 a telegram signed by Jerusalem notables requested the Grand Vizier in Istanbul to prohibit Jewish immigration and land purchase. In 1897 the Mufti, Muhammad Tahir el-Husseini (and father of Haj Amin), set up a commission to persuade landowners

*Arieh L. Avneri, the historian of Zionist land purchasing, has analyzed these transactions, involving a very considerable acreage. The temptation to take profits from such land was high; few if any notables were immune to it. Sellers included the Husseinis and the Nashashibis, the Dajanis, the Abdul Hadis, Saleh Hamdan, Abu Kishek whom Avneri calls "a notorious land speculator," the Shawas in Gaza, the Sursoks, Musa Alami, Sidki Pasha who was the brother of Jamal, one of the Young Turk leaders, and the heir to Emir Abdel Kader of Algeria.

not to sell. Further pressures were applied in Istanbul after the CUP coup of 1908. One of the Palestine deputies to the Turkish parliament, Sheikh Asad Effendi Shuqair, raised the question there of the future of Jewish immigration—he was himself a land seller. In Cairo, Rashid Rida, a pupil of Abdu's and then a teacher of Haj Amin's, made in 1902 what was perhaps the first prediction in print that the Jews were striving through their organizations to achieve statehood. The president of the Jerusalem Municipal Council, Yusuf Diya Pasha al-Khalidi, an eminent notable, wrote to the Chief Rabbi of France that Zionism was "completely natural, fine and just" but feared that it would provoke a popular movement against the Jews and concluded "in the name of God, let Palestine be left in peace." Another member of the Husseini family asked for credit from David Levontin of the Anglo-Palestine Company, and the latter refused with the words, "You are an educated man, yet you deal with us like a fellah from a village." This had happened in the bank before employees, wrote the Arab complaining angrily in a letter to Levontin's superior in London, and it was an insult to him and to all Arabs, and such behavior "shall never be forgotten by me nor by my friends." The shame-honor response was already in play.

Negib Azoury was a Maronite from Beirut who had studied in Paris and wrote in French. In 1898, he was posted as an Ottoman civil servant to Jerusalem. Some mysterious conspiracy occurred, and he fled to Cairo. Tried in absentia, he was condemned to death. Moving on to Paris, he founded his *"Ligue de la Patrie Arabe,"* only a careerist façade, for it consisted of himself and a friend. In 1905 he published *Le Réveil de la Nation Arabe,* the first considered attack on Zionism and one that skirted European anti-Semitic arguments. Obviously addressing the French rather than his compatriots, Azoury was certainly the first to see the careerist possibilities of anti-Zionism. Jews and Arabs, he concluded, were "destined to struggle continuously with one another until one prevails over the other." The Palestinian newspaper *Falastin* published this poem in 1913:

> Jews, sons of clinking gold, stop your deceit;
> We shall not be cheated into bartering away our country. . .
> The Jews, the weakest of all peoples and the least of them,
> are haggling with us for our land;
> how can we slumber on?

We know what they want
—and they have the money, all of it.
Masters, rulers, what is wrong with you?
What ails you?

These, then, were the images and preconceptions to which Haj Amin could appeal once he became the leading Palestinian power holder. In memoirs written at the end of his life, when the bankruptcy of these images and preconceptions was starkly visible, he was still speaking of the Jews as "notorious for perfidy and falsification and distortion and cruelty of which the noble Koran provides the strongest testimony against them." His hatred for Jews was instinctive, tribal; he wished to cut them down, declaring to their face, "Nothing but the sword will decide the future of this country." That this came true amid calamity and ruin was Haj Amin's memorial to posterity.

Reaching toward undisputed power, Haj Amin had first to contend with a Palestinian rival. The Nashashibi family were long-established opponents of the Husseinis, in another example of those dualities that mark the final stage of power challenging. In 1918 the British military authorities had installed Raghib al-Nashashibi mayor of Jerusalem in place of the previous incumbent, Musa Kazem el-Husseini. When Haj Amin was manipulating his election as Mufti, the Nashashibis put up their candidates. In response, a Husseini leaflet accused them of combining with the Jews, and the Nashashibis could be typically branded as "The accursed traitors whom you all know." For a few years, Haj Amin had hopes of recruiting the British as anti-Jewish allies, offering to guarantee law and order in return for their rejection of Zionism. Failure in the attempt determined that for Haj Amin the Palestinian cause and his own interest were identical. He had only his family and retinue to rely on.

In the mid-1920s, Haj Amin enlarged what was in essence a Husseini conspiracy into the so-called Higher Arab Committee. Musa Kazem el-Husseini was its first head but his inclination to caution was a source of friction. When Musa Kazem died in 1934 Haj Amin himself soon replaced him. Correspondingly, Raghib al-Nashashibi formed his Arab National Party in 1923, later called the National Defence Party, for his family and supporters. In private, Raghib el-Nashashibi could explain in 1929 to an official of the Zionist Association that his opposition to Haj Amin "went 10 times further" than the opposition of the Jews to Haj Amin. The more openly the Husseinis were at war with the British or the Jews, the more the Nashashibis adopted the alternative of compromise, pro-British, prepared to treat with Jews at least expediently, therefore branded traitors by the Husseinis at every turn. Municipal elections in 1927 and 1934 were Husseini-Nashashibi tests of strength. Ambition rather than ideology had decided the position taking.

In Ottoman times, a governor would have employed the money-favor nexus to buy off this rivalry, after which there would have been winners enriching themselves in office and losers in a supervised but tolerable exile in Istanbul. Both Husseinis and Nashashibis had had their men in the Ottoman parliament. British rule offered no such familiar option. In view of the anti-French challenging in the adjoining Mandate of Syria, it is only hypothetical to wonder whether over an extended period the British might have learnt the lesson of Egypt, deported Haj Amin as they had deported Zaghlul, but in this instance unrelentingly in order to browbeat and subordinate the Husseinis, finally imposing a constituent assembly upon them, the Nashashibis, and the Jews together. In the event, two external developments finally precluded any participatory resolution of the crisis: in 1924 the United States closed its frontiers to unrestricted immigration, and in January 1933 Hitler assumed control of Germany. Having ebbed during the 1920s, Jewish immigration now shot up—42,359 in 1934 and 61,844 in 1935, when the Nuremberg Laws deprived Jews of civic rights in Germany. No longer some vague national home for the future, Palestine for the Jews was now a rare and necessary haven for safety and survival. Nazism completed the internationalization of the Middle East.

"Tel Aviv 1935" is a period poem by Lea Goldberg, no doubt familiar only in intellectual circles, but it captures the impulses that went into the fulfillment of Zionism, namely fear of what was to come, bitter regret that this should be so, and nostalgia for the passing order. Its final stanza runs:

> And the sound of steps behind your
> back drummed marching songs of
> foreign troops; and—so it seemed—if
> you but turn your head, there's your
> town's church floating in the sea.

Jews in Poland and Rumania, moreover, appeared to be under no less grave a threat from fascist and anti-Semitic regimes. Jewish emigration from Poland, mostly to the U.S., was about 400,000 between 1921 and 1931. Vladimir Jabotinsky, leader of the Revisionists, that is to say the nationalist but nonsocialist Zionists, could predict, "I am sure that elemental floods will soon break out all over Eastern European Jewry, so terribly powerful that the German catastrophe will soon be eclipsed." Zionism was of course part of the human condition and not its cure, as was recognized by the historian Gershom Scholem, one of the most distinguished minds ever to have been a Zionist. As a student in Berlin, he had been struck to hear his philosophy professor express what he called the one unanswerable objection to the Zionists, "These fellows really want to be happy." Emigration to Palestine, in other words, could never be a ticket to Utopia.

In March 1933 Hitler broke the institutions of the Weimar Republic in the process known as *Gleichschaltung* and so confirmed his dictatorship. Millions of Germans, former Communists most prominently, drew the instant conclusion that it was in their interest to become Nazis, earning for themselves the nickname of "March violets." Haj Amin was another March violet. He called on Wolff, the German consul general in Jerusalem. In a telegram of March 31, Wolff relayed to Berlin the Mufti's congratulations, his support for the anti-Jewish boycott in Germany, and his pledge to undertake similar efforts against Jews in Arab countries. A month later, Haj Amin told Wolff of his approval of Nazi measures against the Jews: he was to ask Wolff's successor Döhle for support. Seiler, the German consul in Beirut, and Fritz Grobba, minister in Baghdad and the highest-ranking German in the Middle East, received many similar letters of approval and admiration.

To Arabs, Nazism was readily understandable in terms of the power-challenge dialectic. The Germans were a people with interests against France and Britain. Harmed and shamed in the First World War, as though in a feud, the Germans naturally sought revenge. They had an identity, a language, and a leader. If they chose to call themselves Nazis, that was nobody else's business. Nazi ideology was of concern only to Hitler. Unrestrained application of power as the means to achieve their ends was only normal. Massacre of enemies merely denoted victory and was not in the least shocking, was no moral issue at all. Backing Nazism, Arabs were conscious that the choice might be wrong in the event of

Britain and France proving stronger, but not that Nazism itself was a denial of human rights and values.

To this day, no Arab has written anything like a scholarly study of the Holocaust; and Arab expressions of admiration for it have been frequent, while regret has been perfunctory. A headline in 1961 in a Saudi newspaper "Capture of Eichmann, who had the honor of killing five million Jews" is, in the words of Bernard Lewis, "a fairly typical response." "The worst insult which one Moroccan can offer another is to call him a Jew," a Moroccan wrote under a pseudonym in the French intellectual magazine *Les Temps Modernes* in 1965. "A Hitlerian myth is cultivated at a popular level. Hitler's massacre of the Jews is praised (and the idea has its ecstasy). It is even believed that Hitler is not dead. His arrival is awaited in order to deliver the Arabs from Israel."

Nazism and Arab power challenging had in common the belief that life is an unending struggle in which the victor works his will upon the loser by virtue of his victory. Hitler and his beer cellar cronies were familiar to Arabs as conspirators who had managed to widen their secret society into a mass movement. The Nazi takeover of power was indeed a conspiracy against the nation, and whose ends were not declared until it was too late to be able to impede them. The Party had money-favor aspects about it. The *völkisch* elements of Nazism had an undoubted tribal coloration. But for Arabs, the warm emotional recognition of Nazism began in its perception of Jews.

In *Mein Kampf* Hitler gave his opinion that Zionism was nothing but make-believe, another sly trick on the part of the Jews.

They have no thought of building up a Jewish State in Palestine, so that they might perhaps inhabit it, but they only want a central organization of their international world cheating, endowed with prerogatives, withdrawn from the seizure of others: a refuge for convicted rascals and a high school for future rogues.

This chimed in perfectly with the view endemic to power challenge that ordinary people can act only at the behest of their sponsors, and whether or not they know it, are always the instruments of a conspirator-challenger. What was obviously paranoid nonsense to any European who could see for himself the distressing reasons why Jews would try to reach Palestine, to an Arab was a familiar plot like any other.

So heady was this conviction that it excluded the logical step of inquiring how and why Nazism had at its core a hatred of Jews. Honor, or pride, played its part in preventing Arabs from realizing that the organizing principle of Nazism was race and that they themselves occupied as unfavorable a position as the Jews in the Nazi racist hierarchy. The Islamocentric perception of Nazism, like the response to colonialism, was highly damaging to the Arabs in its indifference to the values really being fought out. Had the Nazis won the war, they would have fitted the Arabs into some brutal *untermensch* servitude.

Confident that the rise of Nazi Germany, and British appeasement of it, offered the right conjuncture for self-assertion, Haj Amin began preparations. He spread the view everywhere in the Arab world that British failure to withstand Mussolini in Abyssinia and to prevent Hitler's rearmament signified a new European arbitrator of power. So he pushed aside other notables, including some of his own kinsmen, and he formed a terrorist group, the Resistance and Jihad Organization, under his nephew Abdel Kader el-Husseini. He stockpiled weapons.

Haj Amin may or may not have incited the outbreak of fighting in 1935. Its leader was Sheikh Ezzeddin Qassam, a man of religion in Haj Amin's mold. Born in Syria, Sheikh Ezzeddin was at least fifty-three at the time, perhaps older. At Al-Azhar, he had been a pupil of Abdu's. Behind him was a record of fighting the Italians in Libya and the French in Syria. Expelled from his own country, he had been given by Haj Amin a post as a preacher in Haifa, where he told his congregation, "You are a people of rabbits, who are afraid of death and scaffolds and engaged in prattle. You must know that nothing will save us but our arms." To the number of about 200, his conspirators formed the "Black Hand," recruited among the poor and religious. Taking to the Judaean hills, the Sheikh and a band of followers spent their days in prayer and in acts of terrorism. They also extorted protection money, as villagers afterward testified. In a shoot-out with British soldiers, Sheikh Ezzeddin and his band were killed, but surviving Qassamites were to commit further sporadic acts of violence, including the murder of a British district commissioner. Other secret societies for terrorism were called "Green Hand," "Young Patriots," and "The Rebellious Youth."

The following April, Haj Amin made his bid to break the British, after which he anticipated becoming the absolute power holder in Palestine and free to deal with the Jews. He declared a general strike and unleashed his terrorists. In August, his auxiliary Fawzi al-Qawukji, also at the head of about 200 men, crossed from Syria, or perhaps Iraq (previously he had been an instructor in the Military College in Baghdad), into Palestine, as self-styled "Commander in Chief of the Revolt in Southern Syria." According to the best Arab authority at the time, Haj Amin could call on about 3000 full-time fighters, another 1000 urban rebels, and in case of need, 6000 villagers.

It came as a disagreeable surprise to Haj Amin and Qawukji to discover that there was in fact little or no solidarity among the Arabs. For all the demonstrations, the murdering, the propaganda and name-calling of traitors, the Husseinis did not command the country. Reluctant strikers at best, ordinary Palestinians preferred caution. They observed that the strike strengthened the parallel Jewish economy and that violence led to Jewish self-defense. Moreover, the Nashashibis saw their opportunity for a rapprochement with the British and the Jews. To stop polarization and to create an appearance of unity, Haj Amin turned more and more on his fellow Palestinians, ordering the killing of everyone who might thwart his ambitions, including Raghib al-Nashashibi (in more than one attempt on his life) and his supporters or moderates, sellers of land, and Arab policemen loyal to the state.

These poor people were not always immediately murdered [writes Y. Porath, the historian of this period]; sometimes they were kidnapped and taken to the mountainous areas under rebel control. There they were thrown into pits infested with snakes and scorpions. After spending a few days there, the victims, if still alive, were brought before one of the rebel courts or commanders, tried, and usually sentenced to death, or, as a special dispensation, to severe flogging. The terror was so strong that no one, including ulema and priests, dared to perform the proper burial services. In some cases, the British Police had to perform this duty; in others, the corpses were left in the streets for several days after a shoe had been placed in the mouth of the victim as a symbol of disgrace and as a lesson to others.

What was called the Great Arab Revolt actually proved to be the victimization of the Palestinian masses by the Husseinis. Firm numbers are hard to establish, but for the scores of British soldiers and Jews who died, there were thousands of Arab victims. In 1938, 69 British, 292 Jews, and at least 1600 Arabs were killed. Between 1937 and 1939, 112 Arabs were sentenced in British courts to death for murder, and almost all were executed. By 1939 Miss M. H. Wilson, a British teacher at Bir Zeit College, was writing that the rebellion was degenerating into squabbles between rival bands. Bir Zeit, like many villages, was "a hornets' nest of long-standing family feuds, stirred up afresh in the hope of getting some advantage through the help of this or that party of rebels." One of his agents at the time was reporting to Haj Amin that the spirit of rebellion was waning. "The behaviour of the fighters towards the villagers is extremely brutal and horrifying: cruel robbery, execution without prior investigation, conflicts without any reason, disorder and inaction. The villagers called upon God for succour against such behaviour." By 1939 Haj Amin and his methods of terror had shaken Palestinian society to its foundations, and he himself had fled into exile in Baghdad. Some 40,000 Arabs had left the country to avoid these events.

The British reaction was exactly what Lord Rosebery had anticipated for Egypt half a century previously—"Commissions, reports and experiments." A rhythm was established of disturbances in Palestine with a commission to report on causes and consequences. Parliamentary government is always in a quandary against undemocratic opponents, and in Palestine the British reluctance to use decisive force further proved an inducement to the alternative of helplessness and chaos. In 1937 Lord Peel headed the most distinguished of these commissions. When one of its members asked Haj Amin whether Palestine was capable of assimilating its 400,000 Jews, the answer was the single word, "No." Tel Aviv, the Mufti liked to repeat, should be established in America. The Peel Commission recommended partition of Palestine into two entities, one Arab and the other Jewish with a reserved portion for the British. By then, no other proposal could have been envisaged. Partition along the broad lines of the Peel Commission was in fact to be realized some ten years later.

Greeted as statesmanlike and realistic, partition as a concept conceded that the British had failed to create intercommunal institutions, and that henceforth Arabs and Jews were destined to relapse each into their own tribal or religious identities.

A conclusion hardened in British government circles between the wars that the crisis in Palestine could be resolved in favor of Arabs or of Jews, but not in a compromise. There was of course nothing predetermined that made Palestine such an either-or issue. Lack of political imagination was responsible for this glib, and in the last resort murderous, oversimplification. Instead, the British imagination was captivated by its peculiar but deep-rooted trait that things different and picturesque should be preserved and cherished. The very separateness of Arabs and Jews attracted most British officials into themselves thinking along confessional lines. Sir Ronald Storrs, governor of Jerusalem in 1920, expressed the trait for himself in words with which Mandate officials almost unanimously could have agreed. Himself not a Jew nor an Arab, Storrs observed, he was for neither but for both. "Two hours of Arab grievances drive me into the Synagogue, while after an intensive course of Zionist propaganda I am prepared to embrace Islam."

The flippancy of Storrs' tone could not be maintained in the 1930s. Clearly the disturbance of the communal balance stemmed from Jewish immigration. British officials more and more came to accept the Arab argument that the Jews were the source of all trouble. Had there been no Jewish immigration at all, Haj Amin would still have made his anti-British power challenge, but this seemed secondary. What finally confirmed Palestine as an either-or issue was guilt, the novel idea that the British were responsible for the Jewish presence in Palestine. This was self-flattering, altogether an imperialist illusion, which ignored the religious and now political impulses giving Jewish immigration its own autonomous motives. If the British had really imported the Jews, as for instance they had imported Indians into Africa or Chinese into other countries, then the Arabs had been deliberately harmed, and amends must be made. Such was not the case.

Out of misplaced guilt, British officials became partisan, in the main pro-Arab, but a handful pro-Jewish, including Orde Wingate, whose impact was crucial in laying the basis of Jewish military training and preparation. "How can we risk prejudicing our whole position in the Arab world for the sake of Palestine?" Evelyn Shuckburgh, then a junior attaché in the British embassy in Cairo, was writing in 1937 to his father Sir John Shuckburgh, colonial under secretary of state. If so, if Palestine was really an either-or issue, then Haj Amin would have his way, and the future of the country would indeed be decided by the sword. "Jew versus Arab—this is what is going on in Palestine now," General Montgomery, soon to be a wartime field marshal, was writing from his command in Palestine in 1939, "And it will go on for the next 50 years in all probability." The White Paper of 1939, setting harsh limits to Jewish immigration at a moment when this was a life-or-death matter, marked the British settling of the either-or alternative in favor of the Arabs. Dealing with illegal Jewish refugees who had to be denied entry into Palestine, Alec Randall of the Foreign Office noted, "We may shortly have to face the choice between raising world Jewish opinion against us and trouble with the Arabs." The British had only themselves to blame that the handling of prewar events in Palestine left them then and afterward deferring to whoever appeared the stronger side, thereby encouraging the violence which was to destroy those for whom they were responsible, and in the end themselves as well.

British military measures in Palestine, however late in the day, were grist to Nazi propaganda. German policy accepted that the Middle East was not a primary area of interest. What Hitler hoped to gain from expansion into Eastern Europe warranted a relationship free from strain with Britain and France over colonial policy. Nonetheless Seiler in Beirut and Grobba in Baghdad listened favorably to requests for arms from the Syrian nationalists and Qawukji in Palestine. Admiral Canaris, head of the Abwehr or German military intelligence, traveled incognito to Beirut in 1938 to meet Haj Amin, and he reported giving financial aid. German and Italian weapons and subsidies reached Palestine and Syria, but in quantities that are still not clear.

Like Haj Amin, sponsor seekers in every Arab country swung to Berlin. Many Arabs, Edward Atiyah has recalled, were so full of disillusion and hatred that "they lapped up Fascist and Nazi lies. They saw the Zionists as the sinister world-menace of the Nazi legend, and England as a puppet-master in their clutches." Bakr Sidqi tried to buy German arms for Iraq. King Abdul Aziz of Saudi Arabia sent his personal physician to Berlin to sound out policy and to request arms. His son, the future King Khaled, dined with Hitler on the night that Czechoslovakia ceded the German claim to the Sudetenland, and joined in the toast of congratulations (and long after the war surprised a foreign diplomat by saying that he believed the Führer to be a maligned man). In 1939, Khalid Bey al-Qarqani, another envoy of Abdul Aziz's, met Hitler to hear him praise the Arab struggle in Palestine and declare that he would drive every Jew out of Germany. Qarqani replied that this had been the Prophet's policy with Jews in Arabia.

Delegations of Syrians and Iraqis attended Nuremberg Party rallies. More than one Arab translated Hitler's *Mein Kampf* into

Arabic, and among them was Yunis el-Sabawi, an Iraqi and close associate of Rashid Ali and later to be hanged by the British for his part in the 1941 pro-Nazi coup in Baghdad. Intellectuals were attracted by "blood and soil" doctrines that stressed power for its own sake. Michel Aflaq, future theorist of Arab nationalism, was in Paris as a student in 1937, and there he became an enthusiastic admirer of Hitler and Rosenberg, whose *The Myth of the Twentieth Century* he read in a French translation. His Syrian friends were as responsive. One of them, Sami al-Jundi, a future politician, in his memoirs has recorded how he was then reading Nietzsche and Houston Stewart Chamberlain and was also interested in *Mein Kampf.* "We were racialists, admiring Nazism" because to the Arab people, he thought, Nazism appeared "the power which could serve as its champion, and he who is defeated will by nature love the victor." (The generalization is revealing, incidentally, for it is valid in terms of the Arab power-challenge dialectic but ridiculous in other belief systems.)

Shakib Arslan, in the judgment of his biographer William L. Cleveland, was "arguably the most widely read Arab writer of the interwar period" as well as the principal liaison between the Axis and the Arabs. The Arslans were hereditary Druze emirs. Shakib Arslan, born in 1869, had attended a Maronite school in Beirut and had been appointed governor of the Shuf region of Lebanon by Sultan Abdul Hamid. In his youth, Arslan had known Afghani and Abdu and Zaghlul. Journeys to London and Paris had strengthened his conviction that Islam alone stood between the Arabs and the loss of their identity. In 1927 he traveled to the tenth anniversary celebrations of the Bolshevik Revolution in Moscow. Three years later, he started his newspaper, *La Nation Arabe,* published in Geneva. In spite of the apparent nationalist and anti-imperialist stance, Arslan was secretly subsidized by the Italians. In 1934 he went to Berlin in the hope of meeting Hitler and explained to Nazi officials that Germany would have to align itself with the Arabs. The Germans financed his newspaper as the leading organ attacking France and Britain. Arslan nurtured conspiratorial contacts all over the Arab world.

Baldur von Schirach, leader of the Hitler Youth, made an extensive tour of the Middle East, and Joseph Goebbels visited Egypt. Mussolini was also promoting his prospective empire in the Mediterranean. Pacifying Libya and conquering Abyssinia, Mussolini had himself declared "Hero of Islam," contrived to form a

Libyan Arab Fascist Party, and on one ludicrous occasion in Tripoli had himself presented with a "Sword of Islam." In 1935 Radio Bari started broadcasting Fascist propaganda in Arabic. The Germans followed four years later with competitive broadcasting in Arabic from the station at Zeesen, outside Berlin. The principal personality at Zeesen, Yunus Bahri, was the Arab equivalent of William Joyce, otherwise Lord Haw Haw, and renowned throughout the Arab world. An Arab language paper, *Barid al-Sharq*, was published in Berlin for dissemination in the Middle East. Millions of *reichsmarks* were poured into the region through a variety of agents, for instance, Dr. Julius Jordan, an archaeologist employed in the Baghdad museum before he was expelled for his political activities. Preposterously, Hitler himself was Islamicized on the radio and by word of mouth as "Abu Ali," and in Egypt at least was referred to as "Muhammad Haidar." As such, he was prayed for in every village, says Grafftey-Smith, who also relates how in Tanta he was shown the house that was claimed to have been Hitler's mother's.

The Young Egypt Party, or Green Shirts, was founded in 1933 by Ahmed Hussein, who proclaimed, "Everyone must believe that the will of the people is the will of God, and that Egypt is above all." The party slogan was "Allah, Fatherland and People." The Wafd imitated the fascist style with its Blue Shirts organization. Even the Muslim Brotherhood pressed Nazi sentiments into service, as in a 1938 publication:

> If the German Reich imposes itself as a protector of everyone who has German blood running in his veins, Muslim faith makes it the clear duty of every strong Muslim whose soul is drenched in the doctrines of the Koran to consider himself the protector of every other Muslim whose soul has also been drenched . . . in Islam.

Building on a conspiracy of five original members bound by an oath, Antun Saada, self-styled "Führer of the Syrian nation," organized a fascist party in his country, called the Syrian National Social Party, with a program that Syrians were "a distinctive and naturally superior race." Another Syrian group was known as the Iron Shirts, and there was also a fascist-inspired League for Arab Action. After a visit to a Nuremberg Party rally, the Maronite Pierre Gemayel started his Phalange in Beirut. In French Morocco, the pro-fascist Diouri family took Italian money for their newspaper, and in Spanish Morocco Abdelhalek Torrès collaborated with Germany through the consul in Tetuan.

In Iraq, Nazism threatened to become institutionalized. Sami Shawkat, director of the ministry of education, was an experienced conspirator, openly admiring Hitler's Germany and creating paramilitary organizations in imitation of the Hitler Youth. In a notorious "Profession of Death" speech to an audience of school children, he declared that it was holy to tear one's enemy limb from limb. His brother Naji Shawkat, a politician, saw career advantages in Nazism. Sati al-Husri, once an Ottoman official and now an Iraqi publicist and official, had attached himself to Feisal in Damascus. Already in 1930 he had written that Arab hopes should be directed to a fascist, not a Bolshevik, system. He and the Shawkats cultivated a mystique of Arab power. In flight from Palestine, Haj Amin arrived in Baghdad with members of his entourage, including Musa Alami in charge of propaganda, and Akram Zuayter, from Nablus, a military organizer. This contingent reinforced the pro-Nazi Iraqis, principally Rashid Ali Gailani and Colonel Salah-eddin Sabbagh, and their associates in the army. Gailani descended from a famous religious forebear in the twelfth century and was an inveterate power seeker, with a long record of conspiracy. Naji Shawkat in 1940 delivered letters from Haj Amin to the German ambassador in Ankara, Franz von Papen, offering support in exchange for diplomatic recognition. Even Nuri Said Pasha decided that it would be expedient to open lines via Turkey to the Germans, but secret overtures from someone so publicly known for British sponsorship were rejected as a British intelligence plot.

Hitler's blitzkrieg victories from 1939 to 1941 attracted favorable opinions throughout the Arab world; and the conviction that the Allies would lose became general and gleeful.

A popular song had a couplet:

> No more Monsieur, no more Mister,
> In heaven Allah, on earth Hitler.

An Algerian historian has written:

The defeat of France in 13 days stimulated the Algerians to look down on the French. On the other hand, the Algerians started to admire Hitler and the Germans. In this respect, Al Akhdar Ibn Tobal stated: "The indigenous Algerians started to . . . declare in the presence of the *pieds noirs* [settlers] that Hitler had taught the French a good lesson." In cinemas, the appearance of Hitler on the screen was greeted with a very long applause.

In Haifa on a Friday in June 1940, P. J. Vatikiotis, the future historian and Arabist, noted that when Italian aircraft flew over to bomb industrial installations, the faithful emerged from the mosque to applaud. Ahmad Shuqairi, son of Sheikh Asad Effendi Shuqairi and the future PLO leader, confirms in his memoirs that the joy and excitement over the bombing of Haifa and Tel Aviv were "indescribable."

The American intelligence agent Kenneth Pendar had the mission of discovering how much the Axis had penetrated and infiltrated into the Arab world. In Marrakesh he met a prince of the royal house who professed "a touching loyalty" to the Allies, but he knew that the prince was reporting back to the Germans. Pendar could always deduce from his talks with the prince what the Germans were doing, and he was amused because the prince believed him to be "on the point of out-bidding the Germans" by offering him a sum of money appropriate to American power. The son of a Caid took Pendar to a local wedding and assured him of his belief in the Allied cause, yet Pendar knew him to be "the most important of the native chiefs in German pay." As a group, the Tunisian Hichem Djait comments,

Arabs admired German courage, daring and know-how; they were impressed by the way Germans fought almost single-handed against a gigantic coalition of enemies.

Bound by the 1936 Treaty with Britain, the Egyptian government in 1939 declared its neutrality. Clandestine German-Egyptian contacts existed at many levels. Through Zulfiqar Pasha, his father-in-law, King Farouk was corresponding with the German foreign minister Ribbentrop to say that he hoped to see German troops liberating Egypt as soon as possible and offering cooperation to that end. Farouk employed seventeen Italians in his palace entourage. His uncle, Abbas Hilmi, the Khedive deposed by the British in 1914, was also a friend of the Nazis. Abbas Hilmi had visited Berlin in 1941, and he was a faithful sponsor of the pro-Nazi journalist Shakib Arslan. Farouk feared that his uncle might begin a power play to regain the throne with Nazi help and clumsily attempted to outbid him. A cousin, Prince Mansour Daoud, joined the S.S. In February 1942 the British decided to put an end to the risk that Farouk might make some open pro-Nazi move. Troops surrounded the palace, and the British ambassador forced Farouk to choose between abdication and a policy of dictated friendship. Having unscrewed his pen to sign the abdication document, Farouk nonetheless decided to opt for retaining his throne.

After the first bombing raids, the sheikh of Al-Azhar (and a favorite of King Farouk's) proclaimed from his pulpit that Egypt had been dragged into the war against its will, and that its rewards for allowing British bases was only "the killing of innocent men, women and children." The popular Egyptian writer Abbas Mahmud al-Aqqad, writing in 1942, could couple the name of Hitler with those of Napoleon and the Prophet Muhammad as military geniuses. When in 1942 the German army reached positions only sixty miles west of Alexandria, an uprising seemed imminent, with pro-Nazi slogans daubed on the walls and students in the street shouting, "Forward, Rommel!" In an attempt to prove to Egyptians that the die might not yet be cast, the British paraded thousands of German prisoners through Cairo and were then amazed by the unexpected and contrary reaction. The Egyptians reasoned that the British would not have staged this display unless they were desperate, pretending to honor because on the point of defeat. The parade almost provoked the violence it was designed to avoid. The event is a cautionary tale about the lack of common ground between outlooks conditioned on the one hand by democracy, and on the other by the power-challenge dialectic. The Battle of El Alamein restored calm.

One prime careerist was Aziz Ali el-Masri, once of the Al-Ahd conspiracy in Istanbul, then with the Sherifians in Mecca, lately inspector general of the Armed Forces and known to the Germans as an agent with the code word "Architect." He had been to Berlin in 1938 on a secret arms buying mission. He had gathered around him a number of pro-Nazi conspirators, the so-called Free Officers, of whom the most noteworthy was Anwar Sadat, then a young lieutenant, but the future president. Sadat claimed to be—and was—in touch with Rommel's headquarters. In May 1941, Aziz Ali received orders to leave for safety, and he tried to fly out to Iraq in order to participate with Rashid Ali Gailani in forging an Arab-German alliance. His pilot, Yusef Zulficar Sabry, was the brother of Ali Sabry, Nasser's future pro-Communist prime minister. The flight was foiled. Aziz Ali spent the rest of the war under surveillance. Sadat and other Free Officers were imprisoned by the British.

In October 1940, Ernst von Weizäcker, secretary of state in the German Foreign Office, gave to Osman Haddad, Haj Amin's confidential agent, an official declaration that the Arabs could count on German and Italian sympathy in their struggle for independence. Sympathy was hardly sufficient. Haj Amin was soon to despatch Haddad back with a proposal that a German-Arab alliance would solve "the Jewish question" on a joint basis. Conspiring with Haj Amin in Baghdad, Rashid Ali Gailani and Sabbagh and other army officers with politicians such as Naji Shawkat mounted a coup on April 1. The Soviet Union recognized this government. British-sponsored Iraqis, including Nuri Said Pasha, fled to Amman. Offers of help arrived from pro-Nazis like Michel Aflaq in Damascus. Against military advice, Churchill insisted that a Nazi regime in Iraq was a risk not to be run. British troops took over the country. British intelligence was to estimate afterward that 95 percent of the Iraqis were pro-German, yet resistance was minimal. No doubt the population and the army recognized that Gailani, power challenging in their name, had actually lost control and endangered them all—a repetition of Haj Amin's experience with the Palestinians. The conspirators fled, some to wander in exile or to be arrested. Others, including Haj Amin and Gailani and Mustapha al-Wakil of the Young Egypt Movement, were reunited again in Berlin at the end of the year after a series of extraordinary escapes in various disguises across numerous frontiers. Passing through Rome, Haj Amin was received by Mussolini, who was paying him a subsidy.

On November 28, 1941, Haj Amin met Hitler. They were in accord about the necessity of destroying Jews everywhere, but Hitler refrained from committing himself to the liberation of the Arabs. That, he said, would have to await the success of his campaigns against the Soviet Union. To both men, the British, the Jews, and the Bolsheviks were common enemies. Making himself a useful ally, Haj Amin became a war criminal. A German-Arab training detachment had already been recruited among Arab volunteers in Germany, wearing the German uniform with an armband *"Frei Arabien."* Haj Amin's military commander Qawukji had also reached Berlin, and with his help the training detachment was enlarged into an Arab legion. The legion was open to other Muslims, for instance Bosnians, and in the end it became an S.S. unit. Haj Amin early appreciated the importance of Himmler and placed himself under his particular sponsorship, prompting him in a series of letters and appeals—superfluous, to be sure—to block escape routes for Jews in the Balkans and elsewhere and to pursue their extermination. In March 1944, Haj Amin was declaring, "Kill the Jews wherever you find them—this pleases God, history and religion." He played his part fully in aiding and abetting mass murder. Hitler came to believe that greater use might have been made of the Arabs, saying in February 1945 with regret that the Arabs might have served as "our best card" because "the Islamic world was quivering in the expectation of our victory."

In Algeria and Tunisia, other Arab auxiliary units were trained and raised for German tasks. The Gestapo chief in Tunisia, Walter Rauff, had been a commander of mobile extermination units in Europe. Jews were rounded up, their homes plundered and their property confiscated, but the Germans did not have time to murder more than a small number. Ra'uf, one of the sons of the Bey of Tunis, wished to enroll in the German army. By December 1943, the returning French had interned 233 Algerians and 352 French citizens on charges of collaboration. Sultan Mohammad V of Morocco, however, insisted that Moroccan-born Jews were his subjects, and they were therefore not persecuted or deported as were French-born Jews in Morocco.

Petty squabbling in Berlin between Haj Amin and Rashid Ali Gailani weakened Arab-Nazi collaboration. As Mufti, Haj Amin controlled the Berlin Mosque. He and Gailani each tried to outbid the other in their approaches to Hitler and Mussolini, and soon they were not on speaking terms. The main content of the clash, says Hirszowicz, was "gratification of personal ambition and thirst for power, for first place in the Fascist protectors' grace."

The influence of Arab Nazi activists enrolled in Germany continued to be felt well into the postwar generation. Qawukji was a commander in the 1948 war against Israel. The Syrian Mahmud Rifai, a paratrooper in the German army, returned to Syria in 1946, joined Qawukji, and then participated in the 1949 coup led by Sami Hinnawi to depose Husni Zaim, the country's first dictator. Muhammad Radwan, an Egyptian, flew an aircraft to the German lines in 1941, and after the war had a senior post in the department of public affairs. Aziz Ali el-Masri was appointed by Nasser in 1954 to be ambassador to the Soviet Union which had an irony all its own. Ahmed Balafrej had spent the years from 1937 to 1943 shuttling between Tangier and Germany, and he became one of the leaders of Moroccan nationalism. Mohamedi Said, an area commander in the Algerian war of independence, had been in Haj Amin's S.S. Arab Legion and had believed, in his words, that "Hitler would destroy French tyranny and free the world." Fighting the French, he still wore his German helmet. Ali Salih Fidama, broadcasting from Aden during the Yemeni civil war, had been awarded the Iron Cross while servicing with the legion on the Russian front. Dr. Maruf al-Dawalibi, described in the German archives by an S.S. Obergruppenführer as "Our man of confidence," was prime minister of Syria in 1950, at which time he declared that the Arabs "would a thousand times rather become a Soviet republic than the victims of Israel." At a United Nations seminar in Geneva in 1984, he raised the medieval libel that Jews kill non-Jews for ritual purposes.

Arab identification with Nazism, and Jewish suffering in the Holocaust, finalized open antagonism between the two communities in the aftermath of the war. The French and the British between them judged it expedient to allow Haj Amin to escape trial as a war criminal. Returning to Cairo, he picked up his anti-Jewish ambitions where he had left off. About half a million Jews had survived genocide in one way or another, and they refused to return to places where they had been persecuted, or to states in eastern or central Europe which no longer existed in their previous form and where Soviet armies of occupation were ominously preparing for "peoples' democracies." The British denied these survivors entry to Palestine, and most of them remained stateless people in camps in Europe. From 1945 to mid–1948, 75,000 Jews did succeed in immigrating, many of them illegally. An estimated 56,000 illegal immigrants were prevented from landing and then escorted to imprisonment in Cyprus. Beginning in November 1945, the Jewish revolt against this harsh policy doomed the Mandate.

Public opinion in the West was influenced by sympathy for Holocaust survivors, ignorance of the desperation of their feelings, and suspicion of Zionism as a political movement, particularly when terrorism started in its name. Of the wartime leaders, only Churchill had declared himself in favor of a Jewish state. Tending to anti-Semitism, Stalin viewed Jewish nationalism as hostile to communism. Roosevelt equivocated. Meeting King Abdul Aziz of Saudi Arabia on his way home from the Yalta Conference in early 1945, Roosevelt on the spur of the moment felt convinced that Zionism was mistaken. His successor, Harry Truman, hitherto uncommitted on the question, was open to pressures for and against Zionism, and he was lobbied accordingly, with changes of mind until shortly before the final recognition of Israel's statehood on May 14, 1948. Among senior American officials Sumner Welles could qualify as pro-Zionist. General Marshall, James Forrestal, the secretary of defense, and the chiefs of staff were strongly opposed to a Jewish state. American business interests, with oil companies to the fore, argued the Arab case. In the State Department, Loy Henderson, the official responsible for the Palestine question, hoped that the Jews would remain a minority in some form of binational state. George F. Kennan, head of the State Department's Planning Staff, thought that with partition, "U.S. prestige in the Muslim world has suffered a severe blow, and U.S. strategic interests in the Mediterranean and Near East have been seriously prejudiced." The newly formed Central Intelligence Agency judged that partition could not be implemented "because of Arab opposition."

In Britain, Clement Attlee had defeated Churchill in the general election of 1945. An unemotional personality, at once doctrinaire and legalist, Attlee was not impressed by Jews or Arabs and was content to leave the issue to officials. The foreign secretary, Ernest Bevin, spoke of "teaching the Jews a lesson" and other fatuities of the sort, but more seriously believed with his advisers in the truth of the either-or alternative that a Jewish victory and the consequent loss of Arab goodwill would eliminate British influences from the Middle East so that only the Soviet Union would benefit. Impatient with the Jews for being in the mess that it had done so much to create, the Foreign Office was by now helpless, and its incoherence inflamed passions, in the end bringing about the very outcomes its policies had been designed to avoid. The War Office anticipated that when it came to fighting, the Jews would lose, after which British forces could intervene to restore a status quo. In February 1947, the British in disarray decided to surrender the Mandate to the United Nations. Amid more surprise and consternation in the Foreign Office where it was erroneously and short-sightedly believed that the Soviets would prove anti-Zionist on all occasions, the Soviet Union now came out in open support of the struggle of the Jews to establish a state of their own. No doubt it was Stalin's belief—as it was that of American and British officialdom—that such a state would antagonize the Arabs and therefore weaken the West, and only the Soviet Union stood to gain.

* * *

The United Nations voted in November 1947 in favor of partition-
ing Palestine into Jewish and Arab sectors. This was the logic of
either-or, but it had a flaw: neither the will nor the mechanics
existed for a peaceful realization of partition. No sooner was the
vote passed than the Arab prime ministers met in Cairo to plan
resistance. By the following March, Fawzi al-Qawukji and Abdel-
Kader el-Husseini had infiltrated into Palestine with 5000 volunteers.
    Palestinian Arabs had been placed in a horrible predicament.
Whatever their feelings toward the Jews might be, they had no
means of expressing them; they also had no means either of rising
en masse behind popular leaders or of electing representative
delegates to argue with Jews, Western governments, or the United
Nations that they were victims of circumstances beyond their control. Haj Amin and his auxiliaries had preempted the Palestine
issue, and its Arab population had already demonstrated that it was
not willing to fight or die on his behalf. Palestinian Arabs well
understood that British soldiers before the war had to some extent
shielded them from the Jews and from Haj Amin's bands, but
would not do so now. Long before the Jews took to active campaigning, the Palestinians had been defeated in fact and in spirit.
That they risked losing something by the establishment of the
Jewish state in their midst was by then virtually certain; but that
they lost almost everything was the direct consequence of the Arab
sociopolitical system.
    Between January and March 1948, according to Jewish sources,
30,000 Arabs from Jerusalem, Jaffa, and Haifa and some villages
left the country, and these included almost all the notables and
their families from whom leadership might have been expected.
On March 30, a Palestinian newspaper reported that "The inhabitants of the large village of Sheikh Munis and of several other Arab
villages in the neighbourhood of Tel Aviv have brought a terrible
disgrace upon all of us by quitting their villages bag and baggage."
Evidently the decision whether to stay or to leave would be influenced by complex psychological reactions of fear and panic, of
the realization that one's fate was in other hands, as well as of
honor and shame. That April, the communal response clarified. In
frustrated mutual bids for supremacy in the field, Abdel-Kader
el-Husseini and Qawukji fell out; when the former requested arms
from the latter, he was told that none could be spared. El-Husseini

was killed and Qawukji driven back by the Jews. Some 250 inhabitants of the village of Deir Yassin were massacred by Jewish terrorists under the command of Menachim Begin: a tribal-religious atrocity of a kind only too familiar to Arabs. About 250,000 Palestinians had already fled before Ben-Gurion declared that the state of Israel had come into existence, and Arab armies had invaded from Egypt, Transjordan, and Syria.

For the second stage of the fighting, between May and November 1948, the Israelis were supplied with weapons delivered on Soviet instructions via Czechoslovakia. This was decisive. The Jordanian Arab Legion occupied the old city of Jerusalem and the U.N.-designated Arab sector, generally known as the West Bank, and the Egyptians held the Gaza Strip along the Mediterranean. Otherwise the Israelis overran what had been allocated to them by the U.N. and more besides. Arabs would henceforth be expected to live under Israeli rule. The loss of any part of the House of Islam to Christians was difficult enough to accept, but such a loss to Jews was inconceivable. In tribal or religious fighting, the alternative to conquest is flight. By the end of the year, out of perhaps 750,000 Arabs who had lived in the territories now Israel, only 69,000 remained, though reunification of families and boundary rectifications increased this total to 167,000 by December 1950. At once, Jewish immigrants took their place. The 1948 Jewish population of 650,000 had more than doubled by 1951. European survivors of genocide were joined by Jews from Turkey, Libya, Yemen, Iraq, and North Africa.

Had the fighting of 1948 been a straightforward conflict of interests, then the reports and commissions beforehand, as well as the armistices and attempted mediations afterward, might have had some hope of success. To this day, the frontiers of Israel are not guaranteed by treaty (with the exception of the 1977 agreement with Egypt), and therefore may be considered negotiable. At one level, it had been a local power challenge; first between Haj Amin and the Jews, then between the Jews and the power holder in the U.N.-designated Arab state, King Abdullah of Jordan, followed by his grandson King Hussein. On a more historical level, it was a tribal-religious clash comparable to the Maronite-Druze clash of 1860, the Ottoman-Armenian confrontation, or even Sunni-Shia hostility. As such, it was inherent in the Muslim political system and beyond resolution unless an outside arbiter of power had intervened. Britain, the obvious outside power, had instead withdrawn, leaving the regional political system to do its best, or its worst.

Tribal-religious boundaries are entirely dependent on conquest. In an image that should be understood as metaphorical, the Arabs have perfectly expressed the inability to define boundaries in this particular instance in the frequent accusation that Israel aims to expand "from the Nile to the Euphrates," and a map of this projected empire has often been alleged to hang in the Knesset, the Israeli parliament. Here is a perfect illustration of customary claims in feuding, whereby what is "hereditary territory" to one party is designated by the other as "expansionism." Put another way, the Israelis ever since 1948 have supposed themselves to be fighting a series of wars which must end in treaties, as wars invariably do in the Western system, but the Arabs have supposed themselves to be about to massacre challengers who happen also to be Jews, adding insult to injury, altogether jeopardizing status. One attempt at massacre may fail, another may succeed; power challenging goes on forever. In a further metaphorical image, the Arabs have captured the repetitiousness of this aspect of power challenging when they claim that they will repel the Jews as they once repelled the Crusaders.

In its assertion of Jewish separatism, the creation of Israel was a piece of business long delayed from the fall of the Ottoman Empire. Like the Greeks, the Serbs, or the Bulgars, and then the Egyptians, the Saudis, and other Arabs, the Jews seized the opportunity to declare their independence in a corner of the empire. Emigrating to Israel from their ancient communities in every Arab country, the oriental Jews proved the confessional point. Without Nazism, it is true, Israel might not have acquired the human and moral impetus necessary to realize statehood. To declare that such statehood is then wrong, inappropriate, or somehow illegitimate is also to ask to be excused from the course of history.

When it comes to interpreting Israel and its creation, the Arabs appear to be substituting wishfulness for evidence. To begin with, other tribal and religious groups have not succeeded in gaining statehood, starting with the Armenians and including the 15 million Kurds (who are Muslim but not Arab) spread between Iran and Iraq and Turkey and into the Soviet Union. National fragmentation becomes an ominous prospect if each people or religious sect is to acquire its own state: Iraq splits between Sunni and Shia and Kurds, for instance, and Syria between Sunni and Druze and Alawi. More fundamentally, the Arabs continue to react in an Islamocentric manner to the Jewish state and its Western component. Unimaginable as a spontaneous mass movement in which hundreds of thousands of people from different backgrounds have had a common political and social interest and behaved accordingly, Zionism has been conceived by the Arabs as though it were a Muslim organization, namely a conspiracy. The weak and despicable Jews could never have established a state by their own efforts; they must have been acting as agents of others, "imperialists," all the more potent because invisible and string-pulling in secret. In the light of hard facts, the actual roles of the United States and the United Nations and the Soviet Union from 1945 to the present, with their manifold reversals and hesitations, have to be forgotten or perverted. In spite of their widely differing background and national experiences, moreover, the Arabs cling with complete uniformity to this unhistoric view of Israel. The more they recite it, the more they repeat their self-defeating political strategy in handling Israel at ever-greater costs to themselves. To date, no Arab anywhere has publicly submitted the Islamocentric interpretation of Israel to scrutiny for the damage that it does to the Arabs. This failure goes to the heart of the dispute. Put another way, Arab sociopolitical culture makes such absolute demands that nobody dares go against them, even in so essential a matter as objective history, without which formulation of policy must be erratic, incoherent, or worse.

Musa Alami, a Jerusalem notable and once Haj Amin's propaganda expert, published in 1949 "The Lesson of Palestine," which tried to explain the catastrophe that had just befallen the Palestinians. The Arabs, he wrote, had had the opportunity to finish with Zionism and its dangers altogether but had failed to take it. The fault lay with the British and other foreigners. Even so, "The Jews were better organised than we were." The Arabs needed to modernize, to introduce a constitutional regime based "on really scientific foundations." If not, they risked becoming "backward human creatures, without honour or spirit." Progress was not for its own sake but had the object of facing the Jewish challenge more appropriately: "Force can only be repelled by force."

At the time, Constantin Zurayk of the American University of Beirut and later president of the Syrian University in Damascus, published *The Meaning of the Disaster,* another analysis of the 1948 developments. He concurred with Musa Alami. Westerners were to blame for what had happened, but there were Arab weaknesses and decay as well. "The Jews are living in the present and the future, while we still dream of the past." Arab society lacked unity; it would have to change, and then it could restore the balance. Although neither writer was very explicit about it, both had grasped that the difference in the organizing principles of the two warring parties fully accounted for Jewish superiority against all odds. How far that lesson sunk in remains questionable. Stereotypes quickly came to hand. Muhammad Kurd Ali in his memoirs quoted with approval a letter he had received from an Arab orientalist in 1949. For 2000 years, this correspondent wrote, the Jews had spread like lice on a healthy body. "In our day they control gold and finance in America. In our own country and in Russia they head many of the public works. . . . Everyone knows the Jew is corrupt and venomous." Al-Hajj Muhammad, the Moroccan street-trader, still speaks for millions of Arabs today when he says, "Whenever I work for a Christian or a Jew, I feel dirty and I go to the *hammam* [public bath]." He adds, "There is nothing worse than the Jews. The Jew is only happy when he has cheated a Muslim."

To Arabs fantasizing along these lines, Israel appears a monstrosity, a cheat, an injection by foreign hands of evil into Arab purity. At heart, this fantasy is inherent in the regional culture of tribe and religion. As though in a feud, there is here an apologia for unacceptable defeat, as well as exhortation to obligatory revenge. The otherness of Jews, as tribe and as religion, is projected so as to place it beyond any incorporation into the social order. That otherness swells into obsession, a sense of unfair victimization by powers or forces too dark to be defined, let alone grappled with. In the forty years of Israel's existence, conspiracy theories have become generalized. Arabs have taken it as axiomatic that Israel was created to serve British interests, and yet, inconsistently, that it is now nothing but an arm of the U.S. As Haj Amin put it, "No one ever thought that 140 million Americans would become tools in Jewish hands." The Saudis alone differ, in recalling the Soviet role and supposing Israel still to be serving Bolshevik purposes. King Feisal, it appears, believed that Party Secretary Leonid Brezhnev was a Jew, though he was unable to adduce what difference that might have made, were it even true. In January 1984, a Saudi newspaper marshaled the conspiracy in this form:

The idea of communism began with the Jew, Karl Marx. The Red Revolution in Russia was begun by the Jews. The communist attack in the Middle East was launched by the Jews who came to Syria, Lebanon, Palestine, and Egypt, in order to propagate communism. . . . We know well that communism and Zionism are two sides of the same coin. From the establishment of Israel up to the present, only the USSR has derived benefit from it.

A chapter of Nasser's Egyptian National Charter ran:

Imperialist intrigue went to the extent of seizing a part of the Arab territory of Palestine, in the heart of the Arab Motherland, and usurping it without any justification of right or law, the aim being to establish a military fascist regime, which cannot live except by military threats. The real danger is the tool of imperialism.

The 1963 Treaty of Unity (actually abortive) between Egypt, Syria, and Iraq, proclaimed:

It was the disaster of Palestine that uncovered the design of the reactionary strata and revealed the shame of the treachery of the anti-national parties, which are foreign agents, and their indifference to the people's aims and aspirations. It was this disaster that demonstrated the weakness and backwardness of the economic and social regimes that reigned in the land then; it was it that liberated the revolutionary energy of the masses of our people and aroused the spirit of revolt against exploiting Imperialism, poverty and backwardness.

Received Arab opinion has been concisely summed up by Saddam Hussein, president of Iraq, "Imperialism uses Zionism as a strategic arm against Arab unity, progress and development. This is a well-known fact." Even a professor like the Moroccan Abdallah Laroui, a Marxist and therefore alert to historical cause and effect, can be found giving credence to such an interpretation. "The bare fact, impossible to deny, is that Israel by its very existence has checked the Arabs' progress and has been one of the determining causes in the process of continuing traditionalization. All liberal, secularizing, and progressive thought appeared as a ruse of Zionist and imperialist propaganda." What liberal and progressive thought did he have in mind? Arabs everywhere have been calling for modernization in order to be better able to resist Israel, so where is the evidence that the existence of Israel has the effect of perpetuating traditionalism? It seems that education in Paris and exposure to Marxism could not displace even an intellectual like Abdallah Laroui from this belief system.

"Tous contre Israel," or All Against Israel, was the call to action in the unadulterated tribal-religious form, uttered by the former Algerian president Ben Bella in 1982. Israel consists of some four million people on little more than 10,000 square miles. How does this infinitesimal part of the Middle East come to resist 180 million Arabs in twenty-one states with far superior resources?

The forces which the Zionists control in all parts of the world [wrote Zurayk] can, if they are permitted to take root in Palestine, threaten the independence of all the Arab lands and form a continuing and frightening danger to their life. The facilities that the Zionist forces have for growth and expansion will place the Arab world forever at their mercy and will paralyze its vitality and deter its progress and evolution in the ladders of advancement and civilization—that is, if this Arab world is permitted to exist at all.

An Egyptian public figure, Muhammad Ali Aluba, could declare, "Zionism aspires to destroy all states and peoples and conspires to dominate the whole world." Throughout the Arab world, it is a commonplace to fantasize and pervert the true relationship in which Jews stood to Nazi Germany, so much so that one Moroccan writer could even assert in 1982 that "Nazism is a creation of Zionism."

To take such sad and ugly exaggeration and hyperbole at face value is to reach the unreasonable conclusion that Arabs, from presidents and scholars to the man on the street, are unable to deal objectively with historical evidence. Privately, many of these same Arabs will speak with knowledge and insight about Israel and its place in the world, and they will concede that Israel, like every country, has qualities both good and bad, and its share of successes and failures, yet not a single Arab has said this in public; opinions offered in private are circumstantial, of course, and carry no commitment. Hundreds of books and thousands of articles and speeches have been published by Arabs on Israel, but none qualify as a contribution to dispassionate study; on the contrary, they mystify and denature the subject. When it comes to public statements, the Arabs have to cover up the shame-honor response released through the loss of Palestine.

Y. Harkabi has collated this set of attitudes toward Israel, and he explains, "The allegation of a bond between imperialism and Israel fulfils the psychological function of protecting the self-respect of the Arabs." The loss of Palestine, in sum, was a public revelation that the Arabs were defeated by the Jews whom they were known to hold in contempt. Resorting to war, and losing, the Arabs were hurt in their self-esteem as warriors, an essential component of the Arab perception of themselves. In their own terms, the Arabs felt at the receiving end of mockery from Jews and Christians; they could not see 1948 as a tragedy for everyone involved and could not imagine that others visualized it thus. Moreover, the whole world had watched, the whole world had the information and was thus co-opted into the response. "Zionism as imperialism" is the metaphor for preserving honor in the face of the world. To have been defeated by Jews is humiliating, but to have been defeated by a conspiracy of all the powers is clearly unavoidable. Reaching Jordan after the 1948 flight, a Palestinian refugee from the village of Saffouriyeh told a sociology researcher, "In 24 hours we were changed from dignity to humiliation." However far away from the experience of Palestine, every Arab was conditioned by his culture to this reaction.

From the moment when Israel could no longer be extricated from the Arab response of shame, Arab self-interest and rationality were forfeit. If honor might be recovered, then any deed or thought was licensed for that purpose, no matter how vicious or suicidal. Shame-honor obliges Arabs to resort to daily subterfuges and pretenses which are exclusions of reality and therefore harmful to themselves. Israel does not appear in Arab maps or reference books; newspapers and even encyclopedias are censured or disfigured if they contain references to it. Arabs will decline to appear with Israelis on television debates or other public platforms. Arab states attempt to maintain a trade boycott with countries or individual companies whose activities are perceived to be aiding the Israeli economy. Arab newspaper cartoons depict Israel and Israelis in the range of anti-Semitic caricatures. Harkabi lists some epithets and insults that aim to keep the tribal-religious distance and defuse shame:

The Zionist monster; the pollution of Zionism; the Zionist plague; the enemy of the peoples; the ally of the murderers; the occupation authorities; the purulent abscess; the illegitimate daughter of Europe; the Zionist cancer; a cancer in the heart of the Arab nation, or in the Middle East; Israel the bleeding thorn; the gang of hypocrites and criminals; the focus of evil; dirt, filth, sewage; the viper State; octopus; spider; the bacillus of evil; claw of a cat; parasite.

In the shame-honor response is the a priori assumption that Arabs are indeed "backward human creatures, without honour and spirit," and that is without doubt its most damaging feature. "Deep in the soul," as Lutfi al-Sayyid put it for the Egyptians, is the sense of inferiority brought on by the events of 1948, requiring the elaborate superstructure of deception and lying in order to conceal the condition. The greater the sense of shame, the more violent the reaction. One of its saddest and most unfair by-products has been the treatment of Palestinians in the Arab countries to which they have scattered. Far from receiving the sympathy due to innocent victims and refugees, the Palestinians have been considered cowards and troublemakers, people who ran away from their homes and brought shame upon themselves and who have therefore shamed all other Arabs.

Profoundly, shame-honor has blocked acceptance of the historic process whereby Jews surviving Nazism turned to Israel for rescue. Shame-honor has prevented the formulation of a rational approach to foreign policy; how to calculate the actual balance of forces in order to be able to take political advantage of Israeli weakness or isolation; how best to advance the Arab case and so to salvage what remains of Palestine. Shame-honor dictates revenge, not compromise. Loss of territory is secondary to loss of honor. No process of negotiation can recover honor, therefore territory has to be relinquished. Without shame-honor, an Arab state of Palestine would have come into existence in 1948, in accordance with the U.N. resolution and sparing further unnecessary and illogical losses. The second and third rounds of fighting, in 1956 and 1967, were triggered by impulses of shame that had become uncontrollable, amid vainglorious boastings of imminent and wholesale massacre of Jews. The fourth round of fighting, in 1973, was prepared in well-laid conspiracy, with the same purpose of avenging humiliation. To the extent that it succeeded, Egyptian honor was restored, and the feuding could cease, and the Camp David agreements be reached between equals.

Seeking to recover honor through war, the Arabs have obliged Israel to become a formidable military power, thus actualizing in a very real army the fears and dreads of their fantasies. Israel in 1984 had an estimated defense expenditure of $5.8 billion, against a gross domestic product of $23 billion (and a foreign debt of $30 billion). Israel has its own armaments industry, exports weapons, and has started manufacturing fighter aircraft. No Arab country has a comparable military-industrial base, though of course Arab resources and foreign military aid provide them in combination with a large numerical advantage in every branch of manpower and weaponry.

Arms and the arms industry are only the technical implements of Israel's survival. What preserves the country and gives it identity is its fully institutionalized pluralism: its soldiers are willing conscripts into a citizens' army. Jews have immigrated from over a hundred countries, bringing with them the widest spectrum of cultural and social attitudes. To deal with this diversity, prestate Zionist organizations transformed naturally into state institutions of a participatory nature, from political parties to the trade union movement and the army. Elections to the Knesset were held on the proportional representation system in force for selecting delegates to the Zionist congresses, and between 1949 and 1987 there have been eleven parliaments. The profusion of parties, some of them with a single parliamentary member, makes for democratic vitality on the one hand and weakness of central government on the other. In the absence of a government likely to be able to command a substantial majority, the conflicting wishes and interests of all sections of the community must be taken into close account.

How the Israelis chose to institutionalize themselves was in a sense no business of the Arabs; the state of Israel could be considered as a reconstitution on a national scale of the old reserved city quarter of the Jews, to which Arabs were immemorially accustomed. Between 1948 and 1967, Israel developed in what was more or less tribal-religious isolation and so was able to put into practice the communal, not to say visionary, ideals of Herzl and the more socialist-minded Zionist founding fathers. The 1967 war put a stop to that period of autonomous construction. In brief but traumatic fighting, the Jordanians evacuated the West Bank, and the Egyptians the Gaza Strip. Once more, the whole of Mandated Palestine, with about 800,000 Arabs, was abruptly and unpredictably reunited, this time under Israeli control. What this implied for the 1947 U.N. vote for partition remained to be seen.

Since the ruin of their society, the Palestinians had been living at the mercy of power holders and of any careerist challengers who might appear. Haj Amin had tried to form a government in exile in 1948, but the Nashashibis and other notables had sought the sponsorship of King Abdullah of Jordan. A willing King Abdullah incorporated the West Bank into his kingdom—and that remains its legal status today. Defeated at last, Haj Amin took the usual revenge by ordering the assassination of King Abdullah in 1951. Eleven years later, Haj Amin died in Beirut. Succeeding his grandfather as King of Jordan, Hussein has ruled over a country now of some two and a half million people, approximately half of them Palestinian, including refugees from 1948 and then from 1967 who have been automatically granted Jordanian citizenship. In the circumstances, Syria and Egypt both decided to sponsor Palestinian careerist challengers, and out of these moves developed the Palestinian Liberation Organization, by 1969 under the leadership of Yasser Arafat.

Whether the PLO or King Hussein commanded the allegiance of the Palestinians, or was entitled to speak for them, has never been settled. An exhausting rivalry has lasted from 1967 until the present between King Hussein and the PLO for authority over the Palestinians. Both of them, acting sometimes in concert, but more usually in antagonism, have extended this power challenge to Israel, which through the fortunes of war has become the actual power holder over Palestinians in the West Bank and Gaza. Through natural increase and schemes for the reunification of families, these numbered 1.34 million at the end of 1985 in the latest figures officially published. Expressed differently, Israel has been defined strictly in tribal-religious terms and drawn against its will, and in defiance of its belief system, into the sociopolitical order of the Arabs.

Theoretically, Israel is in the position of the Mandate authorities in their day and could institutionalize the Palestinians under its control. By way of an encouraging precedent, it has the Israeli Arabs, third-generation descendants of those who remained in the country, now numbering some 700,000. These Israeli Arabs are enfranchised; they share in the rights and duties of all citizens, with the qualification that they are exempt from military service (Druze and Bedouin, however, choose to volunteer). Arabs are members of the Knesset, occupy posts in the bureaucracy including the diplomatic service, publish in Arabic and Hebrew and appear on television, have won prestigious awards and prizes, altogether offering an example of the assimilation of a Muslim minority into a non-Muslim democracy.

In order to institutionalize the remaining Palestinians, however, Israel must first have title to do so, and then the will. Again in theory, it might be possible for Israel to annex the West Bank and Gaza, incorporate these areas, and extend the vote to the inhabitants on equal terms with everyone else in the state. In reality, Israel is not a Mandatory power, and the unilateral action would no doubt be repudiated by every government and international agency. In the event of annexation, moreover, or any political incorporation, the resulting size of the Arab minority would negate the Zionist ideal of a state to redeem the Jews. According to demographic projections from present birthrates, the Arabs would become a majority within a stated period, early in the next century, if not before. Considered a temporary measure at its inception in 1967, Israeli military rule continues to apply *faute de mieux* to the West Bankers, who are Jordanian citizens, and to the Gazans, who are stateless as the law now stands. Municipal elections, which have been held on the West Bank under Jordanian law and Israeli supervision, are not genuine popular expressions of opinion. The franchise is limited, and candidates independent either of Israeli or PLO approval do not dare stand.

So far, all attempts to break the triangular power challenge between Israel, Jordan, and the PLO have been frustrated. Whatever its democratic principles and institutions, Israel has been obliged by this improbable lock to behave like any other Middle Eastern power holder, with divisive social results. On occasion, the security forces and the army have been guilty of arbitrary abuse of power, and there have been attempts to pervert the course of justice in dealing with such incidents. The invasion of Lebanon in 1982 was a glaring example of power challenging as practiced in the Arab system. As though conspiring, the government of Menachim Begin and Ariel Sharon neither consulted the electorate about waging war, nor revealed secret intentions until it was too late for public opinion to change them. During the fighting, several hundred Palestinians were massacred in the Beirut neighborhoods of Shatila and Sabra. Maronite militiamen were responsible for this characteristic confessional atrocity, but it was shown beyond doubt by the Kahane Commission, set up in Israel to inquire into these events, that senior Israeli commanders had been aware of what might happen and so are guilty through connivance or indifference.

To the Westerner, Israel seems in such a case to be enmeshed in geopolitical factors that endanger the whole polity by surrendering to inimical values. To the Arabs, it is historically an exceptional but still recognizable feature of the tribal-religious pattern that Jews should wish to be acting in their own interest, however destructively and even hatefully. Power-asserting behavior such as the invasion of Lebanon in order to destroy the PLO challenge therefore has the contrary and paradoxical effect of revealing that Israel has its own motivation for its actions and is not merely some tool of "imperialist" conspiracy, and so to a certain extent humanizes the Jews. Israel has the strange fate of being the first and only indigenous society in the Middle East to test whether democratic constitutionalism can take root within the all-embracing and ever-flourishing Arab sociopolitical order; and if so, then further testing what the consequences will be for that Arab order.

9

The Impact of Communism

At the close of the Second World War, the British were operating nineteen airfields in the Middle East and maintaining bases at Aden, Bahrain, Malta, and Cyprus, as well as Suez, where a gigantic enclave complete with training area extended almost to Cairo. If the purpose of this presence was the prolongation of the former imperial order, then not much thinking about means and ends had been done. As after the First World War, the British were largely unprepared to deal with Arab demands which they themselves had fostered. The collapse of France in 1940, and the narrow margin by which Britain had survived the blitzkrieg years, had also enabled the Arabs, like everyone else, to predict that these European powers might well no longer have the title to act as final arbiters in Arab affairs.

A number of wartime declarations of promissory intent had once again encouraged Arabs into suppositions about their own strength and European weakness. Not since 1919, then, had there been such prospects for unbridled power challenging among Arabs. A British guarantee had been given for the future independence of the French Mandates of Syria and Lebanon. In May 1941, Anthony Eden, then foreign secretary, promised that Britain would approve and support "any scheme that commands general support" for strengthening ties between Arab countries, whether cultural or economic or political. A year later, he repeated no less publicly that the Arabs were "our friends" and could count on the British supporting their unity. In October 1944, representatives from Egypt, Iraq, Syria, Lebanon, Transjordan, Saudi Arabia, and Yemen met to sign the protocol for just such a form of unity, to be called the League of Arab States. Among its terms was one forbidding the use of force in settling disputes between member states.

In the light of experience, British officials knew that no effective representative institutions of any kind had evolved in any Arab country. How was this Arab League suddenly to be different, a forum in which conflicting interests could be peaceably mediated by agreed procedures of which these countries had not a trace? For the Arab League to succeed, power challenging would have to cease. Although the League in fact continues to exist and has even spawned various sub-bureaucracies, it was still-born from the inception. Far from being the fulfilment of a dream, according to the nationalist historians Nabih Amin Faris and Mohammed Tawfik Husayn, already by 1953 it had become "in the eyes of intelligent Arabs a laughing stock and a farce," or in the words of Khalid Kishtainy, "all that is worst in the Arab World," at best simply another careerist opportunity. These harsh judgments are also Eurocentric. The League was another creation in the most fertile style of power challenging. A device had been improvised for the sake of earning European approval and distributing money and rewards among new officials.

Unity, however heedlessly promoted by the British, was intended as an alternative to Arab nationalism, that bogey with which the British so alarmed themselves. It was vaguely imagined that the Arabs all together might somehow evolve some common aim at least different from the rivalries they pursued individually, and more constructive. Arab nationalism was not seen for the power-challenging call that it was but misconceived as akin to any European nationalism, as a matter of political parties genuinely representing and articulating popular opinions. Should a leader be displaced, in this view, he would be succeeded by another much like him. In fact, each nationalist leader was unique and irreplaceable, mobilizing support around himself and his interests. Eden's reference to "general support" reveals ignorance about leadership as it evolves through power challenging in the Arab tribal-religious collectivity. The element of truth in postwar British perceptions was that more Arabs than previously had begun to realize how they were excluded from political and social life and were tending to shift the blame for this away from their own rulers and on to

Europeans. If traditional despotism were to persist, then the Arabs had their own candidates for the role and were in no need of lessons. If the Europeans still would not provide more reasonable political and social institutions of the type which gave them their strength at home, then they were superfluous, devious, or worse. Leaders advocating nationalism had restricted themselves to the one-dimensional platform of evicting the Europeans. In the well-established mold of Mustafa Kamil, Saad Zaghlul and Dr. Shahbandar, aspiring leaders did not discuss what social and political institutions they might consider appropriate in the event of independence. One and all incited nationalism and then exploited it as the surest way of arousing the mob on their behalf, frightening the authorities, demoralizing the Europeans, and so levering themselves as their successors into the position of supreme power holders. What would actually happen in the event of their seizing the state, they left undefined.

Arab power challengers basing themselves upon nationalism placed European administrations in an unpleasant predicament. It was readily conceded that the Arabs ought to have social and political institutions of their own, and it was further assumed that these institutions should be representative, more or less on European lines. Failure to have evolved in this direction had done much to erode European self-confidence. Playing upon this guilt, nationalist leaders could arouse demonstrations, mob violence, terrorism, to which the only possible response was force. The reluctance of the Europeans as power holders to use force speaks well of them humanly; but there was no way around the fact that the implicit suggestion of weakness only invited further challenging.

In 1945 the French attempted to keep troops in Syria. Fighting broke out until the British intervened, obliging the French to withdraw as they had from Lebanon, and provoking from Georges Bidault, then the French foreign minister, the sibyline warning, *"Hodie mihi, cras tibi"* (me today, you tomorrow). Syria did indeed become an independent republic, with the veteran nationalist Shukri al-Quwatli as president. At the same time, the British accorded independence to King Abdullah in Jordan.

One writer, Patrick Seale, who is an uncritical advocate of Syria and its ambitions, has described the parliamentarians assembling in Damascus in 1947:

Men whom nothing united, sharing no principles, bound by no party organisation, elected to parliament by some mysterious travesty of free and unhampered elections; some were illiterate, others distinguished men of letters; some spoke only Kurdish or Armenian, others only Turkish; some wore a *tarbush*, others a *kafiyeh* [Arab head-dress]; townsmen and bedouin. It was all play-acting.

It was only a matter of time before Quwatli tried unconstitutionally to extend his powers. If he could, so could others. The first coup followed in 1949, initiating a chain of putsches by military officers, which lasted until Hafiz Assad in 1970 proved to have the ruthlessness required for an extended period of despotism.

If Lebanon, Syria, and Jordan (with the exception of a few British army officers on secondment) were unencumbered by a European presence, then challengers elsewhere had the logical argument that military bases must go, as in Egypt and Iraq, and the colonial presence must be finally dismantled, as in North Africa and the Gulf. So it proved. Nasser, capturing power in 1952, negotiated the evacuation of the Suez Canal Zone. Qassem, capturing power in Iraq in 1958, put an end to the British presence there. Once the Algerian war was concluded, and the withdrawal from Aden completed in 1967, nothing but an architectural and civil engineering infrastructure remained as evidence that the British and French had ever incorporated the Arab Middle East within their empires.

Postwar Saudi Arabia, Oman, and the Gulf States continued as the family-based autocracies they had previously been, but every other Arab country, regardless of its colonial and modernizing experience, settled between 1949 and 1970 with startling speed and uniformity into a virtually undifferentiated despotism. Lebanon, the apparent exception, since 1975 has been the arena for a conflicting number of petty despotisms of a family or tribal-religious nature. This complete suppression of popular participation in government no doubt was in accordance with historic Arab norms, but it was also a response to the emergence of the United States and the Soviet Union as the two victorious super powers of the Second World War. This new and overriding balance of forces finally adjusted or arbitrated the relationship of the Arabs to the British and French.

The United States was an unknown quantity to the Arabs, a faraway continent culturally hard to comprehend. In 1947, a single book by an Egyptian existed in Arabic to describe the American political and social system, and to this day little accurate reporting from that country reaches the Arab public. The concept of "life, liberty, and the pursuit of happiness" as legitimate ends of government has no correspondence in the Arab outlook and is almost unimaginable. The key phrase in the Declaration of Independence that all men are equal before "the Laws of Nature and of Nature's God" cannot be translated into Islamic terms but instead conveys blasphemy and heresy. The very few and quite exceptional Arabs who had actually traveled to America were often lonely there, bemused and in two minds about their experiences. One such was Sayyid Qutb, who had been born in Egypt in 1906 and received first a religious and then a modernist education before starting his career in the ministry of public instruction. From 1948 to 1951 he was in America on a scholarship to study its educational system. What he saw of America, its morals, and especially the free conduct of its women, so shocked him that he wrote a book in denunciation of what he took for paganism. Resigning from the civil service, he became the most persuasive publicist for the Muslim Brothers. Only in Saudi Arabia were Americans familiar, as oil company technicians exploiting concessions dating back to 1933.

The Soviet Union, in contrast, has been an imperial power ever since the first Russian conquests and absorption of the Muslim peoples of Asia, and in this century it has cast an ever-approaching shadow over the Sunni provinces of Turkey and the Shia provinces of Iran. In the name of confessionalism, imperial Russia had also appealed to the Orthodox Christian minority. As early as 1910, for example, a Syrian Orthodox Christian who had returned from a course at Moscow University to his hometown of Homs could greet a Russian diplomatic representative there with these words:

> Only when Russian trade spreads throughout Syria will Russian be a useful language. Then Russian will be living and vital in the sense intended by the Arab population. That will be a day of triumph for the Russian schools, for Russian science and culture in Syria and all Turkey. Such are the real results desired by every Russian—Russian by blood or in soul. . . . Let our ill-wishers know that in Russia, which we love for ever, exists a culture which is not inferior to that of Europe, that the future belongs to the great Russian people.

This graduate was expressing an undoubted perception that the Russians and the Arabs had much in common by way of historical and political evolution. The prince of Kiev who founded the

Russian nation in the tenth century is said to have rejected Islam only on account of its prohibition of alcohol. Russia adopted Christianity much as the Turks had adopted Islam and used it similarly to establish and justify despotism. In common with the Turks and the Arabs, the Russians did not experience the Renaissance or the Age of Enlightenment and therefore had no tradition of humanism or respect for the individual, nothing to refine its collectivist culture. Like any Islamic power holder, Peter the Great had not scrupled to use any available means, including murder, to impose upon his people the modernization and militarization which he on his own deemed necessary.

The post-1917 Soviet Union was a despotism immediately recognizable to the Muslim world. Lenin was a consummate example of the careerist conspirator. Capturing the state, he had proceeded to arrange it to suit himself in the manner of any Arab careerist. Law and institutions were decreed through the Communist Party, which was therefore simply the transmission belt for orders from the power holder to the masses below. To claim that the power holder and the Party represented "the will of the people" when actually the people were wholly and forever excluded from participation in decision making was an abuse of fact and of language that conformed to Arab nationalist politics. In the absence of popular participation, the Party bureaucracy acquired a grip on daily life down to the smallest details, with the corresponding growth of a pervasive money-favor nexus of bribery and corruption in order to get anything done. Like Arabs, the Soviet people live in an atmosphere of deliberately contrived unreality and lying, in that the daily practices necessary for survival in no way match the leadership's descriptions and value judgments of them. In both collectivities, transactions among people carry the danger of exposing this mendacious gap, with a constant awareness that the careless or foolhardy are certain to be punished. In the Communist system, individual leaders may be compelled to admit to "mistakes," but the Party can never be wrong; and this in turn acquires an intractability akin to shame-honor. Differences of opinion in both systems therefore become life-and-death matters, with critics blackguarded as "traitors," "agents," and "spies" who have to be eliminated. "Who whom?" in Lenin's brilliantly concise but bloodily ominous phrase reduces to its essential the political terrorism of the Communist system. Who kills whom is also the element of ultimate decision in Arab politics. Succession of power in both systems is always a flashpoint, conducive to conspiracy, and then to armed confrontation of power holder and challenger.

Careerist struggle, however, is not class struggle. Ideology crucially distinguishes the Soviet system from the Arab. Arab power challengers want power for its own sake, for aggrandizement and reward. It seems improbable that any Soviet leaders after Lenin have conscientiously believed in Marxism-Leninism, but nonetheless all have professed this doctrine as a set of historically determined rules whereby those who are "progressive" have the destiny, and therefore the right, to rule over others who are "backward," according to conveniently self-justifying definitions. In the event that Soviet Marxism-Leninism were ever to be applied to them, the Arabs would discover that they are numbered among the unprogressive and backward and can do nothing about it, any more than they could have changed their race for Hitler. Within the Soviet Union, Islam is viewed with unremitting hostility as another "opiate of the people" conditioning this backwardness. The 24,000 working mosques which existed in 1913 have now been reduced to about 300, and Islamic law courts, charitable trusts, and almost all religious schools have been closed since 1928.

Communism, then, has an inbuilt contempt for Muslims, much as Nazism once had. A man of racial prejudices, Stalin in his day moved cautiously. Soviet embassies were opened in 1943 in Cairo, Beirut, and Baghdad. With the example of Hitler as a guide, Stalin no less perversely deployed the Jewish question to introduce Soviet imperialism into the Middle East. Between 1948 and 1953, Stalin proclaimed that Israel was progressive and that the Arabs were backward on two counts, first in their own social forms, and secondly as plain accomplices of the West.

That the Soviets might very well switch this policy and seek a common cause with the Arabs by exploiting anti-Western or "imperialist" arguments was perceived by some British officials—as in this minute of 1946 by a Foreign Office diplomat.

The trouble with the Arab League is that the Russians are to a great extent right. It *is* run at present by a lot of reactionary Pashas and Effendis, and it will never really develop into the progressive, educative and cultural force which it should unless an alliance is made between the Rulers and the rising generation. If we do not fairly quickly promote such an alliance and do not so put ourselves on the side of 'the common man' in the Middle East the Russians will take the lead, and we shall be saddled with a group of old men with cast iron ideas and will go down to defeat with them.

As it happened, the 1945 election in Britain had returned the socialist government of Clement Attlee, and the view was taken that the British position in the Middle East depended in future upon concession and collaboration with "the rising generation," a Eurocentric phrase that had hardly more meaning in the context than "the common man." In the words of Professor William Roger Louis, "The accommodation of moderate nationalism in order to prevent political extremism was the axiom of the Labour government." Like Eden before them, Attlee and his Foreign Secretary Ernest Bevin did not comprehend that if the British refused to use their position as arbiter in the power-challenge dialectic, not only did they forfeit justification for being in the Middle East but they also made their own replacement by a more willing arbiter a foregone conclusion. Through ignorance and sentimentality, British policy actually facilitated Soviet penetration.

These Are the Chains is the title of a book published in 1946 by Abdallah Ali al-Qasimi, originally from Saudi Arabia but living in Egypt, one of several intellectuals who perceived the urgency of modernizing reforms. "Ignorance based on religious doctrine has tied our people with knot on knot," he wrote, and this led to "cultural immobility" which had to be shaken off. The eminent novelist Neguib Mahfouz published *Midaq Alley* in 1947 in which a character is made to exclaim, "What hopeless wretches we are. Our country is pitiful and so are the people." This character goes on to give a glimpse of the submerged national ideal of lost honor and how it might be recovered: "Just imagine what it would be like to be a heroic soldier, plunging from one glorious victory to the next. Imagine being in airplanes and tanks attacking and killing and then capturing the fleeing women."

King Farouk, the actual postwar power holder in Egypt, was indeed pitiful. Born in 1920, he had spent seven months as an officer cadet in England but was temperamentally unsuited to such a discipline. Succeeding to the throne just before he was eighteen, he had entertained characteristic ambitions of becoming leader of all the Arab states and even the caliph of the Muslims. Wartime intrigues with the Nazis had sapped his position and left him at the mercy of particularly venal courtiers and toadies. In 1950 he had been the first postwar Arab ruler to tour Europe, where the royal debaucheries and extravagances, or "melancholy hedonism" in the phrase of one biographer, were mockingly publicized. At home, he maintained his assassination squad (including, it appears, Anwar Sadat) to eliminate enemies, but the will indispensable to his survival had been dissipated. Obese, cunning rather than intelligent, not without humor ("May the British go—but not too far," he is reported to have said), he was surprised on July 23, 1952, to be the victim of a military coup. His life was spared. Rushed to his yacht in Alexandria, he was another—and this time the last—in the line of Muhammad Ali to go into exile. General Neguib, the coup's temporary and nominal leader before Gamal Abdel Nasser declared himself as the real power holder, has recorded that Farouk seemed to have sensed that this ending might have been in store. On the pier before the yacht's departure, Neguib writes, "We were both gripped by a mixture of emotions that brought us close to tears."

No Communist, no Fidel Castro, Nasser at the outset had no clear political perception except that he wanted power. A classic careerist and manipulator, a master of the power-challenge dialectic, he learned quickly how to exploit American-Soviet rivalry and put it to his own ends. By the simple expedient of rejecting the accusation of backwardness and labeling himself progressive and an enemy of the West, he recruited to his cause the Soviet Union and a United States anxious to appease and placate this unknown quantity, proving in the end the ideal instrument for switching much of what had been the British and French colonial Arab world over into the Soviet sphere of influence.

In a little book called *Egypt's Liberation, the philosophy of the revolution,* which he published (and may even have had a hand in writing) in 1955, occurs this suggestive and even wistful passage, which has been much quoted:

I do not know why I always imagine that in this region in which we live there is a role wandering about seeking an author to play it. I do not know why this role, tired of roaming about in this vast region which extends to every place around us, should at last settle down, weary and worn out, on our frontiers beckoning us to move, to dress up for it, and to perform it since there is nobody else who can do it.

The tempting open-ended vista of power challenging could hardly be better described. The role fitted. Arbitrary cruelty was no novelty in Arab history, but to Nasser goes the grisly credit for being the first Arab to have created a police state, complete with arrests at dawn, tribunals to pass predetermined sentences, concentration camps and the secret police, and the whole grim and bloody apparatus of control through bureaucratic terror. That Soviet doctrine and totalitarian practice offered a far more implacable threat to the Arabs than any previous cultural or political concept coming from the West was something Nasser ignored or denied. His Soviet hybrid of a state arose more through personal emotion than calculation.

Born in Alexandria in 1918, Nasser was an ordinary Egyptian in the sense that his father had been a postal clerk and his maternal grandfather a contractor and coal merchant. Sent to school in Cairo, he was only eight when his mother died, and his father then remarried. It has been suggested that this childhood may account for the mistrust in other people which he habitually displayed, a personal style of wary loneliness. Reading Afghani, Abdu, Shakib Arslan, and admiring Ataturk, he absorbed in his youth what was the common stock of ideas about the Arab order and its place in the world. Using the influence of a notable by the name of Ibrahim Khairy Pasha, he had himself sponsored as a cadet in the Cairo Military Academy between 1935 and 1938. At the time, he was an active member of the fascistic Green Shirts, drawing from them his obsession with military measures to overthrow the regime. In 1944 he married, and four years later, as a major, he participated in the fighting in Palestine.

From then on, he devoted himself exclusively to conspiracy. In *Egypt's Liberation,* he gives an artless but vivid account of the hold that conspiracy had acquired over him.

The second World War and the short period before it fired the spirit of our youth, and moved our whole generation towards violence. I confess—and I trust the Public Prosecutor will not take me to task—that to my excited imagination at that time political assassination appeared to be the positive action we had to adopt if we were to rescue the future of our country. I considered the assassination of many individuals, having decided they were the main obstacles which lay between our beloved country and its destined greatness. I began to study their crimes and to take it upon myself to judge the harmfulness of their actions.

Life at the time was "like a thrilling detective story. We had dark secrets and passwords. We lurked in the shadows; we had caches of pistols and hand-grenades, and firing bullets was our cherished hope."

He goes on to describe how he was involved in an assassination attempt, but to his relief it failed, leaving him lying on his bed dreaming of revolution but hearing within himself "echoes of crying and weeping" from the man he had just tried to murder. Carefully he recruited Abdel Hakim Amer, a contemporary at the Military Academy, and others known collectively as the Free Officers, whom he had detected to be discontented and power seeking like himself. One of them, Khalid Mohieddine, gave a journalist a typical description of an undercover rendezvous with Nasser in a room surrounded by books on the third floor of a safe house, where the two men sounded each other out. Later, at a boxing match, Nasser confided that they "had things to discuss," and Mohieddine clinched his own enrollment with the judgment that Nasser "was a proud man, aware of his own dignity and respecting it in others." At the same time, Nasser was recruiting into his conspiratorial coalition the Muslim Brothers and the Communists, and of course the figurehead of General Neguib, a respected senior commander.

According to normal power-challenge practice, Nasser followed the success of the coup by destroying the previous regime, and almost simultaneously the coalition which had brought him where he was but which now threatened him. About five weeks after the coup, two dozen politicians were arrested, due for "purification" before new tribunals. Before these tribunals were to come former notables, senior officials, landowners, industrialists, and businessmen. Five hundred army officers were purged. A law of September 9, 1952, abolished political parties simply by placing them under the control of the army. Peasants were driven in lorries to Cairo, to march and shout in orchestration, "No parties and no parliament; do not abdicate, Gamal; no partisanship and no elections." That December the constitution was abolished, and the republic was proclaimed six months later. An enabling decree then made the power holder's acts sovereign and unaccountable. This was the end of civilian rule. Relying on his friend Abdul Hakim Amer and other Free Officers of proven loyalty, Nasser was now a military despot, with the army as his prime political and social instrument.

The Communists were the first element of the conspiratorial coalition to protest that they were being excluded rather than rewarded as they had expected. Nasser moved against them in January 1954. Hundreds were arrested. That February, Neguib complained that his colleague was too dictatorial and was at once placed under house arrest, where he was to remain for many years. Finally, the Muslim Brothers ill-advisedly hoped to obtain their rewards by attempting to assassinate Nasser in the middle of a speech he was making to a large audience. "Death to the traitors," the crowd dutifully roared, while Nasser immediately shouted into the microphone that he had restored the nation's self-respect. Two days later, at a mass rally, he warned, "The revolution shall not be crippled; if it is not able to proceed white, then we will make it red." Hasan Hudaybi, successor of the murdered al-Banna as Supreme Guide of the Muslim Brothers, was arrested with his closest associates. Hudaybi's death sentence was commuted to life imprisonment, but six leaders of the Muslim Brothers were hanged, others also received life sentences, and about 1000 members were tried. The movement was then dissolved by official decree. Like the Communists, the Muslim Brothers in fact went underground to conspire. A Communist pamphlet of 1955 was already accusing Nasser of having 26,000 political prisoners, and with less exaggeration alleged that there was torture and murder in the concentration camps. Three turbulent years had been enough for Nasser to assume absolute control of Egypt, including "education, the media, professional syndicates, trade unions, the rural structures in the countryside, the religious institutions and orders, the administration and bureaucracy," as listed by P. J. Vatikiotis, the historian of these developments.

In the West, the 1952 coup had been received with satisfaction. Ousting Neguib, Nasser continued to be seen not as the usual despot but as a bright young officer in a hurry to reform. Jefferson Caffery, the American ambassador to Cairo, was soon trumpeting amid the succeeding waves of arrests that in two years Nasser had done more for Egypt than his predecessors in 6000. Visiting Cairo, Secretary of State John Foster Dulles announced that Egypt "is now on the threshold of a great future." At the same time, the Soviet press was castigating Nasser. The Great Soviet Encyclopedia described Nasser and his colleagues in 1952 as "a reactionary officers' group linked to the U.S.A." who had embarked upon severe repression of the workers.

As soon as he was able to do with Egypt what he pleased, Nasser had to decide quite what was the purpose of absolute power. With some part of himself, he may well have been an idealist who would have wished to introduce the "revolution" on which he was so fond of harping, truly aspiring to social justice and better education and medicine. When the British socialist politician Richard Crossman asked him why he did not choose the path of Ataturk and concentrate on the necessary social reforms, he replied that that was all very well for primitive barbarians like the Turks, but would never do for "free Western people" like the Egyptians. Hypocrisy apart, it might have been possible for Nasser to lay social foundations that could indeed have made the Egyptians a free and modern people. In an article designed for Western readers, Nasser defined the ideal:

> Our ultimate aim is to provide Egypt with a truly democratic and representative government, not the type of parliamentary dictatorship which the Palace and the corrupt "pasha" class imposed on the people. In the past, parliament was a body for blocking social improvement. We want to make sure that in the future the senators and deputies will serve all the Egyptians rather than a few.

This task was no doubt formidable, but that still does not explain why Nasser did nothing whatever to undertake it, why on the contrary he in turn deliberately blocked and excluded democratic and representative government. In *Egypt's Liberation,* Nasser complained that the people stood to one side like mere spectators, "observing our revolution, as though they had nothing to do with it. They only waited for the result of a struggle between two opposing forces, neither of which concerned them." Reflecting with hindsight after Nasser's death, no less a person than his Free Officer colleague and successor Anwar Sadat was to point to the helplessness of the majority, the peasants, "an amorphous, passive, dumb mass of people whose chief preoccupation was survival." To many informed Westerners this seemed to be true. "One is struck by the fellah's apparent willingness to accept his existence," wrote one American academic who had done research in rural Egypt under Nasser; "he generally takes for granted that the phenomena of the world around him are arbitrary and not amenable to his efforts. The laws of nature are uncontrollable in his mind unless the spiritual process that determines them can be persuaded to favour him. Thus the incomprehensible aspects of his life are built into a pattern of myths and folk charms." Once again, though, as in the nineteenth century, obscure revolts erupted in the towns and in the countryside, as Egyptians did what they could in the time-honored manner to defend themselves against a tyranny beyond all bounds. Examples exist of villagers who disobeyed the decrees imposed on them and were then surrounded by soldiers and beaten into submission.

Shame-honor ranking made a mockery of any reformist idealism that Nasser might have had. Like all who obey that code, Nasser was unable to value individuals more highly than shame-producing abstractions. Whatever cruelties he imposed on people had no significance so long as he thereby acquired honor. It so happened that his inner feelings and motivations were wholly dominated by the most extreme susceptibility to humiliation and shame. Acquisition of honor was therefore his sole standard, the one justification of his actions. During the Palestine fighting of 1948, he recorded an example of how he could suffer for a shaming cause rather than on behalf of a poor wretch of a man. Questioning a soldier, Nasser had learned that this man believed himself to be on maneuvers near Cairo, having failed to understand that he was at war with Jews. "I wept bitter tears in the headquarters," was Nasser's revealing comment. Appearing on television after the Six Day War, he actually wept for all the nation to witness his humiliation, and perhaps to have their own humiliation expurgated by that means.

"Lift your head, brother, the days of humiliation are over" was the slogan inscribed on banners throughout Cairo and other cities in 1954. Within the optimism of the wording was the admission that the past really had been humiliating, begging the further questions of why and how this had been so. "I saw the British flag," the words of a popular song had run, "A sight that humiliated me and made me cry." The Free Officers shared this outlook. In his memoirs General Neguib often referred to what he took as humiliations by the British, such as assaults on Egyptian men and the molesting of women, acts of vandalism, obscene songs about the very same King Farouk that he was to see off on his yacht: "I was ashamed of the low esteem in which Egyptians were held by Britons and other foreigners, and I was determined to show our cynical rulers that something could and would be done about it."

Nobody spoke this shame-honor language more insistently or at a higher pitch than Nasser. Time after time, in speech after speech, whether in crisis or at a moment of respite, Nasser rubbed away at shame-honor as though it were an open wound that would not heal. "I assure you," he liked to emphasize, "we shall not rest over any social oppression and national humiliation." Responding to such sentiments, Egyptians were prepared to give him the benefit of the doubt and entrust honor to his care. One authority has gone so far as to assert that Nasser took upon himself the whole burden of the national feeling of inferiority. Clever manipulation allowed Nasser to have it both ways. Any success was an honor, but it was shameful even to bring the mind to bear upon defeat.

No landowner or industrialist anywhere gladly sees himself dispossessed and his property nationalized, but if the law of the land, duly established by democratic procedures, so ordains, then he must obey, and he will. Nasser's revolution, imposed from above, was evidently self-serving, and the dispossessed landowner or industrialist could not interpret his own fall and ruin to be anything but a challenge to his status, therefore to his honor. Far from accepting that Nasser's socialist measures were in the national interest, the rest of the population shared the cultural values of the landowner and industrialist, the disgraced officers, the old notables and politicians, and sympathized with them in their humiliation but also perceived exciting opportunities for themselves. Egypt under Nasser therefore broke into a fantastic whirl of submerged intrigue, as people petitioned and intervened and pleaded with the Free Officers, either to acquire property and spoils that had been suddenly released or to defend them, struggling through every means fair and foul over the apportionment of wealth and therefore of honor and shame. It was as though the whole country were nothing but a money-favor nexus temporarily but dizzyingly lurching out of control.

Social justice or egalitarianism were not at issue in these rearrangements. The newly favored possessors stood in exactly the same relationship to superior power holders as their predecessors. Here is what happened to Abd el Baset, the typical fellah, and father of Shahhat, in an example which was reproduced all over the country:

> The land of an old feudal estate, Sombat, which had been seized after the 1952 revolution, was finally redistributed. Abd el Baset, as a former soldier, was eligible, and his many cronies among the petty government officials saw to it that his name was put on the list. He was given title to

two and a quarter acres in two separate fields at Sombat. . . . The government retained the power to tell the new owners what and when to plant. It provided water—not always enough or in time, they soon discovered—and credit for seeds, fertilizer, and labor. The government bought a fixed quota of each harvest at a low price. This meant constant dealings with the village agricultural inspector and so much delay, favoritism, and bribery that most of Abd el Baset's neighbors found it profitable to make sharecropping arrangements.

Ivor Powell was a young Englishman whose experience as a foreign employee in an Egyptian ministry shattered his left-wing illusions.

Although officially no appointment is made without the approval of the Arab Socialist Union, in practice, all appointments stem from the Minister, via his under-secretaries, some of whom are described as permanent. In fact, there is nothing less permanent than an Egyptian ministry; the upper places are the scene of such a coming and going that it is sometimes difficult to keep track of who is in what job, or out of a job altogether. Canvassing and intriguing for higher places occupies a great deal of the time and energies of senior officials. The corruption, embezzlement, and bribery that goes on are staggering; they would not be so surprising, perhaps, in a state which did not make so great a parade of high principles as Nasser's Egypt. Sometimes there are arrests; general directives to improve the tone of public life are issued when a fraud of too great transparency is committed. . . . I have seen, by the use of denunciation, and a talent for loud protestations of political reliability at the right time and in the right place, clerks rise in the space of a year from a job paying E£25 a month to E£200 a month (although officially nobody may have a salary of more than E£120 monthly), together with an official limousine, chauffeur, and any number of perks.

Those such as army officers whose loyalty was necessary to the regime had privileges like cars, social clubs, higher pay, exclusive stores. Nasser's minister of the interior, Sharawi Gomaa, made a speech in 1968 to select police officials in which he specifically stated that "an officer is not barred from promotion because in the past he has accepted a bribe."

As for Nasser himself, he occupied the Kubbeh Palace in Cairo and other former royal residences. At Manshiet-al-Bakri, the Cairo suburb where his family lived, he acquired the houses on either side of his own. At Alexandria, he had a pair of large villas on the seashore, with sixteen chefs and bathrooms lined with Italian marble. His two daughters enjoyed shopping expeditions abroad—

one of them once brought back ninety suitcases of dresses from Paris. Nasser's sons-in-law acquired rapid fortunes, and John Waterbury writes about one of them, Ashraf Marwan: "For years rumors had circulated on Marwan's five-percenting of the flow into Egypt of funds and projects originating in the Arab peninsula." A journalist, Galal al-Hammamsi, accused Nasser of pocketing a $15 million gift from King Saud.

"Furniture, plate, cars, libraries, jewels, vanished like lightning into the possession of the Free Officers and their favourites," comments Ivor Powell, and he tells how Madame Abdul Hakim Amer once arrived at a jeweler's in Switzerland with some diamonds that had belonged to Princess Fawzia, King Farouk's sister, in her handbag. The jeweler identified them. "Call the Egyptian embassy," Madame Amer replied. "You will see that they are mine." The call was made, the sale then took place.

Recovery of honor within Egypt could be finalized only through international recognition. As soon as he was able to do so, Nasser exploited foreign policy as the means to avenge the sense of humiliation which so severely troubled him. To address himself in such a spirit to foreign policy carried a high risk because he was staking his honor upon success in whatever he chose to do and therefore committing himself in the event of frustration to plunge in deeper and deeper, in effect like a gambler doubling his stake. On two particular issues, Nasser felt a humiliation that had absolute priority over rationality. To Nasser, the Palestine battle "was a smear on the entire Arab Nation. No one can forget the shame brought by the battle of 1948." The Arab states, he lamented in *Egypt's Liberation,* had been forced "to bow their heads in humiliation and shame." In addition he was raw with anxiety about the West, impatient for revenge on its supposed slights. As he put it in a speech in 1954, "I assure you that we have been getting ready, ever since the beginning of the revolution, to fight the great battle against colonialism and imperialism until we achieve the dignity the people feel is due to Egypt."

Withdrawal of British troops from the Suez Canal Zone would certify Nasser's nationalist standing and earn honor, and therefore it was a matter of immediate importance to him to begin negotiations on the question. Since 1945 a terrorist campaign to enforce withdrawal had been conducted by the Muslim Brothers, but in secret accord with King Farouk and Wafdist politicians. All were seeking this route to honor. The campaign had culminated in

Black Saturday, a day in January 1952 when the mob in Cairo had destroyed and burned some 700 places associated with Westerners, such as hotels and bars, restaurants, cinemas, department stores. Estimates of damage rose as high as $150 million. Twenty-six foreigners, mostly British, had been killed and 600 people, including Egyptians, were hurt. This unchecked rioting had been a stage play, but it was nonetheless intimidating. Already inverted into guilt after the Palestine fiasco, British confidence never recovered after 1952. Two and a half years later, the British government yielded to Nasser's importunities. Nasser could have his treaty, it was decided in London, on whatever terms could be agreed.

The British had talked themselves into imagining that Egypt at last had a ruler of quite another stripe, who was no longer paying the mob to display violence but rather inspiring nationalism of the kind they too felt. If so, resistance was pointless, doomed. This whole interpretation was Eurocentric and misplaced. What had actually happened was that unresisted force on the part of the Egyptians had enabled them to reverse the power-challenge dialectic, and so to become the arbiters in British affairs. Like Zaghlul thirty years before him, Nasser drew the correct conclusion that he had only to increase levels of violence to demoralize the British still further and so extract more concessions.

Pursuing that logic, Nasser realized that if he could force the British to withdraw not only from Egypt but also from Sudan, Aden, and the Gulf and then aid in pushing the French out of North Africa, he could hope to replace them, and in that event become the unqualified Arab leader and hero, amassing honor enough to sustain him for a lifetime. In doing so, he would be certain to challenge other Arab power holders for supremacy. So it proved. In the course of his career, he challenged Iraq whose Hashemite rulers proposed to join the Baghdad Pact, an alliance designed in 1954 as a barrier to Soviet ambitions; he despatched a force of 70,000 men to wage war in Yemen for five expensive and futile years; he maintained campaigns of subversion against Saudi Arabia and King Hussein of Jordan and President Bourguiba of Tunisia; he backed the Adeni Marxists and Ben Bella in Algeria and Gaddhafi upon the latter's capturing of the state in Libya; and he became enmeshed in the internal politics and fighting of Lebanon and Syria and Iraq. To Arab power holders everywhere, Nasser was an ambivalent figure of the kind invariably thrown up through power challenging and its values, greatly to be admired for the trickiness and the scope of his intrigues and wars, and greatly to be feared for the very same reasons.

Power challenging on these lines, today as in the past, requires the modern armaments that are not manufactured in Middle East societies. To retain absolute power and to exploit it through foreign policy, Nasser had to find a reliable arms supplier. Whether he deliberately or accidentally ensnared the Soviet Union into this role remains an open question. It has been argued that the United States or the European powers would have been willing to deliver arms to Egypt. At any rate, inciting raids on Israel from Gaza and so provoking Israeli retaliation, Nasser as early as 1955 activated the required conditions of regional uncertainty. A Soviet ambassador is supposed to have taken advantage of a social function to mention conversationally that his country was prepared to sell weapons. Afterward Nasser liked to tell anyone who would listen that he was quite the innocent party and had no intention of taking controversial action. That September, the Soviet Union used Czechoslovakia as an intermediary to arm Nasser. A repeat of the 1948 tactic of arming Israel through the Czechs, this was also a reversal of policy. On the common basis of anti-Western sentiment, Nasser had recruited a sponsor, and the Soviet Union had acquired a client. "Reactionary officers" were magically transformed into "enlightened elements." By the same token, Israel was stripped of any progressive character, and ever since has been the object of slander and falsification by Communist parties and their publications worldwide. The process undertaken in Hitler's day of internationalizing the Middle East was extended in the age of Khrushchev and his Soviet successors. In language reminiscent of classical Islam, Khrushchev spoke at the Twentieth Party Congress in 1956 of the division of the world into the "War Zone" of capitalism-imperialism and the "Peace Zone" of the communist countries.

This new sponsor-client relationship became fully forged through the chapter of accidents occurring in 1956. Suspicious of Nasser's real political intentions, neither Britain nor the United States were now willing to finance the construction of the Aswan Dam, a project whose huge scale put Nasser's prestige at stake. Losing honor, Nasser retaliated by nationalizing the Suez Canal. Whether to accept this fait accompli or to insist on the customary arbitration by force of a supposed clash of interests was the choice then facing Anthony Eden, the British prime minister. Had he decided, in the manner of Gladstone before him, that invasion, however ungainly and uncongenial, was the act of arbitration in power challenging and must be pursued to the end, then the Suez crisis of 1956 need never have had such repercussions. As it was, Eden had no sense of the Arab sociopolitical system nor of the values with which he now had to cope; he felt that he had treated the Arabs as "our friends" and was entitled to gratitude; he imagined himself opposing a dictator of the cut of Hitler or Mussolini. Lost in the Arab power-challenge dialectic, he swung the British, the Arabs, and the superpowers about in an absurd ballet of misunderstanding.

That November, the British and the French invaded, in coordination with the Israelis advancing across the Sinai desert. Within a few days, Nasser was paralyzed and Egypt subjugated. To general amazement, the United States then intervened, pressuring the British and French to withdraw, under the threat of financial sanctions. Some months later, the Israeli army also retreated. Nasser was able to claim victory, and the Soviet Union claimed to have promoted it. Almost twenty years later, an Egyptian writer Hussein Dhul-Fiqar Sabri was to sum up exactly what this had achieved for Nasser: "Suez was the turning point. It led him to believe that revolutionary Egypt vanquished Imperialism and that had it not been for Nasser this would not have happened. Victory was his victory, protected by Providence. Everyone forgot Egypt was not victorious in 1956!"

The more intractable Nasser had proved, the greater the concessions he had demanded and obtained against all likelihood, the more a certain kind of British official justified him, wringing his hands in the atmosphere of national guilt that blazed with the Suez crisis. In the years immediately before the crisis, the head of the Middle East department in the Foreign Office was Evelyn Shuckburgh, and in his diaries he has kept a frank record of this peculiar emotion, akin to sadomasochism, distorting the relationship with the Arabs. "How the Arabs hate us really," Shuckburgh could moan about them, flying in the face of the evidence that any such hatred is not some sort of ingrained characteristic but was utterly factitious, something serviceable in power challenging, to be bought and sold.

In 1956 the British ambassador to Cairo was Humphrey Trevelyan, posted on from there to Qassem's Iraq. In his memoirs, he judges that "Revolution is endemic in Iraq" as though it were like the malaria of the Euphrates marshes. If this were correct, then of course Iraqis would be in the grip of some unnatural malevolence, beyond the reach either of logic or of cure, and therefore they would be unlike other human beings. That Trevelyan quite properly might dislike and condemn Arab political practices should nonetheless never have stopped him from realizing that they had dictates and reasons open to analysis and to prevention. When Trevelyan further writes of the British that "We were only retreating from positions which had already been lost," he was exposing how even senior ranks in the Foreign Office, failing to grasp the nature of Arab power challenging and its operation, simply lost heart and so surrendered whole populations to a despotism which they would never have tolerated for themselves.

Anthony Parsons is only another example among scores of such diplomats, and he too has recorded in his memoirs how Nasser's coup meant to him "the dawn of a new era" and that "the Army had lost patience," which are concepts of such ineffable Eurocentricity that they have virtually no meaning in the context. The Suez campaign was seen "by the majority including myself as immoral and inexpedient." Posted in its aftermath to the Cairo embassy, Parsons found himself "basically sympathetic to the aspirations of the regime"—and this at the very moment when Nasser was consolidating under Soviet auspices his absolute tyranny. Far from being the dreaded specter with which Nasser liked to haunt his audiences, imperialism like this was his secret weapon. British panic and defeatism unrolled the red carpet down which Nasser stalked to his artificial triumphs. Unwilling in the years between 1936 and 1956 to pay the price for order, the British handed the costs of disorder to the defenseless Arab masses.

Evidently Soviet sponsorship was a paying proposition, and it seemed a reasonable investment to other Arab power challengers to emulate Nasser by rehearsing anti-Western rhetoric and then await the expected overtures and rewards from Moscow. The Soviets opened their Damascus embassy in 1955 and activated the Baghdad embassy enormously after the 1958 coup there. Offensive and defensive bids for supremacy erupted among the states of the Middle East in a frenzy all the more involved and murderous because of the modern weaponry and communications systems through which it could be fought out. Unlike other colonial arbiters, the Soviet Union was doctrinally able and indeed eager to use force to resolve these rivalries in its favor and impose its version of political settlement. Briefly, Soviet supreme power over the Arabs looked as if it would materialize.

Between 1956 and Nasser's death in 1970, the Soviet Union extended its influence and reach throughout the Middle East, acquiring military and naval bases in the Mediterranean and along the North African coast, stationing a fleet as a counter to the U.S. Sixth Fleet; signing trade and cultural and scientific agreements with Egypt, Iraq, Jordan, Kuwait, Algeria, Tunisia, Morocco, South Yemen, and Syria; converting the former British base at Aden after 1967 into an outright Marxist bastion and Soviet arsenal; financing the Aswan Dam in Egypt and the Euphrates Dam in Syria; creating on its own Marxist-Leninist model the iron and steel complexes at Annaba in Algeria and at Helwan in Egypt; awarding the Stalin Peace Prize to choice Arab sympathizers and the title "Hero of the Soviet Union" to Nasser and Ben Bella; triggering off the 1967 war by false reports of Israeli mobilization and afterward rearming Egypt and Syria; arranging publicized tours of the region by such personalities as Khrushchev, Podgorny, Gromyko, Shepilov, Marshal Grechko, and Brezhnev; summoning Arab leaders openly or in secret for consultation and policy coordination in Moscow; treating Nasser for his deteriorating health in Soviet hospitals and spas; supporting the PLO everywhere and other similiar groups in Oman and Yemen; acquiring its hold through bribery and espionage in virtually every Arab country.

In Egypt alone, by 1965 between sixty and eighty Soviet professors and instructors were teaching at universities, and the Soviet Union was financing at least twenty-four vocational colleges in which 7400 Egyptian students were reported to be trained. Seventeen and a half hours of weekly propaganda in Arabic from Moscow in 1956 had risen by 1970 to seventy-four and a half hours. In that year, the Soviet newspaper printed in Arabic had a circulation of 1.1 million copies. Between 1954 and 1970, writes Jon D. Glassman in *Arms for the Arabs*, Egypt, Syria, and Iraq received more than half of global Soviet military assistance, and in addition Egypt alone received from 3 to 16 percent of total Soviet inventories of various ground and air weapons.

Two constraints operated to prevent the Soviet Union from incorporating, or so to speak balkanizing, parts of the Middle East into its empire in the manner that earlier it had absorbed Eastern

Europe. To its dismay and anger, the Soviet Union was blocked by American determination not to abandon the region. Successive American presidents declared themselves committed to arbitrate in Middle East politics, peacefully if possible, but militarily if need be. President Eisenhower dispatched a force of 18,000 to intervene upon the request of President Chamoun in the Lebanese civil war of 1958. From the mid-1960s, the Sixth Fleet had stations in the Mediterranean. American administrations one and all have judged that Israel is a democracy to be defended on political if not on moral grounds. Humanly, Western public opinion could not tolerate the delayed consummation of the Holocaust through the mass murder by Arab armies of survivors and their descendants in Israel.

In addition, and perhaps more decisively, the Soviet Union has found itself baffled by the Arab power-challenge dialectic. Between themselves, Arab power holders do not and cannot have mutual or agreed ambitions and so are in perpetual and violent flux as they test one another. Soviet ends cannot be reconciled to these temperamental and careerist rivalries. In an exact repetition of the predicament in which the British had previously floundered, Soviet commitment to one Arab power holder by definition has entailed the opposition of that man's rival power holders. In practice it proves impossible to have an assortment of Arab clients, and the Soviet Union accordingly veers from gain to loss and sometimes from loss to gain, like any other external colonial power that has ever been entangled in this system. Moreover the system is all of one piece, as every Arab power holder is employing the same tactics of seeking superior sponsorship, recruiting whom he can into his coalition, however momentarily or mistrustfully, and spiting or damaging internal and external challengers by all available means of conspiracy and murder and war. Marxist-Leninist ideology offers no guide to this, no way of predicting which among the contending power holders is right on the doctrinal level, or which is prospectively the best bet on the tactical level. Arab Communist parties cannot be afforded protection. The division of Arab power holders into "progressive" and "reactionary" or sometimes "moderate" and "extremist" is a completely spurious and deceptive usage for purposes of propaganda. Its translation into "Soviet-sponsored" and "American-sponsored" is not much more realistic because any power holder will switch sponsorship if he sees advantage in it, and of course is vulnerable to a coup by some challenger who might also choose to switch the state over on the spur of the moment, if it suits him.

Soviet limitations became apparent in their handling of Iraq and Syria, both prospective and willing clients. The first military coup in Iraq had been in 1936; in Syria, in 1949. Unlike Egypt, neither of these countries was sufficiently integrated socially or politically for there to be a single power holder who could also hope to have the allegiance of tribes or religions other than his own. Power holding in postcolonial Syria and Iraq has therefore been determined by a deadly fight for supremacy among the component ethnic groups and religions. Local Communist parties, to be sure, had been founded between the world wars and claimed to cut across tribe and religion by means of the class struggle. Since there were no Arab classes as defined in Marxism-Leninism, this struggle was imaginary, and the very small number of Arabs who have also been Communists of genuine Marxist convictions have lived and agitated at a great remove from reality.

Some sort of political party, the Baath (Arabic for Resurrection), for a while promised to be in the process of formation in Damascus. At its heart, fatally, this too was a conspiracy started in about 1941, comprising three friends, Michel Aflaq, Salah al-Din Bitar, and Zaki Arsuzi. Aflaq, a Greek Orthodox, had been born in Damascus in 1910, or perhaps 1912; Bitar was a Sunni Muslim; and Arsuzi was an Alawi from Latakia. "Each was so sure that he was the proper leader of the Arab resurrection," in the words of John F. Devlin, a historian of the Baath, "that neither could defer to the other." Careerist challenging thus opened. Within a year or so, the conspiracy had been enlarged to about two dozen members. At a founding congress in 1947 in a Damascus coffee house, 247 delegates were present. The party was nationalist in outlook, with a belief that the Arabs were one nation and should have a single leader.

Impressed previously with Hitler and Nazism, Aflaq and Bitar now swung toward Soviet-inspired socialism in the manner of Nasser. At least some of the early members of the Baath felt a genuine attachment to a representative system of government, writes Devlin, unfortunately without naming whom he might have had in mind. But as the movement spread into cells in Jordan and Iraq, recruitment along tribal and religious lines proved irresistible. In Syria, the Alawis and Christians and Druze saw their opportunity for assertion against the Sunni majority; in Iraq, in general, the minority Sunnis saw their opportunity for assertion against the Shias and the remainder. All alike were power-hungry men in the usual military idiom. Success in the end depended on the simple fact that in Syria the minorities had previously entered the army as a career and so held a high proportion of senior military posts, enough to command power and to oppress the Sunnis; whereas in Iraq the Sunnis had entered the army and risen accordingly in rank, enough to command power there and to oppress the Shias and other minorities. The contrast was absolute. United in nothing but name, the Baathists in Syria and the Baathists in Iraq were headed for confrontation in the near future on the two counts of religious difference and local power challenging.

Following eagerly the example of Nasser and his Soviet sponsorship after 1955, a Baathist-Communist coalition staked out its ground in Iraq and Syria. In both countries, this coalition unraveled suddenly in 1958, precipitating conditions of widespread tension, as far afield as Lebanon and Jordan, raising for the first time the prospect of superpower clashes in the Middle East. Moving against the Communists that February and also taking precautions against the Iraqis, the Baathists in Syria without warning asked to be united with Egypt. No forethought or preparation preceded this pure power-challenge ploy. The union of Egypt and Syria occurred at a stroke of a pen, without any measures to coordinate banking systems, budgetary practices, exchange controls, import or tariff restrictions, and control of profits. In the political sphere, union involved closing down the Syrian vestigial parties, as had already happened in Egypt, and the arrival in Damascus of Abdul Hakim Amer as Nasser's viceroy, complete with a set of Egyptian decrees. That September, in Iraq Abdul Karim Qassem overthrew the Hashemite monarchy. Some of the Iraqi officers also favored union with Nasser, and overtures were made to that end.

Perhaps Nasser was sincere in his endless exhortations and proclamations of the need for union of this type, for Arab unity in general, its imminent accomplishment and its future glories. It may be that prominent Syrians and Iraqis, parroting those very proclamations in identical language, were also sincere. Nobody in Egypt or Syria or Iraq paused to inquire about the modalities of this unity, to plan the details, to draft working papers and concordances and treaties for establishing who would surrender sovereignty in which field, and to whom. No standing commissions were set up; the services even of the Arab League were never envisaged.

Instead, it was each power holder for himself as usual. Nasser was projecting his wandering role as the sole Arab leader; the Syrians supposed themselves the heirs to a greater Syria; the Iraqi Hashemites had planned for an enlarged Fertile Crescent under their rule, and Qassem was no sooner in power than he rejected proposals for union with Egypt. Not long afterward he preferred instead to launch a local power challenge of his own by laying claim to Kuwait. Nasser's wrath was immediate, and he was to be heard asking, "What's democracy in Baghdad today? It is the democracy of terrorism, gallows, Communist street-courts and the murder of everyone who does not comply with their demands." Qassem, in his opinion, suffered from inferiority complexes. The accusations were generally true, but it was the richest humbug for Nasser to make them with such an air of injured surprise.

Unity, then, was to nations what conspiracy is to challengers, a plot of one power holder to deprive another of his preeminence. Arab unity is clearly incompatible with power challenging; indeed it is its negation; and at best a metaphor for the desire to have done with the whole wearisome and bloody business, and put it aside in favor of more peaceful and productive politics. By 1961, the Egyptian union with Syria had been abrogated as precipitately as it had come about, and by 1963 Qassem had been murdered by his colleague Aref. The free-for-all horror of these events had the sole merit of thwarting the Soviet Union.

Frustrated, Nasser now tried to maximize his Egyptian power base through centralization of national resources. Fully Sovietized jargon emerged in his speeches, as when he spoke of the need "to protect the revolutionary regime from feudalism, monopolies, and exploiting capitalism," or said that "scientific socialism is the suitable style for finding the right method leading to progress." In 1960 he promulgated a National Charter for this socialism. Conscious of the one-man virtuosity of his rule and the distance from it at which the masses stood, he also devised the Arab Socialist Union, intended to be an implement like the Bolshevik Party for mobilization of support and the transmission of orders. In the conditions of Egypt, the A.S.U. became part of the bureaucratic terror apparatus.

Whatever freedom of expression and assembly had survived from the former monarchy was extinguished. Whatever property still remained in foreign or Jewish hands was expropriated. Land-holding was restricted to 100 feddans per man, 300 per family (one feddan is about one acre). Hundreds of Egyptians, Muslims as well as Copts, had their property confiscated. A ceiling of E£5000 was placed on income, and of E£10,000 on shareholding. According to John Waterbury, between 1961 and 1966, 4000 families were af-fected by sequestration measures, and total assets seized in those years may have amounted to E£100 million, including 122,000 feddans of land, 7000 urban properties, about 1000 businesses and stocks and bonds worth over E£30 million. A committee for the liquidation of feudalism was appointed in 1961 to settle rival-ries among contenders for the spoils, and Waterbury adds that it is clear that the victims included the innocent and the poor. Facto-ries and businesses and shops were nationalized, and so were all heavy industries, utilities, pharmaceuticals, large construction firms, some fifty shipping companies, insurance, and the promi-nent Misr Bank and the Ahali Bank and the National Bank of Egypt. All foreign trade, including the cotton crop, was brought under direct state control. Trading agencies were required to have state participation, a measure that hit an estimated 450,000 tradesmen. The first Five Year Plan was proclaimed in 1961 but petered out, and nothing was heard of a second plan.

Real changes occurred, in that by 1970 about one million peo-ple were employed in manufacturing, or more than twice as many as before the world war, and industry's share of the economy had expanded to 23 percent. But in broad terms, Nasser's quasi-Soviet-ization impeded structural reforms which might have tended to popular participation in government and to social and political modernization, while at the same time affirming rooted cultural and psychological assumptions that the leader does as he thinks right. Polarization widened between the elite and the masses. Thoroughly frightened and cowed, the Egyptian people adopted the time-honored strategy for surviving tyranny, of lying low and waiting for it to pass, while loudly and exaggeratedly venerating the tyrant in any sudden emergency. Only the few with the skills or character for it were able to profit from the command economy, and they distanced themselves farther than ever from the man in the street. In a study of the new power elite, R. Hrair Dekmejian numbered 131 men who held the key posts of the country. Of these, forty-four were military officers, and eighty-seven had a civilian background. None of the latter had an independent power base, and however intelligent and efficient they might have been, they displayed what Dekmejian calls "appalling lack of political backbone." Anyone who seemed to be about to dissent was purged at once. For the Free Officers, wrote a Marxist critic Muhammad Hussein, "the masses have only economic and social needs—they require work, bread, amusements," and of course no political activity.

Losers in these careerist proceedings were cast into Nasser's Gulag, only a secondhand replica of the Soviet original, miragelike to be sure, tempered by the compromises and tolerance of the money-favor nexus, yet not merely despotic cruelty on a large scale but rather the first application of mass terror in the Arab world. Tura and Abu Zaabal, the Cairo Citadel, Dakhla Oasis in the Western desert, Khargah oasis, were prisons and camps spoken of with horror. Hans Tütsch, the Swiss journalist, was one of the first to write of "the shocking tortures inflicted on the prisoners surpassing everything yet seen in the Middle East." Sabri Hafiz is an Egyptian who speaks of his generation in the 1960s as "debarred from all political activity, surrounded with a potent and deceptive propaganda, brought up on a diet of illusive slogans and statements, and asked to sacrifice its freedom for a fragile and corrupt establishment."

Mustafa Amin was a journalist who with his brother had run the newspaper *Akhbar al Yawm*. To destroy an independent-minded and influential pair, Nasser accused Mustafa Amin of plotting with the Muslim Brothers and the United States, for which trumped-up charge he served nine years of a prison sentence, subsequently writing a book about it. "The basic rule in those days," Mustafa Amin has explained, "was that if you were found guilty, you went to prison; and if you were found innocent, you went to a concentration camp."

Ahmad Abul Fatih, publisher of the former Wafdist paper *al-Misri*, was tried with his brother before a revolutionary tribunal for "aiming to destroy the government" and "spreading hostile propaganda," for which they received lengthy prison sentences, with the confiscation of their property. Escaping into exile, Ahmad Abul Fatih published a book in Paris to criticize Nasser, and he returned to Egypt only when Sadat was in power. Fathi Abd al-Fattah, author of a two-volume study of the Egyptian village, spent two years in a concentration camp in one of the oases of the Western desert. The writer and critic Louis Awad was similarly detained. With hindsight he summed up, "Nasser first liquidated democracy in Egypt, and later any socialism that may have existed in the country and the Arab world." Yussef Idris, born in 1927 in a village, was the kind of Egyptian that Nasser claimed to be advancing. Becoming one of the best-reputed writers of his generation, Yussef Idris also spent two years in a desert concentration camp. "A hell of hunger, disease, and war!" was how he could describe Egypt at a conference in America, once Nasser was safely dead. A leading Communist writer, Shuhdi Atiyyah al-Shafii, was among those killed in the Abu Zaabal camp. In a recent novel, the Egyptian writer Fawzia Asssad has a character by the name of Mokhtar, a Communist condemned to forced labor at Abu Zaabal, then exiled to Khargah. Tortured as a matter of course, Mokhtar is released as a concession to the Soviets: "he was not brought before a court, in order not to have to admit his innocence." In the present, Fawzia Assaad can speak with hindsight of the "execrated regime."

Free Officers such as Abdul Kader Awda and Salah Salem (nick-named the "dancing major" for his exploits in Sudan) were among those disgraced and arrested. Nasser's chief of intelligence, the sinister Salah Nasr, was finally sentenced to ten years of hard labor for having ordered the arrest and torture of a journalist. As George Ketman, a pseudonym for a writer partly of Egyptian descent, has pointed out, a number of favored officers and conspirators, such as Salah Salem at one time and Khalid Mohieddine, were supported by invisible funds, in other words recruited into Nasser's retinue. But those who were familiar with the likes of Sartre and Abellio and Papini and other fashionable European writers of the moment confused socialism and demagogy. To them, "the Nasserite revolution" was an opportunity for revenge upon the West "to which they had never really succeeded in assimilating themselves."

Not that there was any possibility of dissent or criticism. The Press Law of 1960 brought all publishing houses under the control of the A.S.U. That same year television was inaugurated in Egypt, as another instrument of government control and mobilization. Eleven studios in Cairo employed a staff of 3500. Controlled television of the same type had started in Iraq in 1956, in Syria in 1960. On a visit to Egypt, Jean-Paul Sartre, that veteran apologist of tyranny, asked Tewfik el-Hakim, the doyen of Egyptian writers, why he did not write a book in praise of Nasser. "For there to be a defence there must be an attack and here no one attacks Abdul

Nasser," Tewfik el-Hakim replied. "Nor does anyone in our country dare oppose his view."

Beer in the Snooker Club is an idiosyncratic and courageous novel by Waguih Ghali, a Copt, which he published in London in 1964. Its autobiographical hero, Ram, soon takes the measure of Nasser and joins a secret organization to collect documentary evidence of atrocities in prisons and camps, which will be presented to the United Nations. Once a week, Ram drives to friendly police officers whom he pays in return for an envelope containing pictures and reports by inmates. Speaking to Didi, his girlfriend, he gives this picture of contemporary Egypt:

> Do you know Bobby Malla? He's dead. Killed in a concentration camp. Do you know Hakima Mohammed who used to be with you at school and caused a scandal because she married a Copt? Her husband buried her mutilated body last week. She "committed suicide" they told him. Do you know the number of young men, doctors, engineers, lawyers in concentration camps? Or don't you know that we have concentration camps?

As early as 1955, Nasser had taken the controversial step of suspending the Islamic courts. In another measure to centralize the state, Nasser in 1961 brought under government control Al Azhar and the Muslim trusts that financed the university and its work. In the Soviet manner, he aimed to bring to heel the ulema. To a great extent, he succeeded. Mahmud Shaltut, rector of Al Azhar, stated with the full weight of his authority that Islam and socialism were completely reconcilable, giving the specious reason that Islam was more than just a spiritual religion. Nasser was perceived by the Muslim Brothers and their sympathizers as an apostate, and his socialism as intolerable heresy. Although banned and persecuted, the Muslim Brothers maintained their opposition with consistent bravery and self-sacrifice.

Arresting several hundred Muslim Brothers in 1965, Nasser staged a show trial of their spokesman, Sayyid Qutb, a man of undoubted sincerity. In court, Sayyid Qutb displayed the marks of torture on his body and declared, "The principles of the revolution have indeed been applied to us, Muslim Brothers, in jail." A letter from another prisoner from that roundup contains the sentences, "I am writing to you from the fearful Bastille of Egypt, from that sinful military prison. The whole of Egypt is imprisoned. . . . I was arrested despite my immunity as a judge, without an order of arrest . . . my sole crime being my critique of the non-application of the Sharia (Islamic law)." Sayyid Qutb was hanged in prison along with two of his closest associates. Waterbury tabulates a list derived from official sources of those arrested between 1952 and 1971, including Muslim Brothers, Communists, "feudalists" and politicals, to a total of 14,499. This is a minimum figure. In December 1969 Nasser himself admitted that 18,000 Muslim Brothers had been arrested, and in 1975 a newspaper estimated that 27,000 had been swept into the camps.

Yury Miloslavsky was a Russian Jew who had sought refuge in Egypt and found himself arrested in 1948 and again in 1967. On the latter occasion, as he described in a pamphlet in 1970, he was tortured for twenty days. Like the other inmates of his camp on the outskirts of Cairo, he was obliged to shout, "The Jews are perverts, the Jews are women, the Jews are cowards, long live Arabism, long live Nasser." In his opinion, the camps contained between 20,000 and 30,000 people. Some of the Muslim Brothers on the floor below told him, "You Jews are very lucky, you've never been tortured like us. On our arrival in camp, it was the rule to hang us from the window-bars by the ankles, head down. Then we were dipped alternately into boiling and freezing water. To mock us, urine was brought for us to drink. Not even once was a Red Cross representative allowed to visit." Under Sadat, some families received compensation for members who had died in detention.

The Six Day War of 1967, then, found Egypt an absolute police state. Whether Egyptians actually wished to fight that war is therefore as inscrutable as Nasser's real view of Israel. To a number of Western visitors, at least at the outset of his rule, he had spoken about Israel without rancor. For instance, he allegedly told the French foreign minister Christian Pineau, "I am in favor of maintaining peaceful relations with Israel, but I cannot openly avow that determination for it would embarrass me considerably before public opinion at home and among Arab nations in general." In the light of Sadat's reversal of policy, it may be wondered quite what was this public opinion to which Nasser wished to appear sensitive. Unni Wiken quotes an average Egyptian:

> Once, in a speech, Nasser suggested that all public employees should give two days' wages to the war with Israel. The parliament applauded deafeningly instead of standing up to fight against this suggestion. That is *oppression*. We low-paid public employees were on the verge of tears when pay day came and we found two days' pay deducted from our wages.

After 1955 and the Soviet arms deal, Israel could no longer be extricated from Nasser's power challenging and his shame-honor responses. Soon he was peddling the standard fantasy that Israel was a plot concocted to destroy the Arabs and therefore "the greatest crime in history." When he spoke of "Israel and the imperialism around us," he gave the impression of invoking and naming living people rather than abstract nouns. By 1958 he was advising an Indian journalist that the truth of the Zionist conspiracy to rule the world was to be found in the *Protocols of the Elders of Zion.* Next he was confiding to a German journalist, "Surely nobody still accepts the lie of six million murdered Jews. Even the simplest man in the street here does not believe it." The expression "Zionist Nazism," used in February 1965, may even be his ugly concoction. To Professor Erhard, then chancellor of the German Federal Republic, Nasser wrote in 1963, "Zionist racism exploited the sufferings of the Jews under the Hitlerite regime in order to execute a terrible plot against the Arab nation and tear off part of their territory in order to establish a national home in Palestine." "The liberation of Yemen," he said in 1962, as he dispatched his troops to that inhospitably mountainous country in the opposite direction from Israel, "is a step towards getting rid of Zionism." To take these statements at face value is to suppose that Nasser was unbalanced, aberrant, unable to understand history and even geography. However he may have analyzed the situation to himself, the codes of his culture in fact bound him too tightly to make the public break out into objective analysis which would have been truly revolutionary.

On May 29, a week before the 1967 hostilities, he made a major speech in preparation and exculpation of what was to come.

> We are confronting Israel and the West as well—the West, which created Israel and which despised us Arabs and which ignored us before and since 1948. They had no regard whatsoever for our feelings, our hopes in life, or our rights. . . . We are now ready to confront Israel. . . . If the Western powers disavow our rights and ridicule and despise us, we Arabs must teach them to respect us and take us seriously. . . . We must treat enemies as enemies and friends as friends.

The shame-honor component in Nasser's policy toward Israel could not be clearer or more explicit. His famous threat, "If Israel wishes war, we say to her, 'Welcome, we are ready for you'," is in the purest power-challenge style.

In the event, the outcome of the war dramatized the immobility imposed by shame-honor as well as the urgency of seeking some new device with which to start fresh power challenging. Israeli intelligence intercepted a telephone conversation between Nasser and King Hussein, who had been duped into joining the anti-Israeli coalition and was therefore to suffer the unnecessary loss of the West Bank. Nasser said to the king,

As God is my witness, I tell you that I shall publish a communiqué and that you will publish a communiqué. And we'll see to it that the Syrians also announce that American and English aircraft are attacking us from their aircraft carriers. So, we will publish this communiqué. We'll really emphasise this point and we'll do it together.

Here is a perfect example of concerted lying in pursuit of conspiracy, but it reveals much more besides. The invention allowed for an escape route from humiliation, for clearly no shame could be attached to defeat at the hands of massed Western aircraft carriers. Furthermore, the conspirators could hope to mobilize enough shock and outrage among their people to be able to return to the anti-Israel challenge at a more propitious moment in the future.

In Cairo, the population looked to Nasser to recover from shame, but this actually proved beyond his or anyone's capacities. Nasser's entire justification for the military state had disappeared in a matter of days. Had he emerged with honor from the power challenging with Israel, then much of his Soviet-style police state and his arbitrariness would have been instantly forgiven, welcomed, and admired. As it was, said Nasser's loyal publicist Mohamed Heikal, "nobody had been prepared for defeat on such a shattering scale. Everybody was shocked," and Nasser was left in the midst of the self-induced wreckage, trying to salvage something out of it. A number of senior officers and ministers were arrested and tried. One of them, Field-Marshal Abdul Hakim Amer, was driven to commit suicide in circumstances that suggest compulsion.

In an essay *The Return of Consciousness*, published in 1974, Tewfik el-Hakim tried to come to terms with what had happened.

It was impossible, intellectually or logically, easily to believe that our armies could be routed in a few days. Years had passed during which the regime emphasised the army's marvels and showed us, whenever there was a revolutionary celebration, military reviews which included the latest models of tanks. During those parades we saw rockets called al-Qahir and al-Zafir [meaning Conqueror and Victor] and saw units called al-Saiqah [meaning Thunderbolt], which ran snarling a frightening roar; we saw troops which dropped down from the heights, which hurdled over walls, and which literally tore up and ate snakes. . . .

Concentrating on the personality of Nasser, el-Hakim can go on to say that the man had inundated them with magic and dreams. "We forgot the defeat and began to dance, even in parliament, because of the simple existence of his person among us." Public rallying to the leader concealed or repressed the generalized shame of the moment, for no better reason than that "We are an emotional people." With hindsight, he sadly wondered, "where was I who loved freedom of thought?" and answered that he had been so dazzled by the Free Officers throwing out the king that he "did not pay sufficient attention to the grievousness of the loss of our constitutional life."

More critically, Waguih Ghali wrote in his diary that "Israel just walked all over us."

To cover this utter and complete humiliation Nasser invented the excuse that America and Britain supported Israel's military force. I am no lover of those two countries' policies, but even I felt disgusted, more humiliated and insulted by this cheap lie. And so, after 13 years or more, he has turned out to be unreliable, incompetent, dishonest. It is all disgusting, sad and full of shame. . . . I loathe him absolutely.

In the weeks after the war, Ghali became the first Arab journalist to visit Israel and write what in the circumstances was a dispassionate account. Detaching himself in this way from the tribal-religious outlook, he settled in London, only to commit suicide there some years later.

Three months after the 1967 war, Arab power holders met at a conference in Khartoum. In an illustration of how those who consider themselves to have been shamed are completely unable to accept that fact, they passed a resolution that there would be "no war, no peace, no recognition." The refusal to recognize reality further obligated the combatants to enter once more into power challenging in the hopes of recovery.

The wars with Israel alone are estimated to have cost Nasser $1500 million dollars that could not be afforded. No vital interest was at stake. There was nothing to show for it, except the loss of the Gaza Strip and the Sinai Desert, occupied right up to the Suez Canal by the Israelis. The canal itself remained closed. Dispirited and increasingly ill, Nasser was incapable of further initiative, re-peating and maximizing his mistakes by opening artillery ex-changes across the Suez Canal in what came to be known as the War of Attrition. A point of political no-return was almost reached when Soviet pilots engaged Israeli aircraft but were shot down. An estimated 20,000 Soviet military personnel were then deployed in an Egypt ostensibly on its way to becoming a Soviet satellite. Uncannily, irresistibly, the specter of Muhammad Ali comes to mind. Like him, Nasser had tried to build an Egypt upon a Euro-pean model, to win approval and honor in European eyes. Like him, Nasser wasted the available resources through ambitious schemes of foreign conquest, leaving his people more vulnerable than before to the very foreigners who were to be resisted. E. W. Lane in his day "could not but lament" the difference of the state of Egypt under Muhammad Ali's rule from what it might have been. So it was with Nasser. By the time he died in 1970, he had squandered Egypt's only opportunity so far to reform its inherited absolutism, instead ushering in for Egyptians and the majority of Arabs a period of misery whose end is not in sight. This too can be expressed another way, in that Egypt and the other Arab states did not actually disintegrate by passing under direct Soviet con-trol, but in fact maintained the inner resources to survive such a power holder as Nasser, and even to live in hope that the next might prove less destructive.

10

Arabia and Oil

Since well before recorded history, Bedouin or desert tribes have lived as nomads and herders in Arabia and the Gulf. The Arabian peninsula is between a quarter and a third of the size of the United States, but barren and waterless except around the coastline and in some oases inland. That human beings choose to live—and so tenaciously—in this austere setting is impressive. The supporting continuity of Bedouin custom is no less remarkable, consisting down the centuries of tribal feuding, always with the attached and compelling assertion of honor values. The implacable desert raiding or warfare among the Bedouin, it has been argued, is not humanly haphazard or brutish but a matter of deliberate social organization, either for purposes of population control or for distribution of wealth in a region of such limited resources.

Before the age of modern communications, Westerners who sought out the Arabs of Arabia and the Gulf were exceptional men, explorers with the strength of body and mind to withstand the desert and to survive their own unremittingly hostile reception at the hands of the Bedouin tribesmen. A literature has arisen whose high imaginative impact derives from the epic feats and personalities of these individuals. Instead of being described objectively as people whose poverty and violent ways ensured them a short life expectancy, the Bedouin have tended through this medium to acquire romance. Escaping with relief from their own rapidly industrializing societies, exploring Westerners dramatized the Bedouin as the last free spirits; if wild, then also generous; if primitive, then also warriorlike.

From his extraordinary journey through Arabia starting in 1876, Charles Doughty extracted the resonant poeticism that the Arabs are like "a man sitting in a cloaca to the eyes, and whose brows touch heaven." Just seventy years later, Wilfred Thesiger, one of the very few Europeans to ride by camel across the Empty Quarter of Arabia, could still idealize in much the same terms, "All that is best in the Arabs has come to them from the desert." By means of reports such as these, the Arabs of Arabia, like Maoris or American Indians, seem to inhabit a branch of fiction rather than the real world. Far from being free and noble, Bedouin tribal life was rigidly formalized, first by the extremely harsh conditions imposed by climate and geography, and then by the no less severe obedience to inherited shame-honor codes.

To settled Arabs everywhere, the Bedouin were a menace, backward and uncivilized, thieves and killers, tent dwellers beyond the reach of a mosque, having no tradition of learning or sound religion. Bedouin music and poetry have extensive and fine traditions but have rarely seemed to urban Arabs to be a cultural justification for tribal ways. Before the mechanization of transport, caravans used to set off annually from Cairo and Damascus, conveying Muslims under religious obligation to make the pilgrimage to Mecca, in the heart of Arabia. Into this century, the Bedouin were notorious for their habitual attacks and plunderings of these pious caravans. Until the end of the Ottoman Empire, inhabitants of cities such as Jerusalem, Damascus, or Baghdad were complaining to the authorities about Bedouin marauding. After 1918 British colonial administrators put a stop to it in Iraq, for instance, and the Aden hinterland, only by resorting to the superior force of air squadrons.

Sheltered through their physical remoteness from the Ottoman Turks and the West alike, out of contact with all alien ideas and all alien products except money and rifles, the Arabs of Arabia have modernized only lately and are still doing so in circumstances of particular difficulty and paradox. Disruptions of the kind familiar to the Arabs of the Mediterranean and the Levant have swept in on them like a tidal wave.

The process began as part of the British search for stability in the shipping lanes of the Gulf and the Indian Ocean. Gradually, the British drew tribal leaders and pirates into treaties in which peace was the price for British protection. Such treaties carried indirect benefits in cash or in kind which greatly influenced the leaders who signed them, and they had little or no conception that in fact they were legitimizing their own position in Western eyes and further laying the foundations of a dynasty. As usual, the British believed themselves to be falling in happily with cherished local custom.

Tribal lands and nomadic pasturage do not readily convert into states with defined and recognized boundaries. Any tribal leader who fancies himself in the ascendant will also hope to revive boundary disputes as the surest pretext for power challenging. Should it be suitable or timely, virtually every power holder in Arabia and the Gulf is able to exploit tribal custom to mount a claim upon the territories of his neighbors. As though dealing with European state frontiers, the British expended an immense amount of time and effort adjudicating and regularizing rival claims. Worthy and skillful as this endeavor was, it did not touch the underlying cause, which was tribal power challenging and its nature.

Translated by treaty into the ruler of a new state, the head of a Bedouin family, or tribal sheikh, finds himself an anachronism, accustomed to practices that offer no help in confronting the pressing political and social and economic questions of the present. Despotic authority is no substitute for the technical demands of modern government. But tribal life provides no other form of ruling institution. Saudi Arabia, Bahrain, Kuwait, the seven small entities comprising the United Arab Emirates of the Gulf are tribes and even families writ large and states only in the most tenuous sense of possessing a name and a flag and a vote at the United Nations. Of these states, Kuwait and Bahrain alone have experimented with any form of nontribal or power-sharing legislature, in both cases briefly and pointlessly. At the first clash of interest, the absolute ruler dismissed the parliamentary delegates as rapidly and arbitrarily as he had assembled them in the first place. The impact of the British in Arabia, then, has led to an outward or formal state formation and so to modernization, which is not in accordance with anything known to these tribal societies in the past. What emerges is no longer authentically Arab-tribal and certainly not a Western approximation, but a most unwieldy and unserviceable hybrid.

Thanks to its physical extent and wealth, Saudi Arabia is preeminent among these states. No reliable census exists because considerations of honor dictate inflated estimates of population as far apart as seven and eleven million, when the true figure may well be close to five million, of whom one million at least are immigrants. As the name indicates, the territory belongs to its ruling family, the Al Saud. To this day, there is neither a constitution nor any basic law regulating succession.

The fortunes of the Al Saud illustrate tribal power challenging in all its unpredictable vagaries. Muhammad Ibn Saud was the ruler in the eighteenth century of the oasis of Diriyah. Charles Didier, a Swiss, visited Arabia in 1834 and heard from witnesses how this ruler had used his large family to dominate others: "all power was concentrated in his own hand." In customary style, "expeditions were planned and conducted by Saud or his sons with remarkable skill, and were almost always successful; but the guiding spirit was not one of humanity. No prisoners were taken, and, thanks to the impulse of fanaticism, no quarter was given to the vanquished. Whole populations were put to the sword, as Koranic law decrees." In 1744 Saud entered into a sworn alliance with a religious preacher, Muhammad Ibn Abdul Wahhab, who had then settled in Diriyah. Marriages subsequently occurred between the two families, and from them descend the present Saudi power holders. Through this calculated alliance, the Saudi family was acquiring a religious principle on which to extend challenging, with the particular aim of capturing Mecca and Medina, where the pilgrimages provided the only replenishable source of funds.

Born between 1702 and 1704, the son of a judge, Ibn Abdul Wahhab had studied in Mecca and Medina, and Basra and Qom, and he published a treatise to advocate the stricter practice of Islam. Quite what the Bedouin of his day believed is a subject of debate; to some extent they seem to have remained animists worshipping sacred stones and groves of trees. At any rate, Ibn Abdul Wahhab successfully proselytized doctrines of Islam to which he gave his own name. To qualify Wahhabi doctrines with the Eurocentric appellations of "fundamentalist" or "revivalist" obscures their careerist nature and does nothing to explain the fact that Saudi tribal warriors have campaigned only within the House of Islam. Sunnis themselves, the Saudis have used Wahhabism for purposes of identity and tribal mobilization against other challengers, most particularly the Shia elements steadily infiltrating and encroaching from Persia. According to the twists of local rivalries and ambitions, Saudi tribesmen have pillaged the Shia shrines of Karbala and Najaf, and they have occupied and vandalized their own holy cities of Mecca and Medina.

More than once, the Al Saud appeared to have succumbed irretrievably to other tribal challengers, notably the Rashidis on adjoining lands. Abdul Aziz Ibn Saud (1880–1953), the greatest of the Saudi family power holders, extended his territory at the expense of all his tribal neighbors and rivals, destroying the Rashidis and then the Hashemites of Mecca, capturing Hasa from the Ottomans, and Asir from the Imam of Yemen, pursuing territorial disputes with Oman, Kuwait, and Abu Dhabi, raiding and massacring as far afield as Iraq and Transjordan. Few have shown greater expertise in extracting concessions from the British—then in their heyday as final arbiters of power and therefore able to check him—by the extremely simple expedient of making the greatest possible nuisance of himself to his fellow Arabs. In all his warring, he attracted his tribesmen less with prospects of some sort of purified Islam than through loot and money. When in the late 1920s Abdul Aziz at last became the region's undisputed power holder, his Wahhabi retinue naturally broke up as important personalities within it began to ask for greater rewards. In what amounted to civil war, he was obliged to restore his authority, "breaking the thorns" as he called it, or imprisoning and rendering powerless those who had assisted his rise. From then on, his need to have money and favors to distribute among his Wahhabi tribesmen, and so to pacify them, was imperative.

Greed apart, the money-favor nexus, even in its basic form of gold coins, first integrates and then fulfills the intimate and personal relationship of the ruled to their ruler. A Saudi has described this relationship and how it works to mutual profit:

A given tribe would invite the king and prepare a feast in his honor. The king's advisors estimated the expenses of such a party. Then the expenses would be doubled and handed to the tribe on the spot. The other neighboring tribes did the same and the same was done with them with regard to the expenses. A very limited number of tribal chieftains and tribesmen benefited from such operations simply because only well-to-do persons sponsored those parties and the benefits derived from them were divided among the sponsors, each of whom received an amount of money in proportion to the amount of money he contributed.

While ensuring his absolute authority through these time-honored means, Abdul Aziz also learned the lesson of other despots in his position, that modern technology and communications would centralize and strengthen his power. He began to travel by car rather than camel; he introduced telegraphy and the telephone. Not until about 1950, and the foundation of the Saudi Arabian Monetary Agency, was any distinction drawn between Abdul Aziz's private fortune and the state's revenue.

Earning himself masculine honor, Abdul Aziz fathered forty-seven sons from twenty-two different mothers, and as many daughters again from an ever-wider range of women. Marriage among these descendants is restricted almost exclusively to the handful of notable families of comparable status and honor, the Thunaiyan, Sudairi, Jiluwi. Saudi power holders have subsequently been sons of Abdul Aziz, and what with the honor attached to procreation, the family today may muster as many as 20,000. Numbers on this scale have the defensive purpose of deterring and disheartening possible challengers, and the offensive purpose of monopolizing money and rewards. All family members require palaces, incomes to support their status, and public offices which do them honor. In a process which is invisible to all but themselves, money and appointments are shared out accordingly. "There is no public opposition to government policy," writes Abbas Kelidar, a London-based Arab scholar, "no system of political parties or independent interest groups, and no elected representatives. Politics remain traditional, autocratic, highly personal and extremely centralized, and rather unaffected by the economic transformation which the country is undergoing."

The Al Khalifa family and the Al Sabah family captured Bahrain and Kuwait respectively in the eighteenth century and have ruled it ever since. Sunnis themselves, the Al Khalifas in Bahrain rule over a population of roughly 300,000, over half of them Shia of Persian origins. From time to time, some Shia conspiracy is discovered, and arrests and imprisonments follow. The Al Khalifas control the police and security apparatus on the one hand, and on the other apportion the oil wealth as they see fit. In Kuwait, the foreign colony in 1929 consisted of just eleven British and American residents. According to a census in 1980, the population was 562,065 native Kuwaitis, of whom about 20 percent were Shia, and 793,762 immigrants or non-Kuwaitis, of whom also 20 percent were Shia. The present Al Sabah ruler received secondary education in Kuwait and some police training in England, retaining control of his police and security apparatus and also of the finances. Khrushchev in 1964, in one of his operatic tantrums, characterized the Al Sabah of Kuwait: "There is some little ruler sitting there, an Arab of course, a Muslim. He is given bribes, he lives the life of the rich, but he is trading in the riches of his people." Tribal families, some of them related, similarly rule in Oman, Qatar, Abu Dhabi, Dubai, Sharjah, and the other emirates.

In 1968 the British Labour government of the time took the decision to withdraw from the Gulf within three years. As a prelude, there was one last instance of treaty signing to initiate a federation of the seven Gulf states, to be called the United Arab Emirates. Granted the nature of power challenging, this federation was as purely hypothetical as the unity on which British officials had previously based their expectations for the Arab League. Put bluntly, the federation represented the cynical perception of British officialdom that some apparent Western constitutional form would cover a multitude of sins and soothe liberal consciences in the West while in fact letting the local Arabs return to doing as they pleased to one another. Here is how one authority has described power challenging within these Gulf family emirates:

> Five of the seven emirs in the new federation had come to power through an irregular seizure of power. Sheikh Zayid of Abu Dhabi had overthrown his brother Shakhbut in 1966; Rashid of Dubai had deposed his uncles in 1932; Ahmed of Umm-al-Qaywayn had shot an uncle who had just murdered his father; Saqr of Ras-al-Khayma had expelled his uncle in 1948; and, in the most recent coup, 1972, Sheikh Sultan of Sharja assumed power after his brother Khalid had been shot by his cousin and the former ruler, Saqr ibn Sultan. In Abu Dhabi, the core state of the federation, 8 of the 15 emirs of the Al bu Falah dynasty of the Bani Yas tribe, which had ruled uninterruptedly since the 1760s, have been assassinated.

An influential line of thought—nostalgic, to be sure—runs to the effect that if these people so wish to conduct their affairs, it is nobody's business but theirs. Are other values likely to make them happier, and can these values either be taught or imposed with likelihood of success? What has cut right across the ancestral tribal custom which in its isolation might have continued indefinitely, wrenching it instead out of its historic course, is the discovery of oil in the Arabian peninsula, its extraction by Westerners for Western economic purposes, and its disproportionate rewards. Oil has determined the region's modernization and internationalization. Oil has also confirmed devastating social inequalities and injustices between people within a country, and then between countries with oil and those without it. The seven main Arab oil-exporting states account for about three-quarters of the region's gross domestic product but only about one-quarter of its population. Industry is only about 7 or 8 percent of aggregate GDP. Ninety-five percent of total Arab exports consists of oil, in itself an unbalancing factor socially and economically, with which none of the Arab regimes are able to cope.

No choice was offered to the Bedouin tribes in this matter. It would be absurdly unrealistic, however, to suppose that anyone could ever have contemplated rejecting the unheard-of and unprecedented wealth that suddenly spurted upon Arabia and the Gulf without its inhabitants having to lift a finger for it. At a stroke, as though the tale of Aladdin and his lamp had come true, the inhospitable desert turned effortlessly into what appeared to be riches without end. P. S. Allfree, a British district commissioner, was someone who had the typical experience of explaining to a desert tribe, in this case the Mahra, that an oil concession had been signed for their land. Some tribesmen opposed this, until at a gathering a spokesman by the name of Sulayim came forward to say that "We Mahra are the most God-forsaken people on earth," having nothing but camels and rifles, where other tribesmen had governments and so had prospered. Sulayim went on:

We have all seen, or heard of, Kuwait. Of the land of Ibn Saud. Of Bahrain; of Abu Dhabi. The people there have silver dollars in oil drums under the floors of their houses. And why? Because they have oil under their earth. Can *we* dig it out? Can we even dig out water by ourselves, except in the stream-beds? So we must have an oil company.

Sulayim carried his audience, but in his speech is the characteristic acceptance of traits that can only be psychologically disturbing and frustrating: mockery of tribal capacities, admitted inability to fend for oneself in the new circumstances, wealth unquestioningly desired through the instrumentality of an oil company whose techniques are not to be understood, and voluntary abjection before those very Westerners whom it has been customary to despise. Fed from several sources and from fresh experiences, this woeful loss of confidence is now common and widespread among the Arabs of

Arabia and the Gulf. Defensive xenophobia is only an aspect of the same phenomenon. The speed with which everything has happened leaves the population especially vulnerable. In the nineteenth century, Sir Edwin Pears has recorded, villagers in the Ottoman Empire possessed tin drums in which oil or kerosene had been shipped to them from the United States, the earliest and for a time the sole producer, and this possession was their one and only link in any form with the West. By the first decade of this century, the British were exploiting their first concession in Iran. Between the two world wars, concessions to Western oil companies were granted in Bahrain, Kuwait, and Saudi Arabia, where oil then came on stream. By 1948, the United States had become a large importer of petroleum products, and since then Western capitalist economies have been displaying the vigor and growth that lead to higher energy demands. Saudi Arabia alone is said to have about a quarter of the free world's oil deposits, which becomes a supply factor of economic and perhaps military significance.

Oil statistics and estimates derive from the extracting and marketing companies and must be treated with caution. Standing between Arab power holders and Western consumers, the oil companies are in the peculiar position once occupied by "renegades"; go-betweens or mediators between cultures whose main point of contact is the relaying of money and services. In a scaled-down repetition of what has happened to all other foreign or colonial presences before them, the oil companies have been drawn irresistibly into the Arab power-challenging dialectic, dropping Western commercial standards and practices in order to be integrated into the money-favor nexus. Mystificatory oil company jargon about "phantom freight" and "posted prices" and the rest of it screens who in the West is paying on what terms for which favors.

During the 1970s, known as "the oil years," the Arab countries as a whole exported oil worth $1,207.3 billion, of which $604.2 billion was used to import arms, consumer goods, and commodities. Consequently, the external transformation has been huge, and the visual effect correspondingly shocking. In Riyadh, Jiddah, Kuwait, the Gulf States, fortified city walls and old houses have been pulled down, and everywhere acres of concrete blocks have arisen. Western visitors may be assured of a hotel in familiar style. Even Mecca, the holy city where Westerners are forbidden, "has been overwhelmed by cloverleafs and overpasses, by tall office buildings, supermarkets, parking garages and deluxe hotels," according to a journalist. Soccer began in the 1950s, although opposed by the ulema on the grounds that the exposure of men's thighs was indecent and un-Islamic. Slavery was abolished officially in Saudi Arabia in 1962. Kuwait inaugurated television in 1962; Saudi Arabia in 1964, to be followed within the next seven years by Dubai, Abu Dhabi, Qatar, Bahrain, and Oman. All television stations, like all newspapers, are controlled by the local power holder and his loyal associates to serve and promote his interests. Within the last twenty years, a university has been built in Kuwait, in Abu Dhabi, and in Oman, and no less than seven in Saudi Arabia, three of them for Islamic teaching. The Gulf Telephone Directory lists something as farfetched as a bookstore in remotest Ajman. All urban centers are undergoing the population explosion common to the rest of the Arab world. Shirley Kay, an English woman who recently lived in Saudi Arabia, described the new semi-settlement of the Bedouin: "All around the fringes of the desert one sees villages of huts built of large tins or new breezeblock houses, with a black tent pitched beside each."

Old manners and new externals clash, sometimes painfully and grotesquely. As the steward of King Saud's household, José Arnold witnessed what the Bedouin in the 1950s had made of the trappings of a palace in Taif.

Each cubicle had originally been furnished with two beds and a bureau. New mattresses had to be supplied every year, the previous season's issue having become part of a Bedouin caravan during the winter months. While awaiting delivery of the mattresses, the staff slept on naked springs atop the beds or on the floor. The bureaus had long ago kindled the fires of passing tribes. The wrenched, empty hinges at the entrance way to each room testified to the Bedouin's ability to make a fire out of the doors. The water in the facilities of the community bathroom flowed up instead of down.

Money is no object for the royal family, westernizing today in the old egocentric style of Muhammad Ali in Egypt, Ahmed Bey in Tunis, or Sultan Abdul Aziz in Morocco.

The 12-year-old Prince Mubarak [Arnold again writes] received an elaborate million-dollar palace as a wedding gift. The walls of the majlis [the public reception room] of the new palace were extravagantly decorated with priceless Gobelin tapestries from Paris. Heavy crystal chandeliers swayed from the ceiling in the hallways, the banquet room, and the glass-enclosed terrace. Exotic silk draperies hung in voluminous folds from mahogany wallboards in the master bedroom. Large overstuffed chairs covered in silk brocade were scattered throughout the palace on expensive rugs laid on the marble floors. Silver vases, teak chests inlaid with mother-of-pearl, and mahogany tables added to the lavishness of the 50-room palace. At the far end of the reception room, two full-sized playground swings hung from the high ceiling to provide diversion for the youthful occupants of the palace. Wrought-iron flower baskets lined both sides of the reception room. No one among the palace crowd knew what the purpose of the baskets was, and they finally decided that they were cribs to be filled with royal babies.

Without this show-off, of course, the twelve-year-old prince would be shamed. As it is, he must be allowed to display that he is able to hold his own with Arab and Western counterparts and even to outdo them. In dealing with this outlook, Julio Caro Baroja has emphasized that "wealth, and nothing else, seems an almost physical force against which there is no means of fighting." Oil has had the unexpected consequence of reinforcing shame-honor ranking in all its ramifications, not merely impending reform but certifying and expanding long outdated values. Shame-honor necessitates that every man lay hands on as much of the new wealth as possible, and then flaunt it conspicuously in order to impress others by his status, while doing nothing that might be seen as earning it. Beginning at the top, the Al Saud example percolates downward, to be imitated everywhere. No Western supplier or contractor can operate by law without a Saudi partner; and offering themselves for this role, the Al Saud have a distinct advantage of prominence and influence. According to Said Aburish, a self-confessed practitioner of these arcane arts, a case can be made that "all the members of the House of Saud" are involved in what he calls "skimming," or profitably creaming off into their own pockets the maximum percentages from public contracts, in the awarding of which they themselves have had a hand. Business in Saudi Arabia is a matter of luring some hopeful Westerner and introducing him to those members of the Al Saud family entitled to sign contracts, negotiating and intriguing through sponsors and intermediaries and agency holders, defeating competing networks, depositing secret percentages and bribes into outstretched palms and Swiss accounts, finally bribing signature holders in banks to authorize the remittance abroad of profits. In short, the ancient desert *razzia* or tribal raid has converted into a deadly quagmire of money-favoring.

In an investigative book *The American House of Saud,* Steven Emerson has exposed the processes whereby leading American corporations, lobbyists and businessmen, former diplomats, even the U.S. Corps of Engineers have surrendered to local money-favoring. To move between the Arab and the Western value systems is to create a high and characteristic tragicomedy of limitless wealth one day and disaster the next, with apparent bankruptcy and foreclosure. Someone who seems to have lived this out in full public gaze is Adnan Khashoggi. Born in 1935, the son of a doctor in the royal household of Saudi Arabia, he was educated partly in Paris. According to his biographer Ronald Kessler, Khashoggi had been secretly commissioned by his king to act as middleman for the household's Western clients.

Arabs themselves, and not only the Saudis, reject as Eurocentric any definition that makes money-favoring out to be degrading and corrupt, arguing that this is their tradition, and they are operating comfortably within it. It is harder so expediently to deny or refute the moral and social consequences. Throughout Arabia and the Gulf, oil-inspired rewards have been divorced from work. Hospitals, schools, grants, pensions, municipal services pour out as so many gifts or benefactions from the rulers to the ruled. No man or woman in these countries has a real stake in the sense that he or she could express an opinion, influence a decision, organize and vote; one and all are outside participation in any communal unit superseding family and tribe and religion, and so become pensioners of the ruler, *rentiers* attendant upon the payout.

Forty thousand American and 30,000 British expatriates in Saudi Arabia perform the vital services which actually enable the country to function and modernize. Technical tasks, and of course laboring in all forms, demeaningly connote low status and therefore shame. Hanging around the oil fields, the Bedouin have lost their desert craft but acquired no compensating skills, "corner-boys" in Thesiger's desolating words, "a parasitic proletariat." In these Gulf states, 60 percent of the labor force is estimated to consist of immigrants, and in Saudi Arabia perhaps as much as 80 percent. "Possibly the most devastating negative effect of the oil wealth and its chain reaction," the Egyptian academic Saad Eddin Ibrahim has noted, "has been the near collapse of work ethics in the Arab world. Easily earned and easily spent money undermines the value of productive work."

Here are two advertisements from what may be called the Yellow Pages of the Gulf Telephone Directory.

Al Fateh Manpower Agency Services. We supply all kinds of skilled and unskilled labour to suit your requirements from: India, Pakistan, Philippines, Thailand, Bangladesh.

Hamad Manpower Services Ltd. Profit comes from skilled workers, that is a fact we can prove it. Just write or call us about your requirements of Male or female worker. Our services covers the Asian countries. [Spelling and grammar *sic.*]

This is slaving in modern guise. None of the immigrants have rights of any kind; they are beasts of burden to be shipped in and out again in bulk. Now and then, newspapers in their own countries carry some murky story about how one of their nationals has been abused as an immigrant, beaten, imprisoned, or murdered. Saudi prisons are notorious. In 1986 the U.S. State Department complained to the Saudi authorities about the treatment meted out. One American engineer had had his knees broken by his interrogators; another was tortured; while the head of the Industrial Development Group of California was detained for 130 days for having the temerity to sue a member of the royal household. In November 1986, thirty-five British nurses, radiographers, and medical secretaries, of whom twenty-five were women, were deported merely for attending a party at which alcoholic drinks had been served.

Where once every possession was thriftily cherished, now extravagance, duplication, and wastefulness are norms. Projects are initiated without regard to feasibility or markets but merely because someone has the requisite influence and the will for "skimming." A steel mill was started for which the raw materials had to be imported at prices that excluded profitability in the short and long term. The drawing-board industrialization of the towns of Yanbo and Jubail was undertaken without consideration of the facts that there was neither management nor a work force nor a body of consumers; and in any case, it all faded when the oil price fell. Needless to say, all such schemes depend on extrapolating an ever-rising oil price, a procedure which ignores the likely reactions of foreign oil purchasers and consumers. Wheat is being produced in Saudi Arabia at a cost greatly exceeding world prices; primary foodstuffs have to be imported at dangerously high levels. The cost of constructing anything is three or four times what it would be in the West, writes one authority, J. B. Kelly, and this, he adds, "throws doubts upon the ability of any Saudi Arabian industrial enterprise to compete on economic terms with similar enterprises abroad." According to some estimates, at least half of the entire oil wealth so far may have been frittered and wasted. The assumption remains constant that oil wealth brings no particular responsibility to understand the Western forces and sciences which generated it. As J. B. Kelly summarizes,

the Saudi Arab is convinced of the superiority of his own culture over that of the West and of the industrial world in general. He believes that he can acquire and use whatever the West has to offer in the way of material goods and technological methods, and at the same time reject the culture which produced them. It is, quite literally, incomprehensible to him that the products and skills of the West are inseparable, in their genesis and development, from the West's empirical and scientific traditions.

Sir James Craig was British ambassador in Saudi Arabia, and in a confidential dispatch of June 1984 he too drew attention to this attitude, singling out Saudi insularity and incompetence, which he elaborated as fecklessness and lack of organisation.

Not only do they reject all manual and menial work: they are also reluctant to undertake anything which is tedious or humdrum. Plumbing is manual and roadsweeping is menial: for these tasks they employ foreigners. But whereas taking decisions is noble, the work of preparing to take decisions is ignoble: so the collection of facts, the collation of statistics, the checking of references, the planning of timetables is skimped.

What seems to the Westerner to be arrogance, as ignorant as it is stupid, Craig rightly perceived to be the product of honor values. The tribesman "was arrogant when he was miserably poor." If he had been wrong then, in his opinionated view, he would not have been so rewarded now.

Beyond wastefulness is paralyzing boredom, a stultification impervious to intellectual innovation or creativity. Saudi Arabia is a society with strict segregation of the sexes. At all times, a woman in public must be in her black veil; she may never go out unescorted or drive a car, or attend a class with men in schools or universities; she must use separate elevators in buildings and may go only to banks staffed by female employees. There are no public entertainments, no dancing, no cinemas, no alcohol. Tourism is virtually nonexistent. Initiative may be stifled to the point of surrealism. For instance, a magnificent and expensive bridge has been constructed between Saudi Arabia and the island of Bahrain, but for some time it was kept shut for fear that the Saudis might contaminate themselves through contact with the rather more lax Bahrainis.

Behind closed doors, in silence, hypocrisy breeds and festers. To do shameful things is not of great consequence provided that there is nobody actually to observe or to denounce. It was generally known, for instance, that King Saud was an alcoholic. Westernized Saudis will gladly drink among themselves and in the presence of Westerners and will show obscene videos or pornographic publications and force themselves sexually upon Western women. Anyone in the Western community who might take it upon himself to behave in such ways runs the risk of a public flogging and deportation, while the punishments for Saudis without influence will be merciless. Those Saudis successful in money-favoring are able to escape to the West to buy themselves houses and properties in places like Geneva and Düsseldorf, Brussels and London, where they surrender unabashedly to Western indulgences. Such liberation brings temptation and scandal in its wake. Before taking up his appointment as a doctor in Riyadh, Seymour Gray was asked to treat a Saudi princess for what proved a noncancerous lump in her arm. She was staying in a hotel in the United States. He recalled the scene.

I was ushered into the living quarters set aside for the princes. It had the atmosphere of a bordello. Loud music was blaring from all directions, and white-coated waiters were running back and forth, carrying trays of assorted drinks and snacks. The young princes and their friends were shouting to each other through the walls. There was loud, raucous laughter coming from the rooms, punctuated at times by a female scream. Semi-clad women could be seen darting from room to room, giggling, followed by Saudi princes who were unshaven and dishevelled. Everyone seemed drunk to the gills. It looked as though the bacchanal had been going on for some time.

In April 1986 the Saudi prince Mashur Bin Saud Bin Abdul Aziz was sentenced to prison in London for possession of cocaine. The court heard how "He lavished huge sums of his £250,000 a year allowance on cocaine, vice-girls, night-clubs and accounts at some of London's most expensive hotels." That June, also in London, another Saudi prince, named as Bander Al Jawali, was arrested for drunken driving, to which he pleaded guilty.

At a more mundane level, 20,000 Saudis are estimated to be studying in the West. Around about 1950, the population was 95 percent illiterate, so that these students abroad, as well as the 100,000 or so in Saudi universities, represent change even if its uncontrolled quantitative growth, according to one authority, leads to poor and now declining standards. In any case, home-trained students aspire to honor-bearing and lucrative posts in the bureaucracy, while foreign-trained students not only expect commensurate rewards but also have often acquired Western-type consciousness of their country and their position in it.

Returning home, whether from higher education or profligacy or merely the foreign taste of freedom, Saudis have been westernized enough to be dissatisfied and alienated. An English journalist, Linda Blandford, has described the cultural anomalies through which such people have to find their way.

This wife can't take it [Linda Blandford wrote]. She sits in her living room hooked on cigarettes and tranquillisers. She's in her late twenties, shrinking, wasting away, her face pale and pasty. Her long slender legs hang listlessly below her short Paris couture skirt and skinny T-shirt. In some ways life was easier for her mother. There were slaves then but a wife still had to work. No Californian-style kitchens a generation ago, no air-conditioning, no schooling abroad or glimpses of an alternative life to the prison of the women's quarters. The daughter has lost and gained from progress. Several times a week she covers her face with a mask of make-up, slides into long gowns, mechanically arranges the jewels that label her the possession of a multi-millionaire and they go out together; that's avant-garde for Riyadh.

This Saudi woman of apparent privilege then explains,

I went to a European boarding school with normal girls. Do you know how hard it has been for me to adjust? Women can't drive here so I can't leave the home without a driver for the car. When I do go out I have to put on a long black cloak and cover my face. I suffocate. I know other women say it'll disappear one day. But what about now? It's now that the veil suffocates me, now that I'm humiliated.

Shame-honor inhibits truth telling, and double standards become the rule, as exemplified in this woman's daily life. The word "Christmas" is taboo and may not be used except on December 24, when it is permitted as a description of the following day. A Saudi supermarket dressed up one of its employees as Mickey Mouse to hand out Christmas gifts, whereupon this man was arrested for un-Islamic behavior. Christians may have religious services only by subterfuge within their respective embassies. Jews are altogether forbidden to enter the country, and one British ambassador of Jewish origins proved persona non grata. Yet Prince Faisal of the royal family in June 1987 is reported to have attended a Christian memorial service in Newmarket, England, for an English racehorse trainer.

Hilary Mantel is another English woman who recently lived in Saudi Arabia. The cities are all alike today, she writes, "skyscrapers, fast roads, municipal greenery nourished at vast expense" with "a pervading smell of sewage, a burning, used-up wind." Sometimes, "you might see an old man sitting on the sidewalk, his *thobe* [Arab gown] dirty, his knees pulled up to his ears, staring out at the stream of traffic. The pace of life is murderous. Each intersection has its little massacre." The contrast between what was said and what was done was unacceptable to her. According to the newspapers, there was no crime, no corruption; the women were all chaste, and the families all happy. Actually, amputations of the limbs of criminals were carried out on a Friday after prayers, women were stoned to death for fornication, and in a shabby block of flats an immigrant woman had been found raped and strangled, her children decapitated. She concluded, "The system is cracking up from the inside." This may be a Eurocentric interpretation, however, in that it does not allow for tribal-religious solidarity. Seymour Gray, happening to come upon a public execution in the Riyadh square which once had been the site of the slave market, noted the absence of pity in the spectators. The executioner "took several quick small steps—almost as in a ballet—and then with one long stride he raised the sword high and with a loud whoosh brought the sword down with all his strength, severing the head. . . . For a moment there was a stunned silence, and then a single roar of approval rose from the crowd."

"We believe that it is possible to maintain our traditional Islamic values while creating a modern industrial society with high levels of material welfare available to all citizens." So spoke one of the royal princes, Abdullah Al Saud, at a conference sponsored by Saudi funds in an English university, in itself a notable extension into the West of money-favoring. "Traditional Islamic values" is a piece of mystification for the benefit of credulous Westerners who suppose themselves to be sympathizing with diversity and custom. Such a statement does not refer to Wahhabi devotions, and its primary meaning concerns the determination of the Al Saud to strengthen their stranglehold upon local resources and people. The word "citizens" in this context has no reality for tribesmen who enjoy no rights, who do not participate in political processes or decision-making, and whose sole safeguards are those defensive practices common to tribe or family. No thought has been given to the question whether a modern industrial society is compatible with a tribal order devoid of political institutions to sustain it. Were he sincere, Abdullah Al Saud could not gloss so lightly over the fact that there is no prospect of sharing power. In Arabia and the Gulf states, power holders do meet in public at regular hours with their tribesmen—any one of whom may therefore have direct access to the ruler—and launch into such money-favor proceedings as he is prepared to let the other tribesmen present overhear. Apologists frequently like to call this democracy and even "traditional Islamic values," but clearly a petitioner is in no sense a citizen protected by the law. In his own case at least, a petitioner may on occasion favorably influence decision making or alleviate some grievance, but that is a very different matter from participating on equal and guaranteed terms in debates about social and national issues.

Ghazi Algosaibi has been a minister of industry in Saudi Arabia and is well reputed as a modernist, Western-educated, and an, author. His *Arabian Essays,* published in 1982, covered a number of topics of the day. Somewhere in these essays is an oblique recognition of Saudi reality, as when he writes in "On bribeocracy" that bribery is prevalent. The man who takes bribes, he explains, is active and intelligent, usually enjoying the respect of others. No further information is provided about the way money-favoring legitimizes the general corruption, and no mention is made of the shame-honor ranking that ensures the "bribeocrat" this unusual respect.

In the broadest terms, Algosaibi approves of education, and he scatters about vague phrases like "the new Arab world" that will be socially and economically developed. Nonetheless he can write, "The masses were too uninformed, too excitable and too unreliable to exert any beneficial influence on the making of foreign policy." At what point, one wonders on behalf of this minister, will education be deemed sufficient to have calmed the masses' excitability and allow them to exert influence? Purporting to address America at large, he makes the request, "bring justice to the Middle East." Of course this is the usual plea from a client to an acknowledged sponsor and arbiter of power, but what it might entail in the way of modalities and desired ends, he omits to say. Much more revealing is the depressingly self-doubting implication that the Arabs are unable to bring justice to themselves. For all his position, Algosaibi shares the outlook of Sulayim, the Mahra tribesman in favor of the oil companies because of the rewards they promised.

Too feeble to have practical application, analyses and prescriptions of this sort only serve the existing power holder and his order. A book like *Arabian Essays* therefore takes its place within money-favoring and power challenging, and against reform. Political wisdom for Algosaibi comes down to apostrophizing in time-honored careerist manner, "My God, protect me from the evil of my friends; for their eyes veiled by love see in me only what they want to see. My God, protect me from the evil of my enemies, who suffer because of your gifts to me and who cause me to suffer with them."

The maintenance of "our traditional Islamic values" is another imprecise prescription of the same kind. In theory, Saudi Arabia is a Sunni theocracy in which the ruler has the duty to apply Islamic Law. Outwardly, Islam might appear to be thriving there, in that there are 17,000 mosques, or one for perhaps every 250 people. A Board of Grievances was set up in 1955 to be the forum for cases outside Islamic Law, and in 1971 the whole judicial system was revised. The power holder appointed various quasi-judicial bodies to deal with problems caused by economic, administrative, and social developments. In the absence of formal legislative authority, however, the power holder still needs the ulema to sanction what he is doing. There is an Institute of Religio-Legal Opinions for this very purpose, and between 1965 and 1974, for instance, it issued 675 decrees approving what the power holder had done, but none disapproving. Under this institute, but ultimately responsible to the power holder, is a force to police morals, with the name of "the Committee of Exhortation to Good and Interdiction of Evil." These moral policemen enforce Islamic duties as well as prohibitions, patrolling the streets to stamp down on alcohol and tobacco, gambling, Western entertainments of any sort, prostitution, and ensuring that women are properly veiled and accompanied. They insist on the closure of shops at times of daily prayer, and they carry sticks or truncheons to compel obedience. One authority writes, "Boys hide in side-streets and shops at prayer time for fear of being manhandled. In one case [in 1977], a committee member was stabbed to death when he surprised and tried to arrest some people eating in the month of Ramadan," during which time fasting must be observed in daylight hours.

The maintenance of traditional Islamic values, then, proves in practice to be the maintenance of the Al Saud power holders. The ostentatious, not to say vulgar, behavior of the Al Saud as individuals has long since drained the meaning out of their Islamic pretensions—or as the Arabist Malcolm H. Kerr put it, "the present regime is giving Wahhabism a bad name." Challenges to the Al Saud have come from those Muslims who feel themselves seriously harmed and persecuted by the regime's political exploitation of Islam, and of these the most grave and abiding come from the Shia minority, hardly more than 5 percent of the population, but almost all concentrated in Hasa province. Discrimination in education, housing, and employment keeps the Shia subjugated. Among the immigrant workers, 200,000 or so are Yemeni Zaydis, or Shia, and they too are in constant danger of arbitrary arrest and deportation. Local Sunni prejudices against Shia go to extreme lengths. Some Shia Iranian pilgrims have been banned from entry to the country, and others already in Mecca have been forbidden to hoist placards of Ayatollah Khomeini. In spite of prohibitions, Iranians at the bidding of the Ayatollah often insist on political demonstrations in Mecca, and did so in July 1987 when thousands surged into the streets leading to the Great Mosque, chanting "Death to America, death to the Soviet Union, death to Israel." Whether shooting occurred is not clear, but in the ensuing panic about 400 people were reported dead and many hundreds more injured. (In a normal year, an average of forty pilgrims lose their lives in the crush.)

In November 1979 local Shia in Hasa celebrated their rites in defiance of the law and in an affray killed a National Guardsman, burnt some buildings, and called for the overthrow of the regime. That same month, in an unrelated incident, two brothers-in-law, Juhaiman and Muhammad Al Qahtani characteristically conspired, recruiting a retinue of over a hundred followers. This armed group then seized the great mosque in Mecca, holiest of Islamic shrines.

A drawn-out siege followed, culminating in an assault on the mosque, as a result of which dozens of conspirators were shot and over sixty were executed afterward, including the brothers-in-law. Their motives, as they explained, had been to practice the strict Islam which once had been the Wahhabi justification, but which they and their supporters felt had long since been abandoned in the sinful riches of oil. The ulema, pliant as usual, issued a decree to sanction the killing of these dissidents even within the mosque's precincts.

How long it will remain possible for the Al Saud to defeat power challengers remains uncertain. In 1969 an earlier conspiracy in the air force came mysteriously to a head, and about 200 officers were arrested. Public opinion can be neither expressed nor consulted. In self-defense, the Al Saud have recruited a National Guard some 10,000 strong, consisting of descendants of those loyal tribesmen who once raided and fought with Abdul Aziz ibn Saud. In addition, the armed forces number 52,500, with 450 tanks, 14 SAM missile batteries, the 4 AWACS whose delivery was an American political issue, 7 squadrons of modern fighter and intercepter aircraft, a naval flotilla, and a budget for 1985–86 of $17,777 million. Levels of education and technological skill are poor, and the troops have no compensating combat experience. The vast expenditure on arms that almost certainly could not be used outside their stockpiling warehouses is only the latest instance of military modernization as practiced by Ottoman and Arab despots; and it refers more to values of honor than to actual preparation for battle.

Instead, the Al Saud prefer the technique of using money defensively, thereby hoping to recruit other Arabs into their retinue and to convert possible challengers into clients. Thanks to their oil revenues, the Saudis have been able to extend their particular money-favor nexus over the whole Middle East, enmeshing or entrapping into it the entire spectrum of Arab power holders and challengers. The daily task of the Saudi ruler and his close kinsmen consists in assessing friends and opponents and then buying or holding them off, estimating and apportioning subsidies, bribes, subventions, the whole gamut of open or concealed transfers of money. To whichever palace the ruler happens to be momentarily inhabiting comes the stream of petitioners and clients, heads of Arab states, leaders of underground movements and conspiracies, royalists who seek alliance, republicans who proffer defiance but may be bribed and cheated, those who plead unity and those who plead separatism, intriguers against every Arab power holder and then the agents dispatched with instructions to go one better than the intriguers, murderers who implement policy decisions by means of bomb and bullet; and last and certainly least those venal Westerners who are willing to enrich themselves no matter by what means, but who, perhaps fortunately for all, as often as not are lost and finally impoverished in coils of deception that they do not have the talents to unravel. In this respect too, nothing has changed since Ottoman days, when Sir Charles Eliot put words into the mouth of such a Westerner: "I suppose I might be described as a concession hunter or a commission agent. The essence of my trade is to make Orientals buy what they don't want—anything from matches to railroads. I bribe them to purchase my wares and they bribe me to put down in the bill (which the Ottoman Government pays) a much larger sum than I have actually received. So we both make money."

Plots have plots within them; and no outsider can hope to see his way through them. Rewards are lavishly promised. The monarch nods; his kinsmen adopt a serious demeanor. Gigantic sums are mentioned and sometimes even published in the newspapers. The figures bear no relation to what is actually disbursed. There is neither auditing nor accountability. The anxious petitioner must search out who is obstructing him, and why, where the rake-offs must be diverted, who has become resentful or extra-avaricious, how to turn promise into performance. Documents duly signed and witnessed somehow turn into dead ends, into mere rumors and whispers. Months pass. Something will be done soon, say the intermediaries and middlemen, as they step with dignity from offices into the Mercedes which will sweep them off at high speed into the limbo of their own money-favoring. No appeal is possible. Only occasionally does a hard fact emerge, as when King Saud in 1958 was detected by Syrian intelligence offering a bribe of $2 million for the murder of Nasser; or when in 1975 King Faisal was shot dead by one of his nephews to revenge his brother, himself shot on the king's order ten years previously for an armed attack on the television station in some murky challenge of his own.

Passionate religious prejudice against Israel combines with a fear of the Soviet Union to create a contradiction at the heart of Saudi foreign policy, excitable and unreliable at the best of times. To the Saudis, communism and Zionism are two sides of a coin, and their money-favoring follows this Islamocentric incoherence. The Al Saud have subsidized Egypt to the tune of hundreds of millions of dollars for war against Israel, but they have also subsidized the Yemeni royalists almost as expensively to wage war against Egypt and its clients, the Yemeni republicans; they have subsidized Iraq, a Soviet client, but which is also a Sunni regime fighting Shia Iran; they have paid many hundreds of millions of dollars to Syria and to the PLO, both Soviet clients, but ostensibly killers of the hated Jews. Intimidated or suborned by the Al Saud, the lesser Gulf power holders buy a quiet life by imitation or deference or at least the pretense of doing so. Oil has facilitated each and every one of these maneuvers and mysteries which self-defeatingly neutralize and cancel out one another. But a unique and unrepeatable fortune has been dissipated into gunsmoke in one desert after another.

A few Arab writers have drawn attention to reality, among them the Lebanese Georges Corm, who speaks with eloquence and scorn of "this oil-fired tyranny, the new scourge of the Arabs," judging the society to be "sick with oil." A Kuwaiti professor, Muhammad Ruhaimi, concludes his book *Beyond Oil* somberly. "Vested interests" in the Gulf, he says, oppose social justice and efficiency and "continue to block any rational or open political development." This is about as far as someone in his position can go without bringing down retribution.

Perhaps it is impossible to devise political institutions to deal reasonably with social change in so extreme, yet so immobile, a context. Adding unstoppable impetus to ancient patterns of power challenging and to shame-honor, oil wealth has obstructed any move even to address the question, let alone resolve it. In the absence of such institutions, Western-style buildings and the importation of industrial and consumer goods do not contribute to modernization but to deepening outrage and oppression.

11

The Issue of Palestine

At the onset of industrialization in the nineteenth century, a sense took hold in Europe that a wrong turning was at hand. People of influence believed that in factories and cities the masses were being submitted to a life more abusive than the customary ways. Consequent attitudes of willful pessimism can be seen with hindsight for the romanticism that it was.

After the Second World War, once again people of influence questioned values everywhere in the West, creating another climate of pessimism which was contrary to the evidence. The West, it was widely argued, had acquired scientific and manufacturing power on a scale that was dehumanizing, irresistibly eroding other cultures and even threatening its own progress. In this view, those who opposed the West were to be encouraged and welcomed, no matter what the purpose or motivation might be. Defined simplistically as an assertion of Western power, colonialism was hastened to its close in this climate.

Citizens of democracies incline to attend to their critics and to accommodate through intellectual speculation even the most hostile views. Elements of doubt, therefore self-doubt too, must always be in play within democratic societies in the process of opinion-forming. With hindsight again, the West since 1945 can be seen in reality to have entered a new industrial age of exceptional vitality, leading to increasing choice and freedom. Temporarily, the unexpected confrontation of the Cold War had proved unnerving. To applaud experiments in collective socialism or communism alien to democratic traditions and values, to praise the China of

Mao Ze-dong and the Vietnam of Ho Chi Minh or the expedition of Che Guevara into the Andes, to conceive that the "winds of change" detected by Harold Macmillan in Africa were autonomous and beneficial to Africans, to listen either with fear or joy to Khrushchev's threat that the Soviet Union would bury the West were facets of latter-day romanticism. Imminent doom had its Byronic fascination. In any case, to believe that the blame for the ills and barbarities of other nations or cultures lay with the West was another instance of Eurocentric self-importance, a gratuitous posture.

The Palestine Liberation Organization was a phenomenon of this aberrant period. Restricted in its scope, the PLO was a local power challenge characteristic of Arab politics, but otherwise of little international significance. Thanks to Western confusion, this particular bid for power was magnified out of all proportion, unrecognizably distended to fit into political preconceptions inapplicable to the context. Western societies have been familiar with national liberation movements of their own; the PLO declared itself to be such a movement; the West could accord it a corresponding enthusiasm. This syllogism was false. Far from enjoying popular participation or sanction, the PLO was a strictly careerist grouping around a few ambitious personalities, and it is comparable to other groupings within the Arab order also claiming the right to speak for a nation, for instance the Polisario in the Sahara, the pretenders in Dhofar, Aden, North Yemen, or even Islamic fundamentalists everywhere, whether Sunni or Shia. Their several interests have been rightly perceived in the West as local concerns rather than causes with which to identify. The PLO differs from these other self-proclaimed national movements only in that its challenge is aimed at Israelis, whom it insists on projecting as outsiders and westerners alien to the regional tribal-religious system within which they must operate as others do. Were the PLO to succeed in its declared goal of recovering Palestine, then Israel would cease to exist, and Israelis would undergo the tribal-religious fate of massacre and expulsion. Then, in the Arab perspective, not only Israel but the West as a whole would be judged the loser in a counterassertion of Arab power justified by custom and religion; while in the Western perspective, the either-or logic once so glibly accepted by Mandate officials would be thought to have reached its natural outcome of primitive savagery about which nothing can be done.

In the course of a quarter of a century, PLO leaders and spokesmen have been received and embraced all over the world, addressed the United Nations to a standing ovation, been honored in the Vatican by Pope John Paul II, been official guests or delegates in India and Austria and Greece, Japan and China and elsewhere, and established either diplomatic representation or an office in over a hundred countries. During that same time, the PLO otherwise impinged directly on the West only through its murdering of opponents, the huge majority Palestinian to be sure, but some of them Israelis and other innocent bystanders, including diplomats, and by its hijacking of aircraft and taking hostage more innocent people, all the while persistently threatening to commit more of these crimes. "Palestinian" has become synonymous with criminal, and passengers and travelers have to submit to security routines everywhere involving inconvenience and fear: that is the global memorial to the PLO. No positive achievements, certainly no state-building, make a counterweight. Criminality has nonetheless not negated all prospect for a state. Western governments repudiate the terror without which the PLO would have no political presence, yet regularly declare that the PLO must be a party to peace talks affecting the Middle East. Western media criticize, even sensationalize, the PLO record of crime, yet are prone to underwrite demands for a PLO state.

Governmental as well as personal stances of the kind are inextricably mixed with inherited attitudes toward Jews. Few or none of those Western governments or individuals who veer toward the PLO actually wish to participate in another genocide of Jews or imagine that they will be doing so, preferring to concentrate on Palestinian liberation rather than massacre of Israelis. Yet in such a complacent attitude are assumptions that either-or logic is operative and that Jewish fate is secondary, that Gentiles know best what Jewish interests might be, that Jews must obey the dispensation of others even in matters of life and death. Granted that the state of Israel can defend itself, Israelis and other Jews might well shrug off what is a vacuous contemporary version of anti-Semitism.

For the Palestinian masses, however, the implication of Western support for the PLO is far more immediate and dangerous. Long since led to fragmentation by Haj Amin, Palestinians have no means of mobilizing a national movement or expressing a national will, if indeed such a thing exists. Perhaps five million all told, and altogether a tenacious people of conservative or tribal instincts, Palestinians have spread out in exile as far away as the Gulf, Australia, and South America in the attempt to rebuild a life on the familiar model. Those in the West who indiscriminately advance a Palestinian national movement are first of all patronizing these people for their real and hard-won efforts to normalize, and secondly sentimentalizing them as "freedom fighters" and "guerrillas" in images that would prove suicidal if ever they were to come true. It is romantic fantasy that impels some Westerners to want to march defenseless Palestinians into further murderous fighting in which they themselves would participate at a safe distance only by means of excited shudders about the culpability of their own societies in creating an Arab-Jewish conflict. Victims first of fellow Arabs making careerist claims in their name, and then of Westerners who project them according to their own unfounded notions, ordinary Palestinians have the misfortune to be duped twice over. Since 1965, 650 Israelis have been killed by the PLO (compared with 4464 killed in wars in that period), but the lowest possible estimate of Palestinians who have died by the hand of fellow Arabs in civil disturbances is 35,000, and the true figure may be much higher. Through unrelenting experience of power-challenge politics, from the past era of Haj Amin to the present day of Yasser Arafat, the long-suffering Palestinians have had to perfect the ruses, lies, pretenses, evasions, and switches of allegiance necessary for survival in their world.

In the twilight years after the division of Palestine between Israel, Jordan, and Egypt, nobody had seen fit to speak for the Palestinians or to sponsor a people scattered to make what they could of their ordeal, often as refugees living off United Nations charity. Nasser was the first to perceive this omission, and his sponsorship of the Palestinians in 1964 was in his most deft and self-seeking style. He had in mind the example of the FLN, which had lately come to power in Algeria, in some measure also through his sponsorship. Launching the Palestine Liberation Organization, Nasser hoped for advantages, in that enmity to Israel mobilized other Arab power holders in his support and also attracted arms and subsidies from the Soviet Union. To his cost he had learned that this particular challenge had dangers better passed on to proxies. To head the PLO, Nasser selected Ahmad Shuqairi, son of Sheikh Asad Shuqair, the notable from Acre who had sat in the Ottoman parliament, but himself a man skilled in money-favoring at its most devious. Duly in May 1964, a founding conference of the PLO was held in east Jerusalem, and headquarters established there. A national council was set up, followed by a charter specifying PLO aims.

To prepare for any kind of genuine participatory mass movement was no part of Nasser's intention. Carefully he was to provide subsidies in a measure to ensure that nothing more or less than his orders were obeyed; he was to restrict the supply of weapons and therefore of PLO power. In accordance with current Arab shamebound apologetics, Nasser and Shuqairi too declared Israel to be imperialist and racist and therefore fit to be destroyed and replaced by "a secular democratic state" of Palestine. *Liberation—Not Negotiation* was a booklet published in 1966 by Shuqairi, and the title says all that can be said about the complete and unchanging approach of the PLO.

Further power-challenge responses were at once set in motion, which not even so subtle a manipulator as Nasser could be certain of controlling. The Syrian Baathists who had just seized power in Damascus were not about to allow Nasser to steal a march by this means, and by the end of 1964 they too had recruited their own Palestine Liberation Organization under Yasser Arafat. Here was the usual duality in the struggle for supremacy. By 1965 small squads of Palestinians at the behest either of Egypt or Syria were crossing at night into Israel to lay explosive charges. Hardly any damage was done to life or to property, but a localized power-challenge play had begun to draw in Israel on its terms, so opening the usual hypothetical calculations for assuring profit and laying off losses.

Whether or not this was the deliberate intention of Nasser and the Syrian Baathists, King Hussein of Jordan was also drawn into these moves. The PLO teams chose to operate out of his territory, and Israeli reprisals therefore hit Jordan. On the eve of the 1967 war, King Hussein flew to Cairo, where Nasser deceived him into joining an expedient alliance, dispatching Shuqairi with him on the aircraft back to Amman. Shuqairi's presence in Jordan influenced the king's fatal decision to engage Israel on the opening day of that war, thereby setting in motion the steps that were to lose him the West Bank and enmesh him irretrievably in the PLO play for power that was to follow. A robust defensive power holder himself, the king lacked the offensive resources of Nasser or the Syrians and was unprepared for war. *The Fall of Jerusalem* is an eyewitness account of events on the Jordanian front as seen by Abdullah Schleifer, an American journalist whose conversion to Islam had strengthened an emotional hostility to Israel. Tragicomedy obtained everywhere, in Schleifer's account, as when an elderly notable suffering from gout appeared at a command post, armed with pistols, dagger, and rifle, to assure the others there, "We will dine in Tel Aviv." Afterward the PLO claimed to have been the principal agent unleashing this war. This was vainglory. With a membership of a few hundred at most, under close Egyptian or Syrian supervision, the PLO was in no position to have a military or political role.

In the aftermath of the war, Nasser and the Syrian Baathists and King Hussein shared the common predicament of having wrecked themselves through a misconceived challenge to Israel. Here was one of those moments of vacuum, perplexity, and paradox created by this type of politics. However much the protagonists may have wished inwardly to disengage, none could do so without accepting a fully publicized shame. Recovery of honor was an absolute imperative, and the PLO appeared to be the sole instrument available for the purpose. Shuqairi was dismissed as a scapegoat, and Yasser Arafat soon replaced him, with backing now from Egypt and Syria alike. At a series of meetings of heads of Arab states, Saudi Arabia and Kuwait and the Gulf Emirates and Libya were pledged to subsidize the PLO. In an annual ritual, millions of petro-dollars are promised, but the proportion actually paid is not known. With lack of any title to be doing so, the heads of Arab states further were to endorse resolutions that the PLO was the official representative body of the Palestinians, and then that Palestine was to be "secular and democratic." Every Arab state is a despotism whose constitution specifies that Islam is the state religion, and once again no clue was provided about the modalities of what would have been an unprecedented achievement in Arab nation building, in which secularism and democracy as yet have no reality, let alone institutional dimensions.

Unity itself was a mere appearance, a show for the sake of recovering honor. Far from uniting behind the Palestinian cause as words might indicate, every Arab state in practice discriminated against Palestinians living in its midst and had differing slants upon the PLO. Each Arab power holder was in fact calculating the extent to which the PLO might actually mount a power challenge of its own, and in that case what was the likelihood of its success, and whether this might in turn prove a threat to his security, or on the contrary a useful lever against a rival power holder. Whatever might be publicly declared, weapons and subsidies were doled out according to these private and careerist machinations. Expressed conversely, the PLO found itself presented through the wider Arab disaster with the opportunity for self-assertion. Yasser Arafat's success followed from the speed and maneuverability with which he seized his moment; his failure followed from the fact that he was unable to transcend careerist power challenging, to free the PLO from the incompatible interests of its sponsors, and so create a mass movement for which he would have the right to be spokesman. In capturing the PLO, Arafat had had rivals who no doubt would have acted as he did, with the complete disregard for every larger consideration that accompanies brutally careerist ambition. Beyond that, however, Arafat displays a temperament eager to accept responsibility for killing and bloodshed on an unlimited scale.

Such psychological impulses must lie deep in the personality, and have to remain murky as Arafat has been unusually reticent and mystifying about himself, even about so simple a fact as the place of his birth, although the year, 1929, seems established. For political reasons, he wishes to be thought a native-born Jerusalemite, though from records he appears to have been born in Cairo, or perhaps Gaza. His father was a prosperous merchant. Through his mother, Arafat was a member of the Husseini family, therefore a kinsman of Haj Amin, his mentor. In background and education, he was close to the Muslim Brothers. Thomas Kiernan, his biographer, spoke to several witnesses who had known the youthful Arafat, and from their testimony he credits him with a variety of formative violent activities including the murder of innocent people. In one case, Arafat is alleged to have shot dead a friend, showing no remorse when the man's innocence was then proved. In order to certify himself, a careerist requires past heroics, however mythical, but these deeds of Arafat's hardly seem the kind to vouch for courage or honor. To journalists asking about his private life, Arafat likes to say that he has remained single because he is wedded to Palestine.

Dozens of trivial conspiracies had sprung up in the wake of the 1948 collapse. In power-challenge terms, Palestine had become an arena in which anyone who fancied his skill and ambition could hope to operate. As a student in the 1950s in Egypt or in Europe, Arafat had met Khalil al-Wazir and Salah Khalaf, and these three began to conspire to promote themselves within Palestinian circles. Later they recruited into their conspiracy Khalid al-Hassan and Farouk Qaddumi and two or three more who ever since have been the PLO leadership. "A sacred covenant" between them was sworn one night on a beach in Kuwait.

Arafat distinguished himself from rivals in his ability to persuade current power holders to sponsor him; in succession, Ben Bella, the Syrian Baathists, and Nasser. The Egyptian journalist Mohamed Heikal has described how Arafat contacted Egyptian intelligence in 1966, and how he himself then conducted Arafat into Nasser's presence. On that occasion, Heikal recalls, Arafat typically made an issue of whether or not to wear a revolver. Nasser is quoted as saying to Arafat, "I would be more than glad if you could represent the Palestinian people and the Palestinian will to resist, politically by your presence and militarily by your actions." In democratic terms, this scene and the sentiments are preposterous. No electoral or representative process had legitimized either Nasser or Arafat, and the pair had no title except their guns to be appointing or representing anyone else. Their discourse, so loftily reported, was a matter of conspiration. In reality, Nasser was hoping to enlarge his retinue with a promising ally and therefore to extend his own challenges in the Arab world and elsewhere, while Arafat was expecting to be supplied with whatever help and resources were needed to actualize power for himself. Men and issues are too intractable to be bent to such wishful thinking, of course, and Arafat's relations with Nasser, as with all his sponsors, were to prove equivocal and stormy, a switchback of alternating favor and violence as each sought to subdue the other to his will.

Unchecked by his own people in his careerism, Arafat was able to take up where Haj Amin had left off. Offering in his turn nothing but the sword—or armed struggle, as he more modishly called it—in pursuit of his ambitions, Arafat applied the same terroristic violence of which the Palestinians are the major victims. In the past, Haj Amin had frustrated any possible intercommunal arrangements, and Arafat was to consummate the tribal-religious isolation, reducing Palestinians to a people without sociopolitical institutions either to control or to share, entirely and everywhere at the mercy of power holders who have proved stronger. Far from being some sort of progressive or popular *levée en masse,* the PLO's armed struggle is an example of Arab political careerism at its most reactionary.

The very first test of the PLO's legitimacy as a representative of the Palestinians arose in the hiatus after the Six Day War, as the future of the West Bank and Gaza came into question and was the subject of a United Nations resolution. It is conceivable, in the Eurocentric perspective at least, that a mass movement could have arisen among Israeli-occupied West Bankers and Gazans, spreading to the 100,000 new refugees, as well as to those in exile since 1948. But for the Palestinians to have taken their destiny into their own hands in this manner would have required a leadership willing to analyze political realities and free from shame-honor considerations, in order to be able to act upon a rational policy for limiting damage and loss. For such a leadership to have declared itself would also have been perceived as a fresh power challenge, and nobody apparently had the will or character for it. As it was, rumor and conversation within families was the only method available to Palestinians for balancing arguments between salvaging by means of a compromise with Israel whatever remained of their country, and risking even that rump by the renewal of fighting.

Fully aware of the danger to his standing posed by the formation of a mass peace party, Arafat decided to preempt any such possibility. Within weeks of the ending of the 1967 war, the PLO had initiated a campaign of violence in the occupied territories. The local population was not to be allowed to exercise options on its own behalf. Yet Palestinians, like everyone else, could see for themselves that if Israel had just been able to defeat three combined Arab armies in six days, then it could hardly be much shaken by the PLO and its slender military capacities. So unequal and precipitate was the struggle that by the end of 1967 the Israeli security forces had already cleared any organized PLO presence out of the occupied territories. Driven underground, remaining activists were usually one-man bands or family teams unable to promote actions more effective than the murder of individuals or the placing of an explosive device at random in a public area.

An insuperable difficulty faced Arafat from the moment of his capture of the PLO in 1969, then, because the war of liberation to which he and the PLO were ostensibly committed had already been fought after its fashion, and lost. By fair political means (and occasionally foul ones too, including money-favoring to encourage widespread denunciation), the Israeli authorities took all possible care to drive a wedge of conflicting interests between Palestinians under their control and the PLO. Correspondingly Arafat did what he could to ensure that the population fell into line. On the one hand, he applied whatever terrorist methods were available to him, including the murder of those of independent mind, and on the other hand he used his funds for competitive money-favoring. In 1969 and 1970, 76 West Bankers and Gazans were killed by the PLO, and 1122 were injured. On some mornings, Israeli patrols discovered the corpses of those killed and hung on meat hooks in the Gaza market to intimidate the population. On the strength of such achievements and with oil money to back him, Arafat proclaimed that national liberation was under way, opening offices in Jordan where Palestinian and other Arab or Muslim mercenaries enrolled. At the height of his rise to power, in 1969, Arafat could muster perhaps 20,000 men, slightly more than Haj Amin had disposed of thirty years previously, and whom he was paying between $20 and $30 a month, or more than the local agricultural wage.

Presumably Arafat understood the significance of the PLO failure to mobilize West Bankers and Gazans in 1967, but if so, he did not inform the Palestinians, repeating to whoever would listen the slogans of liberation and armed struggle. His ascendancy to power on the Palestinian issue had naturally provoked rivals to try the same tack in their own interest, and maintenance of his supremacy within the PLO became Arafat's full-time preoccupation. Far from laying the basis for secular or democratic institutions that one day might serve a nation, Arafat recruited Sunni Muslims like himself into a body known as Fatah, loyal to him on confessional lines. Trustworthy uncles and cousins were jobbed into leading and lucrative positions.

A principal contender for power within the PLO was the Popular Front for the Liberation of Palestine, the PFLP, under its leader George Habash and his associate Wadia Haddad. Habash is a doctor originally from Lydda, and a Greek Orthodox. Unlike Arafat and the Fatah, Habash and the PFLP declare themselves Marxists, but more importantly they are Christian, and the division between the PLO and the PFLP follows confessional lines. Yet a third splinter group, the Popular Democratic Front, is led by Nayef Hawatmeh, also a Christian and a Marxist, but with doctrinal differences from Habash. Other aspiring careerists in the grip of this startling outburst of money-favoring and power challenging have sought out and beseeched sponsors among every Arab power holder, each of whom is eager at any prospect of extending his reach, while also anxious at being outwitted in the event of abstention. As a result, Syria and Iraq, Egypt and Libya, even Saudi Arabia and latterly Iran, have all acquired separate purchases on the PLO, backing their men in order to influence the issue in a direction supposedly to their advantage. The multiple betrayals and conspiracies, the turns and turnabouts in allegiance, the doubling of roles in attempts to serve more than one master, the clandestine flitting on undisclosed missions to Arab and European cities, have concluded in interfactional arrests and torturing and lynch-law shootings, all the unresolved barbarities of unrestrained careerist politics. To the outsider, the evolution and history of the PLO seem like a real-life thriller whose plot has run amok; to the insider, each crime and act of terror may be carried out so anonymously that it remains unattributable to any perpetrator, but is nonetheless to be assessed soberly and comprehensibly in the light of the shifting balance of power between groups and promoters. Since 1967, the PLO has been nothing but an amalgamation of mercenary retinues, Muslim or Christian, at the beck of a dozen or so competing power holders, reproducing a microcosm of the Arab world as they fight out in this unlikely forum several conflicting interests which are not related either to Palestine or Israel.

Whether Palestinians outside the occupied territories would in fact accept the legitimacy of the PLO as their representative, and if so, how they would react, was put to the test in Jordan in 1970. Jordanian frontiers had been the product of British mapmaking; half the country's inhabitants were Palestinians by origin. The rapid financing and arming by Arab power holders of Arafat's mercenaries offered these Palestinians in Jordan a chance to repudiate King Hussein and declare themselves nationalists in the new cause. Unexpectedly, Arafat's power challenge threatened to replace King Hussein with a PLO state in Jordan. The more protestations of friendship were made by Arafat, the more cast-iron agreements he signed to limit the scope of the PLO, the less the PLO in fact respected the law in Jordan. Mutual suspicion of intention grew in the course of eighteen tense months as the showdown in this duality approached. In September 1970, the PFLP indulged its speciality of hijacking international airliners, three of which were brought at gunpoint to Jordan. The bid was misconceived. Taking advantage of this example of anarchic jockeying between rival Palestinian groups, King Hussein ordered his army to subjugate the whole movement. As civil war developed, one unit of the army, comprising about 5000 Palestinians, defected to the PLO. A march organized by women set off from one of the larger refugee camps, amid shouts that they were all going to throw themselves at the feet of General Moshe Dayan, then Israeli minister of defense. Otherwise the mass of Palestinians, in Jordan and in the occupied territories, chose to stay quietly indoors or in some cases to flee into the hills until superior force had arbitrated the issue one way or another. Here was a dramatic and bloodier repeat under an Arab power holder of what had happened on the West Bank in 1967 under an Israeli power holder.

"We would rather die in dignity than succumb and fall apart for ever," the PLO proclaimed with a typical shame-honor flourish. At the time, Arafat claimed that 25,000 Palestinians had been killed, and that King Hussein was planning genocide. Inevitably, outside sponsors were not willing to help a challenger who had clearly misjudged the superiority of the local power holder, and it so happened that Nasser died during these events, thus removing the one sponsor who out of shame and chagrin might have intervened. Under gunfire, the PLO evacuated to new bases in Lebanon, while about a hundred men were desperate enough to cross into Israel where they surrendered. PLO revenge took the customary form of assassination. The preferred target, King Hussein, was too security conscious, with the result that gunmen instead shot down his prime minister Wasfi Tal while on a visit to Cairo. For months after the civil war, Palestinians in Jordan and on the West Bank gave evidence of their real thoughts by denouncing PLO and PFLP activists to the authorities and occasionally even helping to round them up.

Lebanon was unprepared to be the terrain where the PLO power challenge would reach its lethal culmination. Prospering through commerce and agriculture, Lebanon had a history of democratic institution-building dating back to the Organic Statute of 1861, whereby intercommunal compromise was practiced. An agreed legal framework reduced tribal-religious and careerist abuses to acceptable levels. Today the country is a particularly horrific example of what happens when institutions are unable to mediate between the predatory strong and the defenseless weak, and therefore careerist politics run unchecked. Ordinary Lebanese of all confessions and ethnic identities had no means of enacting their disapproval of events, no vote or powers of veto that could be put into practical effect, no way of enforcing their undoubted will to continue living as peaceful citizens. Unlike Jordan, Lebanon had no supreme arbiter of power. In an initial period, the eruption into the country of an armed PLO presence was met by compromise and signed agreements. It was not in the careerist nature of the PLO to respect these, as it set about establishing its power base.

Perhaps 300,000 Palestinians lived in Lebanon in 1970, thus making them one of the smaller of the country's component entities. A sizeable minority of them were Christians, and many had been successfully integrated into the professional classes as lawyers, doctors, bankers, and businessmen. These Palestinians now found themselves in the hateful position of having gunmen claiming to be their representatives and liberators. Foreseeing what must lie ahead, some of the best educated and most socially prominent of such people chose to turn their backs on this plight and emigrate. Only Palestinians in Lebanon of exceptional courage and authority could have openly repudiated Arafat and the PLO, and there were none such. On the contrary, their tragedy was hastened implacably by the readiness of Western-educated Palestinian intellectuals in Beirut to extol and to justify PLO terror and crime which could only shred the country's fabric and reduce the Lebanese, in a primitive and retrograde manner, each into his own tribal or religious identity.

Establishing a dominating presence in Sidon and Tyre and the mountainous countryside stretching toward the Lebanese border with Israel, the PLO arrogated to itself the authority to speak for Palestinians there, to treat them as its subjects, to militarize and conscript them, to extort contributions to funds, and to shame the local women. This PLO takeover was arbitrary and cruel, and the Israeli journalists Zeev Schiff and Ehud Yaari give examples of it:

> Major Muin, commander of the Fatah battalion in Nabatiye, collected his own tax from every truck that drove into the town's open-air market. His counterpart in Tyre, Azmi Zerayer, murdered a local soccer player for refusing to join the "Palestinian team." And among the lower ranks, rape and robbery reached epidemic proportions.

The majority of inhabitants in southern Lebanon were Shia, comprising a few rich landowners and a poverty-stricken peasantry. For some years, an Iranian-born leader, the Imam Moussa

Sadr, a careerist but also a charismatic personality, had been organizing this traditional community, recruiting a retinue of his own, gathering arms and money to form Amal, a Shia militia. At first welcoming the PLO into the area, Imam Moussa Sadr changed his opinion as the largely Sunni PLO set about asserting its power so ruthlessly over the local Shia population, in another twist of that ancient schism in Islam. Moreover, PLO attacks across the border were met by Israeli reprisals that destroyed Shia-owned property and ravaged the countryside. Imam Moussa Sadr and the Shia generally perceived the PLO to be at the origin of their misfortune. By May 1970, 50,000 Shia had already fled from their homes. After appealing for help to a government in Beirut which was itself unable to control the PLO, Imam Moussa Sadr then built his Amal militia in self-defense. In a chain reaction every other tribal-religious entity concluded that it must look to its own protection by extensively arming its people.

Since 1970, in a rhythm of ever-deepening civil fighting, each and every one of these entities has had the choice of either attacking other entities preemptively or forming expedient alliances in defense. Eruptions of violence and periods of truce therefore alternate. Those who have been at each other's throats are suddenly reconciled against some third party, only to break away again in yet a further shift of the balance of forces. The untimely strength of one community drives others to combine against it; untimely weakness obliges the victimized community to seek protective allies. As usual, massacre and murder are the means of delineating where the power of one community begins and that of another ceases. Intercommunal killing becomes a ghastly version of determining numbers and therefore power. Atrocities have included the wholesale killing by the PLO of the Maronites in the town of Damour, and the liquidation by the Maronites of the Palestinians in the camp of Tell al-Zaatar. Far from trying to put a stop to such barbarities, other communities observe them keenly in order to make vital calculations about who will emerge as winners or losers, and so which alliances ought to be sought or avoided. Lebanese everywhere have fled from their houses in order to find refuge among their own people in communal enclaves; abandoned villages have been dynamited, and crops and orchards and workplaces have been wantonly destroyed in order to settle communal boundaries as advantageously as possible. Assassination of notables and leading personalities is of course the most effective method of throwing another community altogether into confusion. Beshir Gemayal, Kemal Jumblatt, Rashid Karami, Imam Moussa Sadr, Tony Franjieh, respectively leaders of the Maronites, the Druze, the Sunni, the Shia, the Christians in the north, are among those who have been murdered.

National institutions, fragile at the best of times and dependent on voluntary association, could not survive this sectarian turmoil. The Lebanese army, less than 20,000 strong and recruited on tribal-religious lines, dissolved as soon as soldiers were ordered to perform a national duty involving action against anyone of their own community. The Sixth Brigade, for example, simply converted itself and its weaponry into a unit for Shias who happened to comprise its membership. Pretense at parliamentary government has ceased. Ministers hold titular portfolios but no longer meet in cabinet and are actually mouthpieces for their own tribal-religious entity. Criticism of the conduct of one's own people would be impossible, suicidal. As a nonconfessional institution, moreover with Western affiliations of more than a century's standing, the American University of Beirut has been a special target. Several members of the academic staff, including its American rector, have been murdered, while others have been kidnapped.

How national institutions have withered or been uprooted may be illustrated by the fate of an English-language newspaper, *The Daily Star*, founded in 1952 by the Mrowa family, who are Shia Muslims. When publication ceased in 1986, the senior editor, Robin Mannock, an Englishman, wrote:

> We join those many of our readers who have been driven from this country by the kidnappers, murderers, car bombers and extortioners. Together with petty politicians who feed their followers with lies and lack the guts to lead them, the gunmen have transformed Lebanon into a thugocracy ruled by two-legged wild beasts whose sole reason and law is the gun. Because the overwhelming majority of Lebanon's dead and maimed were innocent men, women and children, we do not feel we are departing in bad company.

However catastrophic, this is by no means the anarchy that it might seem, or that a phrase like "two-legged wild beasts" suggests. Intercommunal warfare has its deadly logic, though the leaders who dictate it are so devious in their careerist conspiracies that they may lose the threads and defeat themselves. Each is seeking to swing the balance of forces in favor of himself and his people.

In the first instance, each communal leader and his trusted associates meet in private conclave, somewhere secret, beyond the reach of opponents who would attempt assassination. Among themselves they conspire, discussing where the advantage lies either in attack or in defense, who needs strengthening or weakening, how the alliances of the hour are shifting according to the latest news and rumors, what the requirements of sponsors might be, whether present rivals are better killed, neutralized, suborned or courted. They debate what targets are available in other communities, whether there are buildings that might be blown up by a car bomb with maximum loss of life, and who is exposed to a kidnapping, and whether it is now opportune to hold hostages, or on the contrary to barter or to sell them outright like a commodity to some other communal leader in need of a means to pressure his opponents, or perhaps to kill them. At no point is there any question of consulting with their people, of referring any matter to them for approval—the mere suggestion that leadership is more than brute strength and assertion would be shame-inducing. Their calculations completed, they telephone instructions accordingly, and the strong-arm bosses of their militias pass on the orders; demonstrators assemble, trucks and cars are fetched from garages, gunmen go out, and the fighting flares until the next session of conspirational appraisal begins or a truce is called to permit lobbying behind the scenes. The anonymous sniper in a stockinged mask who shoots a woman crossing the street to fetch milk for her baby, or the driver who abandons a car packed with explosives to detonate outside a block of apartments, is only the final agent in a chain of commands that compel obedience. Such killers conceive themselves to be enhancing their communal power, a procedure which makes no demand upon conscience.

Power challenges go astray, of course, if someone does not declare his true intention to a fellow conspirator, or betrays him to a rival, or accepts a bribe, or is caught in the unexpected unraveling of some machination. Here is a newspaper report from 1986:

A radical Shia Muslim militia said yesterday that it had "executed" nine men and two women accused of involvement in a lethal series of car bomb blasts in Lebanon dating back to 1978. The pro-Iranian Hizbollah distributed an 86-page document, with photographs of the accused, on its investigation of an alleged bomb ring it said was backed by Christian groups and Army intelligence. The document did not say how, when or where the death sentences were carried out. Video-taped confessions would be shown on Lebanese television. Hizbollah said the 11 were part of a ring responsible for car bomb attacks, including one that killed at least 75 in the Shia suburb of Bir al-Abed in March. The blasts killed 277 people and wounded 1,111. The document said the ringleader, Mahmud Zayyat, had taken refuge in Christian East Beirut.

The incident, like thousands more, cannot be deciphered in full. Car bombs certainly claimed these casualties but nobody is in a position to substantiate whether Christians, civilian or military, were responsible; whether Mahmud Zayyat, in spite of a Muslim name, really is a Christian, a ringleader, a refugee as alleged, or even whether he exists. It is possible only to infer that on this occasion the Shia of Hizbollah saw fit to maltreat eleven people in order to extract their confessions on film, and then to murder them in cold blood, finally choosing to describe them as Christian. Hizbollah power challenging at that moment required this display of faceless killing and conspiracy.

To take these atrocities at face value is to assume that the inhabitants of Lebanon are deranged, largely psychopaths. What has actually occurred is a simple reversion to tribal-religious conditions as they were before the Organic Statute of 1861 was imposed by the European powers. In those days, an Ottoman governor would have arrested and then hanged or exiled the ambitious troublemaking communal leaders to restore the status quo. Superior force alone breaks the tribal-religious deadlock. Separately, the Syrians and the Israelis have supposed themselves to be in a position to apply that superior force, though of course neither party was concerned to reconstruct representative or democratic institutions in Lebanon, but only to exploit the political vacuum for its own ends.

In 1982, the Israelis drove the PLO out of Beirut and southern Lebanon, while the Syrians drove it out of Tripoli and northern Lebanon. In this textbook display of the power-challenge dialectic, two armies too hostile to be able to concert policies nevertheless complemented each other by rounding on a third party for whom they had a still higher level of enmity. Forcible ejection of the PLO put an end to the military play it had launched so rashly in Lebanon, but it came too late to restore national institutions and so put a halt to tribalism. The Israelis found themselves in a challenge with the Shia in the south; the Syrians in a challenge with the Maronites and the Sunnis in the north. Both intervening armies therefore lost the role of supreme arbiter, adding instead two more groupings in the general segmentation of the country. Collapse of any central authority has led to currency decline and inflation, to the destruction of public revenue and to the end of such rational economic measures as a general labor market. Hunger is widespread. Each community now has no choice but to take care of itself by all available means, including fraud and force.

That Lebanese of all persuasions would wish to be free once and for all from these tribalistic horrors in order to enjoy a democratic society is often movingly evident. Here are two newspaper reports from Beirut:

Millions of Lebanese—Christians and Muslims—displayed rare unity Thursday when they joined in a general strike to protest the civil war and worsening economy in the country.

War-weary Christians and Muslims joined hands at Beirut's battlefield barricade yesterday in a rare public protest against Lebanon's 12-year-old civil war. Over 100 white-clad marchers hugged, kissed and held hands as they sang the Lebanese national anthem.

At all times, the main threats to Arafat were on the one hand popular democratic rallies of this type, and on the other the concentration of superior force. One further anxiety was that Arab power holders might be willing to negotiate with Israel, in which case he could take no action beyond accusing them of conspiracy or treason—as was proved in 1977 when Sadat traveled to Jerusalem to initiate the proceedings ending in the Camp David peace agreement. Nobody knew better than Arafat that the PLO's military and diplomatic insignificance had to be screened by processes of politicking and acts of terrorism designed to arouse outrage. In the last resort, the PLO was only a small and uncertain number of mercenaries held together by conspiracy. To have been able to maintain it, and even to familiarize it internationally, required promotion and publicity. In this field, Arafat has shown a special genius.

Somewhat portly and unwarriorlike in person, unshaven, in his dark glasses and his *keffiyeh*, affecting to wear khaki fatigues and a revolver in polite gatherings, Arafat projected an image designed to catch the Western fancy. Here was a figure at once picaresque and esoteric, newest in the line of those sons of the desert who

come riding across the horizon straight out of sentimental literature. No less thrillingly, he was always promising some exploit that
would put paid to the Zionists, to America, to Western interests in
the entire Arab world, to capitalism, to peace itself, thus touching
those in the West who believe that they bear the sins of the world
and so rejoice over prospects of their own merited punishment. In
1969, *Time* magazine devoted a cover story to Arafat, bringing to
birth this media-star peculiar to the times, part hero, part villain,
offering redemption through scourging and bloodshed. Ignorant
fancies are more romantic and captivating when other people can
be found to die of them.

Innumerable Western reporters and commentators have since
done Arafat the inestimable favor of taking literally every least
public-relations pronouncement, alternately fawning upon the
PLO and cringing before it. If such people assure audiences in the
West that the PLO is truly representative and that Arafat is a
statesman, who is a Palestinian farmer or villager or shopkeeper to
be raising an objection, and by what means? Violence and terrorism are sanctioned accordingly, and Palestinians are left to make
whatever they can of it.

In a run-of-the-mill example, John Pilger, an Australian journalist, is only one among many friends more dangerous to Palestinians than an enemy. In 1968 he wrote an account of meeting two
brothers, both PFLP guerrillas, by the name of Salah and Ahmed
Jabit, in order to accompany them on a night expedition into
Israel. Ahmed struck him as "intensely sensitive and shy." Pilger
colors the occasion to make heroes of the PFLP. An Israeli ambush
is fatal to this expedition, and Pilger concludes his reportage, "He
stumbled towards us and into the mud, carrying his brother who
was drenched in blood and crying," in effect congratulating these
poor men on getting themselves pointlessly shot. In a succeeding
article, Pilger describes how he accompanied another Jabit brother
to what had been the family house in Jaffa before 1948. The present Israeli occupant duly abases himself before them, saying, "I am
sorry. I cannot think of what else I should say." Making this Israeli
sound as though he was in Jaffa solely for purposes of stealing Arab
property, Pilger is accepting either-or logic that the rights of the
one community can be satisfied only at the expense of the rights
of the other, and so heedlessly is endorsing tribal-religious identity.

A more prominent case is John Le Carré. Researching for what was to become his bestselling thriller, *The Little Drummer Girl,* he interviewed Arafat:

Briskly he rises from his desk, comes towards me, a busy statesman to his finger-tips. He is neither thin nor fat, his body has the floppiness of unuse [*sic*] and the whiteness of something kept underground. It is said he never sleeps in the same bed twice, that he manages his own security arrangements, that he is abstemious in everything except in his love of Palestine and her people. A bold lady journalist had recently asked him whether he was homosexual. He replied urbanely that he was married to Palestine.

With awe, Le Carré goes on to speak of Arafat's "durability, his dedication, the undeniable love he enjoys among his wretchedly abused people, his talent for diplomacy" and "the mobility and extreme swiftness of his perception." "I fight for love—for love of Palestine," Arafat tells him. In the thriller, PLO agents are described as killing for love as they engage Israeli secret servicemen in internecine conflict. So unspeakably hateful are the Israelis that Palestinians owe it to themselves to kill them. This is hopeless and suicidal in the outcome, not for any moral grounds but only because Palestinians are inferior in power and influence and therefore the losers, shot dead. Palestinians are to understand that they have been selected for premeditated assault by a people too powerful to be defeated, but so inherently evil that peace cannot be made with them. Incited to become aggressive, they also find themselves patronized for being helpless. If Le Carré's view is correct, the Palestinians have nothing to live for, since whatever they do in these frightening circumstances, the Jews will still be the death of them. Tribal-religious power challenging, then, becomes as inevitable as it is right and proper.

Reports continue to be published in which Arafat is recorded speaking as though the sequence of calamities and the number of casualties had no bearing upon his careerism. For instance, an American journalist, Scott MacLeod, interviewed Arafat in 1987, by which time PLO pretensions to power had been cruelly exposed everywhere. "You have not been able to regain one square inch of occupied territory," MacLeod observed correctly, only to hear the following irrelevant apology which he published without comment or refutation.

No, no, no, no. It is not because of their superiority. But because we have our troubles inside our Arab arena. One battle, similar to these battles [between Iran and Iraq] going on in the east side of Basra, will liberate all Palestine. No doubt. Can the Israelis face 60,000 casualties in one battle? Can they? . . . It is not only for their superiority [that we have not regained territory], it is for our troubles inside our Arab field.

The French writer Jean Genet may be characteristic of nobody and nothing except his perverse self. His posthumous memoir *Un Captif Amoureux* is a rhapsodic account of living with Palestinian guerrillas in Jordan, identifying body and soul with their cause. To him, guerrilla songs were "about love, of course. And a bit about revolution." Asking himself questions such as "Had I been in love with Ali? With Ferraj? I think not because I had no time to dream about them," Genet reveals that to him the PLO resolved itself into sexual arousal. The very words "Islam" and "Muslim" brought on pleasurable "giddinesses."

Assorted sentimentalists in the media, Trotskyists, Jew-haters, radical-chic misfits, and masochists could nonetheless never have removed the PLO from its natural context of Arab power challenging and thrust it into the international arena if the Soviet Union had not lent its far greater influence to that end. To recruit the Soviet Union as a sponsor was undoubtedly a great coup for Arafat, because its worldwide propaganda services have ever since been at his disposal.

In the initial stages of the PLO, the Soviet Union was committed to Nasser and hesitant about acquiring a client like Arafat, then still untested, and with Syrian connections which might be prejudicial. In the summer of 1968, Arafat managed to slip on to an Egyptian delegation to Moscow, where he presented his case. From then on, the PLO was upgraded to a "national liberation movement" and Moscow began to insist on this line in policy statements. A second trip by Arafat secured a clandestine supply of weapons through other parties, notably Czechoslovakia. Dismissal of the Soviets by Sadat from Egypt, and then the 1973 war, provided Arafat with his power-challenge opening to place himself at the behest of what he believed to be the ultimate arbiter of force, and therefore certain of promotion. Sponsor and client could agree to sloganize about "the Arab struggle against imperialism and Israel's expansionist policy." Presumably Moscow had its reasons for preferring to back Arafat and the Sunni mainstream of Fatah rather than the PFLP and other declared Marxist revolutionaries.

On a visit to the Kremlin in 1979, Arafat laid out before the Soviet Foreign Minister Gromyko and his deputy Ponomarev the PLO achievements for which they should feel gratitude, interlocking as they did with the wider promotion of Communist aims (and incidentally offering insight into the nature of conspiratorial politics).

We maintain coordination with the Afro-Asian Solidarity Committee, with the World Peace Council and other international institutions, such as the Democratic Lawyers Association [Arafat is naming Soviet front organizations], which some time ago held a symposium in Paris and condemned Camp David from a judicial point of view. We made diplomatic moves in the countries we visited: Vienna, Ankara, Madrid, Lisbon and lately the meeting I had with Marchais [leader of the French Communist Party] in order to obtain an invitation for a visit to France.

To his sympathetic Soviet listeners, Arafat went on to unfold similar worthwhile intrigues: how he had been approached by former U.S. Attorney General Ramsey Clark in the Iran hostage crisis but refused to mediate because he himself supported Khomeini; how he had backed the Soviet line at one conference after another and was standing firm against what he called, in a revealing phrase, the "American-Israeli-Sadat conspiracy." In conclusion, Gromyko thanked him, with the added assurance that the Soviet Union was "a friend of the Arabs," to which Arafat replied, "The PLO has no doubts."

That friendship was put to the test in 1982 when the PLO applied in increasingly urgent and finally plaintive tones for Soviet help against the Israelis and the Syrians in Lebanon. Realistic as ever, the Soviet Union judged that the moment for arbitration by its own superior force was not at hand. With no choice but to withdraw from Lebanon, Arafat was seen by Palestinians everywhere to have been humiliated and so became a disappointment, even an object of execration, until he could rally once more. This setback was a natural and immediate power-challenging opportunity for his rivals. A large faction under Abu Musa, hitherto a PLO officer, defected to Syrian sponsorship. A smaller faction under Atallah Atallah, another PLO officer and one-time military intelligence chief, defected to Jordanian sponsorship. Yet another faction had already formed under Abu Nidal, whose real name is Sabri Khalil Banna (no relation of Hasan al-Banna of the Muslim Brothers). The strife between Abu Nidal and Arafat illuminates the careerism of these politics.

Abu Nidal seems to have been born in Jaffa in 1937, or 1939, or even 1943, according to conflicting sources. Hajj Khalil, his father, marketed 10 percent of the Palestinian citrus crop to Europe and owned houses in Turkey, Egypt, and France. A man of this wealth could afford a succession of thirteen wives, who bore him seventeen sons and eight daughters. After 1948 the family moved from Jaffa to Nablus. Abu Nidal was educated in Jerusalem, later studying engineering in Cairo. A Palestinian witness has described him as a "psychopath and a fascist whose ideology is a hybrid of Marxism, Baathism and gibberish." In the course of a family dispute, he is said to have ordered his men to booby-trap the cooking gas canister in his nephew's house in Amman, killing the nephew's Czech wife and two children. Be that as it may, Abu Nidal enrolled in the PLO, breaking with it in 1972. Two years later, he was condemned to death by Arafat for "armed sedition, murder, provocation." Abu Nidal's own career in gunfire was under way. Opportunity existed at that moment to acquire the sponsorship of the Syrian government, then of the Iraqis. The Camp David agreement of 1977 placed the PLO in a dilemma: was it more advantageous to accept *force majeure* and enter the peace process, or to continue the armed struggle as before? So much hung on this calculation that Arafat remained indecisive, whereupon Abu Nidal quickly preempted him by offering the course of violence. Here was an exact repeat of Arafat's own opportunity and tactics after the Six Day War. Between 1977 and 1984, at the bidding either of Syria or Iraq or Libya, Abu Nidal and his faction murdered some hundreds of Palestinians, among them at least a score of senior PLO officials such as Zuhair Mohsin, gunned down in a luxurious villa in Cannes; Said Hammami, head of the PLO office in London; Ezzeddin Kallak of the PLO office in Paris; the journalist Nazih Matar; Sa'd Sayel, one of Arafat's military advisers; and Issam Sartawi, the only Palestinian to have dared to raise openly in these circles the possibility of some political arrangement with Israel. Nothing like such havoc has been done to Israel, although in 1982 Abu Nidal did succeed in critically shooting Shlomo Argov, the Israeli ambassador to London.

At Ezzeddin Kallak's funeral in Damascus in August 1978, Arafat told the mourners in the customary rhetoric of obfuscation and threat that

The murderers in Baghdad [Iraq was sponsoring Abu Nidal at the time] will not be able to carry out their new plot to liquidate the Palestinian revolution. It is a big and related conspiracy—the murderers in Baghdad will not be able to carry it out while the isolationists [he means the Christians in Lebanon] are plotting against Arab peace-keeping troops.

Interfactional murder, as described here by Arafat, is also not the anarchy it might appear, but in logical accord with careerist politics. Arafat and his original handful of co-conspirators have built the PLO into a vested interest, and they have everything to lose. In the absence of a peace treaty with Israel, who knows how far this particular bid for power might reach? What with petro-dollar subsidies to the tune of hundreds of millions of dollars and Soviet backing as well, there arises the tantalizing open-ended prospect that the political deadlock will somehow be resolved and someone will be able to seize his chance to promote himself from a factional leader into a national power holder.

The fighting ground may be small but the rewards are already gigantic enough to attract every conceivable careerist crime. At stake is a network of assets estimated to be as high as $6 billion, with additional income constantly renewed and enlarged through subsidies from oil states and extortion from Palestinians. In Lebanon at least 10,000 people worked in PLO enterprises from a furniture shop to a textile plant, from a steel mill to food production facilities. There is trafficking in arms, in medical supplies, and in narcotics, with elaborate shelters for laundered money in what amounts to a Mafia-style network complete with protection rackets. Funds go through the Arab Bank in Jordan, the Arab African Bank, and the Arab Bank for Economic Development in Africa, and so into investment accounts and private portfolios and cash reserves in Switzerland that are beyond accurate figures. Wadia Haddad, second in command of Habash's PFLP, was said to have left his sister $140 million upon his death in 1978. Those who shot Zuhair Mohsin claimed to have been disgusted by the man's debauchery and squandering, and such accusations surface continually wherever mysterious murders and suicides occur. Here is a report of the death of a man by the name of Said Moufak Gandoura, who inexplicably fell out of a window in Rome, in an inci-

dent as unpleasant and frightening as it is routine. Tried in an
Italian court for complicity in the hijacking of the liner *Achille Lauro*
in 1985, Gandoura had been convicted of false testimony and
using a false name.

Mrs. Gandoura said Mr. Arafat had telephoned her husband at the
apartment on Wednesday night. "He told me that Arafat wanted him to
leave Italy, to leave me. He was furious with Said because he said he spent
too much money and used the organisation's funds for me," she said.

Like all similarly placed conspirators, Arafat must watch every
single man in his entourage and keep himself informed about the
doings of even such minor thugs as Said Moufak Gandoura. Sharp
attention must be paid to who is spending what, and whether for
authorized purposes. The hundred and more diplomatic missions
or offices abroad, the holders of accounts, those empowered to
sign and to pay, are accountable to Arafat, not to any independent
body or auditor. Petitioners crowd in on him. Arafat has the task
of perpetually estimating who might be receiving too small a reward and therefore contemplating the search for a more profitable
retinue to join, and who might be receiving too much and therefore commanding more attention than is due to someone in that
station, perhaps even planning bids and conspiracies which might
develop into a threat. This fine line in money-favoring is always
hard to draw. On the lookout for telltale indications, Arafat must
study who is encountering whom, and where, and under what
auspices. Of far greater significance than the few hundred reliable
guerrillas now under arms are the loyal informers and security
agents, placed to bring the latest news and rumors about Arab
power holders or rivals like Abu Nidal, Habash, and the leaders of
other breakaway factions. Depending on what he hears in confidence, Arafat telephones his instructions and arranges private
meetings in the small hours in circumstances designed to baffle
hostile informers and security agents known or suspected to be
closing in on him.

None of this is a secret to Palestinians. Wherever they live, they
observe for themselves that the PLO is a means to enrichment and
aggrandizement for the unscrupulous few, but death and destruction for everyone else. With humor and sarcasm, and perhaps the
occasional touch of admiring envy or rage, they will name those of
their friends and relations, and especially their enemies, who are
profiting out of the petro-dollar windfall. They can explain in

detail why one man without apparent means has taken to flaunting silk suits and new limousines; and by what means another, once a landless peasant, has been purchasing real estate in California; and how a third is able to travel comfortably for months on end through the capitals of Europe. But to say such things loudly and clearly not only invites dire reprisal, but also would amount to an inconceivable betrayal of tribal-religious solidarity and identity.

Everywhere Palestinians have little alternative but to cling to this identity, as they continue to seek what freedom they can from power holders of different identity. In Syria, any Palestinian who attempted to form some independent grouping would be seen as a dangerous conspirator and summarily disposed of by Hafez Assad. Arafat himself has been imprisoned in Syria, and once was unceremoniously bundled out of the country on a flight to Tunis as a method of making his inferior status clear. In Jordan, King Hussein has to be continually and delicately appraising his own defensive relationship with Arafat and the PLO, deciding when the limits of tolerance have again been breached. In 1986, for instance, he ordered the police to fire on students demonstrating in Irbid, killing three and wounding sixty, and he then arrested thirty-four Palestinian journalists for writing on behalf of the PLO. King Hussein is also the initiator of a vigorous and effective money-favoring nexus of his own, ensuring that he competes with Arafat in bribery, thereby extending and cementing his retinue among those willing to join. In Lebanon, Palestinians have had to come to terms at gunpoint with the Shia and the Maronites, both tribal-religious enemies who have settled the balance of forces in their favor by means of massacre and murder. Since the enforced evacuation of the PLO in 1982, Palestinians above all have been waiting in the forlorn expectation of an outside arbiter to arrive and impose a centralized authority that might permit the reestablishment of a national identity in some form and save them by a return to the rule of law.

On the West Bank and in Gaza, the unfamiliar spectacle of the Jew as power holder has greatly, sometimes shockingly, complicated the position of Palestinians. Under occupation since 1967, caught between the Israelis and the PLO, the Palestinians have known a daily existence of intrigue and danger, of tacking and trimming, in an atmosphere of plotting and each-for-himself that rapidly turns sinister. Considerations of personal safety naturally come first, as anyone may lose his life on account of an unguarded remark or a hasty deed. The list of those murdered by the PLO extends to many hundreds, including lawyers and intellectuals who floated ideas of compromise, the Imam of Gaza, bankers and businessmen who took some step which the PLO judged to be against its interest, and of course a majority of peasants accused of collaboration and treason, usually on hearsay, always without chance of appeal.

Since the Jordanian civil war of 1970, Palestinians under the Israeli power holders have participated minimally in PLO terror. Now and again a murder has occurred of a lone Israeli, a tourist, or a Palestinian suspected of being a spy or an informer. The killer has usually proved to be a sole operator, often an infiltrator from outside the territories. Quick and adaptable people, Palestinians under occupation have steered a judicious course between the Israelis with whom they have had to do business, and the PLO with whom they have had to do politics. Those who willingly or under blackmailing pressure do indeed assist the PLO bring down upon themselves rough justice from the Israelis, who apply punitive measures such as the demolition of their houses or deportation from the country. In the resulting intercommunal stalemate, Palestinians have been able to summon in aid the resources of the extended family. One member may take it upon himself to befriend the Israelis, so that he is in a position to intercede with the authorities on behalf of anyone in his family in need of a favor or a protection; another member acts likewise by enrolling with the PLO in Beirut or elsewhere; and a third approaches King Hussein in Amman with protestations of loyalty and appeals for help. What might look like servility is actually akin to a wise policy of maximum insurance against the widest possible range of manmade disasters.

In defining these strategies for survival, every Palestinian has to consider where his loyalty and his interests really lie. This is the subject of unceasing conspiratorial discussion and rumor. If someone has been spotted leaving the offices of the Israeli military commander, for example, does it mean that he has gone there to ask for a favor, to protest about something, or to make a denunciation? Is he perhaps feigning to have the right connections, to be a man of influence? Has the man really passed the time of day there over coffee, and if so, then should he be called a traitor? How validly are moral distinctions to be drawn between the various attitudes taken toward self-preservation? Whatever the suspicions and grievances induced by occupation, West Bankers and Gazans are also able to appreciate that the Israeli army has stood between them and horrors committed by fellow Arabs. Virtually every family under occupation has its toll of murdered relations on the far side of the frontier, and episodes to relate of massacre and flight. According to the circumstances of the moment, it is safe to assert, everyone has swung between being in favor of Arafat, resigned to him, scornful of him, and unspokenly grateful to Israel while simultaneously wishing for the end of the occupation.

Well over one hundred thousand West Bankers and Gazans commute every day to work in Israel at jobs in an economy now hard to extricate from their own. These people are also free to travel to Jordan and the wider Arab world, just as other Arabs may visit the occupied territories for three months in each year, and they do so in their hundreds of thousands. The flux of events between 1967 and 1982 offered Palestinians several chances to demonstrate en masse in favor of the PLO, if they had been so inclined. The fact that they refrained was not due to fatalism or cowardice, but substantiates the truism that they cannot suddenly jettison their sociopolitical inheritance. Like other Arabs, Palestinians cannot escape those who power-challenge in their name any more than they can select their own representatives in the absence of electoral machinery for that purpose. Put another way, Arafat has discovered, as Haj Amin did, that the majority of Palestinians may be willing to pay lip service to him, but not more. Intimidation and terror cannot substitute for voluntary association. Failing to address this reality, Arafat emptily adheres to shame-honor rhetoric, declaring to whoever will listen, "Our enemies will suffer from defeat while we shall enjoy victory."

Newspapers are published by Arabs for Arab readers on the West Bank, though they are in receipt of hidden subsidies (the PLO to the fore, but not exclusively), and also subject to a license to print as well as to military censorship. Public opinion, such as it is, finds expression through calculated statements from about a score of notables, usually heads of families or municipal mayors. In September 1986 a poll of 1024 West Bankers was carried out, the first of its kind, by PLO sympathizers. Its conclusions may nevertheless approximate to general attitudes at that time. About 70 percent of those interviewed supported Arafat, it was found, while a slightly higher proportion approved of PLO terrorism. Political outcomes favorable to Arafat will maximize this support, while defeats will diminish it.

Prolonged civil disturbance in Gaza and the West Bank erupted in December 1987. There had been no precedent for it. Throughout the territories, roads were repeatedly blocked by rocks or burning tires, and crowds of youngsters assembled to throw stones first at any trapped vehicles, then at soldiers arriving to clear the passage. Strikes were declared, schools shut, and shopkeepers were compelled to close their businesses in sympathy. Though there was a PLO component among the activists, such leadership as existed was underground and shadowy. Popular participation in the rioting and stone-throwing indicated that the true issue was communal identity, and that for the first time the PLO monopoly claims upon the Palestinians might be questioned.

To begin with, the disturbances had their origins in localized incidents mishandled by the authorities, but they gathered in scope and direction because the wider context of Arab politics at last revealed how irrecoverably the PLO had lost ground since its expulsion from Lebanon. With the PLO embarrassingly unable to translate its slogans of liberation into any meaningful program, the people in the occupied territories could only take their fate into their own hands. Failure to do so could be interpreted as indifference to the Israeli presence, even as compliance with it. The stones thrown at the Israelis were the tribal-religious equivalent of a plebiscite, to the effect that the Palestinians aspired to control their future, to be rid of the occupation in the belief that natural right and justice were on their side.

Once more, the strength of this type of collectivist response proved inseparable from its weakness. With single-minded purposefulness, the activists set about attacking any such intercommunal relations as had existed between Palestinians and Israelis, in a trice undoing the pluralist links that had been so painstakingly forged over the years since 1967. Pressure was exerted on everyone to ignore or repudiate any dealings that they might have had with the Israeli state and its officials, in such matters as taxpaying, social services, the educational system, and most notably the enforcement of law. The lynching in his village of an Arab alleged to have been an informer was an example to Arab policemen, the majority of whom took the warning and resigned.

In general terms, the local Palestinians regrouped in their communal exclusivity. Seeking in this manner to defend their own against neighboring (or encroaching) Israelis, these Palestinians were only following tribal-religious custom. Psychologically satisfying or exhilarating, violence of the kind certainly serves to reinforce identity. Beyond that, violence cannot construct whatever mechanism is required to build the institutions to represent the community, and thus prepare for political processes of actually negotiating and extracting concessions from Israel. In a completely predictable response, communal violence on the one side only arouses communal violence on the other. If the disturbances were to compel the Israelis unilaterally to withdraw from the occupied territories, moreover, careerist power challenging would fill the sudden vacuum, creating conditions truly dangerous to life and property there, until such time as some power holder emerged capable of imposing absolute authority. Far from opening a way to freedom, every stone thrown prepares for self-imposed despotism. The future is thus continuously absorbed into the historic or customary past.

Mahmoud Darwish is one of the best-known contemporary Palestinian poets, and after some months of the disturbances he published a poem in praise of communal exclusivity and the extension of custom from the past into the future. The poem exhorted the Israelis to disappear.

> It is time for you to be gone
> Die wherever you like, but do not die among us
> For we have work to do in our land
> We have the past here
> We have the first cry of life
> We have the present, the present and the future
> We have this world here, and the hereafter
> So leave our country

To the Israelis, Palestinian communal violence and exclusivity implied that the tribal-religious free-for-all raging in Lebanon was moving southward to engulf them as well. Like the Maronites, the Druze, the Shias, the Palestinians themselves, the Israelis are only one Middle Eastern minority among others, all engaged on survival by whatever means are appropriate. At the outset of the disturbances, the Israeli government saw itself before a choice between tyranny and anarchy; between the use of arbitrary and despotic measures to perpetuate its authority, or the abdication to some other authority—in short, initiating a power challenge among the Palestinians. Nobody of influence proposed the pluralist alternative of enfranchising the occupied population, devising a structure whereby these people would be able to elect communal or national representatives on an equal footing. Some such structure certainly converts stone-throwing into a political process, but its realization was doubtful at the best of times, its price deemed too high, and conditions thoroughly unpropitious.

Instead, the Israeli government responded with force, employing live ammunition in crowd control which could only lead to random deaths and casualties, declaring curfews, obliging shopkeepers to ignore strikes, replacing those Arab policemen who had resigned with Israelis, arresting and detaining without trial several thousands of the activists. Strong-arm measures of the kind are day-to-day experiences in the regimes of Arab power holders everywhere, only to be expected, and in Palestinian eyes the customary use of force was not in itself particularly untoward. On the contrary, force has the paradoxical effect of establishing yet again that in communal self-defense Israelis behave as the Arabs do. More than convergence, this is integration. Both the Palestinian stone-throwers and the Israeli soldiers answering with rifle fire imagine themselves to be enhancing their respective community and its power and reach, committing a violence that requires no justification and frees those involved from qualms of conscience, to act as wantonly as need be. What to outsiders looks like deliberate fostering of hate into an indefinite future is to insiders merely another good reason for mobilizing one's own kind. What has resulted may be described in one of two ways: either that at great cost to all concerned the Palestinians have managed to incorporate the Israelis once and for all into Arab power challenging and its values, or that the Israelis are so few and so insecure that they cannot help adopting the customary methods of the region for communal assertion and survival. It is possible to ascribe to human folly, and beyond that to existential tragedy, the long-standing failure to define agreed borders in these small and relatively poor territories, but more realistically the conflict persists because there is no counterweight to the pull of tribe and religion in the Middle East.

Contrary to the simplification in Mahmoud Darwish's poem, the Palestinian future can emerge only through a more exact and objective assessment of the past, and in particular of the roles of Haj Amin and Arafat. Neither of these figures has been subjected to the sort of serious analysis that alone would determine the causes and consequences of their twin careers. A recent biography of Haj Amin by Taysir Jbara had as its conclusion a quotation from a notable who had been his associate for many years: "God gave Palestine, in the twentieth century, Haj Amin." No irony or double entendre was intended. Anwar Nusseibeh was someone who had known Haj Amin, and who subsequently became an elder states-man among Palestinians, living in Jerusalem in the years after 1967; and if any Arab there had freedom of speech, he did. Cam-bridge-educated, Nusseibeh had been a government minister in Jordan, and an ambassador. In an interview shortly before his death, all he could bring himself to say about Haj Amin was that "his opposition to Zionism reflected the consensus among us." Asked why this consensus actually had prompted Arabs to assassi-nate one another, he replied, "I have no ready answer. I can only speculate that those who were concerned with principle could not abide cracks appearing in the Palestinian position." Privately Nus-seibeh understood that terrorism had nothing to do with principle, and he detested it, yet even so privileged and eminent a man could not bring himself to say so aloud, instead concluding the interview with a promotion of the PLO that was certainly insincere. Nobody seems to have gone further than Ahmad Shuqairi, who himself had asked for nothing better than to step into the shoes of Haj Amin and Arafat. Despised and disgraced for his failure to do so, Shuqairi declared truthfully, "The glory of 'His Eminence' came before the glory of the homeland. The homeland fell and with it the glory."

For Palestinians to admit that they have been misled by those who claim to be acting in their name would be a humiliation; and this response may well be as inhibiting as any amount of PLO intimidation. *My Home, My Prison* is a memoir by Raymonda Tawil, a Palestinian Christian from Nablus, where she specializes in es-corting Western reporters on conducted tours of the West Bank in search of oppression. Shame-honor runs through her book, as when she describes how she had once organized a demonstration and sensed "a great feeling of pride" at the sight of housewives and students now "proud, militant champions of our people's dignity and freedom." Why dignity and freedom are incompatible with compromise and peace is something she does not explain.

Wild Thorns is a recent novel by Sahar Khalifah, set in the occu-pied West Bank, and an example of literature that aims solely to bolster honor values and tribal-religious identity. Usama, its hero, returning from abroad to his hometown of Nablus, asks his cousin,

"What's become of you all, of the country? They've stuffed you full and made you greedy. They've absorbed you. And I see no sign of shame in your eyes." The plot glorifies Usama's recovery of honor by means of murdering an Israeli, while at the same time denigrating those characters prepared to lead a quiet life or to collaborate. The isolation of the community thus becomes a value which it is right and proper to perpetuate.

A number of Palestinians are capable of examining and assessing the historical record with the objectivity that alone will permit the formulation of agreed and rational policy for the future. Since 1971, an Institute of Palestinian Studies in Beirut has been publishing a quarterly journal, and there is a body of work from authors such as Walid Khalidi, Yusuf and Faiz Sayigh, Sabri Jiryis, and Edward Said. These—and others—are masters of Western languages and techniques, often contributing at a high level to research in disciplines other than immediate politics. Hamdi Nubani in Jerusalem is one among specialists who have introduced to Arabs the indispensable study of Judaism and Israel, and he has lately published the first Arabic translation of the Mishna, the texts in which Jewish law is codified.

When it comes to the issue of Palestine, not one Palestinian so far has broken tribal-religious identity to consider the role of Arafat and the PLO in finalizing the national catastrophe; not one has queried the retrograde parts played by shame-honor and by PLO corruption and money-favoring; not one has pointed out that private careerism cannot become national liberation, nor put forward proposals for how a movement of popular participation might start, nor submitted to scholarly scrutiny the implications of peace with Israel. Cecil Hourani, Oxford-educated, Lebanese in origin, and for a long time adviser to Bourguiba in Tunisia, is truly exceptional in writing that he always had doubts about the wisdom behind the creation of the Palestinian resistance movement in 1964, which, he says, "time has revealed to be the source not only of many of Lebanon's problems, but also of those of the Palestinians themselves." Among his Palestinian friends, he adds sadly, he often heard repeated a phrase, "the world is ruined, let it be ruined more"—a neat summation of the antisocial sterility of careerist politics.

Edward Said is a Palestinian-American born in Jerusalem between the world wars, and he has made his career in the United States as a professor of comparative literature. A member of the

Palestinian National Council, he is committed to Arafat and the PLO. In *The Question of Palestine* in 1977, Said was nonetheless the first Palestinian author to allow in print that Israel is not a racist society, and that its birth involved factors too complex to be "easily reduced to simple formulation." Jews, he further allowed, have "a long history of victimization and terror behind them." Instead of pursuing the evidence of this to its conclusion, however, in the next breath he said that Zionists were colonizers, "valorizing the white man's superiority and his right over territory." Israel, it seemed to him, was "a device for holding Islam—and later the Soviet Union, or communism—at bay." Inconsistency apart, these are reversions to the usual conspiratorial views. Under the phrase "valorizing the white man's superiority" was the reality of tens of thousands of persecuted men and women driven separately to immigrate from over a hundred countries out of a wish to stay alive in a world hostile to them as Jews. Had white men ever concerted their actions as whites, Jews would not have fallen into the field of persecution in the first place. Nor could there ever be anyone so amazingly capable as to think up an all-purpose device for holding first Islam and then communism at bay, while at the same time being powerful enough to put it into practice. Although living in New York in a position to weigh evidence and also safe to speak his mind, even a man of Said's caliber and standing felt constrained to resort to Islamocentric fantasies in defense of tribal-religious identity; and *The Question of Palestine* accordingly founders in apologetics.

Hope for peace is widespread among the Palestinian masses. If this hope is ever to be realized in institutional form, some Palestinian or other Arab will have first to legitimize it. Unquestioned authority to be doing anything so novel and revolutionary can derive only from an examination of the damage done by careerist power challenging and its supportive values, an examination so scrupulously true to the record that it can be agreed by the victims to be self-evident.

12

Power Holders

Contemporary power holders of note—Anwar Sadat, Muammar Gaddhafi, Hafez Assad, Saddam Hussein, Ayatollah Khomeini— have obviously been very different in personality, without common threads to link them in background or education. The countries in which they have held power—respectively Egypt, Libya, Syria, Iraq, and Iran—are distinct in essentials such as demography, tribal-religious composition, the ratio of Sunni to Shia, natural resources, geography, and historical experience, including exposure to the West and colonialism. For all that, these power holders—and of course others as well—have conducted themselves with a conformity that makes their roles in practice so alike as to be interchangeable. All have risen through conspiracy and employ comparable methods of self-assertion, money-favoring their friends and persecuting their opponents. All have adjusted internal political relationships in their own interest through the secret police, and by means of torture and murder if need be; and all have tried to adjust external relationships by means of tribal-religious mobilization and warfare. In daily life, those who are ruled in these countries experience compulsion and violence as determining constants. To add to bitterness, the ruled everywhere also have to hear power holders and apologists describing as "revolution" what is physically and mentally suffered as tyranny.

ANWAR SADAT

Sadat fired the Western imagination when in 1977 he flew without prior warning to Jerusalem in order to initiate the process that culminated in a peace treaty between Egypt and Israel. Startling and innovative as this move appeared to be, Sadat became the object of admiration and affection as the man who at last had called a halt to forty years of enmity which had proved destructive to the Arabs concerned, had fortified a defensive identity among Israelis, and proved an embarrassment to everyone else. Into the praise crept condescension that was certainly unintentional. Sadat was treated as an Arab who finally had seen sense, as though Arabs generally had not the intellectual capacity to draw reasonable profit-and-loss accounts from their conflicts.

The irony was that Sadat had once been a Nazi sympathizer, and during the Second World War an agent almost certainly in German pay. As late as 1953, he could be found declaring in a Cairo newspaper that he congratulated Hitler with all his heart:

> You are forgiven on account of your faith in your country and people. That you have become immortal in Germany is reason enough for pride. And we should not be surprised to see you again in Germany, or a new Hitler in your place.

Sadat's monotonous menace to kill Jews and to end "the Zionist conspiracy" in the years before 1977 was no doubt as sincere as his repeated promises after 1977 of psychological breakthrough and guaranteed peace with Israel. In Jerusalem in November 1977, and afterward in the United States, he liked to emphasize that the Arab-Israeli conflict must be resolved "as between civilised people." Who had ever doubted it, but how was Sadat to explain away a lifetime of apparent lack of civilization on that score? The only penalty for a total reversal of his attitude toward Israel, he blithely realized, was the disapprobation of other Arab power holders who envied him and resented what they were unable to achieve for themselves, but who could do little about it except try to spoil Sadat's rewards. To have been within a span of thirty years pro-Nazi, pro-Soviet, socialist, capitalist, Jew-hater and peacemaker with Israel may seem evidence of intellectual dishonesty and pure opportunism, but realistically it is an expression of Sadat's instinctive grasp of the power-challenge dialectic and how to work it in order to become the winner in the end.

Succeeding Nasser unexpectedly in 1970 as the Egyptian power holder, Sadat, previously vice-president, had on his hands the makings of a national emergency. Internal and external policies had resulted in bankruptcy and defeat. Police-state repression alone maintained the power holder but simultaneously raised unprecedented frustration and fear, inducing yet more repression in a vicious circle. The first step was to eliminate rivals, especially those who might claim Nasser's doctrines to justify themselves. "I was determined to get rid of all these people," Sadat wrote, "yet I lacked incriminatory evidence." This snag vanished when a young police officer arrived at his palace in the small hours of one night in May 1971, with the most convenient gift of a bugged telephone conversation which "proved clearly" that there was a plot to overthrow him. Sadat's wife, Jehan, has described how the crisis reached its climax with Sadat putting to his commander of the Presidential Guard the crucial question, "if I were to ask you to arrest the Cabinet ministers, could you do it?" On the pretext of forestalling the coup, he then ordered the arrest of Nasser's leading aides, including the former chief of intelligence, whom he now categorized as "Soviet agents." In a broadcast, Sadat announced that he would "grind into mincemeat" any threat, and the crowds massing on the street, recognizing how events were unfolding, were soon chanting, "Grind, Sadat, grind!" By that December, ninety-one of these politicians and officers had been sentenced to lengthy terms in prison. Trusted friends had meanwhile been appointed to run the army and security services. In one of those outcomes habitual in careerist politics, the invaluable commander of the Presidential Guard had also been found mysteriously dead in the course of traveling abroad.

Free to be his own man, Sadat could throw off Soviet sponsorship, that heaviest of Nasser's self-imposed shackles. Ordering some 25,000 Soviet troops and advisers out of Egypt in 1972, Sadat was signaling that a play for new and different rewards was opening, and he was available for offers of backing from the United States. The 1973 war allowed him to select this option safely. The surprise crossing of the Suez Canal was an outcome satisfying honor demands, at last removing that customary barrier to initiative. Peace with Israel and American sponsorship completed the most crystal-clear illustration in recent years of the tortuous peculiarities inflicted on Arab politics by customary values. Neither fresh doctrinal perception nor insight into the nature of Israel had prompted Sadat. Correctly envisaging that the huge majority of his own people, like human beings everywhere, would welcome peace, he could not have brought about the desired end by negotiation as insistently asked by Israel, but only after the usual conflict and violence seemed to certify that he was ceding from a position of superiority.

That he was a peasant, from the Nile delta village of Mit Abul Kom, was Sadat's frequent boast, and he enjoyed escorting visitors, foreigners especially, to the place where he had been born, as though to emphasize the distance he had come. Money-favoring made a showplace of the village, with new houses, including one for himself, and another for his brother Esmat. Brought up in the village school, he had had a traditional Muslim education and had acquired particular sensitivity to shame-honor values. His heroes, he has recorded, were Mustafa Kamil, Ataturk, Napoleon, Gandhi, and a man by the name of Zahran, who had been hanged by the British after the Denshawai incident. Denshawai is in the same province as Mit Abul Kom, and Sadat, by way of certifying his own heroic outlook, could write, "I wished *I* were Zahran."

In 1938 Sadat entered the army and was stationed at Mankabad. Officers there were a "secret revolutionary society." Members used secret signs and passwords: "We swore an oath to remain faithful to our country and to work with all our strength for its regeneration." The hero to be imitated at this point was Aziz Ali el-Masri, already pro-Nazi. Soon Sadat was delegated to contact no less a person than Sheikh Hasan al-Banna of the Muslim Brothers, whose role was purportedly to arouse the masses at the appropriate moment of undoubted Nazi victory. "I felt certain," Sadat writes presciently of al-Banna, "that this man was thinking out grandiose projects which he kept strictly to himself." As a conspirator, Sadat was led to a clandestine rendezvous, to be initiated into the Muslim Brothers, in this scene:

One of the officiants, almost invisible in the dark shadows, then invited him [i.e., the candidate] to sit at a table on which were placed a Koran and a revolver. Placing one hand on the Koran, the other on the revolver, the candidate had to repeat, word for word, the oath of loyalty, obedience and secrecy. The oath bound him as a member of the Brotherhood, and he was henceforward an instrument in the hands of his superior. When this ceremony was over, the officiants left him alone in the room for a few moments, to meditate. Then, fully initiated, he was guided out of the district.

Arrested by the British for his Nazi-promoted activities, Sadat served a short time in prison. According to stories in his memoirs, he performed deeds of bravado, such as escaping and taking a taxi to the Royal Palace to sign the ceremonies book there with comments protesting against prison treatment. Once released, he and his fellow conspirators decided to murder the prime minister, Nahas Pasha. Failing in the attempt, they killed instead Amin Osman Pasha, the finance minister. So certain was he of shame-honor ranking that Sadat boastfully attributed these crimes to himself rather than disclaim them. In another typically Islamocentric passage in *Revolt on the Nile,* he depicts with pride his role in the overthrow of King Farouk. The first abdication document failed to mention the phrase "the will of the people." The document had to be redrafted to say of the conspirators, "We therefore conform to the will of the People," who of course discovered what their will was supposed to be only once the coup was safely over.

Transferring his allegiance to Nasser, joining the Free Officers conspiracy and remaining loyal to it, Sadat took the essential careerist step. Money-favoring promoted him steadily to rewards of wealth and rank and influence, and in return he could publicize the glories of his sponsor Nasser in the approved vein:

Gamal, O Lord, is your magnificent creation, your conquering genius, your true servant, your reliant one, your inspired one, the bearer to his people and his nation of the message of righteousness, dignity and peace.

Once he had succeeded Nasser and was obliged to undo the dire consequences of that regime, he could resort to the truth, rightly accusing Nasser of suspecting everybody and everything, admitting that fear had reigned everywhere, that Nasser had "always left a trail of hatred." All over Egypt, busts and statues and posters in glory of Nasser were dismantled and replaced by others glorifying Sadat. The Nasser years, he was to write, made him realize that "the mistakes made by a democracy in a whole generation do not compare with the mistakes that can be made by a dictatorship in a single day." "We had called for a benevolent dictator, a just tyrant; but when we had one, we realised that the system, though outwardly attractive, was built on sand."

By 1974, *Al-Ahram,* Cairo's leading newspaper, once Nasser's mouthpiece, was acknowledging that peaceful Egypt had been turned by Nasser into "a gloomy scene of torture and punishment, the likes of which was not witnessed even in the darkest days of the medieval ages." The Sudanese Mohammad Ahmed Mahgoub had once had the difficult task of resisting Nasser's ambitions on his country, and in a memoir published in 1974, he could break the silence of complicity by describing how Nasser had plunged "into the disputes and rivalries within the Arab world." Until Nasser's death, it would hardly have been possible for an Arab to have spoken openly, as Mahgoub now did, of how "superficial" his courtship of the Egyptians had been, or how his search for a doctrine was "even more specious."

On the face of it, the 1973 war was a gamble that a power holder could not reasonably have contemplated. So it seemed to the Israeli government, applying Eurocentric thinking to the cost-effectiveness of war, omitting from its calculations the factor of shame-honor. Time and again, Sadat declared in public that "the year of decision" had been reached. No matter how many postponements ensued, no matter what the outcome for Egypt, Sadat could not have survived the shame of failing to attack Israel. In fact, he was conspiring with Hafez Assad, a man with whom he had nothing in common except enmity to Israel. The two then recruited the Al Saud power holder to underwrite the war's financing. The first that the Egyptian and Syrian populations heard of the fighting was when, like everyone else, they were surprised by the news on October 6. Had the Egyptian army been repelled, Sadat's position would have been untenable, his life endangered. As "the Hero of the Crossing" he had legitimized his power holding enough to be able to gloss over the fact that the Israeli army within a fortnight had crossed to the West Bank of the Canal, threatening Cairo.

The profound meaning of October 6, wrote Tewfik el-Hakim, was not merely a military victory or a material crossing as much as it was "a spiritual crossing to a new stage in our history," a stage in which nothing less than Egyptian civilization would be reconstructed. To Mansour Khalid, the importance of the war was in its psychological achievement "restoring the faith of a people in themselves." Yussef Idris wrote a poem, "Deliverance":

> I had never before believed in the role of the
> individual in history
> I did not know that one person alone, in

setting his own will, set that of a Nation, and
the history of a people, and the strength of a
civilization
But the hero, Anwar Sadat, is beyond my ken
He crushed the defeat lying deep within us
all when he resolved upon the crossing
And by his decision not only the army
crossed the canal
But the people crossed with it and trans-
cended their submissiveness and misery
Left behind their humiliation and shame

"The defeat lying deep within us" echoes Lufti al-Sayyid's earlier "Deep in their souls was a feeling of inferiority." No doubt Sadat expertly weighed the shame-honor values to which he was appealing in support of his onslaught against Israel. The impetus of popularity and the association of heroism aroused by the recovery of honor carried Sadat through the reversal of the policy of ending "the Zionist conspiracy" and into peace. By the same token, Sadat was accepting American sponsorship, with its implication that he would replace Nasser's socialism with a local version of capitalism, and in the expectation of rewards. He also appreciated that he would have to break with Hafez Assad, his erstwhile heroic fellow conspirator, who still had little alternative to Soviet sponsorship. By 1977 Egypt and Syria were at loggerheads, exchanging insults and accusations, and American aid to Egypt was greater than to the rest of Africa and Latin America combined.

Realignment of this kind was a considerable achievement, and in that it destroyed measures of state control and planning, it might have had the potential for liberation as well. But Sadat's introduction of Egyptian capitalism had the same personal career-ist character as Nasser's previous introduction of state socialism: neither step took account of popular participation; people were to do as they were told. The Egyptian army, intelligence, and security services continued to enjoy the same preeminent role after 1977 as before. In order to bring their daily problems to the attention of the power holder, people still had little other recourse than rioting: already in January 1977, in riots about the rising price of bread, seventy-nine people were killed, a thousand were wounded, and as many again imprisoned. Those who had enjoyed Nasser's sanction for their own money-favoring were merely replaced by those who enjoyed Sadat's sanction for the same ends. Nasser-backed survivors and Sadat-backed millionaires may have fought each other for spoils, but to the masses they formed a single elite, enviable and remote. As Taha Zaki, minister of industry, put it in 1980 in one of those flashes of truth as memorable as they are rare, "All these debates between capitalism and communism can be reduced to one thing—who gets the money. I don't care about the debates. The question is to get some money first, otherwise the debates are about nothing." Sadat's brother Esmat made a fortune out of privileged money-favoring. Sadat's daughter Huda married the son of Osman Ahmed Osman, the largest contractor in the Middle East and recipient of the most lucrative commissions for public works in Egypt. Another daughter of Sadat's married the son of Sayyid Marei, a minister under Nasser who switched in time to hold office under Sadat. A key Sadat henchman in the People's Assembly was Abu Wafia, married to a sister of Sadat's wife, Jehan, and involved in a scandal about the Suez-Mediterranean pipeline. Mohamed Heikal, once editor of *Al-Ahram* and a witness still eager to defend Nasser, spoke of an emerging picture of "corruption and manipulation on a quite fantastic scale."

In his writings Sadat spoke time and again of the passivity of the Egyptian people, and how rulers could do with them what they liked. In the manner of previous power holders, he gave no thought to what kind of institutions might allow these people to be less passive, to speak on their own behalf, to choose what they might want rather than whatever was wanted for them by the power holder.

Those who felt sufficiently aggrieved by Sadat's realignment as usual broke out of their passivity in order to conspire. Peace with Israel and American sponsorship gave such discontent a natural anti-Western and Islamic slant. Moreover, at the outset of his rule Sadat had deliberately and conspiratorially encouraged the Muslim Brothers as a counterweight to surviving Nasserites who were secular in outlook. As from 1977, ambitious individuals began secretly to recruit their retinues on a basis of Islamic doctrine. Most of these conspirators took their outlook from the Muslim Brothers. One such was Shukri Mustafa, born in 1942, who had been in concentration camps under Nasser. As leader of the so-called Society of Muslims, which in spite of its grandiose name was merely a tiny handful of like-minded friends, he took hostage

Muhammad Al Dhahabi, a religious scholar who had been minister of pious foundations, and shot him dead. For this, Shukri Mustafa was tried in a military court and executed.

Sadat's own careerist rise to power was meeting the challenge it was sure to provoke. In the usual manner, those working to overthrow him were preparing the very methods of terror and murder to which he had himself resorted in his attacks on the British and King Farouk. Just as he had been imprisoned, so now he imprisoned others. Another Islamicist group under the leadership of a Palestinian Salih Sirriya attacked the military academy at Heliopolis. Sirriya and his adjutant were captured and executed, and twenty-nine of his followers jailed.

A devout Muslim himself, Sadat considered that Islamic challenges were particularly unfair and inapplicable to him, the erstwhile conspirator in the Muslim Brothers with Hasan al-Banna. As a gesture of conciliation, he permitted the Muslim Brothers to relaunch their publications. Concessions only created an impression of vulnerability. Informed of the growing numbers of Islamic secret societies, in September 1981 Sadat ordered the arrests of over 1500 men including Umar Tilminsani, the head of the Muslim Brothers, the popular preacher Sheikh Kishk, various leaders of groups uncovered by the intelligence services, and for good measure 150 Copts, with their Pope, 8 bishops and 13 priests among them. Much to their dismay, critics like Mohamed Heikal and the feminist Nawal el-Saadawi were also rounded up.

One group, going under the name of Jihad (meaning war against the unbeliever) had escaped the mass arrest. Its leader, Abdul Salam Faraj, was an electrician and also author of a pamphlet arguing that the present was pagan, to be redeemed by Islamic measures that had been successful fourteen centuries earlier. To him it was a lawful duty to kill a ruler deemed to be un-Islamic. Several members of Jihad were in the army, and four of them shot Sadat dead on October 6, 1981, at a military parade in Cairo to celebrate the crossing of the Canal that had legitimized his rule. The lieutenant in command of the assassination squad is recorded as shouting out an appropriately heroic sentiment at the realization of his deed, "I am Khalid al-Islambuli, I have killed Pharoah, and I do not fear death." In that style Sadat himself had validated his own heroics by wishing that he had been Zahran, hanged at Denshawai. Within months, the busts and statues and posters of Sadat had given way to portraits of his successor, Husni Mubarak, previously vice-president. Esmat Sadat was tried for corruption and found guilty. Al-Islambuli, his three accomplices, and Abdul Salam Faraj were put on trial and executed. Islam, its religious observances and beliefs, had no bearing on the crime but had been exploited to provide a careerist group with justification for murdering the power holder, in the wild expectation of replacing him.

MUAMMAR GADDHAFI

In 1969, Muammar Gaddhafi seized power in Libya, and since then his activities have been observed everywhere with bewilderment and sometimes consternation. In the Eurocentric view, he appears to be little but an adventurer, more and more reckless and sterile in his troublemaking. Libyan troops have fought in neighboring Chad, in Sudan, in Uganda, and they have clashed with both Egyptian and Tunisian forces. Pacts of union variously proposed to Egypt, Morocco, and Tunisia have come to nothing. Libyan subsidies have fueled civil war, revolution, a coup d'état, or some degree of destabilization in countries as far afield as the Philippines, Ireland, Malta, New Caledonia, Surinam, Burkina Faso (formerly Upper Volta), Nicaragua and El Salvador, Eritrea, Ghana and the Canary Islands. Libyan terrorists have exploded bombs fatally in several European cities and have created further outrages by shooting down Libyan dissidents or refugees in Greece, Germany, Britain, and Spain, as well as throughout most of the Arab world. "It is legitimate," Gaddhafi has emphasized, "for our entire people to liquidate its enemies abroad and quite openly." On one occasion, Libyans killed an English policewoman by firing from the windows of their embassy in London—a criminal infringement of diplomatic privilege which is unprecedented.

As the power holder responsible for these acts, Gaddhafi has been widely considered unstable, perhaps deranged. To Sadat, he was "this maniac." President Reagan is among Western statesmen who have called him "mad." Gaddhafi hardly clears the air by responding in kind, for example describing the British and the Americans as "a species which are between pigs and human beings." Needless to say, he is not deranged or mad but merely making what he can of his circumstances, which are as peculiar as they are limited.

Libya has a fertile coastal strip along the Mediterranean but is otherwise a virtual desert. The three million inhabitants of a vast but sparse area are not yet incorporated into social or national institutions other than those of the tribe and of Islam. Between 1911 and 1943, they experienced colonization by the Italians, which reached a climax under Mussolini. The country's first secondary school was opened in 1935. The end of the Second World War and the defeat of fascist Italy assured independence under the rule of Idris al-Sanusi, a religious personality and legitimate claimant to temporal and spiritual power in accordance with Islamic doctrine. Independence in 1951 found Libya with seven college graduates, an administrative structure that one expert has judged "simple in the extreme," and a per capita income of hardly $50 a year. Oil was struck in 1956, however, to come on stream in the 1960s, and by the 1980s to produce an annual revenue of about $30 billion, or far the greater part of the gross domestic product. Agriculture continues to employ a third of the workforce but accounts for a mere 2 percent of gross domestic product and meets only a third of food requirements.

Petro-dollar wealth of this size and suddenness offers each and every power challenger the most irresistible temptation of aggrandizement, but in a country without manpower resources in support. No doubt any other power holder who might have emerged in Libya would have been similarly dazzled by the careerist opportunities of this money and would also have been baffled about how to exploit it in any form more substantial than money-favoring. Gaddhafi's position is comparable to that of the Al Saud in Saudi Arabia, but whereas they tend to proffer money-favors to existing power holders who can return the good deed tangibly, Gaddhafi seeks out underdog challengers like himself, whose full potential remains to be proved. In part, this is a question of who is available to be bought. Influential clients have prior commitments, and therefore Gaddhafi must select those whose sponsorship may one day bring rewards, casting his net as internationally as he can over foreign terrorists, armed groups and likely insurrectionists. In the power-challenge dialectic, what today looks naive and ludicrous may seem viable and far-sighted tomorrow. Incalculable though it must always be, nuisance-value is an essential element in self-assertion like Gaddhafi's, a means of forcing himself upon regional power holders, and beyond that into the focus of the superpowers. These intrigues, however squalid, are intended to transform his sole asset of money into political influence abroad, for purposes of legitimizing his rule and preventing Libyans from asking by what right Gaddhafi is power holder above them. Xenophobia is by no means the controlling factor it might appear to be: foreigners comprise about a third of the active workforce and are indispensable at managerial and professional levels.

Mystifying the date of his birth, which was between 1935 and 1942, Gaddhafi belongs to a desert tribe that is not prominent but proud of its alleged descent from the Prophet. He attended school in the oasis of Sebha, in the eastern Sahara province of the Fezzan. There he met Abdul Salam Jalloud, to this day his close associate. Legend has it that he started conspiring young. Enlisting in 1963 in the army, he seems to have acquired the heroic deeds that generate an aura of fear around oneself; for instance helping to shoot dead a man accused of some sexual offense, possibly homosexuality, and supposedly assassinating the commander of the Benghazi Military Academy. Several months of training courses in England did nothing to familiarize him with Western democracy or to change his outlook. Rising in rank, in 1964 he started in earnest to build a conspiratorial retinue out of officers whom he could trust, including Jalloud, Omar Meheishe, and Abdul Moneim Al Houni. At a meeting on a beach in Talmisa, they held the usual ceremony of induction, with oaths. The actual power holder, Idris al-Sanusi, elderly and increasingly inattentive, uncertain how best to disburse the oil money already amassing, was a natural prey. Gaddhafi and his group were first to stage a coup, in September 1969.

Gaddhafi had modeled himself on Nasser, the obvious precursor as soldier-conspirator. The claim to be imitating Egypt was in itself sufficient to legitimize the coup at the time. Nasserite slogans of socialism and Arab unity served to cover the spoliation of the al-Sanusi regime. Today 100,000 Libyans are in exile, including the Sanusi and their beneficiaries, all of whom have been dispossessed. Land was also confiscated from 30,000 Italian farmers and small-holders, and they were expelled from Libya. As these assets found their way into the hands of Gaddhafi and his retinue and their tribal kinsmen, the whole country suddenly appeared to be up for grabs. This free-for-all pursuit of wealth was further spurred and maximized by Gaddhafi's determination to place at his own disposal the state revenues from oil. In 1971, the oil companies were nationalized, and the oil fields then expropriated.

In the hope of enlarging his Revolutionary Command Council of fellow conspirators into something more like a coalition, Gaddhafi approached the ulema. Islam in Libya had a previous power-challenge complexion, in that the Sanusi had risen to preeminence as religious leaders. Those among the ulema who had opposed the Sanusi, or otherwise been alienated by them, rejoiced in their downfall and were disposed to welcome Gaddhafi. By way of sweetening, Gaddhafi handed over to them mosques and other property confiscated from the Sanusi and promulgated a number of traditionally Islamic measures, such as beheading or amputation of limbs for convicted criminals, and the banning of alcohol.

Favors only encouraged those within the ruling coalition, whether military or religious, to overrate their standing and to demand a larger share of the rewards. The religious were the first to be cut down. In May 1973, Gaddhafi arrested some Muslim Brothers. A challenge developed between him and Sheikh Mohammad al-Bushti, the Mufti of Tripoli, a dominant personality, with an uncompromising nature. The Mufti was finally arrested in 1980 and is reported to have been killed. The original military conspirators broke apart in 1975, when Omar Meheishe vainly attempted a coup, after which he fled to Morocco. Abdul Moneim al-Houni then also escaped into exile. Hundreds of officers were arrested; people's courts were convened in cases sometimes lasting hardly an hour, and death sentences were handed out by the dozen. In April 1977, twenty-two alleged members of the Meheishe coup were executed, and some civilians were publicly hanged. Another coup was suppressed in 1978. In the end, Meheishe himself was forcibly repatriated from Morocco, and according to one account "stomped to death" as he was taken off the aircraft in Libya. In another obscure incident in March 1985, Gaddhafi claimed that there had been a plot, and sixty-five more officers were hanged. That November, he accused another associate, Hassan Ishkar, of conspiracy, summoned him to his headquarters, and had him shot down then and there in the doorway.

Islam, socialism, and Arab unity had evidently failed one after the other to provide a legitimizing doctrine, and Gaddhafi had nothing better to fall back on than justification of his rule on grounds of birth.

The officers have the conscience to recognise the people's claims better than others. This depends on our origin which is characterized by humbleness. We are not rich people; the parents of the majority of us are living in huts. My parents are still living in a tent near Sirte. The interests we represent are genuinely those of the Libyan people.

Eurocentric notions and vocabulary have been incorporated into such a statement to fashion what may well be called mirages. What the country's component tribes have in common politically is only the person of Gaddhafi as power holder, in a position to dispose of them all according to his will. To speak of himself as poor conceals the absolute control he enjoys of the entire resources of the state. To live in a tent, for Gaddhafi as for his parents, is a choice elaborately decked out with helicopters and private aircraft, air conditioning and mobile communications systems, and contingents of bodyguards. Gaddhafi's fellow tribesmen and numerous close relations occupy leading and lucrative posts in the bureaucracy and the army. As for "the people's claims," Gaddhafi alone can define and voice them. No means of expressing popular opinion exists. Newspapers and television, inaugurated in 1968, are state agencies used to control, not to inform. Neither comment nor protest could be articulated when Gaddhafi closed mosques because preachers had delivered equivocal sermons; when he paved over the central square of Tripoli with green cement on the grounds that green is the true color of Islam; or when he decreed that the state is abolished, that a new calendar is henceforth in use and that the economy is in the hands of popular committees. On the contrary, tribalist values and shame-honor ranking accord to certify the actions of the power holder, no matter how whimsical, alarming, or unfathomable these might appear. A frame of mind develops in which virtually everyone within reach comes to admire the power holder for compelling obedience and silence, even by means of outrage.

A quarter of a million Libyans now attend schools at all levels. Large capital sums have been invested in infrastructure. Almost two-thirds of the population is under fifteen, has known nothing but the rule of Gaddhafi, and has rapidly rising expectations. It was for these people that some more permanent legitimizing doctrine had to be devised, if only to nip off those among them who might nurture careerist ambitions. In 1976 and 1977, accordingly, Gaddhafi published a credo, *The Green Book,* in the form of three slender volumes. In these essays, parliamentary democracy and political parties are judged a sham. Voting slips are cast like "papers into the dust-bin." The concept of loyal opposition is evidently too strange to be credible. To Gaddhafi, everyone is born into a class as fixedly as into a tribe, so that party struggle is essentially the same as tribal struggle; "Only blood-relationship distinguishes a tribe from a party." The outcome envisaged is to create "a basic popular congress" as a version of an enlarged tribal gathering, though it is admitted in a final incongruity that "realistically, the strong always rule, i.e., the stronger part in the society is the one that rules." Although *The Green Book* is intellectually feeble or void in its analysis and prescription alike, it nevertheless contains some awareness that force is a cruder and more illegitimate method than popular choice for sanctioning a power holder. A tacit suggestion has been advanced in favor of participation, if only at a primitive level.

For a power holder like Gaddhafi to be promoting "the authority of the People" is a paradox that cannot evolve into a program by publishing a book or issuing a decree. Libyans can see for themselves how an absolute ruler is imposing his will on them even in this. Besides, like a medieval ruler, Gaddhafi has secreted himself within a fortified citadel in Tripoli, protected by an army of 45,000, and a security force of about the same size. Money-favoring with petro-dollars continues to be his sole inspiration. Assorted Europeans and Americans, Yasser Arafat and other Palestinians, renegade CIA agents, arms dealers, IRA and other terrorists have arrived from all over the world to present him with their causes and schemes, from which he picks and chooses. Libya and Saudi Arabia and the Gulf Emirates, in their various offensive and defensive subsidies of others, covert or declared, sometimes pull together, but more generally this way and that in the frantic efforts of those concerned to lay hands on the money.

To the Soviet Union, Libya's own chosen sponsor, Gaddhafi has been a bonus in one respect, purchasing arms in hard currency and either selling them on as war *matériel* requiring replacement or stockpiling them far beyond any capacity for local use. Clearly alarmed by the volatility of Gaddhafi's international money-favoring, the Soviet Union has carefully distanced itself in every crisis, much to Gaddhafi's chagrin.

Detected in a crime such as the killing in September 1986 of an American serviceman in a Berlin nightclub by means of a bomb, for instance, Gaddhafi could only expect an American reaction, though in the event armed retaliation seems to have surprised him. The confrontation was so visible that it triggered shame-honor responses. Gaddhafi was driven to rant with characteristic self-grandeur,

If you continue your tyranny, insolence, madness and foolishness, against the international community and world peace, then I, Muammar Al Gaddhafi, want to state that I can form an international army consisting of fighters against imperialism and against the USA personally. I can form an army outside Libya, and this army will spread to all corners of the globe to destroy the American presence everywhere.

After American aircraft based in Britain had raided Libyan installations, Gaddhafi called a press conference to state that President Reagan "should be toppled and tried," and so Islamocentric a statement calls into question his understanding of the processes of democracy. Safia, Gaddhafi's wife, spoke in the same vein, as though politics was only a combat to the death between power holders.

I didn't believe Mrs. Thatcher was a murderer. She has children. I did not think that she would do this. If the Americans and British are democratic, they should judge Reagan and Thatcher. They should be liquidated.

Speeches of the kind are concealed appeals to the Soviet Union to play its arbitrating and honor-saving role, which once again it declined to do. But such humiliations can be retrieved or at least softened by tribal-religious mobilization. According to a newspaper report,

For his speech in the early hours of Monday morning thousands of Libyan peasants were bussed in from outlying areas to make up the crowd. It was noticeable that armed revolutionary guards, the only people to be trusted with guns in Libya these days, were keeping a close watch on the Libyan military.

No chances are taken, obviously, but those thousands bussed in, like everyone else, knew what their roles were and how to play them as realistically as though in a theater under direction. Ordered to burn an embassy or to kidnap a specific foreigner, they will do so, but their true feelings might well be revealed through displaying personal courtesy to a diplomat or unspecified foreigner actually encountered in pursuit of instructions. Witnessing the public amputations and hangings, they have drawn sad but prudent conclusions. Nothing is offered except the fulfillment of their subservience. In the buses taking them home and every day afterward, they are left to ponder their plight and exclusion. Gaddhafi exemplifies power holding for its own sake, carried aimlessly to such lengths that there have long been shortages of the necessities of life, with empty shops and rationing, smuggling and a black market, as though the Libyans were still truly poor desert tribesmen, without title either to their country's staggering oil wealth or to an agreed and beneficial ordering of society.

HAFEZ ASSAD

Hafez Assad was born in 1928 in the small village of Qardaha, in the mountains above the Syrian port of Latakia. His family were peasants living at subsistence level. The hinterland of Latakia is inhabited by Alawis, who are schismatics from the eleventh century. The million or so Alawis amount to about 12 percent of the country's population, most of whom are otherwise Sunni Muslims who look down on the Alawis as heretics and a people to be considered generally beyond the pale. There are four main tribal confederations of Alawis, and Hafez Assad belongs to the poorest of them, by origin a man at a disadvantage within an already disadvantaged minority. Today Qardaha boasts an opulent palace belonging to Assad, and a visiting reporter recently observed in the village streets, "young men, tall and strong from a good diet, wearing their uniforms, sharply tailored, chatting with the girls with the easy arrogance of power." President of Syria since 1971, Assad has done himself and his Alawi people proud.

It is possible to describe him as Henry Kissinger once did, as "the most interesting man in the Middle East," and possible too to speak of him in the one-dimensional manner of fulsome Western journalists as "a stable and comfortable figure," even "something of a genuine popular hero." This misrepresentation perfectly exemplifies the Eurocentricity which comes so glibly to those fortunate enough to live outside Assad's reach. The price that has to be paid for Assad and Alawi supremacy is the customary one of assault on all other tribal-religious entities within and bordering Syria, by whatever means are appropriate, including murder, massacre and war.

The details of how Assad became—and has remained—power holder cannot be openly aired in a country where the regime owns and controls every medium of communication. Yet each Syrian sifts for himself the slants of news and rumors, weighing personal experiences of tyranny, in the knowledge that the dispossessed Sunnis are eagerly awaiting their moment for revenge and that the

Alawis must take the most extreme dispositions, first to prevent fragmentation among their own four tribal confederations, then to deny Sunnis all openings for conspiracy or mass mobilization. Throughout Assad's rule, Syria has been under Emergency Law, policed by the state security apparatus, which has at least eight separate agencies for intelligence, surveillance, repression, and protection of the power holder to whom alone they are answerable. The total prison population is unknown but runs into many thousands held without trial. Three thousand five hundred individuals are reported to have been arrested between January 1980 and December 1981 alone. In Damascus and Aleppo, the two largest cities, respectively fourteen and nineteen detention centers have been identified, and according to Amnesty International, twenty-three different methods of torture are commonplace. A score of leading personalities, including a former Syrian president, Nour Al Din al-Atassi, and other former colleagues of Assad's, have remained in preventive detention since Assad seized power. Tense with anticipatory fear of whatever the next turn might be in the maintenance of absolute despotism, everyone huddles for protection into his tribal-religious group. To stay alive and at home in the family are grounds for daily gratitude.

Syria has the potential to be self-sufficient in agriculture and to export cotton. Oil was discovered in 1959, in quantities to cater for internal demand, with a small margin for sale abroad. Natural gas reserves are estimated to last into the next century. The Soviet-financed Euphrates Dam has permitted measures of industrial expansion through electrification. Politics prevent the orderly exploitation of these resources to the benefit of all.

Starting afresh, each power challenger has his retinue, which has to be rewarded with public funds. Transformed after a successful coup into the power holder, he has to extend his influence by further challenges at the national level. Sharing frontiers with Turkey, Lebanon, Israel, Jordan, and Iraq, and having Kurds and Druze among the minorities within its borders, Syria is at the center of a round-the-compass maelstrom of power challenging. Since 1948 Syria has been involved in twenty-six interstate disputes that included the threat, display, and use of armed force. Regardless of the power holder's personality or disposition, the same disputes are still pursued. One Syrian power holder after another has exploited these challenges to acquire sponsorship—money, arms, and subsidies—principally from the Soviet Union in a process of continuous careerist influence building. Between 1945 and 1971, most of the dozen regimes were overthrown within months. The government of Adib Shishakli alone lasted as long as four years.

Writing in 1958, one contemporary expert spoke of "the chronic inability" of Syrian governments to maintain themselves, as though the personnel were congenitally incompetent. Quite the contrary, Syrian rulers have proved equally capable and fierce in challenging and power holding, victims not of chronic inability but of one another's ambitions. Lacking the means to create the trust and cooperation to bring tribal-religious groups together for the sake of intercommunal and national purposes, social and political institutions have been mere agencies of control at the service of the power holder. No mechanism is available to question or to obstruct whatever challenges the power holder chooses to make at the national level. Misconceived bids in Lebanon and against Israel have led to squandering of wealth on a massive scale, to diversion of resources into weaponry, finally to armed reprisals, damage, even loss of territory in the Golan Heights, altogether setting back by many years the country's economic base and therefore its real independence.

After 1945, in the early years of independence, the Baath Party in theory seemed to offer some institutional alternative to power challenging. Its founders, Michel Aflaq and Salah al-Din Bitar, had come to an understanding that in a nondemocratic state, force and fear alone will not serve the power holder for effective mobilization of the masses. A positive doctrine is required. Aflaq and Bitar proposed liberation from the West, Arab unity, and socialism. These were concepts grasped by very few people in a society in which Islam alone was a group value. Instead of analyzing whether Baath proposals and Islam were compatible and if so by what means, Aflaq and Bitar lost no chance to praise Islam as though it were some higher form of anti-Western liberation, unity, and socialism. Bitar was a Sunni Muslim, European-educated, and something of an exception among the leading personalities in the Baath who were otherwise members of minorities, Alawis, Druze, Christians. Their promotion of Islam from the outset appeared naive and suspect, and the Baathists themselves oppositional, divisive. Sincere as they may well have been in their intentions, the Baathists succeeded in creating only another means for their own tribal-religious advancement.

Assad joined the party around 1947 when he was an air force cadet in the Military Academy. The armed forces offered career prospects that Alawis were quicker to exploit than Sunnis as a means to redress their lack of privilege and opportunity. Soon the Alawi presence in the officer corps of the armed forces and of the Baath Party merged these two career avenues into one. "The accidents of recruitment," in the words of a historian of the Baath Party, in the case of each individual depended on "the home town, place of education, circle of relatives, and friends," which over the years "led to a predominance of party members from particular towns or districts." This proved the first step in sealing the Sunni fate.

The years of the Syrian merger with Egypt after 1958 threatened minorities with loss of identity under a wider Sunni dispensation. At the time, Assad was stationed in Egypt, and there he began to conspire with two fellow Alawis, Salah Jedid and Muhammad Umran, and a Druze officer Hamad Ubaid. The termination of the merger in 1961 opened up a power-challenge opportunity in Syria, and the Baathists took it in March 1963, mounting a coup. The leaders were disproportionately Alawi, and this marked the second stage of the Alawi takeover.

Sami al-Jundi, who had participated in the founding of the Baath Party, has described how rewards were apportioned on tribal-religious lines after the 1963 coup.

> Three days after my entering the Ministry, the [party] comrades came to ask me for an extensive purge operation. . . . The measure of a minister's success [was determined by] the lists of dismissals, since party members as well as their relatives and the members of their tribes [came to] demand their campaign and kinship rights. From the time the party appeared on the stage, caravans of villagers started to leave the villages of the plains and mountains for Damascus. And while the alarming *Qaf* [Arabic guttural whose pronunciation reveals the rural origins of the person uttering it] started to predominate in the streets, coffee houses and the waiting rooms of the ministries, dismissals became a duty so that [those who had newly come] could be appointed.

Between 1963 and 1970, the Baath-Alawi coalition remained insecure as army officers entered into rivalry among themselves for supreme power. By 1966, Salah Jedid had become the power holder, closely stalked by Hafez Assad. Failing to take advantage of this deadly inter-Alawi duality, the Sunnis finally were condemned to lose the state. During the Jordanian civil war in September 1970, Jedid made a miscalculated play for increased influence by sending Syrian armor across the frontier on behalf of the Palestinians. As commander of the air force, Assad refused to provide air cover, on the grounds—quite possibly correct—that Israel would intervene as the fighting widened. This restraint ensured that the Jordanian army was able to destroy much of the Syrian armor. Blaming Jedid for the fiasco that he had himself largely engineered, Assad arrested his rival and imprisoned him indefinitely. In 1971 he arranged a referendum that gave him a 99 percent vote as the new president. Muhammad Umran was duly murdered in March 1972, and at the end of that year Alawis of Jedid's tribal confederation were arrested en masse on charges of plotting. Assad was ensuring that he could maintain himself as power holder.

Assad inherited Soviet sponsorship. To the anti-Western rhetoric of postcolonial Syria was added the Baathist sloganizing of socialism and unity, altogether making Syria attractive in the worldwide Soviet clientele. Since 1957 the Soviet Union has accepted its role, though with evident anxiety that the next step might follow, which would oblige it to arbitrate in Syrian power challenges against Israel or Lebanon, or even Iraq, thereby risking direct confrontation with the United States. Assad himself had completed a flying course in the Soviet Union, has often visited it openly or secretly, and praised it. Ideology has no part in this; the sponsor has merely to prove his utility. Playing both ends in the 1970s, Assad insinuated that he was willing to entertain a switch, thereby prizing some hundreds of millions of extra dollars out of Washington. But the relentless militarization of the country through its national power challenges and the all-encompassing secret police repression has given Syria the reality of a Soviet satellite. Between 1973 and 1983, Syria received Soviet arms worth $10 billion, without which Assad could neither have remained power holder nor continued his challenges throughout the region. Having stalled to formalize the sponsor-client relationship, Assad finally signed a Soviet-Syrian Treaty of Friendship in 1980.

Cold and calculating, a master of conspiracy, untroubled by conscience, Assad might have built for himself a position of strength greater than the national resources warranted. But in 1973, he proposed a new constitution that specified freedom of worship. The Sunnis saw a chance for a comeback by presenting the proposed constitution as an attack by the heterodox minority against mainstream Islam. In effect, the Sunnis proposed to utilize Islam for self-defense. By law, the president was obliged to be a Muslim, and Assad compounded his difficulties by attending Sunni mosques amid publicity, obtaining a certificate from the cowed and obedient Sunni ulema that as an Alawi he was an authentic Muslim. Perhaps it was hubris, or perhaps he could not bring himself to believe that Baathist slogans of socialism and unity were abstractions, empty and hollow for all but his retainers. At any rate, an undeclared subterranean civil war has been rumbling ever since, in which Assad has almost lost power, and indeed his life, in a lengthening sequence of foiled coups and attempted assassinations, consummating as never before the Alawi-Sunni divide. Without any representative function, the Baath Party mobilizes and controls as the power holder decrees. Aflaq has long since fled to Baghdad, and Bitar was murdered in 1980.

Damascus was a historic center of Sunni worship. Weakened to some extent under the modernizing and secularizing influence of the French, this tradition persisted. In the uprush of postwar independence, a Syrian lodge of the Muslim Brothers opened. Its leader, Mustapha as-Sibai, had been born in Homs in 1915, had attended Al-Azhar where he became a friend of Hasan al-Banna, and had founded a secret society to combat Christian missionaries in Syria. A conspirator of talent, Sibai was the first to mobilize support among the Sunnis. President Shishakli, a self-proclaimed progressive, finding himself opposed by the Muslim Brothers, outlawed the organization in 1952. Sibai died and was succeeded by Marwan Hadid, a friend of Sayyid Qutb's and an advocate of armed resistance in the name of Islam to Nasser in Egypt and then to Assad in Syria. Marwan Hadid died in prison. His successor, Said Hawwa, was imprisoned between 1973 and 1978 but survived to flee into exile in Jordan. Law 49, passed by Assad, has made it a crime punishable by death to be a member of the Muslim Brotherhood, or even be associated with it.

As many as a thousand Muslim Brothers were butchered in one day in Palmyra prison; and 10 percent or more of the 250,000 inhabitants of Hama were killed in 1982 when the regime suppressed a Sunni uprising there, in part provoked by the increasing number of Alawi immigrants into the town; and hundreds more deaths have occurred in actions in Aleppo, Sarmada, and Jisr al-Shughur. In Hama, corpses of ulema were dug out of the ruins and defiled. Prominent Alawis assassinated in this civil fighting have included two brothers-in-law of Assad's, both from the region of Qardaha, as well as the rector of Damascus university, the director of police at the ministry of the interior, and senior officers such as the brigadier commanding the missile corps and the commander of the Hama garrison. Officers and soldiers are frequently purged and executed for sympathy with the Muslim Brothers. Assassins have operated out of Syrian embassies to kill Muslim Brothers abroad.

On behalf of the Brotherhood, a captain by the name of Ibrahim Yusuf led an attack against the Alawi-dominated artillery school in Aleppo in June 1979, as a result of which eighty-three cadets were killed and hundreds more wounded. Typically, the regime covered the tribal-religious complexion of this onslaught with a conspiratorial explanation and shame-honor appeals.

Is it possible to believe that those who killed young men in their prime are training to go to the battlefield shortly, to resist the Israeli aggressions and to be killed by the enemy in defence of our chaste homeland and our nation's dignity? . . . Is it possible to believe that such an action can be anything but a service to Israel and to all the enemies of our nation?

No other idiom can be found for national challenges which do such glaring damage to the real interests of Syria. After attacking Israel in 1973 in what is locally called the Ramadan War, Assad decided to invade Lebanon in 1975, and in his speeches similarly obscured the nature of these challenges:

[The Lebanese invasion, Assad began, recalled Ramadan 1973] these glorious days in which we waged large and honourable battles. The aggression against Lebanon [by the Christians, he means here] began shortly before Ramadan and continued during Ramadan. Your sons have waged the fiercest, bravest and most honourable battles. . . . [In Lebanon] fighting was imposed on us and our army stood up proudly, strongly and honourably. Real epics were recorded. . . . When we fight honourably for martyrdom and when the enemy cannot advance an inch except over our bodies, we will not at all be considered to have lost the battle. . . . We are optimistic about the future and we want to build a strong homeland in which we can live with dignity. We have a right to boast of our steadfastness and of our forces' fighting against the enemy. . . . Man needs dignity and we are determined to defend dignity. We want our dignity and homeland uplifted.

To young paratroopers in a speech in 1983, Assad spoke characteristically:

> We in this country, in Arab Syria, have pledged that there shall be no humiliation, no defeatism, and no capitulation in this land. Only the banners of glory, dignity and pride shall be hoisted in the skies of this noble homeland.

The presumed conspiracy of others and shame-honor discourse have become the sole legitimizing appeals to all elements; nonpolitical but psychological; and a last resort in the impossible task of striving for unity without the enabling institutions. By the same token, the practice of ruling can have no expression but force.

Here are two recent newspaper items:

> A Lebanese national, Ahmad Hasan Id, was executed by hanging at the northern entrance to Damascus, the Syrian agency reported on April 29 [at this same northern entrance a refrigerator truck had earlier been detonated]. The agency said that he had been executed for committing a criminal action which had resulted in the death or injury of a number of citizens, adding that his confession had left no doubt that nobody other than "Saddam Hussein . . . could degenerate to this level of spiteful, foolish crime."

> Syria's Economic Security Court has convicted 65 people of corruption, embezzlement and smuggling, and sentenced five of them to death.

Ahmad Hasan Id and the sixty-five convicted of corruption were in all likelihood ordinary people caught in acts of money-favoring, and unfortunate to encounter a yet more determined careerist whose methods of enforcing his ambitions have behind them the resources of the state. Ahmad Hasan Id was some poor wretch of an agent, employed by Saddam Hussein to blow up the refrigerator truck in the hope of spreading dismay and fear, thus making the task of ruling Syria that much the harder. To have his news agency quite truthfully describe Saddam Hussein as degenerating to spiteful and foolish crime in no way impedes Assad from responding in kind, dispatching his agents to arrange explosions abroad. Such an incident and its repercussions occupy a place in power challenging akin in a democracy to a powerful speech from a parliamentary spokesman in opposition.

Described without reference to careerism and its supportive values, political actions and motivations are lost in some ghostly limbo where states and power holders become indistinguishable, and nothing is what it might seem. This sample is from a speech by the defence minister in 1986, on the anniversary of the 1973 war.

The United States believed that external aggression was the only means to deter Hafez Assad. Therefore, it inspired Iraqi ruler Saddam Hussein to launch an unjust war against the new Islamic Republic of Iran. The plan was a venomous one and the aim was very clear: To engage Iraq and prevent it from assisting Syria if our forces in Lebanon were attacked, by sending the Iraqi forces in the opposite direction and preventing the Iranian forces from assisting the Syrian forces in any war that might erupt in the region. Imam Khomeini's concern was to liberate Iran from its oppressor, and he did so. However, he could not liberate Palestine from its usurper because of Saddam's action. Assad had a clear concept of this barbaric war from the first day. He contacted King Khalid and King Hussein in an attempt to contain it and prevent this dreadful penetration, but Saddam arrogantly refused and continued to implement the US administration's directives to the maximum.

At face value, the defense minister is ignorant about the American body politic and its relations to other states. His view of the world is uninformed and unrealistic, a tragicomedy of lunatic plots in which the actors themselves hardly know which way to stumble. In fact, the minister loses his life if he says plainly that Assad has found it profitable in the political conjuncture of that moment to desert Arab Iraq in order to support Iran. However nonsensical it may sound, this rigmarole is instead concocted, as it were, in a private code to which the audience possess the requisite ciphers. To himself, each listener is silently wondering whether Assad will be able to pull off so high-risk a challenge which defies every Baath slogan, and he is also inwardly applauding the minister's ingenuity in elaborating his fabulous code. Nobody conceives the speech to be the preposterous deception that it is, but merely a routine defensive tactic.

As for corruption, it remains the customary diversion of public wealth into the hands of those who can obtain and keep it—in this case Assad, his family, and Alawis and others in his retinue. The sixty-five singled out in the newspaper item for corruption were doing nothing that those who enforced their conviction had not also done, but they were in a money-favoring nexus not powerful enough to defend them, to plead for mercy, or to bribe to obtain their release.

Investigative reporting is a practice that cannot be entertained within these closed systems, with the result that the deeds of the power holder and the elite remain shrouded in mystery. In spite of the Council of Ministers, the People's Assembly, the Baath Party Command and their subordinate organs, real power is held by Assad and those Alawis who, in the words of the political analyst Hanna Batatu, "control the country's intelligence services and the crucial armoured and air units." These include Assad's younger brother Rifaat, who commands a special paramilitary unit of 25,000 men, with armor; another brother, Jamil, and his cousin Adnan, both commanding other paramilitary units; Ali Haydar, the brother-in-law of Rifaat and commanding yet another unit; Shafiq Fayyad, a brother-in-law of Assad; Adnan Makhluf, chief of the Presidential Guard and a relation of Assad's wife; Muhammad al-Kholi and Ali Aslan, respectively head of intelligence and deputy chief of staff, both from Assad's tribal confederation. Batatu concludes carefully, "Some public figures—civil and military—have waxed rich by creaming off substantial commissions on contracts between nationalised companies and foreign firms." By 1979 a British journalist was writing of "the enormous increase in corruption" and how some of the most prominent of the nouveaux riches were Alawis. "Tales of embezzlement, gigantic rake-offs on Government projects, and racketeering, dissipation in high life are rife. If Syria is still Socialist in name, it has long since ceased to be socialist in spirit."

Toward the end of November 1983, Assad appears to have suffered from a heart illness. The indisposition of the power holder threw the entire state into the suspense that is the preliminary to power challenging. One contender was Rifaat, who ordered his tanks to move on Damascus. Rifaat is alleged to have made a fortune through various enterprises, including smuggling heroin and hashish out of the Bekaa Valley. According to newspaper reports, the drugs are run across various European frontiers in stolen cars in a racket alleged to earn Syria $1 billion a year, under the supervision of Rifaat's son Firaas. When in Paris, Rifaat has an entourage of 200, including two of his four wives, and thirty bodyguards. *Time* magazine has estimated him to be worth $100 million. According to Ion Pacepa, a director of Rumanian intelligence services before he defected to the West, Rifaat has a secret Swiss bank account into which President Ceaucescu of Rumania pays dollars in return for favors and intrigues. "Do I need to have somebody disappear in the West?" Ceaucescu is quoted as saying, "Rifaat will take care of it. Now he can't do without my money." The Al Saud are said to support and finance him as well. This former son of a peasant from Qardaha has acquired a number of houses abroad, including one on the Potomac, a few miles north of Washington, and another in Geneva, and it was to that house that Assad exiled him. Another contender, Mustafa Tlas, the minister of defense, was quoted as saying, "If our President says to anyone 'clear off to Geneva', then that person goes to Geneva. Whoever says no to President Assad will be shorter by a head." As it turned out, Assad recovered; he had no choice but to depend on his brother's loyalty and therefore pardoned him. Rifaat returned to Damascus to consolidate his retinue and his finances, in preparation for the moment favorable to his next bid for power.

Looking back on the careerist politics that have brought the country to this pass, Sami al-Jundi observed in his memoirs how once he and his fellow Baathists had lived as strangers in their own society, "enemies to all the conventions of humanity, rejecting ceremonies, relationships and religions." There was supposedly a spirit of sacrifice in this. "We thought," he says, "that we were the glorious beginnings of a new civilisation, when in fact we were the last exemplars of backwardness and a desolating expression of it." His is a heartfelt confession.

Who among us would have supposed that a day would come when we would be ashamed of our past; would flee from it as from a sin we have deliberately committed and for which we are treated with ignominy; would almost deny having been part of it; and would hide our identity? . . . Our sacrifices, our youth wasted on the roads among the people, our dreams and our faith, were they then all mockery?

Almost nobody credits the fact that we believed in a cause. They insist that we are informers, writers of delations, torturers, killers. They accuse us of treason. They pretend that all that we said was opportunism and trickery, that we so perfected the actor's art that the people were deceived by us.

In exile in Tunisia, Sami al-Jundi practiced as a dentist.

SADDAM HUSSEIN

Iraq, a book about that country by the British journalist Gavin Young, sets a mood in its opening pages with the words, "The

Iraqi charm is one of the natural assets of the place. Any apparent coldness could almost certainly be attributable to shyness," and the author quotes approvingly how in a previous generation Gertrude Bell had found the keynote of Iraq to be "romance." As for politics, Young wafts intimations about "when troubles come" as though the winds blew in such superfluities. In a recent conference paper, Adeed Dawisha, an Iraqi long resident in the West, can summarize the country's evolution with the words, "Iraq has boasted a stable political system that has remained essentially unchanged since the Baathist takeover of power in July 1968," and he ascribes to the present leader Saddam Hussein, "the stability of the recent period." The Iraqi man in the street has charm, may perhaps be shy, and certainly wishes for stability. But how could it be guessed from established commentators such as these that unrelieved terror has held Iraq in thrall for thirty years, or that "stability" is a mealymouthed euphemism for a repressive regime of the utmost cruelty?

In July 1958 Abdul Karim Qassem overthrew the monarchy, in the process murdering the twenty-three-year-old King Faisal II, his uncle the Regent, several women of the royal family, the prime minister Nuri Said Pasha, Nuri's son and others. In the manner of Nasser in Egypt, Qassem had formed a conspiratorial retinue among fellow army officers. From a poverty-stricken background, Qassem was a determined careerist but in circumstances of great tribal-religious complexity. Shias form 60 to 65 percent of the Iraqi population (which today is about 14 million altogether). Numbering 15 to 20 percent, the Arab (as opposed to Kurdish) Sunnis are therefore a minority but have been accustomed since Ottoman days to power holding and supremacy in every respect. The Sunni-Shia divide is felt with keen antagonism as a result. Among other national minorities are Kurds, Christians of Orthodox and heterodox sects that range from the Assyrians and Nestorians to the Sabaeans, and Yazidis, a people with syncretistic creeds of their own.

As the incoming power holder, Qassem appealed for support to these tribal or religious groups historically excluded from access to wealth and privilege. Activists among the minorities had already discovered in the Communist Party some sort of organizational vehicle for their identities and aspirations. How many members the Iraqi Communist Party had enrolled is most uncertain, but to many observers the fact that the Party could recruit at all cast a cold-war shadow that the Qassem regime might be "Communist." Moreover, the destruction of the former power holder and the spoliation of the monarchist retinue released wealth and land to be distributed to Qassem's supporters, in what could be considered an egalitarian policy but more properly was money-favoring. The murder of the Iraqi king—known as a client of the British—in itself supposed that Qassem had switched the country over to the sponsorship of the Soviet Union. For a while, it was feared in the West that Iraq might unite with Syria and Egypt in some combination to form an Arab bloc, federation, or even unitary state of distinct Communist or pro-Soviet complexion. This alarmism arose through the usual misreadings of the power holder's motives and outlook, in another dramatic example of blinkered Eurocentricity.

Ideology was of no concern to Qassem except to the extent that it might be exploited to increase his own power. It may be doubted whether Qassem, or any Iraqi, Communist or Baathist, devoted attention to theories of socialism, nor did any of them require lessons in secret police repression. To Qassem, the novel proposals for Arab unity looked like national challenges on the part of Egypt and Syria against Iraq, with the purpose of bringing him down, and therefore to be firmly resisted. Survival was imperative; his own conspiracy had already begun to break up within days of his coup. His two closest associates were fellow officers, the brothers Abdul Salam Aref and Abdul Rahman Aref, and they were Sunnis, seeing no reason for their personal ambitions to be secondary to Qassem's. The Qassem-Aref duality came to a head when Qassem tried to be rid of Abdul Salam Aref by posting him to Bonn as ambassador. As the Iraqi historian Majid Khadduri writes:

> Conversations continued till the afternoon, but to no avail. Suddenly, while Fuad Arif [another officer, no relation] was standing against the wall and looking at a picture, he turned round upon hearing Qassem saying to Abdul Salam Aref: "What are you up to, Abdul Salam?" Abdul Salam Aref was then sitting on a chair near Qassem's desk and was about to draw his revolver when Qassem quickly grabbed his hand. Fuad Arif immediately took the revolver from Abdul Salam Aref. At this juncture Brigadier Hamid, commander of the Fourth Division, entered Qassem's office to inquire what was going on. "He wanted to kill me," replied Qassem. Aref protested and said that he wanted to commit suicide. "If you wanted to commit suicide," said Qassem, "why did you come to do so in my office; you could have committed suicide in your house." Aref

was in an almost hysterical condition and began to cry and complain about being forced to leave the country.

In fact, Abdul Salam Aref left for Bonn, returned to pursue his takeover, was arrested, put before a tribunal, sentenced to death but released after three years. His turn came in 1963 when he mounted his coup, seized Qassem and put him before a tribunal, and did not repeat the error of showing such mercy as had been shown to him. In the words of Khadduri, Qassem "was then pushed into a small room, where he and the others were shot." This was a prelude to what another authority considers to have been "some of the most terrible scenes of violence hitherto experienced in the post-war Middle East."

In theory, the prolonged civil fighting of the 1960s between Communists and Baathists was about the future social and political orientation of the country. In reality, the two groups were identically matched in outlook and conduct. Mutual accusations of treason and mutual butchery masked a naked power struggle between men each intent upon capturing the state for himself and those prepared to follow him. The Sunni instrument for communal assertion and control of the state was the Baath Party. The influence of Aflaq and Bitar had reached Iraq in the 1950s. The Baath established cells in Iraq to promulgate its ideas of unity and socialism and liberation from the West. One of the moving spirits had been Fuad al-Rikabi, a Shia, who like his counterparts in Syria originally aspired to power sharing. The Party's secretary general, Fuad al-Rikabi, was maneuvered out in 1959 (and ultimately killed in prison by his former colleagues), and with him departed the Shia element. From then on, the Baath had a Sunni leadership. In Iraq, the Sunni had traditionally monopolized the officer corps, treating the army as the natural channel of advancement. By 1968, when the Baath finally had eliminated their opponents so ruthlessly that no further challenges could be mounted, a Sunni-Baath military complex had been established.

Once power challenging is running as openly and brutally as this, nothing can check it except the application of yet greater brutality: the practice of politics descends in ever more vicious spirals. Each tribal-religious group has judged it either vital or opportune to assert itself: the Kurds rebelling for the sake of independence in the north, the Shia mobilizing in the south, the Sunnis monopolizing power by every means at their disposal.

Mosul, Kirkuk, Sulaimaniya, where there are large Kurdish elements, as well as the holy Shia cities of Najaf and Karbala, have consequently experienced one atrocity after another in a succession of attempted coups and uprisings, massacres, assassinations, and communal bloodletting. Prisons and detention centers—Qasr al-Nihaya, or the Palace of the End, for instance—have acquired the most sinister reputation. Nothing limits outrage. In July 1973 no less a person than the head of the state security, Colonel Nazim Kazzar, attempted a putsch. He kidnapped the minister of defense and the interior minister, and when his challenge began to falter, he drove with these two hostages to the border with Iran. There he shot them point-blank in the car. He and his retinue were soon executed. Afterward it was estimated that in discharging his job Kazzar had been personally responsible for murdering 3000 victims. According to Amnesty International in a report in 1983, torture in Iraqi prisons is "widespread," adding that between 1978 and 1981 alone 520 people had been executed for political reasons.

To the Soviet Union, Iraq has appeared to be a country somehow eluding its grasp. The once-promising Qassem was demoted from pro-Communist to being a "bourgeois-nationalist." The Aref brothers and other Baathists continued the anti-Western and socialist rhetoric, yet were at pains to attack the Iraqi Communist Party, in the end killing its secretary general, Hussein al-Radi, and eliminating its influence once and for all. Consequently Baathist-Communist hostility has been exceptionally bitter, and to this day Soviet propaganda and front organizations maintain a worldwide barrage of pamphlets and demonstrations as reminders of Baathist crimes toward Communists. Nonetheless, Moscow cut its losses by signing a Treaty of Friendship with Iraq in 1972 and has continued its aid and supplies of arms.

Whereas in Syria, then, the Baath had been manipulated for Alawi and anti-Sunni assertion, in Iraq the very same set of slogans had been manipulated for quite the opposite, for Sunni and anti-Shia assertion. In Baghdad as in Damascus the Baath has had a power holder with at his service a so-called national command, an assembly, an armed militia, and loyalist organizations for peasants, workers, students, and women to translate his will into the corresponding obedience of the masses. Any Syrian or Iraqi who wished to be upwardly mobile, according to a historian of the Baath, had "the avenue of the party bureaucracy, with its pyramidal structure,

schools for cadres, and rewards for loyal service." Instead of Arab
unity or any approximation of it, what has actually been set up is
a condition whereby Syria and Iraq have tribal-religious grounds
for further mutual challenging as and when either power holder
sees advantage in it.

In a country with a history and social composition like Iraq's,
any autonomous party was likely to have been sucked and absorbed into the prevailing sociopolitical custom, and without exceptional leadership the Baath could probably never have provided a base for intercommunal or participatory politics. The line
of power holders from Qassem, the Aref brothers, and Ahmad
Hasan al-Bakr to Saddam Hussein have behaved identically in the
struggle to capture and hold the state, differentiated only in the
degree of determination that they applied to the killing of rivals.
For all alike, whether members of the Baath or enemies of it, the
gun alone settled the outcome. Whether Saddam Hussein believes
the hour-long speeches he likes to deliver about Baathist virtues
is irrelevant. In his actions, he illustrates how an organization of
the kind is diverted from possible institutional goals to serve personal and tribal-religious careerism. Were he to act otherwise, he
would forfeit his life to whoever has the will to show himself yet
more extreme.

Saddam Hussein was born in 1937, in a village close to the town
of Takrit, which has a population of 30,000. About a hundred miles
from Baghdad, up the river Tigris, Takrit is at the center of the
area inhabited by Arab Sunnis. The family were peasants belonging to a local clan, the Al Bu Nasir. Saddam Hussein never knew
his father, who died, and he was brought up by a maternal uncle,
Khairallah Talfah, an army officer. Heroic deeds are attributed to
him: how as a boy, he allegedly walked to school in Takrit, armed
with a pistol; how he joined the Baath in 1957 and was imprisoned
on a charge of murdering an official; how he was released, only to
be summoned in 1959 to Baath headquarters for an assignment on
a five-man team to kill Qassem by ambushing his car. His biographer writes:

> Two were to fire at the front seat, and two at the back. Saddam
> Hussein was not supposed to fire, just to provide cover for his four
> comrades as they withdrew. But as the operation got under way, his
> excitement mounted and he drew his machine-gun from the folds of a
> long cloak he had borrowed from his uncle Khairallah Talfah, and fired

at Abdul Karim Qassem's car. He withdrew only after covering his comrades' withdrawal. One of them was hit in the chest by a police officer's bullet, and Saddam was wounded in the left leg.

There followed an epic of adventure, according to this biographer, as the wounded Saddam deceived the police searching for him, disguised himself and escaped to Syria, then to Cairo. Returning to Iraq, he attached himself to Ahmad Hasan al-Bakr, a relation and another army officer, also from Takrit. In another intrigue, he was imprisoned again but escaped. At the moment of the Baathist takeover, he is alleged to have bundled a rival at pistol point on to an aircraft. As vice president after 1968, nothing stood in the way of capturing the state except the president, Ahmad Hasan al-Bakr.

The usual duality developed. According to "informed sources in Baghdad," as the Syrians gleefully declared in 1977, the struggle for power between the supporters of Saddam Hussein and the supporters of al-Bakr "was accompanied by frenzied efforts by each side to liquidate the members of the other side." In June 1979, Saddam's men placed al-Bakr under house arrest, and his supporters moved on to seize the broadcasting station, the Iraqi news agency, and the general staff headquarters. "The takeover operation lasted for ten days," according to a Western source. "The remarkable thing is that it was so carefully camouflaged." President al-Bakr in fact announced that he was retiring on grounds of health, and Saddam Hussein has since tried to present this as a rare instance of peaceful change in power holding.

Al-Bakr's loyalists had perceived what their fate would be, and in July they made a last stand. The Baath Revolutionary Council split openly, prompting this typical indictment from the new power holder:

> For several years, this group has been preparing a malicious, conspiratorial design aimed at striking at the Party and the revolution and the socialist and democratic gains of the masses and linking Iraq with the capitulationist design led by U.S. imperialism in the interest of Zionism and the forces of darkness. Throughout the past phase, these plotters were in contact with a foreign side. The Command believes it is not in the national interest to expose that side now. This group received funds from that side, received orders from it, and has coordinated its conspiratorial, criminal efforts with it. [This group comprises] malicious pustules, the remedy for which is achieved by eradicating and eliminating them for ever.

No "foreign side" was ever identified. Within three weeks, the six leading supporters on the command council of the deposed al-Bakr, with sixteen other high-ranking Baathists, had been put before a tribunal consisting of Saddam Hussein's supporters on the command council and executed. Nobody could doubt the merciless ferocity with which Saddam Hussein intended to proceed as power holder. "You all know," Sadat was to say with the usual feigned surprise, "how Saddam Hussein the bloodthirsty hanged 22 of his friends in the government, strung them up before his own eyes."

No matter who the post-1958 power holder had been, Iraq has participated with absolute continuity in national and regional challenges, for instance laying claim to Kuwait; sending troops into Jordan at the time of the 1970 civil war, and exploiting the Palestinian issue by subvention of whichever PLO faction seemed appropriate; deploying against Israel in 1967, and in 1973 when its armor was cut to pieces on the Golan Heights; cyclically suppressing the Kurds, or "the agent reactionary pocket in the North of the homeland," in the words of President al-Bakr. The Kurdish insurrection was promoted by the Shah of Iran in national power challenges of his own. Wishing to acquire title to as much of the Shatt el-Arab waterway as possible, the Shah saw in the Kurds a bargaining counter or lever against Iraq. In 1975, in far-off Algiers, a deal was duly struck between the Shah and Saddam Hussein, then still vice president, whereby Iranian support for the Kurds was halted in a tradeoff against recognition of Iranian territorial and maritime claims in the Shatt el-Arab.

Thanks to climate and the Tigris and Euphrates rivers, Iraq is capable of self-sufficiency in food, with a potentially large margin for export. Iraq's oil reserves are estimated to be second only to those of Saudi Arabia. Nationalization of oil placed this invaluable asset in the hands of the power holder. As a result of oil income, the gross national product had risen by the 1970s to about $30 billion. There has been what one authority calls "the rapid transformation of Iraqi society" in infrastructure, communications, and investment in industry. Nonetheless, much of the oil income so far has been dissipated in the various regional and national challenges, of which the most costly has been the war against Iran.

The tribal-religious nature of this war comes about because the divide between the Sunnis and Shias, however fluid and undemarcated, lies between Iran and Iraq. Shiism has its historic home in

Iran, but its holy cities of Najaf and Karbala are in southern Iraq. None of the various coups since 1958 have offered the Shia of Iraq communal institutions in which to share on equal terms with the Sunnis or other minorities. On the contrary: each coup has served further to exclude the Shia. Baathist slogans about Arab unity have appeared to the Shia to be a cunning justification for a ruling Sunni order everywhere, in which they could expect only a new type of discrimination threatening their very identity. Baathist slogans about socialism appeared equally suspect as a secular attack on Islam. In the aftermath of the Qassem coup of 1958, some of the Shia ulema formed a secret society for the protection of their confession. Ayatollah Muhammad Baqir al-Sadr, then aged about thirty, was its leader and propagandist.

In 1964, Ayatollah Khomeini arrived in Najaf, exiled from Iran by the Shah, and what impression he made upon the Shia of Iraq is far from clear. But Ayatollah Baqir al-Sadr, who may well have influenced Khomeini, was equally opposed to secularism in any form and was committed to a belief in the redemption of Islam through Shia assertion. Gradually the secret society of the ulema widened into a movement, al-Dawa, or Islamic Call, which is for the Shia what the Muslim Brotherhood has been for the Sunnis. Soon, the Baath leadership arrested and executed five Shia ulema in order to stifle this unexpected and unwelcome opposition; and also coopted four pliant Shia on to the command council. The dramatic collapse and downfall of the Shah put paid to this stick-and-carrot approach. A Shia apotheosis appeared to be imminent. In the spring of 1979, Saddam Hussein arrested Ayatollah Muhammad Baqir al-Sadr and a year later executed him, with his sister, for the sake of the exemplary warning. With his death, the Iraqi Shia movements "declined in intellectual significance," as one authority puts it. Thirty-five thousand Shia of alleged Iranian origins were uprooted and driven from the country into Iran. Membership of Islamic Call became an offense carrying a mandatory death sentence on the grounds that this movement "has links with foreign circles and has betrayed the homeland and the Arab nation's objectives and interests. This has been proved by the interrogation of party elements already under arrest."

Islamic Call answered this vituperation in a broadcast from Teheran, which is irrefutably as true about its enemies as it was about itself:

Where is the freedom advocated by the ruling gang's party [i.e. the Baath] in Baghdad? Where is the socialism put forward by this party? Where are the unity and individual rights? The experience of 11 years has proven that this party was founded on pure deception and trickery. This party has used you and has tried to deafen your ears to keep you from hearing the call for help from the oppressed.

In the course of the war between Iraq and Iran, about a million men are estimated to have been casualties, millions of people lost their homes, Basra and Abadan were among the cities annihilated, missile exchanges were directed at civilian populations, and international shipping in the Gulf was wantonly attacked, and seamen of several nationalities were killed. Poison gas was used by the Iraqis, killing an estimated 10,000 Iranian troops, and disabling many more. Some 30,000 Iraqis were said to have deserted and to be in hiding, and those of them who were captured were allegedly shot out of hand. The Iraqi student body of 250,000 was conscripted. Whether out of mortal dread of Saddam Hussein or suspicion of what a victorious Ayatollah Khomeini might demand of them, the Shias of Iraq did not revolt. In a horrible predicament, they had nowhere to turn but were obliged to serve in Iraqi uniform as cannon fodder against others of their confession—cannon fodder in Iranian uniform. Epithets such as "the mummy Khomeini" poured from Saddam Hussein, who was blackened by the Ayatollah Khomeini as "idolator," "heretic," and "the Iraqi Zionist." An Iraqi minister was summarily shot in 1982 for suggesting that Saddam Hussein might temporarily step aside to appease Khomeini.

In the absence of an interest vital to either nation, this war was a duel between power holders, the one claiming that the downfall of the other was the precondition for peace. Neither could negotiate a satisfactory adjudication of the Sunni-Shia relationship, which is the hidden agenda of these mutual challenges as of so many others throughout history in the region. What ensued was reminiscent of the perpetual but aimless fighting between despotic blocs so horrifyingly imagined in George Orwell's *1984*. In the further absence of truthful justification for a bid which had proved so self-destructive, Saddam Hussein had only the final recourse to shame-honor appeal, which loomed larger in his speeches as the war dragged out more and more desperately, as in these examples:

Brothers, great people! Iraq is destined once again to assume its leading Arab role by serving honourably. . . .

Glorious Iraqis . . . You are walking on the road to freedom, dignity and progress. . . . The state in which we are now living, the state of a strong, free and exalted Iraq, over which the banners of justice, prosperity and dignity are fluttering, has become, with God's help and will, a firm state that will continue, despite the conspiracies, difficulties and evil intentions of our enemies.

You, O righteous martyrs, Iraq's dear sons . . . You have embodied the spirit of bravery and chivalry highly valued by your ancestors. Your blood has burned the enemy's remnants and kept your country free from its evil and black ambitions.

Exactly as in Syria, the impossibility of telling the truth obliges those in office to resort to coded speeches, which consist of pure gibberish. Here is the Iraqi deputy prime minister speaking in May 1980 at a moment when he must have known that Saddam Hussein was about to attack Iran, but could not conceivably have explained the real reasons for this imminent challenge:

The area has never before seen a process combining such complexity, blindness, spuriousness and hypocrisy. Who is behind this wide and complicated process which has never before been paralleled? Who is responsible for making Islam reject and clash with revolutionary and socialist Arab nationalism? . . . Why then should anyone wish to distort and destroy Arab nationalism in this way, and in whose interest? How should we understand the alliance, sometimes open and sometimes covert, between movements using religion as a cover and certain parties and communist movements, when they have such obvious contrasts? What united them as one to deal a blow to Arab nationalism, and to entertain misgivings about the methods used for gaining national independence? Why are they rushing along so blindly and with such venom to destroy the national league, which raised the nation, despite its differences, and unified the struggle against Zionism and imperialism?

To strengthen the internal position of the power holder, money-favoring as usual obtains. Said Aburish, the Palestinian businessman and intermediary, has noted that Saddam Hussein believes that people with full bellies do not revolt, and that corrupt generals do not overthrow governments. Consequently, Saddam Hussein "very often lets it be known to companies supplying his army with material that he wishes the generals connected with various projects to receive a fee or commission. It is never a direct request; the President has his ways of transmitting the message. At one time he entrusted the job to his Palestinian intellectual sidekick." Rival money-favoring is of course suppressed, as shown in this typical report:

Seven government employees and businessmen have been hanged for accepting bribes from companies seeking contracts in Iraq, it was reported in Baghdad yesterday.

Those whom Saddam Hussein can rely on loyally to do his bidding are first and foremost family and clan relations, then men from his hometown of Takrit, thus creating a kinship group that is also a tribal-religious elite. Adnan Khairallah Talfah, minister of defense since 1978, is his maternal cousin and also brother-in-law. His half-brother Barzan had been chief of intelligence, responsible for the secret police, until in some obscure conspiracy in 1983 he was dismissed, and is presumed dead. Saadoun Shakir, his right-hand man and minister of the interior since 1980, is another cousin. The director of public security, Ali Hasan al-Majid, and the commander of the Republican Guard, Hamad al-Majid, are paternal cousins. From his clan, the Al Bu Nasir, he has recruited the commander of the Air Force, and the commanders of the 3rd and 4th Army Corps. All these men have been intimately involved in planning and executing the careerist crimes that have brought Saddam Hussein to command the state. Should he fall, they fall too.

AYATOLLAH KHOMEINI

Persia is a nation as ancient as any in the world, with a history and identity of its own, although since its conquest by the Arabs in the seventh century it has shared in the Arab and Muslim sociopolitical system. Persian particularity has always been preserved, most notably by the adoption in the sixteenth century of Shia Islam, much of whose doctrine and practice is defensively aimed against Sunnis, whether Turkish or Arab. Divinity is held to have passed from Muhammad to leaders, or imams, in a line of descendants from Ali, his son-in-law and cousin. When the last of these imams died without posterity, a doctrine was adopted in the tenth century that the imam had gone into hiding but will reappear at the end of time, a belief that seems to derive from Judeo-Christian Messianism. Awaiting his coming, the Shias submit to the rule of the incumbent power holder, keeping their beliefs to themselves and acquiring what one authority has called "the aspect of a secret society." Nine out of ten Muslims are Sunnis, and Shia have always consolidated and defended their minority status by means of vivid reminders of their dispossession and subjection, for instance staging highly emotional and even lachrymose passion plays and such ostentatious demonstrations of religious fervor as self-flagellation in public. A sense of righting historic injustice converts Shia beliefs into an assertive cause.

A Sunni Afghan power holder displaced the Shia Safavids in the eighteenth century. In conditions of unbridled power challenging, the native Qajar dynasty emerged in 1794 as power holders, or shahs. Kurds, Azerbaijani Turks, Lurs, Qashqais, Bakhtiars, Baluchis, Turcomans, and others were tribal peoples in what had essentially been an empire. Into the present day, control and centralization have proved the constant preoccupation of the power holder. To the difficulties of mounting military expeditions in hostile terrain and of finding resources for money-favoring was added the encroachment of the West. Defeats at the hands of Russia galvanized a reaction. The earliest accounts of the West and its characteristics were to be found in books published in 1798 and 1804 by Persians who had traveled to see things for themselves. In 1815, a first group of five students was sent to England, and a second group in 1840, with instructions from the Shah that "they shall study something of use to me, themselves, and their country." Among these students was the remarkable Mirza Mohammad Saleh, the first Persian to attend Oxford University, and who returned to Tabriz to set up a press and the first newspaper in the country. Others studied artillery, engineering, medicine, and chemistry.

A ship of 500 tons was purchased around 1820, the first of its kind in Persia. During the long reign of Nasir al-Din Shah (1848–1896), the country experienced transformations comparable to those of Ottoman Turkey and its Arab provinces, but much less far-reaching. Mirza Taqi Khan, Shah Nasir al-Din's first Grand Vizir, attempted administrative and legal reforms. A European-style technical college, the Dar al-Funun, was started in Teheran in 1853, two years after a similar college in Istanbul. Nonetheless in 1862 Vambéry in Teheran was complaining of "the utter want of cleanliness." Soap was an article of luxury, and to him henna-painting on the visible parts of the body "renders every Persian grandee loathsome." By 1865, British concession holders had laid telegraph lines and were opening railways and mines in the 1870s and a bank in 1889. The British also opened the Karun river to navigation. To bolster his authority, the Shah recruited Russian officers to raise and train a Cossack Brigade. Soon after the turn of the century, the Anglo-Persian oil company launched the industry which above all else was to determine the future. Money-favoring remained the prime governmental instrument, and the search for the necessary funding led the Shah in 1891 to mortgage the future tobacco crop to British concession holders. The Shia ulema used the modern telegraph lines to mobilize opposition and to appeal to the Shah to cancel this measure, in an early illustration that technology is more likely to advance power challenging than to supersede it.

Throughout the nineteenth century, the Shia ulema had been gathering strength. The ulema had pressured successive Shahs to fight Russia and to resist Britain, but then had escaped blame for failures on these scores. Consolidating trust property and religious tax-income into their hands, some ulema were not averse to such practices as hoarding grain during famines and selling it an inflated prices to the starving population. In 1844, in Shiraz, a man by the name of Ali Muhammad had set himself up under the title of the Bab, claiming to be the incarnation of the Hidden Imam, with a new version of the Holy Law. The Bab's teaching was destructive of custom, as when in 1848 a Babi woman publicly tore off her veil. The ulema responded immediately and characteristically to this power challenge against them. Somewhat against his will, the Grand Vizir Mirza Taqi Khan persecuted the movement, and in 1850 he ordered that the Bab be executed and his followers dispersed. In the usual reprisal, he was himself assassinated in 1851. Under the leadership of one of the Bab's successors, Baha-ullah (1817–1892), most surviving Babis formed the sect known today as Bahais, and in effect Shia schismatics. In a move whose long-term consequences could not have been foreseen, the Bahais under Baha-ullah moved their headquarters to Haifa, then an Ottoman town, now in Israel. Spurred on equally by the successes and the failures of their righteous indignation, the ulema strengthened their standing and influence. Unlike their counterparts in Sunni Islam, Shia divines enjoyed a hierarchy of ayatollahs and mullahs. In the later half of the nineteenth century, there developed a practice whereby the foremost ayatollah of the day, distinguished by his learning and piety, became a source of emulation for others. Such a supreme authority, evolving into a figurehead as well as an institution, further served to differentiate Shia Islam from Sunni.

Power challenging within Persia broke into the open with the constitutional crisis of 1906, which bore resemblances to contemporary events in Russia and in Turkey. Nasir al-Din Shah's successor was Mozaffar al-Din, who combined debauchery with lack of political resolution. Secret societies spawned. Popular preachers, or mullahs, seized the moment, and the Shah compromised with an agreement to call a national assembly, dying almost on the day that he ratified it. The historian Hamid Enayat considers that constitutionalism brought Shias "face to face with . . . the modern age," emulating the Sunnis elsewhere. Ulema, in the persons of senior ayatollahs and mullahs, were well represented in the assembly, some supporting the constitution, others against it. Preeminent among the latter was Sheikh Fazlullah, who argued that a constitution could have no place in an Islamic society. Like Sultan Abdul Hamid in Istanbul, Mozaffar al-Din's successor as Shah bided his time, and in 1908 he surrounded the assembly with his Cossack Brigade and artillery, suppressing the constitutional experiment and punishing its initiators. Among those executed by the Constitutional Party was Sheikh Fazlullah, who shortly before his death stated the evident truth that power-challenging motives accounted for the division between him and the constitutional ayatollahs. "It was merely that they wished to excel me, and I them, and there was no question of 'reactionary' or 'constitutional' principles."

Parallels with Turkey were further invited by the military coup of 1921, which put an end to the Qajar dynasty. Reza Khan, leader of the coup, had been born in the 1870s, rising from a humble background to command the Cossack Brigade, the country's most effective institution. The Persia over which Reza Khan declared himself Shah, taking the ancient name of Pahlavi, consisted of peasants in villages belonging to quasi-autonomous landlords, with perhaps a fifth of the population still tribal and nomadic, under tribal chiefs. Paved roads did not yet exist; there was little electrification. Power-challenge conditions applied from the top of the society to the bottom. The English writer Christopher Sykes, on his travels in the 1930s, observed that Reza Shah's Persia was "an utterly atrocious tyranny." To Sykes, the whole country appeared "scattered with wrecks," and from a distance it was not easy to tell whether a particular ruin was Macedonian, medieval or twentieth century.

Like Ataturk, Reza Shah aspired to modernize on Western lines, welding together a nation-state, the new Iran. To that end, he fashioned a national army and campaigned with success against the independence of the tribes. He introduced civil and penal codes which supplanted Islamic law, and in time-honored manner he ordered the assassination of those not otherwise deterred from challenging (notably intellectuals). The attack on the ulema was direct and brutal but incomplete. Reza Shah's personal disposition was displayed in a celebrated incident in the holy city of Qom, when he kicked a mullah who had been complaining that he had caught a glimpse of the face of the Shah's wife (or his mother, in some accounts). The ulema in Iran did not submit to drastic secular reform so supinely as the ulema in Turkey. Reza Shah was forced by the British and the Soviets to abdicate in 1941 for his pro-Hitler stance. Soon afterward a mullah summed up the conventional attitude when he was recorded as commenting, "We were afraid that Farangis [Europeans] would come and desecrate our graves, but our own government turned out to be worse than the heathen Farangi. What is left of our faith now?"

Shame-honor ranking motivated Reza Shah as insistently as it did Ataturk. Emulation of Westerners was less a tribute to their social organization or values than a means of warding them off, of turning their own methods against them for the sake of equal standing, perhaps superiority in the end. At once defensive and offensive, the outlook had its concealed xenophobia.

Already in 1840 Sir Henry Layard was describing the encounter with Persian shame-honor responses.

A Persian will invariably tell a lie, even in a matter which is of no importance whatever to him. He is, moreover, insolent and vain to a degree. Notwithstanding that many Persians of rank have been to England and other parts of Europe, and the Government has adopted many institutions of civilised nations, still its mode of procedure is as barbarous as it was one hundred years ago. In their modes of punishment they exhibit extreme ingenuity.

The presence of the British and Russians as outside arbiters and sponsors could only maximize shame-honor responses. By the end of the century, a couple of British gunboats, operating out of Fao, was enough to keep the peace in the entire Gulf. Mrs. Hume-Griffith, wife of a missionary, noted that Isfahan, a center of Shia worship, had at least fifty Europeans by 1903. Persians tended either to be repelled by the presence of such a community or attracted to the point of imitating foreign ways, and on this topic Mrs. Hume-Griffith commented, "It seems such a pity that Persians of high class are gradually falling into European ways, for they do not suit these Frenchmen of the East half so well as their own manners and customs." The emergence of westernized Persians was rapid. Isa Sadiq was one such. Born in 1895, he received a religious education from the mullahs, entered the Dar al-Funun, and two years later was awarded a scholarship to study in France. After a time at the University of Paris, and then at Cambridge, in England, he went to New York where he wrote his doctorate. Returning to Iran in 1931, he published a book *One Year in America,* from which his compatriots could draw the benefits of his experiences. For him, Western life offered the widest choices to the greatest number of people, and education was the key to it. Minister of education under the Shah, he died in 1978.

Succeeding his father, Mohammad Reza Shah was largely westernized after an education in Switzerland, but he too retained shame-honor ranking as prime motor for his actions. His memoirs are replete with sentiments such as "It was better for us to die in honour and dignity than to lose our birthright" when that birthright was not actually about to be lost. Perhaps it was a sign of inner doubt and weakness that Mohammad Reza Shah was so prone to outbursts of apparently unlimited vainglory, ascribing to himself the traditional title of "King of Kings" and even "Light of the Aryans," as though he were the heir of Cyrus and Darius rather than of a self-made soldier in the Cossack Brigade.

Nationalization of the oil industry in 1951 placed an immense reward in the hands of the power holder. Mohammed Mossadegh, prime minister at the time and by birth a member of the landowning elite, saw his chance to exploit the temptations and passions released by the prospects of this money and power. In a manner reminiscent of Arabi Pasha or Midhat Pasha, who had also challenged royal power holders in the name of constitutionalism, Mossadegh initiated policies which could lead only to the Shah's replacement by himself. Briefly the Shah was in exile, only to return with American and British backing. He then arrested Mossadegh. According to his biographer, Mossadegh had "revitalised the sense of dignity, so essentially a part of the Iranian character." Yet no popular uprising occurred, either in favor of Mossadegh, now banished to his house for the rest of his life, or in favor of the Shah. Persians accepted the Shah's victory for what it was, the resolution of another rival duality for supremacy in a despotism to which they were long and wretchedly accustomed.

The heyday of the Shah's absolute power holding was the decade from 1953 to 1963, otherwise known as the years of his "white revolution." Like his father before him, the Shah determined to force the country into a recognizable Western mold, "force-marched into industrialization" as he liked to put it. Governing by means of ministers whom he alone could appoint and dismiss, the Shah decreed what was to be done. Correction of error would have involved admission of shame, and the country therefore had to persist in the gradual evolution of his autocratic decisions, no matter what the consequences. It was neither reasonable nor likely that the Shah knew best about everything. An army was assembled and equipped out of all proportion to defense requirements, naturally provoking defensive power-challenge reactions in the neighboring Arab states. A large and efficient secret service, known as Savak, protected the power holder and his family and entourage.

In customary style, the Shah extracted for himself a fortune estimated in billions of dollars, much of which he salted abroad, often by means of his private Pahlavi Foundation. Large numbers of well-placed Iranians similarly managed to profit from the money-favoring incited by national oil revenues and the resulting government contracts spreading through the economy. In the custom of the country, none of this was particularly shocking. "There is no such thing as public opinion in Iran," wrote an English commentator in 1956, "there is only public emotion." Public emotion took it for granted that everyone in a position to do so would exploit every careerist means for self-advancement. A single party, the so-called Rastakhiz (ironically meaning Resurrection, as Baath does in Arabic), was supposed to provide an air of legitimacy to the Shah's absolutist ends; but its visible members more often than not were street thugs, paid from secret funds to intimidate other people, and so it was merely another instrument of control. The Shah also maintained the closest hold on the media. The first generation of those exposed to Western education found this a particularly intolerable restriction, and tens of thousands of students preferred to live in Europe and the United States. No institution existed to articulate or mobilize their opposition, and so they loosely affiliated themselves to one or another disgruntled and exiled power challenger. Yet in books and pamphlets written in a Western idiom, these Iranians abroad presented themselves as though they were a democratic opposition in a country suddenly and wickedly denied its historic democratic heritage by a most unexpected and unimaginable despot. These pretensions and misrepresentations were destined to be horribly and cruelly exposed.

The aspiration to become an industrial rival to the West was not founded on the social condition or resources of Iran, and it led the Shah to honor-provoked fatuities such as claiming to be high on the International Monetary Fund's list of the world's richest countries, as though oil wealth were no lucky accident of geology. "I wanted a perfectly modernized Iran, a progressive nation," he wrote in his memoirs, or again, "Iran was earning her place alongside the most advanced states." Implicit in such notions is the admission of backwardness. Iran was now to be a nation like any other, its standing justified in nationalist terms. To nationalist ends, as he defined them, he centralized power in his own hands with far-reaching implications which either he failed to calculate or which he dismissed as backward. This was his undoing. Centralization spelled loss of independence for tribal-religious minorities and for the Shia ulema. In several exemplary measures, the Shah had early persecuted Bahais solely because they were defenseless, and he went on to deal harshly with any assertion of identity other than the highly notional one of Iranian nationalism. The army and Savak, he was sure, would crush these identities.

The evident defense for both the minorities and the ulema was to challenge the Shah on the issue of his undoubted Western sponsors. Sunni Kurds and Azerbaijani Turks and others naturally opted for the competing Soviet sponsorship. Joining the main Soviet instrument in Iran, the Tudeh or Communist Party, they were not convinced converts to Marxist ideology but simple opponents of the Shah. What the Shah might call nationalism to them implied perpetual submission to the Shia Iranians. As for the ulema, they refuted with unfeigned anger any suggestion that they were backward. In their eyes, the Shah was a Muslim failing in his religious duty, an apostate who undermined holy law. In the oil-induced and greedy money-favoring, the ulema had lost ground, and the Shah had taken every opportunity to attack their authority and their sources of income. In defense, they built the Shah's willingness to be an ally of the West into an accusation that he intended utterly to subvert Islam.

Those who sought to challenge the Shah on grounds of religion or leftist convictions drifted into a loose coalition, which was to be further supported, ardently and vociferously, by the numerous Iranians living in the West. According to the Shah's own figures, forty-eight Iranian universities came to have an enrollment of 185,000 students, with another 100,000 in foreign universities, half of those in the United States. This disparate coalition lacked only a leader to embody its discontent. Then in 1961, the chief representative or authority of the Shia ulema, Ayatollah Burujurdi, died. He had been a quietist and a scholar. Here was the opening for a successor, and Ayatollah Khomeini at once moved with passion and persistence to finalize the power challenge against the Shah.

Ayatollah Khomeini hardly seemed a likely person to inflame emotions, to mobilize a mass following, and to become a source either of amazement or dismay the whole world over, prompting wide fantasies about the role of Iran, the Shia confession, indeed of "Islamic revival." Dressed in black robes, with the turban and beard of his rank and beliefs, he had a stately manner, a commanding and charismatic presence. He spoke eloquently and could be most forbidding. He had been born in the village of Khomein, south of Teheran, in 1902, or in some accounts as early as 1899. His grandfather and his father had been mullahs. When Khomeini was a few months old, his father was killed in an obscure dispute, and the boy had been brought up by an uncle. His education was religious, leading to a position as a teacher of jurisprudence and philosophy at Qom. One authority, Shaul Bakhash, has noted how Khomeini's speeches and declarations are sprinkled with "references to the humiliation suffered by the ulema and the willful denigration to which Islam was subjected under Reza Shah." Exactly like the Pahlavi Shahs whom he so resented, Khomeini had an all-embracing shame-honor reaction to the West. Rhetorically he asked, "Is there any people in the world which has tasted the bitterness of humiliation and enslavement like the people of Iran?" Heir to the teachings of Afghani, he also believed that Westerners deliberately planned to oust Islam, though why they should conceive so wanton an idea he too failed to explain. Confronted by the West, he wrote, "people begin to grow smaller and to despise themselves in the face of the material progress of the enemies. When some states advance industrially and scientifically, some of us grow smaller and begin to think that our failure to do the same is due to our religion." Typically he romanticized the founding years of Islam while also holding pessimistically to the belief that Muslims must be punished more and more severely for ever-increasing godlessness. Most exceptionally in the Muslim world, in a book published in 1941, he objected to the "Hitlerite mentality" of justifying the means by the end, as "one of the most poisonous and heinous products of the human mind." Nonetheless, he was a follower (or admirer) of Ayatollah Kashani, whose support for the Nazi cause was such that the British interned him in 1943. But his conception of non-Muslims was entirely traditional and tribal-religious: Christians had the simple objective of destroying Islam, Jews were spies and traitors, and schismatics such as Bahais deserved persecution. Moojan Momen, a historian of the Shia faith, illustrates its introspectiveness when he gives short biographies of fifty-five of the most eminent Shia ulema and some of their descendants over the last eight centuries. Only a single one wrote a commentary touching on anything external to the confession, and that was a refutation of a book by a Christian clergyman.

At the opening of Ayatollah Khomeini's challenge, the American presence in Iran was growing—41,000 Americans were already in the country, largely military personnel training Iranians and servicing aircraft and weaponry. Purchases of American arms were worth $14 billion just in the years from 1972 to 1978 and by then, in the words of a senior American official, "the pipeline was jammed with programs that would extend over decades to come." In 1964 a vote was passed in the Shah-controlled assembly to grant these Americans immunity from prosecution in Iranian courts. "This filthy vote," as the Ayatollah was quick to condemn it, played into his hands.

It has acknowledged that Iran is a colony; it has given America a document attesting that the nation of Muslims is barbarous, it has struck out all our Islamic and national glories with a black line.

By this shameful vote, if an American adviser or the servant of an American adviser should take any liberty with one of the greatest specialists in Shia law . . . the police would have no right to arrest the perpetrator and the courts of Iran have no right to investigate. If the Shah should run over an American dog, he would be called to account but if an American cook should run over the Shah, no one has any claims against him. ... It is America that considers the Koran and Islam to be harmful to itself and wishes to remove them from its way.

The Shah's response was to exile Khomeini, in classic style. A more determined or far-sighted power holder might have ordered the murder of such a challenger, as Saddam Hussein was to do with Ayatollah Muhammad Baqir al-Sadr in 1980. First in Turkey, later settling in Najaf in Iraq and finally in France where he could be in close touch with Western journalists, most of whom were devoid of the experience or knowledge required to pass informed judgments on someone so unusual as a Shia power challenger temporarily in exile, Khomeini skillfully cemented his coalition, gathering the support of all those who opposed the Shah on any grounds, and then forcing the Shah into blunders out of which political capital could be made. Conspiring and intriguing, Khomeini and his loyal ulema were the equivalent of Free Officers planning to transform themselves into a revolutionary command council.

For the Shah, the worst of the dilemma was that he appeared to be unleashing his dreaded Savak not against a ruthless challenger bent single-mindedly on the power holder's downfall and death, but against a dignified and elderly divine, and ranks of the Shia faithful. The more the Shah resorted to secret police repression, the greater the outcry, especially in the West, where he could increasingly be depicted by westernized Iranians as some sort of unique blood-crazed monster. Leniency on his part was therefore mistaken for weakness, and repression served to maximize resistance. As a young Iranian running a bookshop in Teheran remarked to the Englishman Trevor Mostyn as late as 1978, "Either he must abdicate or be prepared to kill up to two million demonstrators." This was an exaggeration; but failure to undertake horrifying exemplary measures of the kind was both a credit to the Shah as a human being and suicidal in effect. At the time, he found himself handicapped by pressure from President Carter to observe human rights, which in the context was an example of insolent and patronizing Eurocentricity without real application. Suffering from the cancer that was soon to kill him, the Shah lost hope. His will to rule ebbed rapidly.

In February 1979, the challenging coalition was so evidently superior in numbers and morale that the Shah abandoned the country, this time forever, and Khomeini duly replaced him as the triumphant power holder. As he had promised, at once he rearranged the state to suit himself, promulgating what he called an Islamic constitution with himself as its head and absolute arbiter. For self-serving purposes of mobilizing the masses on his behalf, he formed a single party, the Islamic Republican Party, and for his own defense as power holder he created the so-called Revolutionary Guards—here was the Rastakhiz and Savak in another guise, and in the case of the secret police even a recruitment of much of the same personnel, simply taking over their premises and their practices unchanged. Careerist sons, brothers, and other relations of Khomeini have obtained well-rewarded posts, which they do not hesitate to abuse, as once the Shah's relations had abused their privileges. A favorite member of Khomeini's family was arrested by West German police for possession of a large quantity of opium (in Iran drugs are illegal and drug traffickers are executed).

In his book *Islam and Revolution,* Khomeini published a prospectus of the state he envisaged. One essential purpose was to justify his own absolutism. "We do not see a single group, nation, or religious community that has ever been able to exist without an individual entrusted with the maintenance of its laws and institutions." "Constitutional" as meaning "based on the approval of laws in accordance with the opinion of the majority" was dismissed outright on the grounds that no one except God has the right to legislate. To him, God's legislation is a matter of revelation, and the power holder's obligation is to put it into effect. "The fact that men in our age live in fear of their rulers is because existing governments are not based on law; they are a form of banditry." Khomeini makes it starkly plain that he believes what he is saying. A theme often repeated in his speeches is that people must participate in the processes of the state, but of course on terms which in actuality transform participation into a matter of obedience willingly accepted. Grim and authoritarian as the Ayatollah's sense of justice and equality may be, it is nonetheless apparent.

Whatever the sincerity and even grandeur of this religious concept of the state, power-challenge practices prevented Khomeini from developing it. Destruction by means of the gallows and firing squad of the Shah's apparatus of defense and control was a priority. General Nasiri, former chief of Savak, was shown on television so badly beaten that he could hardly speak, and then he was led off to be shot. Amir Abbas Hoveyda, prime minister for thirteen years, was shot in prison. Between May and September 1979, 575 people were officially executed. Khomeini saw no obstacle to authorizing the shooting of the only woman to have served in an Iranian cabinet. Somewhere between half a million and one million Iranians fled into exile, and with them the westernized elements of the society largely vanished. Their assets and their jobs became available for money-favoring, in a process of distributing rewards that was widened by the nationalization of foreign banks and companies.

No sooner was this grisly takeover complete than the disparate elements in Khomeini's former coalition began demanding more extensive rewards for their support. There is no doubt that the Soviet-sponsored Tudeh Party and other "progressive" groupings believed that under cover of Shia clericalism they would be able to emerge the ultimate victors. In the usual Soviet jargon of opportunism, the Khomeini regime was "objectively progressive," in other words capable of being exploited. Those westernized intellectuals who had boosted Khomeini on the grounds that any successor must be an improvement on the Shah also began to discourse on the introduction of their version of democracy. One such was the writer Reza Baraheni, who in an intemperate diatribe had accused the Shah of hindering the emergence of "young, dynamic cultural forces of a modern type." What these young dynamic cultural forces might actually be every westernized intellectual could now see for himself, and the prudent among them rapidly returned to safety in the United States and Europe, from where they had arrived in such fond and foolish expectation. Finally, conspiratorial and terrorist groups among the Kurds and Azerbaijani Turks began to arm themselves and prepare for independence.

Uninhibited by a Western education, unfamiliar with Western concepts of human rights, Ayatollah Khomeini quite correctly perceived himself challenged, as once he had been the challenger; and he was determined not to be brought down as the Shah had been but to respond in a manner so exemplary that there could be no mistaking his will. Capturing the state, he had no intention of then allowing it to disintegrate. Whatever terror was employed by his opponents would be returned a hundredfold. Military expeditions nipped in the bud all Kurdish, Turcoman, and Azerbaijani Turk moves for autonomy, and suspected leaders or insurgents among these people were hanged. Teheran radio reported one incident among the Kurds in this language:

> We have witnessed in Urumiyeh a shameful plot by America and the Soviet Union, those international bloodsuckers, a plot engineered by a number of counter-intelligence hirelings which was aimed at undermining the revolutionary morale of the Islamic Army and at sowing discord between the army and the nation.

All that had actually happened, as the broadcast later revealed, was that a Colonel Hushangi and a Warrant Officer Eskandari, both Kurds in Kurdish Urumiyeh, had torn up portraits of Khomeini; and for this they were peremptorily shot. Probably the two men had intended to make a mere gesture of protest, but the occasion was too propitious for Khomeini to miss. The rigmarole about "a shameful plot" serves to emphasize that tearing up photographs is an act to be met with the same degree of repression as a genuine threat to national security.

The process whereby Khomeini had his position first challenged and then confirmed was very close indeed to civil war, as described by the historian Walter Laqueur:

> In 1981 Ayatollah Khomeini's former allies from the left, the mujahedeen [fighters] and some other groups, turned against the new rulers of Iran. They were many and experienced; within three months they succeeded in killing the prime minister, many chiefs of police, half the government and the executive committee of the ruling party, not to mention dozens of members of parliament. Perhaps never before had a terrorist onslaught been so massive and so successful. Yet within another three months, the terrorists either were dead or had escaped abroad. The government acted with great brutality; it killed without discrimination; it extracted information by means of torture; it refused as a matter of principle to extend medical help to injured terrorists.

In his own mind, Ayatollah Khomeini no doubt believed in the natural right of the Shia confession to supremacy. A foregone conclusion from 1979, Shia supremacy was hastened by the opportunistic attack upon Iran by Saddam Hussein in September 1980. Here was confirmation to the Shias that they were on their own, obliged to be at the receiving end of another Sunni challenge, the latest of many in the course of history. Nothing else was to be anticipated. Shia Iranians gathered in a strong defensive reaction. Public emotion was sincere on this score. From the power holder's point of view, any power-challenge scope among tribal or religious minorities had first to be put out of the question, and numerous Christians and Jews and Zoroastrians were hounded to death. The unfortunate Bahais have suffered more than most. Their shrine in Haifa earns them the accusation of being "Zionist," and according to some accounts several thousand out of a community of 400,000 have been killed and imprisoned. Toward the end of 1983, it became clear that internal groups with a potential for challenging Shia supremacy on ethnic or secular or tribal grounds had been smashed, and their leaders were all dead or in exile, their peoples truly cowed. Khomeini could then attend fully to the Sunnis across the frontier.

The price for Shia assertion has been devastating. Nobody can be sure how many political executions and political prisoners there have been. Witnesses to campaigns against the non-Shia peoples are few and unreliable. Dispassionate observers are excluded from most of the country, so that what takes place on the spot goes unrecorded. A United Nations report in 1986 estimated that "At least 7,000 people were executed in Iran between 1979 and 1985, and torture in the country continues to be widespread." Soviet-backed or Tudeh challengers have gone underground and have an interest in atrocity-mongering, but their higher estimates of 15,000 executions and 40,000 political prisoners may nonetheless be true. Prisons like Evin, in Teheran, have a terrifying reputation, and according to a witness of large-scale murdering there in 1983, "Every night you can hear the sound of gunfire." Enormous crowds are mobilized in public arenas to shout prearranged slogans such as "Death to the unveiled" and "Destruction to America," designed to solidify Shia identity. A machine for cutting off the fingers of thieves has been invented, and its inventor personally commended by the Ayatollah. Scenes of revolting brutality are day-by-day matters, as in this newspaper report of the public flogging in Teheran of thirty-four Iranian men and women, each of whom received seventy lashes:

An Islamic court had convicted the 34 for listening to taped music, watching videos and gambling at a private party. The owner of the house where the party was held was jailed for three months.

Anti-Western histrionics is one of the principal instruments of Shia assertion. In language that seems to derive straight from

Afghani a century ago, the Ayatollah addressed his people as "Ye who suffer from Westernization, who love things foreign, ye empty-headed humans, ye humans empty of content." Or again:

We lost ourselves; we lost our independence of thought; we are constantly wondering what the West is doing. Even now that we want, God willing, to set up an Islamic republic and part company with the West, so that an all-round independence may be brought about—even now there is a Western-afflicted group that is planning to bring about a republic, not the Islamic kind but a democratic republic. Even if we do not call them traitors we ought to say they are mistaken. . . . It is true that the West has made material progress and has brought the world up to be a fighter and a beast. Western education has taken the humanity out of humans and created instead a murderous beast.

In repeated images, Khomeini promised that Iran would "strike America in the mouth" or "break America's teeth." Shame-honor ranking is in play, as Ayatollah Khomeini and his officials made evident in their declarations. When American warships escorting tankers in the Gulf had occasion to sink three Iranian patrol boats, the Iranian chief justice gave his reply, induced by shame-honor and a virtual guarantee that the incident would escalate: "America should know that a nation which considers martyrdom an honour and submission a shame cannot be dealt with in this way."

Shia triumphalism is all very well for internal purposes but cannot serve to extend power challenging to the Sunni power holders who are Iran's neighbors. While engaged with Sunni Iraq in a rival duality, Khomeini nevertheless had to calculate the extent to which it was profitable to antagonize other Sunni states. Anti-Western rhetoric will also not serve its purpose in Saudi Arabia and other Gulf states which consider themselves American-sponsored. Cleverly, in an understated yet matter-of-fact style, Khomeini sought to extend his appeal and reach by presenting himself as an Islamic universalist. No such person exists, and if he did, he could hardly be a Shia. Khomeini turned a blind eye to this obvious objection, claiming to speak for all Muslims regardless. Thus in an Army Day speech in 1985, he concealed the Sunni-Shia aspect of the war with Iraq by describing his aims as though embarked upon a religious crusade on behalf of Islam against unbelievers:

We want to attend to the afflictions of the nation of Iraq. . . . They are crying loud: "O Muslims, help us," and we must answer their cry. The

nation of Iraq is being crushed under the jackboot of this evil man. We
have to answer to God on this matter.

No Sunni is even momentarily deceived by such a line. In practice,
this pretense of universalism leads to further division as Shia challenges and money-favoring extend into Sunni Arab countries by
such means as the financing and arming of Shia militia like the
Hizbollah in Lebanon, and the fomenting of terrorist attacks by
Shia minorities in Saudi Arabia, Iraq, Bahrain, and Kuwait.

If their assertion is to be taken at face value, the Shia of Iran
appear to have suffered a complete moral and intellectual collapse.
The world's media report crowds of hundreds of thousands, agi-
tatedly shaking their fists, binding their foreheads with bloodstained bandages and chanting a wish to be martyred for the cause
by throwing themselves against whoever the enemy might be,
whether the greater Satans of the United States and the Soviet
Union, or the lesser Satans of Iraq and Saudi Arabia, Israel,
and Britain. Scenes are photographed and televised of self-
inflicted bloodshed and flagellation. Ten-year-old boys have
been dispatched without weapons to die by the thousand in killing grounds on the Iraqi front, and parents are then found to
proclaim their joy in their son's martyrdom. The death of Iranian
pilgrims in Mecca occasioned a mass demonstration in Teheran
in which the portrait of King Fahd of Saudi Arabia was displayed
upside down, with the eyes gouged out, and the Star of David
scrawled round it. The comedy of such conspiratorial absurdity is
inseparable from the tragedy.

Needless to say, the Shia masses are the people they always
were. Unless ordered to the contrary, these people would gladly
welcome any Westerner who happened to visit their village or
town, as was always the case. No doubt some Shia truly rejoiced
in the supremacy of their Ayatollah, were proud of him as a leader,
and have gloried in the present militancy of Shia assertion. To such
people, tribal-religious persecution and massacring seem only customary. But in all likelihood, precedent also warns even those who
are apparently fanaticized that this condition is temporary, that
other challengers arise, that the sponsorship and arbitration of the
superpowers will not remain suspended forever, that the Sunnis
are numerous and not about to become Shia, that Western education does not breed inhuman beasts and they would like it for their
children if it were possible. Those who are suffering the pitiless

oppression of the present wait in the knowledge that the turn of events may soon throw them a lifeline, an opportunity for a comeback. Bezhad, for instance, the twenty-five-year-old student who escorted V. S. Naipaul in Khomeini's Iran, considered himself a Communist, and he believed his turn would come, stating as though it were obvious, "We too have to do a lot of killing."

Meanwhile in each neighborhood or village, some mullah or revolutionary guard with an automatic weapon on his shoulder is calling for a demonstration, for a display, for the maximum and most spectacular use of whatever symbols of worship and martyrdom will fortify the Shia collectivity. Listening, drawing conclusions, each man has no choice but to fall in at the appointed hour, to parade, to repeat the slogans of the cheerleader with the loudhailer, to pose with his fists in the air for the television cameras. When the mullahs and the revolutionary guards come to the home to demand a boy for their purposes, the parents very well know that a refusal exposes the whole family to reprisals. They sacrifice one of their sons for the sake of the others, and only once they are alone do the grieving mothers and fathers dare to break down and weep in their agony. Witness of gruesome public atrocities, each individual is wary enough to keep to himself just what his inner reservations might be and to conceal the skepticism with which he views the discrepancy between what his leaders ask of him and what he is willing to perform for them. Public emotion is not replaced by public opinion. What Ayatollah Khomeini used to call the "corrupt and murderous rule" of the previous power holder became his own corrupt and murderous rule—a switch of legitimizing doctrine from secular nationalism to Shia assertion, and the power-challenge dialectic switched with it. Absolute control on the one hand and obedience on the other remain unchanged. The projects of the Shah's "white revolution" fall to pieces, building sites are abandoned, cranes rust, sands drift over many a roofless factory into many a derelict machine; and yet another layer of ruins takes shape.

13

Image and Identity

An Arabist from the past, the French General Daumas, who at the height of his career was director of Arab affairs in Algeria, finished his book *La Vie arabe*—published in 1869 and as relevant as ever today—with the reflection that the Arabs had their traditional values but otherwise nothing, and it was this nothingness which so permanently separated them from Europeans. Acquisition of knowledge was in question, and the frame of mind that went with it. Daumas wrote, "We are striding ahead, they move neither forward nor backward. Will they ever begin to do so? I doubt it." Foreboding about the lack of Muslim development spread in that generation among educated and informed Europeans. How were Muslims and Europeans to meet on equal terms? The Muslim's self-image, his identity, was at stake. This was what the Westernized Afghani had been so quick to sense, internalizing it: "Every Muslim is sick, and his only remedy is in the Koran." The diagnosis of sickness is a great deal more traumatizing than the remedial prescription of the Koran. Afghani failed to say to what practical purposes and program the holy text might be put, or in what sociopolitical context. To no better effect, his intellectual successors have repeated him.

"Why are we backward?" Sati al-Husri, later a proponent of nationalism, asked in 1911. Shakib Arslan published in 1930 in Cairo a book with the give-away title, *Why Have the Muslims Become Backward While Others Have Advanced?* An Egyptian, Muhammad Omar, published *The Present Condition of the Egyptians and the Secret of Their Backwardness.* "Why Are They Powerful?" was an article in 1952 by Salama Musa. Sayyid Qutb's brother, Muhammad, wrote a book in 1964, *Are We Still Muslims?* Imam Moussa Sadr, the later leader of the Shia in southern Lebanon before he was murdered in Libya, gave a lecture in 1967, "Why Did the Muslims Fall Behind in the March of Scientific and Material Progress?" and his posthumously published essays have the title, *Islam: Our Choice for Changing Our Backward Condition.* Mehdi Bazargan, one of the successive prime ministers in the contemporary Iranian turmoil, published a booklet *The Causes of the Decadence of Muslims.*

Decadence and backwardness are conceded without ado, even with the self-flagellatory eagerness which stimulates an inferiority complex. To think in these terms is to admit that standards of superiority and progress have been set in the West and that it is against these standards that Muslims are measured and found wanting. Historically, Islam gave the Arabs their uniqueness, and it is therefore supposed to have central causal connections, whether positive or negative, to their present condition. Such an attitude offers no clue toward cultivating a frame of mind more favorable to knowledge. Simplifications follow. If Islam has made the Muslims backward, then it is flawed and should be more suitably reformulated and recast, and that indeed was the policy of Ataturk and all the headlong secularists in his wake: Nasser, the Baathists in Syria and Iraq, and Muhammad Reza Shah in Iran.

Now and again, outright agnosticism or atheism is advocated. Just before the 1967 war, an issue of the Syrian army magazine recommended the abolition of outmoded traditions, including Islam, for the sake of military or socialist modernization. In the face of public outcry, the magazine was withdrawn, and three of the editors were put before a court-martial and sentenced to life imprisonment with hard labor. Publishing a book in 1969, *Critique of Religious Thought,* a Syrian Marxist intellectual, Sadiq al-Azm, had concluded that a modern science-based Israel would not fail to defeat the Arabs so long as they remained conditioned by Islam to be backward, continuing to display "retarded mental habits, bedouin and feudal values, backward human relations, and obscurantist, quietistic world views." Born in 1937 into a famous Damascus family which could to some extent offer protection from the consequences of these opinions, Sadiq al-Azm had studied for a doctorate in America and published a study in English of the philosopher Bishop Berkeley. This westernized outlook only increased the scandal. Tried before a Lebanese court, he was acquitted but deemed it prudent, for a while at least, to live outside his native country.

Those who believe that there is too much Islam have been educated in a rationalist Western mold, and they are in a very small minority, capable of provoking rather than influencing. The majority who believe that there is too little Islam tend to be traditionally or perhaps hardly educated, and they include the Sunni Muslim Brothers in Egypt and Syria, Tunisia and Algeria, and their counterparts who belong to Hizbollah and al-Dawa, the Shia version of the Muslim Brothers in both Iran and Iraq, and the many millions who are sympathizers but may not be activists. Their reasoning has been summarized by the historian Albert Hourani: backwardness in science and civilization is admitted, but it derives from loss of the truth of Islam, and then from bad, that is to say impious, rulers. Islamic civilization was created out of nothing but the Koran and this can be repeated:

> It is irrelevant to say that modern civilization rests on technical advance, and that Islamic civilization cannot be revived so long as the Muslims are technically backward; technical skill is potentially universal, and its acquisition depends on certain moral habits and intellectual principles. If Muslims had these, they would easily obtain technical skill; and such habits and principles are in fact contained in Islam.

If this is so, then the discussion of backwardness is only thrown back to another question: why have these habits and principles remained so completely subdued in Islam as to be invisible? How the Koran will provide the remedy and what the Koran's relationship is or ought to be to scientific principles are philosophical and perhaps political issues that deserve close appraisal rather than the rhetoric they actually receive. Khomeini's Iran is one example of the mindless Islamic affirmation that occurs in practice, and Saudi Arabia is another. The fact that present-day Iran and Saudi Arabia share belief in the all-curative powers of the Koran does nothing to heal the historic and murderous Shia-Sunni detestation in which they hold each other. Among the faithful as among the secular, Islam and what to make of it in today's world lies at the heart of an exploding identity crisis.

Outwardly, verbally, the faithful and the secular appear to be utterly opposed in their prescriptions for the future, to the point of killing or being killed for them. On the one side is the Koran as a total panacea, and on the other is "revolution," which is to the present day what "reform" or "Westernization" were in the last century. Yet the contrasting abstractions share the same vision of a past perfection that in some unspecified way was smashed to pieces, as well as of an idealized future which has been stifled just as unaccountably. Whatever reasons are given for this apocalyptic state of mind, secularists and faithful alike perceive themselves living and enduring in darkness; and they are united in their consequent sense of shame about it. Within the same brief time span in Cairo, Nasser was lamenting that Egypt was "the toy of greed, conspiracy and lust," and the secular journalist Mohamed Heikal was crying out, "O Nasser, the giant, O shatterer of imperialism," and the city's most popular Islamic preacher was saying, "If only we had honoured the Book of God nobody would ever have humiliated us, and the banner of Islam would be all over the world." Recovery of honor is the essential goal on which these voices agree, however they may diverge on the appropriate path to it.

Among contemporary opinions about Arab misfortune and its recovery, those expressed by Muslim Brothers and their fellow travelers like Sheikh Kishk most evidently and ennervatingly combine masochism with boastfulness. To them, the Arabs are fighting hard for their very lives against practically unsurmountable odds and have come to this dreadful plight through their own weaknesses and vices as much as through the depredations of foreigners. To one typical Muslim Brother writer, religious indifference and imperialism have left Egypt in psychological chaos, a prey to "deadly desperation, lethal indolence, disgraceful cowardice, despicable obsequiousness, effeminacy, miserliness, and egotism." Here is Hasan al-Banna, the movement's founder, on how the younger generation was lost and the educated thrown into confusion:

> I saw that the social life of the beloved Egyptian nation was oscillating between her dear and precious Islamism which she inherited, defended, lived with and became accustomed to, and made powerful during 13 centuries, and this severe Western invasion which is armed and equipped with all the destructive and degenerative influences of money, wealth, prestige, ostentation, material enjoyment, power, and means of propaganda.

"I am an Arab: who am I?" was the title of an inquiry in 1981 into identity in the monthly *Middle East* which aims at a westernized

Arab readership. Most of those whose opinion was solicited had come to the conclusion that Arab ideals of unity and nationalism were mythical, or unavailing, and they were Arabs mainly because of "vague, though intense, feelings." According to a spokesman for these feelings, "Being an Arab today on a personal or even a national level means being in crisis in perhaps a more acute form than had ever been the case in the last 50 years." This alarmingly negative formulation is characteristic. The products and values of the Western world are now so pervasive that they are juxtaposed to the products and values of the Arab world at virtually every point, in what is evidently a most unequal competition. Must an Arab who discovers, masters, and enjoys Western values abdicate some part of his Arab personality? If so, does that mean Islam? Conversely, what kind of affirmations or resentments will the Arab feel who deliberately turns his back on Western values? Latitude obviously exists for what must be highly tormenting reactions that flicker and switch in a moment between poles of admiration and repulsion, envy and hatred, friendship and enmity, honor and shame.

Cecil Hourani, like his brother Albert, grew up partly in Lebanon, partly in England. Before he went to Oxford University, he heard his father, a successful businessman, suggest to him that he might change his family name, in the event that it marked him as not English and so proved embarrassing:

He had taken the precaution of giving his children two names, the first English, the second Arabic. . . . To the end of his long life, though attached by sentiment, memory, loyalty to the land of his birth, he remained convinced of the superiority of English life and government, business methods and personal values to those of the East, and even claimed that he owed the healthy ruddiness of his cheeks to the English climate.

To attend a wedding with a bowler hat on what he called his "narrow Semitic head" was more than the young Hourani could manage.

Omar Sharif, not actually an Arab but an Egyptian Copt, is someone from the Middle East who uniquely has become a household name in the West by virtue of his talent as an actor. He explained his predicament to an interviewer.

I am a foreigner everywhere. It would be very difficult for me to go back and live in Egypt because I would miss all the things I've become accustomed to in the Western culture. Emotionally I'm totally Egyptian,

but culturally I've become totally occidental and westernised. My problem as a misplaced oriental is that I cannot sufficiently melodramatise my
feelings the way we do in the Middle East.

Jean Amrouche (1906–1962) was a Kabyle from North Africa who
became a successful writer in the French language, in voluntary
exile in Paris and the son of a convert to Christianity. He said of
himself, "I am a cultural hybrid. Cultural hybrids are very interesting monsters, but monsters with no future. I consider myself,
therefore, condemned by history." In Saudi Arabia, Seymour Gray
had a medical and American-educated colleague from Syria by the
name of Nayef Al-Barras, who asked to be called "Al," declaring,
"I am a United States citizen and hate Syria and Commies."

This is a letter written for publication in 1984 by a young Arab
woman living in the south of England.

My father uprooted us from our home in Egypt more than 18 years
ago. He was searching for Utopia and never really found it. . . . Whenever
my father spoke of our home, he would refer to it with contempt. Even
after so many years away from Egypt, I cannot eradicate those fond
memories I have as a child in the Middle East. I am more or less westernised; however, I still get feelings of rejection and feel I am only tolerated
and never really wanted here.

I have tried to mix with other Arabs, but I found they did not really
want to know. Wherever I go, I keep hearing of Arab brotherhood, of our
common language and the pride we take in being Arab. In reality, we fight
each other rather than get together. . . . If we do not change our present
attitudes to one another and become more united, then one day, in the
not too distant future, we shall all end up like the American Indians, being
confined to small reservations in our homeland.

The novelist Neguib Mahfouz has depicted how the Muslim
today has within himself a tangle of residual responses in conflict
with modern realities.

Life carries him along in its current, and he forgets his misgivings for
a time until one Friday he hears the *imam* [preacher] or reads the religion
page in one of the papers, and the old misgivings come back with a certain
fear. He realizes that in this new society he has been afflicted with a split
personality: half of him believes, prays, fasts and makes the pilgrimage.
The other half renders his values void in banks and courts and in the
streets, even in the cinemas and theatres, perhaps even at home among
his family before the television set.

The uncertainty, the fear, is in the form of a two-fold question as profound as it is beyond answering: granted that the Muslim feelings in oneself cannot help being changed by exposure to Westernization, what is lost and what is gained? To indulge in apologetics is perhaps the primary, and certainly the easiest response. Neither creative nor dynamic, apologetics are satisfying, in the words of the orientalist Wilfrid Cantwell Smith who in 1957 examined the phenomenon in his book *Islam in Modern History*, because they serve "to soothe the conscience of those many thousands who chose to live or found themselves living Westernized lives, and yet would have been unhappy at 'abandoning Islam.' " In *Temperament and Character of the Arabs*, the Lebanese Sania Hamady quotes another Arab writer who puts it more polemically: "The glories of the past often suggest themselves as a comfortable compensation for the humiliation of today, a convenient avenue of escape from the travails of the present and the arduous tasks of the future."

The commonest form of apologetics is to represent the past as a myth of triumph and total victory in all spheres, as when Shakib Arslan (admittedly a Druze whose fervor derived from his wish to identify with the Sunni majority) wrote that thanks to the Koran there was a time of conquest in which "a single Muslim could stand up to 10, and sometimes even 100, non-Muslims." So glorious was the past, the historian Ibraham Abu Lughod considered, that the Arabs had inherited an image of Europeans as barbarians, or dull and backward boors. Philip Hitti, whose *History of the Arabs* has been a standard work in the last two generations, strikes in it the note of purely wishful hope that the present will repeat the past:

> The Arabic-speaking peoples have taken their place among the awakened, forward-marching independent nations of the modern world. With their rich heritage and unmatched natural resource of oil, they should be able to make a significant contribution to the material and spiritual progress of mankind.

A teacher of philosophy at the Higher Teachers' College in Damascus, Dr. Muhammad Kamel Ayyad, is only one among many to make standard claims of this order: "Arab culture has played an important part in the creation of modern civilisation." Europeans, he continues, "derived much of their mathematical science, algebra, physics, medicine, and astronomy from Arabic works." At a recent conference of academics in the United States, Aziz Suryal

Atiya declared, "Americans would not have walked on the moon or reached Mars, if it had not been for Arab contributions to the exact sciences." On the face of it, this amounts to an empty and irrelevant wish to claim honor for the achievements of others, but such romanticizing of the Arab past is also harmful because it invites further questions that destroy self-confidence in the present. What happened, then? Why does Dr. Ayyad, for example, have to sink so swiftly from his grandiloquent claims to conclude in lame and defeatist monosyllables, "We are weak now"? If the Arabs had high scientific achievements to their credit, why did they leave the Europeans exclusively to benefit from them? What kind of a scientific tradition could it have been that apparently stopped dead in its tracks? Do such apologetic sentiments have purposes of self-deception in the face of distressing truth? Is it really the dreadful fate of Arabs not to be the men their fathers were?

In Hamburg in 1983, a body of invited Arabs and Europeans met to discuss cultural ambiguities of mutual interest. The opening address was given by Shedli Klibi, a Tunisian and secretary general of the Arab League. He began by drawing attention to the danger of euphemism and fanciful descriptions but straightaway ignored his own good advice, announcing that the Christian and Jewish minorities had always been able to prosper in the Arab world. "All those cultural centres flourished in the Islamic world, where the right to self-expression was always recognized and safeguarded." Not only Eurocentric in vocabulary and thought, this is foolish sentimentality. Either for Arabs or for minorities in Islam, there has never been anything like a right to self-expression, let alone safeguards for it. Throughout the past, technical limitations alone prevented the power holder from controlling expression absolutely, and today there are no such limitations. Arab civilization, Klibi nonetheless continued, "allowed for an amiable dialectical relation between a core of Islamic values and various nuclei formed by different religious groups." That dialectic in reality consisted of most unamiable discrimination, with massacre as its end resolution, by Muslims of Christians and Jews, and also between Sunnis and Shias in struggles to the death for supremacy. From there, it was a short step for Klibi to expatiate upon Arab scientists and mathematicians, and how "Experiments in medicine and astronomy enabled them to invent new techniques which resulted in an accurate knowledge of the human body and the universe."

Classical Islamic civilization and its achievements are not in doubt. But when Klibi, Philip Hitti, Dr. Ayyad, and the general run of apologists depict the past in this false light as calm, stately, rational and humanly almost transcendent, they take present degeneration for granted, so that all explanation of it becomes immensely more fraught, unconvincing and psychologically unbalancing. Today, Klibi states in his turn, "Arab Islamic culture really faces great danger." How so? Where is the contribution of those scientists and mathematicians with their knowledge of the universe? Evasive and out of touch with reality, this entire discourse soon collapses into ritual cursing of any foreigners at hand to be blamed, Turks, Persians, Mongols, the British and French, "Imperialists," and so the Arabs become the passive objects of other peoples' military feats, not active subjects in their own right. Once again, unspoken but "deep in the soul" and shame-inducing, the inference follows from these apologetics that the Arabs have failed to progress because they really must be backward.

Self-induced misery of this kind erects a boastful screen to hide behind. The historic identity on offer from advocates of Arab nationalism is so abstract that it might more readily pass for prayer, as in this passage by Nasir al-Din Nashashibi, of the Palestinian family:

We are Arabs because we maintain ties with our past, are proud of our traditions, and glory in the heritage of our fathers. Our generation guards this heritage so as to pass it on, pure and complete, to our children and grandchildren. We believe in eternity, the eternity of the spirit and the eternity of the Homeland. We are Arabs because we cherish spiritual values; we shall neither renounce them nor exchange them for others, for the foundations of these values are the true, the beautiful and the good. In these values there is something of God; in them are the attributes of God. We are Arabs because we do not cling to a social philosophical outlook which is taken from beyond our horizons, beyond our borders, beyond our great Homeland, for such outlooks would shatter our existence and strike a blow at all that is sacred to us. We are Arabs because we adhere to Arab Nationalism and are built by it. It belongs to us and we belong to it.

No more firmly grounded either in reality or in meaningful language, the Tunisian historian Hichem Djait writes of "the immense fact of the political renaissance now sweeping the Arab world," although in the next breath he speaks of "the Muslim world's incapacity for self-awareness" (which sad defect, he believes, ended around 1950). Muslims, he goes on, "will be able to create a major alternative form of modernity for our time. Muslims believe they have recovered their Islamic identity; the question is, what will become of it?" Djait's answer to that is, "some kind of feeling of solidarity, a rediscovery of values, an examination of self and the world, with a lesson for everyone." How these grandiloquent words might result in a program he does not say.

To take at face value claims of this kind, with their glories, feelings of solidarity, eternities of the spirit and lessons for everyone, is to ridicule them as bombastic, as lying, deliberately twisting up elaborate fictions like "a major alternative form of modernity" in order to obscure the bloodstained but lasting realities of careerist politics. The need to assert honor has claimed priority once more over dispassionate analysis.

The 1983 Euro-Arab dialogue in Hamburg produced numerous specimens of the morbidly self-pitying sense of shame that fuels these apologetics, as in this example from Mohi ed-Din Saber:

> In the West the Arab is depicted as if he were nothing more than a bedouin leading a camel or sitting on a heap of gold. Or he is simply seen as nothing more than a fat barrel of oil. He is perceived as a blackmailer who only wants to squeeze as much money out of the West as possible. Westerners believe his wealth is fortuitous and due totally to nature, having required no effort at all on the part of the Arab himself. On top of all this the Arabs are viewed as an illiterate and fanatical people.

The former leader of the Muslim Brothers, Hasan al-Banna, put forward the exactly contrary view that the one with the destructive money was the Westerner. But if this picture of the Arabs is a mere caricature, as Mohi El-Dine Saber would have readers believe, then it is not worth a moment's lamenting, as Westerners would only be deceiving themselves about the Arabs. As if this lack of confidence in the figure cut internationally by the Arab was not enough, Mohi El-Dine Saber concludes by bolting into typical Islamocentric conspiracy: "One can but deduce that such deformed images and their like have been propagated by Zionist information services." Shame is seen to be excluding rationality. Any constructive purpose that the speech might have had drains away into cursing.

Omar Farrukh, a scholarly historian of Arab science, writes that the Arabs are in no respects better off today than fifty or a hundred years ago. "Compared with other peoples we have made no advance, we have gained no vital ground; rather we are going backward." Arab states, writes A. B. Zahlan, another well-known historian of Arab science, have "an inability to behave coherently and institutionally" and so scrap entire development programs at the first obstacle. Kateb Yacine is a thoughtful Algerian writer who has fallen foul of his government and been sentenced to internal exile. In a recent interview he said, "We are in a train which is rolling but we have little or no idea where it came from or where it is going. A people fortified by its history is a strong people. But we have lost our way in our history." Ghali Shukri, a prominent Egyptian intellectual, finds that "cultural collapse is imminent." The Lebanese Georges Corm speaks of "the general degradation of cultural life in near-eastern society," to reach the verdict that in the field of education there is "the total absence of a coherent cultural world." "Our culture?" says the Syrian poet Nizar Qabbani. "Nothing but bubbles in washtubs and chamberpots." To the Syrian feminist Ghadah al-Samman, the relationship between the sexes among Arabs can be likened to "ideological venereal disease." "Relations between the Arab and his personality," writes the Algerian Abdelwahab Bouhdiba, "and with nature, with other people, with God, are in a state of total crisis." A Jordanian government White Paper of 1962 postulated, "If we Arabs do not leave behind the reasons for our weakness, then our living in the world of dreams will almost certainly reduce us to the lowest level or to the disappearance of the nation."

In a book *Letters from Hypocrisia*, in 1982, Dr. Ibrahim Abduh wrote that flattery of rulers and hypocrisy had destroyed a realistic outlook in the case of Egypt. Sadat's former foreign minister Boutros Boutros-Ghali judged that "One of the saddest episodes in modern history is that one of the richest and most promising regions of the world, with one of the oldest and most authentic civilizations known to man, is becoming the permanent field for local wars and internal strife because of the lack of imagination, the lack of generosity, and the lack of diplomacy shown by its elite." How, one wonders, is this different from the past, and what suggestions are there for acquiring imagination, generosity, and diplomacy? In contrast, Fouad Ajami speaks of Arabs as living in "the foreigner's universe" and as "losers in the world system." In the eyes of the Lebanese writer and academic Halim Barakat, "The Arab world stretches across continents like a huge stranded octopus, drained of its water of life and indignation. Traditional and authoritarian governments have silenced the Arab people." Even the aspiration to define problems, and so to tell the truth, is thwarted, according to Suhayl Idris, editor of the foremost Lebanese intellectual journal:

> This crisis is one of freedom of expression. Can the Arab writer always stand up and challenge it? Doesn't such a challenge often subject him to pressures, constraints on his livelihood, and a variety of kinds of oppression and terror? . . . What is he supposed to say about other people in the dreadful atmosphere of decline in which the Arab nation finds itself today? Shouldn't he condemn the prevailing authority structures and foundations, and impute to them all the causes of this decline? . . . Where can he find the sphere in which to express this challenge if all the modes of information are in the hands of the official organisations and financed by them?

To self-described "progressives," it follows that the past, the whole culture, must be obliterated rather than venerated: the page must be definitively turned. Article 6 of the Syrian Baath Constitution succinctly asserts that the Party is in favor of "the transformation of the present rotten situation, a transformation which is to include all sectors of life—intellectual, economic, social and political." In a scholarly paper with the title "Impact of Class and Culture on Social Behaviour," the Palestinian academic Hisham Sharabi and his collaborator Mukhtar Ani write:

> We start from questions such as: Why has Arab society failed to modernize? Why have Arab countries failed to cope with some of the most basic social tasks? Why have the Arab people been unable to cooperate, to defend themselves, to organize, to unify? Why is Arab behaviour emotional, unscientific, "irrational"?

In reply, they say that only a change so radical that it will engulf the very structure of society, its values, and its institutions will suffice to put things straight—though they too fail to indicate what practical steps, what modalities, they have in mind for implementing this drastic prescription. Behind such melodrama lies the wish for some quite other Arab culture that could confront the West on its own terms, as well as the shame that this is not actually the case.

Arab culture has been so distorted by political and careerist factors that its true condition is hard to determine. Like so much else, the Islamic tradition of poetry and historical chronicles more or less collapsed under the encroachment of the West. First came newspapers and the theater, then the novel, free verse, abstract art, the isms and affectations each faithfully copied and reproduced after a due delay. Literate Arabs in the recent past, Khalid Kishtainy comments, "must have been stunned by the profound magic of the great European masterpieces of arts and literature. I can draw only on my own personal experience to imagine the impact. As soon as I read Bernard Shaw's *Saint Joan* and Darwin's theory of evolution in my early teens, all the old prose of Arabic literature receded for me into nothing, and the only pressing task I could see ahead of me was to master a European language as soon as possible." R. A. Nicholson, an unqualified admirer of Islam and its works, first published his *Literary History of the Arabs* in 1907 and was already observing that Western culture was a "highly-prized accomplishment of the enlightened and emancipated few," which did not prevent it from being "an object of scorn and detestation to Muslims in general." It was an astute warning of the cultural schism impending in the reaction to Western values.

Music, like science, as Bernard Lewis has aptly put it, "is part of the inner citadel of Western culture," and virtually no Arabs have broached it, or wanted to. Experiments with Western classical music have failed: music festivals at Baalbek or in Tunisia have petered out. Starting in 1959, a Cairo Symphony Orchestra closed after about fifteen years. In contrast to the Japanese, Koreans, and other Asian peoples, no Arab classical musicians, whether as performer or conductor, have proceeded far enough to earn a reputation in the West, with the one exception of the Lebanese composer Anis Fuleihan (1900–1970), whose main career was in the United States. With due symbolism, Khedive Ismail's opera house in Cairo burnt down in Nasser's regime.

Arab music, with its quarter tones, is an experience of an order completely different from melody and harmony, and no doubt it too occupies its inner citadel within Arab or Islamic culture. "To hear a woman sing is like seeing her naked," runs a Muslim adage. According to Ayatollah Khomeini in an interview with the Italian journalist Oriana Fallaci, "Music dulls the mind, because it involves pleasure and ecstasy, similar to drugs," and Western music in particular, he thinks, "has not exalted the spirit." Oriana Fallaci mentioned Bach, Beethoven, Verdi. "I do not know their names," Khomeini replied.

"The treason of an Arab," according to a Tunisian contemporary who puts his finger on the matter, "begins when he enjoys listening to Mozart or Beethoven." When Taha Husayn declared

Beethoven to be his favorite music, or when Tewfik el-Hakim wrote that he had bought a gramophone to play Beethoven as consolation for life in a remote village, they seemed to their critics to be confirming some non-Arab element in their character, something irrevocably and damagingly westernized. Few Arabs in this century have been so widely revered as the Egyptian singer Um Kaltoum. Born in about 1910 in a village, she first sang religious songs, until turning to popular music. In her memoirs she writes with quite unusual appreciation of her father, who was also her impresario: "he gave me his constant life and his undivided attention." She went out of her way to oppose Western music, saying, "What we need is to base ourselves on our ancestral heritage," which also meant the exclusive use of Eastern musical instruments. A child of her times, she was regimented on occasion to sing in her inimitable way songs with titles such as "We Built the High Dam," or "Glory to Gamal Abdul Nasser and Arab Socialism."

Western theater, and following it the cinema, lent themselves readily to importation and mimicry. The Egyptian film industry maintains a high output, and the only producer to have achieved a reputation outside the Arab world is the Egyptian Youssef Shahine. Arab governments have exploited centralized financing and censorship to ensure that plays and films alike are either naive entertainments for the masses, or promotions of regime-approved values and ends. This frequently takes the form of historical or modern apologetics, in which some Arab military or tribal leader is shown in the full careerist triumph of his conquests. Self-appraisal plays no part. In a history written in 1958 of the Arab theater and cinema, Jacob M. Landau put forward the proposition that audiences must be influenced by what he called "one of the most widespread means for the penetration of Western customs and ideas," or in short, that Arabs would soon learn to think critically for themselves as a result of what they were seeing. This has not happened because the power of social mobilization inherent in these media can so easily be manipulated to dominate any educative intention.

Literature as enlightenment, as the play of a free and ranging mind, and the writer as someone distinguished by virtue of his individuality and his thinking, are concepts which hardly exist in the Arab world, being mere tentative grafts from the West. Usually, the very first contact with the West that an Arab might make in the course of his education has been through the translated work of particular writers of international eminence. Some of these writers have naturally acquired paramount prestige and influence among their acolytes. It has been customary to derive and to repeat intellectual genealogies for Arab writers, for example stressing that Lutfi al-Sayyid had read "Comte, Rousseau, Mill, Spencer and Durkheim." Introducing selections from two of the most admired modern Iranian writers, Sadegh Hedayat and Bozorg Alavi, the editors of an anthology felt it right to point to the influence on them of "Marx and Freud, of Poe and Chekhov, of Dostoevsky and Rilke." In the preface to an English-language edition of Mahfouz's *Wedding Song,* the Egyptian editor praised him for having as exemplars "Flaubert, Balzac, Zola, Camus, Tolstoy, and Dostoevsky," and above all Proust. An obituary of Tewfik el-Hakim in the London *Times* mentioned approvingly how he "fell under the spell" of Ibsen, Shaw, and Pirandello. Speaking of the prominent Syrian-born poet Adonis (whose real name is Ahmed Ali Said), the Arabist Jacques Berque thought to be complimenting him with the description "an orphaned Lautréamont."

Modern Arab literature is characterized by a somber and depressing self-hatred, as well as a hatred of the West and all its manifestations. These two tones are sometimes so intermingled that they can hardly be separated, but nonetheless all such hatreds have to be treated cautiously, in view of the hidden meanings and nuances they may contain. Westernized in thought and style, such expressions carry inner falsification from the start, and though they might very well be representative of a genuine reaction, they might also be nothing more than personal, and evidence either of psychological imbalance on the one hand or of careerism on the other. To their detriment, Western conceptions of literature and the role of the writer elide quickly into shame-honor ranking, endowing practitioners with status and therefore encouraging them to restrict themselves to themes and topics of which the power holder will approve, so bestowing honor and monetary rewards too. More insidiously, Western literature itself over the last fifty years has lost touch with the human imagination and narrowed into social criticism. In a highly complex phenomenon involving guilt and aggression and fashionability, Western writing has tended to denigrate and attack the spiritual values, human as well as scientific, which have made Western society what it is. Through distorted and untruthful depiction of reality, literature has forfeited much of its preeminence in the West. Those Arabs who have turned for inspiration and example to the West have encountered the full force of these negative factors, with nothing positive as makeweight. Taught by Westerners themselves to the Arabs, the hate-engendering "radical" and "anti-imperialist" tradition has seemed to offer a high road to advancement and honor and reputation, in London and Paris as much as at home.

Writing in 1913, the Ottoman Celal Nuri considered "the whole world of infidels" as an enemy. "Friendship for the West is the vilest of all crimes I can imagine. A nation incapable of hating the West is doomed to extinction." That was certainly a Muslim and a patriotic reaction to the loss of Macedonia in the Balkan wars of the day. Nonetheless, it did not prevent Celal Nuri dressing like a Westerner, traveling in Europe, and adopting the Western manner of pamphleteering. The Adonis whom Berque likened to Lautréamont wrote in 1967, "We no longer believe in Europe. We no longer have faith in its political system or in its philosophies. Worms have eaten into its social structure as they have into . . . its very soul. Europe for us—we backward, ignorant, impoverished people—is a corpse." This expression of hatred did not prevent Adonis afterward from attending seminars and conferences in the United States where in the radical-chic manner of the period he solemnized about how "revolution is the science of changing reality" and "revolutionary poetry is the linguistic counterpart of this revolutionary science," whatever that might mean. In his adopted city of Beirut, life did not offer metaphorical corpses and worms eating into a social structure, but very real corpses in their tens of thousands and an altogether tragic social disintegration, as a result of which Adonis informed Fouad Ajami in an interview that "Something in the Arab world has died" and he was leaving Beirut to settle in comfortable France. "A deep sorrow and a deep resignation," Fouad Ajami reported, would accompany Adonis into this Europe in which he no longer believed, but which happened to provide a safe haven.

"Come, friends," exclaimed Ali Shariati, an Iranian, "let us abandon Europe; let us cease this nauseating, apish imitation of Europe. Let us leave behind this Europe that always speaks of humanity, but destroys human beings wherever it finds them." Born in 1932, Ali Shariati came from a family of ulema. In 1959 he studied at the Sorbonne for a doctorate in sociology, where according to one commentator, in a typical genealogy, he absorbed "the ideas of Emile Durkheim, Max Weber, Che Guevara,

Albert Camus and Frantz Fanon." Returning to his native country, he used this education to fashion the slogan, "Have faith in God, grab the gun and fight!" What he had done was to draw on Western social critics and advocates of violence in order to find approved arguments for rending his own society. Speaking to audiences in Iran in an idiom apparently certified by the West, he became an instant celebrity in the power-challenging entourage of Khomeini. His death in 1977 was for them no doubt a secret police murder.

Jalal Ali Ahmad was also Iranian, born in a village in 1923, and his book *Occidentosis* is one of the most extreme examples of the pitiful and frantic nihilism whipped up in someone who has the double perspective of looking at his own Islamic society in order to pass Western judgments, and at the West in order to pass Islamic judgments. He descended from a long and distinguished line of ulema, and his uncle was Ayatollah Mahmud Taleghani, a companion and political challenger of Khomeini. At the age of twenty-one, he broke with religion to join the Tudeh Party, or Communists, though not for long. In the 1960s he visited the Soviet Union and the United States, and he made the pilgrimage to Mecca and Medina, where at the tomb of the Prophet he was overcome: "I wept and fled from the mosque." Following Ahmad's somewhat mysterious death in 1969, *Occidentosis* has acquired a cult status. The vivacity of the writing, and its polemic crescendos, are reminiscent of *Les Décombres*, that singular book in which Lucien Rebatet perversely discovered that the cure to the ills of his native France was its occupation by the Nazi Germans.

"Occidentosis" is a disease akin to tuberculosis, whereby the West infects the East. Nothing happens in the East except through the agency of the West, whose countries one and all are plotting ill under cover of local riots and uprisings. The West makes the machines: that is the whole trick of it. He asks in despair, "Why did we utterly fail to develop the machine, leaving it to others to so encompass its development that by the time we awakened, every oil rig had become a nail driven into our land?" Emulation of the foreigner and his machinery is inevitable but vain, producing only neurosis: the Easterner comes to regard himself as nothing, "not to think at all, to give up all reliance on your own self."

We now resemble an alien people, with unfamiliar customs, a culture with no roots in our land and no chance of blossoming here. Thus all we have is stillborn, in our politics, our culture, and our daily life. We are about 19 or 20 million people, 75 per cent of whom live in the country-side, or in tents or huts, following ways from the dawn of creation, ignorant of new values, condemned to the relations of lord and serf, unfamiliar with the machine, having primitive tools and the correspond-ing food, fuel, clothing, and housing: the plow, barley bread, cow dung, tent cloth, and straw huts, respectively. The only things Western that have penetrated this region are the transistor radio and the draft [i.e. instruments of regimentation], and these with more deadly effect than dynamite.

Religion and clericalism were no solution, but a makeshift for which he found one of his favorite images of putrefaction: "When the house has been carried off in a flood or has collapsed in an earthquake, you go looking for a door in the debris to bear the rotting corpse of a loved one to the graveyard". Cruel and alien-ated descriptions of his fellow Iranians are accompanied by further deforming parodies of Western values—for instance, it is his un-derstanding that democratic political parties are "forums to satisfy the melancholia of unbalanced and mentally ill persons." The book culminates in a chapter titled "A Society in Collapse," and its prescription is to await the moment when the machine, in the shape of the atomic bomb, will bring everything to an end.

In societies where high rates of illiteracy obtain, the impact and penetration of such writing must be unfathomable. Its modish and guilt-ridden pessimism is as much a Western import as any ma-chine. At the very least, though, polemicizing in this stereotype further serves to internalize shame and so stimulates the odious climate in which violence is eagerly done to self and to others. In *Journey Among the Believers*, a book with a timely and illuminating account of several present-day Muslim countries including Iran, V. S. Naipaul drew attention to the paradox governing the type of Muslim whose modern education is enough only to equip him for alienation from his own people. This type criticizes the West by means of Western ideas and techniques, thereby extending and magnifying just what he affects to be rejecting. The West, such Muslims are conceding, will go its own masterful and scientifically innovative way regardless, and, Naipaul observes, "That expecta-tion—of others continuing to create, of the alien, necessary civili-zation going on—is implicit in the act of renunciation, and is its great flaw." It may be, of course, that the inarticulate Muslim masses, for whom so very few speak and to whom even fewer listen, in their inner selves ignore alienating and hate-inciting material or treat it as they used to, in the words of R. A. Nicholson, with scorn and detestation. Seething inner confusion and cultural distress may be particularly gleaned from the contemporary Arab novel. The form itself is another Western import, and the first Arab novel is usually considered to be *Zaynab*, dating from 1913. Its author, the Egyptian Muhammad Husayn Haykal, began as a passionate westernizer and a friend of Lutfi al-Sayyid's, though he was to write books glorifying early Islamic history. Between 1913 and 1962, according to Hilary Kilpatrick in *The Modern Egyptian Novel*, Egyptian authors published 438 novels, an output no other Arab country could remotely match. What these, and current Arab writing in general, amount to is a body of social criticism, or as Kilpatrick says, one of the few guides to intellectual and social developments.

To a Western reader, the strength and lasting appeal of the novel as a form lies in its depiction of the choices that a character can take, whether for good or bad, but always through the free exercise of will. Which choices are made and how they have been influenced may well depend on wider social and political factors, but in fiction as in life, the individual is responsible for himself and seen to be so, and this moves the reader to identify.

No such possibility exists for the Arab novelist, who is operating first in a society with tribal and religious constraints which he cannot escape, and then with behavioral codes which block or repress the exercise of free will. To ignore dominant values and their social rigidities removes the writer from reality, and a number of contemporary Arab writers have indeed fled into surrealism, into obscure tales of fantasy and nightmare. In literature as in life, the constraint of tribe and religion for example dictates that a Sunni writer who created a Shia hero would expose himself to ridicule and scandal, and vice versa; while if either of them wished to depict sympathetically some such stranger as a Westerner or an Israeli, he would have to break the agreed code of behavior at great risk that he himself would be rejected, physically attacked, or worse. Within terms of realistic fiction, shame-honor must continue to determine behavior and so excludes any gradual revelation through narrative of how characters by means of personal choices make themselves what they are. Any free-thinking or rebellious hero, who might self-consciously take his destiny into his own hands and defy behavioral codes, invites shame and ostracism. In Arab novels, the stock characters therefore are the young woman who is blocked by shame-honor and has no say in love and marriage; and the young man who is blocked by power challenging and money-favoring and has no say in what to make of his own life. Despair, madness, suicide, and murder are the ends of these characters, and any writer true to reality cannot help pressing against these unhappinesses, sounding strong but mournful notes of pathos. Criticism and perhaps opposition is implicit, no doubt; but proving themselves as much the prisoners of current values as any of their characters, Arab writers have tended to surrender more to self-pity than to the empathy, or pity for others, which alone creates a literature great enough to affect attitudes, and in the long run to change them.

In this world of despotic power holding moreover, the list of Arab writers and journalists who have been murdered or imprisoned on true or false charges is thoroughly intimidating. Outright criticism, if anyone had a mind to it, would be the act of high moral courage. In many cases, the dedication at the front of a book serves as an imprimatur, revealing exactly to whom the author is looking for support and sponsorship, for tribal-religious safeguards and credentials. "I dedicate my book to my native land of Morocco, and to the Moroccan people, my people," Driss Chraibi declares at the front of his novel *Naissance à l'aube.* Sari J. Nasir, in *The Arabs and the English,* puts "To my father and mother in Arab Jerusalem and to all Palestinian fathers and mothers wherever they may be." *Saudi Arabia,* by Fouad al-Farsy, has a whole page laid out ornately "In the Name of Allah the Compassionate the Merciful" to King Feisal, who is floridly called, among other things, "the rejuvenator of the scientific, social and industrial Renaissance." The Egyptian Marxist Anwar Abdel-Malek dedicates his anthology of modern Arab political writings to "the Palestinian Resistance which preserves the honour of the nation," and to be on the safe side he adds Abd al-Moneim Riad, an Egyptian general "who died on the battlefield," and finally to "the workers of Abu Zaabal, our comrades, massacred at work on February 12, 1970 for expressing the national will of Egypt." Ali Shariati's posthumous *Man and Islam* is "In memory of Dr. Mustafa Chamran who, like his beloved friend Dr. Ali Shariati, made the supreme sacrifice in the cause of justice of the world's oppressed people." In absolute symmetry, *The Shah's Story* has "I dedicate this book to the memory of all those Iranian men and women who have suffered and died for their country."

Censorship in this context is merely the visible or formal instrument of control. The novel nevertheless offers the author an alibi: it is only a story, an invention, and he cannot be held to it. Description of some social phenomenon in a factual report or essay sometimes becomes diametrically the opposite when placed in the medium of fiction. In *La Vie quotidienne en Algérie,* for example, the writer Rachid Boudjedra has a sociological account of customs in his native Algeria, courtship, cheerful marriage rites with music, public baths, close ties of kinship, in all of which he appears to delight uncritically. In a novel, *La Pluie,* in contrast Boudjedra puts into the mouth of his heroine a book-length monologue about the horrors of her abuse at the hands of her brother and other men, her hatred of custom, leaving suicide as her likeliest prospect. In another novel *La Répudiation,* Boudjedra's narrator goes over the very same ground of traditional custom, but with overpowering disgust, describing how his father threw out his mother to take instead a fifteen-year-old bride—"the sound of tambourines had hidden the torture of flesh ripped by the patriarch's monstrous organ." "Hate throbbed in us; we wanted to kill him, knock him off then and there, before he had finished with his poisonous fantasies."

Boudjedra's fictional Algiers negates the lively city of his sociology:

At the exit of the souks, we tiptoed among the cunning story-tellers, boring themselves to death by reciting the same old stories to listeners who only react to the obscene bits. Fortune-tellers preferred quieter back-streets in order to attract any pitiful idiots who came to find a buried treasure or a magic potion to bewitch some indifferent woman. Idlers and those with nothing better to do wandered from one group to another, nodded with approval, spat on the ground gobs that were viscous, tubercular. . . . In surrounding streets which seem to lead straight to the sky, blind beggars, their features pock-marked, did what they could to move passers-by to have pity on them, and touted for grim little brothels where the whole population which was accustomed to keep its women secluded, came to make love to unbearable old crones.

He goes on to speak of

> this bankruptcy of the country which might be called a pure fantasy
> if it were not for the thinness of the peasants squatting on their heels in
> circles, their eyes fixed on the nourishing earth wiped clean of its sap, the
> blame lying in the clan's magical links to some occult divinity which allows
> them to stare quietly at the horizon, far away from anger yet secreting a
> terrifying demagogy, of lies, dealings, settling of old scores—to do with
> myth rather than reality.

For these people, he says, "the physical liquidation of those of
another mind had become wholly banal."

Dissatisfaction and pessimism prove to be general. The Turkish
writer Fakir Baykurt makes Turkish villagers say of themselves:

> Life comes and goes, mankind is no different from animalkind. We lay
> and roll, like the village headman's horse, and so spend our lives. We
> were born here. We got sick here. We grew up, got married, dried out
> and rotted, and we are still here. One day we shall not be able to walk
> or even to rot, and will still be here.

When people are shown to be behaving so true to type, characteri-
zation and exposition cannot help becoming bleak and didactic,
mere instruments for the author's point of view. In Mahfouz's
Wedding Song a character says that the 1973 war "should have led
us to a more prosperous life," only to be answered with the remark, "The whole country's become one huge brothel." Someone
else interjects, "Living—reduced to daily encounters with universal blight, the filth and slime of overflowing sewers, and a beastly
transport system—lost all its joy."

In *Blood Feud,* a short story by the well-known Yusuf Sharouni,
a villager says of his home:

> My village, like the rest of the villages of Upper Egypt, is still ailing.
> Water pipes, electric lights and a Collective Unit that includes a hospital
> and school, together with agricultural and social supervisors, have re-
> cently been introduced into it and yet it remains ailing. Its ailment has
> many symptoms, perhaps the most important of which is that of the blood
> feud . . . these brutal people so thirsty for blood.

The unnecessary death of this village's headman proves the story's
point. Yusuf al-Qaid, author of *War in the Land of Egypt,* has a
character say, "When, I wondered, would God release Egypt from
this torment and misery and grief? No one knows the answer, but
things surely can't go on as they are much longer."

Yussef Idris, in his story "The Dregs of the City," sketches the Cairo slums with loathing.

> The winding lanes led to alleys paved with dirt, covered with filth and water and slime. . . . Children and flies swarm in abundance. . . . The slimy ground is the same colour as the dusty walls. The smell of the earth mingles with the smell of humanity. . . . And children. Scores upon scores gather in front and behind and on either side, their eyes bleary with ophthalmia and trachoma, and misery looks out of their haggard faces. Swarms of flies come in their wake. One child shouts as he hurls a stone.

Pursuing social and political commentary at the expense of imagination and universality, even gifted and Western-influenced writers restrict or trivialize their work into something routinely adversarial, a somewhat hopeless version of challenging without real power, from which they are the first to suffer. The Iranian Sadegh Hedayat is a case in point. His country's condition seemed so deplorable to him that he was always searching for satisfactory metaphors to say so, thereby frustrating the widening of his talent, and with sad symbolism he finally committed suicide in Paris in 1951. Local complaints were always breaking through his work, as in a work called "The Message of Kafka" where he suddenly lets go:

> Before the last World War there still existed a vague hope of freedom and respect for the rights of mankind. The supporters of dictatorship had not yet openly replaced freedom by slavery. . . . The masses of the people had not yet been transformed by politicians and robbers into cattle, and living men into half-dead creatures.

In Hedayat's novel *The Blind Owl,* also a cult book, the narrator states that the world has been made for

> a tribe of brazen, money-grubbing, blustering louts, sellers of conscience, hungry of eye and heart—for people, in fact, who had been created in its own likeness and who fawned and grovelled before the mighty of the earth and heaven as the hungry dog outside the butcher's shop wagged his tail in the hope of receiving a fragment of offal.

Halim Barakat, a sociologist at the American University of Beirut, wrote his novel *Days of Dust* around the 1967 war. His young hero is Ramzy, a Beirut student, who "could not forget that the Arab world was underdeveloped and uncoordinated, living in the 20th century only in outward appearance. The worst of it was that it possessed no will power. It could not make up its mind on anything. It did not plan. It glorified in the past and did not dream of the future." So upset was the author by the war and its outcome that a potentially illuminating novel was lost in what effectively proved a series of otherwise unpublishable newspaper editorials. Ramzy and the other characters are given page after page of embittered social criticism in this vein:

> Most of our friends are experts in one field or another. Yet can you tell me what they do? Where are the institutions that know how to benefit from their expertise? Who cares about them? Who wants them to have opinions? And the experts, how in fact do they work? Do they cooperate? No one cooperates with anyone else. Each one lives in his own little world. Tell me about our institutions. Tell me about the organizations and the parties. There's really nothing, nothing at all.

This fear of finding nothing, of being useless, the sense of living in a void for purposes only of dying, crop up nihilistically time and again—a living echo of General Daumas and his pessimism over a century ago. In an autobiographical novel in 1935, Taha Husayn wrote about how he had gone in hope and expectation to the countryside but "I found nothing. Here I shall be, returning to you after a few days, then travelling to Cairo after some weeks, carrying nothing in my soul but tumble-down ruins and two palm trees, standing silent, which feel desolation and spread it around them. How much I wanted, and how little I found!" "I am sodden with some kind of fear" is to be found in the opening paragraphs of Mahfouz's *Wedding Song.* In a Sharouni short story, two brothers quarrel over an inheritance, and "Shafik both wanted and didn't want to kill his brother," only to shoot him in the end. *Aisha,* a collection of gifted stories by the Egyptian Ahdaf Soueif is studded with throwaway lines like "There was just—nothing" or, "And besides, what is there to wait for?" The narrator in Dia el-Sharkawy's story "The Sneak Thief" says, "I look on things detachedly, indifferently, through vacuous eyes, like two empty pools, drained of all interest, of all hope." *Lallia,* a novel by the Algerian Djanet Lachmet, in the setting of the war of independence, has its autobiographical heroine exclaiming, "Deaths, nothing but deaths . . . I had difficulty in understanding how a man could lean over another man and look him in the eye before cutting his throat." Esmail Fassih, who speaks in his novel *Sorraya in a Coma* of his native Iran as "the martyr-begetting country," also has a scene in which Iranian exiles tour Louis XIV's Versailles, and one of them con-

fronts the others: "We're all really miserable. We're all making
fools of ourselves. What do we know about art and civilization?"
He recommends that they should sit in a corner eating gruel, and
belching, "and be beaten on the head. Eat. Sleep. And die."

Abdelhak Serhane is a Moroccan writer, born in 1950, and who
has therefore grown up to know nothing but national independence. A qualified psychologist, he wrote a thesis in France on the
sexuality of young Moroccans from a traditional background; he
teaches in the Moroccan town of Kenitra and edits a highbrow
journal. This career, and these interests, suggest an author who
has prepared himself for insights into his own society. In 1986 he
published a novel *Children of the Narrow Streets*. The setting is the
Moroccan town of Azrou, the writing is completely realistic; and
technically the novel is most accomplished and telling. Its subject
matter and the accompanying commentary upon Arab life and
customs are despairing, violent, without a trace either of humor or
hope, altogether a swamp of negation. In this respect, the novel
may serve as a model at least for this type of Arab self-consciousness.

Rahou, the novel's narrator, is one of the seven children of
Lalla Rabha and Bouchaib, who has part-time employment in a
brickworks. Sharing a small house with three other families, they
all sleep in one room. One of Rahou's earliest memories is of
pretending to be asleep while his naked father steps over him,
frightening him with the sight of his genitals, and dropping urine
on his face. "It's terrible when flies swarm upon human misery! It's
terrible when people look like their flies!" is typical of Rahou's
asides. His dreams are escapist. "You will take revenge upon this
life. You will go somewhere else. You will do like your cousin Ali.
You will study. You will marry a foreign girl and forget yourself in
her white body. You will send money to your mother, but never
again will you set foot in your country."

At school, Rahou is among a class of boys made to undress so
that the teacher can lash their backs with his belt. With his friends
Salah and Brahim, young teenagers like himself, Rahou is part of
a gang out to catch another boy whom they accuse of being insulting, and they then sodomize him one after another. Arrested, they
are treated leniently because Salah's father bribes the police. Nevertheless, they are escorted into the police torture chamber for a
sight of a man suspended there by the arms over three days. Far
from being grateful to his father, Salah feels that he has grown up

in an atmosphere of "indifference and hatred," having in fact been thrown out of the house earlier. Under the mistaken apprehension that Brahim has failed an examination, his father comes for him with a knife, shouting about how he will kill him. As for Rahou, he recalls how his father has mocked the small size of his genitals, and how one day, in the street, in front of a girl, he had opened his trousers in order to draw crude comparisons. "You never again dared to speak a word to that girl. You cried a long time that day. Your father seized every chance to humiliate you. You knew that one day you wouldn't be able to resist the longing to smash in his skull with the copper pestle. How could a child live and grow in this atmosphere of hate and impotence?"

Bouchaib's dreams are also escapist, to leave for Paris "where it rained gold and silver." In the hopes of being sponsored for the requisite passports and work certificates, he flatters the local notable Sid El Haj and bribes him. Sid El Haj is a man characterized as "cheating, giving rise to egoism, corruption, envy, inconsideration and hate." When he comes to the house, his purpose is to eat and drink tea, to break wind openly in his host's face, and to pocket money that cannot be spared. When children chase his departing car, he deliberately brakes so hard that they bang into it. Having no intention of putting himself out for Bouchaib's documents and papers, Sid El Haj is set upon seducing Amina, the fourteen-year-old daughter of the house. He does so, and she commits suicide. In revenge, Bouchaib tries to murder Sid El Haj and is sentenced to twenty years in prison.

At the novel's core is a lengthy train journey in which passengers come together randomly and describe their miseries, in what is an extended and painful metaphor for the national condition. Nothing works. Everything is broken. The train itself runs into a flock of sheep and is then attacked by people with stones. The journey culminates in a stampede, followed by arrests—a literary coding, presumably, for revolution and secret police repression.

Fulfilling his dreams, Rahou at last leaves for France, where he will prepare his university thesis. In the process, he has a harrowing encounter with bureaucracy, waiting futilely in offices, passing bribes to no effect, eventually face to face with a senior official who ought to put his signature to a standard form but instead spends his time telephoning his brother in Canada to ask about the girls there and their seduction. With an emotion that is heart-felt and savage, the mature Rahou in Azrou finds himself amid "walking corpses," pausing at the grave of his sister Amina only to promise himself that he is turning his back on his country for good. General expressions of loathing as well as of self-pity far exceed any narrative demands. Characters marginal to the plot elaborate how they trick boys into pederasty. A ceremony of public storytelling provides the occasion for prostitution. The mosques are filled with hypocrites. Men and women are described as equally sick and sickened with the relationships arising from sexual segregation. "Violence was the universe in which we lived," Rahou sums up his past. "We were children of hate and misery. We knew everything about life. Except whatever might have been useful to us."

Social customs, it is accepted in this angry literature, have become shackles and the source of ills. What is being expressed time and again, with whatever degree of articulation, is dismay at restrictions on the exercise of free will and choice imposed by power challenging in the world at large; and the comparable restrictions imposed within the domestic scene by shame-honor. In both spheres, perfect obedience is called for, or else there will be violence without fail. Shame-honor considerations render it impossible for a son to grow up and assert his own individuality without upsetting, insulting, or otherwise calling into question his father's honor as head of the household and probably his mother's as well. Careerist power challenging at once begins as the father responds, and this shame-rejecting and honor-certifying violence is to be found horrifyingly repeated, as in the scene where Bouchaib asserts superior manhood by physically thrusting out his genitals to threaten his son. Arabs are not unnatural fathers, of course, but even in the parent-child relationship considerations of shame and honor must take precedence over affection or indulgence that might be misinterpreted as weakness, and even over decent or polite conduct. Part of the shock and dismay at this discovery no doubt derives from the fact that it was within the home and family that each and every author was also once socialized, thus carrying from childhood the personal wounds of being humiliated, as well as the appalling knowledge that any exercise of free will certainly entails brutal chastisements. In adulthood, fiction itself appears a medium for relief, for a tentative recovery of honor, and an exercise of free will.

In an issue in 1972 of *Les Temps Modernes,* the prestigious French intellectual magazine, Mohammed Karoui singled out clearly how and why a father's honor converts into his son's hatred. This was, Karoui wrote, a fundamental theme of Arab life and letters.

Who among us Arabs can claim that he was acknowledged, loved, wanted and accepted by the family or atmosphere in which he grew up? None, I am sure. Can anyone be loved who is no more than a useful object, produced to continue the family line, for the troublesome old age of parents, or for the male chauvinist glory of the father who proves what a real man he is by the number of his offspring?

To Karoui, the son has been given life not for his own sake, but for the father's; the son is to that extent castrated, living only through the power of attorney granted by the father. "Shut up, or I'll bash your head in!" a father typically says to his son in Mahfouz's *Wedding Song.* The Sudanese writer El Sir Hassan Fadl, in *Their Finest Days,* a book consisting of two novellas, has one father who swore an oath that "he'd cut off his son's head if he found he were a Communist," and another father who tells his son that if he ever catches him again looking at a woman, "he would gouge your eyes out."

In the story "The Game Is Over," the Iranian Gholamhosein Saedi describes how fathers pass on at home the shame and insult that have been received outside.

Every night when Hasani's father came home, still dressed, face and hands unwashed, he would start beating up on Hasani; he would beat him until it was time to eat, with blows of the fist and with kicks, with a club, with a rope, with a belt. . . . The neighbours would go running up and would free him with pleas of "May we be struck dead if you don't let him go!" Hasani's father would beat him every night but my papa would beat Ahmad and me only once or twice a week when he was out of sorts or his business dealings had gone badly. He would beat me until it was time for dinner. My Ma would begin to weep and cry out, "You bastard, why are you killing my children, why are you maiming them?" My father would turn on her and begin beating her, and she would cry, "Children, get out!"

Here is Rachid Boudjedra, from *La Répudiation:*

Si Zoubir lost all control, became crude, said anything that came into his head. He considered Ma a syphilitic whore. He played with his worry-beads. Asked God for help and protection. His face caved in. We hardly recognised him. He stammered, gesticulated, sat down, stood up again, rambled incoherently, flapped his floppy arms in the air, hit us, panted and whinnied, spat at us, knocked us down, reproached us as cowards.

We were terrified and suddenly had no age, so taken-aback were we by our father's dance in the wreck of our childhood.

Ghassan Kanafani was a Palestinian writer and activist, murdered by a car bomb in Beirut. *Men in the Sun* is his collection of short stories, widely considered to be among the best of modern Arab works. Its title story concerns the driver of a tanker-lorry who is attempting to smuggle some workers across the desert to illicit jobs in the Gulf. This driver has been physically emasculated in some unspecified war, and the workers are all choked to death by heat as they hide inside the lorry: clear metaphorical representations of the impotence and death that Kanafani takes to be the Palestinian condition. In another story, a Palestinian father has been humiliated because he has abandoned his home and fled from the Jews, and he shouts at his children that he wants to kill them and then himself as well. Picking up a revolver, he comes for them. "His eyes glittered as they roamed over our faces," is the commentary of the petrified son. In another Kanafani story, a father says to his son, "If you were a horse I would put a bullet through your brain." In relating the real life of the Egyptian peasant Shahhat, Richard Critchfield describes a scene in which the father, Abd el-Baset, feels himself shamed by Shahhat's behavior in the village; and finding him asleep at home, places a foot on the young man's neck, with the words, "You make me as small as the sesame seed. So small I can no longer show myself before the world." Then he says, "I will kill you, Shahhat." The son promptly runs away.

Shame-honor violence to daughters is parallel. Some of the lasting themes of Western literature—courtship, the gradual realization of mutual love, the development of these intimate feelings, their trials and fulfillments—are of course excluded from Arab literature as from Arab society, with its segregation of the sexes and its arranged marriages. Many an Arab fictional plot turns upon a man spotting a girl at hazard, probably out of his window or in the market, and without a word passing between them, then and there deciding either to seduce or to marry her. Variations of the theme include outright rape, unwilling paternity, impotence, the suicide or murder of the dishonored girls—Yussef Idris and Yusuf Sharouni are masters of these macabre divagations. "The Death of Bed Number 12" is a Kanafani story in which a young man on an errand knocks at a door, is answered by a young girl, finds himself unable to speak but hurries home to ask his sister to arrange a marriage with this apparition of a girl. His untimely death is once again Kanafani's comment on a social predicament. Novels by Arab women contain repeated instances of distressing, and virtually impersonal, physical overpowerings of innocent women. *The Story of Zahra,* by Hanan Al-Shaykh, for example, is set in war-torn Beirut, and its Shia heroine is terrified of her father, sexually abused by her uncle and her brother, obliged to submit to rape and abortion, only to give herself finally to a rooftop sniper for no particular reason, listlessly, as though the only remaining impulse were the wish to hurt herself. At an academic conference in the United States, the well-known critic Sahair El-Calamawy emphasized that "I have not yet read about a truly emancipated woman in any novel by an Arab author."

Some authors continue to subscribe to the customs and values resulting from power challenging and shame-honor ranking and treat them as natural and admirable. Probably the most renowned of these is the Turkish writer Yashar Kemal, whose *Memed My Hawk,* first published in 1955, may well be the best-known novel to have come out of the Middle East. At its center is Memed, a poor boy born in a village belonging to the rich Abdi Agha. Beaten by Abdi Agha, Memed runs away, and the entire story concerns his careerist recovery of honor. Taking to the hills, he becomes a bandit with no compunction about stealing and killing. "Overwhelmed by the hatred he felt, he thought of what it meant to kill a man, to finish him, destroy him utterly." This imperative to hate is a prerequisite if he is to achieve his life's ambition of revenge. In a scene which unconsciously conveys a great deal of social information, he returns to his village at a moment when it is wrongly rumored that he has actually murdered Abdi Agha. At once he is welcomed as the new power holder, and his orders are duly obeyed. Learning that Abdi Agha is still alive, the villagers go into reverse, seeking to escape from the impending trial of strength with Memed, telling themselves "Our Agha would kill 100 dogs like him with one single shot." "Not a soul remained in the alleys as they shut themselves up in their houses. The dogs stopped barking and the cocks crowing. It was as if there were no longer a single living creature in the village." On a national scale, of course, this is what happens when some careerist power challenge comes to its head in a coup. Killing Abdi Agha, Memed becomes a folk hero. The ultimate praise and confirmation of his redeemed and honored status is put into the mouths of the villagers in this collective finale, "Why should he be a villager like us and live miserably? Now the whole world is afraid of him and he's much better off!"

Yashar Kemal was born in 1922, in a village in southern Anatolia. His family were the local landowners—like Abdi Agha—but he has been a lifelong self-declared Communist. For this reason *Memed My Hawk* has been fondly interpreted by Western "progressives" as an epic of rebellion and social justice, translated into European languages, and mentioned for the Nobel Prize. This is a grotesque sentimentalization of a book whose values are thoroughly antisocial and reactionary. Memed takes Abdi Agha's place because he is more effectively ruthless, not because he introduces justice or egalitarian dealings. Far from breaking the old despotic sway of the power holder, he adopts it to advance himself. To justify Memed's career as "heroic" or "legendary" is only the particularly crass form of Eurocentric patronizing whereby barbarous acts by primitive men are excused as folklore and condoned as "custom."

The truly revolutionary act on the part of a Middle Eastern writer would consist in showing pity for his characters, first and foremost realizing them as human beings rather than political and social symbols or vehicles serving those ends he himself approves and predetermines. No Arab writer has taken that first and indispensable step toward democracy more firmly than Mouloud Feraoun, an Algerian from Kabylia. For him, independence involved affection for his own society and people while also seeing their values for what they were. In his diary, kept during the war of independence, he could write, "There is French in me, there is Kabyle in me. But I have a horror of those who kill." This exceptional man was murdered by French extremists in 1962.

Feraoun's finest novel is *Le Fils du Pauvre*, in 1954, in which he deals with the themes to be found in Serhane's *Children of the Narrow Streets*, and indeed in virtually all North African Arab novels. A child, Fouroulou, is caught up in harmful social customs, in fact a lethal blood feud that he accidentally sparks off. He too dreams of escape, and so does his father Ramdane, who longs for the riches of France, "the final hope, the one and only solution." On the eve of Ramdane's departure to work in a French factory, Fouroulou hears him praying aloud. "Then in a flight of despair, he implored God to keep his children safe. In the silence of the

night, the tone was serious and profound. Each request was followed by a moving confession. Ramdane depicted his straitened
circumstances, his wretchedness." Injured by an accident, Ramdane returns from France with insurance compensation and wants
his son to become a fellah with him. To Fouroulou, a life of custom
seems like denial, imprisonment. He has seen for himself the family sufferings, for instance how an aunt died in childbirth and her
sister went mad and was tied down by an ankle rope until she broke
loose to drown herself. He persuades his father to allow him to be
educated in the town of Tizi-Ouzou, in a Protestant mission. Any
sense of inferiority among the Christians is soon overcome. "The
will to succeed" was fierce in the boy: "he knew he was alone in
a struggle which offered no quarter." Fouroulou wins his scholarship to France. As was the case with Feraoun himself in real life,
entry to a fulfilled life does not entail rejection of his background
but greater understanding of the causes of its hardships.

Literature has no means of opposing despotic power holding,
with its apparatus of secret police and torture chambers, but circumstances sometimes impel this human purpose upon it. Unlike
in the Soviet Union, no Arab *samizdat* or underground publications
circulate facts and ideas that are otherwise suppressed. In contrast
to the Soviet public, the Arabs enjoy considerable freedom of
movement; the rich and powerful, at least, are able to travel at will
in the West and so are exposed to its values, while the poor at
home may meet tourists. In a baffled blending of envy and admiration, they can judge for themselves that Western society is organized more effectively to overcome its breakdowns and mistakes
and to produce peace and plenty. In an equally schizophrenic
mood, they look up to the power holder above them with a respect
inseparable from fear of the harm that he might do to them. True
information about the power holder's deeds reaches everyone
through word-of-mouth whispering, and this grapevine may well
be speedier and more reliable than print. Needless to say, every
Arab knows what his society is like, how it fares in comparison to
others, and how wide of the mark are apologetics in all forms. To
articulate this knowledge requires a rare combination of courage,
talent, and opportunity.

An Arab Solzhenitsyn, an Arab Sakharov cannot be conjured
upon request, as though a genie from a bottle. Yet scattered
throughout the West are Arab exiles with the experience and the
abilities to fulfill comparable roles of liberating the spirit through

objective descriptions of present Arab brutality and oppression, its causes and consequences. An Arab Solzhenitsyn is needed to restore to the millions of innocent victims the humanity of which they are robbed. An Arab Sakharov is needed to complete the cross-cultural assessments begun long ago by the likes of Tahtawi and Khayr ed-Din, and so to define what kind of society, which institutions, will sustain their civilization and rescue their identity. In the body of contemporary Arab literature there is already a certain recognition that the exclusive values of tribe and religion, as well as power challenging, maximize hate and injustice and leave the spoils to the strong, and suffering to everyone else. This literature is distressed and distressing through awareness that shame-honor ranking and careerist politics foster activities and values incompatible with equality and freedom. "The Arab despises himself, despises his reality, because he knows that the real facts go against what he is asked to think of them. Politics, news, intellectual life, is a weave of lies," wrote Moncef Marzouki, until then unknown provincial Tunisian doctor, presumably without an audience or influence, in a book in 1982 with the sardonic title *Why the Arabs Will Go to Mars.* If there is hope, it lies in voices like that, at last confident and informed enough to burst through the straitjacket of custom.

Conclusion

The Arab world has no institutions evolved by common consent for common purposes, under guarantee of law, and consequently there is nothing that can be agreed as the general good. No mechanism exists so that people may participate in whatever is being decided and performed in their name, and ostensibly for their sake. Without some such mechanism, presumably electoral but certainly representative, rights and duties cannot be defined, wealth cannot be shared with any degree of fairness, and vital issues of peace and war and life and death are at the sole disposition of whoever has power.

A handful of absolute despots oppress and attack with every available strategem all those within reach. The rich and strong mercilessly bully and exploit their inferiors. Fathers subjugate wives and children. From the proudest power holder down to the humblest family, all are engaged in pillaging whatever they can for themselves, or at best for their tribe and religion, rather than considering the public interest and constructing the commonwealth. Politics in practice is reduced to the black arts of applied force, and in any emergency, of terror. In all relationships, domestic, private and public, internal and external, violence is therefore not only customary but also systematic and utterly impervious to piecemeal reform or amelioration.

Choice, invention, equality, wealth-creation, in a word pluralism, are among the benefits of living under institutions in which citizens participate of their own free will. Mutual agreement by contract, as well as compromise and civility, result of their own accord. As things stand, Arabs are excluded from contractual relationships of this kind among themselves, and this in turn prejudices and handicaps their dealings with outsiders. Foreign affairs, commerce, even acquaintanceships are not conducted as between equals, but as probes conducive to victory or defeat, as though in an extension of feuding. So there is nothing that can yet be properly called Arab society, but only the inherited collectivity.

Voluntary institutions promote justice and equality so self-evidently that in theory imitations ought to arise among people eager for modern society. The United States is the foremost example of a pluralist democracy, and in the heyday of its success may serve at least to impress, much as other Western social models have previously galvanized Ataturk, the Pahlavi Shahs, Nasser. This is perhaps a last chance, but already forlorn, for nothing of the sort yet appears likely to be realized. The customary attachment of notions of honor to status and behavior, leading to pursuit of a military heroism that has long since been obsolete and make-believe in practice, continues to obstruct all reformist thought or experiment throughout the Arab world. Concession of rights to one another, or to members of other tribes and religions, entails loss of supremacy. Anyone who granted equal rights to outsiders and strangers, or who managed to construct participatory institutions to that end, would be considered to have harmed and diminished himself and his own kind quite pointlessly and heedlessly, and he could not survive what would be perceived as humiliation. Promoted and justified by the quest for honor, careerist crime thrives as a routine at all social and political levels, and simple tolerance remains self-defeating, therefore excluded. Lying and corruption remain necessary strategies for survival. Individual Arabs frequently and movingly express grief and dismay at what they have to suffer by way of systematic persecution and rapacity, but not one so far has profoundly analyzed the cause and proposed and published a cure. On the contrary, the Arab collectivity shows more sign of maintaining faith with itself into the indefinite future than of evolving into modern participatory societies. It is as though the Arabs have trapped themselves inside a closed circle from which they sense that they must break out for their own good, but within which identity and its supportive values paralyze endeavors of rescue.

Islam, to which the Arabs have always turned for identity,

ceased in its earliest years to be unitary. Whether Sunni or Shia, ambitious men in all centuries abused the Holy Law they were supposed to be upholding, in sectarian wars and challenges to advance themselves. Religious belief cannot now be conjured in protection. It is not possible to return to ancient simplicities as though science had never questioned nature and the universe, as though the West and its values did not exist. "The good old kernel," in the lament of Ignaz Goldziher over a hundred years ago, is long beyond recall. "Islamic revival" has nothing to do with worship and man's relationship with God or nature, but is a fictitious catch-phrase on which anyone with the will for it may mount a bid for power, either Sunni or Shia, but divisive in any case. Without political form, strictly emotional in thought and practice, the appeal of this alleged revival lies in its apology for weakness, and in the converse of its apparent defiance of Western vitality. Unaffected in any important interest by any such nostalgia or defiance, Westerners take note of it, if at all, as a strange human curiosity, momentarily wondering at the psychological frame of mind in others that calls for hatred and cursing. And indeed it is a morbid symptom that does harm only to those who might otherwise be working for a rational order. What part Islam would finally have in any putative rational order is something a Muslim philosopher has yet to define with authority.

Until such time as the restraining circle is breached, the Arab approach to the modern world must peter out in inadequacy and frustration. The very defensiveness has an obvious and intimate connection with positive envy and temptation. Such envy and temptation have been manifest since Western societies first made their thrust felt in the Arab world. Goods and services, above all arms and armaments, continue to be sucked greedily from the West into the Arab collectivity. Since the days of Selim III and Muhammad Ali, apparent modernization of this type has only been a façade, for in reality the absolute despot thereby acquires ever more efficient means of control and power holding on the one hand, and on the other of circumventing challengers and the mob. As usual, the collectivity still divides as power holder and challenger come to a test of strength, after which it settles for a breathing space until the next man steps forward with ambitions to seize the state and its treasury. Conspiracy, manipulation, and deception of opinion at home and abroad are still the requisite skills of pretenders to power, with exile and death as the fate of losers.

There can be no conception of loyal opposition. To compromise is only to search for advantage by other means. Entire countries are as erratic as their rulers. But thanks to imported arms and communications, the price paid by the masses for these practices is each time costlier and more bloody, ripping away and canceling material progress that has been made, as in Lebanon bringing civilized life to a standstill. Military despotism, pure and simple, is the looming prospect, or the rule of whoever is brutal enough to put a final stop to all ambitions except his own. Consumerism, like colonialism before it, has been able to do no more than decorate (or degrade) the exterior of the Arab collectivity, in a style reminiscent of those expensive but joyous trappings once observed by Walter Harris at the court of Sultan Abdul Aziz in Morocco, the grand pianos and kitchen ranges, the steam launches and false hair and fireworks.

Westerners habitually and ignorantly misconceive the responses they are likely to encounter from the Arabs, unsuitably and even laughably projecting their own political and moral attitudes where these cannot apply. Since the Suez campaign of 1956, there have been several Western expeditionary forces in the Middle East, for instance in the attempt to free American embassy personnel held hostage in Teheran in 1979, in Lebanon in October 1983, and in the Gulf in 1987. Depending on the interests at stake, either such entry into the Middle East should be avoided altogether for the sake of the shame-based hostility it will trigger, or it must be undertaken with inflexible determination to use whatever degree of force is required for supreme arbitration. In Lebanon in 1983, a terrorist sponsored by Syria or Iran drove a truck packed with explosives into a barracks, killing 200 American marines. To abandon Lebanon as a result was a response comprehensible as pragmatic to an electorate, but which in the Islamocentric perspective looks quite different, a shaming of the entire West and an honor to the anonymous terrorist whose bomb, however freakishly, proved to be strong enough for supreme arbitration. As a Western democracy unable by reason of geography to extricate itself from the Arab collectivity, Israel is in a similar predicament, routinely obliged to arbitrate by force while fruitlessly pleading for democratic procedures of compromise and civility to resolve a conflict that would be redundant, indeed would never have assumed its historic form, if such procedures had been available in the first place.

Apparently busy as sponsors and clients, the Arabs are in reality stalemated in intentions and ambitions and rivalries that duplicate, neutralize, and finally oppose one another. A distribution of the once-and-for-all oil wealth follows, but so random that it is often indistinguishable from wastage. How Arabs choose to organize their affairs is naturally their business. For an outsider to prescribe some alternative is vain—even a tentative recommendation of democracy, for example, is evidently Eurocentric as well as wishful in the context. Neither self-confidence nor a scientific outlook can be dispensed. At present, an Arab democrat is not even an idealization, but a contradiction in terms. In the absence of institutions in which otherwise exclusive tribal and religious identities may all partake, however, and pending the introduction of pluralism in whatever form may be suitable, the Arab masses must remain uninvolved in influencing their own fate, unable to exercise the element of choice without which there is neither creativity nor true independence, nor even a genuine nation. In the first instance, the Arabs are the losers, a danger to themselves, dropping out of the making of history, but beyond that the rest of the world is deprived of what ought to be the valuable contribution of these people.

Source Notes

References have been omitted in instances where quotations typify a speaker or a point of view. In addition to the sources cited, I have included a selection of standard works to which I am indebted. For quotations from books with foreign-language titles, the translations are my own.

Introduction

3   "The national movement is . . ." Abd al-Rahman al-Bazzaz, quoted in Sylvia G. Haim, ed., *Arab Nationalism* (Berkeley and Los Angeles: University of California Press, 1976), p. 184.

4   "Give me five years . . ." Husni Zaim, quoted in Eliezer Be'eri, *Army Officers in Arab Politics and Society* (London: Pall Mall Press, 1970), p. 59.

4   "Nationalism Is . . ." Michel Aflaq, quoted in Sylvia G. Haim, ed., *Arab Nationalism*, pp. 242–243.

5   "When I am asked . . ." Michel Aflaq, quoted in Bassam Tibi, *Arab Nationalism* (London: Macmillan, 1981), p. 175.

5   "Almost everyone . . ." "Liberalism is . . ." Jacques Berque, *The Arabs* (London: Faber & Faber, 1964), p. 280; p. 95.

6   "Arab annual per capita income . . ." Samir Amin, *The Arab Economy Today* (London: Zed Books, 1982), p. 41; p. 60.

10   ". . . has been the most important . . ." Abdel Raouf El Reedy, "New Opportunities for Peace in the Middle East" in *Annals of the American Academy of Political and Social Science*, Vol. 482, November 1985, p. 12.

11   The Security Forces . . . Said K. Aburish, *Pay-Off* (London: Unwin, 1985), p. 79.

12   "In Tripoli on December 18 . . ." *Middle East and Mediterranean Outlook* (MEMO), No 37, February 1987, p. 1.

12   "Fifty-seven boxes . . ." *Observer,* 15 March 1987.

12   "There was never . . ." Kamal Zaki Mostapha, quoted in *Observer,* 19 October 1986.

13   "Kuwait's State Security Court . . ." *Arab Times,* 19–20 February 1987, p. 4.

13   "This means that . . ." Saif Ali Al-Jarwan, quoted in *Arab Times,* 19–20 February 1987, p. 6.

14   "The long winter . . ." Abdallah Laroui, *The Crisis of the Arab Intellectual* (Berkeley and Los Angeles: University of California Press, 1976), p. 177.

14   "The chaos of . . ." Malek Bennabi, *Vocation de l'Islam* (Paris: Editions du Seuil, 1954), p. 68.

14   "From the Arab Gulf to . . ." Jabra Ibrahim Jabra, quoted in Roger Allen, *The Arabic Novel* (Manchester: University of Manchester Press, 1982), p. 50.

14   ". . . a chronicle of . . ." Fouad Ajami, *The Arab Predicament* (Cambridge: Cambridge University Press, 1985), p. 4.

14   ". . . sons of a bitch . . ." Khalid Kishtainy, *Independent,* 23 February 1987.

16   ". . . really believe in their . . ." Morroe Berger, *The Arab World Today* (London: Weidenfeld & Nicolson, 1962), p. 388.

16   "In plain words . . ." Frantz Fanon, *The Wretched of the Earth* (New York: Grove Press, 1968), p. 97.

16   ". . . to manage as best . . ." Mouloud Feraoun, quoted in Alistair Horne, *A Savage War of Peace* (Harmondsworth, Middlesex: Penguin Books, 1985), p. 507.

16   "In those days . . ." Al-Hajj Muhammad, quoted in Henry Munson, Jr., ed., *The House of Si Abd Allah* (New Haven: Yale University Press, 1982), p. 21.

17   "For all the indisputable diversity . . ." Ernest Gellner, *Muslim Society* (Cambridge: Cambridge University Press, 1981), p. 99.

18   ". . . the Governmental System . . ." *Traveller's Guide to Yemen* (Sana'a: North Yemen Tourist Company, n.d.), p. 5.

18   ". . . a people's democratic republic . . ." *Iraq, A Tourist Guide* (Baghdad: State Organisation for Tourism, 1982), p. 20.

1: Tribal Society and Its Legacy

22   ". . . by which groups constrain . . ." Ernest Gellner, "Cohesion and Identity" in *Muslim Society,* p. 97.

22   "Once victory . . ." Jacob Black-Michaud, *Cohesive Force: Feud in the Mediterranean and the Middle East* (Oxford: Blackwell, 1975), p. 26.

22   "What fools you . . ." Isabel Burton, *The Inner Life of Syria, Palestine and the Holy Land* (London, 1876), Vol. I, pp. 323–326.

23   "There are many ways . . ." Om Naeema, quoted in Nayra Atiya, ed., *Khul-Khaal* (Cairo: American University in Cairo Press, 1984), p. 149.

23   "A Syrian tried . . ." Kamal S. Salibi, *Crossroads to Civil War: Lebanon 1958–1976* (London: Ithaca Press, 1976), p. 122.

25   "The fabric of life . . ." Andrea B. Rugh, *Family in Contemporary Egypt* (Cairo: American University in Cairo Press, 1985), p. 167.

26   "We are all members . . ." John Waterbury, *Commander of the Faithful* (London: Weidenfeld & Nicolson, 1970), p. 123.

27   "The family is . . ." Pierre Bourdieu, *The Algerians* (Boston: Beacon Press, 1962), quoted in John F. Entelis, *Algeria: The Revolution Institutionalized* (Boulder: Westview Press, 1986), p. 71.

27   "When faced with . . ." Hisham Sharabi and Mukhtar Ani, "Impact of Class and Culture on Social Behaviour" in L. Carl Brown and N. Itzkowitz, eds., *Psychological Dimensions of Near Eastern Studies* (Princeton, N.J.: Darwin Press, 1977), p. 244; p. 255.

29   "There are no parliaments . . ." Bernard Lewis, "Communism and Islam" in Walter Laqueur, ed., *The Middle East in Transition* (London: Routledge & Kegan Paul, 1958), pp. 318–319.

30   "They hate one another . . ." Isabel Burton, *The Inner Life* Vol. I, pp. 105–106.

30   "But they will remain Saar . . ." P. S. Allfree, *Hawks of the Hadhramaut* (London: Robert Hale, 1967), p. 192.

31   "The Ruler of Bahrain . . ." David Holden, *Farewell to Arabia* (London: Faber & Faber, 1966), p. 159.

31   "Kuwaitis think . . ." Sheikh Hafiz Wahba, *Arabian Days* (London: Arthur Barker, 1964), p. 12.

31   "The Palestinians loathe . . ." Said Aburish, *Pay-Off*, p. 8.

31   "Then one night . . ." Sir Edwin Pears, *Turkey and Its People* (London: 1911), p. 39.

32   "It's a Babi-killing! . . ." Mohammad Ali Jamalzadeh, *Isfahan Is Half the World* (Princeton, N.J.: Princeton University Press, 1983), pp. 56–57.

32   "Because he used to play . . ." Alistair Horne, *A Savage War*, p. 135.

32   "Atrocious crimes . . ." Gilles Kepel, *The Prophet and Pharoah* (London: Al Saqi Books, 1985), p. 166.

32   "Such deeds, such certainties . . ." For a general account from an anthropological viewpoint, see Daniel G. Bates and Amal Rassam, *Peoples and Cultures of the Middle East* (Englewood Cliffs, N.J.: Prentice-Hall, 1983).

2: Shame and Honor

34   ". . . the heaviest chains . . ." Ernest Renan, *L'Islam et la science* (Paris, 1883), quoted in Elie Kedourie, *Afghani and Abduh* (London: Cass, 1966), p. 43.

36   "To an Arab, honor . . ." Mansour Khalid, "The Sociocultural Determinants of Arab Diplomacy" in George N. Atiyeh, ed., *Arab and American Cultures* (Washington, D.C.: American Enterprise Institute for Public Policy Research, 1977), p. 128.

36   "It is shameful . . ." Al-Hajj Muhammad, quoted in Henry Munson Jr., ed., *The House of Si Abd Allah*, p. 79.

37   "The world of the Arab . . ." Khalid Kishtainy, *Arab Political Humour* (London: Quartet Books, 1985), p. 113.

37   ". . . raised his voice . . ." Suda, quoted in Nayra Atiya, ed., *Khul-Khaal,* pp. 56–86.

38   ". . . the exact definition . . ." Leonardo Sciascia, quoted in John Haycraft, *Italian Labyrinth* (Harmondsworth, Middlesex: Penguin Books, 1986), p. 119.

38   ". . . no dishonor attaches to . . ." Pierre Bourdieu, "The Sentiment of Honour in Kabyle Society" in J. G. Peristiany, ed., *Honour and Shame: The Values of Mediterranean Society* (Chicago: University of Chicago Press, 1966), pp. 228–229.

38   "Everyone knew I'd killed . . ." Patrick Meney, *Même les tueurs ont une mère* (Paris: La Table Ronde, 1986), p. 124.

39   In Syria between 1946 and 1958 . . . Gordon H. Torrey, "Aspects of the Political Elite in Syria" in George Lenczowski, ed., *Political Elites in the Middle East* (Washington, D.C.: American Enterprise Institute for Public Policy Research, 1975), p. 154.

39   In Iraq . . . Phebe A. Marr, "The Political Elite in Iraq," ibid., p. 109.

39   "There are 40 national elite families . . ." James A. Bill, ibid., p. 33.

39   ". . . the ruling elite of contemporary Morocco . . ." John Waterbury, *Commander of the Faithful,* p. 86.

39   "Every sultan had . . ." Salah Khalaf, "Changing forms of political patronage in Lebanon" in Ernest Gellner and John Waterbury, eds., *Patrons and Clients in Mediterranean Societies* (London: Duckworth, in association with the Center for Mediterranean Studies of the American Universities Field Staff, 1977), p. 200.

42   "In many respects . . ." Lucie Duff Gordon, *Letters from Egypt* (London: Virago Press, 1983), p. 140.

42   "The Moors are children . . ." Sir John Drummond Hay, quoted in Douglas Porch, *The Conquest of Morocco* (London: Cape, 1986), p. 32.

42   "The narrowness of his experience . . ." James Bruce Mayfield, *Rural Politics in Nasser's Egypt* (Austin: University of Texas Press, 1971), p. 73.

42   "What sparked off . . ." Tewfik el-Hakim, *Un Substitut de campagne en Egypte* (Paris: Plon, 1974 and 1982), p. 168. The English version of 1947 is less widely available.

42   ". . . techniques of fear . . ." Hamad Ammar, *Growing Up in an Egyptian Village* (London: Routledge & Kegan Paul; International Library of Sociology, 1954), pp. 42–43.

43   "Society persecuted us . . ." Sami al-Jundi, quoted in Elie Kedourie, *Arabic Political Memoirs* (London: Cass, 1974), p. 200.

43   "What is produced . . ." Unni Wiken, *Life Among the Poor in Cairo* (London: Tavistock Publications, 1980), p. 143.

43   "He mercilessly tyrannizes . . ." Piot Bey, *Causerie ethnographique sur le fellah*

(Paris, 1900), p. 34, quoted in Gabriel Baer, *Studies in the Social History of Modern Egypt* (Chicago: University of Chicago Press, 1969), p. 93.

43 "It was quite normal . . ." Salama Musa, *The Education of Salama Musa* (Brill: Leiden, 1961), p. 7.

44 ". . . a man's adopted 'mask' in the end . . ." Haig Khatchadourian, "The Mask and the Face: a study of make-believe in Middle Eastern society," *Middle East Forum*, Vol. 37, 1961, pp. 15–18.

44 "But they are slaves . . ." Jean-Pierre Péroncel-Hugoz, *Le Radeau de Mahomet* (Paris: Flammarion, 1984), p. 88.

44 "The green band . . ." Michael Gilsenan, *Recognising Islam* (London: Croom Helm, 1982), p. 9 ff.

45 "Arab psychology is . . ." Kenneth Pendar, *Adventure in Diplomacy* (New York: Dodd, Mead and Co., 1945), p. 38.

46 ". . . at once oblique . . ." Henry Kissinger, *Years of Upheaval,* pp. 658–659, quoted in Daniel Pipes, *In the Path of God* (New York: Basic Books, 1983), p. 303.

46 "People who believe . . ." Abd al-Mohsin Fadlallah, quoted in London *Times,* 4 March 1987.

48 ". . . the universal appearance of . . ." C.-F. Volney, *Travels in Egypt and Syria* (English translation 1787), Vol. I, p. 188.

48 "Cairo is apocalyptic . . ." Sami Nair, *Le Caire* (Paris: Denoël, 1986), p. 15.

48 ". . . divided into four quarters . . ." W. G. Palgrave, *Narrative of a Year's Journey through Central and Eastern Arabia 1862–3* (London, 1865), Vol. I, pp. 392–393.

48 ". . . another English rolling-stone" Trevor Mostyn, *Coming of Age in the Middle East* (London: KPI, 1987), pp. 72–73.

49 ". . . junkyards of rotting automobiles . . ." Seymour Gray, *Beyond the Veil. The Adventures of an American Doctor in Saudi Arabia* (New York: Harper & Row, 1983), p. 151.

50 "After a revolution . . ." Ihab Hassan, *Out of Egypt* (Carbondale: Southern Illinois University Press, 1986), p. 14.

50 "Egypt, Iraq, Morocco and . . ." Saad Eddin Ibrahim, "Urbanisation in the Arab World" in Nicholas S. Hopkins and Saad Eddin Ibrahim, eds., *Arab Society* (Cairo: American University in Cairo Press, 1985), p. 133.

52 "This increase in scientific and . . ." Richard Critchfield, *Shahhat* (Cairo: American University in Cairo Press, 1982), p. xiii.

52 "There are no doctors . . ." P. W. Harrison, *The Arab at Home* (London: Hutchinson, 1925), p. 306 ff.

53 ". . . largely failed to . . ." James Bruce Mayfield, *Rural Politics,* p. 184.

53 "Pictures of dirt . . ." Ian Young, *The private life of Islam* (London: Allen Lane, 1974), p. 50.

54 "He shook me . . ." ibid., p. 120.

54 "How it pained him . . ." ibid., p. 121.

54 "Illiteracy is . . ." Samuel M. Zwemer, *Childhood in the Moslem World* (New York: Revell, 1915), p. 33.

55 "In the last few years . . ." Charles Issawi, *An Economic History of the Middle East* (London: Methuen, 1982), p. 114.

55 ". . . around a trillion dollars" A. B. Zahlan, *Science and Science Policy in the Arab World* (London: Croom Helm, 1981), p. 127.

55 "What will become of . . ." Ismail Kemal Bey, *Memoirs* (London: Constable, 1920), p. 57.

55 "And what will happen if he stays here?" Zia Gokalp, see Uriel Heyd, *Foundations of Turkish Nationalism* (London: Luzac & The Harvill Press, 1950), p. 22.

55 "If I educate my sons . . ." Hugh Boustead, *The Wind of Morning* (London: Chatto & Windus, 1971), p. 119.

56 ". . . contact between the two cultures . . ." Malcolm H. Kerr, "Egypt" in James S. Coleman, ed. *Education and Political Development,* quoted in Mahmud Faksh, "The Consequences of the Introduction and Spread of Modern Education" in Elie Kedourie and Sylvia G. Haim, eds., *Modern Egypt: Studies in Politics and Society* (London: Cass, 1980), p. 43. ". . . it would be safe . . ." ibid. p. 52.

57 ". . . the mannerisms of modern life . . ." Kepel, *Prophet and Pharoah,* p. 235.

3: Western Approaches

58 "Original scientific ideas . . ." Kurt Mendelssohn, *Science and Western Domination* (London: Thames & Hudson, 1976), p. 18.

59 "The practice of the arts . . ." Ibn Khaldun, quoted in Alfred Bonné, *State and Economics in the Middle East* (London: Routledge & Kegan Paul; International Library of Sociology, 1948), p. 227.

59 "Philosophical thought . . ." Ibn Khaldun, quoted in Daniel Pipes, *Path of God,* p. 81.

60 "Caravan of the Grand Signor to Mecca," Paris, *Bulletin de la Société d'histoire de l'art français,* 1962.

61 "We are meditating . . ." quoted in Stanford J. Shaw, *Between Old and New. The Ottoman Empire Under Sultan Selim III, 1789–1807* (Cambridge, Mass.: Harvard University Press, 1971), pp. 15–16.

62 "But a few months ago . . ." James Morier, *The Adventures of Hajji Baba of Isfahan* (London, 1824), LXXIV.

63 For al-Jabarti, see Ibrahim Abu-Lughod, *Arab Rediscovery of Europe* (Princeton, N.J.: Princeton University Press, 1963), p. 21.

63 For Hassan al-Attar, see Afaf Lutfi al-Sayyid Marsot, "The Beginnings of Modernization among the Rectors of al-Azhar, 1798–1879" in William R. Polk and Richard L. Chambers, eds., *Beginnings of Modernization in the Middle East* (Chicago: University of Chicago Press, 1968), pp. 269–270.

63 "We longed for you . . ." quoted in Jamal Mohammad Ahmed, *The Intellec-*

tual Origins of Egyptian Nationalism (London: Oxford University Press, 1960), p. 94.

63 ". . . almost as a demi-god" Gustave Flaubert, Francis Steegmuller, ed., *Flaubert in Egypt* (London: Michael Haag, 1983), p. 82.

64 "I came to . . ." Muhammad Ali, quoted in Consul-General John Barker, *Syria and Egypt Under the Last Five Sultans of Turkey* (London, 1876), Vol. II, p. 48.

64 "I collected all power . . ." Muhammad Ali, quoted in Mayfield, *Rural Politics*, p. 27.

64 "The Fellah is an animal . . ." Nassau Senior, *Conversations and Journals in Egypt and Malta* (London, 1882), Vol. I, p. 273.

65 ". . . a system reminiscent of . . ." Charles Issawi, *An Economic History*, p. 19.

65 ". . . inflicted terrible or . . ." Nada Tomiche, "The Situation of Egyptian Women in the First Half of the Nineteenth Century" in William R. Polk and Richard L. Chambers, eds., *Beginnings of Modernization*, p. 181.

67 ". . . could not but lament . . ." E. W. Lane, *Manners and Customs of the Modern Egyptians* (London, 1908), p. 25.

68 "Do not borrow from . . ." Prince Metternich, quoted in Niyazi Berkes, *The Development of Secularism in Turkey* (Montreal: McGill University Press, 1964), pp. 148–149.

68 "I want to see the Porte . . ." Stratford Canning, quoted in Lee Gerald Byrne, *The Great Ambassador* (Cleveland: Ohio State University Press, 1964), p. 136.

68 ". . . the filth is not to be imagined . . ." Ian H. C. Fraser, *The Heir of Parham: Robert Curzon* (Harleston, Norfolk: Paradigm Press, 1986), p. 105.

69 "Two of the major-generals . . ." Helmut von Moltke, quoted in Eliezer Be'eri, *Army Officers*, p. 302.

70 ". . . hating them particularly . . ." Adolphus Slade, *Turkey, Greece and Malta* (London, 1837), Vol. I, p. 470.

70 ". . . trying to acquire . . ." Armin Vambéry, *Life and Adventures* (London, 1884), pp. 20–21.

70 For general accounts of the impact of European technology at the time, see Daniel R. Headrick, *The Tools of Empire* (New York: Oxford University Press, 1981); Roger Owen, *The Middle East in the World Economy* (London: Methuen, 1981).

71 For a general account of cultural interaction between Muslims and Christians at the time, see Bernard Lewis, *The Muslim Discovery of Europe* (London: Weidenfeld & Nicolson, 1982).

72 "I have only to repeat . . ." George Sadlier, quoted in Kathryn Tidrick, *Heart-Beguiling Araby* (Cambridge: Cambridge University Press, 1981), p. 38.

74 "Any Muslim who revolts . . ." Emir Abdel-Kader, quoted in Robert Montagnon, *La Conquête de l'Algérie* (Paris: Editions Pygmalion, 1986), p. 219.

74   "The native Muslim is French . . ." ibid., p. 396.

75   "O my God! . . ." ibid., p. 98.

75   ". . . barbarian state . . ." "the high-pitched antagonism . . ." Shlomo
       Avineri, ed., *Karl Marx on Colonialism and Modernization* (New York: Double-
       day, 1968), p. 43; p. 398.

76   "Tanyus Shahin gathered . . ." quoted in Kamal S. Salibi, *The Modern History
       of Lebanon* (London: Weidenfeld & Nicolson, 1965), p. 86.

77   "Ahmed wanted so much . . ." L. C. Brown, *The Tunisia of Ahmed Bey,
       1837–1855* (Princeton, N.J.: Princeton University Press, 1974), p. 315.

79   "They each exhausted their body . . ." Prisse d'Avennes, quoted in Anouar
       Louca, *Voyageurs et écrivains égyptiens en France au XIXe siècle* (Paris: Didier,
       1970), p. 80.

79   ". . . favouritism in promotion . . ." James A. Field Jr., *America and the
       Mediterranean World, 1776–1882* (Princeton, N.J.: Princeton University
       Press, 1969), p. 396.

82   For Celebi Mehmed, see Bernard Lewis, *The Muslim Discovery,* pp. 114–116,
       pp. 239–242; for Sadik Rifat Pasha, see Bernard Lewis, *The Emergence of
       Modern Turkey* (London: Oxford University Press, 1961), p. 129.

82   For Rifaa al-Tahtawi, see C. Ernest Dawn, *From Ottomanism to Arabism: Essays
       on the Origins of Arab Nationalism* (Urbana: University of Illinois Press, 1973),
       p. 123 *ff.*

82   ". . . had no channel . . ." al-Tahtawi, quoted in John J. Donohue and John
       L. Esposito, eds., *Islam in Transition* (New York: Oxford University Press,
       1982), pp. 12–13.

82   ". . . that the secret of . . ." Albert Hourani, *Arabic Thought in the Liberal Age,
       1798–1962* (Cambridge: Cambridge University Press, 1984), p. 82.

83   "Here we found a judge . . ." Assad Khayat, *A Voice from Lebanon* (London,
       1847), p. 123. On the title page the name has been transcribed as Assaad
       Y. Kayat.

83   ". . . but he must not try . . ." ibid., p. 410.

83   For Muhammad Bin Diyaf, see L. C. Brown, *The Tunisia of Ahmed Bey,* p. 331.

83   For Shah Nasir al-Din, see *Diary During Tour Through Europe, 1873* (London,
       1874), and *Diary During His Journey to Europe, 1878* (London, 1879).

84   For Khayr Ed-Din, see his *Mémoire de ma vie privée et politique* (Revue Tuni-
       sienne, 1934), and *The Surest Path,* trans. L. C. Brown (Cambridge, Mass.:
       Harvard University Press, 1967).

84   "I also assert . . ." Khayr Ed-Din, *The Surest Path,* p. 178.

85   "How can you assemble . . ." quoted in N. Berkes, *Development of Secularism,*
       p. 227.

85   "I maintained that . . ." Ismail Kemal Bey, *Memoirs,* p. 137.

85   Midhat Pasha, "The Past, Present, and Future of Turkey," in *The Nineteenth
       Century,* June 1878, p. 985; p. 992.

87   For Afghani in general, see Nikki R. Keddie, *Sayyid Jamal ad-Din "al-Afg-*

hani" (Berkeley and Los Angeles: University of California Press, 1972), and Elie Kedourie, *Afghani and Abduh* (London: Cass, 1966).

87 "It is amazing that . . ." quoted in Be'eri, *Army Officers*, p. 6.

87 "The Europeans have now . . ." Afghani, quoted in John J. Donohue and John L. Esposito, eds., *Islam in Transition*, p. 17.

88 "Here a white dog . . ." C. Snouck Hurgronje, *Makka in the Latter Part of the 19th century*, trans. J. H. Monahan (Brill: Leiden and Luzac of London, 1931), p. 185.

89 "How Can the East be True to Itself?" Abdallah al-Nadim, quoted in Anwar Abdel Malek, ed., *Contemporary Arab Political Thought* (London: Zed Books, 1983), pp. 89–92.

90 "Look at Morocco . . ." Mehmed Akif, quoted in N. Berkes, *Development of Secularism*, p. 343.

90 "We were defeated . . ." Zia Gokalp, quoted in Uriel Heyd, *Turkish Nationalism*, p. 79.

90 "This talk of Oriental culture . . ." Husseyin Cahit, quoted in N. Berkes, *Development of Secularism*, p. 298.

4: The Consequences of Careerism

92 "No Turk dare associate . . ." Sir Charles Eliot, *Turkey in Europe* (London, 1908), pp. 138–39.

94 "The contractor bribed the Minister . . ." Earl of Cromer, *Modern Egypt* (London, 1907), Vol. II, p. 421.

95 "Disorder has reached . . ." Pierre de Vaucelles, *La vie en Iraq il y a un siècle* (Paris: Editions A. Pedone, 1963), pp. 23–24.

95 "To get paid . . ." Unni Wiken, *Life Among the Poor*, p. 160.

96 "We do not want to make enemies . . ." Desmond Stewart and John Haylock, *New Babylon: A Portrait of Iraq* (London: Collins, 1956), p. 201.

96 "You are not going to waste . . ." Tewfik el-Hakim, *Un Substitut*, p. 247.

96 "X, Y and Z are prominent . . ." John Waterbury, "Endemic and Planned Corruption in a Monarchical Regime," *World Politics*, Vol. XXV, October 1972–July 1973, p. 544.

97 "There are even civil servants . . ." Abdelaziz Dahmani, *Jeune Afrique*, 12 March 1986, p. 51.

97 "It is more or less the same . . ." Louis Awad, "Freedom and Ideology," *MESA Bulletin*, Vol. 18, No. I, July 1984, pp. 11–21.

97 "This sort of popular release . . ." Kepel, *Prophet and Pharoah*, pp. 232–233.

98 ". . . no matter what the minister says . . ." William Golding, *An Egyptian Journal* (London: Faber & Faber, 1985), p. 179.

99 "If it's a question of . . ." quoted in Neville J. Mandel, *The Arabs and Zionism before World War I* (Berkeley and Los Angeles: University of California Press, 1980), p. 19.

99 "We spend it on . . ." Roger Owen, *Middle East in World Economy*, p. 19.

100   "Gaddhafi: 'If we are faced . . .'" quoted in Mohamed Heikal, *The Road to Ramadan* (London: Collins, 1975), p. 100.

103   "The Arabs are always the same . . ." Burhan Cahit, quoted in Andrew Mango, "Turkey and the Middle East" in Walter Laqueur, ed., *Middle East in Transition*, p. 188.

105   "The form of initiation . . ." Charles Roden Buxton, *Turkey in Revolution* (London, 1909), pp. 45–47.

106   "The Khedive and Mustafa Kamil . . ." Afaf Lutfi al-Sayyid, *Egypt and Cromer: A Study in Anglo-Egyptian Relations* (London: John Murray, 1968), p. 186.

106   "Nationalism is a sentiment . . ." Mustafa Kamil, quoted in Nadav Safran, *Egypt in Search of Political Community* (Cambridge, Mass: Harvard University Press, 1961), p. 87.

107   "No truly patriotic Egyptian . . ." from "Open Letter to the Khedive" 26 May 1907, quoted in ibid. p. 89.

107   ". . . an atmosphere of . . ." in Abu Khaldun Sati al-Husri, *Three Reformers*, (Beirut: Khayats, 1966), p. 58.

108   "Only 126 men . . ." C. Ernest Dawn, *From Ottomanism to Arabism*, p. 152.

110   "In Mecca, below his Palace . . ." Laurence Grafftey-Smith, *Bright Levant* (London: John Murray, 1970), p. 157.

111   "We know not the practical way . . ." Richard P. Mitchell, *The Society of the Muslim Brothers* (London: Oxford University Press, 1969), p. 8.

111   "At last it has become clear . . ." Nadav Safran, *Egypt in Search*, p. 235.

111   "The Western way of life . . ." John L. Donohue and John L. Esposito, eds., *Islam in Transition*, p. 79.

112   "To the honourable Iraqi people . . ." quoted in Majid Khadduri, *Republican Iraq* (London: Oxford University Press, 1969), p. 130.

113   "At 09.15 today . . ." British Broadcasting Corporation Summary of World Broadcasts (abbreviated to BBC in future references) ME/7961/A/2, 27 May 1985.

113   ". . . people who had infiltrated . . ." Fuad Matar, *Saddam Hussein, The Man, the Cause and the Future* (London: Third World Centre, 1981), p. 61.

113   "A group of people . . ." Ayatollah Khomeini, *Islam and Revolution* (Berkeley, Ca.: Mizan Press, 1981), p. 126.

114   ". . . a limited liability company . . ." Nasser, quoted in Mayfield, *Rural Politics*, p. 103.

115   "Soon after that, my uncle . . ." Fawaz Turki, *The Disinherited* (London and New York: Monthly Review Press, 1972), pp. 83–84

116   "To my brothers, the sons of . . ." Mohammed Neguib, *Egypt's Destiny* (London: Gollancz, 1955), p. 120.

116   "Egypt was now . . ." "We have not been beaten . . ." ". . . the family of traitors . . ." Nasser, quoted in P. J. Vatikiotis, *Nasser and His Generation* (London: Croom Helm, 1978), p. 276; p. 341; p. 281.

116   "Bourguiba is a traitor . . ." Ahmed Shuqairi, quoted in Cecil Hourani, *An Unfinished Odyssey* (London: Weidenfeld & Nicolson, 1984), p. 89.

117 "Our sister is betraying us . . ." Mostyn, *Coming of Age*, p. 65.

117 "The traitors opened fire . . ." London *Times*, 22 June 1987.

117 "As to the existence in Syria . . ." Abdul Karim Qassem, "Objectives of Iraq's Revolution" (Baghdad: Iraqi Ministry of Guidance, n.d.), quoted in George Lenczowski, ed., *The political awakening in the Middle East* (Englewood Cliffs, New Jersey: Prentice-Hall, 1970), p. 156.

119 ". . . a very peaceful . . ." Peter Clark, *Marmaduke Pickthall: British Muslim* (London: Quartet Books, 1986), p. 25.

119 "A long enslaved nation . . ." Cromer, *Modern Egypt*, Vol. I, p. 343.

119 "The Orient needs a despot . . ." Muhammad Abdu, quoted in Anwar Abdel Malek, ed., *Contemporary Arab Political Thought*, p. 40.

120 "We felt in our souls . . ." Hifni Bey Nasif, quoted in C. C. Adams, *Islam and Modernism in Egypt* (London: Oxford University Press, 1933), p. 212.

120 "The novelty of the procedure . . ." Majid Khadduri, *Independent Iraq, 1932-1958* (London: Oxford University Press, 1960), p. 93.

120 "There is an almost nostalgic . . ." Majid Khadduri, "The Army Officer: His Role in Middle Eastern Politics" in S. N. Fisher, ed., *Social Forces in the Middle East* (Ithaca: Cornell University Press, 1955), p. 163.

120 "Arabs yearn for . . ." Majid Khadduri, *Arab Contemporaries* (Baltimore: The Johns Hopkins University Press, 1973), p. 231.

120 ". . . the honest governor . . ." Khalid Muhammad Khalid, *From Here We Start* (Washington, D.C.: American Council of Learned Societies, 1953), p. 102.

120 "The Worshipped One! . . ." Tewfik el-Hakim, quoted in Safran, *Egypt in Search*, p. 147.

120 ". . . who would glow with defiance . . ." Halim Barakat, *Days of Dust* (Washington, D.C.: Three Continents Press, 1983), p. 27.

120 "We had called for . . ." Anwar Sadat, *In Search of Identity* (London: Collins, 1978), p. 84.

120 "I would have a sword . . ." Daniel Lerner, *The Passing of Traditional Society* (New York: Free Press, 1964), p. 282.

121 "What system?" Habib Bourguiba, quoted in John F. Entelis, *Comparative Politics of North Africa* (Syracuse, New York: Syracuse University Press, 1980), p. 127.

121 "Pluralism for us . . ." Hedi Nouira, quoted in Lisa Anderson, *The State and Social Transformation in Tunisia and Libya, 1830-1980* (Princeton, N.J.: Princeton University Press, 1986), p. 243.

5: Men and Women

123 "I think it is a form of . . ." Mai Yamani, London *Times*, 15 August 1986.

123 "Two little girls watched . . ." Margaret Luce, *From Aden to the Gulf* (Wilton, Salisbury: Michael Russell, 1987), p. 127.

123 "I wouldn't play . . ." Djanet Lachmet, *Lallia* (Manchester: Carcanet Press, 1987), p. 40.

125 For Hindal, see Zahra Freeth, *Kuwait was My Home* (London: Allen & Unwin, 1956), p. 135.

125 For Fajar Salem al-Sabah, see *Daily Mail,* 4 September 1987.

125 ". . . marriage means you are establishing . . ." Ommohamad, quoted in Critchfield, *Shahhat,* pp. 29–31.

125 "My mother had tried . . ." Ibrahim Souss, *Loin de Jérusalem* (Paris: Editions Liana Levi, 1987), p. 11.

126 ". . . in Arab society love must always be restrained . . ." Abdelwahab Bouhdiba, *La Sexualité en Islam* (Paris: Presses Universitaires de France, 1975), p. 140 *ff.* The English translation, *Islam and Sexuality* (London: Routledge & Kegan Paul, 1985), appears less readily available.

126 ". . . the norms of buying . . ." Nawal el Saadawi, *The Hidden Face of Eve: Women in the Arab World* (London: Zed Press, 1980), p. 78.

126 "Arranging marriages is . . ." Hildred Geertz, quoted in Dale F. Eickelmann, *The Middle East: An Anthropological Approach* (Englewood Cliffs, N.J.: Prentice Hall, 1981), p. 124.

126 "Marriage today in my opinion . . ." Ghadah al-Samman, in Elizabeth Warnock Fernea and Basima Qattan Bezirgan, eds., *Middle Eastern Muslim Women Speak* (Austin: University of Texas Press, 1977), pp. 395–96.

127 "The Gaza Strip's oldest resident . . ." *Jerusalem Post,* 31 January 1987.

127 "Forty-year-old Salem Jemaa Mabruk . . ." *Independent,* 1 December 1986.

127 "The Moroccan woman . . ." Al-Hajj Muhammad, quoted in Henry Munson, Jr., ed., *The House of Si Abd Allah,* p. 90.

127 Abdelwahab Bouhdiba quotes an Egyptian colleague . . .: see his "Child and Mother in Arab-Muslim Society," in L. C. Brown and N. Itzkowitz, eds., *Psychological Dimensions,* p. 135; and his *La Sexualité en Islam,* p. 112; p. 273.

127 "Nothing can equal the disgrace . . ." Khalid Kishtainy, *Arab Political Humour,* p. 139.

128 "An 85-year-old merchant . . ." *Independent,* 11 January 1988.

128 "Before he would consent . . ." José Arnold, *Golden Swords and Pots and Pans* (London: Gollancz, 1964), p. 73.

128 "But once I arrived . . ." Unni Wiken, *Life Among the Poor,* p. 11.

128 "In such cases, sexuality . . ." Juliette Minces, *The House of Obedience* (London: Zed Press, 1982), p. 38.

129 "In most cases, a girl's parents . . ." Lois Beck and Nikki Keddie, eds., *Women in the Muslim World* (Cambridge, Mass.: Harvard University Press, 1978), p. 18.

129 "A man will think . . ." Dale F. Eickelmann, *The Middle East,* p. 181.

130 ". . . the names of 175 girls who . . ." Fadela M'Rabet, *Les Algériennes* (Paris: François Maspero, 1967), p. 88.

130 ". . . while grandmothers and . . ." Germaine Tillion, *Le Harem et les cousins* (Paris: Editions du Seuil, 1966), p. 127.

130   "It is no longer possible to . . ." Nawal el Saadawi, *The Hidden Face of Eve*, p. 1; p. 7.

130   ". . . tells of an Egyptian villager who . . ." J.-P. Péroncel-Hugoz, *Le Radeau de Mahomet*, pp. 180–182.

130   "The midwife again delved . . ." Laila Abou Saif, *A Bridge Through Time* (London: Quartet Books, 1986), p. 278.

131   "My people do this . . ." Om Gad, quoted in Nayra Atiya, ed., *Khul-Khaal*, p. 11.

131   "It is the custom . . ." Egyptian woman, quoted in Minces, *The House of Obedience*, p. 101.

131   ". . . like a vaccination . . ." Abdelwahab Bouhdiba, *La Sexualité en Islam*, pp. 225–237.

131   "Brutally and swiftly deflowering . . ." Rachid Boudjedra, *La Vie quotidienne en Algérie* (Paris: Librairie Hachette, 1971), p. 5.

131   ". . . little is known . . ." "Impotence and related problems . . ." John Racy, "Psychiatry in the Arab East" in L. C. Brown and N. Itzkowitz, eds., *Psychological Dimensions*, p. 287; p. 321.

132   ". . . to see who was the strongest . . ." Critchfield, *Shahhat*, p. 17.

132   ". . . two of my four remaining . . ." Mohammed Neguib, *Egypt's Destiny*, p. 71.

132   "We were inundated . . ." Seymour Gray, *Beyond the Veil*, p. 293.

132   "His penis won't rise . . ." Raja Shehadeh, *The Third Way* (London: Quartet Books, 1982), pp. 78–80.

133   "My grandmother . . ." "What is feared . . ." Fatima Mernissi, *Beyond the Veil: Male-Female Dynamics in Muslim Society* (London: Al Saqi Books, 1985), p. 48; p. 8.

133   "Until a radical reform is effected . . ." Sir Henry Layard, *Autobiography* (London, 1903), Vol. II, p. 101.

133   "Because of early marriage . . ." Samuel M. Zwemer, *Childhood in the Moslem World*, p. 63.

134   ". . . nothing but a legal fiction . . ." Qasim Amin, quoted in Safran, *Egypt in Search*, p. 152.

134   "Look at the eastern countries . . ." Qasim Amin, quoted in Albert Hourani, *Arabic Thought*, p. 168.

134   For Huda Shaarawi, see her *Harem Years* (London: Virago Press, 1986), ". . . intense love of country . . ." ibid. p. 84.

135   ". . . the Gulf's token Emancipated Woman . . ." Jonathan Raban, *Arabia Through the Looking-Glass* (London: Flamingo, 1979), p. 180.

136   "Paper legislation . . ." Noel Coulson and Doreen Hinchcliffe, "Women and Law Reform in Contemporary Islam" in Lois Beck and Nikki Keddie, eds., *Women in the Muslim World*, p. 49 *ff.*

136   For Salman Abu Jildan, see London *Times*, 17 June 1987.

136   "Women have an advantage . . ." Andrea B. Rugh, *Family in Contemporary Egypt*, p. 286.

6: The Turkish Example

139 "Constitution is . . ." Halide Edib, *Memoirs* (New York: Century, 1926), p. 260.

139 "A parliament! . . ." Peter Clark, *Marmaduke Pickthall*, p. 26.

140 For the Armenians, see Elie Kedourie, "Minorities" in his *The Chatham House Version* (London: Weidenfeld & Nicolson, 1970), p. 286 *ff.*

142 "After that a revolver . . ." Patrick Kinross, *Ataturk: The Rebirth of a Nation* (London: Weidenfeld & Nicolson, 1964), p. 25.

143 "I shall follow . . ." ibid., p. 187.

143 "After the Greeks . . ." Ataturk, quoted in Halide Edib, *The Turkish Ordeal* (London: John Murray, 1928), p. 355

143 ". . . a few heads . . ." N. Berkes, *Development of Secularism*, p. 450.

144 ". . . cruel, vicious . . ." H. C. Armstrong, *Grey Wolf* (London: Arthur Barker, 1932), p. 301.

144 "I don't mean to be . . ." ibid., p. 21.

144 "I don't want any . . ." Halide Edib, *The Turkish Ordeal*, p. 188.

144 ". . . an inflated and grandiose . . ." Vamik D. Volkan and Norman Itzkowitz, *The Immortal Ataturk: A Psychobiography* (Chicago and London: University of Chicago Press, 1984), p. xxiii.

144 "What does this word . . ." Kinross, *Ataturk*, p. 379.

145 "And all that will still be . . ." ibid., pp. 342–343.

145 "Gentlemen, the Turkish people . . ." ibid., p. 415.

145 "In some places . . ." ibid., p. 420.

145 ". . . a matter of pride—to look modern" Aziz Nesin, *Istanbul Boy* (Austin: University of Texas Press, 1977), Vol. I, p. 144.

146 "The suit was dark green . . ." Kinross, *Ataturk*, pp. 42–43.

147 "The platform was lined . . ." David Hotham, *The Turks* (London: John Murray, 1972), p. 36.

147 ". . . a miserable reactionary movement . . ." quoted in Safran, *Egypt in Search*, p. 243.

148 "economic and social evolution . . ." David Barchand, *Turkey and the West* (London: Chatham House Papers, No. 27, 1985), p. 89.

7: Colonialism

149 "Only force and terror . . ." Alexis de Tocqueville, "Notes du voyage en Algérie en 1841," J.-P. Mayer, ed., *Oeuvres* Vol. II, pp. 216–217, quoted in David C. Gordon, *North Africa's French Legacy, 1954–1962* (Cambridge, Mass.: Harvard University Press, 1962), p. 24.

150 "This good weak people . . ." Raphael Patai, trans. and ed., *Ignaz Goldziher and His Oriental Diary* (Detroit: Wayne State University Press, 1987), p. 149.

150 ". . . the utter incapacity . . ." Cromer to Salisbury, quoted in Philip Magnus, *Kitchener* (London: Grey Arrow, 1961), p. 83.

150 "I must say I had..." Attlee, quoted in Paul Johnson, *A History of the Modern World* (London: Weidenfeld & Nicolson, 1983), p. 486.

151 "...a thumbnail sketch of a character..." Humphrey Bowman, *Middle-East Window* (London: Longmans, Green, 1942), p. 97 *ff.*

151 "Commissions, reports and experiments" Lord Rosebery, quoted in Gordon Martel, "The Near East in the Balance of Power," Elie Kedourie and Sylvia G. Haim, eds., *Modern Egypt: Studies in Politics and Society* (London: Frank Cass, 1980), p. 33.

152 "...the balance sheet shows..." Charles Issawi, *An Economic History*, p. 220.

153 "Grand pianos and kitchen ranges..." Walter Harris, *Morocco That Was* (London: Eland Books, 1983), p. 79.

154 "The advent of the French..." ibid., p. 237.

154 "The concept of the Protectorate..." Lyautey, quoted in John P. Halstead, *Rebirth of a Nation: Origins and Rise of Moroccan Nationalism, 1912–1944* (Cambridge, Mass.: Harvard University Press, 1967), p. 34.

157 "Ferhat Abbas and Sheikh Ben Badis, quoted in John Obert Voll, *Islam: Continuity and Change in the Modern World* (Boulder: Westview Press, 1982), p. 211.

159 "Gathered together were..." Philip Khoury, *Syria and the French Mandate: The Politics of Arab Nationalism, 1920–1945* (London: I. B. Tauris, 1987), p. 335.

159 "Paid agents protected..." Khoury, ibid., p. 366.

160 "...their deference to other religions..." Margaret Luce, *From Aden*, p. 4.

160 "In the evenings..." Wilfred Thesiger, *The Life of My Choice* (London: Collins, 1987), p. 191.

161 "...one of the most remarkable..." "How is it that you..." Barry Carman and John McPherson, eds., *Bimbashi McPherson: A Life in Egypt* (London: British Broadcasting Corporation Publications, 1983), p. 40; p. 237.

161 "...a peaceful law-abiding and..." Sir Thomas Russell Pasha, *Egyptian Service, 1902–46* (London: John Murray, 1949), pp. 31–32.

162 "The Egyptian fellah is..." "Tawwaf" (pseudonym), *Egypt, 1919, Being a Narrative of Certain Incidents of the Rising in Upper Egypt* (Alexandria: Whitehead Morris, 1925), p. 8.

162 "The Gypo as we call him..." Andrew Motion, *The Lamberts* (London: Chatto & Windus, 1986), p. 71.

162 For a general account of Saad Zaghlul, see Elie Kedourie, *The Chatham House Version*, pp. 82–159.

163 "You can win him..." quoted in Janice J. Terry, *The Wafd, 1919–1952* (London: Third World Centre, 1982), p. 165.

164 "They are both sons of dogs" Grafftey-Smith, *Bright Levant*, p. 57.

164 "Has Mahmud Pasha Sulayman distributed..." quoted in Gabriel Baer, *Studies in Social History*, p. 101.

164 ". . . composed of several thousands . . ." Thomas Russell Pasha, *Egyptian Service,* p. 203.

165 "It was not his business . . ." John Marlowe, *Anglo-Egyptian Relations, 1800–1953* (London: Cresset Press, 1954), p. 246.

166 "The 1923 constitution . . ." Grafftey-Smith, *Bright Levant,* pp. 124–125.

166 "I let people vote . . ." Tewfik el-Hakim, *Un Substitut,* p. 99.

166 ". . . might as well be a storm . . ." Neguib Mahfouz, *Midaq Alley* (Cairo: American University in Cairo Press, 1975), p. 128 *ff.*

167 "I seriously recommend that . . ." Sir Ronald Storrs, *Orientations* (London: Nicholson & Watson, 1943), p. 219.

168 "The Iraqi wanted a Monarchy" Mrs. Steuart Erskine, *King Feisal of Iraq* (London: Hutchinson, 1933), p. 110.

168 ". . . both groups were ignorant . . ." Elie Kedourie, "The Iraqi Shi'is and Their Fate" in Martin Kramer, ed., *Shiism, Resistance and Revolution* (Boulder: Westview Press, 1987), p. 149.

168 "It doesn't happen often . . ." Gertrude Bell, *Letters of Gertrude Bell* (London: Ernest Benn, 1927), Vol. II, p. 463.

169 "The true ruling elite of Iraq . . ." Reeva S. Simon, *Iraq Between the Two World Wars* (New York: Columbia University Press, 1986), p. 56.

172 ". . . great gifts . . ." Vincent Sheean, *Personal History* (London: Hamish Hamilton, 1969), p. 373.

173 ". . . the countless parties with . . ." Walid Khalidi, "Political Trends in the Fertile Crescent" in Walter Laqueur, ed., *Middle East in Transition,* p. 122.

174 "It was impossible for Egyptians . . ." for Faris Nimr, see Jamal Mohammad Ahmed, *Intellectual Origins,* p. 83.

175 "In a truly free country . . ." Qasim Amin, quoted in Hisham Sharabi, *Arab Intellectuals and the West: The Formative Years, 1875–1914* (Baltimore and London: The Johns Hopkins University Press, 1970), p. 94.

175 "The West is our teacher . . ." Abdulla Cevdet, quoted in N. Berkes, *Development of Secularism,* p. 357.

175 "What good would it do . . ." Abdel Djelil Zaouche, quoted in Leon Carl Brown, "Stages in the Process of Change," in Charles A. Micaud with L. C. Brown and Clement Henry Moore, *Tunisia: The Politics of Modernization* (London and Dunmow: Pall Mall Press, 1964), p. 36.

175 "The dominant civilisation of today . . ." Ahmad Lutfi al-Sayyid, quoted in Jamal Mohammad Ahmed, *Intellectual Origins,* p. 97.

176 ". . . a programme of national instruction" C. E. von Grunebaum, *Essays in the Nature and Growth of a Cultural Tradition* (London: Oxford University Press, 1961), p. 209.

176 "Day by day . . ." Taha Hussein, quoted in Donohue and Esposito, eds., *Islam in Transition,* p. 76.

176 "Our real national duty . . ." Taha Hussein, quoted in Albert Hourani, *Arabic Thought,* p. 329.

176 "Deep in their souls . . ." Jamal Mohammad Ahmad, *Intellectual Origins*, p. 93.

177 "The cup of humiliation . . ." Tewfik el-Hakim, *Un Substitut*, p. 121.

177 "They are the coming rulers . . ." Theodor Herzl, *Diaries* (London: Gollancz, 1958), pp. 381-382.

178 ". . . our miserable kill-joy policy . . ." Carman and McPherson, eds., *Bimbashi McPherson*, p. 222.

178 "I never fully understood . . ." Muhammad Kurd Ali, *Memoirs* (Washington, D.C.: American Council of Learned Societies, 1954), p. 67; p. 87; p. 96; p. 129.

179 "Like some invisible worm . . ." Ihab Hassan, *Out of Egypt*, p. 25.

179 "Help us to reconquer our dignity . . ." Ferhat Abbas, quoted in David C. Gordon, *North Africa's French Legacy*, p. 44.

179 "We had freed ourselves . . ." Mouloud Feraoun, *Les Chemins qui montent* (Paris: Editions du Seuil, 1957), p. 126

180 Salama Musa, *Education of Salama Musa*, p. 41; p. 59.

180 ". . . he was attracted in particular . . ." Majid Khadduri, *Arab Contemporaries*, p. 121.

180 ". . . that brings disgrace . . ." Rudolph Peters, *Islam and Colonialism: The Doctrine of Jihad in Modern History* (Hague: Mouton, 1979), pp. 118-119.

180 "It was taken for granted . . ." "I need no longer . . ." Edward Atiyah, *An Arab Tells His Story* (London: John Murray, 1946), p. 28; p. 124.

181 "My whole life went . . ." ibid., p. 148.

181 ". . . mental and emotional stability . . ." ibid., p. 164.

181 "The Egyptians always recall . . ." Emile Sage, *Voyage en Egypte* (Fontenay-le-Comte, 1900), p. 55.

181 "Don't argue, you!" Salama Musa, *Education of Salama Musa*, p. 149.

182 "It is always the Frenchman who . . ." Joachim Durel, quoted in L. C. Brown, *Tunisia: The Politics of Modernization*, p. 51.

8: The Impact of Nazism

185 "Look at medicine . . ." C. Snouck Hurgronje, *Makka in the 19th Century*, p. 171.

185 "A Jewish beard would defile . . ." E. W. Lane, *Manners and Customs*, p. 561, n. 1.

185 "May God curse me like a Jew" M. J. E. Daumas, *La Vie arabe et la société musulmane* (Paris, 1869), p. 95.

185 "If a Jew enters . . ." Edward Westermarck, *Ritual and Belief in Morocco* (London: Macmillan, 1926), Vol. I, p. 229.

185 "It is characteristic of the Jews . . ." Abd al-Latif Sharara, quoted in Yehoshofat Harkabi, *Arab Attitudes to Israel* (Jerusalem: Israel Universities Press, 1971), p. 153.

185 For a general account of the importation from Europe of anti-Semitism, see Bernard Lewis, *The Jews of Islam* (Princeton, N.J.: Princeton University Press, 1984); also Jacob M. Landau, "Ritual Murder Accusations in Nineteenth Century Egypt" in his *Middle East Themes* (London: Cass, 1973).

186 "32 repetitions of blood-libels . . ." Bernard Lewis, *Jews of Islam*, pp. 156–158.

186 For the Baal Shem Tov and Rabbi Nahman, see Arthur Green, *Tormented Master: A Life of Rabbi Nahman of Bratslav* (Alabama: University of Alabama Press, 1979), pp. 63–86.

186 For Crémieux, Graetz, etc., see Martin Gilbert, *Jerusalem: Rebirth of a City* (London: Chatto & Windus, 1985).

187 "I would clear out . . ." Herzl, *Diaries*, p. 284.

188 ". . . the private property of . . ." Ismail Kemal Bey, *Memoirs*, pp. 204–05.

189 For a general account of land purchasing in Palestine, see Arieh L. Avneri, *The Claim of Dispossession. Jewish Land-Settlement and the Arabs 1878–1948* (New York: Herzl Press, 1982).

189 ". . . an atmosphere of suspicion . . ." Y. Porath, *The Palestinian Arab National Movement* (London: Cass, Vol. I, 1974, Vol. II, 1979) Vol. II, p. 86.

190 ". . . completely natural, fine and just . . ." Yusuf Diya Pasha al-Khalidi, quoted in Neville J. Mandel, *Arabs and Zionism*, pp. 47–48.

190 "You are an educated man . . ." ibid., p. 43.

190 ". . . destined to struggle continuously . . ." Negib Azoury, *Le Réveil de la nation arabe* (Paris: Librairie Plon, 1905), p. v.

190 "Jews, sons of clinking gold . . ." Neville J. Mandel, *Arabs and Zionism*, p. 175.

191 "Nothing but the sword . . ." J. B. Schechtman, *The Mufti and the Führer* (New York: Thomas Yoseloff, 1965), p. 18.

191 "The accursed traitors . . ." Elie Kedourie, "Samuel and the Government of Palestine" in *The Chatham House Version*, pp. 62–63.

192 "Tel Aviv 1935" Lea Goldberg, in *Penguin Book of Hebrew Verse*, trans. and ed. T. Carmi (Harmondsworth, Middlesex: Penguin Books, 1981), pp. 553–554.

193 "I am sure that elemental floods . . ." Jabotinsky, quoted in Michael R. Marrus, *The Unwanted: European Refugees in the Twentieth Century* (London: Oxford University Press, 1985), p. 142.

193 "These fellows really want to be happy . . ." Gerschom Scholem, *Von Berlin nach Jerusalem* (Frankfurt am Main: Suhrkamp, 1977), p. 91.

193 For general accounts of the Arabs and Nazism, see Lukasz Hirszowicz, *The Third Reich and the Arab East* (London: Routledge & Kegan Paul, 1965); Francis R. Nicosia, *The Third Reich and the Palestine Question* (London: I. B. Tauris, 1985).

194 "Capture of Eichmann, who . . ." al-Bilad, 31 May 1960, quoted in Bernard Lewis, *Semites and Anti-Semites* (London: Weidenfeld & Nicolson, 1986), p. 162.

194 "The worst insult which . . ." Said Ghallab (pseudonym), quoted in J.-P. Péroncel-Hugoz, *Le Radeau de Mahomet*, p. 74.

194 "They have no thought of building up . . ." Adolf Hitler, *Mein Kampf* (London: Hurst & Blackett, 1939), pp. 447–448.

195 For Sheikh Ezzeddin Qassem, see Shai Lachman, "Arab Rebellion and Terrorism in Palestine, 1929–39" in Elie Kedourie and Sylvia G. Haim, eds., *Zionism and Arabism in Palestine and Israel* (London: Cass, 1982), pp. 52–99.

195 "You are a people of rabbits" Y. Porath, *Palestinian Arab Movement*, Vol. II, pp. 135–136.

196 "These poor people were not always . . ." ibid., p. 250.

197 ". . . a hornets' nest . . ." Miss M. H. Wilson, quoted in ibid., p. 255.

197 "The behaviour of the fighters . . ." ibid., p. 266.

197 "No." Haj Amin, quoted in Nicholas Bethell, *The Palestine Triangle* (London: Deutsch, 1979), p. 28.

198 "Two hours of Arab grievances . . ." Sir Ronald Storrs, *Orientations*, p. 340.

198 "How can we risk . . ." Evelyn Shuckburgh, *Descent to Suez: Diaries 1951–56* (London: Weidenfeld & Nicolson, 1986), p. 212.

198 "Jew versus Arab . . ." General Montgomery, quoted in Bethell, *Palestine Triangle*, p. 74.

199 "We may shortly have to face . . ." Alec Randall, quoted in ibid., p. 119.

199 ". . . so full of disillusion . . ." Edward Atiyah, *An Arab Tells His Story*, p. 202.

199 ". . . the future King Khaled dined with Hitler" David Holden and Richard Johns, *The House of Saud* (London: Pan Books, 1982), pp. 384–385.

199 For Khalid Bey al-Qarqani, see Robert L. Melka, "Nazi Germany and the Palestine Question," *Middle Eastern Studies* 5, (1969), pp. 221–233.

200 Michel Aflaq, future theorist . . .: Elie Kedourie, *Arabic Political Memoirs* (London: Cass, 1974), p. 201; see also Bassam Tibi, *Arab Nationalism*, p. 174.

200 "We were racialists, admiring Nazism . . ." Sami al-Jundi, quoted in Kedourie, *Arabic Political Memoirs*, pp. 200–201.

200 ". . . arguably the most widely read Arab writer . . ." William L. Cleveland, *Islam Against the West: Shakib Arslan and the Campaign for Islamic Nationalism* (London: Al Saqi Books, 1985), p. xxi.

201 ". . . he was prayed for . . ." Grafftey-Smith, *Bright Levant*, p. 218.

201 "If the German Reich imposes . . ." quoted in Manfred B. Halpern, *The Politics of Social Change in the Middle East and North Africa* (Princeton, N.J.: Princeton University Press, 1963), p. 147.

202 For Sami Shawkat, etc., see Elsa Marston, "Fascist Tendencies in Pre-war Arab Politics," *Middle East Forum*, No. 35, 1959, pp. 19–22.

202 "No more Monsieur . . ." J. B. Schechtman, *The Mufti and the Führer*, p. 84.

202 "The defeat of France . . ." Salah el Din el Zein el Tayeb, "The Europeanised Algerians and the Emancipation of Algeria," *Middle Eastern Studies*, Vol. 22, No. 6, April 1986, p. 218.

203 In Haifa on a Friday . . .: P. J. Vatikiotis, "The Rise of the Clerisocracy"

in *Arab and Regional Politics in the Middle East* (London: Croom Helm, 1984), p. 60.

203   ". . . indescribable . . ." Shuqairi, quoted in Elie Kedourie, *Arabic Political Memoirs*, p. 190.

203   ". . . on the point of out-bidding . . ." ". . . the most important of the . . ." Kenneth Pendar, *Adventure in Diplomacy*, p. 40; p. 57.

204   For the sheikh of Al-Azhar, see Martin Kramer, *Islam Assembled: The Advent of the Muslim Congresses* (New York: Columbia University Press, 1986), p. 163 *ff.*

204   For Abbas Mahmud al-Aqqad, see Safran, *Egypt in Search*, p. 214.

206   "Kill the Jews . . ." Haj Amin, quoted in J. B. Schechtman, *The Mufti and the Führer*, p. 151.

206   ". . . our best card . . ." *Hitlers Politisches Testament. Die Bormann Diktate vom Februar und April 1945* (Hamburg: Albrecht Knaus, 1981), p. 85.; see also Robert Wistrich, *Hitler's Apocalypse* (London: Weidenfeld & Nicolson, 1985), p. 60.

206   ". . . gratification of personal ambition . . ." Hirszowicz, *The Third Reich*, p. 259.

207   "Hitler would destroy . . ." quoted in A. Horne, *A Savage War*, p. 131; for Mohamedi Said, see also Paul Johnson, *History of the Modern World*, p. 497.

207   For Maruf al-Dawalibi, see Bernard Lewis, *Semites and Anti-Semites*, p. 194; p. 271, n. 2.

207   ". . . would a thousand times rather . . ." Maruf al-Dawalibi, quoted in Pierre Rondot, *The Changing Patterns of the Middle East* (London: Chatto & Windus, 1961), p. 136.

208   For a general account of American and British attitudes at the time, see William Roger Louis, *The British Empire in the Middle East, 1945–1951* (London: Oxford University Press, 1985), p. 395; pp. 481–504.

208   "U.S. prestige in the Muslim world . . ." George F. Kennan, quoted in Peter Grose, "The President versus the Diplomats," in William Roger Louis and Robert W. Stookey, eds., *The End of the Palestine Mandate* (London: I. B. Tauris, 1986), p. 48.

209   "30,000 Arabs from Jerusalem . . ." Rony E. Gabbay, *A Political Study of the Arab-Jewish Conflict* (Geneva: Librairie E. Droz, 1959), p. 66.

209   "The inhabitants of the large village . . ." *Al-Sarih*, quoted in ibid., p. 66.

209   See Musa Alami, "The Lesson of Palestine", *Middle East Journal*, October 1949, Vol. 3, No. 4, pp. 373–405.

213   "The Jews are living in the present . . ." Constantin Zurayk, *The Meaning of the Disaster* (Beirut, 1948), quoted in a review by Cecil Hourani, *Middle East Journal*, ibid., p. 470.

213   "In our day they control gold . . ." Muhammad Kurd Ali, *Memoirs*, p. 187.

213   "Whenever I work for a . . ." Al-Hajj Muhammad, quoted Henry Munson, Jr., *The House of Si Abd Allah*, p. 83.

213 "No one ever thought that . . ." Haj Amin, 1 March 1944, quoted in J. B. Schechtman, *The Mufti and the Führer*, p. 150.

214 "The idea of communism began . . ." quoted in David K. Shipler, *Arab and Jew: Wounded Spirits in a Promised Land* (London: Bloomsbury, 1987), p. 258.

214 "Imperialist intrigue went to the . . ." Y. Harkabi, *Arab Attitudes*, p. 70.

214 "It was the disaster of . . ." Y. Harkabi, ibid., p. 382.

214 "Imperialism uses Zionism . . ." Saddam Hussein, quoted in Fuad Matar, *Saddam Hussein*, p. 234.

214 "The bare fact, impossible to deny . . ." Abdallah Laroui, *Crisis of the Arab Intellectual*, p. 172.

215 *"Tous contre Israel"* Ben Bella, quoted in Bat Ye'or, *The Dhimmi: Jews and Christians under Islam* (Cranbury, N.J.: Associated University Presses, 1985), p. 114 and footnote, p. 125. For another general account of Jews under Islam, see Norman A. Stillman, *The Jews of Arab Lands* (Philadelphia: Jewish Publication Society of America, 1979).

215 "The forces which the Zionists control . . ." Constantin Zurayk, quoted in Y. Harkabi, *Arab Attitudes*, p. 66.

215 "Zionism aspires to destroy . . ." Muhammad Ali Aluba, *Palestine and the Conscience of Mankind* (1964), pp. 195–196, quoted in Y. Harkabi, ibid., p. 29.

215 "Nazism is a creation of Zionism" Bougenaa Amara, *Le Monde*, 2 June 1982, quoted in Pierre Vidal-Naquet, *Les Assassins de la mémoire* (Paris: La Découverte, 1987), p. 208 n. 44.

215 "The allegation of a bond . . ." Y. Harkabi, *Arab Attitudes*, p. 159.

216 "In 24 hours we were changed . . ." Rosemary Sayigh, "Palestinians in Camps: The New Reality, 1948–65" in Talal Asad and Roger Owen, eds., *Sociology of Developing Societies: The Middle East* (London: Macmillan, 1983), p. 196.

216 "The Zionist monster . . ." Y. Harkabi, *Arab Attitudes*, p. 345. The full list has been condensed here.

9: The Impact of Communism

223 ". . . in the eyes of intelligent Arabs . . ." Nabih Amin Faris and Mohammed Tawfik Husayn, *The Crescent in Crisis, An Interpretative Study of the Modern Arab World* (Lawrence, Kansas: University of Kansas Press, 1955), p. 83.

223 ". . . all that is worst in the Arab World" Khalid Kishtainy, *Arab Political Humour*, p. 133.

225 "Men whom nothing united . . ." Patrick Seale, *The Struggle for Syria* (London: I. B. Tauris, 1986), p. 32.

225 In 1947, a single book . . . (by Farhat Ziyadah): see George N. Atiyeh, ed., *Arab and American Cultures*, p. 38.

226 "One such was Sayyid Qutb . . ." see his *Social Justice in Islam* (Washington

D.C.: American Council of Learned Studies, 1953); also Kepel, *Prophet and Pharoah*, p. 40 *ff.*

226 "Only when Russian trade spreads . . ." Derek Hopwood, *The Russian Presence in Syria and Palestine 1843–1914* (London: Oxford University Press, 1969), p. 212.

228 "The trouble with the Arab League . . ." Minute by J. Thyne Henderson, quoted in William Roger Louis, *British Empire in the Middle East*, pp. 18–19.

229 "The accommodation of moderate nationalism . . ." William Roger Louis, ibid., pp. 46–47.

229 "Ignorance based on religious doctrine . . ." Abdallah Ali al-Qasimi, *These Are the Chains* (1946), quoted in Raphael Patai, *The Arab Mind* (New York: Charles Scribner's Sons, 1983), p. 252.

229 "What hopeless wretches we are . . ." Neguib Mahfouz, *Midaq Alley*, p. 213.

230 ". . . melancholy hedonism" Hugh McLeave, *The Last Pharoah: The Ten Faces of Farouk* (London: Michael Joseph, 1969), p. 232.

230 "We were both gripped . . ." Mohammed Neguib, *Egypt's Destiny*, p. 139.

230 "I do not know why I always . . ." Gamal Abdul Nasser, *Egypt's Liberation, the Philosophy of the Revolution* (Washington, D.C.: Public Affairs Press, 1955), pp. 87–88 in a slightly variant translation.

231 "The second World War . . ." Gamal Abdul Nasser, ibid., p. 51.

232 ". . . had things to discuss . . ." "was a proud man . . ." Khalid Mohieddine, quoted in Georges Vaucher, *Gamal Abdel Nasser et son équipe* (Paris: Julliard, 1959), Vol I, p. 142.

233 "Death to the traitors" Richard P. Mitchell, *The Muslim Brothers*, pp. 151–152.

233 ". . . education, the media, . . ." P. J. Vatikiotis, *Nasser and His Generation* (London: Croom Helm, 1978), p. 127.

233 ". . . is now on the threshold . . ." John Foster Dulles, quoted in Jean and Simonne Lacouture, *Egypt in Transition* (London: Methuen, 1958), p. 213.

234 ". . . free Western people" Richard Crossman, *A Nation Reborn* (London: Hamish Hamilton, 1960), p. 67.

234 "Our ultimate aim is . . ." Gamal Abdul Nasser, "The Egyptian Revolution," *Foreign Affairs* Vol. XXXIII, No. 2 (January 1955), p. 208.

234 ". . . observing our revolution . . ." Gamal Abdul Nasser, *Egypt's Liberation*, p. 63–64.

234 ". . . an amorphous, passive, dumb mass . . ." Anwar Sadat, *Revolt on the Nile* (London: Allen Wingate, 1957), p. 17.

234 "One is struck by . . ." Mayfield, *Rural Politics*, p. 59.

235 "I wept bitter tears . . ." Gamal Abdul Nasser, *Toute la vérité sur la guerre de Palestine* (Cairo: Direction des relations publiques des Forces Armées, 1955), p. 18.

235 "Lift your head, brother . . ." Vaucher, *Nasser et son équipe*, Vol. I, p. 7.

235 "I was ashamed of . . ." Neguib, *Egypt's Destiny*, p. 19; p. 84.

236 "I assure you . . ." Nasser, quoted in Vatikiotis, *Nasser and His Generation*, p. 168.

236 "the whole burden of the national feeling . . ." Vatikiotis, ibid., p. 322.

236 "The land of an old feudal estate . . ." Critchfield, *Shahhat*, pp. 15-16.

237 "Although officially no appointment . . ." Ivor Powell, *Disillusion by the Nile* (London: Solstice Productions, 1967), pp. 29-30.

237 ". . . an officer is not barred" Sharawi Gomaa, quoted in Raymond William Baker, *Egypt's Uncertain Revolution Under Nasser and Sadat* (Cambridge, Mass.: Harvard University Press, 1978), p. 58.

238 "For years rumors had . . ." John Waterbury, *The Egypt of Nasser and Sadat* (Princeton, N.J.: Princeton University Press, 1984), p. 256.

238 For Galal al-Hammamsi, see John Waterbury, ibid., p. 338.

238 "Furniture, plate cars . . ." Powell, *Disillusion*, p. 81.

238 ". . . was a smear on the entire . . ." Nasser, *Egyptian Gazette*, 12 August 1963, quoted in Harkabi, *Arab Attitudes*, p. 72.

238 ". . . to bow their heads . . ." Gamal Abdul Nasser, *Egypt's Liberation*, p. 95.

238 "I assure you that we have . . ." Vatikiotis, *Nasser's Generation*, p. 288.

241 "Suez was the turning point" Husein Dhul-Fiqar Sabri, quoted in Vatikiotis, ibid., p. 290

241 "How the Arabs hate us really . . ." Evelyn Shuckburgh, *Descent to Suez*, p. 311.

241 "Revolution is endemic in Iraq" Humphrey Trevelyan, *The Middle East in Revolution* (London: Macmillan, 1970), p. 134.

242 "We were only retreating . . ." Trevelyan, ibid., p. 13.

242 ". . . by the majority . . ." ". . . basically sympathetic . . ." Anthony Parsons, *They Say the Lion* (London: Cape, 1986), p. 34; p. 58.

243 For the Soviet role in this period, see Baruch A. Hazan, *Soviet Propaganda: A Case Study of the Middle East Conflict* (Jerusalem: Israel Universities Press, 1976); Oles M. Smolansky, *The Soviet Union and the Arab East Under Khrushchev* (Cranbury, N.J.: Associated Universities Press, 1964); Galia Golan, *Yom Kippur and After: The Soviet Union and the Middle East Crisis* (Cambridge: Cambridge University Press, 1977); Mark V. Kauppi and R. Craig Nation, eds., *The Soviet Union and the Middle East in the 1980s* (Lexington, Mass.: Lexington Books, 1983); Amnon Sella, *Soviet Political and Military Conduct in the Middle East* (London: Macmillan, 1981).

243 "more than half the global Soviet military . . ." Jon D. Glassman, *Arms for the Arabs* (Baltimore: Johns Hopkins University Press, 1975), pp. 197-98.

245 "Each was so sure . . ." John F. Devlin, *The Ba'ath Party* (Stanford: Hoover Institution, 1976), p. 11.

247 "What's democracy in Baghdad today?" Nasser, quoted in Walter Laqueur, *The Struggle for the Middle East* (London: Routledge & Kegan Paul, 1969), p. 233.

248 It is clear that the victims . . . Waterbury, *The Egypt of Nasser and Sadat*, p. 73 *ff.;* pp. 339-341.

249 ". . . appalling lack of political backbone" R. Hrair Dekmejian, *Egypt Under Nasir* (Albany: State University of New York Press, 1972), p. 171.

249 ". . . the masses have only . . ." Muhammad Hussein, quoted in Hilary

Kilpatrick, *The Modern Egyptian Novel* (Oxford: St Anthony's Middle East monographs, No. 1, 1974), p. 169.

249   "... the shocking tortures inflicted ..." Hans E. Tütsch, *From Ankara to Marrakesh: Turks and Arabs in a Changing World* (London: Allen & Unwin, 1964), p. 87.

249   "... debarred from all political ..." Sabri Hafiz, quoted in Roger Allen, *The Arabic Novel,* p. 91.

249   "The basic rule in those days ..." Mustafa Amin, quoted in Waterbury, *The Egypt of Nasser and Sadat,* p. 340.

249   For Ahmad Abul Fatih, see William A. Rugh, *The Arab Press, News Media and the Political Process in the Arab World* (Syracuse, New York: Syracuse University Press, 1972), p. 62.

249   For Fathi Abd al-Fattah and Louis Awad, see Waterbury, *The Egypt of Nasser and Sadat,* p. 338.

250   "Nasser first liquidated democracy ..." Louis Awad, quoted in Vatikiotis, *Nasser and His Generation,* p. 329.

250   "A hell of hunger ..." Yussef Idris, quoted in Amos Elon, *Flight into Egypt* (New York: Doubleday, 1980), p. 58.

250   "... he was not brought before ..." Fawzia Assad, *Des Enfants et des Chats* (Lausanne: Faure, 1987), pp. 124–129.

250   "... the Nasserite revolution ..." Georges Ketman (pseudonym), "The Egyptian Intelligentsia" in Walter Laqueur, ed., *Middle East in Transition,* p. 486.

250   For the press and television in Arab countries generally, see William A. Rugh, *The Arab Press.*

250   "For there to be a defence ..." Tewfik el-Hakim, *The Return of Consciousness* (New York: New York University Press, 1985), p. 27.

251   "Do you know Bobby Malla?" Waguih Ghali, *Beer in the Snooker Club* (London: Deutsch, 1964), p. 205.

251   "The principles of the revolution ..." Sayyid Qutb, quoted in Emmanuel Sivan, *Radical Islam: Medieval Theology and Modern Politics* (New Haven: Yale University Press, 1985), p. 42.

251   "I am writing to you ..." Emmanuel Sivan, ibid., p. 43.

252   "a total of 14,499 ..." Waterbury, *The Egypt of Nasser and Sadat,* p. 341.

252   "The Jews are perverts ..." Yuri Miloslavsky, *Les Camps de Concentration pours Juifs de 1948 à 1970* (Jerusalem: The Israel Council for Jews in Arab Countries, n.d.), p. 9.

252   "I am in favour of ..." Nasser, quoted in Edmond Taylor, *The Real Case Against Nasser* (pamphlet. Washington, D.C.: Atlantic Features, n.d.), p. 13.

252   "Once, in a speech, Nasser ..." Unni Wiken, *Life Among the Poor,* p. 162.

253   "an Indian journalist ..." R. K. Karanjia, in Gamal Abdul Nasser, *Speeches and Press Interviews During the Year 1958* (Cairo: State Information Department, 1958), p. 30. Quoted in Harkabi, *Arab Attitudes,* p. 235.

253 "Surely nobody still accepts . . ." *Deutsche National und Soldaten-Zeitung*, Munich, 1 May 1964, quoted in Be'eri, *Army Officers* p. 49.

253 "Zionist Nazism . . ." Letter to Erhard, quoted in Y. Harkabi, *Arab Attitudes*, p. 176. "Zionist racism . . ." ibid., p. 178.

253 "The liberation of Yemen . . ." Y. Harkabi, ibid., p. 431.

253 "We are confronting . . ." Gamal Abdul Nasser, speech of 29 May 1967, quoted in Walter Laqueur, *The Road to War, 1967* (London: Weidenfeld & Nicolson, 1968), Appendix 7, p. 308.

253 "Welcome, we are ready . . ." Laqueur, ibid., p. 292 for another expression of it.

254 "As God is my witness . . ." King Hussein of Jordan, *My "War" with Israel* (London: Peter Owen, 1969), p. 83.

254 ". . . nobody had been prepared . . ." Mohamed Heikal, *Road to Ramadan*, p. 46.

254 "It was impossible, intellectually . . ." Tewfik el-Hakim, *The Return of Consciousness*, pp. 40–41.

255 "We forgot the defeat . . ." "Where was I who . . ." Tewfik el-Hakim, ibid., p. 42; p. 8.

255 "To cover this utter . . ." Waguih Ghali, quoted in Diana Athill, *After a Funeral* (London: Cape, 1986), p. 138.

10: Arabia and Oil

258 ". . . a man sitting in a cloaca . . ." Charles Doughty, *Arabia Deserta* (Harmondsworth, Middlesex: Penguin Books, 1956), p. 20.

258 "All that is best in the Arabs . . ." Wilfred Thesiger, *Arabian Sands* (London: Longmans, 1959), p. 82.

260 ". . . all power was concentrated . . ." Charles Didier, *Sojourn with the Grand Sharif of Mekkah* (Cambridge: Oleander Press, 1985), pp. 97–98.

261 "A given tribe would invite . . ." T. O. el-Farra, "The Effects of Detribalising the Bedouin on the Internal Cohesion of an Emerging State: The Case of Saudi Arabia," quoted in Tim Niblock, ed., *State, Society and Economy in Saudi Arabia* (London: Croom Helm, 1982), p. 105, n. 85.

262 "There is no public opposition . . ." Abbas Kelidar, "The Problem of Succession in Saudi Arabia" in J. E. Peterson, ed., *The Politics of Middle Eastern Oil* (Washington, D.C.: Middle East Institute, 1983), p. 250.

263 "There is some little ruler . . ." Khrushchev, quoted in Aryeh Y. Yodfat, *The Soviet Union and the Arabian Peninsula* (London: Croom Helm, 1983), p. 9.

263 "Five of the seven emirs . . ." Michael C. Hudson, *Arab Politics: The Search for Legitimacy* (New Haven: Yale University Press, 1977), p. 198.

264 "We Mahra are the most God-forsaken . . ." P. S. Allfree, *Hawks of the Hadhramaut*, pp. 103–104.

265   For a general account of the economics of oil, see Yusef Sayigh, *Arab Oil Policies in the 1970s* (London: Croom Helm, 1983); Rodney Wilson, *The Economics of the Middle East* (London: Macmillan, 1979).

265   ". . . has been overwhelmed by cloverleafs . . ." Thomas Abercrombie, *National Geographic Magazine*, Vol. 168, No. 4, October 1985.

266   "All around the fringes of the desert . . ." Shirley Kay, "Social Change in Modern Saudi Arabia," in Tim Niblock, ed., *Saudi Arabia*, p. 172.

266   "Each cubicle had originally . . ." José Arnold, *Golden Swords*, p. 162.

266   "The 12-year-old Prince . . ." Arnold, ibid., p. 236.

267   ". . . wealth, and nothing else, seems . . ." Julio Caro Baroja, "Honour and Shame" in J. G. Peristiany, ed., *Honour and Shame*, p. 124.

267   ". . . all the members of the House of Saud . . ." Aburish, *Pay-Off*, p. 52.

268   For a general account of the Saudi money-favour nexus, see Steven Emerson, *The American House of Saud* (New York: Franklin Watts, 1985); Ronald Kessler, *Khashoggi* (London: Bantam Books, 1986).

268   "corner-boys" "a parasitic proletariat" Wilfred Thesiger, *Arabian Sands*, p. 310; *Daily Telegraph Magazine*, No. 265, 7 November 1969.

268   "Possibly the most devastating . . ." Saad Eddin Ibrahim, "Oil, Migration and the New Arab Social Order" In Malcolm H. Kerr and El Sayed Yassin, eds., *Rich and Poor States in the Middle East: Egypt and the New Arab Order* (Boulder: Westview Press, 1982), p. 50.

269   "the U.S. State Department complained . . ." see MEMO No. 36, January 1987, for abuses as detailed.

270   ". . . throws doubt upon the ability . . ." J. B. Kelly, *Arabia, The Gulf and The West* (London: Weidenfeld & Nicolson, 1980), p. 247.

270   ". . . the Saudi Arab is convinced . . ." J. B. Kelly, ibid., p. 250.

270   "Not only do they reject . . ." Sir James Craig, *Glasgow Herald*, 9 October 1980.

271   "I was ushered into . . ." Seymour Gray, *Beyond the Veil*, p. 12.

271   For Prince Mashur Bin Saud Bin Abdul Aziz, see *Daily Mail*, 12 March 1986.

272   For Bander Al Jawali (*sic* in the report), see *Daily Telegraph*, 4 June 1986.

272   "uncontrolled quantitative growth . . ." Mordechai Abir, "Modern Education and the Evolution of Saudi Arabia," in Edward Ingram, ed., *National and International Politics in the Middle East. Essays in Honour of Elie Kedourie* (London: Cass, 1986), p. 239.

272   "This wife can't take it . . ." Linda Blandford, *Oil Sheikhs* (London: Weidenfeld & Nicolson, 1977), p. 51.

273   ". . . The word 'Christmas' . . ." *Independent*, 23 December 1986.

273   "Prince Faisal of the royal family . . ." *Daily Telegraph*, 23 June 1987.

273   ". . . skyscrapers, municipal greenery . . ." Hilary Mantel, "Last Morning in Al Hamra," *The Spectator*, 24 January 1987, pp. 23–26.

273   ". . . took several quick small steps" Seymour Gray, *Beyond the Veil*, p. 145.

273   "We believe that it is . . ." Abdullah al-Saud, quoted in Tim Niblock, ed., *Saudi Arabia*, p. 303.

274 "The masses were too uninformed . . ." Ghazi Algosaibi, *Arabian Essays* (London: KPI, 1982), p. 36.

275 ". . . bring justice to . . ." Algosaibi, ibid., p. 116.

275 "My God, protect me . . ." Algosaibi, ibid., p. 61.

275 For a general account of Islamic Law in Saudi Arabia, see William Ochsenwald, "Saudi Arabia and the Islamic Revival" *International Journal of Middle Eastern Studies* 13, No. 3 (1981), pp. 271–286; Herbert J. Liebesny, "Judicial Systems in the Near and Middle East," *Middle East Journal*, Vol. 37, No. 2, 1983.

276 "Boys hide in side-streets . . ." Aharon Layish, "Ulema and Politics in Saudi Arabia" in Metin Heper and Raphael Israeli, eds., *Islam and Politics in the Modern Middle East* (London: Croom Helm, 1984). p. 36.

278 "I suppose I might be . . ." Sir Charles Eliot, *Turkey in Europe*, p. 5.

279 ". . . this oil-fired tyranny . . ." Georges Corm, *Le Proche Orient éclaté* (Paris: La Découverte, 1983), p. 67.

279 "Vested interests continue to . . ." Muhammad Ruhaimi, *Beyond Oil* (London: Al Saqi Books, 1986), pp. 140–141.

11: The Issue of Palestine

285 "We will dine in Tel Aviv . . ." Abdallah Schleifer, *The Fall of Jerusalem* (New York: Monthly Review Press, 1972), p. 174.

285 For a general account, see Jillian Becker, *The PLO: The Rise and Fall of the Palestine Liberation Organisation* (London: Weidenfeld & Nicolson, 1984).

286 ". . . spoke to several witnesses . . ." Thomas Kiernan, *Arafat: The Man and the Myth* (New York: W. W. Norton, 1976), p. 108; p. 163.

287 "A sacred covenant" Thomas Kiernan, ibid., p. 218.

287 "I would be more than glad . . ." Mohamed Heikal, *Road to Ramadan*, pp. 62–64.

292 "Major Muin, commander of . . ." Ze'ev Schiff and Ehud Yaari, *Israel's Lebanon War* (New York: Simon & Schuster, 1984). p. 80.

292 For a general account of Imam Moussa Sadr, see Fouad Ajami, *The Vanished Imam* (London: I. B. Tauris, 1986); Peter Theroux, *The Strange Disappearance of Imam Moussa Sadr* (London: Weidenfeld & Nicolson, 1987).

294 "We join those many of . . ." *Daily Telegraph*, 3 June 1986.

295 "A radical Shia Muslim . . ." London *Times*, 4 March 1986.

297 "Millions of Lebanese . . ." *International Herald Tribune*, 4 July 1986.

297 "War-weary Christians and Muslims . . ." London *Times*, 21 August 1987.

298 ". . . intensely sensitive and shy . . ." John Pilger, *Heroes* (London: Cape, 1986), p. 367 ff.

299 "Briskly he rises . . ." John Le Carré, *Observer*, 13 June 1982.

299 "No, no, no . . ." Scott MacLeod, *New York Review of Books*, 11 June 1987.

300 "About love . . ." Jean Genet, *Un Captif Amoureux* (Paris: Gallimard, 1986), p. 58.

300   "Had I been in love . . ." Jean Genet, ibid., p. 361.

301   "We maintain coordination with . . ." Yasser Arafat, quoted in Raphael Israeli, ed., *The PLO in Lebanon: Selected Documents* (London: Weidenfeld & Nicolson, 1983), p. 43.

301   "a friend of the Arabs" Raphael Israeli, ed., ibid., p. 55.

302   For a general account of Abu Nidal, see Yossi Melman, *The Master Terrorist* (New York: Adama, 1986).

302   ". . . psychopath and a fascist . . ." *Sunday Times,* 9 December 1984.

303   "The murderers in Baghdad . . ." *Morning Star,* 7 August 1984.

303   For PLO finances, see *Der Spiegel,* No. 44, 1985; London *Times,* 9 December 1985; Walter Laqueur, *The Age of Terrorism* (London: Weidenfeld & Nicolson, 1987), p. 102.

304   "Mrs Gandoura said . . ." *Independent,* 28 July 1987. Said Moufak *sic* in the report but probably more correctly Said Mouafak.

307   "Our enemies will suffer . . ." BBC ME/8469/A/9, 19 January 1987.

307   For poll of West Bankers, see *International Herald Tribune,* 10 September 1986.

309   "It is time . . ." Mahmoud Darwish, "Those Who Pass Between Fleeting Words," *Jerusalem Post* International Edition, 2 April 1988.

311   "God gave Palestine . . ." Taysir Jbara, *Palestinian Leader: Hajj Amin Al-Husayni* (Princeton, N.J.: Kingston Press, 1985), p. 192.

311   ". . . his opposition to Zionism . . ." Anwar Nusseibeh interviewed, *Jerusalem Post* International Edition, 19 April 1986.

311   "The glory of . . ." Shuqairi, quoted in Elie Kedourie, *Arabic Political Memoirs,* p. 191.

311   ". . . a great feeling of pride . . ." Raymonda Tawil, *My Home, My Prison* (New York: Holt, Rinehart and Winston, 1979), p. 139.

312   "What's become of you all . . ." Sahar Khalifah, *Wild Thorns* (London: Al Saqi Books, 1985), p. 27.

312   ". . . time has revealed . . ." Cecil Hourani, *Unfinished Odyssey,* p. 189.

312   "The world is ruined . . ." Cecil Hourani, ibid., p. 190.

313   ". . . easily reduced to . . ." Edward Said, *The Question of Palestine* (London: Routledge & Kegan Paul, 1977), p. 100.

313   ". . . a long history of . . ." Edward Said, ibid., p. 119.

313   ". . . a device for holding . . ." ". . . valorizing . . ." Edward Said, ibid., p. 29.

12: Power Holders

315   "You are forgiven . . ." Sadat, quoted in Bernard Lewis, *Semites and Anti-Semites,* p. 161.

315   ". . . as between civilised people . . ." Sadat, quoted in Georges Corm, *Le Proche Orient éclaté,* p. 133.

316   "I was determined to get rid . . ." Anwar Sadat, *In Search of Identity* (London: Collins, 1978), p. 223.

316   "If I were to ask . . ." Jehan Sadat, *A Woman of Egypt* (New York: Simon & Schuster, 1987), p. 267.

316   ". . . grind into mincemeat . . ." Jehan Sadat, ibid., p. 270.

317   "I wished *I* were Zahran" Anwar Sadat, *In Search of Identity*, p. 6.

317   ". . . secret revolutionary society" Anwar Sadat, *Revolt on the Nile*, p. 14.

317   "We swore an oath . . ." Anwar Sadat, ibid., p. 15.

317   "I felt certain that . . ." Anwar Sadat, ibid., p. 29.

317   "One of the officiants . . ." Anwar Sadat, ibid., p. 80.

318   "We therefore conform to . . ." Anwar Sadat, ibid., p. 127.

318   "Gamal, O Lord, is . . ." Sadat, quoted in David Hirst and Irene Beeson, *Sadat* (London: Faber & Faber, 1981), p. 83.

318   ". . . always left a trail of hatred . . ." Anwar Sadat, *In Search of Identity*, p. 155.

318   ". . . the mistakes made by . . ." Anwar Sadat, *Those I Have Known* (London: Cape, 1985), p. 130.

319   ". . . a gloomy scene of torture . . ." *Al-Ahram*, quoted in Alvin Z. Rubinstein, *Red Star on the Nile* (Princeton, N.J.: Princeton University Press, 1977), p. 317.

319   ". . . into the disputes . . ." "even more specious" Mohamad Ahmed Mahgoub, *Democracy on Trial* (London: Deutsch, 1974), p. 64; p. 73.

319   ". . . a spiritual crossing to . . ." Tewfik el-Hakim, quoted in Raymond William Baker, *Egypt's Uncertain Revolution*, p. 131.

319   ". . . restoring the faith of . . ." Mansour Khalid, in George N. Atiyeh, ed., *Arab and American Cultures*, p. 139.

319   Yussef Idris, "Deliverance," quoted in John Waterbury, *The Crossing* (Hanover, New Hampshire: American Universities Field Staff Report Vol. XVIII No. 6, 1973), p. 2.

321   "All these debates between . . ." Taha Zaki, quoted John Waterbury, *The Egypt of Nasser and Sadat*, p. 252.

321   ". . . corruption and manipulation . . ." Mohamed Heikal, *Autumn of Fury* (London: Corgi Books, 1984), p. 204.

322   For a general account of Islamicist groups and their beliefs in Egypt, see Gilles Kepel, *The Prophet and Pharoah* (1985); Johannes J. G. Jansen, *The Neglected Duty* (New York: Macmillan, 1986).

322   "I am Khalid . . ." Kepel, *Prophet and Pharoah*, p. 192.

323   "It is legitimate for . . ." Gaddhafi, quoted in MEMO No. 18, May 1985.

323   ". . . a species which are . . ." London *Times*, 28 April 1986.

324   ". . . simple in the extreme" Lisa S. Anderson, "Libya and American Foreign Policy" in J. E. Peterson, ed., *Politics of Middle Eastern Oil*, p. 332.

325   For a general account of Gaddhafi, see David Blundy and Andrew Lycett, *Qaddhafi and the Libyan Revolution* (London: Weidenfeld & Nicolson, 1987); John Davis, *Libyan Politics: Tribe and Revolution* (London: I. B. Tauris, 1987).

326   ". . . stomped to death . . ." MEMO No. 25, January 1986. John Davis, *Libyan Politics* reports Meheishe to be alive in exile.

326   "The officers have the conscience . . ." quoted Lisa S. Anderson, "Religion and Politics in Libya," *Journal of Arab Affairs* (Fresno, Ca) Vol. I, No. 1, 1987, p. 67.

327   ". . . papers into the dust-bin . . ." Muammer Gaddhafi, *The Green Book*, Part 1 (London: Martin Brian & O'Keeffe, 1976), p. 8.

327   ". . . only blood relationships" Muammer Gaddhafi, ibid., p. 13.

328   ". . . realistically, the strong always rule . . ." Muammer Gaddhafi, ibid., p. 32.

329   "If you continue your tyranny . . ." Colonel Gaddafi (*sic*), "My army against Imperialism," London *Times*, 3 September 1986.

329   "I didn't believe Mrs Thatcher . . ." Safia Gaddhafi, quoted in London *Times*, 22 April 1986.

329   "For his speech in . . ." *Daily Telegraph*, 3 September 1986.

330   ". . . young men, tall and . . ." *International Herald Tribune*, 7 January 1987.

330   ". . . a stable and comfortable . . ." Robert Fisk, London *Times*, 5 March 1987.

331   ". . . the total prison population . . ." for a general account, see *Report from Amnesty International to the Government of the Syrian Arab Republic* (London, November 1983), pp. 12–17; pp. 29–30 for statistics cited.

331   "twenty-six inter-state disputes . . ." Ze'ev Ma'oz, "The Evolution of Syrian Power," in Moshe Ma'oz and Avner Yariv, eds., *Syria Under Assad* (London: Croom Helm, 1986), p. 80.

332   ". . . the chronic inability . . ." Daniel Lerner, *Passing of Traditional Society*, p. 265.

333   "The accidents of recruitment . . ." John F. Devlin, *The Ba'ath Party*, p. 38.

333   "Three days after my entering . . ." Sami al-Jundi, quoted in Nikolaos Van Dam, *The Struggle for Power in Syria: Sectarianism, Regionalism and Tribalism in Politics, 1961–1978* (London: Croom Helm, 1979), p. 99.

335   For a general account of Mustapha as-Sibai and his successors, see Umar F. Abd-Allah, *The Islamic Struggle in Syria* (Berkeley, Ca: Mizan Press, 1983).

336   "Is it possible to believe . . ." BBC ME/6150/A/2, 25 June 1979.

336   "The Lebanese invasion . . ." Assad, quoted in BBC ME/7083/A 11 & 12, 21 July 1982.

337   "We in this country . . ." Assad speech to paratroopers, quoted in BBC ME/7455/A/1, 4 October 1983.

337   "A Lebanese national, Ahmad Hasan Id . . ." BBC ME/8247/i, 1 May 1986.

337   "Syria's Economic Security Court . . ." *Independent*, 9 September 1987.

338   "The United States believed . . ." General Mustafa Tlas, speech of 6 October 1973 anniversary, BBC ME/8385/A/15, 9 October 1986.

339   ". . . control the country's intelligence services . . ." Hanna Batatu, "Political Power and Social Structure in Syria and Iraq" in Sami K. Farsoun, ed., *Arab Society: Continuity and Change* (London: Croom Helm, 1985), p. 37.

339   "... the enormous increase in corruption ..." *Guardian*, 26 June 1979.

339   "Do I need ..." Ion Pacepa, *Red Horizons* (London: Heinemann, 1988), p. 188.

340   "If our President says ..." Mustafa Tlas, quoted in London *Times*, 12 September 1984.

340   "Who among us would have supposed ..." Sami al-Jundi, quoted in Elie Kedourie, *Arabic Political Memoirs*, p. 202; see also Fouad Ajami, *The Arab Predicament*, p. xii; pp. 40–50.

341   "The Iraqi charm ..." Gavin Young, *Iraq* (London: Collins, 1980), p. 16.

341   "Iraq has boasted ..." Adeed Dawisha, "The Politics of War," in Frederick W. Axelgard, ed., *Iraq in Transition* (Boulder: Westview Press, 1986), p. 21.

342   "Conversations continued till the afternoon ..." Majid Khadduri, *Republican Iraq*, p. 96.

343   "... some of the most terrible scenes ..." Marian Farouk-Sluglett and Peter Sluglett, *Iraq Since 1958* (London: KPI, 1987), p. 85.

344   "Torture in Iraqi prisons ..." see *Report and Recommendation of an Amnesty International Mission to the Government of the Republic of Iraq, 22–28 January 1983* (London, October 1983), p. 2; p. 21.

344   "... the avenue of the party bureaucracy ..." John F. Devlin, *The Ba'ath Party*, p. 312.

345   "Two were to fire at ..." Fuad Matar, *Saddam Hussein*, p. 32.

346   "... informed sources in Baghdad ..." BBC ME/5562/A/5, 14 July 1977.

346   "The takeover operation lasted ..." *Economist* Foreign Report 1593, 1 August 1979, p. 3.

346   "For several years, this group ..." BBC ME/6180/A2 & A3, 30 July 1979.

347   "You all know how ..." Sadat, quoted in David Hirst and Irene Beeson, *Sadat*, p. 340.

347   "... the agent reactionary pocket ..." BBC ME/4959/A/3, 19 July 1975.
       "... the rapid transformation ..." Marian Farouk-Sluglett and Peter Sluglett, *Iraq Since 1958*, p. 232.

348   "... declined in intellectual significance" Hanna Batatu, "Shi'i Organizations in Iraq" in Juan R. I. Cole and Nikki Keddie, eds., *Shi'ism and Social Protest* (New Haven: Yale University Press, 1986), p. 182.

348   "... has links with foreign circles ..." BBC ME/6392/A/1, 11 April 1980.

349   "Where is the freedom ..." BBC ME/6392/A/2, 11 April 1980.

350   "Brothers, great people! ..." BBC ME/6398/A/3, 18 April 1980.

350   "Glorious Iraqis ..." BBC ME/7081/A/4, 19 July 1982.

350   "You, O righteous martyrs ..." BBC ME/8314/A/7, 18 July 1986.

350   "The area has never before seen ..." Speech by Tareq Aziz, quoted in Tareq Y. Ismael, *Iraq and Iran: Roots of Conflict* (Syracuse, New York: Syracuse University Press, 1982), p. 99.

350   "... very often lets it be known ..." Aburish, *Pay-Off*, p. 50.

351   "Seven government employees and ..." *Daily Telegraph*, 4 October 1986.

352 ". . . the aspect of a secret society" Maurice Gaudefroy-Demombynes, *Muslim Institutions* (London: Allen & Unwin, 1950), p. 38.

352 ". . . they shall study something of use . . ." Hafez Farman Farmayan, "The Forces of Modernization in 19th century Iran" in William R. Polk and Richard L. Chambers, eds., *Beginnings of Modernization*, p. 120 *ff.*

352 ". . . the utter want of cleanliness . . ." Vambéry, *Life*, p. 80.

354 ". . . face to face with the modern age . . ." Hamid Enayat, *Modern Islamic Political Thought* (London: Macmillan, 1982), p. 163.

354 "It was merely that they wished . . ." quoted in Roy Mottahedeh, *The Mantle of the Prophet: Religion and Politics in Iran* (London: Chatto & Windus, 1986), p. 222.

354 ". . . an utterly atrocious tyranny . . ." ". . . scattered with wrecks . . ." Christopher Sykes, *Four Studies in Loyalty* (London: Century Hutchinson, 1986), p. 59; p. 41.

355 "We were afraid that . . ." Amin Banani, *Impact of the West on Iran, 1921–1941*, Stanford University Ph.D. dissertation. Stanford, Ca., 1959, p. 232.

355 "A Persian will invariably tell . . ." Sir Henry Layard, *Autobiography*, Vol. II, p. 5.

356 "It seems such a pity . . ." Mrs M. E. Hume-Griffith, *Behind the Veil in Persia and Turkish Arabia* (London, 1910), p. 81

356 ". . . Isa Sadiq was one such . . ." see Roy Mottahedeh, *The Mantle*, pp. 60–67.

356 "It was better for us . . ." Muhammad Reza Shah, *Mission for My Country* (London: Hutchinson, 1961), p. 124.

356 "revitalised the sense of dignity . . ." Farhad Diba, *Mossadegh: A Political Biography* (London: Croom Helm, 1986), p. 202.

357 ". . . force-marched into industrialization . . ." Muhammad Reza Shah, *Shah's Story* (London: Michael Joseph, 1980), p. 94.

357 "There is no such thing as . . ." Mollie Panter-Downes, "Letter from Teheran," *The New Yorker*, 21 April 1956.

358 "I wanted a perfectly . . ." "Iran was earning her place . . ." Muhammad Reza Shah, *Shah's Story*, p. 11; p. 112.

359 ". . . references to the humiliation suffered . . ." Shaul Bakhash, *The Reign of the Ayatollahs* (London: Unwin, 1985), p. 22.

359 ". . . people begin to grow smaller . . ." Khomeini, quoted in Tareq Y. Ismael, *Iraq and Iran*, p. 106.

360 ". . . one of the most poisonous and . . ." Ayatollah Khomeini, *Islam and Revolution*, p. 170.

360 "short biographies of fifty-five of the . . ." Moojan Momen, *An Introduction to Shii Islam* (New Haven: Yale University Press, 1985), pp. 310–323.

360 "Kashani, whose support for the Nazi cause . . ." Roy Mottahedeh, *The Mantle*, p. 130.

360 ". . . the pipeline was jammed . . ." Gary Sick, *All Fall Down: America's Fateful Encounter with Iran* (London: I. B. Tauris, 1985), p. 18.

360 "It has acknowledged that . . ." Khomeini, quoted in Roy Mottahedeh, *The Mantle*, p. 245.

361 "Either he must abdicate or . . ." Trevor Mostyn, *Coming of Age*, p. 160.

362 "We do not see a single group . . ." Khomeini, *Islam and Revolution*, p. 52.

362 ". . . based on the approval of laws . . ." Khomeini, ibid., p. 55.

362 "The fact that men in our age . . ." Khomeini, ibid., p. 90.

363 ". . . young, dynamic cultural forces . . ." Reza Baraheni, *The Crowned Cannibals* (New York: Vintage Books, 1977), p. 108.

364 "We have witnessed in Urumiyeh . . ." BBC ME/6191/A/6, 11 August 1979.

364 "In 1981, Ayatollah Khomeini's former allies . . ." Walter Laqueur, "Reflections on Terrorism," *Foreign Affairs*, Vol. 65, No. 1, Fall 1986, p. 94.

365 ". . . political executions and political prisoners: see *Amnesty International File on Torture No. 7*, April 1985.

365 "Every night you can hear . . ." *Amnesty International Newsletter*, February 1983, p. 18.

365 "An Islamic court had convicted . . ." *Daily Telegraph*, 12 December 1985.

366 "Ye who suffer from . . ." Khomeini, BBC ME/6135/A/12, 7 June 1979.

366 "We lost ourselves . . ." Khomeini, BBC ME/6140/A/3, 13 June 1979.

366 "America should know that . . ." Abdelkarim Mousavi Arbedili, quoted in *Independent*, 10 October 1987.

366 "We want to attend to . . ." Khomeini, BBC ME/7930/A/4, 20 April 1985.

368 "We too have to do a . . ." V. S. Naipaul, *Among the Believers: An Islamic Journey* (London: Deutsch, 1981), p. 390.

13: Image and Identity

369 "We are striding ahead . . ." M. J. E. Daumas, *La Vie arabe*, p. 586.

369 "Every Muslim is sick . . ." Afghani, quoted in Hisham Sharabi, *Arab Intellectuals and the West*, p. 26.

370 ". . . retarded mental habits . . ." Sadiq al-Azm, quoted in Donohue and Esposito, eds., *Islam in Transition*, p. 113.

371 "It is irrelevant to say . . ." Albert Hourani, *Arabic Thought*, p. 228.

372 ". . . deadly desperation . . ." quoted in Richard P. Mitchell, *The Muslim Brothers*, p. 224.

372 "I saw that the social life . . ." Hasan al-Banna, quoted in Raymond William Baker, *Egypt's Uncertain Revolution*, p. 8.

372 "I am an Arab: who am I?" *The Middle East*, May 1981, pp. 6–9.

373 "He had taken the precaution . . ." ". . . narrow Semitic head . . ." Cecil Hourani, *Unfinished Odyssey*, p. 9; p. 8.

373 "I am a foreigner everywhere . . ." Omar Sharif, interviewed in *Sunday Times Magazine*, 13 October 1985.

374 "I am a cultural hybrid . . ." Jean Amrouche, quoted in David C. Gordon, *North Africa's French Legacy*, p. 52.

374 "I am a United States citizen . . ." Nayef al-Barras, quoted in Seymour Gray, *Beyond the Veil,* p. 56.

374 "My father uprooted us . . ." *The Middle East,* December 1984, p. 3.

374 "Life carries him along . . ." Neguib Mahfouz, *Al-Ahram,* 17 May 1977, quoted in Donohue and Esposito, eds., *Islam in Transition,* p. 240.

375 ". . . to soothe the conscience of . . ." Wilfred Cantwell Smith, *Islam in Modern History* (Princeton, N.J.: Princeton University Press, 1977), p. 86.

375 "The glories of the past . . ." F. A. Sayegh, quoted in Sania Hamady, *Temperament and Character of the Arabs* (New York: Twayne, 1960), p. 217.

375 ". . . a single Muslim could . . ." Shakib Arslan, quoted in William L. Cleveland, *Islam Against the West,* p. 116.

375 "So glorious was the past . . ." Ibrahim Abu-Lughod, *Arab Rediscovery of Europe,* p. 6.

375 "The Arab-speaking peoples . . ." Philip K. Hitti, *History of the Arabs* (London: Macmillan, 1970), p. 757.

375 "Arab culture has played . . ." Muhammad Kamel Ayyad, "The Future of Culture in Arab Society," in Walter Laqueur, ed., *Middle East in Transition,* p. 469.

376 "Americans would not have . . ." Aziz Suryal Atiya, *Arab and American Cultures,* p. 28.

376 "All those cultural centres . . ." Shedli (*sic* but more usually Chedli) Klibi, in Derek Hopwood, ed., *Euro-Arab Dialogue: The Relations Between the Two Cultures,* Hamburg Symposium, 11–15 April 1983 (London: Croom Helm, 1985), p. 23 *ff.*

377 "We are Arabs because . . ." Nasir el-Din Nashashibi, quoted in Y. Harkabi, *Arab Attitudes,* p. 356.

377 ". . . the immense fact of . . ." Hichem Djait, *Europe and Islam,* p. 131.

378 "In the West the Arab is depicted . . ." Mohi El-Dine Saber, *Euro-Arab Dialogue,* p. 41.

378 "Compared with other peoples . . ." Omar Farrukh, quoted in Raphael Patai, *The Arab Mind,* p. 253.

379 ". . . an inability to behave coherently . . ." A. B. Zahlan, *Science and Science Policy,* p. 184.

379 "We are in a train . . ." Kateb Yacine, *Jeune Afrique,* 8 January 1986, p. 40.

379 ". . . cultural collapse is imminent" Ghali Shukri, quoted in Emmanuel Sivan, *Radical Islam,* p. 156.

379 ". . . the general degradation of . . ." Georges Corm, *Le Proche Orient éclaté,* p. 238.

379 "Our culture? . . ." Nizar Qabbani, quoted in Jacques Berque, *Cultural Expression in Arab Society Today* (Austin: University of Texas Press, 1978), p. 197.

379 ". . . ideological venereal disease" Ghadah al-Samman, quoted in Fernea and Bezirgan, eds., *Muslim Women Speak,* p. 394.

379 "Relations between the Arab and his . . ." Abdelwahab Bouhdiba, *Sexualité en Islam,* p. 299.

379   "If we Arabs do not leave . . ." quoted in Y. Harkabi, *Arab Attitudes*, p. 418.

379   ". . . one of the saddest . . ." Boutros Boutros-Ghali, *Arab and American Cultures*, p. 236.

379   "The Arab world stretches . . ." Halim Barakat, quoted in Emmanuel Sivan, *Radical Islam*, p. 157.

379   "This crisis is . . ." Suhayl Idris, *al-Adab*, February–March 1980, quoted in Roger Allen, *The Arabic Novel*, p. 89.

380   ". . . the transformation of the . . ." Ba'ath Constitution, quoted in John F. Devlin, *The Ba'ath Party*, p. 27.

380   "We start from questions . . ." Hisham Sharabi and Mukhtar Ani, in L. C. Brown and N. Itzkowitz, eds., *Psychological Dimensions*, p. 240.

381   ". . . must have been stunned . . ." Khalid Kishtainy, *Arab Political Humour*, p. 69.

381   ". . . highly prized accomplishment . . ." R. A. Nicholson, *Literary History of the Arabs* (London: 1907), p. 470.

381   ". . . is part of the inner citadel . . ." Bernard Lewis, *The Emergence of Modern Turkey*, p. 436.

381   For a general account of Arab culture today (and Anis Fuleihan in particular), see Cecil Hourani, ed., *The Arab Cultural Scene: A Literary Review* supplement (London: Namara Press, 1982).

381   "The treason of an Arab . . ." Norman Daniel quoting al-Wasti, *Euro-Arab Dialogue*, p. 88.

382   "He gave me his constant . . ." Um Kaltoum, quoted in Fernea and Bezirgan, eds., *Muslim Women Speak*, p. 163.

382   ". . . one of the most widespread means . . ." Jacob M. Landau, *Studies in the Arab Theater and Cinema* (Philadelphia: University of Pennsylvania Press, 1958), p. 205.

383   "Comte, Rousseau, Mill . . ." P. J. Vatikiotis, *The History of Egypt from Muhammad Ali to Mubarak* (London: Weidenfeld & Nicolson, 1985), p. 240.

383   "Marx and Freud . . ." Leo Hamalian and John D. Yohannan, eds., *New Writing from the Middle East* (New York: Frederick Ungar Publishing, 1978), p. 274.

383   "Flaubert, Balzac . . ." Mursi Saad El Din, preface to Neguib Mahfouz, *Wedding Song*, p. x.

383   ". . . fell under the spell . . ." Tewfik el-Hakim obituary, London *Times*, 28 July 1987.

383   ". . . an orphaned Lautréamont . . ." Jacques Berque, *The Arabs*, p. 208.

384   "Friendship for the West . . ." Celal Nuri, quoted in N. Berkes, *Development of Secularism*, p. 357.

384   "We no longer believe in . . ." Adonis, *Lisan*, May 1967, quoted in Hisham Sharabi, *Arab Intellectuals and the West*, p. 136.

384   ". . . revolution is the science . . ." Adonis, quoted in Jacques Berque, *Cultural Expression*, p. 47.

384   "Something in the Arab world . . ." Fouad Ajami, "The Silence In Arab Culture," *The New Republic*, 6 April 1987, p. 29.

384   "Come friends . . ." Ali Shariati, "On the Sociology of Islam," quoted in
      John L. Esposito, *Islam and Politics* (Syracuse, New York: Syracuse University Press, 1984), p. 184.

384   ". . . the ideas of Emile Durkheim . . ." ibid., p. 183.

385   "Have faith in God . . ." Ali Shariati, *Man and Islam.* Trans. with a preface
      by Fatollah Marjani (Houston: Free Islamic Literature, 1981), p. xvii.

385   "I wept and fled . . ." Jalal Ali Ahmad, *Occidentosis: A Plague from the West*
      (London: Al Saqi Books, 1984), p. 18.

385   "Why did we utterly fail . . ." Jalal Ali Ahmad, ibid., p. 35.

385   "We now resemble . . ." Jalal Ali Ahmad, ibid., p. 64.

386   "When the house has . . ." Jalal Ali Ahmad, ibid., p. 118.

386   "forums to satisfy . . ." Jalal Ali Ahmad, ibid., p. 125.

387   "That expectation . . ." V. S. Naipaul, *Among the Believers*, p. 19.

389   ". . . the sound of tambourines . . ." Rachid Boudjedra, *La Répudiation*
      (Paris: Denoël, 1969), p. 71.

389   "Hate throbbed in us . . ." Boudjedra, ibid., p. 97.

389   "At the exit of the souks . . ." Boudjedra, ibid., p. 65.

390   ". . . this bankruptcy . . ." Boudjedra, ibid., p. 273.

390   "Life comes and goes . . ." Fakir Baykurt, quoted in Kemal H. Karpat,
      "Social Themes in Contemporary Turkish Literature" Part II, *Middle East
      Journal*, Vol. XIV, Spring 1960, p. 153.

390   ". . . should have led us to . . ." Neguib Mahfouz, *Wedding Song*, p. 15.

390   "Living—reduced to . . ." Neguib Mahfouz, ibid., p. 89.

390   "My village, like . . ." Yusuf Sharouni, *Blood Feud* (London: Heinemann,
      1984), p. 120; p. 136.

390   "When, I wondered . . ." Yusuf al-Qaid, *War in the Land of Egypt* (London:
      Al Saqi Books, 1986), p. 126.

391   "The winding lanes . . ." Yussef Idris, "The Dregs of the City" in his *The
      Cheapest Nights* (London: Heinemann, 1983), pp. 111-113.

391   "Before the last World War . . ." Sadegh Hedayat, "The Message of Kafka,"
      quoted in H. H. Kamshad, *Modern Persian Prose Literature* (Cambridge: Cambridge University Press, 1966), p. 200.

391   ". . . a tribe of brazen . . ." Sadegh Hedayat, *The Blind Owl* (London: Calder,
      1986), p. 99.

391   ". . . could not forget that the . . ." Halim Barakat, *Days of Dust*, p. 18.

392   "Most of our friends . . ." Halim Barakat, ibid., p. 18.

392   "I found nothing . . ." Taha Husayn, *Adib*, quoted in Hilary Kilpatrick,
      Modern Egyptian Novel, p. 37.

392   "Shafik both wanted and . . ." Yusuf Sharouni, "Flesh and the Knife" in
      Blood Feud, p. 48.

392   "There was just nothing . . ." "And besides . . ." Ahdaf Soueif, *Aisha*
      (London: Black Swan Books, 1985), p. 41; p. 61.

392   "I look on things . . ." Dia el-Sharkawy, "The Sneak Thief," in A. Man-

zalaoui, ed., *Arabic Short Stories, 1945–1965* (Cairo: American University in Cairo Press, 1985), p. 374.

392 "Deaths, nothing but . . ." Djanet Lachmet, *Lallia,* p. 123.

392 "We're all really miserable . . ." Esmail Fassih, *Sorraya in a Coma* (London: Al Saqi Books, 1985), p. 252.

393 "It's terrible . . ." Abdelhak Serhane, *Les Enfants des rues étroites* (Paris: Editions du Seuil, 1986), p. 19.

393 "You will take revenge . . ." Serhane, ibid., p. 14.

394 "You never again dared . . ." Serhane, ibid., p. 47.

394 ". . . where it rained gold . . ." Serhane, ibid., p. 14.

394 ". . . cheating, giving rise to . . ." Serhane, ibid., p. 25.

395 "Violence was the universe . . ." Serhane, ibid., p. 86.

396 "Who among us Arabs . . ." Mohamed Karoui, *Les Temps Modernes,* September–October 1972, quoted in Hisham Sharabi and Mukhtar Ani "Impact of Class and Culture" in L. C. Brown and N. Itzkowitz, eds., *Psychological Dimensions,* p. 243.

396 "Shut up, or . . ." Neguib Mahfouz, *Wedding Song,* pp. 72–73.

396 ". . . he'd cut off . . ." ". . . gouge your eyes out . . ." El Sir Hassan Fadl, *Their Finest Days* (London: Rex Collings, 1969), p. 34; p. 74.

396 "Every night when . . ." Gholamhosein Saedi, "The Game is Over" in Leo Hamalian and John D. Yohannan, eds., *New Writing,* p. 354.

396 "Si Zoubir lost control . . ." Rachid Boudjedra, *La Répudiation,* p. 96.

397 "His eyes glittered . . ." Ghassan Kanafani, "The Land of Sad Oranges" in his *Men in the Sun* (London: Heinemann, 1982), p. 61.

397 "If you were a horse . . ." Ghassan Kanafani, ibid., p. 63.

397 "You make me as small as . . ." Critchfield, *Shahhat,* p. 65.

398 Hanan Al-Shaykh, *The Story of Zahra* (London: Quartet Books, 1986), p. 127.

398 "I have not yet read . . ." Sahair El-Calamawy, "The Impact of Tradition on the Development of Modern Arabic Literature," in George N. Atiyeh, ed., *Arab and American Cultures,* p. 52

398 "Overwhelmed by the hatred . . ." Yashar Kemal, *Memed My Hawk* (London and New York: Writers and Readers Publishing Cooperative, 1981), p. 184.

398 ". . . our Agha would kill . . ." Kemal, ibid., p. 264.

398 "Not a soul remained . . ." Kemal, ibid., p. 263.

399 "Why should he be a . . ." Kemal, ibid., p. 343.

399 "There is French in me . . ." Mouloud Feraoun, quoted in A. Horne, *A Savage War,* p. 518.

399 "Then in a flight of despair . . ." Mouloud Feraoun, *Le Fils du pauvre* (Paris: Editions de Seuil, 1954), p. 101.

400 "The will to succeed . . ." Feraoun, Ibid., p. 124.

401 "The Arab despises himself . . ." Moncef Marzouki, quoted in J.-P. Péroncel-Hugoz, *Le Radeau de Mahomet,* p. 227.

Index

Abaza, Fikri, 164
Abbas, Ferhat, 157, 179
Abbas (Imam), 72
Abdel-Kader (Emir of Algeria), 73, 74, 87
Abdu, Muhammad, 103, 104, 119, 174, 231
Abduh, Ibrahim, 379
Abdullah (King of Jordan), 112, 210, 218–19, 224
Abdel-Malek, Anwar, 174, 388
absolutism: and Arab collectivity, 402, 404; and conspiracies, 102; defense of, 64; and democracy, 15, 102–3; and justice, 28–29; and modernization, 71, 112–13; and power challenges, 26, 104; and religion, 29, 34–35; and shame and honor, 402; and socialism, 7, 15, 17; and wealth, 65; and Westernization, 65–66. *See also name of specific person or country*
Abu Dhabi, 126–27, 261, 263, 266. *See also* Arabia; United Arab Emirates
Aburish, Said, 11, 31, 267, 350
Adam, Juliette, 106–7, 153
Adonis (aka Ahmed Ali Said), 383, 384
adventurers/explorers, 71–77, 257–58. *See also name of specific person*
Afghani, Jamal al-Din al-, 86–88, 103, 104, 231, 359, 369
Aflaq, Michel, 4, 5, 15, 200, 205, 245, 332, 335, 343
Aga, Achmed, 73
Aga, Khalil, 73
Aga, Mehmet, 147
agnosticism/atheism, 370–71
Ahmad, Jalal Ali, 385

Ahmed, Mohammed, 80
Ahmed Bey (ruler of Tunisia), 77–78, 79
Ajami, Fouad, 14, 379, 384
Akif, Mehmed, 90
Al-Ahd (conspiracy group), 108, 109
Alami, Musa, 202, 212, 213
Alavi, Bozorg, 383
Algeria: adventurers/explorers in, 72, 73; and anti-Semitism, 186; and colonialism, 73–75, 149–50, 156–57, 173; and deception/facades, 53–54; and Egypt, 239; *évolués* in, 156–57; and France, 73–75, 149–50, 156–57, 173; and image/identity, 389–90, 399–400; and independence, 4, 7, 173, 225; insulation of, 60; and Jews, 156; leadership in, 60, 73–75; literature about, 389–90, 399–400; and the military, 75; and modernization, 47, 53–54; and Morocco, 10; and the Muslim Brothers, 371; and nationalism, 7, 156–57, 173; and nazism, 202–3, 206; and the Ottoman Empire, 60; and the PLO, 287; and politics, 17; power challenges in, 73–75, 115–16; public health in, 53–54; religion in, 74, 156–57; sexual practices in, 7, 130, 135, 389–90; and shame and honor, 53–54, 179; and the Soviet Union, 243; and terrorism/violence, 7, 117; and treason, 117; and tribalism, 32, 60, 74, 156; and Westernization, 62; and World War I, 156; and World War II, 206. *See also name of specific person*
Algosaibi, Ghazi, 274–75

445